ITALIAN SYNTAX

STUDIES IN NATURAL LANGUAGE AND LINGUISTIC THEORY

Managing Editor

FRANK HENY, *Dept. of Linguistics, University of Minnesota,*
142 Klaeber Court, 320 16th Avenue S.E., Minneapolis, MN 55455, U.S.A.

Editor

JOAN MALING, *Linguistics Program, Dept. of Psychology, Brandeis University,*
Waltham, MA 02254, U.S.A.

LUIGI BURZIO

Department of Romance Languages and Literatures
Harvard University

ITALIAN SYNTAX

A Government-Binding Approach

D. REIDEL PUBLISHING COMPANY

A MEMBER OF THE KLUWER  ACADEMIC PUBLISHERS GROUP

DORDRECHT / BOSTON / LANCASTER / TOKYO

Library of Congress Cataloging-in-Publication Data

Burzio, Luigi, 1943-
    Italian syntax.

    (Studies in natural language and linguistic theory)
    Bibliography: p.
    Includes index.
    1. Italian language–Syntax.   2.   Italian language–Grammar,
Generative.   I.   Title.   II.   Series.
PC1369.B87   1986   455   85-31251
ISBN 90-277-2014-2
ISBN 90-277-2015-0 (pbk.)

Published by D. Reidel Publishing Company,
P.O. Box 17, 3300 AA Dordrecht, Holland.

Sold and distributed in the U.S.A. and Canada
by Kluwer Academic Publishers,
190 Old Derby Street, Hingham, MA 02043, U.S.A.

In all other countries, sold and distributed
by Kluwer Academic Publishers Group,
P.O. Box 322, 3300 AH Dordrecht, Holland.

Printed in The Netherlands

Alla memoria di mia madre

TABLE OF CONTENTS

PREFACE

In the course of our everyday lives, we generally take our knowledge of language for granted. Occasionally, we may become aware of its great practical importance, but we rarely pay any attention to the formal properties that language has. Yet these properties are remarkably complex. So complex that the question immediately arises as to how we could know so much.

The facts that will be considered in this book should serve well to illustrate this point. We will see for example that verbs like **arrivare** 'arrive' and others like **telefonare** 'telephone', which are superficially similar, actually differ in a large number of respects, some fairly well known, others not. Why should there be such differencces, we may ask. And why should it be that if a verb behaves like *arrivare* and unlike *telefonare* in one respect, it will do so in all others consistently, and how could everyone know it? To take another case, Italian has two series of pronouns: stressed and unstressed. Thus, for example, alongside of reflexive **se stesso** 'himself' which is the stressed form, one finds *si* which is unstressed but otherwise synonymous. Yet we will see that the differences between the two could not simply be stress versus lack of stress, as their behavior is radically different under a variety of syntactic conditions. Again, why should this be the case, and how does every speaker know it? The list could continue at length: as facts of this nature abound, many more will be found through these pages.

Among the phenomena we will consider, only a small number have ever been noted by even the most thorough of traditional or pedagogical grammars. But, if the knowledge that speakers have thus exceeds — and by far — the contents of grammar books, then it could not be claimed that this knowledge is merely a reflex of what grammar books say, induced by some form of instruction. It would seem more plausible to hold the opposite view, that it is grammar books that represent some reflection of what we know, and a dim one at that. But even more significantly, it could not be claimed that the knowledge of language is, in any reasonable sense, derived by 'induction' from the linguistic facts that language learners are exposed to. For instance, many of the facts we will address, though conforming with the intuitions of all speakers, are very exotic from the point of view of normal life situations, as they can only be assembled artificially, through the painstaking work of the linguist. It is simply unimaginable that such facts could have occurred with sufficient frequency or consistency to provide an adequate inductive basis for what is a complex system of knowledge, so remarkably uniform among speakers. The much richer character of the knowledge attained, compared with the experience required to attain it, compels us to postulate that the structure of the human mind is itself contributing significantly to that knowledge.

The research of Noam Chomsky and of the school of Generative Grammar focuses attention precisely on the human mind. It studies language phenomena for the purpose of determining the nature of the system of knowledge involved, and what aspects of this system must be taken to exist above and beyond experience. This book falls within the tradition of that school. In it, we consider various syntactic phenomena of Italian, sometimes comparing this language with others. The analyses of these phenomena which we propose constitute hypotheses on the system of mental representation to which these phenomena are due.

Although some parts of the discussion reach considerable degrees of technical and theoretical complexity, a great effort has been made to render the discussion accessible to a wide audience and to those whose familiarity with Generative Grammar is limited. With the aid of the introductions to each of the two parts, I trust that at least the essence of the discussion will be within the means of most patient readers.

A few words are in order to situate the book within the context of generative research and to give credit to those who contributed the most. In a more direct way, this book and my doctoral dissertation on which it is based owe the greatest debt to the work of Luigi Rizzi and Richard Kayne. It was Rizzi's article 'Ristrutturazione', the first of a series of rather brilliant contributions, that sparked my interest in the issues that were to become the core of the book. Most of his later work also exerted great influence, as will be evident throughout. As my work progressed and branched out into several directions, I found that the system I was elaborating was becoming increasingly comparable, if not in insight, at least in empirical coverage to that of Kayne's *French Syntax*, which soon became an invaluable point of reference for facts, observations, and for the high standards of research it inspires.

In a more indirect, but also all-pervasive way, the greatest recognition goes to Noam Chomsky. As everyone knows, linguistics could not be what it is today without him. In this respect, his influence on this book is obvious enough. But the impact of his way of thinking on my own has been great in many ways which will not be obvious from this book. To thank someone for having the intellect they have is an odd thing to do. But Noam Chomsky must at least be thanked for the sincerity with which he cares about his students, as he did in my case, and for going through the various stages of the manuscript — and there were many — with the greatest of care, pointing out errors and suggesting improvements.

I must thank David Perlmutter for suggesting to me the single most important idea in this book, the one that he later termed the "Unaccusative Hypothesis".

I must also thank Adriana Belletti, Guglielmo Cinque, Richard Kayne, Luigi Rizzi for their expert and friendly advice at various points.

Finally, much credit must be given to Frank Heny for an editorial effort of very impressive proportions.

PART I

VERB CLASSES

VERB CLASSES

I.0 INTRODUCTION TO PART I

I.0.1 *Overall Organization*

The division of this book into two parts is not meant to suggest two independent inquiries, but only some respects in which the material we discuss, while being all interrelated, seems to cluster around either one of two major concerns: the study of the different classes of verbs, and the study of certain constructions which all involve a main verb and an infinitival complement, but which differ in significant ways from the norm. This first part is devoted to the first of these concerns: the different classes of verbs. We will claim that apparently intransitive verbs actually comprise two different classes.

Chapter 1 is devoted to laying out this claim and to some topics which relate to it more or less directly. Since a very important role in identifying the different classes of verbs is played by "inversion" constructions, that is constructions in which the apparent subject occurs after the verb, a study of inversion is highly relevant to the more general goal. This study we undertake in chapter 2, where we contrast the inversion of languages that allow null subjects, like Italian and the Piedmontese dialect, with that of languages that do not, like French and English. Chapter 3 deals with three different topics, which are in part subsidiary to the first two chapters, and in part related to later discussion.

I.0.2 *Notational Conventions*

In this work we will adopt all of the usual symbols, such as *N, A, V, P* for the lexical categories of noun, adjective, verb, preposition, and correspondingly *NP, AP, VP, PP* for the phrases that have such categories as heads. We will adopt all the current assumptions regarding the internal structure of sentences. In particular we take sentences to be introduced in general by a 'complementizer' or 'COMP' position (the position occupied by English *that*). We assume that COMP and S together form an $\bar{S}$, and that S consists of a subject NP and a VP. Structural analyses will be indicated in tree notation or equivalently in bracketing notation. Note however that especially when they use bracketing these analyses will often be incomplete, and will provide only those elements which are of immediate relevance. For example, while we take infinitivals to have 'null' subjects,

3

these subjects will sometimes be omitted, and brackets will sometimes not be labelled. Note also that since we will in general not be concerned with the syntax of complementizers, we will for the most part ignore the distinction between S and $\bar{S}$ in the analyses, and use the symbol S ambiguously for both.

Unless we use them in quotes or with qualifications like 'apparent', terms like SUBJECT, OBJECT will be taken to be defined configurationally, rather than in terms of either 'thematic' considerations or considerations of Case. Thus, a subject will be the NP in a structure like (1a), while an object (direct or indirect) will be the NP in either of (1b, c).

(1) a.   SUBJECT

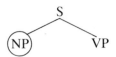

b.   DIRECT OBJECT

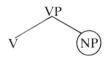

c.   INDIRECT OBJECT

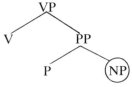

Non English examples will be accompanied either by word-for-word English glosses or by English translations or both, as required by our expository objectives. In general, glosses will be given when translations would be insufficient for the necessary understanding of the internal structure of the example, and translations will be omitted when the gloss is sufficiently transparent. Glosses without translations will also be given in many ungrammatical examples which would only have non-sentences as translations. The exact style of both glosses and translations will also be determined by the expository objectives at hand and will therefore be less than perfectly consistent. Thus, certain translations will be more literal than others, and certain glosses will also be more detailed than others.

I.0.3 *The Government-Binding Framework*

The various hypotheses about the syntax of Italian and other languages that we will present in the course of this work will be formulated within the framework of a larger hypothesis about the nature of the language faculty known as the Extended Standard Theory (EST). This is the theory which has been advanced in several variants over the past ten years or so by N. Chomsky and his associates. Of these variants, we will adopt in particular the one called *Theory of Government and Binding* (GB) first formulated around 1979–80, and then presented in Chomsky (1981a) (*Lectures on Government and Binding,* henceforth "LGB"). In what follows, we present a rough outline of this theory, returning to specific aspects of it later in the discussion.

The GB theory, and the EST in general, postulate a system of mental representation that has four different levels, one that provides an abstract characterization of sound: the level of Phonetic Form (PF); another that provides an abstract characterization of the interpretation: the level of Logical Form (LF); and two other levels: D-structure and S-structure, all interconnected as in (2).

(2)   D-structure

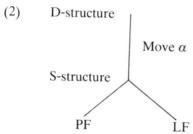

Move α

S-structure

PF   LF

Each of the levels in (2) expresses certain specific aspects of our knowledge of language. To illustrate the function of D-structure, we may consider (3).

(3) a.   John reads **the book**.
    b.   **The book** was read.
    c.   John seems to read **the book**.
    d.   **The book** seems to have been read.

As speakers, we know that *the book* stands in the same semantic or THEMATIC relation with the verb *read* in all of (3a, b, c, d). We could say that this NP is the PATIENT of action in all four cases. The relation between *the book* and *read* is marked by selectional dependency. Thus, if we replace *the book* with *the cat*, all of (3) become semantically deviant, and all in the same way. We also know in analogous fashion that *John* stands in the same relation to *read* in both of (3a) and (3c). We might say here that *John* is the AGENT of the action in both. This relation too is marked by selectional dependency. Thus, replacing *John* with, for example, *the tree*, brings about the same deviance in both (3a, c). From the point of view of how we understand these sentences, it is therefore as if *the book* was the direct object of *read* not only in (3a, c), but in (3b, d) as well. It is also as if *John* was the subject of *read* not only in (3a), but in (3c) as well. This aspect of our knowledge is expressed by the D-structures in (4), in which each [e] is an empty position.

(4) a. John reads **the book**.
   b. [e] was read **the book**
   c. [e] seems John to read **the book**
   d. [e] seems [e] to have been read **the book**

The D-structures of (4) will also allow us to define very simply the syntactic context in which *read* occurs as '___NP', something which we would not have been able to do on the basis of (3). The context '___NP' is the SUBCATEGORIZATION FRAME of *read*. D-structure is therefore an immediate projection of the lexicon, in the sense that it is the level at which each lexical item appears exactly in its subcategorization frame. And it is the level at which there is a one-to-one correspondence between thematic relations (such as agent, patient), and grammatical functions like *subject, object*. To put it slightly differently, it is the level at which grammatical functions are 'thematically relevant'.

D-structure as we have just characterized it is fairly similar, though not identical, to the 'deep' structure of earlier theoretical models, in particular of the 'Standard' theory (ST) as formulated in Chomsky (1965). Analogously, S-structure corresponds to the former 'surface' structure, but with some significant differences. While surface structure was intended to represent rather closely the audible signal, S-structure representation contains elements that do not have an audible counterpart. Thus, consider the S-structures in (5). These are derived from the D-structures in (4) via the rule Move α, to which we will return.

(5) a. John reads the book
   b. The book$_i$ was read t$_i$
   c. John$_i$ seems t$_i$ to read the book
   d. The book$_i$ seems t$_i$ to have been read t$_i$

The symbol t_i in (5b, c, d) stands for TRACE and is meant to represent an empty category (analogously to "[e]" of (4)) which has arisen via movement of a certain element: the one that bears the same index. The claim that mental representation at the level of S-structure includes such null elements as the traces of (5) is supported empirically by the fact that certain aspects of interpretation which must be attributed to S-structure, such as pronominalization, anaphora, and coreference in general, detect, as it were, these empty categories. The same kind of empirical justification can be given for the other null element PRO of (6) (meant to suggest a special kind of null "pronoun": compare (6) with *John$_i$ hopes that he$_i$ will leave*).[1]

(6)   John$_i$ hopes [PRO$_i$ to leave]

The two levels of D-structure and S-structure, mediated by Move α, constitute the syntactic component.

In broad conceptual terms, the justification for the PF and LF components is analogous to the justification we gave for the syntactic component.[2] Just as postulating Move α allows us to express certain generalizations by means of the D-structures in (4), so, postulating phonological rules that change, say, /elektrik-iti/ into [elektrisiti], and /elektrik-ian/ into [elektrišen] will enable us to maintain that there is one single underlying lexical element, /elektrik-/, in both of of these words as well as in the adjective [elektrik], which − it is plausible to assume − is part of our knowledge of English.

Analogously, since it seems to be the case that speakers know that 'quantifiers', i.e. elements like *every, some*, have scope over certain domains which are not identified by the S-structure position of the quantifier, we will be justified in postulating a rule that assigns scope to these elements, giving rise to a level of LF distinct from S-structure. (We will see that there are other processes that occur in the LF branch.)

Consider now how the three branches: Syntax, Phonology and LF are interconnected in (2). In essence, the interconnections express two facts. First, it is S-structure rather than D-structure that provides the basis for both the representation of sound and the interpretation. Secondly, no operation occurring in the PF component affects interpretation, and conversely no operation occurring in the LF component affects sound. Concerning the first fact, it is trivially obvious that sound is determined by S-structure. Thus, the sound of *The book seems to have been read* corresponds to (5d) above, and not to (4d). It is less obvious however that interpretation is also determined by S-structure.

Recall that part of the function of D-structure was precisely to represent certain aspects of meaning: the 'thematic' relations between verbs and NPs. Yet on the one hand there are certain aspects of meaning, such as coreference, that *must* rely on S-structure, as we mentioned above, and on the other we note that the thematic relations of D-structure are essentially preserved in S-structure, given the traces of (5) above. Thus, in (5b) *the book* can still be regarded as the thematic object of *read* as in the corresponding D-structure (4b), if we take account of its relation with the trace in object position.[3] Therefore, S-structure is in effect not only necessary, but also sufficient for interpretation.

As for the second fact, i.e. the independence of PF and LF, this seems true too. It is clear that when a phonological rule changes, for example, /elektrik/ to [elektris] in the context ___/iti/, it does not alter the meaning of this item, whatever exactly that meaning is (it is precisely the identity of meaning that leads us to postulate one underlying form for different surface realizations). Conversely, if there is a rule that operates on S-structure to assign a certain interpretation to quantifiers, we know that this rule has no effect on sound, which is determined solely by S-structure.

Having thus reviewed the various levels of representation and the way in which these are interconnected, it remains to consider exactly which classes of structures appear at each level. With respect to the syntax, which is what concerns us most directly, the traditional assumption was that the set of possible D- (or *deep*) structures is characterized by a Phrase Structure (PS) Grammar, called the "Base", while the set of possible S- (or *surface*) structures is characterized by a set of "transformations" performed on the available D-structures. Under this view, for example the structure of (7a) would be due to application of the PS rules in (7b). (Other rules could be postulated, to provide the internal analysis of the NPs, or of the tensed verb, but these will suffice for our purposes).

(7) a.

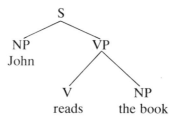

    b. S → NP VP
         VP → V NP

A structure like (7a), whose terminal string can be analyzed as 'NP$_1$ V NP$_2$', could then be subject to a transformation that (omitting inessential details) would turn that sequence into 'NP$_2$ be V-en (by NP$_1$)' where *-en* designates a passive participial suffix, thus giving rise to the passive sentence in (8).

(8)   The book was read (by John)

This characterization of the set of well-formed structures in terms of systems of rules (PS rules and transformations) which generate the relevant structures at each level, has progressively given way in recent years to a characterization in terms of well-formedness conditions and principles which apply at the various levels.[4] The conditions and principles postulated by the GB theory can be grouped into the subtheories in (9), which we will review in this order.

(9) a.   Case theory
    b.   Binding theory
    c.   θ-theory

    d.   Government theory
    e.   Control theory
    f.   Bounding theory

CASE THEORY consists of mechanisms for the assignment of Case and a well-formedness condition applying at S-structure which requires that NPs with phonological content must have Case. This is the so-called "Case Filter" of (10).

  (10)   CASE FILTER
          *NP, if NP has phonological content and no Case.

Case is assigned in various ways. In particular it is assigned by verbs and prepositions to their objects, or more generally to elements that they govern, where the notion of GOVERNMENT is defined as in (11).

  (11)   GOVERNMENT
          α governs β if and only if:
          i) α is one of the lexical categories (N, A, V, P)
          ii) α c-commands β
          iii) Any maximal projection (i.e. NP, AP, VP, PP, $\bar{\text{S}}$) dominating β also dominates α

The notion of *c-command* referred to in (11ii) can be defined as in (12a), and illustrated as in (12b) (the linear order in (12b) is irrelevant however).

  (12)a. C-COMMAND (non-extended notion)
          α c-commands β if and only if there is a γ which immediately dominates α and which dominates β, and α does not dominate β.

     b.

While (12) is adequate for most cases, we must note that there is also an extended notion of c-command, which is required by some of the cases we will discuss. Under the extended notion, γ in (12b) need not *immediately* dominate α, provided that the intervening nodes are of the same category as γ. If the path connecting γ and β in (12b) does not cross any maximal projection, and α is a lexical category, then, by (11), not only c-command, but also government obtains.

Such configurational conditions on Case assignment correctly allow Case to be assigned not only to objects, but also to certain subjects of infinitives, such as those in (13a, b).

(13)a. For **John** to leave would be rude
     b. I expected **John** to leave

In (13a), *John* receives Case from the complementizer/preposition *for* in the structure [$_\bar{S}$ *for* [$_S$ *John* ...]]. In (13b), a case of Exceptional Case Marking (ECM), it is the main verb which assigns Case, in the structure ... *expected* [$_S$ *John* ...]. Notice that it must be assumed that infinitival complements like the one in (13b) have no $\bar{S}$: a maximal projection that would prevent government. We return to this matter and to the whole typology of infinitival complements in the introduction to Part II.

Outside of such cases as (13a, b), which are somewhat peculiar to English, subjects of infinitivals will not be in Case assigning environments however, so that given (10) they will in effect be required to be phonologically null, like the trace in (14a) or PRO in (14b).

(14)a. John$_i$ seems [t$_i$ to leave]
     b. John$_i$ hopes [PRO$_i$ to leave]

Another Case marking provision must be added to those we have already mentioned, to account for the fact that, unlike subjects of infinitivals, subjects of tensed clauses generally *are* phonologically realized. Here Case assignment is attributed to the inflectional element of the tensed verb: INFL. We take the Case assigned by INFL to be nominative, in contrast with accusative (or 'objective') assigned by verbs, and still some other Case, perhaps 'oblique' assigned by prepositions. Since, in general, Case assignment requires government, it is natural to presume that it does so also when INFL is involved. This and other considerations lead us to postulate that at S-structure INFL is represented as in (15), and that a later (PF) rule moves it onto the verb.

(15)

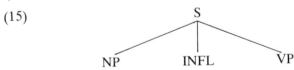

In (15), the element INFL will govern the subject under (11), assigning nominative Case, provided that we add this element to the list of governors in (11i). (See however the discussion of proper government below.)

The overall effect of Case theory is thus that of predicting when an NP will be phonologically realized or 'lexical', and when it will be null.

The BINDING THEORY, (9b), is the theory of coreference, or of referential dependence among syntactic constituents. With respect to coreference, there appear to be three different types of elements: ANAPHORS, i.e.

elements that do not have independent reference, like *each other, himself,* etc.; R-EXPRESSIONS (to suggest 'referential'), which do have independent reference, like for example *John, the men, sincerity,* and PRONOMINALS, whose status is intermediate between the other two. These three classes behave in accordance with the three generalizations of (16), each illustrated in (17).

(16) a. An anaphor must be locally bound.
    b. A pronominal must not be locally bound.
    c. An R-expression must not be bound.

(17) a. The men$_i$ knew **each other**$_i$
    b. * The men$_i$ knew **them**$_i$
    c. * They$_i$ said that John knew **the men**$_i$

We will interpret *bound* in (16) as: "having a c-commanding antecedent". Thus, each of the phrases in boldface in (17) is bound. As for the qualification "locally" of (16a, b), we will define it on the basis of the notion GOVERNING CATEGORY of (18).

(18)   The GOVERNING CATEGORY for α is the minimal category of the type NP or S that contains both α and the governor of α.

We can how translate each of (16a, b, c) into a corresponding principle of the binding theory in (19) (where *free* means 'not bound').

(19)   BINDING THEORY
    (A) An anaphor is bound in its governing category.
    (B) A pronominal is free in its governing category.
    (C) An R-expression is free.

For the time being, we will take the binding theory to apply to both S-structure and LF, returning to this question in Part II.

The definition of *governing category* in (18) correctly accounts for the apparently exceptional behavior of subjects of infinitives with respect to coreference. Let us first consider tensed Ss. With these, both the subject and any object will have the S itself as a governing category, as in (20), whence the ungrammaticality of both of these cases.

(20) a. * They$_i$ expected that [$_{gc}$ John would see **each other**$_i$]
    b. * They$_i$ expected that [$_{gc}$ **each other**$_i$ would see John]

The tensed complement is the governing category for the anaphor *each other* in both of (20a, b) because, beside the anaphor, it also contains its governor in both cases: the verb *see* in (20a), and the tensed inflection (INFL) in (20b). But with infinitival Ss, only objects will have the S itself as their governing category, as in (21).

(21)a. * They$_i$ expected [$_{gc}$ John to see **each other**$_i$]
      b.   [$_{gc}$ They$_i$ expected **each other**$_i$ to see John]

In (21a), *each other* is governed by *see*, just as in (20a), whence the parallel results. But in (21b) *each other* is governed by the main verb *expect* (just as *John* is in (13b) above). The governing category will therefore be, not the complement, but the main clause, whence the grammaticality of this case.

The category of anaphors, subject to principle A of the binding theory, also includes NP-traces. The well-formedness of 'raising' cases like (14a) above is therefore analogous to that of (21b) (whereas for instance the ungrammaticality of (20b) would correspond to that of *$John_i$ seemed that t_i would leave*). In contrast, Wh-traces, which are identified with the category of 'variables', appear to behave like R-expressions with respect to coreference, falling under principle C of the binding theory.[5] (They also differ from NP-traces in requiring Case and in receiving a θ-role.)

The binding theory of (19) has (roughly) the same empirical coverage as its various predecessors.[6] Thus, the framework of Chomsky (1973) excluded (20a) and (21a) by means of a condition that prohibited crossing a subject: the "Specified Subject Condition" (SSC), while it excluded (20b) by means of the "Tensed S Condition", which stated that the boundaries of a tensed clause could not be crossed. The latter condition also ruled out (20a), redundantly with the SSC. This redundancy concerning cases like (20a) was eliminated in Chomsky (1980) by replacing the Tensed S condition with the "Nominative Island Condition" (NIC), a condition that made only *subjects* of tensed clauses inaccessible (that framework also introduced the term "Opacity" to refer sometimes to the SSC, sometimes to both SSC and NIC).

However, (19) has conceptual advantages over its predecessors. Note in particular that within the model of Chomsky (1980) it seemed accidental that two different subtheories both singled out subjects of infinitives: Case theory, to account for Case assignment from outside the clause as in (13b) (*I expected John to leave*); and binding theory, to account for binding from outside the clause as in (21b). This is no longer accidental in the GB framework, since the two theories of Case and binding are now integrated, so that both (13b) and (21b) follow from the single fact that the subject of the infinitival is *governed* from outside the clause.

θ-THEORY, (9c), is the theory of "thematic" relations. Formally, θ-theory is somewhat similar to Case theory. It has certain provisions for the assignment of θ- ("thematic") roles, and a well-formedness condition ensuring that all θ-roles have been properly assigned. Like Case assignment, θ-role assignment too requires government.

As far as objects are concerned, θ-role assignment is taken to be directly entailed by the subcategorization frame, in the sense that a verb will automatically assign a θ-role to objects it is subcategorized for. As for subjects, θ-role seems also to depend on lexical specifications, given that some verbs have subjects with a θ-role, while others do not (for instance, *it* of *It seems that . . .* has no θ-role.) However, there is reason to believe that lexical specifications concerning the subject are not part of the subcategorization frame. The reason is that, while subcategorized objects are invariably required, thematic subjects are not. Thus for example in *The city was destroyed* and in *The destruction of the city*, the agent is not expressed. We will thus postulate that the lexicon provides two independent pieces of information: a subcategorization frame, which directly translates into assignment of θ-role to the objects; and the ability to assign subject θ-role, which may or may not translate into assignment of θ-role to the subject, depending on various factors.

The general well-formedness condition on assignment of θ-roles is the "θ-CRITERION" of (22).

(22) θ-CRITERION
        Each θ-role must be assigned to one argument, and each argument must receive one θ-role.

The notion "argument" in (22) refers to phrases that have a certain semantic content, thus all NPs that can potentially refer (not excluding anaphors) and clauses, but not pleonastic elements like *there* and *it*, which will be "non-arguments". The θ-criterion in (22) will be satisfied at D-structure essentially by the definition of D-structure as an immediate projection of the lexicon and a direct representation of thematic relations.[7] But we have already seen how traces make it possible for thematic relations to be expressed at S-structure and LF as well. The θ-criterion can therefore also be satisfied at those levels. The GB theory in fact explicitly requires that it be satisfied at those levels, by means of the principle given in (23).

(23)   PROJECTION PRINCIPLE
        Representations at each syntactic level (D-structure, S-structure, LF) are projected from the lexicon.

Now consider again passive cases, like (24b), whose D-structure is (24a).

(24)a. [e] was read the book
    b. The book$_i$ was read t$_i$

The D-structure (24a) is well-formed with respect to (22)–(23). The passive form *was read* assigns a θ-role to the object it is subcategorized for, just as its active counterpart would, but does not assign θ-role to the subject. We take this to be a general property of all passive forms. The subject position will thus be allowed to remain empty, which will make it

possible for the object to move, giving rise to the S-structure (24b). In
(24b), the object θ-role is assigned to the trace, which 'transmits' it to the
argument *the book*. Alternatively, we may slightly reinterpret (22), and
assume that θ-roles are assigned not only to NPs or Ss, but more generally to CHAINS, where a chain is a sequence of coindexed elements that
contains exactly one argument, like the sequence 'the book$_i$ t$_i$' in (24b).
Single NPs and Ss will also be chains (with only one member). Like
(24a), (24b) will thus also be well-formed with respect to (22) (under the
reinterpretation), and (23).

The principle in (23) has the desirable effect of imposing severe restrictions on the mapping from D-structure to S-structure, since this
mapping must preserve the network of thematic relations in its entirety.
To the extent that it is 'natural' the projection principle provides the conceptual justification for the existence of traces, and quite analogously for
the existence of PRO (which is always associated with a θ-role), both of
which were initially justified by empirical considerations.

We have seen how there is a certain degree of integration between
Case theory and binding theory. Chapter 6 of LGB attempts to further
integrate the subtheories of (9) above, by reducing the Case filter of (10)
to the θ-criterion. The basis for this attempt is provided by the observation that the notion of chain will enable us to maintain a one-to-one association between Case and θ-roles. Thus, in the chain in (24b) there is one
θ-role: the one assigned to the object, and one Case: the one assigned to
the subject. It is thus possible to entertain the idea that Case is a condition for θ-role assignment to chains.[8]

We can see, even on the basis of the three subtheories considered thus
far, of Case, binding, and θ-roles, how this system of conditions and
principles supplants the traditional systems of rules, by taking on the
empirical content of those systems. Consider D-structures, formerly attributed to the 'base'. The portion of D-structures that concerns heads of
phrases and their objects can now simply be attributed to the fact that
subcategorized objects must be assigned a θ-role under government by
their heads. Thus, no base rule like (25a) will have to be resorted to, to
account for (25b).[9]

(25)a. VP → V NP

   b.

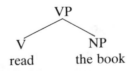

At most, what needs to be specified is whether objects will appear to the
left or to the right of their head: a respect in which languages differ. The

typology of complementation seems to be also to a large extent predict-able without recourse to base rules. For example, the fact that verbs have a very small number of direct objects: essentially one, aside from some rare constructions, can be naturally attributed to Case theory. That is, objects additional to those that can receive Case from the verb will be excluded unless they occur with a preposition that can assign Case to them.

Unlike objects however, the presence of a subject position does not seem predictable from lexical specifications. Thus, in *It seems that . . . ,* there is a subject, *it*, and yet *seem* does not assign subject θ-role. The very existence of pleonastic elements like *it* forces us to still postulate a rule like (26).

(26)   S → NP VP

We may regard (26) as a base rule, or perhaps as a general structural principle requiring that sentences have subjects.[10] When no subject θ-role is assigned, (26) will give rise to D-structure subjects which are either empty, like the one in (24a), or filled by a non-argument like *it*. Neither possibility will exist for objects. But despite (26), we have reasons to believe that the 'base' component can now be largely dispensed with. (Terms like "base-generated" etc. will be used in this work only for expository convenience, to refer to structures which are non-distinct from D-structures; they should not be taken to reflect a commitment to the more traditional view.)

Like base rules, transformations are also undercut by the proposed well-formedness conditions. Consider the passive in (24b), formerly derived from the corresponding active via a complex transformation. As it appears that passive verb forms do not assign Case, movement of the NP *the book* into subject position will in effect be required to ensure Case assignment (by INFL). Were such a structure to be embedded into a larger sentence, principle A of the binding theory would ensure that NP-movement would always be 'local', as it is in (24).

As we will discuss in more detail below, all that needs to be said about passives in the present framework is that they do not assign subject θ-role. From this, the D-structure in (24a) and then the S-structure in (24b) will follow automatically.

While it is still necessary to postulate the existence of movement oper-ations in the syntax as in the transformational framework, it is now other theoretical devices rather than those operations themselves that provide the characterization of the class of possible structures. Thus, all move-ment operations can now be subsumed under one optional and uncon-strained rule: 'Move α', where α is any category.

Turning now to GOVERNMENT THEORY, (9d), we have seen how the notion of government enters crucially into each of the three subtheories we have discussed. However, there are other conditions beside those we have already seen that rely on the notion of government. In particular, there are two that aim to capture the exact distributions of the two types of null elements, trace and PRO. Both of these elements appear to be asymmetrically distributed over subject and object positions, but in opposite ways. Thus PRO is only found in subject position, as shown by (27).

(27) a.   John$_i$ hopes [PRO$_i$ to leave]

b. * John$_i$ watches PRO$_i$
(i.e. *John watches himself.*)

On the other hand traces occur freely in object positon, provided that none of the independent conditions (binding or θ-criterion) are violated, as in (28a), but they do not occur as freely in subject position, as shown by (28b) (Passivization of *hope* is otherwise unproblematic, as in *It was hoped that John would leave.*)

(28) a.   John$_i$ was invited t$_i$
b. * John$_i$ was hoped [t$_i$ to leave]

A similar asymmetry us also found with Wh-traces, as in (29).[11]

(29) a.   The girl that$_i$ you know that [John likes t$_i$] is here
b. * The girl that$_i$ you know that [t$_i$ likes John] is here

These facts are captured by the condition in (30a), which must be interpreted as not referring to PRO, and the one in (30b), which does refer to PRO.

(30) a.   EMPTY CATEGORY PRINCIPLE (ECP)
An empty category must be properly governed.

b.   PRO THEOREM
PRO must be ungoverned.

The notion of PROPER GOVERNMENT that enters into (30a) is a notion of government that *excludes* government by INFL. (Thus, (11) above is in effect the definition of *proper* government.) In general, subjects of tensed clauses are thus governed (by INFL) so as to receive Case, but are not *properly* governed. Given (30a), both (28a) and (29a) will be well-formed since the traces are properly governed by the verb, while both (28b) and (29b) will be ruled out since the traces are not properly governed. Note that this requires postulating that, unlike complements of other verbs, the infinitival complement of *hope* in (28b) does have an $\overline{S}$ (like the tensed complement in (29b)), so that government by the main verb will be blocked (again, we will examine the typology of infinitival complements in more detail in the introduction to Part II.)

In contrast with the trace in (29b), the one in (28b) is not only not properly governed, but is in fact ungoverned, since there is no INFL in the infinitival (at least no tensed, governing INFL). We will then expect that PRO should freely occur in that position, given (30b). And (27a) shows that this is true. At the same time (27b) is correctly excluded by (30b).

While (30a) is postulated as an independent condition of the theory, (30b) is actually derived from the binding theory in the following fashion. If we take the element PRO to be both an anaphor and a pronominal at the same time, as seems plausible given its semantics, then it might fall under both (A) and (B) of the binding theory in (19). But this would give rise to a paradox, since (A) and (B) impose incompatible conditions. The only possibility to avoid the paradox will be that PRO have no governor (i.e. (30b)) and therefore no governing category. Then neither (A) nor (B) would be applicable.

On CONTROL THEORY and BOUNDING THEORY, (9e, f) we will not say much. control theory should account for the range of relations that one finds between the element PRO and its antecedent (when there is one). At present, several issues are still unsettled however. For a valuable attempt to solve some of the problems, see Manzini (1983). We will merely note here, that the behavior of PRO is ambivalent in that, while there are cases of 'long distance' Control like (31a), 'Control' verbs like *hope* never permit long distance Control, as shown by (31b).

(31) a.   They$_i$ thought it would be difficult [PRO$_i$ to see each other]
      b. * They$_i$ said it was hoped [PRO$_i$ to see each other]

PRO of (31b) thus seems to behave just like an anaphor in requiring a local antecedent: a fact which does not immediately follow from the GB approach.[12]

In contrast, the bounding theory is a full-fledged theory with a considerable degree of predictive power. However, since it will not be crucial to our discussion, we will sketch it only very briefly.

This theory includes the SUBJACENCY condition, which holds that any movement operation can cross at must one 'bounding' node, as well as a characterization of the bounding nodes. These seem to vary from language to language: S and NP being proposed for English, $\bar{S}$ and NP for Italian. This very simple system accounts for rather complex sets of data relative to Wh-movement constructions, under the assumption that Wh-movement can make use of all COMP positions, in successive cyclic fashion. In particular, it accounts for various well-known generalizations such as the impossibility of extractions from sentential structures embedded in NPs (the Complex NP Constraint), and from indirect questions (the "Wh-island constraint" of Ross (1967)).[13]

The general formulation of this theory first appeared in Chomsky (1977). Rizzi (1978b) applied the theory to Italian and achieved additional results of considerable theoretical importance (cf. Note 5).

In conclusion, from a broader historical perspective, the GB theory is the result of a gradual conceptual shift from a characterization of grammar in terms of systems of rules to one in terms of systems of principles: a process whose origin can be traced — I believe — to Chomsky's 1973 article 'Conditions on Transformations'. With respect to its immediate predecessor (i.e. Chomsky (1980)), the most salient innovations of the GB theory are: the formulation of the binding principles in terms of the notion of government, the introduction of the θ-criterion and the projection principle, the reduction of the Case filter to the θ-criterion, the ECP and the PRO theorem.

Notes

[1] The role of traces and PRO in determining coreference can be illustrated by the examples in (i).

(i) a.   They$_i$ seem to me t$_i$ to like $\left\{ \begin{array}{l} \text{each other.} \\ \text{*myself.} \end{array} \right\}$

   b.   They said to me that PRO to see $\left\{ \begin{array}{l} \text{each other} \\ \text{them} \end{array} \right\}$ would be difficult.

If the trace is present, the account of (ia) is straightforward. Since we independently know that elements like *each other* and *myself* must have *local* antecedents (see discussion of the binding theory below), the local antecedent available in (ia) will be t_i, which is necessarily interpreted with *they*, whence the impossibility of having 'myself'. On the other hand if there were no trace, it would be very surprising indeed that the object of *like* may only have the more remote *they* as an antecedent, and not the less remote *me*.

As for (ib), note that the subject of the infinitival (PRO) is interpreted differently in the two variants. If *each other* is selected, then the subject of the infinitival is taken to be *they*, while if *them* is selected, the subject is taken to be *me*. If the subject of the infinitival is a real element as in (ib), this fact will receive exactly the same account as the facts in (ii) (on the exact details, see discussion of the binding theory below).

(ii) a.   They said to me that for **them**$_i$ to see $\left\{ \begin{array}{l} \text{each other}_i \\ \text{*them}_i \end{array} \right\}$ ...

   b.   They said to me that for **me**$_i$ to see $\left\{ \begin{array}{l} \text{*each other}_i \\ \text{them} \end{array} \right\}$ ...

But if there is no PRO, this fact would be very mysterious. Also very mysterious would be the coocurrence of *each other* and the pronominal *them* in the same structural position, never possible otherwise (see below).

This kind of observation goes back at least to Chomsky (1973), in which the idea that there are traces was first proposed. The idea was then developed in Fiengo (1974) and other work.

There are also other empty categories being postulated, beside trace and PRO. See in particular the discussion of null subjects and cliticization below (especially chapter 2) and the references cited.

[2] Since we are already using the terms PF and LF to refer to levels, it may be more appropriate to refer to the components or 'branches' as "PF-component" and "LF-component" respectively.

[3] That S-structure is required to express significant aspects of the interpretation has been clear since the late 60's and early 70's. It was this fact that brought about the demise of the ST model, which had semantic interpretation derived from deep structure. Of central importance in this development was Jackendoff (1972).

[4] The underlying motive for this change was the desire to restrict the power of the theoretical apparatus so as to achieve a higher degree of explanatory power. The systems of rules were too rich in the number of options that they allowed in principle, and in this sense they did not provide an explanatory account of language acquisition, which must involve selecting among relatively few options, given the relatively limited amount of evidence it requires.

[5] This difference between NP-traces and Wh-traces has been established only relatively recently, to a large extent as a result of the discussion in Rizzi (1978b).

[6] The basic understanding of the mechanisms of coreference dates back to the mid 70's. Among the most important contributions to such an understanding are Reinhart (1976), Lasnik (1976).

[7] Note that the θ-criterion by definition has to be satisfied at LF too, to the extent that LF provides the interpretation and that thematic relations are part of the interpretation.

[8] Some different provision must be made for chains headed by PRO however, which never require Case, although they have a θ-role.

[9] Even prior to this development, one major simplification of the base component was introduced by the $\bar{X}$-theory (of Chomsky (1970), Jackendoff (1977) and others), which expresses the idea that base rules are categorially neutral. This idea captures the fact that there are significant similarities between the structures associated with different categories (typically, a head plus certain complements and a system of specifiers).

The exact theoretical status of PS rules with respect to the current model is examined in Stowell (1981).

[10] The conjunction of (26) and (23) is sometimes referred to as the "Extended Projection Principle".

[11] We will return later on to the fact that (29b) becomes grammatical if *that* is deleted.

[12] On the other hand, an approach that regards PRO simply as an anaphor (like the one of Chomsky (1980)) fails to account for (31a).

[13] It is assumed that subjacency applies not only to Wh-movement, but to NP-movement as well. However, its effects on NP-movement cannot be (easily) verified empirically since (A) of the binding theory already imposes conditions that are generally tighter than subjacency (recall that Wh-movement does not fall under (A).)

CHAPTER 1

INTRANSITIVE VERBS AND AUXILIARIES

1.0. INTRODUCTION

In Italian there are two particularly striking facts, originally brought to my attention by D. Perlmutter, which suggest that the class of verbs traditional grammar refers to as 'intransitive' is not homogeneous, and in particular that there exist important structural differences between sentences like (1a) and (1b).

(1) a. Giovanni arriva.
        Giovanni arrives.

    b. Giovanni telefona.
        Giovanni telephones.

One of these facts is represented by the grammaticality of (2a) versus the ungrammaticality of (2b).

(2) a. **Ne**   arrivano molti.
        of-them arrive   many.

        Many of them arrive.

    b. * *Ne*   telefonano molti.
        of-them telephone   many.

        Many of them telephone.

The second fact is represented by selection of the aspectual auxiliary, illustrated by (3), and by its exact correlation with the contrast in (2) (i.e. all verbs that pattern as in (2a) also pattern as in (3a).[1])

(3) a. Giovanni è arrivato.
        Giovanni is arrived.

        Giovanni has arrived.

    b. Giovanni **ha** telefonato.
        Giovanni has telephoned.

The material of this chapter will provide several arguments, some directly related to Perlmutter's observations, for the idea that the superficial subject of verbs like *arrivare* in (1), (3), is the D-structure direct object: an idea which corresponds to the "Unaccusative Hypothesis" of Perlmutter

20

(1978) and other related work in Relational Grammar.[2] Other points of central importance in this chapter are the analyses of reflexive, impersonal, and other cosntructions involving the morpheme *si*.

I will begin by addressing the contrast in (2).

1.1. FREE INVERSION

In Italian, virtually any type of sentence with pre-verbal subject has a counterpart in which the 'subject' appears to the right of the verb, as illustrated by the following contrasts.

(4) i.a. **Molti esperti**   arriveranno.
         Many   experts   will arrive.

   b. Arriveranno **molti esperti**.
      will arrive   many   experts.

   Many experts will arrive.

  ii.a. **Molti esperti**   telefoneranno.
         Many   experts   will telephone.

   b. Telefoneranno   **molti   esperti**.
      will telephone   many   experts.

   Many experts will telephone.

 iii.a. **Molti esperti**   esamineranno il caso.
         Many   experts   will examine   the case.

   b. Esamineranno il caso   **molti   esperti**.
      will examine   the case   many   experts.

   Many experts will examine the case.

Let us note the obvious similarities between the (a) and the corresponding (b) cases above. First, they are essentially synonymous. Second, the verb agrees with the phrase in boldface in both cases. Third, the latter phrase bears nominative Case in both, as can be easily shown: for example, with personal pronouns one consistently finds nominative forms *io, tu,* rather than non-nominative *me, te,* e.g.: **Io telefonerò/Telefonerò io** 'I will telephone'. The facts exemplified in (4), have often been characterized by saying that Italian has "free (subject) inversion". This characterization, which has been used sometimes theoretically, and sometimes as a descriptive device, reflects the fact that, given the (a)—(b) parallelism noted, one is tempted to assume the existence of a (presumably late) unconstrained rule that postposes the subject.

Our claim here will be that 'inversion' in Italian is not a unitary phenomenon, and specifically that, while the phrase in boldface in (iib) and (iiib) results from rightward NP-movement, the one in (ib) is simply base-generated in its position, with (ia) being the derived form in this case, obtained by (leftward) NP-movement. On the formal similarities between (a) and (b) noted, we assume, deferring relevant discussion to chapter 2, that the mechanisms which account for nominative Case and verb agreement in (iib), (iiib), will work in the same fashion in (ib), in spite of the different derivations involved. The synonymy of (a) and (b) will also follow from our analysis.

In the following discussion and through the rest of this work I will refer to phrases like the ones in boldface in the (b) examples above, as 'i-subject'. This is meant to suggest 'inverted subject,' but only in the descriptive sense of the latter. We thus intend to avoid implying that a rule of subject-inversion must have applied. The descriptive sense of 'inverted subject' that we thus wish to convey is the obvious one, resting on the noted parallelism between (a) and (b) above, so that a definition of *i-subject* would be something like "The NP_i in a form ... V_j ... NP_i ..., such that the verb V_j agrees with NP_i and such that there is a near-synonymous form NP_iV_j ...". As we noted, NP_i of the latter definition bears nominative Case. I will also use the term *inversion* in the descriptive sense parallel to that of *i-subject*. The terms *subject* and *direct object* continue to refer to configurational notions, as defined in Subsection I.0.2. The superficial similarity of the (b) cases in (4) breaks down with quantified i-subjects, when the quantified NP is pronominalized in the form of the clitic pronoun **ne**, meaning 'of it, of them', stranding a quantifier element (such as **molto, poco, alcuno, due, tre** 'much/many, little/few, some, two, three' etc.). This fact is illustrated by (2) above, and by the following, corresponding to the (b) cases of (4).

(5) i. **Ne**   arriveranno molti.
         of-them   will arrive   many.

   Many of them will arrive.

   ii. *** Ne**   telefoneranno molti.
         of-them   will telephone   many.

   iii. *** Ne**   esamineranno il   caso molti.
         of-them   will examine   the   case many.

We will refer to whatever process is responsible for relating (in the obvious sense) clitic *ne* to the 'gap' which immediately follows the quantifier element, as 'Ne-Cl', for '*Ne*-cliticization', returning in Section 1.4 below to the exact nature of this process.

We will argue that, even aside from their correlation with auxiliary selection which we noted, the different results concerning Ne-Cl must reflect structural differences involving the i-subjects and cannot be attributed merely to lexical properties of the verb. Namely, we will argue that the view that verbs like *arrivare* are somehow lexically marked to allow Ne-Cl from an i-subject (or, alternatively, that *telefonare* etc. are lexically marked to not allow it), would be extremely implausible. Our argument is based on the fact that over a number of syntactically well-defined domains Ne-Cl is absolutely regular: a rare accident if lexical factors played any role.

1.2. THE DISTRIBUTION OF *NE*

To begin, we note that outside of the domain of i-subjects Ne-Cl is entirely predictable, as described informally in (6).[3]

(6)   Ne-Cl is possible with respect to all and only direct objects.

The validity of (6) is briefly illustrated by the following examples.

(7) a.   Giovanni   ne   inviterà   molti.   (dir. object)
         Giovanni   of-them   will invite   many.

         Giovanni will invite many of them.

   b. *Giovanni   ne   parlerà   a   due.   (indir. object)
         Giovanni   of-them   will talk   to   two.

   c. *Molti   ne   arriveranno.   (subject)
         Many   of-them   arrive.

   d. *Molti   ne   telefoneranno.   (subject)
         many   of-them   will telephone.

Furthermore, even within the domain of i-subjects, the possibility for Ne-Cl is entirely uniform over certain subdomains. One such subdomain is that of transitive verbs. With transitive verbs Ne-Cl from an i-subject is always impossible as in (5iii) above, the choice of verb having no effect on this result. In addition, there are three subdomains within which Ne-Cl from an i-subject is systematically possible. The first one is represented by the passive construction, as illustrated in (8).

(8) a.   Molti esperti saranno invitati.
         many experts will be invited.

   b.   Saranno invitati molti esperti.
         will be invited many experts.

   c.   Ne   saranno   invitati molti.
         of-them   will be   invited many.

Again, the choice of verb plays no role here. The second subdomain is represented by one variant of the construction with impersonal-*si*. Consider the following alternation.

(9) a. Si   leggerà   volentieri alcuni   articoli.
     one will read (sg.) willingly a few   articles.

   We will be eager to read a few articles.

   b. Alcuni articoli si   leggeranno   volentieri.
      a few articles one will read (pl.) willingly.

   A few articles will be read eagerly.

As will be argued in 1.6 below and as has been widely assumed in the literature, we take (9b) to be derived from a structure like (9a) via preposing of the object into subject position (NP-movement), much as in passive cases like (8a). As for (9a), we assume that it is a transitive structure, in which the subject role is played by the clitic *si* and the empty category in subject position. Again, a more detailed discussion will be presented in 1.6 below. Since we assume that inversion is always a possibility in Italian, we will expect the form in (10) as the i-subject counterpart of (9b).

(10)   Si   leggeranno   volentieri alcuni   articoli.
       one will read (pl.) willingly a few   articles.

   A few articles will be read eagerly.

By virtue of the plural verb agreement of (10) versus the singular verb agreement of (9a), the phrase *alcuni articoli* will be an i-subject in (10), though not in (9a) (analogous plural agreement occurs in (8a,c)). The variant of the impersonal-*si* construction in (10) systematically allows Ne-Cl from its i-subject (there are three variants: (9a), (9b), (10); only the last has an i-subject), as in (11).[4]

(11)   Se   ne   leggeranno   alcuni.
       one of-them   will read (pl.) a few.

   A few of them will be read.

Once again, the choice of verb has no effect on the result. Ne-Cl will also be possible in the variant (9a) as in (12), but this requires no comment since it follows from the established direct-object status of the phrase *alcuni articoli* in the latter case, under generalization (6).

(12)   Se   ne   leggerà   alcuni.
       one of-them   will read (sg.) a few.

   We will read a few of them.

A third subdomain can be defined by considering alternations like the one in (13).

(13)a. L'artiglieria affondò   due   navi   nemiche.
       The artillery sank   two   enemy   ships.

   b. Due   navi   nemiche affondarono.
      Two   enemy   ships   sank.

We might refer to cases like (13) as "AVB/BV" surface-structure pairs, where V is a verb and A, B are noun phrases (respectively *l'artiglieria* and *due navi nemiche* in (13)). The number of verbs that pattern like *affondare* is rather large.[5] With the BV versions of these verbs Ne-Cl from an i-subject is again always possible, as in (14).

(14)   Ne   affondarono due.
       of them sank   two.

       Two of them sank.

The absence of any lexical variation over these domains makes it seem extremely unlikely that lexical factors could be involved in Ne-Cl at all. (Why should they not affect these domains?) On the other hand the fact that such domains seem to be readily defined syntactically strongly suggests that Ne-Cl should be characterized solely in syntactic terms. Pursuing this possibility, we note that in each of the three cases just discussed, i.e., passives, impersonal-*si* construction, verbs like *affondare* of (13b), the i-subject is rather clearly related to a direct object, as we can see by considering each of the following pairs.

(15)i. a. Il   governo   invitò   **molti esperti**.
          The government invited many experts.

     b. Furono invitati **molti esperti**.
        were   invited many experts.

        Many experts were invited.

  ii. a. Si leggerà   **molti articoli**.
          one will read (sg.) many articles.

         We will read many articles.

     b. Si leggeranno   **molti articoli**.
        one will read (pl.) many articles.

        Many articles will be read.

 iii. a. L'artiglieria affondò **due navi**.
          The artillery sank   two ships.

    b. Affondarono **due navi**.
      sank   *two ships.*

    Two ships sank.

In each of (i), (ii), (iii), the phrase in boldface in (a) is rather unquestion-
ably the direct object of a transitive verb, while the one in (b) (i-subject)
is related to it in at least two ways. In some 'semantic' sense. Thus we
might say that such a phrase is roughly the 'patient' in each (b) case, just
as it is the 'patient' in the corresponding (a) case. And in a 'distributional'
sense, since it is exactly the same class of NPs that can occur in both
members of each pair. We may therefore attempt a second generalization
on the distribution of *ne*, along the lines of (16), where the italicized
portion refers to the relation we have just described.

    (16)   Ne-Cl is possible with respect to an i-subject *related to* a
           direct object.

But of course (16) could not be true by accident, and is in fact too
similar to (6) to be an independent generalization. Let us then take
the passive case in (15ib) and consider exactly how the 'semantic' and
distributional link alluded to above would be expressed.

    Within the theoretical framework we are assuming, S-structure subjects
of passives are D-structure direct objects. From this it follows that such
S-structure subjects will obey the selectional restrictions characteristic of
the direct object of the relevant verb, and that they will be interpreted
as 'semantic' objects.[6] We now clearly want this to be true also
of *i-subjects* of passives, such as the one in (15ib). Namely, we want to
assume that the latter too is a D-structure direct object. One could now
point out that such an assumption would suffice to account for Ne-Cl
in passives like (8c) if the generalization in (6) was taken to refer to
D-structure direct objects. However, if interpreted in this sense, the
generalization would be false, given cases like (17), in which the phrase
affected by Ne-Cl is a direct object in D-structure, but not in S-structure
(thus contrasting with (8c)).

    (17)   *Molti ne   saranno   invitati.
           many of-them will be   *invited.*

    Many of them will be invited.

Clearly the S-structure position must be relevant, and (6) must be taken
to refer to S-structure direct objects, thus excluding (17). We will thus
make the additional assumption that the phrase in boldface in (15ib) has
never been moved from its D-structure position, so that even in S-structure it will be in direct object position. Ne-Cl with i-subject of passives
will now fall directly under the scope of (6). This proposal leaves open
some questions which — as mentioned above — will be addressed later.

In particular, the question of verb agreement in such cases as (15ib), as well as the question of nominative Case (cf. **Fui invitato io** 'was invited I'). The difference betwen Italian and English with respect to cases like (15ib) will also be addressed later (see chapter 3).

Considering now (15iib) (equivalent to (10)) we will claim that there, too, the phrase in boldface has never been moved from its direct object position, so that Ne-Cl from i-subjects in the impersonal-*si* construction (e.g. (11)) will also fall under (6) as is. With respect to base-forms like the one underlying (9a) we are thus assuming that there are three derivational options, corresponding to the three variants of the construction. In one, the direct object is accusative and does not trigger verb agreement, as in any transitive construction (9a)). In the second, the direct object is moved into subject position, where it becomes a nominative subject triggering verb agreement (9b)). In the third, the direct object is assigned nominative Case and induces verb agreement ((10), (15iib)) as a result — we assume — of the same mechanisms that are operative in (15ib) etc. If this is correct, what remains to be accounted for is therefore not only why nominative Case assignment and verb agreement can each operate with respect to a phrase in direct object position, but also why the two *must* go together (as in (10) or (15iib)), versus (9a).

The identification of i-subjects with a direct object position proposed for passives and *si*-construction would be applicable as well to the case in (15iiib), if we could claim that its D-structure is as in (18).

(18)   [e] affondare   due navi.
             sink   two ships.

This kind of D-structure would then give rise to cases like (13b) when NP-movement applies, and to (15iiib) when it fails to apply: the same option we have appealed to for (15ib), (15iib). Ne-Cl as in (14) would then once again fall under generalization (6).

1.3. ERGATIVE VERBS

There are certain advantages in assuming — as we will — that cases like (19) have the structure indicated, namely that they are derived via NP-movement.

(19)   [$_i$Due navi] affondarono t$_i$.
             Two ships sank.

Consider the relation between the subject of (19) and the direct object of (15iiia): *NP affondò due navi.* As we noted above (for the i-subject counterpart of (19), (15iiib)) this relation is quite analogous to the one found between subjects of passives and objects of the corresponding active forms. This relation is also analogous to the one found between the S-structure subject of Raising verbs and the subject of their infinitival complements.[7] Under our analysis of (19), the theory will handle all of these descriptively analogous relations, in analogous fashion, namely by NP-movement (or 'Move α'). If we reject the NP-movement analysis, some lexical mechanism will have to be resorted to, to express the relation in question, namely the identity between the object of transitive and the subject of 'intransitive' *affondare*. But then it will be rather curious that the properties of such a mechanism should match so closely those of a quite unrelated one, namely Move α. Notice in particular that, within the class of *AVB/BV* alternations (like (13)), there is no case where *B* is an *indirect* object, i.e. there is no case of the type **Giovanni pensa spesso alle vacanze** 'Giovanni often thinks about a vacation' which has a counterpart like ***Le vacanze pensano spesso** presumably meaning roughly 'A vacation is often thought about'. While this follows if Move α is involved, since we independently know that the latter operation only moves NPs, not PPs, into subject position, we see no reason why some lexical mechanism should also have the same property.

Notice that this and other considerations are in no way specific to Italian, and suggest the same conclusion for English and other languages. We can thus relate the two verbs *affondare* of (15iii) above, in a minimal fashion. They will in fact have identical subcategorization frames and differ by exactly one lexical parameter, namely by whether or not they assign a θ-role to the subject position.[8] The verb in (20a) will assign such a θ-role so that − given the θ-criterion of subsection I.0.3 above − the D-structure representation will require presence of an argument. The verb in (20b) will not assign such a θ-role, and correspondingly no argument will be found. (In fact there is no need to assume two different verbs: we could assume one verb which assigns subject θ-role optionally.)

(20) a. [L'artiglieria]   affondare due navi.
          $(+\theta)$ *the artillery   sink*   *two ships.*

      b. [e]   affondare due navi.
          $(-\theta)$ *sink*   *two ships.*

Application of Move α to (20b) will then yield (19).

The possibility for non assignment of θ-role to the subject position is established independently of this discussion for various verbs taking sentential complements: Raising verbs, as in the derivations of (21), and others, like those of (22).

(21) a. [e] seems [John to leave] → John seems to leave.
      b. [e] seems [that John left] → It seems that John left.

(22) a. It remains [PRO to talk about John's situation].
      b. It suffices [PRO to talk about it].

But there is nothing in the present theoretical framework that makes such failure to assign *subject θ-role* (henceforth "$θ_s$") contingent on the presence of a sentential complement, or that relates it to the subcategorization frame in any fashion. Therefore we expect such a parameter to vary among verbs which are subcategorized for NP objects, just as much as it does among verbs subcategorized for sentential complements. This is to say that we expect a class of D-structures like (18), i.e. of the type '[e] V NP'.[9] From this point of view it is thus the absence, rather than the presence of such a class of D-structures which would have to be justified (and, again, English and Italian are identical in this respect).

Since *AVB/BV* pairs are thus determined by lexical factors, namely by the double possibility for the value of $θ_s$, we will not expect such pairs to appear with full productivity. Thus, on the one hand we will expect cases like (23a) lacking the counterpart (23b).

(23)a. Giovanni legge il   libro.
        Giovanni reads the book.

  b. *[e] leggere il libro →   Il libro   legge.
                                 the book reads.

On the other hand we will expect verbs that appear in a D-structure frame "[e] V NP" and which lack a transitive counterpart. Our claim is now that a verb like *arrivare* represents just such a case, whence (24).[10]

(24)a. [e] arrivare molti esperti   → Molti esperti   arrivano.
            arrive   many   experts   many   experts   arrive.

  b. *Giovanni arriva molti esperti.
      Giovanni arrives many experts.

Concerning (23), (24), notice that no systematic $[+θ_s]/[-θ_s]$ pairing is found with verbs that take sentential complements either. Thus for example the verbs in (21), (22) do not have $[+θ_s]$ counterparts (cf. '*Bill seems that John left', '*Bill suffices to talk about it'). Correspondingly *expect* of *Bill expects that John will leave* lacks a $[-θ_s]$ counterpart (cf. **It expects that John will leave*). Occasional pairs do exist however, as we might expect, as in (25).

(25)a. John proved [the problem to be unsolvable].

  b. [e] proved [the problem to be unsolvable] →
      [$_i$The problem] proved [t$_i$ to be unsolvable].

The sentences in (25) would constitute an *AVB . . . /BV . . .* pair in the sense of (13) above, where *B* is the D-structure subject of the infinitival.

I will henceforth refer to verbs which are subcategorized for a direct object and which do not assign $θ_s$, such as *affondare* of (19) and *arrivare* of (24a) as "ergative" verbs.[11] Instead of the two classes 'transitive' and 'intransitive' of traditional grammar, I will thus assume the three classes illustrated below.[12]

(26) a. Transitive   Giovanni esamina il   caso.
                         Giovanni examines the case.

    b. Intransitive   Giovanni telefona.
                         Giovanni telephones.

    c. Ergative   [e] arriva Giovanni
                                        arrives Giovanni

                    ($\rightarrow$ Giovanni$_i$ arriva t$_i$).
                                        Giovanni arrives.

It may be worth noting for the sake of clarity that the above classification refers to θ-structure information and not for example to Case marking properties. Thus, by 'transitive' verbs, we do not mean to refer to all and only those verbs that can assign accusative Case. (On the correlation between θ-structure and Case-marking properties, see Section 3.1 below).

The simple assumption that Move α may fail, combined with the ergative hypothesis, will now enable us to maintain (6), repeated here below, as an *exhaustive* characterization of the distribution of *ne*, and correspondingly to explain the noted regularities over certain domains.

(27)   Ne-Cl is possible with respect to all and only direct objects.

Thus, the systematic possibility for Ne-Cl from i-subjects of: passives, impersonal-*si* constructions, and verbs like *affondare* of (13b), will follow from the assumption that in all of those cases the i-subject *is* a direct object, due to non application of Move α.

The possibility for Ne-Cl in these cases will in fact confirm D-structures that we would be independently assuming. In particular we note that Ne-Cl provides evidence for the syntactic (versus lexical) analysis of passives since it distinguishes passives from even the superficially most similar of the copula-adjective constructions, i.e. the so-called "unpassives" (cf. Siegel (1973), as in (29), related to (28).

(28) a. Molte vittime sarebbero riconosciute dalle famiglie.
         Many victims would be recognized by their families.

    b. Molte vittime sarebbero sconosciute alle autorità.
         Many victims would be unknown to the authorities.

(29) a. Ne   sarebbero   riconosciute molti.
         of-them would be   recognized   many.

Many of them would be recognized.

b. *Ne   sarebbero sconosciute molte.
    of-them would be   unknown   many.

The case in (29b) will be ungrammatical because there is no verb **sconoscere** 'to unknow', so that in the latter the i-subject could not be a direct object as it is in (29a).[13]

Let us finally return to the contrasting cases in (5), repeated here.

(30)a. Ne   arriveranno molti.
        of-them will arrive   many

        Many of them will arrive.

  b. *Ne   telefoneranno molti.
        of-them will telephone many

  c. *Ne   esamineranno il   caso molti.
        of-them will examine   the   case   many

The grammaticality of (30a) will follow from the assumption that *arrivare* is an ergative verb, as in (24) above, just like *affondare* of (13b). From now on we will in fact take Ne-Cl as in (30a) to be a diagnostic for ergativity. As for the ungrammaticality of (30b,c), it will follow from the assumption that *telefonare, esaminare* are not ergative verbs (which is transparent for the latter verb), and that i-subjects that arise from movement are not 'direct objects' in the sense that is relevant for (27).

There appear to be two possibilities to ensure this result. One is to assume that such i-subjects are not sisters of V like direct objects as in [$_{VP}$V NP], but rather adjoined to VP, as in [$_{VP}$[$_{VP}$V . . .]NP], and that the syntax of *ne* is such as to discriminate betwen these two positions. Another is to assume that Ne-Cl applies only to those NPs which are direct objects *at all levels.* In this case i-subjects of transitive and intransitive verbs would be excluded regardless of their exact position in S-structure. We will discuss these two (not mutually exclusive) possibilities in the next section. Assuming for the moment that either approach will prove viable, another one of the regularities noted, the impossibility of Ne-Cl from i-subjects of transitive verbs, will also be accounted for.

To conclude: since the hypothesis that there exists a class of verbs with the syntactic characteristics indicated in (26c) (ergative verbs) allows us to express the superficially complex distribution of clitic *ne* by means of the simple statement in (27), we must hold that hypothesis to be true.

1.4. ON THE SYNTAX OF *NE*

The ,exact characterization of the syntax of *ne* will depend on how one treats cliticization in general. On the nature of cliticization, I will start by assuming, as in Chomsky (1981c), that clitics are arguments, bearing θ-roles. This assumption is supported by the difference between cliticization and Wh-movement with respect to the possibility of 'parasitic' gaps: a phenomenon discussed at length in Taraldsen (1979), Engdahl (1983), Chomsky (1981c). Consider the contrast in (31) (adapted from Chomsky (1981c).[14]

(31)a. ?I   libri   **che**$_{op}$ gli   dobbiamo far   mettere **e**$_1$
    the books that$_{op}$ to-him (we) must   make   put

    The books that we should make him put

    nello   scaffale [per non lasciare **e**$_2$ sul   tavolo] . . .
    in-the shelf   for not to leave   on-the table

    on the shelf so as not to leave on the table . . . .

b. *Glieli$_{cl}$ dobbiamo far   metter **e**$_1$
    to-him-them$_{cl}$ (we) must   make   put

    We must make him put them

    nello scaffale [per non lasciare **e**$_2$ sul tavolo]
    in-the shelf   for not to leave   on-the table.

    on the shelf so as not to leave on the table.

The two examples in (31) are parallel, yet while the relation between the relative operator ("op") *che* and the Wh-trace e_1 marginally allows the presence of (or 'licenses') the second gap e_2, the relation between the clitic *li* and the corresponding empty category (henceforth *ec*) e_1, will not analogously allow the second gap e_2. Chomsky accounts for the contrast by assuming that, while the relation between a clitic and an *ec* is a chain (in the sense of Subsection I.0.3 above), and as such involves one and only one θ-role, the one between an operator and a Wh-trace is not. Thus in (31b), e_1 is in a position which is assigned a θ-role, and will transmit this θ-role to the clitic which fulfils it. If the bracketed portion is omitted, (31b) is grammatical. However, if it is not omitted, e_2 will transmit a second θ-role to the clitic, thus violating the θ-criterion. But in (31a), it is not the operator which fulfils the θ-role assigned to the position e_1, but rather the *ec* itself, functioning as a variable. The presence of a second variable related to the same operator will thus cause no violation of the θ-criterion.[15]

With respect to θ-role transmission, clitic-*ec* relations are thus like NP-trace relations, which also — as expected — do not allow parasitic gaps, as shown in (32).[16]

(32)   *Quel libro$_i$ fu   messo t$_i$ nello   scaffale.
    that book   was put   in-the shelf.

[per non lasciare **e** sul   tavolo].
for not to leave   on-the table.

Given our assumption that clitics must bear a θ-role, the projection principle will then require that they do so at every level. This leaves two possibilities concerning derivation of clitics:

(i) Cliticization by movement. In this case the clitic fulfils a θ-role, in D-structure by occupying a θ-marked position, and in S-structure by entering into a chain with the latter position.

(ii) The clitic is base-generated in clitic position, but then it must be related to (say, coindexed with) a θ-marked position even in D-structure.

What the projection principle excludes is that a base-generated clitic may be related to a θ-marked position only late in the derivation (say, in S-structure or LF). Later in the discussion we will see that both of the above possibilities, and only those, are instantiated: the first by impersonal subject clitic *si*, the second by object clitics rather generally. Our task here will then be to determine to which of the existing possibilities *ne* corresponds.

There are theoretical reasons, discussed in van Riemsdijk (1978), as well as empirical reasons which we will come to, to assume that rightward movement of the subject results in adjunction to VP. If this is correct, then the cases in (4ib) and (4iib) above will have the analyses in (33).[17] We ignore for the moment the status of the subject position.

(33)a.

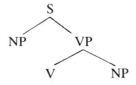

arriveranno molti esperti
will arrive many experts

b.

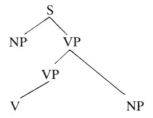

telefoneranno   molti esperti
will telephone   many experts

Since the two post verbal positions of (33a, b) are structurally distinguishable, one might appeal to such a distinction in accounting for the
contrast in (34) (which is that of (5) and (30)).

(34) a. Ne   arriveranno molti.
         of-them   will arrive   many.

     b. *Ne   telefoneranno molti.
         of-them   will telephone many.

However, consider the fact that clitics like *ne* relate to object, or post-
verbal position exlcusively, while others, like impersonal *si* relate to
subject, or pre-verbal position exclusively, as we shall see. Any theory
will then have to specify at least of which kind each clitic is.[18] The
question is whether more is required.

   If we assumed that *ne* was base-generated, nothing more would be
required, and the distinction in (33) would not need to be resorted to.[19]
This is because the proper relation between *ne* and the *ec* would obtain
at all levels in (34a), where no movement has occurred, but would not
obtain at all levels in (34b). In particular it would fail to obtain with
respect to its D-structure (35).

(35)   [molti e_i] ne_i telefoneranno.
         many   of-them   will telephone.

In (35), *ne* would fail to receive a θ-role since, while it can only be
related to a post verbal position, there is no *ec* in such a position to
transmit θ-role. But if we assumed that *ne* cliticizes by movement, the
D-structure for (34b) would be (36), presumably well-formed since *ne* is
itself in a position where θ-role is assigned.

(36)   [molti ne]   telefoneranno.
         many of-them   will telephone.

Further specifications would then have to be added to a characterization
of the syntax of *ne* to the effect of distinguishing between the two post-
verbal positions in (33). The view that *ne* is base-generated would thus
seem to have advantages over the alternative, and I will in fact assume it
is the correct one, even though on closer scrutiny the advantages become
less obvious.

   A movement analysis of *ne* has been developed in Belletti and Rizzi
(1981) (henceforth B&R). B&R also assume the two different structures
in (33), although they assume that they are both derived by postposing
the subject. (Notice that this would eliminate the possibility for our
solution of (34) relying on base-generation of *ne*.) They argue that the
theoretical provision required to prevent Ne-Cl (in 34b) is independently
required to prevent both Ne-Cl and Wh-movement from adverbial
phrases, such as the ones bracketed in (37).

(37) a. i. Mario ha   studiato [due ore].
       Mario has studied   two hours.

   ii.*Mario ne$_i$ ha   studiate [due e$_i$].
       Mario of-them has studied   two.

   b. *Il   premio che$_i$ Mario ha   rimproverato Francesco
      The prize   that Mario has reproached   Francesco

      [per ottenere e$_i$] . . .
      for obtaining . . .

There clearly is a generalization to the effect that certain syntactic processes apply only to positions that bear grammatical relations (subject, object etc.), in the terminology of LGB: "A" positions. The view of B&R that the ungrammaticality of (34b) above falls under such a generalization seems rather plausible and may be correct.[20] In fact, within our discussion, exactly such a distinction between the two i-subjects of (33) in terms of A versus non-A ($\overline{\text{A}}$) positions will be appealed to independently, in′ connection with our rule of auxiliary assignment (cf. 2.2). The advantage of choosing the base-generation analysis of *ne* thus seems to disappear. In addition, it may be argued that there are even disadvantages, on the basis of B&R's account of the ungrammaticality of (38b) parallel to (38a) (and analogous to (7b) above).

(38)a.   Ho   telefonato [a   due amici].
         (I) have telephoned to two friends.

      I telephoned two friends.

   b. *   Ne$_i$ ho   telefonato [a   due   e$_i$].
         (I) of-them have telephoned to two.

B&R suggest (Appendix 2) that the impossibility of cliticizing *ne* from indirect objects, as in (38b) is a reflex of subjacency, assuming (as in van Riemsdijk (1978); Baltin (1978)) that PP is a bounding node. In (38b), Ne-Cl would cross two bounding nodes: NP and PP. But, if *ne* is base-generated, subjacency is likely to become irrelevant since the latter is currently regarded as a conditon on movement, not as a condition on representation (cf. Chomsky (1981c)).[21]

   While we have no alternative to the subjacency account of (38b), we note however that certain other evidence, exemplified in (39), seems to provide further support for our proposal.

(39)a. *   Ne   inviterò   quante   conosci.
         (I) of-them will invite how many (you) know.

   b.   Ne   inviterò   quante   pensi.
         (I) of-them will invite how many (you) think.

      I will invite however many of them you think.

The contrast in (39) must be partly qualified since, while the source for (39b) is perfect, the one for (39a) is somewhat marginal, as in (40).

(40)a. ?   Inviterò   quante   ragazze   conosci.
            (*I*) *will invite how many girls*   (*you*) *know.*

    I will invite however many girls you know.

    b.   Inviterò   quante   ragazze   pensi.
            (*I*) *will invite how many girls*   (*you*) *think.*

    I will invite however many girls you think.

However, even with this qualification, the contrast seems significant. It follows rather naturally from the base-generation hypothesis for *ne*, given the assumption that the phrase *quante ragazze* is moved to its position in (40a), while it is base-generated in place in (40b), an assumption supported by the presence of a corresponding gap in (40a) (cf. 'you know *so many girls*'), but not in (40b) (cf. '*you think *so many girls*'). (For a discussion of similar alternations involving comparatives in English see LGB, p. 81 ff.[22]) If *ne* is base-generated, the ungrammaticality of (39a) will be expected, as analogous to that of (34b), and will be due to the fact that *ne* fails to be related to the corresponding *ec* in the D-structure (41).

(41)   Ne$_i$ inviterò . . . [$_S$ . . . conosci [$_{NP}$ quante   e$_i$]].
            (*I*) *of-them   will invite*   (*you*) *know*   *how many*

It seems natural to assume that locality requirements on the relation between *ne* and its *ec* are violated in (41). We return to the exact nature of such requirements in Subsection II.0.3 below. But in (39b), the phrase [*quante e$_i$*] being base-generated in place, the *ec* can be locally related to *ne* at all levels. The availability of an account of (39) under a movement analysis of *ne* seems much more unlikely, although it cannot be ruled out in principle: it will depend on the exact analysis of free relatives like (40a) and of cases like (40b): a question which we will not address (on free relatives see Bresnan and Grimshaw (1978), Groos and van Riemsdijk (1979)).

    Bearing in mind that arguments against the alternative are not very strong, we will nevertheless assume that clitic *ne* is base generated, like other object clitics, so that the contrast in (34) will be due to the ill-formedness of the D-structure (35).[23]

1.5. REFLEXIVE, ERGATIVE AND INHERENT-REFLEXIVE *SI*

In this section we will provide analyses for the constructions exemplified in (42).

(42) a. Maria si   guarda.
         Maria herself watches.

         Maria watches herself.

     b. Il vetro   si   rompe.
         the glass itself breaks.

         The glass breaks.

     c. Giovanni si   sbaglia.
         Giovanni himself mistakes.

         Giovanni is mistaken.

By doing so, we will in part extend the discussion of ergative verbs
of Section 1.3, and in part prepare the ground for the discussion of
auxiliary assignment in Section 1.7: since all the constructions in (42)
systematically require auxiliary **essere** 'be', we must know exactly what
their syntactic properties are, before we can attempt to characterize the
mechanisms of auxiliary selection.

The three constructions of (42) differ in certain respects, but they are
alike in that they involve the same clitic element which agrees with the
subject according to the paradigm in (43).

(43)	pers.	sing.	pl.
	1	mi	ci
	2	ti	vi
	3	si	si

From now on I will refer to a form in (43) simply as "*si*", for ease for exposition, but it should be borne in mind that there is person and number
agreement.

Beginning with the case in (42a), I will assume that *si* here is a reflexive
object clitic, base-generated in clitic position, and forming a chain with an
empty category in object position, exactly as a non-reflexive clitic would,
whence the parallel analyses of (44).

(44) a. Maria si guarda [e].

         Maria watches herself.

     b. Maria lo guarda [e].

         Maria watches him.

In both (44a), (44b), the object position is assigned a θ-role by the verb,
and this θ-role is transmitted to the clitic, at all levels, thus satisfying the
projection principle. We also assume, as we discuss in more detail in Part

II, that the clitic is a spell-out of the Case-marking features of the verb (as proposed by Aoun (1979), Borer (1981), and others), so that in each case the chain has both Case and θ-role. The difference between *si* and *lo* in (44), will be that the former but not the latter has an antecedent, here *Maria*. The presence of both Case and θ-role in contexts like (44a, b) accounts for the fact that such clitics alternate with lexical NPs as in (45), where both Case and θ-role are borne by *se stessa/Giovanni*.

(45)   Maria   guarda $\left\{ \begin{array}{l} \text{se stessa} \\ \text{Giovanni} \end{array} \right\}$

       Maria   watches $\left\{ \begin{array}{l} \textit{herself} \\ \textit{Giovanni} \end{array} \right\}$

I will refer to the *si* of (42a), (44a) as "reflexive *si*".

In contrast to reflexive *si*, the *si* of (42b) does not have reflexive meaning and does not alternate with an object. We note however that, in a sense, it alternates with a subject, as shown by (46).[24]

(46) a.   Il   vetro si rompe.
       The glass breaks.

    b.   Giovanni rompe il   vetro.
       Giovanni breaks the glass.

Pairs of sentences like (46), we note, are just like the *AVB/BV* pairs of Section 1.3 above, except for the fact that *si* appears in the 'BV' form. We will then assume that verbs like *rompersi* of (46a) are ergative verbs, and will regard clitic *si* of such cases as a morphological reflex of the 'loss' of subject θ-role which marks the derivation of ergative entries from transitive ones: a lexical process, as we have assumed. We will refer to such occurrences of *si* as "ergative *si*". We will assume for the moment that ergative *si* plays no syntactic role at all, being simply an affix. On the difference between *rompersi* and *affondare* of (13b) above, we find no principled way to predict when in a transitive-ergative alternation *si* will appear. We may regard this as governed by lexical idiosyncrasies.[25]

As we now expect, verbs like *rompersi* pass all the tests for ergativity. In particular, they allow Ne-Cl from an i-subject, as in (47), and share with ergative verbs other relevant syntactic properties as we will see.

(47)   Se   ne   rompono molti.
       themselves óf-them break   many.

    Many of them break.

We note that the ergative analysis of verbs like *rompersi* of (46b) is also confirmed by the existence of alternations like (48).

(48)a. Il   governo   ha $\left\{\begin{matrix}\text{dimostrato}\\\text{rivelato}\end{matrix}\right\}$

The government has $\left\{\begin{matrix}\textit{demonstrated}\\\textit{revealed}\end{matrix}\right\}$

[che il blocco degli affitti contribuisce alla crisi edilizia]
that rent-control contributes to the building slump.

 b. [Il blocco degli affitti]$_i$ si   è $\left\{\begin{matrix}\text{dimostrato}\\\text{rivelato}\end{matrix}\right\}$

  rent-control   *itself is* $\left\{\begin{matrix}\textit{demonstrated}\\\textit{revealed}\end{matrix}\right\}$

  Rent-control has $\left\{\begin{matrix}\text{proved}\\\text{turned out}\end{matrix}\right\}$

 [$_S$t$_i$ contribuire   alla crisi edilizia]
  to contribute to the building slump

 to contribute to the building slump.

It would be easy to show that the analysis given in (48b) is correct,
namely that these are indeed cases of Raising.[26] If this is true, then the
cases in (48) share subcategorization specifications: they are all subcategorized for an S-complement, and differ by whether they assign subject
θ-role: those in (48a) do, while those in (48b) − with which we note the
presence of *si* − do not.[27] Plainly, given the exact descriptive parallelism,
we want the same account to carry over to (46). That is: same subcategorization (in this case for a NP-object), and difference with respect to
subject θ-role assignment, which means that *rompersi* is an ergative verb.
    The case of *si* in (42c), which following established terminology we
will call "inherent (-reflexive) *si*", differs from both the reflexive and the
ergative *si*. This can be illustrated by considering (49).[28]

(49)a. Giovanni si   sbaglia.
        Giovanni himself mistakes.

 Giovanni is mistaken.

 b. *Giovanni sbaglia   Piero.
     Giovanni mistakes Piero.

Example (49b) shows that the *si* of (49a) does not alternate with an overt
direct object. This correlates with the fact that it is not interpreted as a
reflexive object. But (49b) also shows that *si* of (49a) does not alternate
with a subject in the sense in which ergative *si* did: compare (49) with
(46).
    We may begin our attempt to analyze (49a) by saying that, unlike
(44a), it is not a transitive structure, thus accounting for the non-object

status of *si*. It must then be either intransitive or ergative. Ne-Cl as in (50) suggests in fact the latter.

(50)   Se   ne   sbaglieranno molti.
        themselves of-them   will mistake   many.

        Many of them will be mistaken.

But what about the difference we noted with respect to ergative *si*? This can in fact be accommodated rather straightforwardly. Recall that among those ergative verbs that do not exhibit the affix *si*, some have a transitive alternant (e.g. *affondare* of (13b)), while some do not (e.g. *arrivare* of (24a)). It is then rather natural to assume that the same situation exists among those ergative verbs that do exhibit the affix *si*, so that a class of cases like (49a) will be expected. If this view is correct, then the *si* of (49a) will be just like the one of (46a), namely a marker associated with lack of θ-role assignment to the subject position, and there will be no difference between the two classes represented by *rompersi* and *sbagliarsi* other than the fact that only the members of the former have transitive alternants in the way we discussed.

We note that, if the ergative analysis of (49a) is correct, we should find no case of inherent-reflexive *si* with an overt direct object, just as we find no ergative verbs with overt direct objects (aside of course from i-subjects). That is to say, at the level of phonologically realized constituents we ought to find only cases of the type "Giovanni si-V (PP)", and no case of the type "Giovanni si-V NP". The latter case would in fact be in violation of a very solid factual generalization to the effect that verbs may have at most one direct object (the second direct obejct here would be the trace of *Giovanni*). Some cases seem particularly revealing in this connection. For instance, there is a verb *sbagliare*, that can take direct objects, as in (51a). Yet its inherent-reflexive counterpart *sbagliarsi* can only take prepositional objects, as in (51b) versus (51c).

(51) a.   Giovanni sbaglia   tutto.
          Giovanni mistakes   everything.

          Giovanni does everything wrong.

     b.   Giovanni si   sbaglia   su tutto.
          Giovanni himself mistakes on everything.

          Giovanni is mistaken on everything.

     c. *Giovanni si   sbaglia   tutto.
          Giovanni himself mistakes everything.

Another case is that of transitive *interessare* versus *interessarsi*, the latter again taking only PP objects, as in (52). (Note however that one might perhaps classify the *si* of (52b) as ergative rather than inherent-reflexive

since the alternation in (52) is rather similar to the *AVB/BV* alternation
we found with *rompere/rompersi* of (46) above).

(52)a. Il   dibattito interessa Mario.
      the debate   interests   Mario.

b. Mario si   interessa $\left\{ \begin{array}{l} \text{al dibattito} \\ \text{del dibattito} \\ \text{*il dibattito} \end{array} \right\}$.

    Mario himself interests $\left\{ \begin{array}{l} \textit{to the debate} \\ \textit{of the debate} \\ \textit{the debate} \end{array} \right\}$.

Mario takes an interest in the debate.

Yet another case is represented by the difference between transitive
ricordare and *ricordarsi* in (53).

(53)a. Giovanni ricorda   la guerra.
       Giovanni remembers the war.

b. Giovanni si   ricorda   della guerra.
    Giovanni himself remembers of-the war.

Giovanni remembers the war.

While these cases thus seem to confirm our ergative analysis, there is
actually a small number of apparent counterexamples, in which *si* is
indeed found in the presence of a direct object. One is represented by
ricordarsi, which can not only appear with a PP object as in (53b), but
also with a NP object as in **Giovanni si ricorda la guerra** 'Giovanni
remembers the war'. (The contrast with transitive *ricordare* remains however, since the latter does not appear with a PP object). In the latter case
si might perhaps be analyzed as a real reflexive: an indirect object, on a
par with the indirect object of (54).

(54)   Giovanni gli   ricorda la guerra.
     Giovanni to-him reminds the war.

Giovanni reminds him of the war.

However there are other cases also involving an overt direct object, in
which *si* does not alternate with a non-reflexive pronoun, such as those in
(55), (56).

(55)a. (Le vacanze) Giovanni se   le   sogna.
      (the vacation) Giovanni to-himself them dreams.

(As for a vacation) Giovanni dreams about it.

b. *Giovanni gliele   sogna.
    Giovanni to-him-them dreams.

(56)a.   (La spiaggia) Giovanni se   la immagina.
         (*the beach*)   *Giovanni to-himself it imagines.*

         (As for the beach) Giovanni imagines it.

   b. *Giovanni gliela   immagina.
      Giovanni to-him-it imagines.

Given their relative rarity, it may not seem too implausible to treat these cases as idiosyncratic, essentially like idioms. I will thus suggest that (55a), (56a) involve an indirect object, specifically a benefactive dative, which must obligatorily be realized as a reflexive clitič. Since an ergative analysis of (55a) and (56a) is thus not tenable, we will correctly expect Ne-Cl as in (57), to be impossible.

(57)a. *Se   ne   sognano le   vacanze   molti.
       to-themselves of-them dream   the vacations many.

   b. *Se   ne   immaginano la   spiaggia molti.
      to-themselves of-them imagine   the beach   many.

To conclude, we reviewed three major classes of cases involving the morpheme *si*. We referred to these three different instances of *si* as "reflexive", "ergative" and "inherent-reflexive" *si*. We argued that reflexive *si* is an object clitic, bearing object θ-role, and that both ergative and inherent-reflexive *si* are affixes with no other syntactic function than marking the lack of θ-role assignment to the subject position, so that the verbs that take this affix are ergative verbs. Ergative and inherent-reflexive *si* are therefore assigned identical analyses. The two classes of verbs will be distinct only in so far as the members of one class (e.g. *rompersi*), but not of the other (e.g. *sbagliarsi*) have transitive alternants in the sense of *A VB/BV* pairs. We further postulated the existence of a small class of verbs like *sognarsi, immaginarsi* of (55), (56), which are transitive and obligatorily require the presence of a reflexive dative benefactive. We may refer to the latter cases as 'obligatory reflexives'.

1.6 IMPERSONAL *SI*

1.6.0. *Introduction*

In this section, we deal with impersonal *si*, some instances of which were encountered in Section 1.2. Like the previous section, this one too relates partly to Section 1.7, devoted to auxiliary assignment (like the cases of Section 1.5, constructions with impersonal *si* also require auxiliary *essere*). However, it also relates to later parts of the discussion, as well as to the previous section in that we examine the differences between impersonal *si* and the other *si*'s.

Our view will be that impersonal *si* differs radically from the other *si*'s: a view defended extensively in Napoli (1973). The analysis we will propose can be seen as an extension with respect to Case theory of the one in Rizzi (1976b).

The type of constructions which exemplify impersonal *si*, are those in (58).

(58) a. Gli   si   telefona   spesso.
      to-him one telephones often.

      We phone him often.

  b. Si   leggerà   volentieri alcuni articoli.
     one will read (sg.) willingly a few articles.

     We will be eager to read a few articles.

  c. Alcuni articoli si   leggeranno   volentieri.
     a few   articles one will read (pl.) willingly.

     A few articles will be read eagerly.

  d. Si   leggeranno   volentieri alcuni articoli.
     one will read (pl.) willingly a few articles.

     A few articles will be read eagerly.

Unlike the *si*'s of Section 1.5, which vary according to the paradigm in (43), the *si* of (58) is invariant. I will henceforth refer to the *si* of (58) simply as SI, thus distinguishing it from the *si*'s of Section 1.5. (I will also give it as SI in the glosses.)

1.6.1. *SI as a Subject Argument*

We begin by considering the cases in (58a, b). It is clear that in such cases, SI plays the role of subject: It is understood as a subject (meaning 'people/one/we'). It is incompatible with an overt subject (cf. ***La gente si leggerà** . . . 'People SI will read . . .'). It is also clear that SI is a clitic, given the following observations: it can occur between other clitics and the verb, as in (58a); it will follow the negation, as in **Non si leggerà quegli articoli** 'Not SI will read those articles', whereas a non-clitic subject will precede it, as in **La gente non leggerà quegli articoli** 'People not will read those articles'; it will resist coordination with an NP, as in ***[Maria e si] leggerà quegli articoli** 'Maria and SI will read those articles', just as clitics do, as in ***Vorrei invitar [lo e Maria]** 'I would like to invite him and Maria'.

We thus take SI to be a subject clitic, so that the analysis for example of (58b), will be as in (59).

(59)   [e] si leggerà   volentieri alcuni articoli.

SI will read willingly   a few   articles.

The natural assumption that the chain *ec*-SI in (59) has subject θ-role,
will account for the fact that SI is in complementary distribution with
other subjects. The thesis of LGB, Chapter 6, that there is systematic
correspondence between θ-role and Case requirements (more precisely,
that all chains — except those headed by PRO — must be Case-marked in
order to bear θ-role), will then lead us to correctly expect that the chain
ec-SI will not occur in environments that fail to assign Case to the
subject, namely in infinitivals, as in (60) (clitics are enclitic to infinitives,
in Italian).

(60) a.   E' necessario $\left\{ \begin{array}{c} \text{telefonare} \\ \text{*telefonarsi} \end{array} \right\}$ a Giovanni.

      It is necessary $\left\{ \begin{array}{c} to\ phone \\ SI\text{-}to\ phone \end{array} \right\}$ *(to) Giovanni.*

    b.   La possibilità di $\left\{ \begin{array}{c} \text{trovare} \\ \text{*trovarsi} \end{array} \right\}$ quei libri è remota.

      The possibility of $\left\{ \begin{array}{c} finding \\ SI\text{-}finding \end{array} \right\}$ *those books is remote.*

    c.   Si è detto quelle cose senza $\left\{ \begin{array}{c} \text{pensare} \\ \text{*pensarsi} \end{array} \right\}$

      SI said those things without $\left\{ \begin{array}{c} thinking \\ SI\text{-}thinking \end{array} \right\}$

What remains to be determined is whether the *ec*-SI chain of (59) arises
via movement (cliticization of SI by movement), or whether it is a base-
generated chain as in the case of *ne* or of object clitics *lo, si* of (43)
above. Recall that what we are excluding is the possibility that a clitic
may be base-generated in clitic position and linked with its *ec* only in the
course of the derivation (cf. 1.4).

    What is relevant to decide between the two options is to note that, as
a subject, SI can be a 'derived' subject. Consider the cases in (61).

(61) a.   [e]   si   è stati   invitati   t

        SI is been invited
        We have been invited.

    b.   [Giovanni] è stato invitato   t

        Giovanni has been invited.

If in (61a) the *ec*-SI chain was base generated, a violation of the projection principle would ensue, since SI would fail to receive a θ-role in the
D-structure (62).

(62)   [e]   si è stati invitati [e]
        └────┘

This is so because, while the passive verb assigns θ-role to the object
position, the relation between object and subject positions does not exist
at D-structure: plainly we want to assume that such a relation is of the
same nature in (61a) as in (61b), namely that it arises by application of
Move α. Notice that any possibility of linking SI with the object position
directly so as to ensure θ-role assignment even in (62) seems precluded,
as SI never bears object θ-role when NP-movement is not involved, i.e. it
is never an *object* clitic, as (63) shows.

(63)   *Giovanni si   prende in giro.
         Giovanni SI ('people')   takes   for a ride.

We thus have to assume for SI a constraint to the effect that it can only
be related to a subject position. This constraint (implicit in our claim that
SI is a *subject* clitic) is the symmetrical counterpart to the one we are
assuming for *ne*, which as we recall, can only be related to direct object
positions.[29] Cases like (61a) thus exclude an analysis of clitic SI as base-
generated in clitic position. On the other hand they do not raise any
problem for a movement analysis. Under the latter, (61a) will have the
D-structure (64a) and the intermediate structure (64b).

(64) a.   [e] è stati invitati [si].

     b.   [si] è stati invitati   t
          └────────────────────┘

Both (64a, b) are well-formed with respect to the θ-criterion and the
projection principle: object θ-role is borne directly by SI in (64a), and by
the chain SI-*t* in (64b).

    We will thus assume that this is the correct analysis, and that SI can
be inserted under any NP-node so long as it cliticizes from subject position. Our argument for a movement analysis of SI has been based on the
observation that the latter appears to interact with movement rules (NP-
movement). Recall that we argued for base-generation of *ne* precisely on
the basis of its failure to interact with movement rules (cf. discussion
of (39) above). Interaction of SI with NP-movement, can indeed be
observed consistently, as with the ergative verb in (65a), and with the
Raising case in (65b).[30]

(65) a.   [e$_i$] si$_i$ è arrivati t$_i$ stamattina.
              SI is arrived   this morning.

        We have arrived this morning.

b. [e_i] si$_i$ stava   per t$_i$ vincere.
    SI   stood   for   to win.

We were about to win.

We now turn to the other variants of the construction with SI.

1.6.2. *Object Preposing*

Let us consider the two remaining variants (58c,d), alongside of (58b) which has already been discussed, as in (66).

(66) a. Si leggerà   volentieri [alcuni articoli].
         Si will read (sg.) willingly   a few articles.

     b. [Alcuni articoli] si leggeranno   volentieri.
         a few articles SI will read (pl.) willingly.

     c. Si leggeranno   volentieri [alcuni articoli].
         SI will read (pl.) willingly   a few articles.

The three variants in (66) are essentially synonymous: (66a, b) are synonymous roughly in the manner in which actives and their corresponding passives are;[31] while (66b, c) are synonymous in the manner in which sentences with pre-verbal subjects and their counterparts with i-subjects are. In fact, since it is rather obvious that the relation between (66b) and (66c) is one of inversion (cf. verb agreement), we can put (66c) aside till we deal with inversion systematically, and concentrate on the analysis of (66b).

As was implicit in some of the preceding remarks, it is quite clear that the bracketed phrase in (66b) is in subject position: it triggers verb agreement; it can undergo Raising, as we will see (cf. (77) below); it can be replaced by a null pronominal ('Null Subject') as in (67a), just as happens with subjects in general, as for example in (67b).

(67) a. (Quegli articoli) Si   leggeranno   volentieri.
         those articles (they) SI will read (pl.) willingly.

As for those articles, they will be read eagerly.

     b. (Quegli articoli) Mi   interessano molto.
         those articles (they) to-me interest   much.

As for those articles, they interest me very much.

It is also quite clear that such a phrase has been moved from object position, as all of the usual diagnostics for movement apply: there is a gap in direct object position; the phrase in question always meets the selectional restrictions that the verb generally enforces on its direct object (a subcase within this generalization is the fact that one can find idiom chunks in the position of *Alcuni articoli* in (66b). For extensive discussion of this and relevant examples, see Rizzi (1976b), and − on the corresponding French cases − Ruwet (1972, p. 3)). There is little controversy on this point, and I will thus assume without further ado that NP-movement is involved in the derivation of cases like (66b).[32] For expository convenience I will refer to this specific instance of NP-movement as "O.P." (Object Preposing).

The question that arises now is whether in the O.P. variant, (66b), SI is derived as in (66a) and the cases of 1.6.1 above, namely whether it is cliticized by movement. The answer appears to be yes. First, one would tend to assume so, just on grounds of theoretical simplicity, but furthermore O.P. cases do exist in which SI itself must have undergone NP-movement. Consider (68).

(68)   [$_i$e] si$_i$ andrà t$_i$ [a comprare quei libri]   appena   possibile.
        SI will go (sg.)   to buy   those books as soon as possible.

Main verb *andare* of (68) is an ergative verb (by all the relevant diagnostics; e.g. Ne-Cl). This means that its subject, here SI, must have undergone NP-movement as the analysis in (68) indicates. Yet at the same time O.P. can occur, as in (69).

(69)   [$_i$quei libri] si andranno ... [a comprare t$_i$] appena   possibile.
        those books SI will go (pl.)   to buy   as soon as possible.

Example (69) thus represents a case where both O.P. has occurred, and SI has undergone NP-movement. By our reasoning in 1.6.1 above, SI must have cliticized by movement in (69). We must note that cases like (69) are rather peculiar: normally extraction of an object from an infinitival complement is not possible, given the binding theory. In Chapter 5 below we will discuss the 'restructuring' process, which makes such extractions possible, and under our analysis of restructuring our point here will stand: that is, it will be the case that *andare* is still an ergative verb even under restructuring, from which it follows that SI must have undergone movement in this case.

If one could maintain that, contrary to our claim, at least in the O.P. variant (66b), SI is base-generated as a clitic, one might then assume that SI 'withholds' subject θ-role, so that the subject position is never θ-marked, and the object is thus moved into a non-θ position. Under this view, the situation in (66b) would be rather analogous to the one we find with passives and with ergative/inherent-reflexive *si* of 1.5 above. But, since base-generation of SI cannot be maintained ever (given (69)), we are forced to assume that the O.P. variant of the SI construction is somewhat unique with respect to the general theory and the θ-criterion in par-

ticular, since what one finds in such cases is two chains, each with one
θ-role, but intersecting in subject position, as indicated in (70).

(70)   [Alcuni articoli] si leggeranno volentieri t

That is, in these cases the subject position will be associated both with
object θ-role, because of O.P., and with subject θ-role because of SI-cliti-
cization. To put it differently, the chain consisting of subject position
and SI will have two arguments in it: the preposed object and SI. This
situation is generally disallowed by the θ-criterion and the projection
principle, which require exactly one argument and one θ-role per chain.

Two points can be made regarding the analysis in (70). The first is
that such an analysis violates more the letter than the spirit of the projection principle. The second is that there are empirical reasons to believe
that such constructions are somewhat exceptional, so that the exceptional
character of the analysis may well seem appropriate. Regarding the first
point, it seems to me reasonable to view the projection principle, namely
the requirement that the θ-criterion hold, not only in D-structure and LF
(here it holds essentially by definition), but — in a certain well-defined
manner — in S-structure as well, as a condition on recoverability of
thematic relations from surface-structure. Let us refer to a representation
of such relations as "θ-structure". From this point of view, the projection
principle ensures that there is always a straightforward algorithm to
derive θ-structure from 'surface' structure, i.e. the structure at the level of
phonetically realized constituents. This algorithm would not be straightforward if chains with more than one argument, or intersecting chains
were generally allowed. As an illustration of this, consider for example a
hypothetical case in which the subject was moved to the right and the
direct object was then moved into subject position, so that from a structure like (71a), one would derive (71b).

(71) a.   Giovanni leggerà   quei   libri.
           Giovanni will read those books.

     b. *[Quei libri]   leggeranno t [Giovanni].

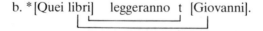

           those books will read   Giovanni.

The surface-structure for (71b) would provide little clue for the recovery
of θ-structure. Compare it with (70). While we have intersecting chains in
both cases, the fact that SI is unambiguously a subject clitic (aside from
the *si*/SI ambiguities which we will discuss below) provides the clue that
the phrase *Alcuni articoli* does not fulfil the subject θ-role. Not so with
the phrase *Giovanni* in (71b), which is not unambiguously a subject.

Also, such information concerning the subject is provided locally by the presence of SI, for SI is always present locally with respect to the subject position, since as a clitic it is part of the verb morphology. Not so with the phrase *Giovanni* in (71b). Furthermore, in spite of the fact that (70) has intersecting chains, one can think of an algorithm to determine θ-structure in (70), analogous to the corresponding algorithm for a passive case (e.g. **Alcuni articoli saranno letti volentieri** 'A few articles will be read keenly'), which has no intersecting chains. In both cases one can determine by looking at the verb morphology that the surface-structure subject does not fulfil subject θ-role and must therefore be linked to the direct object position: in (70) because subject θ-role is fulfilled by SI; in the passive case because passive morphology implies no subject θ-role.

Turning now to our second point, we note that the O.P. variant is limited to third person objects, as in (72).

(72) a. I Rossi / ?Loro } si inviterebbero volentieri.

the Rossi's / they } *SI would invite (pl.) willingly.*

The Rossi's / They } would be eagerly invited.

b. *Io si inviterò volentieri.
   I SI will invite willingly.

*Tu si inviterai volentieri.
   you SI will invite willingly.

*Noi si inviteremo volentieri.
   we SI will invite willingly.

*Voi si inviterete volentieri.
   you (pl.) SI will invite willingly.

The ungrammaticality of (72b) contrasts with the grammaticality of the corresponding cases in which O.P. has not occurred (e.g. **Ti si inviterà** 'SI will invite you', where *ti* is an object clitic, or **SI inviterà anche te** 'SI will invite you too', where *te* is a non-clitic object). The i-subject counterparts of (72b), i.e. the variants analogous to (66c) above, are equally ungrammatical. This suggests that it was indeed correct to regard (66c) as more closely related to (66b) than to (66a). Although there is as yet no precise understanding of why the O.P. variant should be constrained in this particular fashion, the fact that it is not fully productive is not too surprising if it is anomalous with respect to general principles, as we are claiming.[33] No analogous constraints exist in fact for the passive construction which does not share such theoretical anomaly (cf. **Io fui invitato** 'I was invited').[34]

We have seen in 1.6.1 above that in the variant exemplified by (66a)
(*Si leggerà alcuni articoli*), SI is associated with nominative Case, whence
its non-occurrence in infinitivals (e.g. as in (60)). We now consider Case
requirements for SI in the O.P. variant. We note that the analysis in (70)
suggests that even in the latter variant, SI continues to be associated
with nominative Case. Indeed, this seems correct, since SI cannot occur
in infinitivals even if O.P. has applied. Thus, in (73) the O.P. cases are
ungrammatical, just like the simple SI cases of (60) above, whereas the
corresponding passives are grammatical.

(73)a. Sarebbe   bello $\left\{ \begin{array}{l} [PRO_i \text{ essere invitati } t_i \text{ a quella festa}] \\ \quad\quad\quad to\ be\quad invited\quad\quad to\ that\ party \\ *[PRO_i \text{ invitarsi } t_i \text{ a quella festa}] \\ \quad\quad SI\text{-}to\ invite\ \ to\ that\ party \end{array} \right\}$
        (*it*) *would be nice*

It would be nice to be invited to that party.

   b. La possibilità $\left\{ \begin{array}{l} [\text{di } PRO_i \text{ essere accettati } t_i] \text{ è remota} \\ \quad of\quad\quad\quad to\ be\ accepted\quad\quad is\ remote \\ *[\text{di } PRO_i \text{ accettarsi } t_i] \text{ è remota} \\ \quad of\quad\quad SI\text{-}to\ accept\ \ is\ remote \end{array} \right\}$
       the possibility

The possibility of being accepted is remote.

   c. Giovanni parlò $\left\{ \begin{array}{l} \text{senza } [PRO_i \text{ essere interrogato } t_i] \\ \quad without\quad\quad to\ be\quad asked \\ *\text{senza } [PRO_i \text{ interrogarsi } t_i] \\ \quad without\quad\quad SI\text{-}to\ ask \end{array} \right\}$
       Giovanni spoke

Giovanni spoke without being asked.

These facts support the analysis in (70), since it is only by assuming
intersecting chains as in (70) that we can regard SI as receiving Case
from the subject position and thus explain (73).[35,36]

Since the SI of (66b) appears identical in the ways we have discussed
to the one of (66a), we thus conclude that the construction in (66b) is
simply derived from the one in (66a) by NP-movement.

The ungrammatical cases in (73) bring us to a significant difference in
the distribution of SI and *si*. O.P. cases are superficially parallel to cases
involving *si* (in all of its variants). In fact it is well known that there are
classes of sentences which are systematically ambiguous between the '*si*'
and the 'SI' reading (cf. for example Ruwet (1972) for a discussion of the
corresponding French data). One such class is provided by verbs taking
animate direct objects. With such verbs, O.P. will typically give rise to a
sentence identical to a possible instance of reflexive *si*. An example of
this is (74).

(74)   I nuovi assunti   si   presenteranno al   direttore

    the new hired $\left\{\begin{array}{l} SI \\ themselves \end{array}\right\}$ *will introduce   to   the director*

appena   possibile.
as soon as possible.

  i. The newly hired will be introduced to the director as soon as possible.

  ii. The newly hired will introduce themselves to the director as soon as possible.

A second class is provided by the cases of ergative *si* of 1.5 above, which will rather systematically also allow a SI reading. This is due to the fact that, under our definitions of 1.5, verbs taking ergative *si* (e.g. **Il vetro si è rotto** 'The glass broke') are verbs which have transitive counterparts (e.g. **Giovanni rompe il vetro** 'Giovanni breaks the glass'). Since the O.P. variant of the SI-construction is always possible with a transitive verb, we will systematically have the ambiguity of (75).[37]

(75)   Quel vetro   si   è rotto per la   seconda volta.

    that   glass $\left\{\begin{array}{l} SI \\ itself \end{array}\right\}$ *broke   for the   second   time.*

  i. That glass was broken for the second time.

  ii. That glass broke for the second time.

No analogous ambiguity will arise with inherent-reflexive *si*, since we defined inherent reflexives as verbs that lack a transitive counterpart.

In spite of the superficial similarity, all instances of *si* differ from SI in that they can freely occur in infinitivals. Contrasting with the ungrammatical cases in (73), one thus finds the grammatical ones in (76).

(76)a. *Reflexive (reciprocal)* **si:**
    Sarebbe bello [PRO vedersi$_i$ [$_i$e] più spesso]
    It would be nice to see each other more often.

   b. *Inherent-reflexive* **si:**
    Non c'è possibilità [di PRO$_i$ sbagliarsi t$_i$]
    There is no possibility of being mistaken.

   c. *Ergative* **si:**
    Quel vaso era già rovinato anche prima [di PRO$_i$ rompersi t$_i$]
    That vase was already ruined even before breaking.

This difference follows from our analyses. In particular, the grammaticality of (76) follows from the fact that, unlike SI, *si* is never associated

with nominative Case, but either with objective Case (76a), or with no
Case when it is an affix (76b,c). This difference of course implies that
the infinitival counterparts of (74) and (75) will no longer be ambiguous.
Thus, **E' meglio presentarsi subito al direttore**, only means 'It is better to
introduce oneself immediately to the director', and not 'It is better to be
introduced immediately to the director'. Correspondingly, the 'SI' reading
is impossible in (76c).

   Beside accounting for the difference between O.P. cases and the corresponding passives (i.e. the contrasts in (73)) and for the difference
between SI and *si* (i.e. the contrast between (73) and (76)), our analysis
will account for a class of well-known Raising/Control alternations. Consider the result of embedding an instance of O.P. such as (77a) under a
Raising predicate, as in (77b).[38]

   (77)a.   [Questi articoli] si sono già   letti t
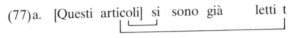

             these   articles SI are   already read
          These articles have already been read.

      b.   [Questi articoli] risultano [t' essersi già   *letti t*]

             these   articles turn out   SI-to be already read
          These articles turn out to have already been read.

The grammaticality of (77b) follows from the same assumptions we made
to account for (77a). In (77a) Case requirements for SI are satisfied in
that SI is in a chain with a position that is assigned Case. This is true in
(77b) too, where the matrix subject is assigned Case.[39,40] If we now select,
in a configuration like (77b), an embedded verb that takes animate direct
objects, we will produce cases like (78a), which have superficially similar,
and yet ungrammatical, Control counterparts like (78b).

   (78)a   [$_i$*Quei* prigionieri] risultavano [t'$_i$ essersi già   liberati t$_i$]
             those prisoners   turned out   SI-to be already freed
          Those prisoners turned out to have already been freed.

      b. *[$_i$Quei prigionieri] vorrebbero [PRO$_i$ essersi già   liberati t$_i$]
             those prisoners   would want   SI-to be already freed
          Those prisoners would like to have already been freed.

The ungrammaticality of (78b) will be due to the fact that, unlike ([Quei
prigionieri], t'$_i$) of (78a), the corresponding sequence ([$_i$Quei prigionieri],
PRO$_i$) does not constitute a chain, since the two elements involved have

independent θ-roles. SI in (78b) will thus fail to be associated with nominative Case, and the ungrammaticality of (78b) will be exactly analogous to that of the cases in (73). Once again, the corresponding passive **Quei prigionieri vorrebbero essere già stati liberati** 'Those prisoners would want to have already been freed' is grammatical, like its English counterpart.[41]

In this section we have thus provided an analysis of two variants of the construction with (impersonal) SI. We argued that the variant we referred to as "O.P." is derived from the other via movement of the direct object into subject position. We argued that in both variants SI must be cliticized by movement, since in some cases it appears to undergo NP-movement in the course of the derivation. We also argued that, in both variants, SI is associated with nominative Case. This accounts for the fact that both variants are limited to finite clauses: a respect in which superficially similar instances of SI and *si* differ.[42] O.P. cases will differ in this respect also from parallel passive cases.

We have seen that precisely those considerations that lead to an explanation for the distribution of the O.P. variant, namely the assumption that SI must be linked to a position receiving nominative Case, give the analysis an apparently anomalous character with respect to general principles. In this connection we noted that O.P. constructions are limited to third person derived subjects (a second major difference with respect to *si* and passives) and suggested that this limitation may in face be related to the anomalous character of the construction which our analysis expresses.

1.7. AUXILIARY ASSIGNMENT

In this section, we will discuss the general distribution of the two aspectual auxiliaries **essere** 'be' and **avere** 'have' (henceforth 'E', 'A' respectively), and provide a theory of auxiliary selection. As we noted in 1.0 above, one of the most striking facts suggesting that verbs like *arrivare* are not simply 'intransitive' is the difference in auxiliary selection of (79).

(79) a.   Giovanni è arrivato.
   Giovanni has (E) arrived.

    b.   Giovanni ha telefonato.
   Giovanni has (A) telephoned.

In its rough form, an argument for the ergative analysis of *arrivare* based on the contrast of (79) is rather analogous to the one of 1.2 above based on Ne-Cl. That is, the view that *arrivare* and *telefonare* of (79) are both intransitive verbs would imply that auxiliary selection must be determined by lexical factors, and we would then be at a loss to account for the regularities observable over syntactically well-defined domains: always E with passives and with all constructions involving *si* or SI (relevant data will be given below); always E with the second member of the *AVB/BV* pairs we discussed in 1.2 (cf. (13)) and always A with transitive verbs, so that within such *AVB/BV* alternations one will systematically observe the auxiliary switch of (80).

(80) a.   L'artiglieria **ha** affondato due navi nemiche.
          The artillery has (A) sunk two enemy ships.

      b.   Due navi nemiche **sono** affondate.
          Two enemy ships have (E) sunk.

In the next few pages, this and related arguments will be presented in more detail, bringing into the discussion as well the distribution of past participle agreement ('pp agreement'), which appears closely related to that of the auxiliaries. We begin with a systematic review of the facts.

Auxiliary E overlaps rather conspicuously in its distribution with pp agreement. In particular, one finds both E and pp agreement in the following cases: passives, cases of reflexive *si*, and ergative verbs, where we define such a class in terms of the possibility of Ne-Cl discussed in 1.2, 1.3 above. In such cases, illustrated in (81), the pp agrees in gender and number with the subject.

(81) a.   Passive: Maria è stata accusata.
                        Maria is been accused (fem.)   (E; pp ag't)
          Maria has been accused.

      b.   Reflexive *si*: Maria si   è accusata.
                        Maria herself is accused (fem.)   (E; pp ag't)
          Maria has accused herself.

      c.   Ergative V: Maria è arrivata.
                        Maria is arrived (fem.)   (E; pp ag't)
          Maria has arrived.

Auxiliary E and pp agreement appear dissociated in two cases. The first dissociation, involving pp agreement but no E, is found with (non-reflexive) direct object clitics, where the pp will agree in gender and number with the clitic, as in (82).[43]

(82)   Giovanni la   ha   accusata.
          Giovanni her has accused (fem.)   (A; pp ag't)
          Giovanni has accused her.

The second dissociation, involving E but no pp agreement, is found with one variant of the SI-construction, as in (83).

(83)   Si è telefonato a Giovanni.
        SI is telephoned to Giovanni   (E; no pp ag't)
        We have phoned Giovanni.

We note however that, if intransitive *telefonare* of (83) is replaced by an ergative verb like *arrivare*, then pp agreement will be found, as in (84), where we assume plural agreement is with SI.

(84)   Si è appena arrivati.
        SI is just   arrived (pl.)   (E; pp ag't)
        We have just arrived.

The descriptive generalization behind the contrast between (83) and (84) is that pp agreement in this variant of the SI-construction will appear in all and only those cases which require pp agreement independently of the presence of SI, namely in passive, reflexive and ergative cases as in (81). Thus we do not find pp agreement in (83) since we do not find it in **Maria ha telefonato a Giovanni** 'Maria has telephoned Giovanni', but we do find it in (84) since we find it in (81c). Correspondingly we will find it in (85a, b), since we find it in (81a, b) (assuming *si si* → *ci si.*)

(85)a. Si è stati accusati.
        SI is been accused (pl.)   (E; pp ag't)
        We have been accused.

   b. Ci   si era accusati
       themselves SI was accused (pl.)   (E; pp ag't)
       We have accused ourselves/each other.

We put aside the O.P. variant of the SI-construction for the moment.

Our analyses of the various constructions involved will now allow us to express rather simple generalizations regarding the distribution of both E and pp agreement. In particular it appears that in all the cases requiring E the subject enters into a certain relation with another element, while in all the cases requiring pp agreement it is the direct object that enters into a certain type of relation. Specifically, we propose the two rules of (86).

(86)a. ESSERE ASSIGNMENT: The auxiliary will be realized as *essere* whenever a '*binding relation*₁' exists between the subject and a 'nominal contiguous to the verb'.

   b. PAST PARTICIPLE AGREEMENT: A past participle will

agree (in gender and number) with an element holding a
'*binding relation*₁' with its 'direct object'.

By "*binding relations*₁," we mean a subset of the binding relations in the
usual sense: a matter to which we will return. Provisionally we may
assume this to refer to binding relations, generally. The other two phrases
enclosed in quotes in (86) are defined in (87).

> (87) a. A 'nominal contiguous to the verb' is a nominal which is
>   either part of the verb morphology, i.e. a clitic, or a 'direct
>   object'.
>
>   b. A 'direct object' is an NP in an A-position governed by the
>   verb.

As in LGB, we identify as A-positions those positions that bear grammatical relations, like those of subject or object, to the exclusion of
adjuncts. The notion of direct object of (87b) may thus simply be
regarded as a technically more precise version of the notion we have
been using in general. However, (87b) actually makes the non-trivial
claim that the subjects of certain infinitivals, which are governed by the
verb, should behave analogously to direct objects with respect to E
assignment and pp agreement. But we put this claim aside for the
moment.

The rule in (86a), given the definition (87a), will allow for two subcases of E assignment: in one subcase there is a binding relation between
the subject and a clitic, in the other there is a binding relation between
the subject and the direct object, as in (88) (where the NPs do not necessarily have phonological content).

> (88)   ESSERE ASSIGNMENT
>
>   i. NP cl-V . . . .
>
>   ii. NP V NP . . .

Since, due to extrinsic factors, an element binding a direct object can
only be either a clitic or a subject, the rule in (86a) will also allow for
two subcases: in one there is a binding relation between a clitic and the
direct object, in the other a binding relation between the subject and the
direct object, as in (89).

> (89)   PAST PARTICIPLE AGREEMENT
>
>   i. . . . cl-V NP . . .
>
>   ii. NP V NP . . .

The idea behind (86) is that E assignment and pp agreement are essentially symmetrical systems: compare (88i) with (89i), overlapping in part: note the identity of (88ii) and (89ii).

We will now see how the system works in the cases we reviewed. Consider those in (81), where E and pp agreement cooccur, in the analyses we are assuming, given in (90).

(90)a. [Maria] è stata accusata t

      Maria   is been accused (fem.)

  b. [Maria] si   è accusata [e]

      Maria   herself is accused (fem.)

  c. [Maria] è arrivata t

      Maria   is arrived (fem.)

The passive in (90a) and the ergative case in (90c) are, for our purposes, identical: they instantiate (88ii)–(89ii), whence both E and pp agreement.[44] As for the reflexive case in (90b), the relation between the clitic and the *ec* will trigger pp agreement, as an instance of (89i), while the relation between the reflexive clitic and its antecedent will trigger E assignment, as an instance of (88i).

The account we just gave of (90c) provides the first argument within this section for the ergative analysis of verbs like *arrivare*: if the latter verbs were intransitive, there would be no reason why they should fall together with passive and reflexive constructions with respect to auxiliary assignment.

Our proposal, of 1.5 above, that verbs taking ergative and inherent-reflexive *si* should be analyzed as ergative verbs like *arrivare* of (90c) will account for the fact that those verbs, too, systematically exhibit both E and pp agreement, as in (91).

(91)a. [La tazza] si   è rotta t

      the cup   itself is broken (fem.)   (E; pp ag't)
      The cup has broken.

  b. [Maria] si   è sbagliata t

      Maria   herself is mistaken (fem.)   (E; pp ag't)
      Maria has been mistaken.

Note that our discussion is thus giving different reasons for E and pp agreement with reflexive *si* on the one hand, and with ergative and inherent-reflexive *si* on the other. This matter will be partially reconsidered in 6.3.1 below.

Consider now the cases (82), (83) above, in which E and pp agreement are dissociated, in their analyses, as in (92).

(92)a.   Giovanni la   ha   accusata [e]

       Giovanni her has accused (fem.)   (pp ag't only)

    b.   [e] si è telefonato a   Giovanni

        SI is telephoned to Giovanni   (E only)

The cases in (92) instantiate respectively the configurations of (89i) and (88i). The facts are therefore as expected.[45]

The common account of pp agreement in (90c) (*Maria è arrivata*) and (92a) will represent a second argument for the ergative analysis of verbs like *arrivare*, since it is only if we accept the latter analysis that those two instances of pp agreement can be collapsed.[46]

The difference in pp agreement between (92b) and the cases in (84), (85), repeated here below with their analyses, will also follow from (86).

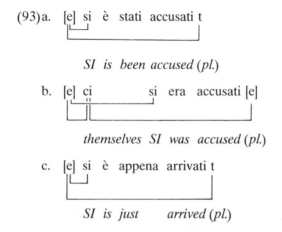

(93)a.   [e] si è stati accusati t

       SI is been accused (pl.)

    b.   [e] ci   si era accusati [e]

       themselves SI was accused (pl.)

    c.   [e] si è appena arrivati t

       SI is just   arrived (pl.)

The cases in (93) are the 'impersonal' counterparts to those in (90). As such, their analyses involve the same relations as those of (90), in addition to a relation between the empty subject position and clitic SI. Thus, pp agreement in each of (93), contrasting with the lack of it in (92b), will be due to the fact that in each of (93), though not in (92b), there is a relation involving the direct object position, just as in (90). Regarding assignment of E in (93), we note that — according to our account — it is actually overdetermined since there are now two relations involving the subject position: one as in (90), the other due to the clitic status of subject SI. No difficulty arises in this connection.

There is an apparent paradox in the fact that SI appears plural for pp agreement (cf. *accusati*, etc.) but singular for verb agreement (cf. *è*), as in (93). We suggest the following account of this. Let us assume that SI only bears gender and number features, in particular that it is plural and either gender (the feminine counterpart to (93) will be *Si è state accusate*, etc.), but lacks the feature 'person', as implicit in the definition 'Impersonal *si*' which we are using. Past participle agreement (recall: in gender and number) will thus be able to operate correctly, yielding plural inflection. However verb agreement will fail if we suppose that such agreement always requires both person and number features. The verb will thus remain in its neutral, third person singular form.[47]

A partially parallel account can be given of the fact that, while third person clitics always induce pp agreement as in (92a), first and second person clitics optionally fail to induce agreement, as for example in (94).

(94) a. Maria,
       Maria,

   i.   ti   ho   visto
      (I) you have seen   (no ag't)

   ii. ti   ho   vista
      (I) you have seen (fem.)   (ag't)

b. Maria e Paola,
   Maria and Paola,

   i.   vi   ho   visto
      (I) you have seen   (no ag't)

   ii. vi   ho viste
      (I) you have seen (fem. pl.)   (ag't)

We will relate this to the fact that, unlike third person forms, first and second person direct object clitics are not differentiated for gender, as in the paradigm (95).

(95)   DIRECT OBJECT CLITICS (NON-REFLEXIVE)

pers.		sg.	pl.
1		mi	ci
2		ti	vi
3	*masc.*	lo	li
3	*fem.*	la	le

Specifically, we will assume that first and second person clitics are ambiguous as to whether or not they bear abstract gender-features, whereas third person clitics always do bear them, as they overtly show. Let us say tht such ambiguity arises from the option of assigning abstract gender features contextually. If this option is taken, then pp agreement will unproblematically occur, as in (94ii). If the option is not taken, the clitic will lack gender features, and pp agreement, which we assume requires both gender and number features, will fail, leaving the past participle in its unmarked, masculine singular form as in (94i), even though the clitic may be plural, as in (94bi).[48]

Returning to the contrast in pp agreement between *Si è telefonato* and *Si è arrivati* ((92b)−(93c), or (83)−(84)), we note that our account of the latter provides a third argument for the ergative analysis of *arrivare*, since if both *arrivare* and *telefonare* were intransitive verbs, one would see little reason why they should differ in this respect.

We have thus accounted for all of the cases which we reviewed at the outset, as well as for some facts directly related to them. We now turn to a few other cases. One of these is the O.P. variant of the SI-construction, which always exhibits both E and pp agreement (with the preposed object) as in (96), given in the analysis of 1.6.2.

(96)   [Quegli articoli] si sono già   letti t
        |___|
        |_____|

        those   articles SI are   already read (pl.)   (E; pp ag't)
        Those articles have already been read.

This example is as predicted, since the relation between subject and object will trigger both E assignment and pp agreement. Redundantly, E will be determined by the relation between SI and the subject position.

Another case that appears to fall within our predictions is that of clitic *ne*, which induces pp agreement as in (97).

(97)   Ne   ho   visti   molti [e]
        |_____|

        (I) of-them have seen (pl.) many   (ag't)
        I have seen many of them.

Such cases will follow if we adopt the assumption of Belletti and Rizzi (1981) that the *ec* in (97) is governed by the verb (an assumption required by the Empty Category Principle), as well as their assumption that this *ec* is essentially a NP, not a PP. Then the latter would be a direct object in the sense assumed in (86b) (given (87b)), whence pp agreement.[49]

Further comment, however, is required by the case of pp agreement with indirect object reflexive clitics, illustrated by the following contrast.

(98) a. Giovanni le   ha $\left\{\begin{array}{c}\text{comprato}\\ \text{*comprata}\end{array}\right\}$ un libro.

Giovanni to-her has $\left\{\begin{array}{c}\textit{bought}\\ \textit{bought (fem.)}\end{array}\right\}$ *a book*   (no ag't only)

Giovanni has bought her a book.

  b. Maria si   è $\left\{\begin{array}{c}\text{??comprato}\\ \text{comprata}\end{array}\right\}$ un libro.

Maria to-herself is $\left\{\begin{array}{c}\textit{bought}\\ \textit{bought (fem.)}\end{array}\right\}$ *a book*   (ag't only)

Maria has bought herself a book.

Regarding the lack of agreement in (98a), we assume that the *ec* to which the clitic is related is a PP, not an NP, so that pp agreement as in (86b) will be inapplicable (given (87b)). But the same considerations ought to apply to (98b). It seems reasonable to attempt to relate the contrast in (98) to the fact that, unlike non-reflexives, indirect object reflexive clitics are systematically non-distinct morphologically from their direct object counterparts. Thus, while the paradigm in (95) contrasts with the one in (99) at least in the third person, the one in (43) above (*mi, ti, si; ci, vi, si*) is equally relevant to both direct and indirect objects. (On the fact that pp agreement always occurs even though reflexive clitics are not overtly marked for gender, cf. Note 48).

(99)   INDIRECT OBJECT CLITICS (NON-REFLEXIVE)

pers.		sg.	pl.
1		mi	ci
2		ti	vi
3	*masc.*	gli	gli (loro)
3	*fem.*	le	gli (loro)

However, rather than attempting to build these considerations into (86b) so as to extend it to cover cases like (98b), we will note that the latter cases of pp agreement do not have the same status as the cases covered by the non-extended rule in (86b). Consider in fact (100), where both a reflexive indirect object clitic and a non-reflexive direct object clitic are present.

(100) Maria se   li   è $\left\{\begin{array}{c}\text{comprati}\\ \text{*comprata}\end{array}\right\}$

Maria to-herself them is $\left\{\begin{array}{c}\textit{bought (pl.)}\\ \textit{bought (fem.)}\end{array}\right\}$ (ag't with *them* only)

Maria has bought them for herself.

In (100), while agreement with the direct object clitic as prescribed by (86b) is obligatory and unproblematic, agreement with the indirect object reflexive is impossible. The case in (100) contrasts with the one in (101), a case of 'restructuring' in which, as will be clear from the discussion in 5.7 below, the past participle ought to agree with both the subject (*Maria*) and the clitic *li*, by rule (86b).

(101)   Maria li   è $\left\{ \begin{array}{l} \text{?andata} \\ \text{??andati} \end{array} \right\}$ a comprare.

Maria them is $\left\{ \begin{array}{l} \textit{gone (fem.)} \\ \textit{gone (pl.)} \end{array} \right\}$ *to buy*   (? ag't with *Maria*;
                                                                                                   ?? ag't with *them*)

Maria has gone to buy them.

These facts suggest that, while cases directly covered by (86b) have roughly equal status, agreement with indirect object reflexives is some-what weaker. If we were to extend the formulation of pp agreement to the latter case, we would thus have to build into the formulation an ap-propriate hierarchical condition to the effect that in the case of conflict, agreement with an indirect object reflexive can be overruled as in (100), while other agreements cannot, as in (101). Rather than attempting to extend the formalism with this added condition, we will leave (86b) as is and simply assume that it refers to the cases of agreement at the top of the hierarchy, leaving the (weaker) agreement of (98b) unexpressed.[50]

Let us now turn to the definition of *binding relation$_1$* in (86). Among binding relations, namely relations between an antecedent and an anaphor, some do not trigger the system in (86). Thus, while we regard the element **se stesso** 'himself' as an anaphor, just like its English coun-terpart, neither E nor pp agreement occurs in (102).

(102)   Maria ha   accusato se stessa.
        Maria has accused   herself   (A; no pp ag't)

In general, the binding relations which determine either E or pp agree-ment, seem to be those which involve transmission of θ-role or, even more accurately, those which constitute chains, in the sense of LGB. There is one problem however in assuming that *binding relations$_1$* are all and only the chain-forming relations. The problem is that the relation between the subject and reflexive *si* in (90b) (*Maria si è accusata*) is presumably not a chain in the usual sense since *Maria* and *si* do not share a θ-role. We might attempt to circumvent this difficulty by assum-ing (103) under a certain interpretation.

(103)   A *binding relation*₁ is a binding relation other than a relation
between elements of independent θ-roles.

While *si* in (90b) has a θ-role transmitted by the *ec* in object position, it
does not have one which is independent in absolute terms. Its θ-role is
only independent of the NP in subject position. Under this interpretation
of 'independent' in (103), the relation between *Maria* and *si* in (90b) is a
*binding relation*₁, just like the various clitic-*ec* and NP-trace relations of
(90)—(93) etc., while the one between *Maria* and *se stessa* is not. The issue of the exact nature of the bifurcation which E assignment/pp agreement produce within the set of binding relations is an important one, to
which we will return (cf. 4.6, 6.1). For the moment, let us assume (103),
under the interpretation discussed.

In this section we have thus argued that the ergative analysis of verbs
that select auxiliary *essere* permits us to capture important generalizations
about auxiliary assignment and past participle agreement. In particular, it
permits us to hold the view that selection of *essere* and past participle
agreement are due to certain well-defined aspects of syntactic representation at the S-structure level.

The discussion in this section, combined with the one in 1.2, 1.3
above, accounts for the exact correspondence between Ne-Cl from an
i-subject and selection of auxiliary *essere* brought to light by Perlmutter.
Both of these are now properties of ergative verbs, and will in fact serve
as our two major diagnostics distinguishing ergatives from intransitives.

The account of *essere* assignment and past participle agreement we
provided rests on the existence of empty categories in S-structure. Therefore, to the extent that it is adequate, it provides evidence for the
existence of such empty categories. In particular, we note that the rules
we formulated appear to cut across empty and non empty elements: thus
the subject-trace relation of (90a) will trigger E assignment, just like the
subject-*si* relation of (90b). The factual parallelism would not be equally
expected if there was no trace in (90a).

1.8. LINEAR ORDER

We will conclude this chapter, essentially devoted to establishing the
difference between ergative and intransitive verbs, by reviewing a few
more differences observable between the two classes. These, like Ne-Cl
and auxiliary selection, will support our analysis. The general thrust of
our observations in this section is that if one considers cases of inversion,
the i-subject of an ergative verb will precede certain complements of the
verb, whereas the i-subject of an intransitive verb will follow them. This
is predicted under our hypothesis, as we will see.

Our first case concerns sentential complements. As we discussed in 1.3 above, we assume that in D-structure intransitive verbs appear as in (104a), while ergative verbs will appear as in (104b) (where NP's are arguments).

(104) a. NP V   (Intransitive)

    b. [e] V NP   (Ergative)

If we now consider the counterparts to (104) that take sentential complements, we will have the D-structures of (105).[51]

(105) a. NP V S

    b. [e] V NP S

Cases which must originate from D-structures like (105a, b) are those in (106a, b), where the (unanalyzed) S-complement is within brackets.

(106) a. Giovanni sperava [di risolvere il   problema]
         Giovanni hoped   to solve   the problem

    b. Giovanni interverrà   [a risolvere il   problema]
         Giovanni will intervene to solve   the problem

It is clear that *intervenire* of (106b) is an ergative verb, while *sperare* of (106a) is not (cf. **Giovanni è intervenuto . . .** 'Giovanni has intervened . . .' (aux. E), **Giovanni ha sperato . . .** 'Giovanni has hoped . . .' (aux. A)). We now note that the superficial similarity of the examples in (106) gives way to the contrast in (107).[52]

(107) a. ?? Sperava Giovanni [di risolvere il problema]
          hoped   Giovanni to solve   · the problem

    Giovanni hoped to solve the problem.

    b.   Interverrà   Giovanni [a risolvere il problema]
          will intervene Giovanni to solve   the problem

    Giovanni will intervene to solve the problem.

This contrast follows from our assumption that *pensare* and *intervenire* are associated with the two different D-structures of (105). In the case of *intervenire*, the i-subject will be expected to appear in its D-structure position, as in the cases discussed in 1.3 above, a position which precedes the S-complement as (105b) indicates. In the case of *sperare*, we expect an i-subject to arise only by rightward movement to a VP external position (VP-adjunction cf. (33b) above). The sequence in (107a) is therefore excluded, the expected order being the one in (108).

(108) ? Sperava [di risolvere il   problema] Giovanni
      hoped   to solve   the problem Giovanni

On the marginality of (108) we note that, quite generally, VP-final position of the i-subject yields unnatural results when a 'heavy' complement precedes: perhaps a reflex of a general condition requiring that heavy phrases follow less heavy ones. (Examples like (108) will in fact improve if the i-subject is heavier, e.g. **la sorella di Giovanni** 'Giovanni's sister.)

Like ergative verbs, passives also allow the i-subject to precede a sentential complement, as in (109).

(109)   Fu   mandato Giovanni [a risolvere il   problema]
        was sent   *Giovanni   to solve   the problem*

Giovanni was sent to solve the problem.

This will follow from the same considerations discussed for (107b), namely from the assumption that i-subjects can appear in their D-structure position. The phrase **Giovanni** will thus be in the same position in (109) as in its active counterpart (110).[53]

(110)   Ho mandato Giovanni [a risolvere il   problema]
        I have sent   Giovanni   to solve   the problem

Note that the similarity in linear order between (109) and (110) provides evidence that NP-movement can fail, and in turn that NP-movement exists. That is, in **Giovanni fu mandato [a risolvere il problema]** 'Giovanni was sent to solve the problem' the phrase *Giovanni* must be base-generated in direct object position (and then moved), since there is a corresponding case (i.e. (109)) in which it in fact appears in such position. A quite parallel point was made in 1.3 on the basis of Ne-Cl (cf. (28), (29) and discussion).

Contrasts between ergative and non-ergative verbs like (107) are rather typical. A sample of verbs which pattern like *sperare* and *intervenire* respectively is given in (111).

(111) a. NON-ERGATIVE: pensare, pretendere, affermare, cercare,
                       think   *pretend*   *affirm*   *seek*

                       odiare, esitare, desiderare
                       hate   *hesitate* *wish*

      b. ERGATIVE: venire, tornare, andare, scendere, salire, uscire,
                   come   *return* *go*   *descend*   *climb* *go out*

                   accorrere, correre, riuscire
                   rush in   *run*   *succeed*

However, there are a few exceptions. While ergative verbs pattern quite generally like *intervenire* in (107b), there are a few non ergative ones, like those in (112) which allow the order *i-subject, S-complement* rather freely.

(112) a. Ha $\left\{\begin{array}{l}\text{provato}\\\text{provveduto}\end{array}\right\}$ Giovanni [a telefonare al   medico]

   has $\left\{\begin{array}{l}\textit{tried}\\\textit{provided}\end{array}\right\}$ *Giovanni [to telephone to the doctor]*

Giovanni has tried/taken steps to phone the doctor.

b. Ha $\left\{\begin{array}{l}\text{cominciato}\\\text{continuato}\end{array}\right\}$ Giovanni [a mettere in ordine]

   has $\left\{\begin{array}{l}\textit{begun}\\\textit{continued}\end{array}\right\}$ *Giovanni to put   in order*

Giovanni has begun/continued to straighten things up.

Considering their rarity, it seems plausible to assume that the cases in (112) will not invalidate the generalization illustrated by (107), although it remains unclear how these cases are to be accounted for.[54]

It is not always impossible, even aside from the exceptional cases in (112), for the i-subject of a non-ergative verb to precede a complement of the verb. For example, in cases like (113), (114) involving a NP and a PP complement (in brackets), both orders seem equally acceptable.

(113) a. Ha esaminato [il   caso] Giovanni.
         has examined   the case   Giovanni

   Giovanni has examined the case.

   b. Ha esaminato Giovanni [il caso].

(114) a. Mi   ha   parlato [di   te]   Giovanni.
         to-me has   spoken   about you Giovanni

   Giovanni has spoken to me about you.

   b. Mi ha parlato Giovanni [di te].

We suggest that cases like (113b), (114b) are derived from the corresponding (a) cases via a rule that permutes the two post-verbal constituents: a rule which seems independently required to account for alternations like (115).

(115) a. Ho   scritto una lunga lettera a Giovanni
         (I) have written a   long letter   to Giovanni

   b. Ho   scritto a Giovanni una lunga lettera
      (I) have written to Giovanni a   long   letter

We may refer to this rule as "C-shift" (Complement Shift). Given (107a), it must be the case that — for some reason — C-shift is (near) inapplicable in cases like (108) involving S-complements. It is precisely this impossibility that provides the evidence distinguishing ergative from non-ergative verbs which we just discussed. There are other cases in which the latter rule apparently fails to apply, thus providing further evidence for the distinction.

Consider (116).

(116)   Un carabiniere ha   sparato addosso al   dimostrante.
         a   policeman   has fired   upon   to-the demonstrator

A policeman has fired on the demonstrator.

The dative phrase *al dimostrante* of (116) can be cliticized, thus leaving the preposition *addosso* stranded, as in (117).

(117)   Un carabiniere gli ha sparato addosso.
         A policeman has fired on him.

We now note that under inversion the i-subject must follow the stranded preposition, as in (118).

(118) a.   Gli ha sparato [addosso] **un carabiniere**.

      b. ?? Gli ha sparato **un carabiniere** [addosso].

The case in (118b), involving non-ergative *sparare* will now contrast with the one in (119) involving ergative *cadere*, where the same linear order turns out perfectly grammatical.

(119)   Gli   è caduto **un carabiniere** [addosso]
         to-him is fallen a policeman   upon

A policeman has fallen on him.

The contrast between (118b) and (119) is parallel to the one between (107a) and (107b) and supports our account in the same fashion. That is, (119) is expected since the i-subject *un carabiniere* may occur in direct object position, while (118b) is excluded since rightward movement will place the i-subject in a VP-external position (and C-shift is apparently inapplicable). Only the order in (118a) will be expected, the latter thus being analogous to (108). Beside providing evidence for ergative verbs, such contrasts as (107), (118b)−(119) will thus also confirm our assumption that i-subjects derived via movement are adjoined to VP (rather than placed in a VP internal position).

The contrast in (118) weakens if the dative phrase is not cliticized, as in (120).

(120) a. (?) Ha sparato [addosso al   dimostrante] **un carabiniere**
             has fired   upon   to-the demonstrator a   policeman

       b. ? Ha sparato **un carabiniere** [addosso al dimostrante].

Regarding the difference between (118) and (120) we may assume, in line with some of the previous remarks, that the prepositional complement is more easily permuted with the i-subject if it is phonologically heavier, as it is when cliticization has not occurred.[55]

Returning to the contrast between (118b) and (119), we note that passives once again give the same results as ergative verbs, as predicted. This is shown by (121a), parallel in linear order to its active counterpart (121b).

(121) a. Gli   fu   spinto **un carabiniere** [addosso]
      to-him was   pushed a   policeman   upon

      A policeman was pushed over him.

  b. La folla   gli   spinse **un carabiniere** [addosso]
     the crowd to-him pushed a   policeman   upon

     The crowd pushed a policeman over him.

Such similarity in linear order provides evidence for the NP-movement derivation of passives with pre-verbal subjects, in the same manner as the similarity noted between (109) and (110) does.

We have so far discussed two cases in which a linear order *i-subject, complement* is found only with ergative verbs, while with non-ergative verbs only the order *complement, i-subject* occurs. What we have not discussed is the possibility for the latter order to occur with ergative verbs also, as in (122) (cf. (107b) and (119).)

(122) a. ? Interverrà   [a risolvere il   problema] **Giovanni**.
      will intervene   to solve   the problem   Giovanni

  b. Gli   è caduto [addosso] **un carabiniere**.
      to-him is fallen upon   a   policeman

      A policeman has fallen on him.

Cases like (122) are not problematic for our analysis: we assume they arise by rightward movement from the forms with pre-verbal subject (i.e. *Giovanni interverrà . . .*, etc.), just like the cases involving non-ergative verbs (i.e. (108), (118a)).

In contrast with (122), there are some cases in which the order *complement, i-subject* is impossible with ergative verbs, and with ergative verbs only. Let us first consider the fact that dative benefactives occur in a fixed position, to the immediate right of a direct object as in (123), (124), where the dative benefactive is within brackets, and the direct object is in boldface.[56]

(123) a.   La mareggiata ha capovolto **la barca** [a Giovanni]
      the sea storm   has capsized   the boat   to Giovanni
                                  . . . Giovanni's boat

  b. ?? La mareggiata ha capovolto [a Giovanni] **la barca**.

(124) a.   Giovanni ha rotto   **la gamba** [al   tavolo]
           Giovanni has broken the leg   to-the table
                              . . . the leg of the table

b. ?? Giovanni ha rotto [al tavolo] **la gamba.**

Now we note that the transitive verbs in (123), (124) have ergative counterparts. With these, one observes the pattern illustrated by (125), (126).

(125) a.   Si   è capovolta **la barca** [a Giovanni]
           itself is capsized   the boat   to Giovanni

           Giovanni's boat has capsized.

b. ?? Si è capovolta [a Giovanni] **la barca.**

c.   ? **La barca** si è capovolta [a Giovanni].

(126) a.   Si   è rotta   **la gamba** [al   tavolo]
           itself is broken the leg   to the table

           The leg of the table has broken.

b. ?* Si è rotta [al tavolo] **la gamba.**

c. ?* **La gamba** si è rotta [al tavolo].

Under our analysis, the facts in (125), (126) are directly accounted
for by assuming that direct objects and dative benefactives must occur
contiguously and in that order, as is independently required by the cases
in (123), (124). On the other hand, if (125a), (126a) were the result of
rightward movement of the subject, then the parallelism with the transitive cases in (124), (125) would be a rather curious accident. In particular it would have to be the case not only that inversion is semi-obligatory
here (given the status of (c)), but also that permutation of the i-subject
and the dative is required exactly in these cases (given the status of (b)).
In contrast, i-subjects of non-ergative verbs appear to the right of datives
rather unproblematically, as in (127).[57]

(127)   Ha telefonato a Giovanni suo fratello.
        has telephoned to Giovanni his brother

        His brother has phoned Giovanni.

Once again passives exhibit the same pattern as ergatives, with the
usual implications for the correctness of our analysis of ergatives, as in
(128).

(128) a.   Fu capovolta **la barca** [a Giovanni].
           was capsized the boat   to Giovanni

           Giovanni's boat was capsized.

b. ?? Fu capovolta [a Giovanni] **la barca**.

c. ? **La barca** fu capovolta [a Giovanni].

The last difference between ergative and non-ergative verbs we will discuss in this section and in this chapter concerns pronominalization of sentential complements. We note that, while among non-ergative verbs we find S-pronominalization in the form of a direct object in some cases, and in the form of an indirect object in others, with ergative verbs only indirect object pronominalization of S-complements is ever found. This situation is illustrated below, where the verbs in (129) are non-ergative and those in (130) ergative, *pentirsi, arrangiarsi* of (130b,c) being inherent-reflexives.[58]

(129) a. (Di vincere la gara) Giovanni **lo** sperava davvero
       (*To win the race*)   *Giovanni it   hoped   truly*

           Giovanni truly hoped it

     b. (Ad occuparsi del problema) Giovanni **vi**   acconsentì
        (*To deal with the problem*)   *Giovanni there consented*

           Giovanni consented to it

(130) a. (A prendere il giornale) Giovanni **ci**   va
       (*To fetch the newpaper*) *Giovanni there goes*

           Giovanni goes there

     b. (Di aver smesso di studiare) Giovanni se   **ne** pentirà
        (*Giving up studying*)   *Giovanni himself of-it will repent*

           Giovanni will be sorry for it

     c. (A riparare la finestra) Giovanni **ci**   si   è   arrangiato
        (*To repair the window*) *Giovanni there himself is managed*

           Giovanni has managed it

We can easily show that, under our analysis, this difference between ergative and non-ergative verbs follows from the independently established generalization that no verb can have more than one direct object. Later on we will return to the exact theoretical characterization of such a generalization. For the time being, let us just assume its factual truth, which we may express as in (131).

(131) *... V NP NP ...

One of the predictions of (131) is the impossibility of direct-object pronomirtalization of S-complements with verbs which already have a direct object NP, as in (132).

(132) (A prendere provvedimenti) *Giovanni **lo** persuase Piero
     (*To take action*)   *Giovanni it persuaded Piero*

Direct object pronominalization of the sentential complement in (132) gives rise to a second direct object beside the phrase *Piero*, whence a violation of (131) (we assume that clitic *lo* would be related to a null NP to the immediate right of *Piero*). The kind of pronominalization that is impossible in (132) is possible, as expected, in (133), where the verb does not have a direct object beside the S-complement, but only an *indirect* one.

(133) (Di prendere provvedimenti) Giovanni **lo** promise a Piero
     (*To take action*)   *Giovanni it promised to Piero*

The ungrammaticality of (132) persists under passivization, as in (134).

(134) (A prendere provvedimenti) *Piero **lo** fu persuaso
     (*To take action*)   *Piero it was persuaded*

Under the analysis of passives which we are assuming, the impossibility illustrated by (134), which is systematic, is exactly analogous to the impossibility of having active counterparts like (132): since we assume the existence of a null direct object to the immediate right of the past participle in (134) (i.e. the trace), direct object pronominalization of the S-complement will give rise to a second direct object, violating (131), just as in (132). The case of ergative verbs will now be quite analogous to the one in (134): since, like passives, ergative verbs have one direct object (either a trace, if NP-movement has applied, or an i-subject, if it has not), direct object pronominalization of the complement would give rise to a second direct object, whence the contrast between (129) and (130).[59] Once again ergative verbs and passives fall together as we expect.

In the course of this section, we have thus seen that only i-subjects of ergative verbs precede S-complements and certain prepositional complements, that only i-subjects of ergative verbs are found associated with dative benefactives in a way which is typical of direct objects, and that direct object pronominalization of S-complements is systematically impossible with ergative verbs. We have argued in each case that the facts support the distinction between ergatives and intransitives, and the hypothesis we put forth in 1.3 above.

1.9. CONCLUSION

In this chapter we have argued that there is a class of verbs, which we referred to as "ergative", whose surface structure subject is a D-structure direct object. In essence, our arguments can be summarized as follows: Such a class of verbs is theoretically expected (i).[60] This hypothesis allows us to express in maximally simple terms the relation between pairs like *The artillery sank the boat/The boat sank* (ii). It allows us to capture a sweeping generalization regarding the distribution of clitic *ne* (iii), an equally sweeping generalization about the distribution of auxiliary *essere* (iv), and to account for the correspondence between the distribution of these two elements (v). The last three points are due to D. Perlmutter. Also, under inversion, such verbs differ from others, not only with respect to *ne*, but with respect to linear order of constituents (vi). Furthermore, sentential complements of such verbs are consistently analogous to indirect objects, never to direct objects (vii).

Beside providing evidence for the existence of ergative verbs, in this chapter we put forth specific proposals on several aspects of the grammar of Italian. In particular, we provided analyses of the constructions involving *si* and SI, and formulated a two-part rule for the assignment of auxiliary and past participle agreement.

NOTES

[1] The inverse correlation is slightly less than general, due to Raising verbs like *sembrare*, which take auxiliary *essere* but do not allow *ne* in the manner of (2a), as in (i).

(i) a.   Molti studenti erano   sembrati superare l'esame
          Many students were ('had') seemed   to pass   the exam

     b. * **Ne** sembrano $\left\{ \begin{array}{l} \text{superare l'esame molti} \\ \text{molti superare l'esame} \end{array} \right\}$

          Many of them seem to pass the exam.

The lack of correspondence in (i) is irrelevant to our discussion in this chapter, and will be accounted for by the discussion in chapter 2.

[2] We note in particular the discussion in Rosen (1981).

[3] There are (at least descriptively) three types of *ne*, only one of which will be considered in the text. Beside the cases of quantified nominals of the text, we find cases of cliticization of an adnominal complement like (i), and cases of cliticization of **di** 'of' PP-complements like (ii).

(i)   Ne   conosco l'autore
             (I) of-it know   the author

(ii)   Ne   ho parlato   a lungo
             (I) of-it have spoken   at length

The type in (i) exhibits the same pre-verbal/post-verbal asymmetry as the type of the text (and so does the type in (ii), for obvious reasons), as shown by (iii).

(iii)   * L'autore   ne   conosce Giovanni
           the author of-it knows   Giovanni

However the impossibility of (iii) has a class of apparent exceptions in French (and, marginally, perhaps also in Italian), an instance of which is (iv).

(iv)   L'auteur   en   est célèbre
         the author of-it is famous

(iv) is a case of "En-avant" ("En forward"), a phenomenon discussed in Ruwet (1972), Kayne (1975), and more recently in Couquaux (1981). On (iv) I will assume that Couquaux (1981) is correct in concluding that *en* cliticizes from a position to the right of *be*, and that *ne/en* is a post verbal clitic without exception.

[4] Here and elsewhere I assume the existence of minor phonological rules, changing, for example, the sequence *si ne* into *se ne*, as in (11).

[5] A small sample is given in (i).

(i)   migliorare, peggiorare, aumentare, diminuire, ingrassare, raffreddare,
       improve   worsen   increase   diminish   fatten   cool

       consumare, sprofondare, congelare rinverdire, annerire, ispessire
       wear out   sink in   freeze   turn green blacken   thicken

On these verbs, see also 1.5 below.

[6] Specifically, as we saw in I.0.3, the identity in selectional restrictions follows from the assumption that selectional restrictions are imposed in D-structure, which we regard as the most immediate projection of the lexicon. The 'semantic-object' status follows from the assumption that in LF the subject of a passive bears object θ-role because it is in a chain with a trace in object position.

[7] I.e., in *John seems to leave, John* is 'semantically' the subject of *leave,* and the class of NPs that can replace *John* is exactly the class of NPs that *leave* selects as a subject (cf. discussion of (5c) in I.0.3.

[8] Chomsky (LGB), as well as Marantz (1981) argue that what assigns subject θ-role is not really the verb, but the whole predicate, compositionally. We will assume that their conclusion is correct. It seems clear however that the verb alone determines whether or not θ-role is assigned. For our purposes here we can thus assume inconsequentially that V assigns subject θ-role.

[9] On the basis of our discussion so far, one may also expect D-structure forms like '[e] V PP'. In general, these would not seem to exist, for reasons I discuss in Note 4, ch. 3. However, I do find one candidate in Italian, exemplified in (i).

(i)   Si   tratta di tuo   figlio.
       (*it*) *itself treats of your   son*

       It's about your son.

The semantics, as well as the presence of *si* (on this see 1.5 below) indicate that the subject in (i) does not have θ-role. *Trattarsi* of (i) is in fact quite plausibly the $-\theta_s$ counterpart of *trattare* of (ii).

(ii)   Questo libro tratta della sua famiglia.
       this book   treats of-the his family

       This book deals with/is about his family.

[10] The only way to introduce an agent with *arrivare* which thus lacks a lexical causative counterpart, will be to resort to the syntactic constructions with *fare,* as in (i).

(i)   Giovanni fa   arrivare molti esperti.
       Giovanni makes arrive   many experts

       Giovanni makes many experts arrive.

This construction will be discussed in detail in Part II.

[11] The term ERGATIVE has often been used to refer to verbs like *affondare* of (19), namely to verbs that have a transitive counterpart. In using it to refer to verbs like *arrivare* as well, we thus extend a more or less established use. The corresponding terminology in

Relational Grammar is UNACCUSATIVE for our ergative class, and UNERGATIVE for our intransitive class.

[12] While our hypothesis regarding ergative verbs derives directly from the "Unaccusative Hypothesis" of Perlmutter (1978) as stated in the text, we must note that other claims to various degrees similar to ours in postulating a class of verbs whose surface subject is the underlying direct object have also appeared in the literature. In particular we note: Hall (1965); Fillmore (1968); Bowers (1973), (1981); Napoli (1973); Fiengo (1974), (1980); Herschensohn (1979), (1982); Couquaux (1981), den Besten (1981), (1982). Also closely related to our hypothesis is Stowell (1978), which provides an 'ergative' or 'Raising' analysis of *be*, and Borer (1980), which extends Stowell's analysis to other verbs in Hebrew. All of these proposals are independent of Perlmutter (1978), so far as we know.

[13] Notice that the configuration in (29b) involving Ne-Cl appears impossible with all adjectives. As will become clear below, this fact is — in the context of our discussion — parallel to the failure of all adjectives to enter into the French *il*-construction (e.g., *Il est heureux beaucoup de monde* 'It is happy many people'). This suggests that there are no ergative adjectives, namely no adjectives appearing in the D-structure '[e] be-Adj NP'. If any existed, they should allow Ne-Cl with respect to the NP, and should give rise to instances of the *il*-construction by insertion of pleonastic *il*. At this point I know of no clear theoretical reason for the non-existence of such a class of adjectives.

[14] The complexity of the examples in (31) is required (as discussed in Chomsky (1981c)) to comply at the same time with both the constraints on the occurrence of parasitic gaps and the constraints on cliticization. Clitic *gli* (*gli li* → *glieli* in (31b)) is the dativized subject of the embedded verb *mettere*. On the 'causative' construction of (31), see Part II.

[15] The mild ungrammaticality of (31a) and of all such cases can be attributed to violation of a general principle requiring one and only one operator for each variable and one and only one variable for each operator. this is the BIJECTION PRINCIPLE of Koopman and Sportiche (1981).

[16] The contrast between (32) and (31a) correlates with the fact noted in I.0.3 that, while NP-trace relations fall strictly under Opacity (i.e., Principle A of the Binding Theory), operator-variable relations do not, as first noted in Rizzi (1978b). The case in (i) would in fact be a violation of Opacity (by 'che$_i$ - e$_i$').

(i)   Il libro [che$_i$ sai [chi$_j$ e$_j$ mi ha regalato e$_i$] . . .
           The book that you know who gave me . . .

We thus have two independent pieces of evidence for the distinction between NP-traces (anaphors) and variables.

[17] The transitive case in (4iiib) (*Esamineranno il caso molti esperti*) will be relevantly analogous to the one in (33b), namely it will be a case of adjunction to VP.

[18] I am thus assuming that, given a certain clitic, the grammar must fix two independent parameters. One: base-generation versus cliticization by movement. Two: subject versus object cliticization. The independence of the two parameters is attested by the movement analysis of impersonal subject *si* (cf. 1.6 below) versus the base-generation analysis of pleonastic subject *ci* (cf. 2.5.3 below).

[19] I am thankful to D. Sportiche for pointing this out to me.

[20] We note that if B&R are correct in claiming that the ungrammaticality of (34b) falls under the same generalization as the cases in (37), one would then expect that in cases like (34) Wh-movement should give the same results as Ne-Cl. However such a test is not applicable to this particular kind of configuration, since Wh-extraction from quantified nominals is generally impossible, as discussed in Belletti (1980). But the test can be applied to the configuration in (i) of fn. 3 above (*Ne conosco l'autore*), in which *ne* cliticizes an adnominal complement. The results are as follows.

(i) a. ?? Le ditte delle quali$_i$ hanno scioperato [gli operai e$_i$] . . .
   the firms of   which   have   struck   the workers

   . . . the workers have struck

 b. ?* Ne$_i$ hanno scioperato [gli operai e$_i$]
   of-them have   struck   the workers

 Their workers have struck.

(ii) a. (?) Le ditte delle quali$_i$ sono arrivati [i dirigenti e$_i$] . . .
   the firms of   which have arrived the managers

 b.   Ne$_i$ sono arrivati [i dirigenti e$_i$]
   of-them have arrived the managers

 Their managers have arrived.

The contrast between (ib) and (iib) is analogous to the one in (34), confirming that this type of Ne-Cl is equally relevant to our discussion. The contrast relative to Wh-movement between the (a) cases is perceptibly weaker than the one between the (b) cases, yet some contrast seems to be present. The facts thus seem open to either interpretation.

[21] The subjacency account predicts that Wh-extraction should produce similar results. Once again it is not clear whether this is in fact the case, given (i) compared with (38b).

(i) ?(?) Il paziente di cui$_i$ hai   parlato [alla figlia e$_i$] . . .
   the patient of whom (you) have talked   to the daughter . . .

[22] As we would expect, a parasitic gap will be possible in one case but not in the other, cf. (i).

(i) a. ? Inviterò quante ragazze conosci senza aver mai visto
   I will invite however many girls you know without having ever seen.

 b. * Inviterò quante ragazze pensi senza aver mai visto
   I will invite however many girls you think without having ever seen.

[23] Several aspects of the discussion in B&R are compatible with our view that *ne* is base-generated and will be assumed to be essentially correct. In particular, their assumption that the *ec* related to *ne* (in the case of quantified nominals) is governed by the verb (on this cf. discussion of (97) below); and their view that the null phrase following the quantifier in (i) (where there is no *ne*) is to be assimilated to PRO.

(i)   Molti hanno telefonato.
   Many (of them) have telephoned.

[24] A small sample of verbs that pattern like *rompere* in (45) is the following.

(i)   accumulare, radunare, allargare, capovolgere, muovere, sviluppare,
   accumulate gather   widen   capsize   move   develop

   dividere, riempire, laureare, liquefare, sporcare, rovesciare, attorcigliare
   divide   fill up   graduate liquefy   dirty   spill   twist

[25] With regard to these two different classes of ergative verbs, we may note that some verbs appear in both classes. For example both **indurire** and **indurirsi** 'harden' exist as ergative counterparts to transitive **indurire**. Also, it appears that across Romance languages, cognates do not systematically belong to the same class. This would suggest that no principle of Universal Grammar is directly involved.

[26] Let it suffice to apply the test in (i), as in (ii).

(i)   The winner $\left\{\begin{array}{l}\text{seemed}\\ \text{*tried}\end{array}\right\}$ to be John.   (Raising)
                                                                                          (Control)

(ii)   Il vincitore $\left\{\begin{array}{l}\text{si è rivelato}\\ \text{si è dimonstrato}\end{array}\right\}$ essere Giovanni.

           The winner has $\left\{\begin{array}{l}\text{proved}\\ \text{turned out}\end{array}\right\}$ *to be Giovanni.*

[27] The sentential complements of (48a, b) differ in that one is tensed, the other an infinitival. But this is predictable from independent considerations. The complement must be tensed in (48a) since Italian lacks the so called 'Exceptional Case Marking', a fact to which we will return (cf. the case of English *prove* in (25) above), but it must not be tensed in the Raising case (49b) for familiar reasons (binding theory). In fact this confirms the Raising analysis.

[28] Like *sbagliarsi* of (49) are the following:

(i)   pentirsi, risentirsi, arrampicarsi, rinfrancarsi, sbrigarsi, stancarsi, riposarsi,
           repent   resent   climb   hearten   hurry   get tired   rest

           suicidarsi,   accorgersi, fidarsi, arrabbiarsi, arrangiarsi, congratularsi,
           commit suicide notice   trust   get angry   manage   congratulate

           vergognarsi, interessarsi, ricordarsi, perdersi, offendersi
           be ashamed take interest remember get lost   get offended

We may note that in some cases the English equivalent consists of a passive participle form (cf. *be mistaken, get lost, get offended*). This seems to support the ergative analysis of this class we will propose in the text, since passive forms are analogous to ergative verbs in failing to assign subject θ-role.

[29] In the case of SI, it may be reasonable to express the constraint by saying that SI must be nominative (in (63) it would be accusative). One might then wonder whether this provision would not be sufficient to account for the difference between (61a) and (63) even compatibly with a base-generation analysis of SI: in (61a) the latter would be linked with the object position at D-structure; the object position would then be linked with the subject by Move α (movement of an *ec*), so that the resulting chain, containing SI, would have nominative Case due to assignment of such Case to the subject. Example (63) would remain excluded. This account however would not extend to cases like (i).

(i)   [e] si stava per [t essergli   presentati t]

           SI   stood for   to be to-him introduced
           We were about to be introduced to him.

Here, at D-structure SI would have to be linked with the obejct of the embedded verb. This seems rather implausible: we surely expect whatever relations are established at D-structure to obey reasonable locality conditions (on this see II.0.3). The base-generation analysis of SI thus continues to be ruled out.

[30] Rizzi (1976b, fn. 18) notes that with some Raising verbs, Raising of SI as in (65b) produces less than acceptable results. The reasons for this remain unclear. Passives and ergative cases like (61a), (65a), on the other hand are always perfect.

[31] Differences in meaning betwen (66a) and (66b) are carefully noted by traditional grammars. But these seem to be roughly of the same order as those between actives and passives. For a discussion of some of the differences, see also Cinque (1976).

It may also be worth noting here that the facts we assume are somewhat idealized, since we ignore the general preferability of (66b, c) over (66a) in most dialects.

[32] The only analysis I am aware of in which cases like (66b) (actually the French equiva-

lents) are not derived via NP-movement, is the one in Grimshaw (1980) who assumes a framework without NP-movement (Bresnan's Lexical Functional Grammar). Aissen and Perlmutter (1976) assume the Relational Grammar equivalent of NP-movement for the Spanish counterparts to (66b).

[33] There is one other case in which first and second person NPs behave differently from third person NPs, though it remains unclear if it is related to (72). This cocnerns the possibility for verb agreement to fail in **C'è molti studenti** 'There is many students' though not in ***C'e io** 'There is I', etc., as we will discuss in 2.5.4 below.

[34] An extreme version of the view that cases like (66b, c) are theoretically anomalous has been given in Otero (1972), (1976) who goes as far as claiming for the Spanish counterparts that they cannot possibly be characterized by a grammar of Spanish and concludes that such sentences are "acceptable ungrammatical", namely that they are not part of the relevant corpus. Otero's position, though in partial agreement with our discussion in the text, seems to us excessive, and is certainly not shared by Italian grammars, which consistently report such sentences as part of the language, or by the many generative linguists who have proceeded to characterize them in theoretical terms (cf. Aissen and Perlmutter (1976) for Spanish; Napoli (1973), (1976), Rizzi (1976b), Cinque (1976), Belletti (1982) for Italian. See also Contreras (1973) for a specific citique of Otero (1972).)

[35] Nominative Case on the derived subject in O.P. cases cannot be verified directly by using first or second person pronouns which are differentiated for Case, because of the prohibition illustrated by (72). Nominative Case here is inferred on the basis of the assumption (discussed in chapter 2) that the NP that induces verb agreement is always nominative.

[36] There are some cases, noted in Belletti (1982), in which SI can appear in infinitivals. These are "Tough Movement" and infinitival relative constructions, exemplified in (i).

(i) a. Questo libro è difficile da legger**si**
    this   book is difficult SI-to read

  b. Sono   cose da far**si** al più presto
    (they) are things SI-to do as soon as possible

Although I will have no precise proposal for cases like (i), it seems to me that they do not threaten the generalization that SI cannot occur in infinitivals which our analysis expresses. First, they represent the only instances in which SI thus alternates with lack of SI (cf. . . . *difficile da leggere*, etc.). Second, they seem to be of limited productivity. Thus, while (i) corresponds to (ii), there is no case like (iv) corresponding to (iii).

(ii) a. Si legge questo libro.
    SI reads this   book

  b. Si fa   queste cose.
    SI does these   things

(iii) a. Si comincia a leggere questo libro.
    SI begins to read this   book

  b. Si comincia a fare queste cose.
    SI begins to do these   things

(iv) a. ?* Questo libro è difficile da cominciar**si** a leggere.
      this   book is difficult SI-to begin   to read

  b. ?* Sono   cose da cominciar**si** a fare al più presto.
      (they) are things SI-to begin   to do as soon as possible

Notice that both cases in (iv) are grammatical if SI does not appear. These facts may suggest that the forms in (i) are (at least in part) lexicalized. If this is the case we may then expect SI not to play any syntactic role, which would account for the alternation with lack of SI, and also that it should fail to appear in more complex structures like (iv).

[37] It would be inaccurate to say that every individual sentence involving ergative *si* is ambiguous between *si* and SI, however. For reasons which remain unclear, O.P. cases often require the presence of an adverbial phrase (analogously to English 'middle' verbs discussed in Keyser and Roeper (1984), cf. *Beaurocrats bribe* **easily**). The case in (75) is thus hardly ambiguous with the phrase *per la seconda volta* omitted. Aside from these considerations, there are systematic ambiguities, as assumed in the text.

[38] As L. Rizzi has pointed out to me, cases like (77b) have a reasonable level of acceptability only if the embedded verb has an aspectual auxiliary. The nature of this constraint remains unclear.

[39] The grammaticality of (77b) in fact confirms the relevance of the chain *subject-SI* in (77a): as N. Chomsky points out to me, one might have assumed that the peculiarity of cases like (77a) was nominative Case being assigned twice separately: to the subject position and to SI, rather than intersecting chains, as we assumed. But this alternative will not account for (77b), since the infinitival to which SI is cliticized does not assign nominative.

[40] Under the terms of our discussion, we may expect that, just as embedding of (77a) under a Raising predicate gives rise to (77b), embedding of (i) should give rise to (ii).

(i)   [e] si è letto questi articoli.

        SI is read   these   articles

        We have read these articles.

(ii)   ?(?) [e] risulta [t   essersi già   letto questi articoli]

        (*it*) *turns out SI-to be already read   these   articles*

In (ii) SI would presumably receive nominative Case at a distance, much as in (77b). Recall that Raising can also give rise to the variant in (iii) (cf. (65b)).

(iii)   (?) [e] si risultò [t aver   già   letto quegli articoli]

        SI turned out to have already read   those   articles

The reason why both (ii) and (iii) are expected lies in the lack of relative ordering between cliticization of SI and NP-movement. Cliticization of SI before Raising will give rise to (ii). The inverse order will give rise to (iii). Our discussion will not account for the less acceptable status of (ii) compared with (iii) (on the latter, cf. Note 30). However, it will account for the fact that (ii) contrasts with superficially similar cases involving Control verbs, which are totally impossible, e.g. ***Vorrebbe essersi già letto questi articoli**. 'Would like SI to have already read these articles' (cf. the contrast in (78) below in the text). Cases analogous to (ii) involving pleonastic *ci* instead of SI are perfect as we will see.

[41] Contrasts of the same nature as (78), noted in the generative literature at least since Napoli (1973) were to my knowledge first attributed to the Control versus Raising character of the verbs involved in Rizzi (1976b) and independently in Aissen and Perlmutter (1976). Both of those references considered the lack of Control counterparts to cases like (77b) and attributed it to the fact that Control verbs take only animate subjects. As was noted in Radford (1977), as well as in Burzio (1978), the latter solution is not tenable precisely because of cases like (78). The more recent attempt of Rizzi (1982a) attributes

the ungrammaticality of (78b) to a violation of the condition that PRO be ungoverned, by assuming that SI in fact governs the subject position. The latter proposal differs in empirical predictions from ours. Consider (i).

(i) a. Per ottenere il rimborso, bisogna [PRO$_i$ $\left\{\begin{array}{l}\text{*essersi invitati}\\ \text{esser stati invitati}\end{array}\right\}$ t$_i$]
         To obtain a refund it is necessary to have been invited

     b. Giovanni parlava senza [PRO$_i$ mai $\left\{\begin{array}{l}\text{*essersi interrogato}\\ \text{esser stato interrogato}\end{array}\right\}$ t$_i$]
         Giovanni would talk without ever having been asked

     c. Quei prigionieri vorrebbero [PRO$_i$ $\left\{\begin{array}{l}\text{*essersi già liberati}\\ \text{essere già stati liberati}\end{array}\right\}$ t$_i$]
         Those prisoners would want to have already been freed

If the SI cases in (i) were ungrammatical because PRO is governed by SI, then the ungrammaticality ought to disappear if PRO underwent Raising, leaving a trace. On the other hand, if they are ungrammatical because SI fails to be associated with a nominative phrase, then the ungrammaticality ought to persist if PRO is Raised (into a higher infinitival). Consider now (ii).

(ii) a. Per ottenere il rimborso, bisogna
          To obtain a refund   it is necessary

          [PRO$_i$ risultare [t$_i$ $\left\{\begin{array}{l}\text{*essersi invitati}\\ \text{esser stati invitati}\\ \text{to have been invited}\end{array}\right\}$ t$_i$]
          to appear

      b. Giovanni parlava
          Giovanni would talk

          senza [PRO$_i$ mai risultare [t$_i$ $\left\{\begin{array}{l}\text{*essersi interrogato}\\ \text{esser stato interrogato}\\ \text{to have been asked}\end{array}\right\}$ t$_i$]
          without ever appearing

      c. Quei prigionieri vorrebbero
          Those prisoners would want

          [PRO$_i$ risultare [t$_i$ $\left\{\begin{array}{l}\text{*essersi gia liberati}\\ \text{essere gia stati liberati}\end{array}\right\}$ t$_i$]
          to appear to have already been freed

The passive cases in (ii) are actually mildly ungrammatical, due to a general prohibition on sequences of infinitives discussed in Longobardi (1980a) (see 5.4 below). However, the ungrammaticality of the SI cases is much more severe, and although the contrasts of (ii) are thus slightly less clear, perhaps also because of the complexity of the examples, in my view there is little reason to believe that such contrasts are anything other than those in (i), as our analysis would predict.

[42] Ruwet (1972) discusses the corresponding French data and notes a number of syntactic differences between superficially identical pairs. In particular he notes that *se-moyen* (corresponding to Italian SI, as we will assume), but not 'neuter' *se* (our ergative *si*) can serve as an antecedent to various kinds of phrases. A typical case among those he cites is the unambiguous one in (i).

(i)   Une branche comme ça,   ça **se** casse [d'une seule main]
         a   branch   like   that, that one breaks with one hand

Another difference between *si* and SI (noted in traditional grammars, in Napoli (1973) and elsewhere) concerns the position within clitic clusters. Thus we find **Giovanni se lo compra** 'Giovanni buys it to himself', but **Lo si compra** 'SI buys it'.

[43] This discussion will not consider pp agreement in the case of Wh-movement, as in (i), which has a stylistically rather marked character.

(i) a. Le ragazze che hai   viste . . .
          the girls   that (you) have seen (fem. pl.) . . .

     b. Quante   ragazze hai   viste?
          how many girls   (you) have seen (fem. pl.)

          How many girls have you seen?

This kind of agreement is more common in French. For relevant discussion see Note 4, ch. 6.

[44] In 2.7.1 below, we will actually revise the analysis of passives, differentiating the latter from ergative verbs, and accounting for a difference between Italian and French with respect to auxiliary selection in passives, as well as for the agreement of the past participle of passive 'be', *stata*, in (90a). That revision will not affect the essence of our discussion here.

[45] Notice that we have not made clear which of the two elements in (92b) ([e], *si*) is binding the other. From one point of view it should be *si* that binds the *ec*, since the latter is in effect its trace. From another it should be the *ec* that binds *si* since it c-commands it. The case in (ii), Note 40 above, repeated in (i) suggests that the second point of view is correct (however marginal such examples may be).

(i) ?(?) [e] risulta [e']   esser**si** già   letto questi articoli.
          (it) turns out SI-to be already read those articles

     It turns out that we have already read those articles.

In (i), we clearly want *e'* to be the trace of *e*, and we would hardly expect *si* to bind the latter, or *e'* to have two antecedents. We therefore assume that *e* binds *e'* and that the latter binds *si*, and in general that the *ec* in subject position binds *si* (SI). We will assume that this is a particular type of binding, analogous to that found with inversion, where we also have an *ec* in subject position (cf. chapter 2). We note however that in cases like (ii), the *ec* in subject position would be binding two elements: SI and the object position.

(ii)   [e] si fu   invitati [e]

        SI was invited

        We were invited.

We return to this matter in Note 57, ch. 2.

[46] Notice that this second argument would disappear if one could claim that pp agreement in cases like *Maria è arrivata* simply reflects the presence of *essere*, as with — presumably — *essere*-adjective constructions, e.g. **Maria è malata** 'Maria is ill (fem.)' However, aside from the doubts that would be raised by thus treating auxiliary *essere* and main verb (copula) *essere* alike, the view that pp agreement is a reflex of *essere* is untenable empirically. Specifically it is falsified by (92b) (*Si è telefonato . . .*) and by cases of indirect object reflexives, as will be pointed out in Note 50 below.

[47] SI occurs with third person reflexives, as in **Si loda spesso se stessi** 'SI praises often themselves (i.e. oneself)', but as G. Cinque points out to me, it does not occur with coreferential possessives, as in *Si ama i suoi/loro eroi 'SI loves his/their (i.e. SI's) heroes' (cf. **Il popolo ama i suoi eroi** 'The people love(s) his (i.e. their) heroes'). These facts

support our view that SI lacks person features, under the assumption that *se stessi* (though not *suoi/loro*) is not only a third person, but also an impersonal form. In this respect SI is analogous to instances of 'arbitrary' PRO, given **Lodare se stessi è indice di vanità** 'To praise themselves (i.e. oneself) is a sign of vanity' versus ***Adorare i suoi/loro eroi è segno di ingenuità** 'To worship his/their heroes is a sign of naiveté'. We note however that such occurrences of PRO can contextually be made not 'impersonal', as in **Vedere i suoi amici fu il primo desiderio di Giovanni** 'To see his friends was Giovanni's first wish', whereas SI appears in non impersonal uses only dialectally (Tuscan dialects, mostly). In such uses SI has the force of a first person plural pronominal, which sometimes appears overtly in addition to SI, as in **(Noi) si vorrebbe vedere i nostri amici** '(We) *si* would like to see our friends' (notice that whereas *nostri* agrees with *noi*, the verb still fails to agree: a fact for which we have no account).

With respect to clitic reflexives, I will assume that SI selects the form analogous to *se stessi* of the above examples, namely third person plural *si*, and that a phonological rule changes *si si* into *ci si* (as stated in the text for (85)). We do not assume (except for Tuscan dialects) that SI selects first person plural *ci* (cf. paradigm (43)). Our assumption is supported by the fact that when the reflexive does not cluster with SI, it shows up as *si*, not as *ci* (again Tuscan aside), as in **SI sperava di vederSI** 'SI hoped to see each other'.

[48] The analogy with the case of SI appears to be only partial since the latter too is undifferentiated for gender and we may thus expect – falsely – that pp agreement could fail with SI also (cf. ***Si è arrivato**). We must therefore assume that SI always bears *abstract* gender features, unlike *mi*, *ti*, etc., a fact to which we return. I am grateful to G. Cinque for bringing to my attention the facts in (94).

L. Rizzi has pointed out to me some related facts, in particular that pp agreement with first and second person clitics cannot fail if the latter are reflexive, in spite of the fact that these are morphologically identical to their non-reflexive counterparts. The cases in (94) will thus contrast with the following.

(i)   Maria (tu)   ti   sei $\left\{ \begin{array}{l} \text{vista} \\ \text{*visto} \end{array} \right\}$

Maria, (you) yourself are $\left\{ \begin{array}{l} seen\ (fem.) \\ seen \end{array} \right\}$ (ag't only)

Maria, you have seen yourself.

We will account for this contrast by assuming that the relation between the subject and the reflexive clitic always forces the contextual determination of features discussed in the text, which is otherwise optional. Notice that in order for this contextual determination to occur as desired we must further assume that subjects (unlike clitic objects) always bear *abstract* gender features even though such features do not show up overtly (cf. *io*, *tu*, or the null subject of pro drop, which are undifferentiated for gender). The latter assumption is not at all ad-hoc, but is clearly required independently, given for example **(Maria) tu sei arrivata/*arrivato** '(Maria) you have arrived (fem).' This assumption will now subsume the one we made with respect to SI, if we simply regard SI as a subject.

[49] Notice that since *ne* is undifferentiated for gender and number we may expect agreement to be optional as in (94). This is in fact correct for cases like (i) in which the quantifier phrase is not overt.

(i)   a.   (Birra)   ne ho $\left\{ \begin{array}{l} \text{bevuta} \\ \text{bevuto} \end{array} \right\}$

(Beer (fem.)) (I) of-it have $\left\{ \begin{array}{l} drunk\ (fem.) \\ drunk \end{array} \right\}$ (optional ag't)

I have drunk some of it.

b.   (Spaghetti)   ne   ho $\left\{\begin{array}{l} \text{mangiati} \\ \text{mangiato} \end{array}\right\}$.

(*Spaghetti (pl.)*) (*I*) *of-them have* $\left\{\begin{array}{l} eaten \ (pl.) \\ eaten \end{array}\right\}$ (optional ag't)

I have eaten some of it.

For the case in (97) (**Ne ho visti molti**) in which agreement is actually obligatory, we assume that the overt quantifier forces contextual determination of features for *ne*, just as the subject does with the reflexive clitic in (i) of Note 48. Note that there is always agreement between quantifier and quantified phrase (cf. **molta birra** (fem.), **molto vino** (masc.) etc.)

Our system also accounts directly for the lack of agreement in cases like **(Della tua domanda) ne abbiamo parlato/*parlata** '(Of your application (fem)) (we) of-it have *spoken* (no ag't)' mentioned in Note 3, since here *ne* is related to a PP object (thus not a direct object under (87b)).

As for the case of Ne-Cl in (i) of Note 3 (**Ne conosco l'autore**), we correctly expect lack of agreement as in (**Di quella villa) ne ho conosciuto/*conosciuta i costruttori** '(Of that villa (fem.)) (I) of-it have *known* (no ag't) the builders'. This will follow from the fact that here *ne* cliticizes a PP, as in the previous case (cf. **I costruttori [di quella villa]** versus **Molti [articoli]**), and also from the assumption that the cliticized phrase is not governed by V, but rather by the head *i costruttori*. What will remain unaccounted for is the optional agreement with the head in these cases, as in **Ne ho conosciuto/conosciuti i costruttori** '(I) of-it have *known* (optional ag't) the builders (pl.)'.

[50] The weaker status of this kind of agreement is also underscored by the fact that it does not exist in French, as it is clear that French has a system of E (*être*) assignment and pp agreement quite similar to that of Italian, but of a more restricted scope (cf. later discussion).

Notice that this is another case of dissociation between E and pp agreement analogous to that of (92b) (**si è telefonato . . .**) since, while pp agreement is weaker in Italian and non-existent in French, E (i.e. *essere/être*) appears in both languages and in Italian there is no sense in which the latter is 'weaker'. Thus, like the case in (92b), this case too falsifies the conjecture that pp agreement may simply be a reflex of E, which we rejected in Note 46 above.

[51] While we will refer to the verbs of both (104b) and (105b) as ergative, it would not be appropriate to refer to those of (105a) as intransitive, like those of (104a). The reason is that, at least some of the verbs occurring as in (105a) are actually transitive in relevant respects. Consider cases of S-pronominalization like **Giovanni lo sperava** 'Giovanni it hoped' meaning "Giovanni hoped *S*". In these cases, since we assume that *lo* is related to an empty NP as usual, the verb is transitive by definition (i.e. by the definition of transitive structure as "NP V NP" implied by (26a) above). This issue is purely terminological.

[52] There are a few cases of inherent-reflexives that take S-complements. With these, results are rather similar to those provided by ergative *intervenire* in (107b), as we would expect, but not quite identical as, in (i).

(i) a. (?) Si è ricordato Giovanni [di comprare il giornale]
        Giovanni has remembered to buy the newspaper.

     b. ? Si è pentito Giovanni [di aver smesso di studiare]
        Giovanni has repented for giving up studying.

The less than perfect status of (i) would not seem to bear on the point at issue however, since it appears that with these verbs inversion is not very natural in general, for reasons that remain unclear. Cf. **? Si è pentito Giovanni** 'Giovanni has repented'. The contrast between (i) and (107a), both involving preposition *di*, and the one between, for example

?? **Ha esitato giovanni [a partire]** 'Giovanni has hesitated to leave' and (107b) both involving *a* will indicate that there is no correlation between the possibility for the linear order in question and the preposition introducing the infinitival (on related matters, cf. Note 59).

[53] The same behavior noted for passives can be observed, as expected, with SI cases. Thus, analogous to (109) we find **Si mandarono alcuni esperti [a risolvere il problema]** 'SI sent (pl.) a few experts to solve the problem'. And quite generally throughout this section, our observations regarding passives carry over to the O.P. variant of the SI construction.

[54] It may be relevant to note that the verbs in (112) differ from those of (111a) also in that they allow ellipsis of the complement, e.g. as in (i).

(i)   (A telefonare al medico)   Ha   provveduto   Giovanni
        (*To call the doctor*)   *has   provided   Giovanni*

        Giovanni has seen to it.

If the possibility for ellipsis is related to some notion of syntactic distance from the verb, as argued in Williams (1975), then (112) may not be too surprising since the i-subject can also be interpolated in other cases in which an S-complement is not contiguous to the verb, as in (ii), in which the verb has a direct object (related to clitic *lo*), and which also permits S-ellipsis with reasonable results.

(ii)   ? Lo   ha   costretto   Giovanni   [a rimandare la   partenza]
        him   has   forced   Giovanni   to delay   the   departure

        Giovanni has forced him to delay the departure.

The idea that the complements in (112) are in some sense 'distant' from the verb is confirmed by the fact that they do not pronominalize as direct objects. Rather, those of (112a) pronominalize as quasi-locative *vi*, while those of (112b) do not pronominalize at all. We may then suggest that both (ii) and (112) are due to a rearrangement in linear order late in the derivation (the rule of Complement Shift suggested below in the text), and that both the latter process and S-ellipsis are sensitive to some notion of distance from the verb along the lines of Williams (1975).

[55] L. Rizzi (p.c.) suggests a — perhaps more principled — alternative to this. In particular, he suggests that preposition stranding as in (117) requires some form of reanalysis as has been proposed for English (cf. in particular Hornstein and Weinberg (1981)), and that such reanalysis can occur only if the stranded P is in the VP (VP minimal). Then in (118b) *addosso* would necessarily be outside of VP since the i-subject is itself VP external, but in (118a) it could be within the VP since the i-subject is VP internal, whence the contrast. The contrast between (118b) and (120b) would follow from the fact that in the latter case no reanalysis is necessary.

Other prepositions that can be stranded like *addosso* in (117) are those in (i).

(i)   dietro, davanti sopra, sotto, dentro, accanto
        behind before   above   below   within   near

[56] Examples like (123a), (124a) are actually slightly odd unless the dative is cliticized, as in **Una mareggiata gli ha capovolto la barca**. For a discussion of the analogous but much stronger requirement in French, see Kayne (1975, ch. 2). The contrasts within (123), (124) are however quite noticeable, as indicated.

[57] The pattern of (125), (126) can be observed with all the various subclasses of ergative verbs we have considered. For example with *arrivare* **Sono arrivati dei parenti a Giovanni** 'have arrived some relatives to Giovanni' and with inherent-reflexive *stancarsi* **Si è stancato il cavallo a Giovanni** 'got tired the horse to Giovanni'.

[58] With some verbs like **esitare** 'hesitate' or **cercare** 'seek' pronominalization of the sen-

tential complement does not seem possible at all. The reasons for this remain unclear. Cf. Note 54.

[59] As L. Rizzi has pointed out to me, there appears to be a one way correspondence between S-pronominalization and the preposition that introduces the infinitive: direct object pronominalization always corresponds to *di*, while the inverse is not true, given (130b). Notice in any case that an account of S-pronominalization based on the preposition selected would not provide a solution and thus an alternative to the text discussion: it would merely change the problem to how to account for selection of the preposition.

[60] This is even clearer in English than in Italian. Given the derivational parallelism between (i) (lacking in Italian) and (iii), which differ with respect to passive morphology, there is no reason for the lack of (iv), derivationally parallel to (ii) and differing from the latter with respect to passive morphology.

(i)   John$_i$ was expected [t$_i$ to leave].
(ii)   John$_i$ was invited t$_i$.
(iii)   John$_i$ seemed [t$_i$ to leave].
(iv)   The boat$_i$ sank t$_i$.

CHAPTER 2

THE SYNTAX OF INVERSION

2.0 INTRODUCTION

In this chapter, we will attempt to provide a characterization of inversion, namely of the set of constructions with i-subjects, comparing Italian with some other languages. Our first step will be to assume, following a well established line of research, that inversion in Italian is closely related to another property of this language: the pro-drop, or null-subject (henceforth NS) property. Namely, we assume that the existence of the type in (1a), is strictly related to the existence of (1b).

(1) a. Ha parlato Giovanni.
         has spoken Giovanni

     b. Ha   parlato.
         (he) has spoken

This assumption is supported by typological evidence: most Romance languages are like Italian in having both (1a) and (1b), while French, English and other languages lack both. Furthermore, it is supported by the following consideration: since Italian allows 'null' subject pronouns as in (1b) in general, it is natural to expect that it also allows 'null' non-argument subjects corresponding to French *il* and English *there*, an assumption under which we can regard Italian as analogous to English and French, in the manner illustrated by (2), where ø is a null NP.

(2) a. There have arrived three girls.

     b. Il est   arrivé   trois filles.
         it is('has') arrived three girls

     c. ø sono   arrivate tre   ragazze.
         (it) are('have') arrived three girls

If the parallelism between Italian and English-French of (2) is real, then the existence of (1a) does depend on the NS property of Italian, the property that makes (1b) possible. We will assume that all cases in (2) are indeed to receive parallel analyses. We put aside for the moment the well known differences between the three languages in question: the difference in productivity, the constructions with *il* and *there* each being possible only with a restricted class of verbs, while Italian inversion is possible with any verb; the difference with respect to verb agreement, the verb agreeing apparently with the i-subject in both the English and the Italian examples in (2), though not in the French example;[1] and the difference with respect to the so-called "definiteness restriction", which appears to hold in English and French, as in *There has arrived John, *Il est arrivé Jean, though not in Italian, as in (1a).[2]

Once we have made the assumption that inversion is related to null subjects, the next logical step will be to provide a characterization of the NS property. This we will do in 2.1, returning in 2.2 to inversion and the relation between the non-argument subject and the i-subject. In 2.3 we will point to an analogy − in Italian − between the latter relation and the one holding between a subject and an emphatic pronoun. Some not well understood limitations on inversion will be addressed in 2.4. In the last two sections (2.6, 2.7) we will discuss inversion in French and in English, preceding this (2.5) by a discussion of inversion in the Piedmontese dialect, which appears to have a dual inversion strategy, combining the strategy of Italian with one closely resembling that of French.

2.1 NULL SUBJECTS AND CLITICIZATION

The characterization of the NS property which we will adopt is the one provided in Rizzi (1982b, IV). With Rizzi, we will follow Taraldsen (1978) in assuming that null subjects are analogous to cliticized objects, and specifically that the inflectional morpheme of the verb can function as a subject clitic. We thus assume a parallelism between the two cases in (3).

(3) a.   Giovanni la vede [e]
                     ⌊_____⌋

          Giovanni sees   her.

    b.   [e]   ved-e Maria
          ⌊_____⌋

          He sees   Maria.

This view aims to capture on the one hand analogies in distribution between null subjects and cliticization, and on the other the correlation between the NS property and richness of inflection (Italian contrasting with French in having a richer inflectional system).[3]

As we saw in I.0.3, within the GB framework it is supposed that the inflectional element of tensed verbs generally assigns nominative Case to a subject under government. The inflectional element (INFL) will govern the subject position, since at syntactic levels of representation it is taken to occur as in (4), moving onto the verb after S-structure, in the phonology.

(4)

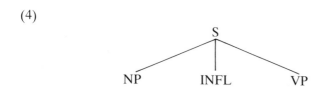

While INFL thus governs the subject position for purposes of Case assignment, it is also supposed that, in English, the relation of INFL to the subject does not satisfy the more restrictive notion PROPER GOVERN-MENT required by the ECP.[4] This accounts for well-known subject-object asymmetries like (5), (6).

(5) a.   The girl that$_i$ you know [that John likes t$_i$] . . .

   b.   *The girl that$_i$ you know [that t$_i$ likes John] . . .

(6) a.   ?*The book that$_i$ you know [who$_j$ t$_j$ bought t$_i$] . . .

   b.   **The man that$_i$ you know [what$_j$ t$_i$ bought t$_j$] . . .

The cases in (5) illustrate the so called "*that-trace" phenomenon, and the cases in (6) a phenomenon that seems closely related. Together, (5) and (6) point to the general impossibility of Wh-extracting the subject over a filled complementizer. We will refer to this (following Rizzi) as "COMP-trace" effect (or phenomenon). Within the GB framework, such phenomena fall under the ECP. Thus (5b) and (6b) are ruled out because the subject position is not properly governed, while the object position in (5a), (6a) is (by the verb.) We will abstract away from the fact, irrelevant here, that both (6a, b) are Wh-island (subjacency) violations. Wh-extraction of the subject will be possible (in English) when the COMP position is not filled, such as when *that* is deleted in (5b), since this will allow the intermediate trace in COMP (not shown in (5b)) to properly govern the subject position, satisfying the ECP (cf. Note 4). Analogously, *who$_j$* will properly govern t$_j$ in (6a).

It has been known, since it was noted in Perlmutter (1971), that NS languages do not manifest the COMP-trace effect, so that Italian sentences apparently identical to (5b), (6b) are grammatical. (Italian also does not observe Wh-island conditions. Cf. Rizzi (1978b).) While only partly related to the rest of our discussion, this third difference between NS and non-NS languages (beside null subjects and free inversion) plays a major role in Rizzi's theory, which we are adopting, and in much of the literature on the subject. It therefore seems appropriate to address it briefly.

As Rizzi points out, the apparent immunity of NS languages to the COMP-trace effect could follow directly from the assumption that in those languages INFL not only governs, but *properly* governs the subject position, an assumption which seems required in any case by the well-formedness of (3b), given the ECP. Under this view, cases analogous to (5b) would be well-formed, the ECP being satisfied just as in (3b). However, Rizzi has shown — conclusively, I think — that the immunity of Italian to the COMP-trace effect is only apparent, and that in Italian examples superficially identical to (5b), (6b) it is not the subject which is Wh-extracted, but rather (in our terms) the i-subject. Wh-extraction thus leaves a trace in post verbal position, where it is properly governed by the verb, on a par with traces of objects. From this point of view the third difference between NS and non-NS languages is a direct reflex not of the first, i.e. null subjects, as one might have thought, but rather of the second, i.e. free inversion. The Italian equivalent of *Who do you think that came is thus grammatical only because Italian has *Came John.[5] This represents an important reinterpretation of the cluster of properties of NS languages, previous attempts having invariably related both free inversion and lack of COMP-trace effect directly to null subjects.[6]

Under Rizzi's reinterpretation, the impossibility of Wh-extracting the subject over a filled complementizer holds quite generally, for NS and non-NS languages. But languages will differ in the strategies they use to overcome this prohibition. In languages like Italian, which have a fully productive inversion strategy, inversion will suffice, while other languages will need additional devices. (Notice that inversion in English also bypasses the prohibition in question. Compare *How many people do you think that were in the room and How many people do you think that there were in the room). Thus English has deletion of that in cases like (5b), and French has a rule changing que to qui in similar configurations. (For discussion and further references see Chomsky and Lasnik (1977), Pesetsky (1979), Kayne (1980a)).

Granting that only i-subjects (not subjects) can be extracted over a complementizer in Italian, the question at this point — as Rizzi points out — is how to allow an ec in subject position in cases of null subjects, as in (7a), while disallowing it in cases of extraction, as in (7b).

(7) a.   [e]   parla
         He speaks.

    b. *Chi   credi   [che   [e]   parli]
                        ⟵_____⏌

         Who do you   think   that speaks?

Government versus *proper* government by INFL will not distinguish the two cases in (7). What will distinguish them, is our initial assumption that in cases like (7a) INFL has a pronominal character, like a clitic; (7b) will then be ruled out on a par with (8).

(8)   *Chi$_i$ credi   che   Giovanni la vede [$_i$e]

Who do you think that Giovanni sees   her?

It is reasonable, even at a pre-theoretical level, to assume that an object cannot be interpreted in conjunction with both a clitic and a Wh-phrase (aside perhaps for some cases of clitic doubling, cf. Note 10). Specifically, we will assume that an *ec* related to a clitic is an anaphor (falling under principle A of the Binding Theory, see II.0.3 below), while an *ec* related to a Wh-phrase must be a variable.[7] Example (8) is thus excluded, and so is (7b).[8]

We therefore assume that INFL in NS languages has the option of being either just like INFL in English (non-pronominal and not a proper governer), or just like a clitic, namely pronominal. In this latter case (and only in this case) it will be a proper governer.[9] The first possibility will account for the cases in which the subject is not null. The second possibility will be responsible for the NS phenomena, i.e. for null subjects, whence free inversion, whence the apparent lack of COMP-trace effect. Availability of the second possibility represents the NS (or pro-drop) parameter.

A characterization of the NS parameter partly similar to Rizzi's, which shares Rizzi's reinterpretation of the distribution of COMP-trace phenomena, has been given by Chomsky in LGB, following in part Jaeggli (1980). Chomsky also assumes that the empty position of NS sentences is related to the inflectional element of the verb, but he assumes that such a position is not an instance of [e], as in Rizzi's theory, but an instance of PRO, the element that enters into Control. Under Chomsky's formulation, the *plus* value of the NS parameter consists of the possibility for INFL (in (4)) not to govern the subject position at all, an idea which is implemented by assuming that in NS languages INFL can either move to the verb in the phonology, as in English, or in the syntax, thus leaving the subject position ungoverned at S-structure. Under the second option, the element PRO will be allowed in subject position, and in fact required, since [e] will be ruled out by the ECP, and lexical NPs and variables will fail to receive Case.

The parallelism between NS and cliticization is preserved in Chomsky's discussion, which assumes, following Jaeggli (1980), that null objects related to clitics are also instances of PRO. Within our account however, there will be no motivation for assuming PRO in the case of clitics, an assumption that leads to the undesirable conclusion that clitics must 'absorb' government by the verb (in addition to Case).[10] Rather, we assume that null objects related to clitics are quite analogous to traces (though they do not arise from movement), transmitting a θ-role to their antecedents. Since we assume the analogy between NS and cliticization and since we assume [e] not PRO for the case of cliticization, it follows that we must adopt Rizzi's, not Chomsky's formulation.[11]

We note that within a framework in which null elements are intrinsically defined there would be a certain argument in favor of the PRO hypothesis. Consider cases combining NS and NP-movement, like (9).

(9)   [$_i$e]   sono stato invitato [$_i$e]
         (I) have been invited.

Within the framework in question, the θ-criterion would force us to assume that the D-structure direct object in (9) is not [e] but PRO, since this is the only null element that can receive a θ-role, and therefore that the S-structure subject is PRO. However, the argument disappears in the framework of LGB, Chapter 6, which we are adopting. In this framework [e] and PRO do not differ in content, but only in the contexts where they can occur at S-structure (governed versus ungoverned ones). The D-structure object in (9) would now be PRO, if by *PRO* we identify the null element that has an independent θ-role, but could become [e] linked with inflection once it is moved into subject position, since the two are not distinct in content.

While we thus assume that INFL is analogous to clitics (an assumption supported also by the fact that in certain Italian dialects there are real subject clitics functioning as inflection; cf. 2.5 below), comparison between (9) and the corresponding case involving subject clitic SI in (10), will require further discussion.

(10)   [$_i$e] si è stati   invitati [$_i$e]
          SI has been invited

In 1.6 above, we assumed that in cases like (10), SI is in object position in D-structure, later undergoing NP-movement, and finally cliticizing from subject position. This analysis was required by our assumption that clitics are arguments, and as such must, by virtue of the projection principle and the θ-criterion, be associated with a θ-role at all levels. The question now is whether such considerations relative to subject clitic SI carry over to the inflectional element INFL, which we are also taking to be a subject clitic. We note that, if they did, we would be led to the rather strange conclusion that INFL too must be base-generated in object position in (9), in order to receive a θ-role, undergoing NP-movement in the course of the derivation. This would conflict with our previous assumption that the structural position of INFL at all syntactic levels is the one indicated in (4) (i.e. the one in [$_S$NP INFL VP]). However, there is reason to believe that the considerations in question do not carry over to INFL.

Note that we are independently assuming that INFL in Italian is ambiguously either a clitic, as in (11a), or just like INFL in English, as in (11b).

(11) a. [e]   ved- e   Maria

     (*he*) *se-   es Maria*

     He sees Maria.

   b. Giovanni ved- e   Maria

     Giovanni se-   es Maria

     Giovanni sees Maria.

But we must assume further that this ambiguity of INFL, i.e. the possibility of being either plus or minus pronominal, holds not only across different sentences, as in (11), but also within the same sentence, across different derivational levels. Consider (12), where (b) derives from (a) via rightward NP-movement.

(12) a. Giovanni telefon-   a
     Giovanni telephon- es

     Giovanni telephones.

   b. [e] telefon-a Giovanni

Clearly, in the D-structure (12a), INFL cannot be pronominal, since it has no *ec* to be associated with. Yet it must be pronominal (a non-argument pronominal in this case) in the S-structure (12b), where it is associated with the *ec*. This assumption that the pronominal status of INFL need not be determined till late in the derivation will now suffice to account for (9) ([$_i$ *e*] *sono stato invitato* [$_i$ *e*]) under our general assumptions. In this case, INFL will be non-pronominal in D-structure (as in the English [*e*] *have been invited I*). There will therefore be no requirement that it be associated with an *ec*. The *ec* in object position will be assigned a θ-role in D-structure as we discussed above (in this respect it will be PRO), and then moved into subject position. Once object θ-role is thus associated with the subject position (as in I_i *have been invited* t_i), INFL will — necessarily — become pronominal (an argument pronominal in this case), so as to be associated with the subject position and the θ-role which is transmitted to that position by the object. Therefore, although sometimes a clitic, the element INFL is thus effectively exempted from the requirement that it be associated with a θ-role at all levels.

While our view of SI therefore does not carry over to INFL, we may still ask whether our view of INFL could carry over to SI: if SI could function just like INFL, then in (10) it would not need to be generated in object position at all, contrary to our analysis of 1.6, and just like INFL. The question in essence is whether it would be appropriate to analyze SI as a special inflectional element.[12] The answer to this seems to be no. The motivation that led us to assume ambiguity with respect to pronominal or nonpronominal status for INFL, is lacking in the case of SI. In particular, there is no alternation like (11) in the case of SI. Thus, while we have **[e] si vede Maria** 'SI sees Maria', possibly parallel to (11a), we do not have ***La gente si vede Maria** 'People SI-see Maria' or anything of the sort, parallel to (11b). We must therefore assume that SI is un-ambiguously pronominal, and that our conclusions of 1.6 above stand.[13]

There are two other respects in which the inflectional element differs from subject clitic SI. The first difference is that, unlike SI, INFL does not allow Object Preposing, as in (13).

(13) a. Maria$_i$ si vede spesso t$_i$
   Maria SI sees often

  b. *Maria$_i$ vede spesso t$_i$
   Maria (he) sees often

The ungrammaticality of (13b) follows straightforwardly from the θ-criterion and from the fact that there is only one INFL. Assuming that the verb must always obligatorily agree with the subject (when the latter has person features, cf. 1.7), INFL in (13b) must be non-pronominal, since it must agree with *Maria* which however has object θ-role. Thus, there remains no element analogous to SI of (13a) to bear subject θ-role. Notice that in (13a), although we assume SI to be related to the subject position (cf. 1.6.2), there is no question of conflict of verb agreement (between *Maria* and SI), since we have argued that, being impersonal, SI does not induce any verb agreement at all — and that it does not induce third person singular agreement. (cf. 1.7.) In this respect we predict (cor-rectly) that O.P. should be possible with a subject clitic only if this is also impersonal, i.e. if it leaves the verb free to agree with some other NP.

The second difference between INFL as a clitic and SI is that only the latter induces auxiliary **essere** (E) as in (14).

(14) a. [e] si è mangiato bene

   SI has eaten well

  b. [e] h-o mangiato bene

   (I) have eaten well

Recall that a relation between the subject position and a clitic is one of the cases that trigger the rule of E-assignment (cf. 1.7.) Yet in the case of INFL, we find auxiliary *avere*, as in (14b).

A plausible account of this apparent discrepancy in our theory can be given by regarding E-assignment/pp agreement on the one hand, and verb agreement on the other as analogous but complementary systems. That is to say, both as systems through which certain relations between constituents are given morphological manifestation, and yet as systems whose domains do not overlap. Then, since the relation between the subject and INFL is part of the verb agreement system, we will expect that it should not induce auxiliary E. But we will then also expect that a subject clitic should induce E just in case it does not also induce verb agreement. And this seems to be true as SI does not induce verb agreement (cf. 1.7.)

In this section we have provided a characterization of the null subject property of Italian, adopting the theory of Rizzi (1982b, IV), which appears quite compatible with the rest of our discussion. Under this characterization, the inflectional element of the verb binds the *ec* in subject position in the same manner as an object clitic binds an *ec* in object position.[14] The inflectional element in Italian thus alternates between being a pronominal, in which case it will *properly* govern the subject position, and not a pronominal, in which case it will govern the subject position, assigning nominative Case to it, but not *properly* governing it. We assume that when INFL is a pronominal it is sometimes an argument (as in (3b), (11a)), and sometimes a non-argument (as in (12b)) just like other pronominals such as French *il* or English *it*.

2.2 NULL SUBJECTS AND FREE INVERSION

We will argue that, in inversion sentences, a certain relation holds between the non-argument in subject position and the i-subject, as in (15), where the relation is expressed by coindexing.

(15)   There$_i$ have arrived [$_i$three men]

We will also argue that an analogous relation holds between the non-argument in subject position and the sentence in cases like (16).

(16)   It$_i$ seems [$_i$that John is here]

Existence of such a relation in cases like (15), (16) is supported by a number of considerations. First there is the distribution of these pleonastic elements. *There* is only found when there is an NP in post verbal position, and correspondingly pleonastic *it* is only found when there is an S.[15] This follows if *there* must in fact be coindexed with an NP, and *it* with an S, but it would be an accident if the latter elements did not bear any relation to the post verbal argument. Another piece of evidence is plural verb agreement in (15): if the relation in question exists, we can assume that in (15) the i-subject transmits plural features to the subject position, and we thus avoid duplication of verb agreement mechanisms.[16] We can also naturally assume that in (15) *there* transmits Case to the i-subject (or forms a chain with it. See below.)

A rather ingenious argument for coindexation in both *there* and *it* cases, which we will attempt to reproduce succinctly, is given in LGB, 3.2.3, on the basis of observations of D. Sportiche and T. Stowell. Chomsky points out the quasi-grammaticality of cases like (17a, b) despite the fact that in these cases the relation between antecedent and anaphor seems even less local than in fully ungrammatical cases like (17c).

(17) a. They$_i$ expected [$_S$that [pictures of *each other$_i$*] would be on sale]

b. They$_i$ think [$_{S_1}$ it is a pity [$_{S_2}$ that [pictures of *each other$_i$*] are hanging on the wall]]

c. *They$_i$ expect [$_S$that *each other$_i$* will come]

Chomsky proposes to account for these facts in a way which we may summarize as in (18).

(18) a. An anaphoric relation is possible only if there is no accessible SUBJECT different from the antecedent. Where SUBJECT is either a subject or INFL.[17]

b. There is a general condition "*[$_i$ ... α_i ...]" disallowing coindexation between a category and one of its constituents.

The generalization in (18a) is implied by the binding theory under a further elaboration that Chomsky proposes. The claim in (18b) appears to have independent justification (see LGB for details). Under (18), (17c) will be correctly ruled out as there is an accessible SUBJECT, namely the INFL relative to the tensed complement, intervening to rule out the anaphoric relation. In contrast, (17a) will be allowed since the same INFL is not accessible, by virtue of (18b). In particular, since it is assumed that INFL is always coindexed with the subject, and thus with *pictures of each other* in (17a), further coindexation between INFL and *each other* would violate (18b). This makes INFL not accessible in the relevant sense, and thus leaves *each other* free to be coindexed with an NP outside the clause. Turning now to (17b), here *each other* will be free to have an antecedent outside S$_2$ for precisely the same reasons as those discussed in connection with (17a). But in order to have an antecedent outside S$_1$ as well, it must be the case that neither the element *it*, nor INFL relative to S$_1$ (INFL$_1$) are accessible. This in fact follows from coindexation between *it* and S_2, which is what we are trying to prove: the element *it* is the subject of S_1 and is thus coindexed with $INFL_1$; S_2 is coindexed with *it* and thus with $INFL_1$ as well; since *each other* is a constituent of S_2, its coindexation with either *it* or $INFL_1$ would violate (18b). Thus neither *it* nor $INFL_1$ are accessible SUBJECTS, and *each other* can have the more remote antecedent *they*.[18]

As Chomsky notes, it would not be possible to claim that pleonastic *it* is not an accessible SUBJECT in general, since it must be in (19), where it does disallow a more remote antecedent.

(19)   *They$_i$ think it bothered *each other*$_i$ [$_S$that . . .]

The case in (19) is as expected under (18), since *each other* is here out-side the clause coindexed with *it*, and (18b) will thus play no role.

Parallel evidence for coindexation in the case of *there* is provided by examples like (20) (from LGB).

(20)   They$_i$ think there are [some letters for *each other*$_i$] at the post office.

Again, *each other* will be allowed (by (18b)) to have the remote antece-dent *they*, since it is contained within a phrase coindexed with the inter-vening subject *there*.

Implicit evidence for coindexation between *it*, *there* and the post verbal argument is also provided by the discussion in LGB, Chapter 6. As we mentioned in I.0.3, in this chapter Chomsky attempts to reduce the Case Filter to the θ-criterion, by appealing to the notion of chain. For example, in *John$_i$ was invited t$_i$*, the chain (*John$_i$*, t_i) has one Case, assigned to the subject position, and one θ-role, assigned to the object position. Given such one-to-one correspondence between Case and θ-roles, one can adv-ance the hypothesis that Case assignment is always a prerequisite for θ-role assignment (except for the case of PRO however, which does not require Case, cf. Note 8, I.0.)[19] But pleonastic elements like *it* and *there* would falsify this hypothesis unless they formed chains with post verbal arguments. That is, taken in isolation, pleonastics have Case, as can be shown since they do not occur in general as subjects of infinitives, but have no θ-role, since they are non-arguments. It is only if they are taken in conjunction with a post verbal argument that the association between Case and θ-roles holds. A chain formed by the pleonastic and an argu-ment will have one Case: assigned to the pleonastic, and one θ-role: ful-filled by the argument.

On the basis of the several arguments we have given, we thus conclude that elements like *there* and *it* are coindexed with post verbal phrases, NPs or Ss.

We will now claim that, for the aspects we just discussed, Italian is analogous to English, namely that in Italian too one finds non-argument subjects coindexed with a post verbal NP or S. Before turning to Italian however, we consider the fact that there are two different types of cases in which the configuration 'It . . . that S' is found. In one, exemplified by (21a) (and presumably (16)), the clause has object θ-role, and in the other, exemplified by (21b), the clause has subject θ-role.

(21) a. It was expected [that John would leave]
   b. It bothers me [that John left]

That the clause in (21a) bears object θ-role is obvious from the parallelism with *Someone expected [that John would leave]*, where it clearly does. That the clause in (21b) bears subject θ-role is obvious from the fact that, while the active verb *bother*, assigns subject θ-role in general as in *Bill bothers me*, it does not itself fulfil that θ-role. Thus, if we replace the element *it* with an element that will necessarily fulfil the θ-role, the example will be ungrammatical unless we eliminate the clause: *Bill bothers me (*that John left)*. In (21b) *it* must thus transmit subject θ-role to the clause, which — incidentally — is further evidence for coindexation.

If we take D-structure — as usual — to be a pure representation of θ-structure (or of "thematically relevant grammatical functions", in Chomsky's terms), with all the arguments in the position in which they are assigned θ-role, it will follow that the clause is base-generated in its position in (21a), but moved from subject position in (21b).[20, 21] Both constructions in (21) are generally labelled "extraposition". Given the preceding discussion, this may not seem too appropriate for referring to the type in (21a). But we can use the term in a manner parallel to our use of *inversion*, namely to identify a certain configuration descriptively, while remaining neutral on the derivational history.

Given the two types of extraposition we have characterized, the parallelism we are assuming between extraposition and inversion (i.e. between (15) and (16)) will lead us to expect that, at least in principle, there should be two types of inversion as well. Existence of these two types in Italian is in fact precisely what we argued for in chapter 1. The two types are exemplified in (22).

(22) a. [$_i$e] arriv- a   Giovanni$_i$
           arriv- es Giovanni

   Giovanni arrives.

   b. [$_i$e] telefon- a   Giovanni$_i$
           telephon- es Giovanni

   Giovanni telephones

As we argued, we take the i-subject in (22b) to be derived by movement, but the one in (22a) to be base-generated. Then, while the coindexation of (22b) may be due to movement, that of (22a) must be due to some other procedure. But the existence of such a procedure is now established independently of our discussion of Italian, by extraposition cases like (21a). We thus assume the same coindexation relation between a non-argument subject and a post-verbal argument, NP or S, whether the latter has undergone movement, as in (21b), (22b), or not, as in (21a), (22a). We put aside for the moment the question of whether English also has both types of inversion. Pursuing the analysis of Italian inversion, we assume that in both examples of (22) the null subject falls under the characterization of 2.1 above. The *ec* is thus properly governed by INFL under the pronominal option for INFL. In these cases INFL will be a non-argument pronominal element, like *it* and *there*.

We may note that the two types of both extraposition and inversion emphasize the relevance of the notion of chain. Thus, while the argument has subject θ-role in one case ((22b), (21b)), and object θ-role in the other ((22a), (21a)) the two cases appropriately fall together in terms of chains, since there is exactly one chain, with one argument and one θ-role, in both cases.

Continuing to extend to Italian the analyses we outlined for English, we will assume that, as in English, the relation between subject and i-subject is responsible for transmitting Case to the i-subject, as well as transmitting the features of the i-subject to the subject position.[22] We then correctly expect that the impossibility of lexical subjects with infinitivals, illustrated by (23a) should carry over to i-subjects, as in (23b).

(23) a. *La speranza [(di) Giovanni arrivare] è svanita
         the hope   (of) Giovanni to arrive is vanished

     b. *La speranza [(di) arrivare Giovanni] è svanita
         the hope   (of) arrive Giovanni is vanished

Both (23a, b) will be ruled out by lack of Case on the NP *Giovanni* (or the chain containing it), analogously to corresponding English cases, cf. *The hope some men to arrive . . . /*the hope there to arrive some men . . . .*[23] On the assumption that not only Italian inversion, but Italian extraposition, too, is analogous to its English counterpart, we will predict the ungrammaticality of the infinitival version of (24a) in (24b).

(24) a. Mi è capitato   di nuovo [di vedere Maria]
        (it) to-me is happened again   of to see Maria
        It happened to me again to see Maria.

     b. *La probabilità di capitarmi   di nuovo [di vedere
         the probability of (it) to happen-to-me again   of to see

        Maria] è scarsa
        Maria is scanty

Notice that the ungrammaticality of (24b) and the parallelism with its English counterparts, cf. the gloss or, for example, *It to seem that John is incompetent would be embarassing*, provides a fairly strong argument for the existence of the subject position in these cases. For cases of inversion, one could have tried to argue that the inflectional element simply assigns nominative Case to the right rather than to the left, and correspondingly agrees with a post-verbal rather than a pre-verebal NP. The parallel ungrammaticality of (23a, b) might thus have been accounted for under this view, without invoking the presence of a subject position. But a similar approach to extraposition cases would fail to account for (24b). In fact there is little reason to believe that the sentential complement in (24b), or that Ss in general, require Case. The ungrammaticality of (24b) will thus only follow if we assume the existence of a subject analogous to English *it*.

Notice that the account of (24b) we are thus providing assumes that the subject of the infinitival cannot be PRO: since chains headed by PRO never require Case, (24b) ought to be grammatical if PRO was allowed. But that PRO cannot occur in such cases is established independently of Italian: *To seem/To happen that S would be embarrassing*. What must be assumed is that PRO cannot be a non-argument, quite generally. As far as I can see, at the present stage of understanding, this condition must be stipulated.

Returning to inversion and to the relation between subject and i-subject, we note that, in Italian, evidence for such a relation is also provided by the system of auxiliary assignment and past participle (pp) agreement of 1.7 above. Consider the identity in auxiliary and pp agreement in (25a, b), under the analyses we are now assuming.

(25) a.   Maria è   arrivata t
          |_____|

     Maria is arrived (fem.)
     Maria has arrived

     b. [e] è arrivata   Maria
         |_____|

         is arrived (fem.) Maria

Under the formulation of 1.7 above, in (25a) both **essere** (E) and pp agreement are determined by the relation between the subject and the direct object. In particular the pp will agree with the element that serves as the antecedent in the relation (i.e. *Maria*). It must then be the case that an analogous relation between the subject and the direct object exists in (25b), just as we are assuming. (Specifically, a *binding relation*₁ must be involved, given our formulation of 1.7. We will return to the exact status of these relations with respect to the binding theory). As in (25a), the pp will agree with the element coindexed with the direct object, namely the subject. Since the subject bears the traits transmitted by the i-subject, pp agreement is as expected. Notice that we do not assume that the pp agrees directly with *Maria* in (25b), and we thus predict that, under inversion, verb agreement and pp agreement will always go together. This is correct, as shown for example by French, which lacks both verb agreement and pp agreement in corresponding cases, as in (2b) (*Il est arrivé trois filles*). Cf. also Note 60.

Having thus considered auxiliary and pp agreement in one subcase of inversion, involving ergative verbs like **arrivare**, we must consider the other subcase, involving non-ergative verbs. This is illustrated by (26).

(26) a. Maria ha   telefonato
         Maria has telephoned

b. [e] [$_{VP}$[$_{VP}$ ha   telefonato] Maria]

has telephoned Maria

Under our discussion of 1.7, the lack of both E and pp agreement in (26a) is due to the lack of any relation involving either the subject or the direct object. The identical results in (26b) will follow from our definition of direct object as "an NP in an A-position governed by the verb" (cf. (86), (87), ch. 1). Since the i-subject in (26b) is adjoined to VP, it is not in an A-position, and it is thus not a direct object under the definition. Its relation with the subject will therefore not trigger either E or pp agreement. The system of E assignment/pp agreement thus appears to be sensitive only to relations between elements which are especially 'close' to the verb.

Notice that in 2.1 above, in adopting Rizzi's theory of NSs, we have committed ourselves to the view that all i-subjects can undergo Wh-movement, which in turn implies — given the ECP — that all i-subjects must be governed. Thus, the i-subject in (26b) must be governed like an object, and yet it must be distinguishable from a direct object for E assignment and pp agreement. These two constraints force us in effect to conclude that rightward moved i-subjects are adjoined to VP, just as we have been assuming: in order to be governed by the verb, such i-subjects must be within VP, but in order to be distinguished from direct objects at S-structure, where E assignment/pp agreement applies, they must only be *adjoined* to VP. They will then be governed under the 'extended' notion of c-command (cf. (12) in I.0.3 and discussion).

The difference with respect to auxiliary assignment that we find between the two subcases of inversion is reproduced within cases of extraposition, as in (27).

(27) a. [e]   mi   è   capitato   [di rivedere   Maria]

      (it) to-me is happened   of to see-again Maria   (E)

      It happened to me to see Maria again.

   b. [e]   mi   ha   seccato   [rivedere   Maria]

      (it) me has bothered   to see-again Maria   (A)

      It bothered me to see Maria again

The contrast in (27) follows (under a straightforward extension of the formalism of 1.7) from the assumption that in (27a) the clause has object θ-role, i.e. it is the analogue to the direct object NP of (25b), while in (27b) it has subject θ-role and is thus analogous to the VP adjoined i-subject of (26b).[24] The distribution of auxiliaries thus confirms the similarity between inversion and extraposition and provides evidence for the existence of the subject position in both cases.

     We can now address the questions which were left open in chapter 1. One question concerned the essential synonymy of inverted and non-inverted forms. This synonymy follows rather obviously from the fact that inverted/non-inverted pairs have identical θ-structures, i.e. originate from one D-structure. Thus (25b) is in its D-structure configuration while (25a) derives from the same structure via leftward NP-movement, and (26a) represents the D-structure configuration while (26b) is derived from it. Another question concerned the fact that the verb appears to agree with a post verbal NP if and only if the latter NP receives nominative Case (cf. discussion in 1.2 above). This will follow from the fact that both agreement traits and nominative Case are transmitted by the same relation. If that relation exists, both properties obtain; if it does not exist, neither property obtains. It is useful in this connection to consider each of the variants of the SI-construction, as in (28).

(28) i. a.   [e] si   leggerà   volentieri [alcuni articoli]
             SI will read (sg.) willingly   a few articles

     b.   [e] li   si   leggerà   volentieri [e]

        them SI will read (sg.) willingly

   ii. a.   [Alcuni articoli] si   leggeranno   volentieri t

        a few   articles SI will read (pl.) willingly

     b.   [$_i$e]   si   legger-anno   volentieri t$_i$

        (they) SI will read (pl.) willingly

iii. a. [e] si leggeranno   volentieri [alcuni articoli]

        SI will read (pl.) willingly   a few   articles

  b. *[e] li   si leggeranno   volentieri [e]

        them SI will read (pl.) willingly

In (ia), the verb does not agree with *alcuni articoli*, and the latter is not nominative. This is directly established by (ib), where the phrase pronominalizes as accusative *li*. The variant in (i) is therefore a normal transitive construction, with clitic SI as a subject. In (iia) the phrase *alcuni articoli* has been moved into subject position, where it triggers verb agreement, and where we assume it receives nominative Case. As we expect, (iia) has the NS counterpart (iib). Derivation of (iib) is parallel to that of (iia), with [e] replacing [alcuni articoli]. Because of the *ec* in subject position linked to object θ-role, verb inflection (INFL) must take the pronominal option to fulfil the θ-role. In (iib) INFL is thus the nominative counterpart to accusative clitic *li* of (ib). In (iiia) the subject-object relation is established not by movement as in (iia), but in the same way as in *Arriva Maria*, etc. INFL is also pronominal here, as in (iib), but non-argument pronominal in this case (like *it, there*). The relation indicated in (iiia) will cause transmission of the direct object (i-subject) features, resulting in verb agreement, and transmission of nominative Case to *alcuni articoli*, which therefore fails to pronominalize as accusative *li* in (iiib).[25]

Still in connection with the SI-construction, consider now the paradigm in (29), and the parallelism between (29b, c), which will further confirm our analysis.

(29) a. [e] ci   si   [molte cose inutili]   a Natale
        to-themselves SI buys   many useless things at Christmas

    We buy ourselves many useless things at Christmas.

  b. *[Molte cose inutili]   ci   si comprano t a Natale

    many useless things to-themselves SI buy   at Christmas

  c. *[e] ci   si   [molte cose inutili]   a Natale
        to-themselves SI buy   many useless things at Christmas

In (29a), a reflexive clitic coreferential with SI is possible, but in (29b) it is not. We can rather naturally account for this by assuming that only the subject position, and not SI itself, can be the antecedent for a reflexive clitic. Thus, in (29a) the reflexive can be coreferential with SI because the subject position is (solely) related to SI. But in (29b) the subject position is occupied by the phrase *molte cose inutili*, so that the reflexive can no longer be related to SI.[26] Given verb agreement, (29c) is the 'inverted' counterpart of (29b) (same relation as between (28iia) and (28iiia). Our analysis can rather naturally account for (29c), in terms of the subject position being occupied by the agreement features of the phrase *molte cose inutili*. In contrast, if inversion consisted of the possibility for nominative Case assignment and verb agreement to operate with respect to a post verbal position directly, this should cause no interference with the relation between subject position and a reflexive clitic, and there would then be no reason at all why (29c) should be ungrammatical.[27]

In this section we have claimed, based on the discussion in LGB, that English pleonastic subjects *there, it* are coindexed with a post verbal argument. We have further claimed that, once we abstract away from the fact that Italian allows null subjects, Italian is just like English, so that in Italian, too, we have coindexing between a non-argument subject and a post-verbal argument, NP or S. In support of our claim, we noted the impossibility of both inversion and extraposition occurring in infinitivals, which — especially in the case of extraposition — would not be predicted if the coindexing relation did not exist. We noted that the latter relation is in fact detected by the system of E assignment and pp agreement of 1.7. We further noted a similarity between the O.P. variant of the SI-construction and its 'inverted' counterpart which can only be accounted for if the non-preposed object is linked with the subject position as we assume. The conclusion that the post verbal argument is related to the subject position implies that the subject position exists, from which it is natural to deduce that in NS sentences in general the subject position exists, as in Rizzi's theory.

If our discussion is at all correct, then inversion in Italian is not a non-configurational aspect of that language. That is, Italian inversion does not consist of the option to have the subject position to the right of the verb rather than to the left. If the subject position were indeed on the right of the verb, inversion would be dissociated from the possibility of having null subjects.

2.3 INVERSION RELATIONS AND EMPHATIC PRONOUNS

In this section we will consider the exact nature of the relation between a non-argument subject and a post verbal argument. We will claim that such a relation is in important respects analogous to anaphoric relations, and that the binding theory must be modified in order to capture this fact. We will then consider the syntax of Italian 'emphatic' pronouns, which appears to have certain points in common with that of inversion.

As both Chomsky in LGB and Rizzi (1982, IV) note, the unqualified view that there is coindexing between the subject and the post-verbal NP in (30a, b) is problematic with respect to the binding theory of (31).

(30) a.   There$_i$ arrived [$_i$three men]

    b.   [$_i$e]   arriva   [$_i$ $\left\{ \begin{array}{l} \text{Giovanni} \\ \text{lui} \end{array} \right\}$]

             arrives $\left\{ \begin{array}{l} \textit{Giovanni} \\ \textit{he} \end{array} \right\}$

(31) a.   (A) An anaphor is bound in its governing category
         (B) A pronominal is free in its governing category
         (C) An R-expression is free

    b. α is bound by β if and only if α is c-commanded by β and coindexed with β. 'Free' equals 'not bound'.

The post verbal arguments in (30) are bound within their governing category (i.e. their S), given the coindexing, in violation of (B) and (C) of (31a).[28] Both Chomsky and Rizzi suggest that the coindexing of (30) is irrelevant to (31), though they do so in different ways. Chomsky supposes that a special type of indexing is involved, one which does not fall under the definition of 'bound' in (31b). Specifically, that co-superscripting rather than co-subscripting is involved, and that (31b) must read "co-subscripted", rather than "coindexed". Rizzi, on the other hand, suggests that the qualification that α not be 'θ-dependent' on β must be added to (31b), and he assumes that i-subjects always receive θ-role from the subject position, thus being 'θ-dependent' on the subject. Ignoring the fact that the latter assumption could not be made within our discussion since we assume that i-subjects of ergative verbs appear in a θ-marked position and are therefore assigned θ-role directly, under Rizzi's proposal the coindexing of (30) would not qualify as binding in (31b) (much as in Chomsky's system). The conditions in (31a) would then be irrelevant.

    The problem with this kind of solution, which removes inversion entirely from the scope of (31), is that it fails to express the fact that inversion relations are subject to precise locality conditions, as we will now try to show.[29]

    It is well known that the *there* construction gives rise to Raising/Control contrasts like (32).

(32) a.   There **seemed** to be several people at the meeting
    b.   *There **tried** to be several people at the meeting

The French *il*-construction is quite analogous in this respect, as in (33).

(33) a.   Il **semblait** venir   beaucoup   de monde
        it seemed   to come many people

    b.   *Il **voulait** venir   beaucoup de monde
        it wanted to come many people

At a superficial glance, the corresponding contrasts in Italian seem to be much weaker, as in (34).

(34) a.   **Sembrava** intervenire Giovanni
          seemed   *to intervene* *Giovanni*

   b.   ?**Sperava** di intervenire Giovanni
          hoped   *to intervene*   *Giovanni*

However, under special conditions the contrast appears very vividly in Italian too, as in (35), (36).

(35) a.   Sembravano intervenirne   molti
          seemed   *to intervene-of-them* *many*

   b.   *Speravano di intervenirne   molti
          hoped   *to intervene-of-them* *many*

(36) a.   Sembrava intervenire Giovanni [a risolvere il   problema]
          seemed   *to intervene* *Giovanni* *to solve* *the problem*

   b.   ?*Sperava di intervenire Giovanni [a risolvere il   problema]
          hoped   *to intervene*   *Giovanni* *to solve*   *the problem*

The reason for the difference between (34b) and (35b), (36b) is that in the latter cases the i-subject is necessarily within the infinitival complement which contains the ergative verb *intervenire*, and is actually the direct object of *intervenire*. Recall how Ne-Cl as in (35), and occurrence before a sentential complement as in (36) were two of the criteria given above (see 1.3, 1.8) to determine whether the i-subject was in direct object position (rather than adjoined to VP). Thus in (35) and (36) the matrix subject and the i-subject are effectively separated by a clause boundary, as for example in (37a) below. But in (34) the i-subject could simply be derived via rightward movement from matrix subject position (i.e. from *Giovanni sembrava/sperava di intervenire*) with adjunction to the matrix VP, so that no clause boundary would intervene, as in (37b).

(37) a.   [e] sperava [di intervenire Giovanni . . .]

   b.   [e] sperava [di intervenire] Giovanni

We will return to the fact that while the additional measures of (35), (36) are required to bring out the contrast in Italian, nothing is required in the case of English or French (see 2.6, 2.7 below).

At a certain descriptive level, we could then say that inversion appears bounded with Control verbs (let us say *clause*-bounded) but unbounded with Raising verbs. One can in fact have inversion over any number of

Raising verbs, without significant changes in the results (cf. *There seemed to be likely to be a riot*, etc.).

The apparent unboundedness with Raising verbs has a rather obvious explanation. It is clearly due to the fact that the non-argument subject undergoes Raising, so that the analysis of, for example, (36a) is as (38).

(38) $[_i e]$ sembrava $[t_i$ intervenire Giovanni$_i$ . . .]

Thus there is good reason to believe that there is, not a direct connection here between the subject and the i-subject in the embedded clause, but rather a two-step connection, each step having a character of locality. Before turning to Control verbs, we note that configurations like (38) support our view that the verb never agrees directly with a post-verbal NP. In fact in such cases the NP in question could be arbitrarily far away from the verb (given an arbitrarily long sequence of Raising verbs). Direct verb agreement would thus imply, rather implausibly, that the verb agreement rule is subject to no locality conditions at all. Under our assumption that the traits of the i-subject are transmitted to the subject position via the chain that links the two, nothing has to be added for (38).

Beside cases involving Raising verbs, in Italian there are actually other cases in which inversion seems to have an unbounded character. Consider (39).

(39) a. **Lui** sperava di intervenire a risolvere il   problema
         he   *hoped*   *to intervene*   *to solve*   *the* *problem*

     b. Sperava di intervenire **lui** a risolvere il   problema
         hoped   *to intervene*   *he*   *to solve*   *the* *problem*

The grammatical case in (39b), which is the inverted counterpart to (39a) by our descriptive criteria, seems to differ from the ungrammatical case in (36b), only in that the pronoun *lui* replaces the R-expression *Giovanni*. To give a descriptive characterization of the facts, we would thus have to say that inversion is bounded, except when the i-subject is a pronominal. But we will see below that even this second curious exception is only apparent, so that the bounded character of inversion is in fact quite general.

Let us then consider the typical violation of such boundedness, as in (40), in the analysis we assume.

(40)   *[e] sperava [di [e] intervenire Giovanni [$_S$ . . .]]

The question now is: Is (40) ruled out by independent principles, and is the bounded character of inversion thus merely a reflex of those principles, or do we have to assume specific locality conditions on the relation diagrammed in (40)? For cases like (40), independent principles, such as the θ-criterion, seem to suffice. In fact, the complement verb *intervenire* assigns a θ-role to its object — here *Giovanni* — but no θ-role to its subject which must therefore be interpreted as a non-argument, i.e. differently than PRO. Main verb *sperare* on the other hand does assign a θ-role to its subject. The latter will thus be interpreted as an argument, i.e. as a null subject analogous to *he*, and the sentence could thus only have the interpretation 'He hoped that Giovanni would intervene' (not 'Giovanni hoped to intervene'). But (40) is ungrammatical under such an interpretation as well, since even aside from the unresolved status of the embedded subject, the NP *Giovanni* has no Case.[30]

However, while the θ-criterion may thus be sufficient for (40), it will not be for other cases. Consider in particular the parallelism between (41) and (42), involving the SI-construction.

(41) a. *I sindacati si speravano [di convincere t a fare ulteriori

the Unions SI hoped (pl.) to convince to make further

concessioni]
concessions

b. I sindacati si vorrebbero [convincere t a fare

the Unions SI would want (pl.) to convince to make

ulteriori concessioni]
further concessions

(42) a. *[e] si speravano [di convincere i sindacati a fare

SI hoped (pl.) to convince the Unions to make

ulteriori concessioni]
further concessions

b. [e] si vorrebbero [convincere i sindacati a fare

SI would want (pl.) to convince the Unions to make

ulteriori concessioni
further concessions

The contrasts in (41), (42) are due to the restructuring process (of Rizzi (1978a) and ch. 5 below) applying in the (b), but not in the (a) cases. Since *sperare* is not a restructuring verb, the phrase within brackets in (41a) is sentential, and O.P. as in (41a) is thus ruled out by locality conditions on NP-trace relations (principle (A) of (31a)). But in (41b), where *volere* is a restructuring verb, the infinitival complement has been reanalyzed, so that the relevant locality conditions are no longer violated. The exact nature of the restructuring process need not concern us here. What is relevant is to note that inversion in (42) behaves exactly like NP-movement in (41).

Unlike (40) above and other cases, (42a) can be ruled out only by invoking locality conditions on the inversion relation. This is for two reasons. First, no problem arises with respect to the θ-criterion. Both the subject and the object positions involved have exactly the same status as their counterparts in the simple case **Si convinsero i sindacati a . . .** 'SI convinced (pl.) the Unions to . . .', or for that matter in (42b). Secondly, we cannot claim that in (42a) (and (41a)) SI can no longer be a controller for the embedded subject PRO on the grounds that the subject position is now related to (and, in (41a), occupied by) the object, as illustrated in (43).

(43) NP_j si_i speravano [di PRO_i . . .]

In fact, a relevantly analogous configuration is otherwise possible, as in (44).[31]

(44) $[_i$Certe cose] si_i dicono spesso t_j senza [PRO_i pensare]
           certain things SI say   often   without   thinking

   We often say certain things without thinking

Notice further that it would be both false and irrelevant to claim that (42a) is derived from (41a) via rightward NP-movement and is therefore ungrammatical for the same reason that (41a) is. False, because in (42a, b) the i-subject occurs in its D-structure position, preceding the sentential complement *a fare* . . . (Recall that the order 'i-subject, S-complement' is a diagnostic for base-generation of the i-subject.) Irrelevant, because the question would remain as to why (42a) should be impossible when there is no movement at all, as in *Arriva Maria*, etc.

   We thus have several reasons at this point to assume that the inversion relation is analogous to the relation between an NP and its trace. One reason is that, just like NP-trace relations, inversion relations trigger the system of E-assignment/pp agreement of 1.7, as we saw in 2.2. A second reason is that both NP-trace and inversion relations must fall under a common notion of 'chain', if Case-theory and θ-theory are to be unified along the lines of LGB, 6, as we discussed in 2.2. A third reason is that, as we just saw, the two appear subject to analogous locality conditions.[32]

   Let us then return to our initial problem, posed by (45) with respect to the binding theory in (46).

(45) a.   There$_i$ arrived [$_i$three men]

b.   [$_i$e] arriva   [$_i$ { Giovanni / lui }]

            arrives   { *Giovanni* / *he* }

(46) a.   (A) An anaphor is bound in its governing category
          (B) A pronominal is free in its governing category
          (C) An R-expression is free

   b. α is bound by β if and only if α is c-commanded by and coin-
        dexed with β. 'Free' equals 'not bound'.

It is intuitively clear that the binding theory is a mechanism regulating
coreference. As such, it prescribes that, of two coreferential NPs one of
which c-commands the other, the one which is c-commanded will never
be an R-expression, but will be either an anaphor or a pronominal,
depending on its 'distance' from the one which c-commands it. We may
schematically represent this as in (47).

(47)

The demarcation line between anaphors and pronominals in (47) is
determined by the governing category for NP'_i, for example by the clause
boundary in *John$_i$ said to himself$_i$ [that he$_i$ would leave]*. We thus have a
class of expressions which have local antecedents: anaphors; a second
class which have remote antecedents: pronouns; and a third class which
have no antecedents at all: R-expressions.

If we take (46) as saying something about coreference, it is clear why
R-expressions are required to never have antecedents (on a path of
c-command, which is what seems to be relevant). It is because they independently refer, unlike anaphors and pronouns. But if the purpose of
(46) is that of regulating coreference, we have no reason to expect that
the same formal principles should hold in cases like (45), where the
antecedent (NP$_i$ of (47)) is not an argument, and hence is not referential.[33] Both Chomsky and Rizzi implement the assumption that (46)
should not apply to (45), by reconsidering (46b). Under their reconsider-
ation, the cases in (45) do not fall within the definition 'bound' of (46b),
and (46a) is thus irrelevant. We will pursue the alternative, which consists
of leaving (46b) as is, and reconsidering (46a) instead.

Let us assume that 'free' of (B), (C) in (46a) means 'argument free'.
Under this assumption, (45) will not violate (46a) since the i-subjects in
(45) are only *non-argument* bound within their governing category.
Assuming naturally that the same qualification ought to be extended to
(A), i.e. that 'bound' in (A) should be interpreted as 'argument bound',
we will predict the ungrammaticality of cases like (48).[34]

(48)   *There$_i$ arrived [$_i$each other]

The anaphor in (48) is in fact not *argument* bound (only *non-argument* bound). As both Chomsky and Rizzi note, non arguments like *there*, which are not proper antecedents in cases like (48), are however proper antecedents in cases like (49), with respect to their own traces.

(49)   There$_i$ seemed [t$_i$ to arrive three men]

This suggests that the proposed qualification 'argument' (bound/free) in (46) only holds for arguments, i.e. for elements that bear θ-roles, not for traces, which do not. We will assume that this is correct. Principle (A) will thus read as in (50), and (B), (C) will have analogous expansions.[35]

(50) a.   An argument anaphor is argument bound in its governing category.

b.   A non-argument anaphor is bound in its governing category.

Principle (50a) will thus rule out (48), while (50b) will allow (49).

We must now ensure that locality conditions hold on the relations in (45). We will assume the following:

(51)   An argument bound by a non-argument, is bound in its governing category.

The advantage of this approach is that the relations in (45) are now binding relations, so that both the system of E assignment/pp agreement of 1.7 and the definition of 'chain' can refer simply to binding relations rather than to two types of relations. We also note that within Chomsky's and Rizzi's solutions, locality conditions on inversion (which they do not provide) would necessarily remain unrelated to the conditions in (46a), while this is not true in our case. In fact, although (51) is a separate condition, the similarity with (46a) raises the possibility — which we will not pursue here — that the former could be collapsed with the latter. Note in particular that the effect of (51) is exactly complementary to that of (B) and (C). That is, while pronominals and R-expressions must be free within their governing category with respect to arguments, they must be bound within their governing category with respect to non-argments, suggesting that the binding theory actually reverses itself when the antecedent changes from argument to non-argument.[36]

We now turn to the class of exceptions noted above, i.e. to (52).

(52)   [$_i$e] sperava [di intervenire lui$_i$ a risolvere il   problema]
             hoped   to intervene   he   to solve   the problem

If (52) were a case of inversion in the theoretical — not just the descriptive — sense, namely if the pronoun *lui* was non-argument bound by the matrix subject, this case would violate the locality condition in (51). However, there is good reason to believe that (52) is not a case of inversion in the theoretical sense.

We note first that such pronouns as *lui* in (52) occur in cases where there is no inversion, as in (53).

(53)   Giovanni interviene lui.
         Giovanni intervenes himself.

In (53), *lui* is understood as coreferential with the subject *Giovanni*, analogously to *himself* of the English translation. This means that, though formally a pronoun, *lui* of (53) is not a 'pronominal' in the sense of (B) of the binding theory (46a). Rather, such emphatic pronouns (henceforth 'ep's') must be regarded as anaphors. (We will argue for this below.) If (53) thus suggests that (52) *need* not be case of inversion, (54) suggests that in fact it *cannot*.

(54) Persuase   Maria [PRO a intervenire $\left\{ \begin{array}{c} \text{*lui} \\ \text{lei} \end{array} \right\}$

     (he) persuaded Maria   to intervene $\left\{ \begin{array}{c} he \\ she \end{array} \right\}$

     a risolvere il problema]
     to solve   the problem

     He persuaded Maria to intervene $\left\{ \begin{array}{c} \text{himself} \\ \text{herself} \end{array} \right\}$ to solve the problem.

If (52) were a case of inversion, there would be no reason why masculine pronoun *lui* should not occur in (54), just as it does in (52). This contrast between (52) and (54) indicates that the pronoun in these cases is related not to the *matrix* subject, but rather to the embedded subject PRO, controlled in (54) by *Maria*, whence feminine *lei*. The possibility for ep's to be related to PRO is also established by (55), in which the ep has no other possible antecedent.

(55)   [PRO andarci   noi] sarebbe un grave   errore
              to go-there we   would be a   serious mistake
         To go there ourselves would be a serious mistake.

The exceptionality of (52) will then disappear under the analysis in (56), once *lui* is interpreted as an ep.

(56)   [$_i$e] sperava [di PRO$_i$ intervenire lui$_i$ . . .]
              He hoped   to intervene himself

In (56) the matrix null subject will be an argument (analogous to *he*) and the pronoun in the complement will be an ep related to PRO. There will, therefore be no direct relation between the matrix subject and the pronoun.

Although the occurrence of an ep, which we may refer to as '(subject) doubling', and inversion are different phenomena as we have just argued, there are (in Italian) some striking similarities between the two, which we will discuss in the remainder of this section.

First, the constrast in (57) relative to i-subjects, appears duplicated in the case of ep's as in (58).[37]

(57) a. ??Sperava Giovanni [di risolvere il   problema]
         hoped   Giovanni to solve   the problem

    b.   Interverrà   Giovanni [a risolvere il   problema]
         will intervene Giovanni to solve   the problem

(58) a. (?)?Giovanni sperava lui [di risolvere il   problema]
        Giovanni hoped   he to solve   the problem

        Giovanni hoped himself to solve the problem.

    b.   Giovanni interverrà   lui [a risolvere il   problema]
         Giovanni will intervene he to solve   the   problem

        Giovanni will intervene himself to solve the problem.

In 1.8 above we argued that the i-subject in (57b) can unproblematically occur before the complement only because it is base-generated in that position, and that the contrast in (57) is therefore due to the fact that unlike *intervenire, sperare* is not an ergative verb. The parallelism of (57) and (58) will now suggest that the ep in (58b) is in the same position as the i-subject of (57b), namely in trace position (the same would hold in (52), and for *lei* in (54)). Examples (57b) and (58b) would thus be equally possible because *Giovanni* and *lui* occupy a base-generated position, while (57a), (58a) would both be problematic because with non-ergative *sperare* there is no such position, so that both the i-subject and the ep would have to be interpolated in some fashion.

That the i-subject and the ep make use of the same position here (that of direct object of the matrix verb), is confirmed by the fact that when such a position seems no longer available for the i-subject, as in (59c) contrasting with both (59a) and (59b), the ep is also barred, as in (60b) contrasting with (60a).

(59) a. Viene Giovanni [a prenderlo]
         comes Giovanni   to fetch-it

    b.   Giovanni lo viene [a prendere]
         Giovanni it comes to fetch

        Giovanni comes to fetch it.

    c. *Lo viene   Giovanni [a prendere]
        it   comes Giovanni   to fetch

(60) a. Giovanni viene   lui [a prenderlo]
        Giovanni comes   he   to fetch-it

Giovanni comes himself to fetch it.

    b. *Giovanni **lo** viene   lui [a prendere]
        Giovanni it   comes   he   to fetch

In (59), (60), *venire* is an ergative verb, like *intervenire* of (57), (58), whence the grammaticality of (59a), (60a). In addition however, *venire* can trigger the restructuring process. One of the indicators that restructuring has occurred is the cliticization of embedded objects to the matrix verb; (59b,c) and (60b) must therefore be cases of restructuring. What (59c) then indicates is that the NP position which separates the main verb from the complement in the absence of restructuring as in (59a) is no longer there once restructuring occurs. In chapter 5 below, we will consider how the restructuring process produces this effect. Here, it is sufficient to note that it does. But, given the parallelism between (60b) and (59c) we must conclude that the ep in (60a) does indeed occupy the same position as the i-subject in (59a), i.e. that *lui* in (60a) is in trace position.

While we thus have reason to assume that ep's can occur in trace position, it is clear that they do not occur only in trace position. In fact they are found not only with ergative verbs or passives, but also with other forms, as in **Giovanni ha telefonato lui** 'Giovanni has telephoned himself', etc. It may then seem reasonable to assume that when ep's are not in trace position, they are adjoined to VP, so that the parallelism with i-subjects becomes rather general. Occurrence in non VP final position, as in **Giovanni esaminerà lui il caso** 'Giovanni will examine himself the case' could then be accounted for by the same rule (discussed in 1.8), which we assume produces a similar order with i-subjects, as in **Esaminerà Giovanni il caso** 'Will examine Giovanni the case'. (As suggested in Note 37 we may assume that ep's can be permuted with other constituents slightly more freely than i-subjects).

But the formal similarity between inversion and doubling goes beyond the range of positions in which i-subjects and ep's can occur. We must assume in fact that a binding relation exists between the subject and the ep, just as it exists between the subject and the i-subject. This assumption is implicit in our conclusion that ep's sometimes occur in trace position, and is confirmed by cases like the following, which do not involve a trace position.

(61) Giovanni voleva [che Maria telefonasse { lei / *lui } a Piero]

    Giovanni wanted that Maria should phone { herself / himself } Piero

The grammatical variant of (61) shows that an ep is possible in this position. Since *telefonare* is not an ergative verb, this is not a trace position,
and is thus not independently coindexed with the nearest subject. In
order to rule out the ungrammatical variant we thus have to appeal to
locality conditions on the relation between an ep and its antecedent. The
most reasonable assumption is indeed that, while they are intrinsically
pronominals, functionally ep's are anaphors, just like traces, with which
they overlap in distribution. Principle A will then apply. Undoubtedly,
the functionally anaphoric status of these pronouns must be due to the
fact that they are not arguments.[38]

In so far as they are non-arguments, ep's are thus analogous to the null
subject of inversion. Compare the following two cases.

(62) a. [e] viene Giovanni

       comes Giovanni

  b. Giovanni viene lui

     Giovanni comes he

The null subject in (62) is interpreted as a non-argument pronominal.
Since the i-subject *Giovanni* transmits agreement traits to the subject
position, the latter is in effect a third person pronominal, just like *lui* of
(62b). The two cases in (62) are thus virtually symmetrical. The only
respect in which the symmetry breaks down is in that the pronominal of
(62a) is a clitic (as we saw in 2.2, 2.3 above), whereas the one in (62b) is
not. We may ask whether this difference is accidental. The answer is no.
Thus, *lui* of (62b) could not be a clitic, precisely because it is an
'emphatic' pronoun. As such, it carries emphatic stress, and lack of stress
is one of the conditions that characterize cliticization. Cf. **Ho invitato
LUI/*LO ho invitato** 'I invited HIM', where capital letters indicate stress.
On the other hand, the pronominal of (62a) *must* be a clitic. We note in
fact that non-arguments will never carry emphatic or contrastive stress,
presumably because they are semantically empty. (Cf. **It seemed that
John was incompetent, but IT never seemed that he was dishonest.*) Given
the relation between stress and cliticization just noted, we then naturally
expect that, in a language that has subject clitics, non-argument subjects
will always be clitics. Thus, aside from a predictable difference, the two
cases in (62) are exactly symmetrical.

The symmetry in (62) becomes identity of surface forms if we replace
Giovanni in (62a) with a pronoun, as in (63a), and *Giovanni* in (62b)
with the pronominal of NS sentences, as in (63b).

(63) a. [e] viene lui

      comes he

b. [e]   viene   lui

He comes himself

A sentence like *Viene lui* is thus ambiguously a case of inversion or of doubling. But the identity of the two cases in (63) goes in fact beyond the surface. In both cases we have a binding relation between the subject position related to a clitic pronominal (INFL) and a non clitic pronominal in post verbal position. The only difference between the two cases will concern which element bears the θ-role. In (63a) the i-subject *lui* bears the θ-role, whereas in (63b) the null subject does.[39]

The ambiguity between inversion and doubling of cases like (63) disappears in infinitivals however, which allow doubling as we have seen, and as in (64a), while not allowing inversion, as we saw in 2.2, and as in (64b).

(64) a. [PRO andarci   noi] sarebbe   un errore

to go-there we   would be a   mistake

To go there ourselves would be a mistake.

b. *[[e] andarci   Giovanni] sarebbe   un errore

to go-there Giovanni would be a   mistake

In (64a) we have a chain with one θ-role and one argument, namely PRO. We are independently assuming that quite generally there are no Case requirements for PRO. We further assume that there are no Case requirements for ep's. In the framework of LGB, 6, in which Case requirements are a reflex of θ-role assignment, this follows naturally from the fact that ep's have no θ-role, that is, they are non-arguments. Example (64a) will thus be well formed. (The fact that ep's are formally nominative (i.e. identical to nominative argument pronouns), forces us to assume that nominative is the unmarked form in Italian.) In (64b), as in (64a), we have a chain with one θ-role and one argument. However in this case the argument is not PRO but the phrase *Giovanni*, with respect to which Case requirements hold. Consequently (64b) is ungrammatical and (64a) unambiguously a case of doubling.

In this section we have thus argued that there are locality conditions holding on relations between a non argument subject and a post verbal argument. We have further argued that such conditions are best characterized by an appropriate extension of the binding theory. This allows us to regard inversion and extraposition relations as binding relations, like NP-trace relations. To the extent that they appear to exist, the locality conditions discussed provide further evidence for our claim of 2.2 above that the relations themselves exist.

We have also considered the case of emphatic pronouns in Italian, relevant to account for the apparent existence of a class of unbounded cases of inversion. We noted that the two strategies of inversion and doubling, which bear some analogy at the descriptive level in that both allow the presence of a NP with subject traits in post verbal position, appear to be in certain respects analogous at the formal level as well. In particular this is so with respect to the structural positions used, the relation linking the subject position and the post verbal NP, and the use of a non argument pronominal. Doubling becomes in fact superficially nondistinct from inversion when it occurs with a null subject.

2.4 RESIDUAL QUESTIONS

In this section we discuss certain cases with respect to which the theory of inversion we have proposed seems to be deficient.

One such case is exemplified in (65a,b), in which an i-subject occurs within a PP.[40]

(65) a. *[e] furono parlate [de   [le   vacanze]]
         were   talked   about   the vacations

    b. *[e] si parlano spesso [de   [le   vacanze]]
         SI talk   often   about   the vacations

Nothing in our discussion so far rules out such a case. The relation in (65) is legitimate from the point of view of the locality conditions we are assuming (i.e. (51)), and it therefore ought to be possible both for nominative Case to be transmitted to the post verbal NP, and for agreement traits to be transmitted to the subject position. Also, it seems unlikely that (65) could be ruled out in terms of Case conflict arising from both transmission of nominative Case from the subject position and assignment of ('oblique') Case by the preposition.

In fact other cases which are in this respect analogous, such as (66), are grammatical.

(66) a. [e] se ne$_i$ leggeranno   volentieri [alcuni [$_i$e]]
         SI of-them will read (pl.) willingly   a few
    We will eagerly read a few of them.

    b. [e] ne$_i$ furono fatti   leggere [alcuni [$_i$e]]
         of-them were   made to read   a few
    A few of them were made to be read.

According to our discussion of Ne-Cl in 1.4 above, the phrase *alcuni [e]* in (66a, b) must be in its D-structure position, and is therefore the direct object of *leggere* in both (66a, b). In terms of our discussion of the SI-

construction, the verb in (66a) can assign accusative. The direct object
here is therefore in a context of accusative Case assignment, and yet it is
nominative (cf. the discussion of (28) above, and Note 25). The same is
true in the 'causative' construction in (66b), where, while the matrix verb
fare has passive morphology and is therefore not a Case assigner (as we
discuss in 3.1), the embedded verb *leggere* can assign Case (we discuss
the causative construction in chapter 4 below). While (66b) is perhaps a
little odd, it is not at all comparable to either of (65). We must therefore
assume that Case assignment is obligatory not intrinsically, but only in so
far as NPs must receive Case. Under this assumption, accusative assignment in (66a,b) will freely fail, and the i-subject will correctly be assigned
nominative (recall that we are assuming on the basis of the discussion
in 2.2, that a post verbal NP will transmit agreement traits only if it is
nominative).

In 2.3 above, we stressed the similarity in the distribution of inversion
relations and NP-trace relations. Note that the similarity continues to
hold with respect to (65), given (67).

(67) a. *Le   vacanze   furono   parlate [di   t]

　　　 the   vacations   were   talked   about

　　 b. *Le   vacanze   si   parlano   spesso [di   t]

　　　 the   vacations   SI   talk   often   about

Presuming that the parallelism between (65) and (67) is not fortuitous,
one may wonder whether any of the existing theories of preposition
'stranding', which would account for (67), might be extended to cover
(65).[41] However, in contrast to the parallel status of (65)–(67), (68a, b)
exemplify a configuration in which an NP-trace relation is possible, while
an inversion relation is not, a fact again not predicted by our theory.[42]

(68) a.   Giovanni   sembrava [t   conoscere   la strada]

　　　 Giovanni   seemed   to know   the way

　　 b. *[e]   sembrava [Giovanni   conoscere   la strada]

　　　 seemed   Giovanni   to know   the way

Despite this breakdown in parallelism, there seems to be no reason to
dissociate the locality conditions on inversion from the binding theory. In
fact the ungrammaticality of (68b) is duplicated in the case of ep's, for
which it is fairly clear that the binding theory is involved, as in (69).

(69)   *Giovanni sembrava [lui conoscere la strada]

     Giovanni seemed   he to know   the way

Recall that we have argued that ep's can generally occur in trace position. From this point of view, the ep of (69) should then be unproblematic. Some other consideration would thus have to be appealed to in order to exclude this example, and we may plausibly expect that this will rule out (68b) as well. Notice that while both (69) and (68b) are unaccounted for, they represent yet another respect in which the distributions of inversion and of doubling are analogous.

There is one possibility that comes to mind, to exclude uniformly all the ungrammatical cases we just reviewed, which I will now briefly consider, even though it turns out to be incompatible with the rest of our discussion. This consists of supposing contrary to what has been assumed in the previous sections, that both i-subjects and ep's must be assigned nominative Case under government by a verb, tensed or infinitival.[43] Under this proposal, the cases in (65) would be ruled out because the intervening PP boundary blocks government by the verb, preventing the NP *le vacanze* from being assigned nominative Case. Example (65) would thus in effect be excluded quite analogously to (67) if we adopted the account of preposition stranding of Kayne (1981b). Kayne argues − on the basis of a proposed elaboration of the ECP − that in languages that do not allow preposition stranding, cases like (67) are excluded because the ec fails to be governed by the verb, whereas in languages that do allow preposition stranding, verb and preposition are 'reanalyzed' (as in Hornstein and Weinberg (1981)), so that government by the verb will in fact obtain.

For the cases in (68b) and (69) one could assume that the notion of government which is relevant for nominative assignment is a particularly restrictive notion, such that government here is blocked by intervening clause boundaries even though these are not maximal projections. Thus, *Giovanni* in (68b) and *lui* in (69) would fail to receive Case. This idea would not be too implausible since, within our discussion notions of government more restrictive than the one entering into the ECP are independently required to account for the lack of Exceptional Case Marking in Italian (see 4.1.3), and for the lack of assignment of auxiliary *essere* with some Raising verbs (see 2.6.2). That Case assignment is involved may seem to be supported in part by the fact that 'small clauses' (sc's), which − unlike Ss, as we assume − generally allow Case assignment across their boundaries as shown by (70), yield slightly different results in the configurations of (68b) and (69), as (71) shows.

(70) a. Ritengo [sc Giovanni   ammalato]
     I believe   Giovanni   sick

b. *Ritengo [$_S$ Giovanni essere ammalato]
  I believe   Giovanni to be   sick

(71) a.   Giovanni$_i$ sembrava [t$_i$ ammalato]
       Giovanni   seemed   sick

  b.   ?*[$_i$e] sembrava [$_{sc}$Giovanni$_i$ ammalato]
          seemed   Giovanni sick

  c.   ??Giovanni$_i$ sembrava [$_{sc}$lui$_i$ ammalato]
       Giovanni   seemed   he sick

The fact that the sc and S examples in (71b, c), and (68b)–(69) contrast
only weakly, thus mirroring (70) only in part, would remain problematic,
however.

But whatever exactly its intrinsic merits, the above proposal conflicts
with some of our other assumptions, in particular the following.

I. Under this approach, the Case Filter is no longer derivable from the
θ-criterion (as in LGB, 6). This is because, in order to block infinitival
cases of inversion like (72a), and appropriately distinguish them from
other cases like (72b), it will no longer be sufficient to require that the
chain be Case marked since we would be assuming that the i-subject in
(72a), just like the one in (72b), has Case.

(72) a. *[[e] andare Giovanni] sarebbe   un errore

        to go   Giovanni would be a   mistake

  b. [e] sembrano [t intervenir ne$_i$ [molti [$_i$e]]

        seem   to intervene-of-them many

Within this system we could not assume that nominative assignment to
the right is limited to tensed verbs, both because of the well formed
(72b) and because of infinitival cases with ep's such as *Andarci noi . .*
'To go there ourselves . . .' discussed in 2.3. In order to rule out (72a) we
would thus have to appeal to Case requirements on the non-argument
subject (which is in a Case assigning position in (72b), but not in (72a)),
even though the latter has no θ-role.[44] Such dissociation of Case requirements from θ-roles would also be implied by the assumption under this
hypothesis that ep's require Case.

II. In order to avoid arbitrary assignment of nominative Case to post
verbal NPs (cf. ***Giovanni invita io** 'Giovanni invites I' versus **Giovanni
viene lui** 'Giovanni is coming himself'), a requirement to the effect that a
post verbal nominative must be coindexed with a subject would have to
be added to our grammar.

III. While independent Case assignment to both subject and i-subject would thus be postulated, Case transmission by coindexing would still have to be allowed, for cases like (73a) contrasting with (73b) (cf. 1.6.2).

(73) a. [$_i$Quegli articoli] risultano [t$_i$ esser**si**   già letti t$_i$]
        those articles   turn out   SI-to be ('have') already read

    Those articles turn out to have already been read.

    b. *Sarebbe   bello [PRO$_i$ esser**si**   invitati t$_i$]
       (it) would be nice   SI-to be ('have') invited

               . . . to have been invited.

As we discussed in 1.6.2 above, we assume that (73a) is grammatical because SI is related to the subject position within its clause, which is in a chain bearing nominative Case, whereas there is no corresponding nominative Case in (73b). But given that Case transmission across clause boundaries is thus possible in (73a) (as well as in other cases involving subject clitic *ci* to be discussed below), nothing seems to prevent it in (68b), (69), in which *Giovanni, lui* should therefore have Case regardless of whether the preceding verb can assign it.

This kind of solution thus seem essentially incompatible with the assumption that Case is a property of chains or of indices: an assumption which we will continue to adopt, both because of conceptual advantages (it allows us to deduce the Case filter from the θ-criterion), and because of empirical advantages (it allows us to give an account of (73) and other cases.) We will thus leave the problems of (65), (68b), (69) (and (71b, c)) unsolved, simply keeping in mind their existence.

2.5 PIEDMONTESE *YE*

2.5.0 *Introduction*

In the preceding sections we provided a theoretical characterization of inversion in Italian. We claimed that i-subjects are linked to a non-argument in subject position and that the relation between the i-subject and the non-argument falls under locality conditions parallel to those which hold of antecedent-anaphor relations. We began our discussion by regarding inversion in Italian as essentially analogous to inversion in French and English, once we make allowance for the existence of empty subjects in Italian. In doing so we put aside a number of well-known differences. It is to those differences that we now turn, especially to the difference in the productivity of inversion. In this section we consider null subjects and inversion in the Piedmontese dialect (in the variety spoken in the Turin area), one of Italy's many regional languages. Piedmontese is of particular interest since it provides an almost perfect link between Italian and French, as we will see. The discussion of Piedmontese also provides a natural basis for dealing with Italian pleonastic subject **ci** 'there', which we thus also consider in this section.

2.5.1 *Inflectional Clitics*

Like Italian, Piedmontese is a NS language, as (75) below will illustrate. It differs from Italian in having a series of overt subject clitics. These are given in (74), along with the corresponding non-clitic nominative pronominal (with which they can coocur, as we see directly).[45]

(74)   Subject Pronouns
                          Non-clitic   Clitic

Sg. 1	mi	e
2	ti	t
3	chiel/chila	a
Pl. 1	nui (autri)	e
2	vui autri	(e)
3	lur	a

In tensed sentences, these clitics always occur, regardless of whether or not the subject position is filled, as in (75), where 'CL' in the glosses is a clitic in (74).

(75) a. $\left\{ \begin{array}{l} \text{Giuanin} \\ \text{Chiel} \end{array} \right\}$ **a** mangia

$\left\{ \begin{array}{l} \textit{Giuanin} \\ \textit{he} \end{array} \right\}$ *CL eats*

b.   **A** völ [mangé]
(he) *CL wants to eat*

Furthermore, such clitics occur *only* in tensed sentences, never in infinitivals, as in (76).

(76)   Giuanin **a** völ [mangé]
Giuanin CL wants to eat

This distribution follows if we regard these elements as part of a tensed inflection, namely as forming a discontinuous inflection with verb-inflection proper.[46] If this analysis is correct, it will lend further plausibility to our assumption that the inflectional element in Italian has clitic properties.

However, since Piedmontese allows 'Clitic Doubling', namely coexistence of a clitic and a non-clitic phrase related to it (with dative objects), one might suggest that (75a) should be regarded as a case of Clitic Doubling. Under this view, the alternation in (75) would be analogous to the one in (77).

(77) a.   E y_i parlava [$_i$ a Giuanin]
             (*I*) *CL to-him spoke   to Giuanin*

   I spoke to Giuanin.

   b.   E y_i parlava [$_i$e]
             (*I*) *CL to-him spoke*

   I spoke to him.

The conclusion that the clitics of (74) are inflectional elements may thus not seem required: they would simply be the subject counterparts to object clitics, allowing doubling, like the latter. The alternation in (75) would thus follow, and the absence of these elements in infinitivals, as in (76) could be handled by supposing that subject clitics require nominative Case. However, further considerations support the analysis of these elements as part of inflection over the alternative, as we will show.

Corresponding to Italian impersonal SI and pleonastic **ci** 'there' respectively, Piedmontese has the two subject clitics *se* (henceforth 'SE') and *ye*. In the presence of either SE or *ye*, the relevant element in (74) still appears, as in (78).[47]

(78) a. **A   s**   mangia bin
           CL SE eats   well

   We eat well.

   b. **A   y**   era   tanta   gent
           CL there was much people

   There were many people.

This is expected if *a* of (78) is part of inflection, since there is no reason, under our assumptions, why verb inflection should disappear in the presence of subject clitics like SE, *ye*. But it is unexpected if *a* in (78) is truly analogous to the dative clitic in (77), since Clitic Doubling never involves coexistence of two clitics, only of a clitic and a non-clitic phrase.[48]

Also, under Raising, subject clitics like *ye* of (78b), (79a) remain stranded in the infinitival, as in (79b), whereas clitics like *a* never do, as in (80).

(79) a. [$_i$e] a y_i é   tanta   gent
                  CL there is much people

   There are many people.

b. [$_i$e] a   püdria [t$_i$ esye$_i$ tanta gent]
         CL could   be-there much people

There could be many people.

(80) a. Giuanin **a**   mangia
         Giuanin CL   eats

b. Giuanin$_i$ **a**   püdria [t$_i$ mangé]
         Giuanin CL could   eat

Again, this follows if *a* in (80) is part of the tensed inflection, but not if it is a subject clitic unrelated to inflection. We will thus assume that the clitics of (74) are indeed part of inflection, and will refer to them as "inflectional clitics". We now turn to inversion.

2.5.2 *Inversion*

Piedmontese has two inversion strategies. One is exemplified in (81) and is quite analogous to the Italian strategy. The other is exemplified in (82) and involves the use of the pleonastic clitic *ye*.

(81) a. I   client a   telefunu
         the clients CL telephone

b. A   telefunu i   client
         CL telephone the clients

(82) a. I   client a   rivu
         the clients CL arrive

b. A   y   riva   i   client
         CL there arrives the clients

Beside differing with respect to the presence of *ye*, (81b) and (82b) also differ with respect to verb agreement: plural in (81b), singular in (82b). For the analysis of (81b) we assume complete analogy with corresponding Italian cases, regarding clitics like *a* now as part of INFL. For the analysis of (82b), we assume that *ye* is the clitic analogue to English *there*. Like the latter, *ye* can also be a locative pronoun. That *ye* of (82b) is related to the subject, can be easily shown. It is clear that it is not a locative here since, unlike the locative in (83a), *ye* of (82b) can cooccur with a locative expression, as in (83b).

(83) a. *   A   y   purtava sempre i cit
         (he) CL there took   always   the kids

al Valentin
         to the 'Valentin' (a public park)

b. A   **y**   riva   i   client ntel negosi
CL   there   arrives the clients in the store

Also, *ye* of (82b) cannot appear if the subject position is occupied as in (82a), so that *ye* of (84) will necessarily have a locative reading.

(84)   I   client   a   **y**   rivu
the clients CL there arrive

The clients arrive there.

We therefore take the analysis of (82b) to be essentially as in (85), where the relation between *ye* and the subject position is analogous to the one we have with the subject clitic SI of 1.6 above. We will return to the difference in agreement between (82b) and (81b).

(85) $[_i$e] a   y   riva $[_i$ i client]

CL   there   arrives   the clients

We now consider the distribution of the two inversion strategies. It is clear that the two types of inversion in (81b), (82b) correspond exactly in their distribution to the two types of inversion we claimed exist in Italian since, aside from some apparent exceptions to which we return, inversion with *ye* as in (82b) appears possible with all and only the verbs which we would analyze as ergative on the basis of independent criteria. The relevant criteria are the same as those we employed for Italian, in particular, alternation with a transitive form, as in (86) (on euphonic *l*, see Note 47), cliticization of *ne* as in (87) (see Note 47 on *na*), and auxiliary selection, as in (88) (cf. also the auxiliary alternation in (86)). With respect to both the syntax of *ne* and auxiliary selection, Piedmontese is indeed just like Italian.[49]

(86) a.   A   lan   chersü   tüti i   presi
        (they) CL have increased all   the prices

    b. A   lé chersüye   tüti i   presi
       CL is increased-there all   the prices

       There has increased all the prices

(87) a. A   y   **na**   riva   tanti
       CL there of-them arrives many

       There arrives many of them

    b. *A   **na**   telefunu tanti
       CL of-them telephone many

(88) a. I client   a   **sun**   rivà
    the clients CL are ('have') arrived

   b. I client   a   **lan**   telefunà
    the clients CL have telephoned

The class of apparent exceptions alluded to above is represented by ergative verbs that take the clitic *se*, equivalent to Italian *si* of 1.5 above. With these verbs, *ye* does not appear, as in (89).

(89)   A   lé rumpü**se**   due fnestre
    CL is broken-themselves two windows

   Two windows have broken.

Regarding this fact, we note first that in cases like (89), just as in cases in which *ye* does appear, and unlike those involving non-ergative verbs, there is lack of verb agreement; and second that there is reason to think that *ye* is actually deleted in the presence of some clitics (not all, given (87a)), as (90) illustrates. Notice the lack of verb agreement in (90c).

(90) a. A   lé riva**ye**   dui regai
    CL is arrived-there two presents

   There has arrived two presents

   b. *A   lé riva**mye**   dui regai
    CL is arrived-to-me-there two presents

   c. A   lé riva**me**   dui regai
    CL is arrived-to-me two presents

   (There) has arrived to me two presents

It is thus rather natural to assume that in cases like (89), (90c), *ye* is present underlyingly and is later deleted in the presence of *se, me*, let us say by a phonological rule. This will account for lack of verb agreement in such cases, and our generalization on the distribution of *ye* will hold in full.

Piedmontese thus strongly supports our view of chapter 1 that in Italian there are two different types of inversion, related to the two different classes of verbs (ergatives and non-ergatives), a view under which the superficial uniformity one observes in Italian is somewhat fortuitous.

Let us now consider what exactly determines the distribution of *ye*. The most natural assumption, and the one we will adopt, is that pleonastic *ye* is only available for insertion in D-structure. If *ye* cliticized by movement, this assumption would suffice to exclude it with non ergative verbs since, in D-structure, the subject position of a non-ergative verb will contain an argument, and *ye* could thus not be inserted. However, we must assume that *ye* is introduced as a clitic, to account for its failure to undergo Raising in cases like (79b), a consideration to which we will return in connection with Italian *ci*. Some further assumption will then be required to rule out the coexistence of a full subject NP and *ye* in D-structures like (91a), which would give rise to the ungrammatical S-structure (91b).[50]

(91) a. *I   client   a   y   telefunu
        the   clients CL   there   telephone

    b. *[$_i$e] a   y$_i$ $\left\{ \begin{array}{l} \text{telefunu} \\ \text{telefuna} \end{array} \right\}$ i   client

        CL   there $\left\{ \begin{array}{l} \textit{telephone} \\ \textit{telephones} \end{array} \right\}$ *the   clients*

We can naturally rule out D-structures like (91a) by postulating that *ye*, which is a subject clitic, must be related to an empty category, and not to a full NP. This condition is required independently, though at S-structure, by the ungrammaticality of (92b) (which corresponds to the impossible interpretation of *ye* as a pleonastic in (84)) derived from the well-formed (92a).[51]

(92) a. [$_i$e] a   y$_i$ riva   [$_i$ i client]   ntel negosi
            CL   there   arrives   the clients   in the store

    b. *[$_i$ I client]   a   y$_i$ rivu t$_i$ ntel negosi
            the clients   CL   there   arrive   in the store

The extension to D-structure of the condition required by (92b) is a rather natural one. Recall that, as we discussed in 1.4, we assume that if a clitic is base-generated, it must be related to its *ec* at all levels, thus also in D-structure. This conclusion was required by the projection principle for those clitics which we take to be arguments (i.e. those which correspond to *him*, etc.). What is required for *ye* is that this conclusion be generalized to all clitics, even those that are not arguments. Such a generalization seems reasonable, and we will assume it is true. Thus, while the projection principle gives us (93) with the parenthesized portion included, we will assume (93) holds even with that portion omitted.

(93)   A base-generated (argument) clitic must be associated with the relevant *ec* at all levels.

The condition in (94), required for (92b), will thus hold at all levels as a result of (93). This will rule out the D-structure (91a).

(94)   *NP$_i$ ye$_i$ ...
        where NP$_i$ is not an *ec*.

Occurrence of *ye* is thus limited to ergative verbs by postulating that it can only be inserted in D-structure and that once inserted it behaves as a subject clitic, requiring an *ec* in subject postion. Although insertion of *ye* is thus possible with ergative verbs, we assume of course that it is not necessary, to account for cases in which NP-movement applies (like (82a)).

2.5.3 *Italian ci*

Italian *ci* has a more limited distribution than its Piedmontese counterpart *ye*, but its syntactic behavior is otherwise quite analogous.

We have noted that Piedmontese *ye* selects ergative verbs. We now note that it also occurs with 'be' of existential and locational sentences as in (95a) (also as in (79) above). This is the domain in which *ci* is also possible, as in (95b).

(95) a.   A   y   é tanti client   ntel negosi   (Piedmontese)
          CL there is many clients in the store

          There are many clients in the store.

   b.   **Ci**   sono molti clienti nel negozio   (Italian)
          there are   many clients in the store

(We will return to the difference with respect to verb agreement between (95a) and (95b).) Occurrence of *ye* with 'be' suggests that the latter verb is relevantly analogous to ergative verbs, which means that the i-subjects of (95) are base-generated in post verbal position. If this is correct, it would then be perfectly natural to suppose that the cases in (96) are derived via leftward NP-movement from the same base forms, as the analyses indicate.[52]

(96) a.   [$_i$ Tanti client] a sun t$_i$ ntel negosi   (Piedmontese)
          Many clients are in the store.

   b.   [$_i$ Molti clienti] sono t$_i$ nel negozio   (Italian)
          Many clients are in the store.

This would in effect reverse the traditional view of the corresponding English cases (cf., in particular, Milsark (1974), (1977)) under which the forms of (96) are basic and those of (95) are derived via rightward movement. There are good reasons to believe that this reinterpretation, first proposed on independent grounds in Stowell (1978), is correct. One reason is precisely the occurrence of 'be' with Piedmontese *ye*, which we just noted.

Another reason is that there are cases of *ci/ye* which would have no source under a rightward movement derivation, such as for example (97a), given the ungrammaticality of (97b) (It is quite clear that (97a) represents the same construction as (95); a number of relevant facts will appear in the ensuing discussion).[53]

(97) a. Ci   vogliono altri   soldi.   (Italian)
         there want   other moneys

         It takes more money.

     b. *Altri soldi   vogliono.   (Italian)
         other   moneys want

Yet another reason is represented by Ne-Cl as in (98a, b). Ne-Cl is also possibile in (97a), as shown in (98c).

(98) a. A   y   **na**   ié tanti   ntel negosi.   (Piedmontese)
         CL there of-them is many in the store

         There are many of them in the store.

     b. Ce   **ne**   sono molti nel negozio.   (Italian)
         there of-them are   many in the store

         There are many of them in the store.

     c. Ce   **ne**   vogliono altri.   (Italian)
         there of-them want   others

         It takes more of them.

Recall that under our analysis of 1.4, Ne-Cl is only possible if the quantified phrase is base-generated in post verbal position, as with ergative verbs. The evidence for an ergative analysis of 'be' is, we find, rather strong, and we will review it more systematically in 2.7 below. Under such an analysis, appearance of *ye* as in (95a) is expected.

We will take Italian *ci* to be subject to exactly the same syntactic constraints we proposed for *ye*, in particular insertion only at D-structure, as in (95b). In addition however, we must presume that *ci* is subject to a lexical constraint allowing its occurrence only with 'be' (and some idioms, like the one in (97a)).

While our proposal that *ye/ci* can only be inserted at D-structure thus accounts for the fact that inversion with these elements is not possible with non-ergative verbs, we must note that a stronger condition seems to hold, in particular that if a verb allows *ye/ci*, then inversion without the latter elements is not possible, or is at least awkward, as in (99), (100).

(99) a. Tanti curidur a sun rivà.   (Piedmontese)
          Many   racers   have arrived.

      b. A   lè riva**ye**   tanti   curidur.   (Piedmontese)
          CL is arrived-there many   racers

          'There has arrived many racers.'

      c. ?*A   sun rivà   tanti   curidur.   (Piedmontese)
          CL   are arrived many   racers

(100) a.   Una lettera è   nella busta.   (Italian)
           A   letter   is   in the envelope.

   b.   C'è   una lettera nella busta   (Italian)
        there is a   letter   in the envelope

   c. ?*È $\left\{ \begin{array}{l} \text{nella busta una lettera} \\ \text{una lettera nella busta} \end{array} \right\}$ (Italian)

        is $\left\{ \begin{array}{l} \textit{in the envelope a letter} \\ \textit{a letter in the envelope} \end{array} \right\}$

It is not too clear how this fact could be expressed formally: since in chapter 1 we argued that inversion by rightward movement was always possible, even with ergative verbs (see the discussion of (122), ch. 1), the (c) cases above would be expected to be derivable from (a). We must therefore suppose that there is some hierarchy within the two inversion strategies, whereby inversion with *ye/ci* must be chosen if it can.

However exactly it is to be accounted for, the ungrammaticality of (c) in (99), (100) is of interest, because it gives rise to a situation in which inverted forms are necessarily distinguished from their non-inverted counterparts by the presence of an overt pleonastic element. This will enable us to test rather directly the claim of Rizzi (1982b, IV) that only i-subjects and not subjects can be Wh-moved in Italian (and, we assume, in Piedmontese, given its NS language status). The test gives the results in (101), (102).

(101) a. ??Vaire curidur t las dit ch'a sun rivà?   (Piedmontese)
          'How many racers did you say that have arrived?'

   b.   Vaire curidur t las dit ch'a lé riva**ye**?
         'How many racers did you say that there has arrived?'

(102) a. ??Che cosa hai detto che è nella busta?   (Italian)
          'What did you say that was in the envelope?'

   b.   Che cosa hai detto che **c**'è nella busta?
         'What did you say that there was in the envelope?'

The good cases of extraction, those in (b), are the ones that have the pleonastic element, whereas those in (a), that do not, are bad. The results are therefore as predicted by Rizzi's theory.[54]

Sentences with an *ec* in subject position, but with subject clitics like *ci* or SI raise the question of whether inflection (and, correspondingly, Piedmontese inflectional clitics) play any role in these cases. So far, we have been tacitly assuming that subject clitics are simply related to an *ec*, in the way in which object clitics are, as in (103), and that nothing else is involved.

(103) a. [$_i$e] **si**$_i$ costruisce molte case   in questa città   (Italian)
           SI builds   many houses in this city

  b. [$_i$e] **c**$_i$**'è**   del pane   sul tavolo   (Italian)
           there is some bread on the table

It is clear however that the possibility of having an *ec* in subject position here is determined by the NS property of Italian, since there appears to be no such possibility in French, which we will maintain is not a NS language. Thus, while we assume that French *se-moyen* (henceforth *SE*) corresponds to Italian SI, and that French *y* of the *Il y a*-construction corresponds to Italian *ci*, French cases like (104) would be ungrammatical with an empty subject position, as in **Se construit . . . , *Y a . . . .* ((104a) from Kayne (1975, p. 330)).

(104) a. Il **se** construit beaucoup d'immeubles dans cette ville (French)
        it SE builds   many buildings   in   this   city

  b. Il **y**   a   du pain   sur la table   (French)
      it there has ('is') some bread on the table

Recalling that we characterized the NS property as the possibility for inflection to perform as a subject clitic, two hypotheses come to mind to account for (103) versus (104):

I. The NS property is as we defined it: the *ec* in (103) is allowed because it is related to inflection (INFL), as in other NS sentences. Under this view, there are then two subject clitics in (103), SI/*ci* and INFL.

II. The NS property must be redefined to allow an *ec* in subject position when this is related not only to INFL, but also to other subject clitics, like those of (103). (French lacks this property.)

There are several considerations leading to the conclusion that I, not II is true. The first consideration has to do with the already noted fact that in the presence of clitics like SI/*ci*, inflection − in particular the inflectional clitics of Piedmontese − does not disappear, as in (78) above: **A s mangia bin** 'CL SE eats well'. If II were true, one might expect that the inflectional clitic *would* disappear, since it would be unnecessary. A second consideration relates to the fact that there is 'pro drop' only pre verbally, not post verbally, as in (105) versus (106) (analogous facts hold in Piedmontese).

(105) a.   Io sono alla festa.   (Italian)
       I am   at the party

  b.   Sono   alla festa.   (Italian)
       (I) am at the party

(106) a.   Ci   sono io alla festa.   (Italian)
         there am   I   at the party

     b. *Ci   sono   alla festa.   (Italian)
         there am (I) at the party

If SI/*ci* in (103) could satisfy well-formedness requirements on the empty subject, then perhaps inflection (which as we have just said does not disappear) would be free to be related to the post verbal nominative in (106b), exactly as it is related to the pre verbal nominative in (105b). Thus, II does not — at least not obviously — account for (106b), but I does: under the latter, since there is only one INFL, there can be only one empty position.[55]

A third consideration has to do with the stranding of these clitics under Raising as in (107) (analogous to the Piedmontese case in (79).)[56]

(107) a. [$_i$e] pareva [t$_i$ esser**ci**   del pane   sul tavolo]
          seemed   to be-there some bread on the table

    There seemed to be some bread on the table.

     b. [$_i$e] parevano [t$_i$ voler**ci**   altri   soldi]
          seemed (pl.) to want-there other moneys

    It seemed to take more money.

We note that, in this configuration, French differs from Italian not with respect to the *embedded* subject, which is contiguous to *ci*, but with respect to the *matrix* subject, which is contiguous to the tensed inflection, as in (108).

(108)   Il$_i$ semblait [t$_i$ **y**   **avoir**   du pain   sur la   table]
         it   seemed   there to have ('be') some bread on the table

    There seemed to be some bread on the table.

This shows that I, not II, must be correct: if II were true, and if (103) were grammatical because SI, *ci* can 'properly govern' the *ec* (or whatever the right local condition is), we would not expect (107) to be equally grammatical since the relevant configurational relation between SI/*ci* and the subject of the tensed verb — say, proper government — is certainly lost in (107). However, if I is true and if tensed inflection is thus what is relevant to the occurrence of the *ec* in (103), then the grammaticality of (107) is expected since, in the latter, tensed inflection — unlike *ci* — is indeed on the main verb.

We must therefore conclude that I is correct, and thus that there are two pronominals related to the subject position in (103): SI/*ci* and INFL. This is hardly surprising since we must in any case make a similar assumption for French, where we find both subject clitic SE/*y* and non-argument subject *il*, as in (104) above. Thus INFL in (103) and (107) (like the inflectional clitic of (79) above) will be the clitic analogue to French non-argument *il*.[57]

Cases like (107) provide us with the opportunity to draw a few other conclusions regarding the syntax of *ci/ye*. It is clear that, under Raising, pleonastic *ci/ye* not only *can* be stranded as in (79b), (107), but in fact *must*, as illustrated by ***Ci pareva essere del pane sul tavolo** in contrast with (107a). Apparent exceptions like **Ci dovrebbe essere del pane sul tavolo** 'There should be some bread on the table' are irrelevant here since we will see that the higher position of *ci* in these cases is due not to Raising, but to the process of Clitic Climbing characteristic of restructuring verbs like *dovere* (see ch. 5). Pleonastic *ci* and *ye* thus differ from the other subject clitic SI (Piedmontese SE is like SI) which, as we saw, can undergo Raising. This difference is accounted for by our assumption that *ci* and *ye* are base generated in clitic position, whereas for SI we assumed cliticization by movement. Since *ci* and *ye* are never in NP position, NP-movement will never affect them.

Notice however that, while we thus predict that Raising of *ci/ye* should not be possible, nothing we have said so far rules out insertion of *ci/ye* directly on the matrix verb in cases like (107). The phrase *del pane/altri soldi* would perhaps have to move first to embedded subject position, and then back to post verbal position if there were no other way to establish the appropriate coindexing with that position, but none of the conditions we have so far proposed would be violated.[58] What seems to be required to rule out generation of *ci* in the matrix is that not only the relation between *ci* and the *ec*, but also the inversion relation of *ci* be established at D-structure under appropriate locality conditions. These conditions would then be violated, for example, in $[_i e]$ ci_i *pareva* $[[e]$ *essere* NP_i ...]. We will assume that this is correct, returning in 2.7.2 below to discuss other facts that support it, and to consider its exact theoretical status.

As with other cases of inversion discussed in 2.3, in (standard) Italian cases like (107), the main verb obligatorily agrees with an i-subject which is actually within a sentential complement. Thus we find plural agreement in (107b), and **Parevo/*Pareva esserci io** ... 'seemed (1st sg.)/seemed (3rd sg.) to be-there I ...'. This shows that Raising here is obligatory. If it were not, the matrix subject ought to be interpretable as a non-argument related to the clause, like *it* of *It seems that* ..., and third person singular agreement ought to be possible. The obligatoriness of Raising in these cases, and analogously in the cases discussed in 2.3 (e.g. (38)) follows from Case theory. It is only if Raising applies that the chain containing the i-subject is extended to a Case-marking position. The *ci*-construction is in fact impossible in non-Raising infinitivals, like the other cases of inversion discussed above (cf. (23)), and as in (109) (analogous facts hold, of course, for Piedmontese *ye*).[59]

(109) *La probabilità $\left\{ \begin{array}{l} \text{di esser}\mathbf{ci}\text{ Giovanni} \\ \text{di voler}\mathbf{ci}\text{ le chiavi} \end{array} \right\} \ldots$

The probability $\left\{ \begin{array}{l} \textit{there to be Giovanni} \\ \textit{it to take the keys} \end{array} \right\} \ldots$

Notice that in infinitivals, instances of the *ci*-construction involving a pronominal i-subject like (110a) contrast with superficially similar cases like (110b).

(110) a. *[Non esserci   **noi** all'inaugurazione] sarebbe   un
            not *to be-there* *we* *at the inauguration* *would be*   *a*

          errore.
          mistake

     b. [Non andarci   **noi**] sarebbe   un errore.
          not *to go-there* *we*   *would be*   *a*   *mistake*

          Note to go there ourselves would be a mistake.

As we pointed out in 2.3, the grammaticality of (110b) is predicted under the analysis of *noi* as an emphatic pronoun, that is, as a non-argument. The argument here is the PRO subject of the infinitival, which does not require Case. But in (110a) the analysis of *noi* as an *ep* is impossible: while *ci* of (110b) is a locative, the one in (110a) is necessarily a pleonastic subject, given the presence of an overt locative phrase. Because of *ci*, the null subject of the infinitival in (110a) can therefore not be interpreted as an argument (cf. Note 57). The argument must then be *noi*; hence Case is required and ungrammaticality results, just as in (109).

2.5.4 *Verb Agreement*

We will conclude this section with some considerations on verb agreement and the 'definiteness' restriction. We have seen that the various inversion constructions of the languages we are dealing with exhibit differences in verb agreement. The case of Piedmontese will suggest that these differences are at least in part predictable from the nature of the non-argument subject involved.

    Like Italian, Piedmontese has systematic verb agreement with the i-subject when the empty subject is related only to inflection (cf. (81b)). However, things are different when *ye* is present. With *ye*, there is no verb agreement when the i-subject is third person (cf. (82b)), but agreement is required when the i-subject is first or second person (singular or plural), as for example in (111).

(111) a.   E seve riva**ye** vui autri.   (Piedmontese)
            There have arrived you-pl

b.   *A lé rivaye vui autri.   (Piedmontese)
     There has arrived you-pl

The facts of Piedmontese are actually duplicated by Italian at a substandard level. Thus, at that level, verb agreement can fail with ci as in
(112a), but not in the absence of ci, as in (112b).[60]

(112) a.   C'era molti clienti nel negozio.   (Substandard Italian)
           There was many clients in the store

    b. $*\begin{Bmatrix} \text{Arriva} \\ \text{Telefona} \end{Bmatrix}$ i clienti   (Substandard Italian)

        $\begin{Bmatrix} \text{arrives} \\ \text{telephones} \end{Bmatrix}$ *the clients*

But again, agreement cannot fail, even with ci, for first and second person i-subjects, as in (113).

(113) a.   C'eravate voi nel negozio.
           There were you-pl in the store

    b.   *C'era voi nel negozio.
           There was you-pl in the store

Since agreement can fail in English too (especially in spoken English)
as in *There's many people*, it would seem that for those constructions that
employ pleonastic *there* or its equivalents, the differences separating
Piedmontese, Italian and English are indeed minimal. Once we put aside
the difference between first-second and third person of Piedmontese and
Italian, not verifiable in English because of the definiteness restriction (see
below), we can regard standard Italian as identical to standard English,
while substandard Italian is identical to spoken English and Piedmontese.

Thus, while language specific idiosyncrasies must play some role, so as
to distinguish standard Italian from Piedmontese over otherwise identical
constructions (cf. (95)), the qualitative differences across the two types of
inversion suggest that a major role is played by the non-argument subject.
We may assume that the presence of lexical material such as *there* and its
equivalents interferes with the transmission of agreement to the subject
position, which is automatic and necessary in simple NS cases of inversion. For first and second person i-subjects, we must assume that somehow they transmit agreement traits more 'strongly', though we have no
explanation for this. For elements like *it* and its French counterpart *il*,
which *never* allow transmission of agreement (as noted in Note 22, cf. *It is/
are my friends, etc.) we may assume that they do not simply interfere in
the manner of *there*, but that — unlike *there* — they have third person singular agreement properties of their own (like argument *it/il*) which trigger
normal subject-verb agreement.

Turning now to the definiteness restriction, it is known from the literature that both the *there*-construction of English and the *il*-construction of
French are ungrammatical with i-subjects like *the dog, my dog, John, he,*
etc. As some of our examples have shown, this is not true of any case of
inversion in Italian or Piedmontese. However some form of restriction
along the lines of the one holding in English and French appears to hold
for the constructions with *ci* and *ye*, though apparently not for the other
inversion strategy.

Thus, quantifier phrases like 'everyone', which are impossible in English and French, appear to be impossible with *ci/ye* too, as in (114),
though they are not in (115).

(114) a. ?*A lé riva**ye** tüti.   (Piedmontese)
              '*There has arrived everyone*'

      b. ?*C'erano tutti nel negozio.   (Italian)
              '*There was everyone in the store*'

(115) a.   A   lan telefunà   tüti.   (Piedmontese)
           CL have telephoned all

      b.   Sono arrivati tutti.   (Italian)
           have arrived   all

It would thus seem that with respect to the definiteness restriction also,
the lexical versus non-lexical nature of the non-argument subject plays a
role, but we have no specific proposal to make regarding this. (For discussion of the definiteness restriction see the references of Note 2.)

2.5.5 *Conclusion*

In this section we have seen that Piedmontese has two different inversion
strategies, one for ergative verbs, the other for non ergative verbs. Both
strategies rely on the NS property of Piedmontese, but in different ways.
The strategy relative to non ergative verbs requires the NS property because no element is inserted with respect to the subject position. The
other strategy requires it because, although the element *ye* is inserted, the
latter is a clitic and does not therefore properly govern the subject position, so that the governing property of INFL must again be resorted to.

We thus predict that if a language had an element like Piedmontese *ye*
that was not a clitic, then only one of the two strategies would rely on the
NS property. Our predictions can in fact be sharpened further. Recalling
how we suggested in 2.3 above that the non-argument subjects of inversion and extraposition are clitics in Italian because they never carry stress,
we propose a general principle to the effect that a non-argument subject
will be a clitic whenever it can. In a NS language it always can. But not

so in a non NS language, since clitics do not govern the subject position. If we then consider a hypothetical language which differs minimally from Piedmontese in being a non NS language, this language will have an element analogous to *ye* which is not a clitic. It will then have inversion with ergative verbs since the NS property will no longer be involved, but will lack inversion altogether with non ergative verbs. In the next section we argue that French is exactly such a hypothetical language.

2.6 FRENCH *IL*

2.6.1 *Subject Pronouns*

We will begin by claiming that French is a non-NS language. This claim is superficially challenged by the fact that French subject pronouns *je, tu, il/elle/*non-argument *il, nous, vous, ils/elles* exhibit some of the properties of clitics. This fact is discussed in Kayne (1975, pp. 83–86). Kayne notes that these pronouns behave like object clitics in that: (i) They cannot be separated from the verb by intervening material, as in ***Il, souvent, mange du fromage** 'He often eats cheese', (ii) they cannot be modified, as in ***Ils deux partiront bientôt** 'The two of them will leave soon'; (iii) they cannot be conjoined, as in ***Il et Jean partiront bientôt** 'He and Jean will leave soon; (iv) they cannot be contrastively stressed, as in ***IL partira le premier** 'HE will leave first'; (v) they behave differently from other subject NPs with respect to certain phonological rules.

Nevertheless we will assume, unlike Kayne (1975), but in agreement with Kayne (1982) that the subject pronouns of French are not clitics at syntactic levels, and that the correct way to account for (i)–(v) above is to regard them as 'phonological clitics', i.e. clitics with respect to aspects of the phonology only, perhaps by assuming that they cliticize in the phonology.

There are several arguments against an analysis of French subject pronouns as (syntactic) clitics. Note first that they cannot be inflectional clitics, like those of Piedmontese, since they do not cooccur with a subject NP as in ***Jean il mange du fromage** 'Jean he eats cheese'. But they must also not be real (i.e. non-inflectional) subject clitics since they cooccur with subject clitics like SE and *y* as in *Il se construit . . . , Il y a . . .* of (104) above and (116a), (117a) here below. If *il* is in subject position, then there is a precise reason for its occurrence in these cases: to fill that position. But if it is a clitic, then there is no reason: why should there be two clitics? Secondly these pronouns undergo Raising, just like other subject NPs, and unlike subject clitics SE, *y*, which remain stranded, as is illustrated by (116) and (117).

(116) a. **Il se** construit beaucoup d'immeubles.
    it SE builds   many buildings

b. **Il** semble **se** construire beaucoup d'immeubles.
it seems SE to build   many buildings

(117) a. **Il y**   a   du pain.
it there has ('is') some bread

b. **Il** semble **y**   avoir   du pain.
it seems   there to have ('be') some bread

There are only two possible reasons for the appearance of *il* on the higher verb in (116b) and (117b): (i) It is an inflectional clitic; or (ii) It has undergone Raising. But (i) is false, as we have just argued. Therefore (ii) must be true and *il* must be in subject position at least when Raising applies. But French subject pronouns must be in subject position even in S-structure, given that, as Brandi and Cordin (1981) note, they allow coordination as in (118a), a kind of coordination which is impossible with subject clitics, whether inflectional as in (118b), or not, as in (118c).

(118) a.   Tu manges et   bois   (French)
you eat   and drink

b.   *   T   mange e   beive   (Piedmontese)
(you) CL eat   and drink

c.   *Si mangia e   beve   (Italian)
SI eats   and drinks

The different results of (118) follow only if French *tu* is in subject position. VP coordination will then be unproblematic in (118a), just as in its English translation, while in (118b, c) it will be excluded, presumably by general constraints on coordination, since only one of the VPs has a subject clitic in it.

Arguments against a clitic analysis of French subject pronouns are also given in Couquaux (1981) who notes that the negation *ne* follows subject pronouns, as in **ELLE N'aime pas les épinards** 'She does not like spinach', while it precedes clitics, as in **Elle NE LES aime pas** 'She does not like them' (even *subject* clitics, as in **Il N'Y a pas . . .** , **Il NE SE construit pas . . .**).

We conclude therefore that French subject pronouns are in NP position (at syntactic levels), and therefore that French is a non-NS language.

2.6.2 *Il-inversion and Auxiliary Assignment*

In French there are two types of inversion. The first type involves non-argument *il* as in some of the examples we have seen above. The second type does not involve *il* and only occurs in conjunction with Wh-movement, as in **Quand partira ton ami**? 'When will leave your friend?' (from

Kayne and Pollock 1978). We will not deal with the latter type of inversion, generally referred to as "Stylistic Inversion" (see Kayne and Pollock (1978), a characterization of which falls outside the scope of our
discussion. We will only consider inversion not specific to Wh-movement
contexts, namely *il*-inversion (including the *Il y a* construction).

Il-inversion discriminates between certain verbs and others, as in
(119).

(119) a.   Il est   arrivé   trois amis.
          it ('has') arrived three friends

    b. ??Il a   téléphoné trois amis.
        it has telephoned three friends

The contrast in (119) recalls of course other familiar ones, especially
once we note that *il*-inversion quite generally allows cliticization of *en*,
which we assume is just like Italian and Piedmontese *ne* (i.e. is derived
from base-generated, direct object positions only).

(120)   Il **en**   est   arrivè   trois
      it of-them is ('has') arrived three

Indeed (119) suggests that our expectation of 2.5.5 is fulfilled, that as we
move to a non-NS language we may find inversion with ergative verbs
only. This is in fact our claim. Specifically, we are claiming that, like
Piedmontese *ye*, French *il* is only available for insertion in D-structure,
from which it should follow that *il*-inversion is possible with all and only
those constructions that allow an empty subject in D-structure. Thus it is
possible with ergative verbs and impossible with non-ergative verbs. (The
claim that the *il*-construction is base-generated has been independently
made by Herschensohn (1979), (1982).)

Our claim will be supported by two arguments. One argument is more
strictly empirical: by reviewing the verbs which can appear in *il*-inversion,
we will see that there are independent reasons to assume that they are
ergative. The other argument is more conceptual: it derives from the fact
that *il*-inversion has uniform distribution over certain syntactically well
defined domains. This suggests that the bifurcation of (119) is indeed
along syntactic, not lexical, lines. (This argument is of the same kind
as the ones we presented in chapter 1, in connection with the distributions of *ne* and of auxiliary *essere*.) Let us begin with the first, empirical
argument.

If we assumed, as may seem reasonable, that the two auxiliaries of
French, **être** 'be' and **avoir** 'have' (henceforth "E" and "A", respectively),
reflect exactly the same system of auxiliary assignment we postulated for
Italian, then we would expect *il*-inversion to be possible with all and only
the verbs that take auxiliary E. One half of this expectation seems to be

fulfilled unproblematically: it seems to be the case, as noted for example in Obenauer (1976), that verbs that take E, like *arriver* of (119), allow *il*-inversion rather generally. The other half of the expectation is not entirely fulfilled however, since there are cases of *il*-inversion with verbs that take A, like those in (121) (also due to Obenauer (1976)).

(121) a. Il **a**   manqué   trois élèves.
     it has been missing three pupils   (A)

  b. Il **a**   disparu   plus de   sept   cents   sucettes.
     it has disappeared more than seven hundred lollipops (A)

  c. Il **a**   surgi   d'autres   correspondances.
     it has arisen some other correspondences   (A)

We note that with the majority of such cases, the corresponding verbs in Italian take auxiliary E (as is true of **mancare, sparire, sorgere** 'be missing, disappear, arise', the verbs of (121)). There are two ways to account for the difference in auxiliary with this class of verbs: (i) French has a different class of ergative verbs (the verbs in (121) are ergative in Italian, but not in French). (ii) French has a somewhat different system of auxiliary assignment. Although (i) and (ii) are not logically incompatible, we clearly want to assume that only one of them is true, not both, to keep theoretical differences between Italian and French to a minimum. If (ii) rather than (i) was true, cases like (121) would pose no problem for our hypothesis since such verbs would in fact be ergative (and we would also account for the fact that these cases too allow *en*, as in **Il en a manqué trois** 'It has been missing three of them').

There is independent reason to believe that (ii) is indeed true: there is at least one case in which we are most likely to be dealing with the exact same syntactic configuration, and in which French has auxiliary A, while Italian has E. This is the passive construction, as in (122).

(122) a. Jean **a**   été   invité.   (French)
     Jean has been invited   (A)

  b. Giovanni **è**   stato invitato.   (Italian)
     Giovanni is ('has') been invited   (E)

Given (122), (ii) must be true, and we thus proceed to assume that (i) is false, and that French has the same class of ergative verbs as Italian.

To account for auxiliary A in (121), we would have to say that in the configuration in (123), which is the one relevant to ergative verbs both under inversion and not (cf. 1.7, 2.2), lexical factors are allowed to play a role in French, though not in Italian.

(123)   NP   V   NP

Due to such lexical factors, E will be assigned to *arriver* of (119), but not to the verbs of (121), while in Italian all of the corresponding verbs will be assigned E. Let us put aside for the moment auxiliary assignment in (122), to which we return in 2.7.

It is clear that auxiliary assignment in French is in any event only partly lexical, since there are, as in Italian, syntactic regularities: always A with transitive verbs, and always E with *se*-moyen and reflexive constructions as in (124).

(124) a. Il s'**est**   vendu beaucoup de livres.   (French)
     it SE is ('*has*') *sold   many books*   (E)

  b. Jean s'**est**   regardé.   (French)
     Jean himself is watched   (E)

     Jean has watched himself.

Notice that although we have so far assumed that auxiliary assignment in Italian is *entirely* predictable from the syntactic configuration, this is not quite true. Italian also has an area of idiosyncrasy, like French. This is represented by Raising configurations like those in (125).

(125) a. Maria **ha**   potuto [t risolvere il   problema]   (Italian)

     Maria has been able to solve   the problem   (A)

  b. Maria **è**   sembrata [t risolvere il   problema] (Italian)

     Maria is ('*has*') *seemed   to solve the problem* (E)

In our discussion in 1.7 we distinguished two cases in which E was assigned, (126a) and (126b) below. But it now appears that we must consider three, thus also (126c), interpreting the latter as distinct from (126b).

(126) a. NP   cl-V

  b. NP   V   NP

  c. NP   V   [s NP . . .]

French never allows E in the configuration (126c), as shown by the contrast between (125) and (127).

(127) a. Marie **a**   pu   résoudre le   problème   (French)
     Marie has been able to solve   the problem   (A)

  b. Marie **a**   semblé résoudre le   problème   (French)
     Marie has seemed to solve the problem   (A)

However, French always requires E in the configuration (126a). This is shown by (124) (we assume that as with SI (cf.1.6) SE holds a relation with the subject position). What emerges is therefore a general picture in which the Italian system has (126a) and (126b) as the core cases, and (126c) as the periphery, while French has (126a) as the core case, (126b) as the periphery, and (126c) outside the system altogether, as in (128).[61]

(128)   Assignment of Auxiliary *Essere/Etre*

	Italian	*French*
a. NP cl-V	core	core
b. NP V NP	core	periphery
c. NP V [$_S$ NP . . .]	periphery	——

Recalling how we defined relations that trigger E assignment as relations between the subject and an element contiguous to the verb (cf. (86), ch. 1), we note that the three cases of (128) are ordered precisely according to the degree of proximity of the relevant element to the verb: since clitics form one morphological unit with the verb, the clitic of (128a) is plainly 'closer' to the verb than the direct object of (128b); and the latter is in a reasonable sense closer to the verb than the subject of the complement in (128c), given the intervening clause boundary. It thus appears that the rule of E assignment is parameterized with respect to the degree of contiguity it requires, with not only Italian and French differing in the value of the parameter, but also with each language having a stronger and a weaker version of the rule depending on the degree of contiguity.

From the point of view of our formalism of 1.7 and of our definition of *element contiguous to the verb* as "either a clitic or an NP in an A-position governed by the verb" ((87), ch. 1), it would seem that what is parameterized is the notion of government that enters into the system. At least two different notions seem to be needed, to appropriately distinguish the governed NP in (128b) from the one in (128c), both internally to each language, and across languages. We may refer to them as STRONG GOVERNMENT, obtaining in (128b), and WEAK GOVERNMENT, obtaining in (128c). Perhaps the relation between the verb and the clitic in (128a) could also be captured in terms of government: a third and the strongest notion (call it SUPERGOVERNMENT).

Recall, too, from 1.7 that in Italian the relation of (128b) triggers not only E assignment, but pp agreement as well, since a 'direct object' (defined as "an NP in an A-position governed by the verb") is involved. This is true of (128c) as well, but only in the sense that *if* the relation triggers E it will trigger pp agreement, and vice-versa (compare feminine *sem-*

brata of (125b) versus masculine *potuto* of (125a)). The same is true of (128b) for French: pp agreement is found with all and only the ergative verbs that take E (as with *arriver*, etc., never with *manquer*, etc.). The generalization is therefore that, although in a periphery configuration E assignment can either succeed or fail, pp agreement must either succeed or fail with it. We take this to mean that although E assignment and pp agreement are two different rules, as we argued on the grounds that pp agreement is not predictable in general from the auxiliary, there being no pp agreement in (128a), they are nevertheless part of a closely integrated system. This fact is important for some of our later discussion.

While either auxiliary can thus be assigned in the periphery, it appears that even in the periphery there are important subregularities. In particular, a principle seems to be operative to the effect that if a verb, in its various modes of complementation, ever falls into the core of the system, then the auxiliary assigned in the core is maintained in the periphery. This explains in particular the difference between the two verbs of (125). *Sembrare*, unlike *potere*, occurs not only with Raising, but also as in (129).

(129)   [e] **sarebbe**   sembrato [$_S$ che Maria   (Italian)

        (*it*) *would be* ('*have*') *seemed*   *that Maria*   (E)

        risolvesse   il   problema]
        would solve the problem

The case in (129) is a core case. Indeed it falls under (128b), once we simply generalize the latter to S complements. (This generalization was already implied by our discussion in 2.2 above.) *Sembrare* therefore *must* take E in (129) and then appears to maintain it in the periphery case (125b).

But the corresponding French case in (127b) is outside the periphery. Therefore it is in effect a core case for the assignment of A. The configuration of (129), corresponding to (128b) is a periphery case for French, but since French *sembler* takes A in a core case, as in (127b), we expect it to maintain it in cases like (129). This is correct (Cf. *Il a semblé que* . . . 'It has seemed that . . .') This principle also allows us to correctly predict that all French ergative verbs that have transitive alternants in the manner of (130) and (131), ought to take A. They do — another important subregularity.

(130) a. Jean **a**   coulé le   bateau.
         Jean has sunk   the boat   (A)

      b. Le bateau **a**   coulé t

         the boat   has sunk   (A)

(131) a. La chaleur **a**   étouffé plusieurs personnes.
       the heat   has choked several   people   (A)

b. Plusieurs personnes **ont**   étouffé t

several   people   have choked   (A)

Since in the transitive configuration of (130a), (131a) *couler* and *étouffer*
fall outside of the system in (128) and are therefore core cases for A, they
will maintain A when they occur as periphery cases, as they do in (130b),
(131b).

The ergative verbs of (130b), (131b) differ from those ergative verbs that
take the morpheme *se*, which always take auxiliary E, like *se casser* in (132).

(132) a. Jean **a**   cassé   la fenêtre.
       Jean has broken the window   (A)

b. La fenêtre s'**est**   cassée t

the window itself is broken   (E)

The window has broken.

The difference between (132) and (130)—(131) leads us to believe that
(132b) must be a core case in (128), in particular that the subject position
in (132b) must be linked with *se*. This suggests a revision of our analysis
of 1.5 above, which assigned no syntactic role to 'ergative' *si*: a point to
which we will return. The conclusion of immediate relevance is that there
is no reason at all to believe that French and Italian have different classes
of ergative verbs, only differences in auxiliary assignment.

While cases like (121) are thus accounted for, our hypothesis regarding the distribution of *il*-inversion still faces some problems of empirical
adequacy. One problem is represented by the class of ergative verbs like
those of (130b), (131b), which do not readily allow *il*-inversion, as shown
in (133).

(133) a. ??Il a   coulé deux bateaux.
       it has sunk   two boats

b. ??Il a   étouffé plusieurs personnes.
       it has choked several people

This is quite general for this class, while the class of verbs like *se casser*
of (132b) appear with *il* rather freely, as we predict. The nature of the
difficulty in (133) is not very clear, but it may be related at least in part
to the fact that unlike the *se casser* class these verbs give no overt indication that the subject position lacks a θ-role, so that cases like (133)
would be essentially ambiguous, *il* being interpretable as an argument as

in *It/he has sunk two boats.* (With the *se casser* class, the overt indication is *se*, and no ambiguity can arise.)[62]

Other apparently problematic cases are represented by isolated instances of *il*-inversion with verbs that cannot reasonably be characterized as ergative, which have appeared in the literature, such as (134) (from Grimshaw (1980)).

> (134) Il mange beaucoup de linguistes dans ce   restaurant.
>   *it eats   many linguists   in   this restaurant*

Verbs like *manger* are in fact not ergative by any of the criteria that our discussion provides or suggests. A few instances of *il*-inversion involving transitive verbs, like (135) (from Kayne (1979)), are also attested.

> (135) Il prend corps   dans ce pays   une grande espérance.
>   *it is taking shape in   this country a   great   hope*

We have nothing to say about these cases beyond noting that they are rare (speakers differ on the acceptability of (134).) We will thus assume that our hypothesis provides an acceptable approximation to the empirical facts.

We now turn to the second argument that we promised for our analysis of *il*, noting that *il*-inversion is distributed quite uniformly over some syntactic domains: systematically impossible — with very few exceptions like (135) — with transitive verbs, systematically possible with passive and *se*-moyen (SE) constructions, as in (136).

> (136) a. Il a   été   construit beaucoup d'immeubles dans cette ville.
>   *it has been built   many buildings   in   this   city*
>
>   b. Il se   construit beaucoup d'immeubles dans cette ville.
>   *it SE builds   many buildings   in   this   city*

Since the class of verbs that appear in sentences like (136) is exactly the class of transitive verbs (on the distribution of SE, see below), *il*-inversion is either systematically possible or systematically impossible over the same class of verbs, depending on the syntactic configuration. This clearly stresses the syntactic, non-lexical, character of the factors that determine its distribution. Also, the facts of (136) support our claim that *il*-inversion is base-generated, since the cases in (136) are exactly those which we have independent grounds for believing are base-generated in that configuration. (The grounds for this are independent not only of this discussion of *il*-inversion, but even of the ergative hypothesis.) Thus, as is standard within the literature (cf. Note 32, ch. 1), we take cases like (137) to be derived from the same base forms as (136), via NP-movement.

(137) a. [*i* Beaucoup d'immeubles] ont été   construits t*i* dans cette ville.
          many buildings   *have been built*   *in   this   city*

   b. [*i* Beaucoup d'immeubles] se   construisent t*i*   dans cette ville.
          many buildings   *SE build ('are built') in   this   city*

The existence of the D-structures in question is clearly not incidental to
the fact that *il* can appear as in (136): if we take 'be' adjective constructions, which differ minimally from passives like (136a) precisely in that
they do not have that D-structure, we find that they cannot appear with *il*.
In fact there are minimal pairs like (138).

(138) a.   Il a été   achevé   plusieurs constructions cette année.
           it has been finished many buildings   this   year

   b. *Il a été   inachevé plusieurs constructions cette année.
        it has been unfinished many buildings   this   year

The contrast in (138) is, in this context, the exact counterpart to the one
we noted for Italian in 1.3, relative to Ne-Cl (cf. (29), ch. 1). Of course
cliticization of *en* is analogously possible in (138a): **Il EN a été achevé
plusieurs . . .** 'It has been finished several of them . . .'.

   Note however that, in order for our claim to be true that both examples of (136) represent D-structure configurations, and that *il* is inserted
in D-structure, it must be the case that French SE, unlike Italian SI, is
base-generated in clitic position. We believe that this is the case. This
conclusion is independently required by the systematic failure of SE to
undergo Raising, as in (116b) above, and (139).

(139) a.   Il semble **se** construire beaucoup d'immeubles.
           it seems   SE   to build   many buildings

   b. *Il **se** semble construire beaucoup d'immeubles.
        it   SE   seems   to build   many buildings

We will return to this difference between Italian and French.

   We conclude that, in French, the non-argument subject of inversion, *il,*
can only be inserted in D-structure, like Piedmontese *ye.* Because of this,
il-inversion is only possible with ergative verbs, passive and *se*-moyen
constructions.[63] The impossibility of inversion in other cases and thus the
more limited scope of French inversion compared with inversion in Italian and Piedmontese, is due to the non-NS character of French. Since
INFL cannot properly govern the subject position, in French, insertion
is always required, but no element is available for insertion after NP-
movement.

   Notice that we find no deeper reason why insertion of *il* or *ye* should
be constrained to D-structure. However, since it is a fact that the distribution of these elements is restricted, any theory is bound to have some

condition on their occurrence: the condition we are assuming is maximally simple, and empirically adequate.

We can now account for the Raising/Control contrast of (33) above: **Il semblait/*voulait venir beaucoup de monde** 'It seemed/wanted to come many people': while *il* is Raised into matrix subject position with *sembler*, with the Control verb *vouloir* it cannot be Raised and it can also never be inserted since such verbs require an argument subject in D-structure. *Il*-inversion will thus be impossible with Control ('Equi') verbs altogether. This is not true of Italian inversion, as we noted in 2.3. We saw in fact that in Italian, inversion with Control verbs was impossible only if the i-subject was within the complement, but possible (though perhaps marginal) otherwise, as in (34) above: **Sembrava/?Sperava di intervenire Giovanni** 'seemed/hoped to intervene Giovanni'. This follows from the fact that in Italian no insertion into subject position is required, which is to say it follows from the NS property of Italian.[64]

2.6.3. *Se moyen*

In this subsection, we will argue that, like the more limited distribution of French inversion compared with Italian inversion, the more limited distribution of *se*-moyen ('SE') compared with that of Italian SI, is also predictable from the NS property.

As is well known (cf. for example Rizzi (1976b)), SE differs from SI in that it essentially only occurs with transitive verbs, either as in (136b), or as in (137b), repeated as (140a), (140b) respectively.

(140) a. Il$_i$ se construit [$_i$ beaucoup d'immeubles] . . .   (French)
     it SE builds   many buildings

   b. [$_i$Beaucoup d'immeubles] se construisent t$_i$ . . .   (French)
     many buildings   SE build
   Many buildings are built . . .

While the cases of (140) can be duplicated in Italian, as we know from 1.6 (cf. **Si costruiscono molte case . . .** 'SI build many houses . . .', **Molte case si costruiscono . . .** 'Many houses SI build ("are built") . . .') none of the Italian cases in (141) can be duplicated in French.

(141) a. [$_i$e] si$_i$ mangia bene qui   (Italian)
     SI eats   well here
   We eat well here.

   b. [$_i$e] si$_i$ è appena arrivati t$_i$ (Italian)
     SI is just   arrived
   We have just arrived.

c. [$_i$e] si$_i$ è stati invitati t$_i$ (Italian)
        SI is been invited

    We have been invited.

This divergence is of interest because of course we assume that SE and SI are fundamentally the same element. This assumption rests on obvious morphological, semantic and syntactic similarities. Note in particular how SE fails to appear in infinitivals, in either one of the variants of (140), just like SI, as shown in (142).

(142) a. *La possibilité [de **se** construire des immeubles] est
          the possibility of SE to build any buildings is

        limitée.   (French)
        limited

    b. *Beaucoup de livres s'achètent sans   [**se** lire]   (French)
        many books   SE buy   without SE reading

        Many books are bought without being read.

This contrasts with the possibility for all *se*'s (reflexive, inherent reflexive, ergative) to appear in infinitivals, as in (143).

(143) a. Il serait   agréable [de **se** voir   plus
          It would be pleasant to see each other more

        souvent]   (French)
        often.

    b. Jean a   passé la nuit sans   [**s'** endormir]   (French)
        Jean has spent the night without falling asleep.

    c. Le verre est tombé sans   [**se** casser]   (French)
        The glass has fallen without breaking.

The contrast between (142) and (143) is identical to the one noted for Italian in 1.6. Within our theory, such contrasts are due to the fact that SI, SE require that Case be assigned to the subject position, unlike *si, se*.

    Let us then consider how the French counterparts to (141) can be excluded. Under the assumption, which we have already made, that SE is base-generated in clitic position, (141b,c) are excluded directly. In fact these are exactly the cases which we claimed required a movement analysis of SI.[65] What about (141a)? It would seem that by simply inserting *il* into the empty subject in D-structure it ought to be possible to derive the French counterpart of (141a), (144).

(144) *Il se   mange bien ici.
       it SE eats   well here

However there is reason to believe that, at least in languages like French, Italian and English, non-argument subjects must always be linked with an S or NP argument, as *il* is in (140a). This assumption is required by the fact (to which we will return) that these languages do not have passives with intransitive verbs, i.e. the so called 'impersonal' passives, like *It was danced by everyone*. French has some impersonal passives, such as **Il sera parlé de vous par tout le monde** 'It will be talked about you by everybody' (from Kayne (1975)), but there are also some corresponding cases of SE: **Il se réfléchit à de drôles de choses ici** 'SE thinks about funny things around here' (from Kayne (1975, p. 397, Note 64)). It therefore seems reasonable to assume that cases like (144) ought to be ruled out only to the extent that impersonal passives are. We suppose therefore that what accounts for the contrast between (144) and (140a) is the fact that in (144) there is no post verbal argument to which *il* could be related.

Yet the problem of (144) is not entirely solved: In 2.5.3, we concluded that in Italian cases like (141a) (**Si mangia bene qui**) INFL plays the role of a non-argument pronominal, just like French *il*. Since, in Italian, impersonal passives are at least as unproductive as in French, we must assume for Italian too that non-argument subjects are linked to arguments, from which it follows that the Italian equivalent of *il* in (141a) must be linked to argument SI (cf. Note 57). But why is the same not sufficient for *il* in (144)?

A plausible solution to this problem is provided by recent work of M. R. Manzini (1982), suggesting that the difference between French and Italian here is a reflex of the definiteness restriction. Since it is an independent fact that French *il* only occurs with 'indefinite' arguments, unlike the corresponding non-argument subject of Italian, we may assume that SE/SI is definite in the relevant sense, whence the difference between (144) and (141a). The analogue to (141a) will thus be ruled out differently from the analogues to (141b,c). But this seems correct since, while the prohibition excluding (141a) in French is sometimes relaxed, as in Kayne's example **Il se réfléchit à de drôles de choses ici**, the one excluding (141b,c) is not.

The above discussion has accounted for the differing distributions of SI/SE by appealing to two differences between Italian and French: the definiteness restriction, and the fact that SE is base-generated as a clitic, unlike SI. Although we have no precise understanding of the definiteness restriction, we have suggested in 2.5.4 that it is related to the presence of lexical elements like *there, il* (and *ci/ye*), as it never appears with null subjects related only to INFL. If this is correct, then one of the two differences simply derives from the NS property.

Let us consider the second difference and see whether it too can be derived. As we argued in 1.6, cases of the type '$[_i e]$ si$_i$ ... t$_i$ ...' like those in (141b, c) are possible because SI cliticizes by movement, so that it can undergo NP-movement before it cliticizes. But suppose SE cliticized by movement, like SI. Could corresponding French cases, which would be of the type 'Il$_i$ se$_i$ ... t$_i$ ...', be derived? Not if *il* can only be inserted in D-structure as we claim, since NP-movement of SE would be blocked. Thus, while cliticization by movement of Italian SI gives rise to sentences that could not exist otherwise, cliticization by movement of French SE would not. On the contrary, cliticization by movement of SE would exclude all sentences of the type 'Il se ...' which are possible under a base-generation analysis, like (140a) above. Thus, if we simply postulated that the choice between the two possible analyses of these elements is determined by a principle that aims at maximum productivity, which is not unreasonable, it would automatically follow from the NS property holding in Italian but not in French that Italian SI should be analyzed as moved, while French SE is analyzed as base-generated. Assuming that something along these lines is correct, then the different distributions of SI/SE will now be *entirely* predictable, like the difference in the productivity of inversion, from the different status of the two languages with respect to the NS property.

Notice that our discussion of SE confirms the analysis of SI as a case of cliticization by movement: if SI were base-generated like SE, it would remain a mystery why French and Italian should have such different configurations of data.

2.7. ENGLISH *THERE*

2.7.0 *Introduction*

In this section we consider inversion in English, namely constructions with pleonastic *there*. We will distinguish two subcases: *there* with *be*, and *there* with other verbs: the so called 'presentational' sentences. We will try to account for a number of differences between inversion in English and inversion in the other languages we have considered. In the case of inversion with 'be' in particular, we will maintain that virtually all the observable differences are reducible to the fact that the Romance counterparts to *there* are clitics.

Given our previous discussion, one might expect that, like *ye/ci* and French *il*, English *there* may also be restricted to insertion in D-structure. We will argue that this is true, or at least is a strong tendency. We will begin by arguing that this view is tenable when *there* occurs with *be*.

2.7.1 *'Be' as a Raising Verb*

Consider the two forms in (145).

(145) a. There is a man on the roof.

  b. A man is on the roof.

If we accept the idea, convincingly argued for in Milsark (1974), that pairs like (145) originate from a common D-structure, there will be two ways of expressing this idea. One is to assume that (145a) is representative of the D-structure configuration, the other that (145b) is. Under the first possibility, derivation of (145a,b) will be as in (146), where both (b,c) are derived from (a).

(146) a. [e] is [a man] on the roof →

  b. There$_i$ is [$_i$ a man] on the roof

  c. [$_i$ A man] is t$_i$ on the roof

Under the second possibility, (145a) is derived from (145b) via rightward movement of [*a man*] and insertion of *there*. Early analyses, including Milsark's, assumed that the second possibility was true. As far as we can make out, this assumption rested on two considerations:

I. A base form like (146a) would be implausible since the existence of complements, or even phrases, corresponding to some of the material that can follow *be*: our X of (147), is not independently attested.

$$(147) \quad \text{There was } [_X \text{a man} \left\{ \begin{array}{l} \text{arrested} \\ \text{singing} \\ \text{drunk} \\ \text{on the roof} \end{array} \right\}]$$

II. A syntactic rule permuting the subject and *be* in linear order has the right properties since it appears to operate quite mechanically with respect to any instance of *be*, whether copular, progressive, or passive, as (147) illustrates.

However, Stowell (1978) has shown that both I and II are crucially flawed. In particular, with respect to II, it is not true that rightward movement would treat all instances of *be* alike, since — as Milsark himself notes — it must fail with 'semi-modal' *be*, as in *A man is to leave at noon* → **There is a man to leave at noon*. With respect to I, complements such as X of (147) are indeed attested. In particular by the cases in (148).

$$(148) \text{ a. } \left\{ \begin{array}{l} \text{We had} \\ \text{We needed} \end{array} \right\} [_X \text{the car painted green}]$$

$$\text{b. We} \left\{ \begin{array}{l} \text{like} \\ \text{want} \\ \text{keep} \end{array} \right\} [_X \text{the hens} \left\{ \begin{array}{l} \text{locked up} \\ \text{in the barn} \\ \text{pecking at dirt} \end{array} \right\}]$$

The existence of such phrases as X of (147) is attested, not only in cases like (148) noted by Stowell (which are somewhat peculiar to English), but rather massively by complements of verbs like *believe, consider* and by 'reduced' relatives, if we give up the idea, which was common in earlier literature, that there is a process of *be* deletion, specifically, if we *do not* regard cases like (149b), (150b) as derived from the corresponding (a) cases by deletion of the portions in boldface.

(149) a. I consider [him **to have been** accepted in the program]

b. I consider [him accepted in the program]

(150) a. A student [**who has been** accepted in the program] has arrived

b. A student [accepted in the program] has arrived

There are good arguments in the literature to the effect that there is no process of (*Wh-*)*be* deletion. In this work, we will simply take that conclusion for granted, noting in passing how some arguments arise specifically from the material we will be discussing. For more extensive discussion of (*Wh-*)*be* deletion, see in particular Williams (1975), Burzio (1981, 3.3). Rather than (*Wh-*)*be* deletion, we will postulate the existence, alongside of tensed and infinitival clauses, of a third type of clause, which, following Williams (1975), we refer to as a SMALL CLAUSES. The complement in (149b) will then be a small clause ('sc'). The alternation of (149a, b) will now be due to the fact that different types of clauses freely alternate as complements of a verb, in the unmarked case. As for relatives like the one in (150b), the most natural assumption is that they have a PRO subject controlled by the head of the relative, as in (151), so that they too will be small clauses. We will refer to these as SMALL CLAUSE RELATIVES.

(151)   A student$_i$ [PRO$_i$ accepted . . .] . . .

Relativization in (150b) therefore does not involve Wh-movement as in (150a), but Control.

The complement in (147) (X) will thus be a sc, and so will those in (148). The four possibilities of (147) are indeed found with sc's in general as in (152), although present participles do not occur freely with complements of *believe, consider,* for reasons which remain unclear.[66]

$$(152)\ a.\ I \left\{ \begin{matrix} \text{believe} \\ \text{consider} \end{matrix} \right\} [_{sc}\ \text{him} \left\{ \begin{matrix} \text{accepted in the program} \\ ??\ \text{applying to the program} \\ \text{proud to be here} \\ \text{on the committee} \end{matrix} \right\}]$$

$$b.\ A\ \text{student}_i\ [_{sc}\ \text{PRO}_i \left\{ \begin{matrix} \text{accepted in the program} \\ \text{applying to the program} \\ \text{proud to be here} \\ \text{on the committee} \end{matrix} \right\}] \ldots$$

A sc will thus have a subject, and a predicate ranging over past participle, present participle, adjective, PP.

On the one hand there will therefore be no argument against the
derivation in (146). On the other there will be good arguments for it.
In particular — as Stowell notes — the impossibility of *There is a man to
leave at noon, no longer requires a special stipulation to the effect that
rightward NP-movement must fail with semi-modal be (the "Semi-Modal
Restriction" of Milsark (1974)). The independent assumption that semi-
modal be is a modal, and as such does not take sc complements, will suffice. Also, leftward movement as in (146c) is far preferable to the
rightward movement of the alternative. Note in particular that within our
framework we would expect rightward movement to place the i-subject
into a VP final position (cf. 1.8), which is clearly not the case here (cf.
(147)). Following Stowell (1978), we will thus analyze be as a Raising
verb taking a sc complement.[67] We will then slightly revise our analysis of
Italian and Piedmontese locational constructions to include the sc boundaries, so that for example Italian (103b) above is now **C'è** [$_{sc}$ **del pane sul
tavolo**] 'There is some bread on the table'.

Notice that the fact that the subject of passives is the 'semantic' object
of the verb, will follow much as in the traditional analysis of passives,
since we assume that when the predicate of the sc is a past participle,
NP-movement occurs internal to the sc as in (153a), while no analogous
movement occurs with present participles, as in (153b).

(153) a. [e] was [John$_i$ invited t$_i$] → John was invited.

b. [e] was [John walking] → John was walking.

We assume, specifically, that past participles fail to assign a θ-role to
their subject: the same property which we had been attributing to the
passive morphology as a whole. Therefore John in (153a) could only be
linked with object θ-role. For present participles, we assume that they
maintain the same properties of θ-role assignment as the corresponding
verb, so that John in (153b) will have subject θ-role. Analogously for
complements of believe, consider, as in I consider [John$_i$ invited t$_i$ to the
party].

The same considerations will hold for sc relatives, so that we will have
the two different cases in (154).

(154) a. A student [PRO$_i$ accepted t$_i$ in the program]

b. A student [PRO applying to the program]

Our analysis of sc relatives will thus predict correctly that the relativized
element will always be the subject of the corresponding verb with present
participles, as in (154b), while with past participles it will never be the
subject, as (155a) shows. Rather, with past participles, it will be either the

direct object, as in (154a), or the object of a preposition in cases in which the preposition can be stranded, as in (155b), or in general some NP that can move into subject position.[68]

(155) a. *A student [PRO applied to the program] has arrived.

   b. The rights [PRO$_i$ infringed upon t$_i$] were mine.

To avoid confusion we note here that the property of the past participles in (153a), (154a) which we have been discussing, is not to be extended to past participles of active complex tenses, such as the one in *John has walked.* The latter will be regarded as forming a verbal unit with the aspectual auxiliary, a unit which is identical to the corresponding verb with respect to assignment of θ-roles. Where confusion may arise, we will refer to the past participles of (153a), (154a) as PASSIVE (PAST) PARTICIPLES.

While it could be shown that it does not incur any of the problems of (*Wh-*)*be* deletion, the analysis we are proposing will account precisely for the parallelism between sc's and *be* clauses that (*Wh-*)*be* deletion analyses aimed to capture. The relation has simply been reversed: *Be* clauses (for example, (153)) are now essentially 'augmented' small clauses, whereas under (*Wh-*)*be* deletion sc's were 'reduced' *be* clauses.

Romance provides further evidence that Stowell's analysis of *be* is correct. First, we recall from 2.5.3 that both the distribution of Piedmontese *ye* and the possibility for Ne-Cl point to the existence of D-structures like (146a) (i.e. of the type '[e] be NP . . .'), thus confirming the analysis in question. Then, we note that the differences between French and Italian in the cases in (156), (157) provide further confirmation.

(156) a. Marie a   été [$_{sc}$ t à la mer]   (French)

   Marie has been   at the sea   (A; no ag't)

   b. Maria è   stata [$_{sc}$ t al mare]   (Italian)

   Maria is ('has') been ('fem.') at the sea   (E; ag't)

(157) a. Maria a   été [$_{sc}$ t invitée t]   (French)

   Marie has been   invited (fem.)   (A; no ag't; ag't)

   b. Maria è   stata [$_{sc}$ t invitata t]   (Italian)

   Maria is ('has') been (fem.) invited (fem.)   (E; ag't; ag't)

The distribution of auxiliaries and agreements in (156), (157) follows straightforwardly from our discussion of 2.6.2, but crucially only under the Raising analysis of 'be', not under the traditional analysis. Let us first consider the Raising analysis, the one given in those examples. The relation in (156) is a periphery case for Italian (cf. (128c), assuming that sc boundaries are just like S boundaries for E assignment); therefore we expect E to be possible in (156b). But if we also consider the principle we discussed in 2.6.2, we can actually predict that E should be not only possible, but necessary here. The reason is that 'be' also occurs in existentials (in Italian; French uses 'have' of *Il y a . . .*) like (158), which are core cases for Italian, since no clause boundary is involved (cf. (128b)).

(158) $[_i e]$ c_i'è   stato [un terremoto]   (Italian)

       there is ('has') been   an   earthquake   (E)

While E is thus assigned in (156b), A is assigned in (156a), since the configuration is outside of the system for French (cf. (128c)). The distribution of pp agreement in (156) follows in the same way as that of E.

In (157), the relations involving the matrix subject are identical to those in (156). Auxiliary and agreement on the main verb are thus correctly predicted, as in (156). As for the relation internal to the complement, the latter will give rise to a core case for Italian, and a periphery case for French. No auxiliary will appear here, since there is no auxiliary in sc's, but pp agreement will. The agreement of (157b) is thus predicted to be necessary, the one in (157a) to be possible.[69]

Let us now consider the traditional analysis of 'be'. The latter would fail in particular with respect to (156b) and (157a), given in that analysis in (159).

(159) a. Maria è   stata   al mare   (Italian)
         Maria is ('has') been (fem.) at the sea   (E; ag't)

     b. Marie a ˙ été   invitée t   (French)

         Marie has been invited (fem.)   (A; no ag't; ag't)

In (159), since there is no binding relation, auxiliary E and pp agreement are quite unexpected. In (159b), since the configuration would be a periphery case for French, auxiliary A is predicted possible, but what is curious is that the rightmost past participle (the passive participle) should exhibit agreement. As we saw in 2.6.2, we never find any case in which the same subject-object relation triggers either one of E assignment or pp agreement without triggering the other. This would be the only case. The distribution of E and pp agreement thus provide evidence that the Raising analyses in (156), (157), rather than the traditional analyses in (159) are correct.

Further support for the Raising analysis of 'be' is provided by reflexive/reciprocal *si/se*. The latter quite generally fails to occur with derived subjects, a fact to which we will return, and it also fails to occur with 'be', including copular 'be', which has a derived subject only under our analysis. We thus find the contrast of (160). (French cases like (160) were noted in Kayne (1975, 5.1)).

(160) a. *Essi si erano fedeli.   (Italian)
          They were faithful to each other.

      b. Essi gli erano fedeli.   (Italian)
          They were faithful to him.

The hypothesis that 'be' is a Raising verb, has also been put forth independently in Couquaux, (1981), on the basis of a discussion of *Enavant* phenomena (e.g. *L'auteur en est célèbre*; cf. Note 3, ch. 1). Couquaux argues that a Raising analysis of 'be' makes it possible to reduce such apparent cases of rightward *en*-cliticization to the standard case of leftward cliticization. We will assume that Couquaux' proposal is essentially correct.

The Raising analysis of 'be' which we will thus adopt will not (as far as I can see) invalidate any of the results we obtained prior to this point by assuming the traditional analysis (for example of passives).

2.7.2 *Inversion with 'be'*

We now consider some differences among the various cases of inversion with 'be' that one finds among the languages under consideration. We distinguish two cases of inversion with *be* in English: one in which NP-movement has occurred within the sc, as in (161a), i.e. passive cases, and one in which movement has not occurred, as for example in (161b), or analogously in cases involving present participles or adjectives.

    (161) a. There were [several houses$_i$ built t$_i$]

           b. There was [some bread on the table]

Let us see how our Romance languages pattern with respect to the two subcases of (161). We bear in mind that those languages lack the English use of present participles, the progressive form, as in *There was a man singing*. Descriptively, the general situation can be represented as in A, B, C, D below.

    A. The configuration of (161a) is impossible with the Romance counterparts of *there*, as in (162).

    (162) *Ci   furono [molte case$_i$ costruite t$_i$]
           there were   many houses built

As we have already noted, French uses **avoir** 'have' with clitic *y*. Aside from this, Italian *ci* and French *y* behave quite analogously, so that corresponding to (162) we find ***Il y avait beacoup d'immeubles construit** 'There were many buildings built' (*ci* and *y* behave also analogously with respect to the facts of Note 59). We will thus regard French *y* as essentially the same element as Italian *ci*, in spite of its occurrence with *avoir*, for which we have no account. To represent this relationship descriptively, we may postulate the existence of an abstract verb 'be', which is realized as **avoir** just in the presence of *y* in French, and as *be* or its equivalents otherwise. By 'be' we will henceforth mean such an abstract verb, thus covering the relevant cases of **avoir** as well.

B. The configuration of (161a) is also impossible with French *il*, and with the null subject (related only to INFL) of Italian (and Piedmontese), as in (163).

(163) a. *Il a été [beaucoup d'immeubles construit t_i] (French)
        it has been many buildings built

   b. *[e] furono [molte case$_i$ costruite t_i] (Italian)
        were many houses built

In fact, the only type of inversion possible with passives in French and Italian, is as in (164).

(164) a. Il$_i$ a été [t_i construit beaucoup d'immeubles] (French)
        it has been built many buildings

   b. [$_i$e] furono [t_i costruite molte case] (Italian)
        were built many houses

Unlike (161a), in which *there* is inserted into matrix subject position, (164a) must have *il* inserted into embedded subject position and then Raised. The *ec* in (164b) is also analogously Raised. Use of *ci/y/ye* remains impossible even in the configuration of (164), as in (165).

(165) a. *Il$_i$ y avait [t_i construit (French)
        it there had ("was") built

        beaucoup d'immeubles] (French)
        buildings

   b. *[$_i$e] ci furono [t_i costruite molte case] (Italian)
        there were built many buildings

Having noted A, B for the configuration (161a), we now turn to (161b).

C. The configuration (161b) occurs with *ci/y/ye*, as in (166), as we have already seen.

(166) a. Il y avait [du pain sur la table] (French)
        it there had ("was") some bread on the table

b. [e] c'era   [del pane   sul tavolo]   (Italian)
    there was   some bread   on the table

D. The latter configuration is impossible however with any other type
of inversion, as suggested in (167) (and as we have seen in (99), (100)
above).

(167) a. *Il était [du pain   sur la table]   (French)
          it was   some bread   on the table

      b. *[e] era   [del pane   sul tavolo]   (Italian)
          was   some bread   on the table

Concerning A–D above, one may suppose that, over such frequently
used constructions, the different distributions we have just noted, merely
reflect language specific idiosyncrasies. However, we will suggest that
there are more principled reasons for the differences.

With regard to point A, if 'be' is a Raising verb, then ci, y, ye are presumably excluded from sentences like (162) by the same factors that exclude them from other Raising structures. In 2.5.3 above, we claimed that
with ci the inversion relation must be established at D-structure, subject
to locality conditions. Under this view, (162) will be ruled out because
the inversion relation of its D-structure (168) is 'non-local'.

(168) $[_i e]$ ci_i furono [e] costruite [molte case]]   (Italian)

            there were   built   many houses

A D-structure condition ruling out the relation of (168) is thus empirically supported by the ungrammaticality of cases like (162) involving 'be'
and by the non appearance of ci on Raising verbs in general, discussed in
2.5.3, but we may ask what the theoretical status of such a condition is.
Our idea is that *all* relations involving base-generated clitics must exist at
D-structure. This would follow from the projection principle for a core
number of cases, namely for clitic-ec relations, in the manner we discussed in 1.4. However, our claim is that this reflex of the projection
principle is in effect generalized to an operative principle that deals with
all relations involving base-generated clitics in the same fashion. This
would also explain (by replacing (93) above) the fact noted in 2.5.3 that
pleonastic ci must be linked with a non-argument subject even at
D-structure, and the fact noted just above, that reflexive si cannot occur
with a derived subject. The latter follows because si must have an antecedent even at D-structure. If relations that involve clitics *must* obtain at
D-structure, it is natural to assume that they will have to obey locality
conditions, even at D-structure, and we will then consider what these
conditions are. In Part II, where we return to these issues, we will claim
that it is the usual binding conditions that apply at D-structure. Example

(168) is then ruled out by the binding principle we proposed for inversion: (51) above.[70]

The same considerations ruling out (162), namely the ill-formedness of D-structures like (168), will rule out the cases in (165) as well.[71] The cases in (164) will be allowed in contrast with (162) and (165) because the non-argument subjects *il* and the *ec* of Italian are Raised, so that there will be no violation of locality conditions here. Notice that there will never be an analogous possibility of Raising applying in *ci/y* cases, since *ci/y* is inserted directly as a clitic and not in NP position.

The impossibility of (162) will contrast with the possibility of superficially similar cases in which an adjective rather than a passive participle is involved, like (169).[72]

(169)   C'erano   [molte case   disabitate]
        there were   many houses   uninhabited

The grammaticality of (169), like that of (166), will be due to the fact that the S-structure subject of the sc is in that position at all levels, so that locality conditions on the inversion relation will never be violated.

We have so far covered A and C above. We now consider D before turning to B. As we discussed in 2.5.3, the ungrammaticality of (167b) seemingly forces us to assume that inversion possibilities are hierarchically ranked and that inversion with *ci* is higher in the hierarchy; (167b) will thus be impossible because (166b) is possible. Similar considerations for French will rule out (167a) given (166a).[73] We are thus left with B and the cases in (163).

It would seem reasonable to suppose that the impossibility of (163) is related to that of (167). Let us then suggest that in the context (170), where NP is lexical, *ci/y/ye* is required not only if it is possible as we assumed in the preceding paragraph, but even if it is not.

(170)   ___ be NP . . .

The configuration of (170) will then be ruled out altogether in the case of passives since, though *ci/y* is required, the latter cannot be successfully inserted, for the reasons we discussed. We may regard the condition requiring insertion of *ci/y/ye* in (170) as universal over the languages in question, thus affecting English *there* as well, although English has no alternative inversion strategy. We may then further assume that in (standard, contemporary) English the relevant conditional is strengthened to a biconditional, i.e. that not only will (170) require *there*, but that *there* (when it occurs with *be*) will require the context in (170) as well. This will rule out ?**There were built several houses*, parallel to (164) and contrasting with (161a) (*There were several houses built*).

Although a few things have been left vague at the formal level, we take this discussion to provide some explanation for the distribution of the various inversion strategies with 'be'. In essence, our thesis is that the distribution reflects, not so much a difference between English and the Romance languages under discussion, but rather a difference between the type of inversion with *there/ci/y/ye* and all other types. As for the differences between *there* and *ci/y/ye*, these appear predictable from the fact that *ci, y, ye* are clitics. This will itself be predictable on the basis of the principle mentioned in 2.3 and 2.5.5 above, which we may regard as universal, a principle prescribing that non-argument subjects (which cannot receive stress) will be clitics whenever they can. Thus, English *there* cannot be a clitic, since English has no clitics, while Italian and Piedmontese will have clitics *ci/ye* since these languages do have clitics and furthermore since in these languages INFL can properly govern the subject position. French will have clitic *y* because it too has clitics and because, although INFL is not a proper governer in this language, it has another non-argument subject (beside *y*) which is not a clitic and which can thus fill the subject position, namely *il*. Our principle predicts in fact that in a non-NS language that has clitics, like French, any non-argument subject 'can' be a clitic, so long as there is one which is not, like *il*.

We now note that some of the configurations possible with 'be', such as the one in (171a) (relevantly analogous to (161b)), are not possible with other verbs, as shown in (171b).

(171) a.   There are [many people sick]

b. ?*There seem [many people sick]

Be and *seem* do not differ if instead of *there* insertion, NP-movement occurs, as in (172).

(172) a.   Many people$_i$ are [t$_i$ sick]

b.   Many people$_i$ seem [t$_i$ sick]

The ungrammaticality of (171b) is unlikely to be related to the occurrence of *there* (although *ci/y/ye* give the same results). More likely, it is related to the ungrammaticality of the cases in (173), noted in 2.4 above.

(173) a. ?*Sembrava [Giovanni ammalato]
         seemed   Giovanni sick

b. ??Giovanni sembrava [lui ammalato]
    Giovanni seemed   he sick

Since we lack a precise understanding of (173), we will not be in a position to account for the contrast in (171). It may seem reasonable to suggest however that the grammaticality of (171a) and analogous cases is related to the fact that *be* also occurs in existentials (as in *There is a Santa Claus*), whereas *seem* does not.[74]

We now turn to instances of *there* with verbs other than *be*, that is, presentational *there*.

2.7.3 Presentational there

English *there* is not restricted to 'be' like Italian *ci*, yet its distribution is clearly more limited than that of Piedmontese *ye* or French *il*. There are two ways in which we may attempt to account for this difference. One is to assume that, while *there* can be inserted with *all* ergative verbs, English has a different, more restricted class of ergative verbs than the Romance languages we have discussed. The other is to assume that, while English has the same class of ergative verbs, additional constraints account for the limited distribution of *there*.

Now note that the existence of 'semantic' restrictions — limiting occurrence of *there* roughly to verbs of appearance — is independently established, by minimal pairs like (174) (from Kayne (1979)).

(174)   There has just $\left\{ \begin{array}{c} \text{appeared} \\ \text{??disappeared} \end{array} \right\}$ another book by Smith.

It is in fact very unlikely that *appear* and *disappear* of (174) could differ with respect to whether they are ergative or not. We thus assume that the rather limited productivity of presentational *there* is due to semantic factors, which we will not attempt to define precisely, referring for this to relevant literature, in particular to Milsark (1974), Stowell (1978), Kayne (1979), Guéron (1980). If we assume no other difference between *there* and *ye/il*, we will predict *there* to be possible *only* with ergative verbs, though not with all of them. This prediction is fulfilled in some respects, but not in others. We first consider the respects in which it is.

The majority of verbs with which *there* can appear most naturally, such as those in (175), are indeed verbs that we would independently assume are ergative.

(175)   arise, emerge, develop, ensue, begin, exist, occur, arrive, follow

The verbs in (175) will in fact be ergative under our assumption that English has roughly the same class of ergative verbs as Italian, since the Italian equivalents *sorgere, emergere, svilupparsi, succedere, cominciare, esistere, accadere, arrivare, seguire* are all ergative, taking auxiliary E (on *cominciare, seguire* 'begin, follow' see below).

The correctness of the hypothesis that *there* occurs only with verbs whose Italian counterparts take auxiliary E, is suggested by the fact that it solves some problems noted in Milsark (1974). Consider the contrast between (176) and (177).

(176) a.   A rainstorm followed.

b.   There followed a rainstorm.

(177) a.   A taxicab followed.

b.   *There followed a taxicab.

The two different meanings of *follow* pointed out by Milsark, i.e. 'occur after' and 'move in the same direction as, but behind', are also found with its Italian counterpart *seguire*, but are associated with different auxiliaries, as in (178).

(178) a. Alla bella giornata **era** seguito   un temporale.   (Italian)
      to the nice day   was followed a   storm   (E)

A rainstorm had followed after the nice day.

b. L'auto   si   era mossa   ed   il tassí **aveva** seguito. (Italian)
   the auto itself was moved and the taxi had   followed(A)

The auto had moved and the taxicab had followed.

This suggests that the verb of (176) is ergative, whereas the one of (177) is intransitive. The contrast between (176b) and (177b), a rather curious fact in the context of Milsark's discussion, is thus accounted for by our hypothesis. A similar case noted by Milsark is represented by the contrast between *start* and *begin* in (179), (180).

(179) a.   The riot began.

b.   There began a riot.

(180) a.   The riot started.

b.   *There started a riot.

In Italian we find only one verb corresponding to both *start* and *begin*, but again one featuring two different auxiliaries, as in (181).

(181) a. Gli operai   avevano appena cominciato (i   lavori) (Italian)
      the workers had   just   started   (the works) (A)

b. I   lavori erano   appena cominciati   (Italian)
   the works were ('had') just   begun   (E)

The contrast between (179b) and (180b) would then follow if we assumed that only *begin*, not *start* is ergative, like *cominciare* of (181b).[75]

The correctness of the hypothesis that *there* only occurs with ergative verbs can be partially confirmed, even independently of any Italian facts, by noting that if we take the class of verbs which we assume are ergative because they have transitive alternants, such as *spill, assemble, circulate, roll*, etc., results with *there* are rather systematically on the good side, too systematically to be accidental:[76, 77]

(182) a. (?)There spilled large amounts of wine over the floor.

    b. (?)There assembled a large number of people in the square.

    c. (?)There circulated many crazy ideas at the conference.

    d. (?)There rolled a big boulder into the lake.

In so far as the aspects of the distribution of *there* just noted can be accounted for along the lines discussed, they provide evidence for the existence of a class of ergative verbs in English. We may note a few further reasons for assuming that English has such a class of verbs. One reason is theoretical. As we noted in 1.3 above, within our theoretical framework, such a class is expected, in English as well as in Italian. A few other reasons of a more empirical nature are discussed in Burzio (1981). These concern in particular -*er* affixation, as in (183), and the distribution of 'expletive' objects, as in (184).

(183)   killer, walker, *arriver

(184) a.   He walked [the hell out of those shoes]

    b.   *They arrive [the hell out of those bus terminals]

A most natural assumption regarding -*er* affixation is that it requires that the verb assign subject θ-role. Nominals in -*er* in fact specifically refer to that θ-role, i.e. a *killer* is one who kills (not one who is killed). The contrast in (183) will then follow from the assumption that *arrive* does not assign subject θ-role, i.e. is ergative, unlike *kill* and *walk*.[78] As for the contrast in (184) it will follow from the same assumption in conjunction with the descriptive generalization introduced in 1.8 above that verbs have one direct object at most. In (184b) there are two: the trace of *they* and the phrase within brackets. (We will see how this descriptive generalization follows from Case theory.) Notice that both -*er* affixation and expletive objects are impossible with the verbs of (175), as well as with those of (182) at least in their ergative use. Thus *developer* cannot refer to the idea of *A brilliant idea developed; beginner* cannot be the riot of (179); and while *follower* can perhaps refer to the taxicab in (177), it can never refer to the rainstorm of (176).

Turning now to the respects in which our prediction is not fulfilled, we note that cases involving non ergative verbs also exist, as in (185), from Milsark (1974).

(185) a. There walked into the bedroom a unicorn.

      b. There ambled into the room a frog.

However, Milsark distinguishes cases like (185) from cases involving the verbs in (175). He notes that with verbs like *walk* the i-subject (our terminology) occurs in VP final position, (cf. (185)), whereas with the verbs of (175) it occurs VP internally, adjacent to V, as for example in (186) (also from Milsark).

(186)   There arose **many trivial objections** during the meeting.

The V-adjacent/VP final distinction noted by Milsark, which has no explanation within his discussion, seems to me to follow rather closely an ergative/non ergative distinction made on independent bases, and is then exactly what we would expect if *there* constructions could be derived not only by inserting *there* in D-structure, but also by insertion after rightward movement of the subject. The difference in linear order between, say, (185) and (186) would then simply be the counterpart to analogous differences we noted for Italian in 1.8 above.[79]

Cases like (185) therefore do not challenge the existence of ergative verbs in English. If Milsark is right they in fact confirm it. What they challenge is the assumption that insertion of *there* is limited to D-structure. At this point we thus have to choose between relinquishing the latter assumption and losing those explanations which it provides, or maintaining it and regarding cases like (185) as somewhat outside of the core system. The second alternative would also be suggested by the fact that, at least for many speakers, such cases are on a lower scale of acceptability. It seems clearly preferable.

We have argued in this section that the cases in which *there* occurs most productively, namely those involving *be*, are clearly cases of base-generation. A Raising analysis of main verb 'be' is in fact supported by a number of convincing and quite independent arguments. Internal to English we have Stowell's arguments and the explanation for the Semi-Modal Restriction. Within Romance we have the distribution of Piedmontese *ye*, the possibilities for Ne-Cl, the distribution of reflexive *si/se*, the distributions of auxiliaries and pp agreement in Italian and French. Internal to French we have Couquaux' discussion of *En-Avant* to which we made reference.

Furthermore, we have seen how some superficial differences between *three* and its Romance counterparts *ci, y, ye* are predictable from the fact that the latter are clitics, a difference which is itself reasonably well predicted by independent considerations.

Finally, we have considered occurrences of *there* with other verbs and noted that while some evidence indicates that *there* selects ergative verbs, just as *ye* and *il* do, the occurrence of *there* with some non-ergative verbs seems to falsify this view. We suggested that a way to avoid the paradox is to assume that instances of *there* with non-ergative verbs fall on a lower scale of grammaticality.

Our discussion leaves a residue of idiosyncratic differences among the various elements that correspond to *there*, represented by the fact that while Piedmontese *ye* is not constrained by any extrasyntactic factors, Italian *ci* and French *y* are *lexically* constrained to occurring with 'be' (realized as *avoir* in French), and English *there* is *semantically* constrained to presentational contexts, or verbs of appearance.

2.8 CONCLUSION

In the first part of this chapter, we characterized both inversion and extraposition as consisting of a relation between a non-argument subject and a post verbal argument NP or S. We argued that the latter relation is subject to locality conditions analogous to those holding for NP-trace relations, and attempted to capture such conditions under an extension of the binding theory.

If our claim is true that this characterization is to apply equally well to Italian and to English or French, then it must be the case that Italian employs empty subject positions in the way that English and French employ overt pleonastic subjects like *there* and *il*, so that the type of inversion one finds in Italian is strictly contingent on the Null Subject property. On the one hand, such a claim was supported by the fact that the relevant evidence cuts across the two types of languages. In particular we noted that evidence for coindexation between subject and post verbal argument arises both in English and in Italian. On the other hand, the claim seemed challenged by the more limited distribution of inversion in English, French than in Italian.

Since in chapter 1 we had argued for the existence of two types of inversion in Italian (a conclusion corroborated by the existence, even in English, of two kinds of extraposition), a natural way to address the more limited productivity of inversion in French and English is to ask whether these languages may not simply lack one of the two types. In essence, this is the question we considered in the second part of the chapter.

What has emerged is that this is indeed true, and that inversion by rightward movement is — to a very good approximation — missing in these languages. We have attributed this fact to a constraint limiting insertion of pleonastics like *il* and *there* to D-structure. NS languages like Italian will always allow inversion since they allow null subjects, and thus do not *require* insertion, though they may allow it. The view that it is insertion versus non-insertion of a pleonastic element that plays the major role in limiting the productivity of the construction is confirmed by the fact that, if we look only at inversion *with* insertion of a pleonastic ele-

ment, then the differences among the languages become of a smaller order, and indeed no longer follow the distinction between NS and non-NS
languages. Thus inversion with *ye* in Piedmontese (a NS language) has
approximately the same distribution as inversion with *il* in French (a non-
NS language) and Italian *ci* has an even more limited distribution than its
English equivalent *there*.

   If this account is correct and if in fact the complete productivity of inversion in Italian is itself a reflex of the NS property, then our earlier assumption that Italian inversion shares essential properties with inversion
in English and French, is not only no longer challenged, but is in fact
supported, since it is precisely the latter assumption that allows us to predict the difference in distribution.

   While we assume that, with respect to inversion, insertion of pleonastic
elements is constrained to D-structure as we said, we must mention that
no analogous restriction appears to exist with respect to extraposition
(see, however, Note 63). Thus, for example, English *it* is not limited to the
base-generated type of extraposition. We have no formal proposal to account for this difference, but we may informally relate it to the rather
general tendency to place heavier phrases last. Since sentences are generally heavier than NPs, we may suppose that the lack of extraposition by
rightward movement would run counter to the latter tendency to a greater extent than the absence of the corresponding type of inversion would.

NOTES

[1] Given cases like (2b) and others that will come up in this chapter, the definition
of i-subject that was given in 1.1 above (p. 22), which was "The NP_i in a form . . . V_j . . .
NP_i . . . , such that the verb V_j agrees with NP_i and such that there is a near-synonymous
from NP_i V_j . . .", will have to be slightly modified. In particular we will have to assume
that the portion of the definition which refers to verb agreement holds only sometimes.
We will continue to make reference to verb agreement in connection with i-subjects where
this is applicable, as we did above.
[2] For discussion of the definiteness restriction, see Milsark (1974), Stowell (1978),
Kayne (1979), Guéron (1980), as well as Safir (1980).
[3] On the distributional analogies between clitics and null subjects, note that languages
that have null subjects also have clitics; both null subjects and cliticization correspond to
lack of contrastive stress; syntactic constructions that require cliticization for objects
correspondingly require null subjects. An illustration of this is the strategy to form relative clauses by resumptive pronouns, discussed in Rizzi (1978b). Under the latter
strategy it is null subjects and object clitics that can function as resumptive pronouns.
   On the correlation between the NS property and richness of inflection, cf. Note 46
below.
[4] The class of proper governors, which contains the lexical categories (N, A, V, P), excludes INFL, as we mentioned in I.0.3. However, it must include elements in COMP
which are coindexed with the *ec*, to account for the phenomena we discuss shortly below
in the text. For further details, see LGB 4.4 (Cf. also Notes 8, 9).
[5] Rizzi comes to this conclusion by noting that Italian is just like French (and English) in

not allowing wide scope interpretation of quantifiers in subject position, as in (ib) compared with the French counterpart (ia).

(i) a.   *Je *n*'ai exigé que *personne* soit arrêté.

           I have NOT required that ANYBODY be arrested.

     b.   *(in the interpretation)
           Non pretendo che *nessuno* sia arrestato.

           I do NOT require that ANYBODY be arrested.

Both cases in (i) are ungrammatical under a reading in which the quantifier is in the
scope of the negation (i.e. under the 'nobody' reading), although for the Italian case there
is one grammatical reading, for reasons which Rizzi discusses. The corresponding cases
involving objects are (near) grammatical, as in (ii).

(ii) a.   ?Je *n*'ai exigé qu'ils arrêtent *personne*.

           I have NOT required that they arrest ANYBODY.

      b.   *Non* pretendo che arrestino *nessuno*.

           I do NOT require that they arrest ANYBODY.

Assuming, as seems plausible, that the subject/object asymmetry of (i), (ii) must be accounted for in the same manner as the one in (5), (6), by postulating a rule that moves
the quantifier to the higher S in LF, thus mimicking Wh-movement, it must be the case
that Italian also disallows extraction from subject position; hence the hypothesis that Wh-
movement never occurs from subject position. Rizzi's hypothesis can be tested directly in
cases like (iii), where the inverted and the non-inverted forms differ by more than the position of the 'subject', as Rizzi discusses.

(iii) a.   **Ne**   arrivano [molti]
           of-them   arrive   many

                       [Quanti] credi che **ne** arrivino?
                       How many of them do you think will arrive?

      b.   [Molti]   arrivano
           many (of them)   arrive

                       *[Quanti] credi che arrivino?
                       How many of them do you think will arrive?

The fact that only the inverted form (iiia) has a Wh-moved counterpart confirms Rizzi's
hypothesis (on *ne* and the null partitive phrase of (iiib) see 1.2, 1.4 above, Note 23 ch. 1,
and Belletti and Rizzi (1981)).

[6] See in particular Chomsky and Lasnik (1977), Taraldsen (1978), Pesetsky (1979),
Kayne (1980a).

[7] Cases like (8) (and analogously cases involving null subjects like (7b)) become possible
where clitics can function as resumptive pronouns (cf. Note 3), e.g. as in **Chi credi che ab-
bia sparso la voce che Giovanni la vede?** 'Who do you think has spread the rumor that
Giovanni sees her?' It is easy to show that in these cases there is no movement, and the
pronoun functions as a variable.

[8] However, it appears that not only movement of the subject *over* an adjacent complementizer as in (7b) is impossible, but even movement *into* such a position. Compare the
ungrammaticality of ***[Quanti] arrivano?** 'How many (of them) arrive?' with (iiib) of Note

5. Italian thus appears to have an even stronger prohibition than English, as Rizzi notes. Two possibilities come to mind to account for this fact, not accounted for in the text (i). Somehow, in Italian an *ec* in subject position must always be interpreted as related to INFL (i.e. as a pronominal, never as a variable). (ii) Proper government of the subject by an element in COMP (cf. Note 4) is a marked option, taken only by those languages that do not have an alternative such as a productive inversion strategy. Italian would thus differ from English not only in not allowing proper government from COMP under *that*-deletion, but in not allowing proper government from COMP altogether. Of these possibilities Rizzi assumes (i), but it seems to us that (ii) might be more principled.

[9] Under the pronominal option, INFL will be a proper governer just like a noun (cf. Note 4).

[10] Government absorption, unlike Case absorption, sems suspicious because, whereas Case can reasonably be regarded as a feature, which *can* thus be absorbed, government is a certain type of configurational relation, which we expect to change only when the configuration changes. The conceptual difficulties associated with government absorption are paralleled by empirical difficulties. Consider for example (i).

(i) a.   Giovanni *la* fa   riparare |e|

   Giovanni it   makes repair
   Giovanni has it repaired.

   b.   Giovanni *gli*   butta   l'acqua |addosso |e||

   Giovanni to-him throws the water upon
   Giovanni throws water on him.

There is reason to believe that in the causative construction of (ia) both verbs govern the embedded object. It would thus be unclear how the clitic could absorb government from both. Analogously in (ib), it seems at most plausible that the clitic could absorb government from the verb, but government by the preposition would remain, still incorrectly barring PRO.

As empirical evidence for the governed status of the object position, Jaeggli cites Spanish cases like (ii) involving Wh-movement in so called "Clitic Doubling" constructions.

(ii)   *¿A quien la   viste?
        to whom her (you) saw
        Who did you see?

If clitic *la* made the object position ungoverned, then indeed (ii) would be excluded by the ECP. However, the status of sentences like (ii) seems to be tied to dialect specific factors rather than to the ECP. For example, Borer (1981) reports that in certain dialects of Spanish such sentences are acceptable.

[11] But there are stronger reasons for rejecting the PRO hypothesis, acknowledged in Chomsky (1981c). One is the difference in syntactic/semantic properties between established instances of PRO and NSs: while PRO is only definite in interpretation when it is controlled, as in *Mary hopes [PRO to go]*, and is otherwise 'arbitrary', as in *[PRO to leave] would be rude*, a NS is always definite and never controlled. This difference can be accommodated under the PRO hypothesis, but not very naturally. Another reason for rejecting the hypothesis relates to the cases of inversion in Spanish discussed in Torrego (1984), which provide rather convincing evidence for government of NSs, a conclusion also suggested by the class of Italian gerundive constructions of Rizzi (1982b, III, IV).

[12] Cf. Belletti (1982).

[13] The point of the text seems to me to stand in spite of cooccurrence of SI with first person plural *noi* in Tuscan dialects (cf. Note 47, ch. 1), as in *Noi si va* 'we-SI goes'.

As Belletii (1982) notes, the view that SI is an instance of INFL seems supported by the fact (discussed in 1.7) that SI does not induce verb agreement, i.e. one could suppose that with SI the verb is not inflected since SI itself *is* the inflection. However, this interpretation seems to me challenged by the fact that in Italian dialects in which INFL has overtly the form of a clitic, such a clitic does appear with SI, as in the Piedmontese example (i).

(i)   A   s   mangia bin.
         clitic SI eats   well

         We eat well.

If SI was INFL, one might expect third person singular clitic *a* of (i) not to appear. For further discussion, see 2.5.1.

[14] While INFL can bind the subject position because it c-commands it, as in (4), the same is not true of subject clitics like SI. For the latter, we assume as discussed in Note 45, chapter 1, that the binding relation is essentially reversed, the subject position binding the clitic. We will be more explicit on these matters in 2.5.3 below, where we extend the discussion to the other subject clitic *ci* (cf. Note 57). In this respect the two relations in (14) actually differ, so that, as an alternative to the solution proposed in the text, one might consider accounting for the difference in auxiliary by sharpening up the formulation of the E assignment rule.

[15] Actually there are a few cases in which non-argument *it* occurs in conjunction with NPs as in *It is John, It is time to go.* As for weather *it*, we assume with LGB, 6 that the latter is a 'quasi' argument, therefore not a non-argument. The (near-)argument status of weather verb subjects is stressed (somewhat theory internally) by the fact that in Italian these verbs take either auxiliary. Under our proposals, the possibility for auxiliary E corresponds to a possiblity for the verb to be ergative, and thus have a D-structure direct object. But by the projection principle, direct objects — unlike subjects — cannot fail to have a θ-role, from which we infer that the NP associated with a weather verb has some θ-role, i.e. is not a non-argument.

[16] Milsark (1974) has noted a certain peculiarity in this kind of agreement, illustrated in (i).

(i) a.   [A chimp and a gorilla] $\begin{Bmatrix} ?*\text{was} \\ \text{were} \end{Bmatrix}$ in the cage.

    b.   There $\begin{Bmatrix} \text{was} \\ ??\text{were} \end{Bmatrix}$ [a chimp and a gorilla] in the cage.

The contrast between (ia) and (ib) argues against the view that in *there*-constructions the verb agrees directly with the i-subject. However, we have no explanation for the effect in (ib). This effect is also found with Italian constructions employing pleonastic subject *ci* 'there' though not with other instances of inversion in Italian.

[17] In Chomsky's discussion INFL contains the feature [± tense] as well as the agreement element AGR. It is actually the latter element rather than INFL which is referred to in Chomsky's version of (18a). Our discussion slightly simplifies Chomsky's by not distinguishing AGR from INFL.

[18] There is some conceptual analogy between such a discussion of cases like (17b) (and (20) below) and the discussion of 'reconstruction in LF' which we will present in 3.3 below, in the sense that one can view the grammaticality of, for example (17b) in terms of reconstruction of S_2 into the position occupied by non-argument *it*. One thus wonders whether phenomena exemplified by (17b) (and (20)) and reconstructions phenomena may in fact not be of one kind. But we will not pursue this question here.

[19] The view that Case is necessary for θ-role assignment goes under the name of the VISIBILITY HYPOTHESIS and was first advanced by Y. Aoun.

[20] We must note however that the requirement that all arguments must be in a θ-position at D-structure is relaxed for base-generated clitics.

[21] Notice that the hypothesis that the clause is moved rightward even in cases like (21a) (from *That John would leave was expected*) is untenable (even aside from the unnecessary complexity of having movement first to the left and then to the right) since, as is noted in Williams (1980), some such cases would then fail to have a source, cf. *It was felt/reasoned that S* vs. **That S was felt/reasoned*; analogously with *It seems that S* vs. **That S seems*.

[22] In the case of Italian we must assume that person, number, and gender features are transmitted. Person and number features are required by verb agreement, e.g. **Siamo arrivati noi** 'Have arrived we'. Number and gender features are required by part participle agreement (which we assume is with the subject position). In English only transmission of number features is attested, since *there* only occurs with third person i-subjects, and since English has no past participle agreement.

We will see in 2.5.4 below that while the general case of inversion in Italian differs somewhat from *there*-constructions with respect to verb agreement, there is essentially no difference between English and Italian if we consider constructions that involve the equivalent of English *there*, namely *ci*. Where they exist, differences between English and Italian seem therefore predictable from the constituency of the non argument subject. This gives us reason to believe that contrasts like (i) are also predictable along the same lines.

(i) a.   It is $\left\{ \begin{array}{c} \text{me} \\ \text{I} \end{array} \right\}$.

   b.   Sono io.
         am I

We may in fact assume that it is a general property of non-argument subjects like *it* that they do not allow transmission of features. (Compare French *il*, which never does.) Agreement will thus occur in (ib) because Italian does not require an element like *it*, presumably a reflex of the NS property.

[23] Note that if the discussion in Rizzi (1982b, IV) is correct, in Italian infinitival inflection can also be a proper governor, like tensed inflection (Rizzi points to a class of infinitivals that have some of the properties of NS sentences). If this is true, then (23b) will be ruled out only by lack of Case marking and not also by the ECP, since the subject position will be governed.

[24] The auxiliary is therefore a diagnostic for subject versus object θ-role of sentential arguments. Another diagnostic is provided by the observation of Radford (1977) that complementizer *di* only occurs with complements (i.e. Ss) that have object θ-role (cf. (27)). The correctness of Radford's observation is emphasized by the contrast between passives like **Mi fu proibito di posteggiare** 'It was forbidden to me to park' and superficially similar adjectival cases like **Era proibito (*di) posteggiare** 'Parking was forbidden'. The same facts do not seem to hold however in French, which allows **Il est facile de chanter** 'Singing is easy'.

[25] Cases like (28iiib), i.e. ***Li si leggeranno volentieri**, are actually reported as uncommon, rather than as totally impossible, by some descriptive grammars (cf. in particular Lepschy and Lepschy (1977, p. 218). Within our proposal, such marginal possibility, contrasting with the absolute impossibility of, for example, ***Li arriveranno** 'Them will arrive' is to be related to the fact that the transitive verb *leggere* in (28iiib) can assign accusative whereas ergative verbs like *arrivare* cannot (as we will discuss in 3.1 below). Notice in fact that our discussion in the text does not make clear what exactly would exclude (28iiib), it assumes only implicitly that non nominative NPs cannot enter into a chain with the subject position.

The account of failure of pronominalization of i-subjects which we are providing here thus differs from the one given in Kayne (1979). Kayne assumes that French cases like (i) are ruled out by the definiteness restriction.

(i)   *Il l'est arrivé.
        It has arrived him.

For us, (i) is ruled out by the hypothesis that clitics like *le* are exclusively accusative. The superiority of our account is established by the fact that a 'definiteness' account of (i) fails to carry over to Italian cases, in which the definiteness restriction is inoperative.

[26] In this respect clitic reflexives differ from non clitic ones and from other elements like PRO, which can still take SI for an antecedent even after Object Preposing: **Queste cose si dicono sempre di se stessi** 'These things SI always say about themselves' (for an example with PRO see (44) in 2.3 below). Cf. also Note 42, chapter 1.

[27] Also, the exclusion of non third person objects in both of (b) and (c) below, which we noted in 1.6, is likely to be better captured under our analysis of inversion than under the alternative we are dismissing. (Only under our analysis are (ib, c) structurally parallel).

(i) a.   Si   invitò   voi.
          SI invited (3rd sg.) you (pl.)

    b.   *Voi   si   invitaste.
          you (pl.) SI   invited (2nd pl.)

    c.   *Si invitaste   voi.
          SI invited (2nd pl.) you (pl.)

[28] The same considerations and the whole discussion carry over to the assumption that there is coindexation between the subject and INFL (cf. discussion of (17a) above). Thus in, for example *John arrived* such coindexation would violate C of (31a), since *John*, an R-expression, ought to be free in its S.

[29] In the following discussion we will deal only with inversion, which provides the relevant evidence, not with extraposition. But we will assume, as seems natural, that the conclusions regarding locality conditions hold for extraposition as well.

[30] Actually, (40) is ruled out by more subtle assumptions than those discussed in the text, in particular by the assumption that chains cannot intersect. If they could, there would be one chain transmitting embedded object θ-role to the embedded subject, which would thus be PRO, and another transmitting matrix subject θ-role to the embedded object *Giovanni*, and (40) would be well-formed with respect to the θ-criterion. To the extent that our discussion provides instances of intersecting chains (cf. 1.6), the θ-criterion account of (40) may be weakened, strengthening the need for the locality conditions we will discuss below.

[31] The relevance of SI as an antecedent for PRO in (44) is enphasized by the fact that corresponding passive cases like (i) are ungrammatical.

(i)   ?*Queste cose sono state dette senza pensare.
        These things have been said without thinking.

We must note however that there are cases of Object Preposing, like (ii), discussed in Burzio (1981, 6.4), in which Control by SI is not entirely felicitous.

(ii)   ??[$_j$ Gli operai] si$_i$ informarono t$_j$ [di PRO$_i$ voler   chiudere la fabbrica]
        the workers SI informed   (of)   to want to close down the plant

Yet even such cases contrast with (42a), so that the point of the text remains. The reasons for the difference between (ii) and (44) are not entirely clear but are at least in part due to the fact that the animate phrase *Gli operai* of (iii), unlike the inanimate *Certe cose* of (44), is also a potential antecedent for PRO.

[32] Recall, also, that the coindexing of inversion (and extraposition) must play a role with respect to the binding theory to allow remote antecedents in cases like (i) discussed in 2.2 above.

(i)   They$_i$ think there$_j$ are [$_j$ some letters for **each other**$_i$]

Rather than the simpler version of (31), the formulation of the binding theory which is relevant here is the one that incorporates the notion 'accessible subject' in the manner of (18) above (i.e. the formulation of LGB, p. 220). As discussed in 2.2, Chomsky argues that *there* in (i) is not an accessible subject for *each other* because it is coindexed with a phrase containing the latter. But if such coindexation and the relation *there$_j$-NP$_j$* in (i) was not a binding relation, one would see little reason why it should be relevant to the binding conditions. Note in particular that the independent motivation for the condition *[$_i$ ... a_i ...] of (18c) above comes from cases like (ii), where binding relations would be involved (cf. LGB, p. 212)).

(ii)   *[$_i$ the friends of **each other**$_i$'s parents]

[33] Notice that whereas the non-argument status of *there* is established by its intrinsic content (i.e. by the fact that subject *there* is never an argument), the non-argument status of the null subject in (45b) is determined only contextually, and in particular by the fact that the latter does not bear a θ-role. This is true of other cases, for example of English *it*, which is intrinsically ambiguous as to whether or not it is an argument, and is thus unambiguous only contextually.

[34] Within Rizzi's proposals (48) would be ruled out by the assumption that *each other* is θ-dependent on *there*, so that the relation between the two would not count for the binding theory and *each other* would be free in violation of (A) of (31). Under Chomsky's account, (48) would be ruled out in a rather analogous fashion if co-superscripting is involved, but some additional assumption would be requried to avoid permitting the two elements in (48) to also be co-subscripted.

[35] This may seem to give rise to a paradox with respect to cases like (i).

(i)   a.   *There$_i$ seem [t$_i$ to arrive **each other**$_i$]

     b.   They$_i$ seem [t$_i$ to like **each other**$_i$]

If traces are non-arguments, then both (iab) ought to be ruled out on a par with (48). Notice however that some distinction is required independently of our discussion: It is a fact that in (i) we cannot determine locally whether *each other* has the proper antecedent, but must know what the antecedent of the trace is. A natural way to capture this is to assume that the antecedent in (i) is not the trace itself, but rather the chain containing it. But then the chain in (ib) is in effect an argument, while the one in (ia) is not, and the contrast in (i) will correctly follow from (50). One may then expect that the same considerations applying to NP-trace chains may apply to inversion (and extraposition) chains. This expectation is fulfilled for example by (ii).

(ii)   [$_i$e] si   è comprato la   macchina anche [$_i$Giovanni]
            to-himself is bought   the car   also   Giovanni

        Giovanni also has bought himself a car.

As we will discuss later on, reflexive *si* requires an argument antecedent at all levels. We must conclude therefore that the chain is what counts in (ii).

Incidentally, some of the above considerations may shed light on the fact that, while NP-trace relations allow VP coordination as in (iiia), inversion (and extraposition) relations do not, as in (iiib).

(iii) a.   John$_i$ [$_{VP}$ was arrested t$_i$] and [$_{VP}$ was later released t$_i$]

b.   *There$_i$ [$_{VP}$ arrived *three men$_i$*] and [$_{VP}$ will arrive *three women$_i$*]

If we assume, as seems reasonable, that in (iiib) *there* forms chains with both *three men* and *three women*, and if we regard chains as non-distinct from their members (along the lines suggested above), then in effect the two post verbal NPs in (iiib) c-command each other, since *there*, which is a member of a chain containing either one, c-commands the other. Since the two NPs in question are coindexed, and since they c-command each other under the 'chain' notion, (C) of (31a) is violated. Notice that if this or any account of (iiib) in terms of the binding theory is correct, then it must be the case that the coindexing of inversion is indeed relevant for the binding theory as we are claiming in the text.

[36] Formally, what is thus suggested is that each principle of the binding theory should be parameterized as in (i), where α ranges over *plus* and *minus*.

(i)   (A) An anaphor is α argument α bound in its governing category
        (B) A pronominal is α argument α free in its governing category
        (C) An R-expression is α argument α free (in its governing category)

While (i) seems rather straightforward, it is inadequate as it stands, and would have to be complicated in two ways: to express the fact that reference to "argument" must be dropped from (A) when the anaphor is a trace, as we discussed in the text (cf. (49)); and to express the fact that (B), (C) for the minus value of α (covering the inversion cases) apply only if a non-argument antecedent is in fact present.

[37] In the case of ep's, contrasts are somewhat weaker and, in general, there is a higher degree of freedom in the position in which ep's can occur than there is with i-subjects. We may plausibly attribute this to the fact that ep's are less 'heavy' and are thus more susceptible to being moved by late reordering rules, say by the rule of Complement Shift of 1.8 above. However, to the extent that contrasts like the one in (58) are noticeable, passives predictably pattern analogously to ergative verbs, while *be*-adjective constructions do not, as shown in (i).

(i) a.   Giovanni fu   mandato lui [a risolvere il   problema]
           Giovanni was sent   he to solve   the problem
           Giovanni was sent himself to solve the problem.

b.   (?)?Giovanni era contento lui [di risolvere il   problema]
           Giovanni was happy   he to solve   the problem

[38] English ep's like *himself*, etc. will differ from Italian ones in that they are anaphoric not only functionally, but also intrinsically.

Notice that if the anaphoric rather than pronominal status of Italian ep's is indeed due to their being non-arguments as supposed in the text, then one might consider the fact that with such elements the binding theory seems to reverse as we pass from arguments to non-arguments. That is, while argument *lui* is subject to (B) of (46), non-argument *lui* is subject to its converse, namely (A). This recalls in part the reversal we noted with respect to the non-argument subjects of (45) above (cf. Note 36). At the present time however, we see no enlightening way to relate the two phenomena.

[39] There is no intonational difference between the doubling and the inversion interpretations of, for example, *Viene lui*. Every such sentence is thus perfectly ambiguous. The ambiguity may only be theoretical however since speakers seem to have no intuition that such cases are ambiguous. This is not surprising given the essential formal identity of the analyses.

[40] We will not be concerned here with the still ungrammatical but much better variant *Fu pensato alle vacanze* '(it) was thought about the vacations' (with no verb agreement

and no pp agreement), which would be a case of impersonal passive (see 3.2.2 below), with no i-subject.

[41] If the same principles that rule out preposition stranding in (67) are involved in (65), then cases like (65) ought to be grammatical in languages that allow preposition stranding. This prediction cannot be tested in English however, since English requires the i-subject to appear between *be* and the past participle, as in *There were several people arrested* versus *??There were arrested several people.* Cases like (65), e.g. **There were talked about many people*, are thus independently excluded.

[42] The impossibility of inversion as in (68b) holds in English and French also. Cf. some of 2.7.2 below.

[43] The assumption that a verb can assign nominative to its right would seem to be required independently by cases like (i), if the analysis of Rizzi (1982, III) is correct.

(i)   Ritengo   [[$_{COMP}$ esser] lui partito]
         (*I*) *believe*   *to be*   *he* *left*

         I believe him to have left.

Rizzi argues that in such cases the auxiliary is moved into COMP and assigns nominative to the subject under government.

[44] The non-argument subject would naturally fall under the original version of the Case Filter because it is phonologically realized, as INFL (on infinitival INFL cf. Note 23), analogously to other clitics. Recall that the assumption that such non-argument subjects cannot lack phonological realization (i.e. cannot be PRO) is required independently (cf. 2.2).

Some evidence for formulating the Case Filter independently of the θ-criterion is suggested by the impersonal passives, which we will discuss in 3.2.2 below. With such passives the pleonastic subject is apparently not linked to any argument, and hence to any θ-role, and yet it still appears to require Case.

[45] Since Piedmontese is mostly a spoken language, it does not have a well established orthography. The one used in the text will be partly arbitrary.

[46] As noted in Kayne (1983), languages like Piedmontese show that the link between the NS property and richness of inflection is to be interpreted with respect to the *extended* notion of inflection, which includes inflectional clitics: in Piedmontese inflection proper is no richer than in French and yet Piedmontese is a NS language.

[47] A number of phonological rules will be at work in the forthcoming text examples. In particular we will have to assume: (a) In certain environments *ye* turns to *y* (*ye* is also a dative clitic either gender either number, whence the possibility of a dative reading in some cases as will be mentioned); (b) In certain environments *se* (all cases: reflexive, impersonal, etc.) turns to *s*; (c) A euphonic *l* is inserted between clitics and 'be' or 'have' in certain cases, whence for example *lan, lé* (as in (86a), (89)). The latter is realized as a glide in some environments, whence *ié*, etc, as in (98a); (d) Clitic *ne* is realized as *na* when proclitic.

[48] Coexistence as in (78) will then also suggest that *se/ye* are not part of inflection, as we noted in Note 13.

[49] As some of the next few examples show, in auxiliary-past participle structures, clitics are enclitic to the past participle in Piedmontese, unlike in Italian.

[50] The status of (91) would change of course if *ye* were interpreted as a dative object (cf. Note 47).

[51] Notice that in so far as it does not allow movement into subject position, as in (92b), *ye* differs from SI of 1.6.2' (and its Piedmontese counterpart) which does allow such movement. The behavior of *ye* is not surprising, since we regarded the possibility for Object Preposing with SI as exceptional.

[57] On the basis of the analysis in (96) we correctly expect ep's to be possible as in (i).

(i)   Giovanni era lui nel negozio.
         Giovanni was himself in the store.

On the other hand, the assumption that (95) and (96) have common D-structures may seem to be challenged by the fact that the corresponding French cases exhibit two different verbs, as in (ii).

(ii) a.　Il　y　a　　du pain　　sur la table.
　　　　it there has some bread on the table

　　　There is some bread on the table.

　b.　Le pain　est　sur la table.
　　　The bread is on the table.

However, this is not particularly problematic, as we show in 2.7.2 below.

[53] Idiom *volerci* of (97) is quite analogous to English *It takes* of the gloss. In both cases we have a verb which is normally transitive, but ergative in the idiom. As we expect, *volerci* takes auxiliary *essere* in contrast to *volere*, which takes *avere*. Italian and English differ in the choice of pleonastic element. This difference may in a sense be predictable from the fact that English *there*, unlike Italian *ci* is constrained to presentational contexts, as we see in 2.7.3. Notice that we must assume that *ci* is obligatory with *volere* here, to account for the lack of (97b). This is quite natural given that the expression is an idiom. Analogously with English *it*, to rule out *More money takes*, etc.

[54] Note that the less than complete ungrammaticality of (101a), (102a) would indicate that extraction from subject position is not completely impossible, only to the extent that these cases are better than the inverted forms without overt pleonastics in (99c), (100c). But the difference, if any, is too narrow to draw any conclusion.

Note also that the ungrammaticality of (101a), (102a) remains even when 'short' movement is involved, as in **?? Che cosa è nella busta?** 'What is in the envelope?'. This too agrees with Rizzi's findings. Cf. Note 8.

[55] Cases like (106b) will also argue against any rule of 'nominative pronoun drop' that one may propose to account for NS sentences.

[56] Stranding of SI is more problematic, as we noted in Note 40, ch. 1.

[57] This conclusion requires a number of minor readjustments to our previous discussion.

In Note 45, chapter 1, and in Note 14 above, we assumed that the *ec* in subject position binds the clitic. We have now seen that the *ec* is itself bound by INFL. Thus, in effect it is the chain INFL-*ec* (which is the clitic equivalent to French *il*) that binds the clitic. Relations between a non-argument subject and a subject clitic are therefore essentially analogous to inversion relations.

Consider now now cases like (i), examined in Note 45, chapter 1.

(i)　　[e]　si　fu　　invitati [e]

　　　SI was invited

The correct interpretation of such cases seems to me to be that the chain represented by INFL and the *ec* in subject position, which does not have argument status (like French *il*), binds SI, whereas the same chain extended to SI, which does have argument status since SI is an argument, will bind the object position.

A slight reinterpretation will also be required for the cases in (28) above repeated here below.

(ii) a.　[e]　si　leggerá　　　volentieri　[alcuni articoli]
　　　　　SI will read (sg.) willingly a few articles

　b.　[e]　si　leggeranno　　volentieri　[alcuni articoli]
　　　　　SI will read (pl.) willingly a few articles

In our previous discussion we assumed that only in (iib) was there a non-argument subject due to the pronominal option for INFL. We assumed that such non-argument subjects were linked to the post verbal NP, whence plural agreement. For (iia) we tacitly assumed that the *ec* was solely related to SI. Since we are now assuming that a non-argument subject is present in (iia) also, we must then regard alternations like (ii) as due to the fact that the non-argument subject can be linked either with argument SI, as in (iia), or with the post verbal argument, as in (iib). Note that we assume that SI is coindexed with the subject position even in cases like (iib). This situation is no different from the one which arises in Object Preposing cases discussed in 1.6.2. As in those cases, we have in (iib) two interesecting chains: A subject-SI chain, and an INFL-subject-object chain. Note that we have claimed that there are intersecting chains in (i) too: An INFL-subject-SI chain, and a SI-subject-object chain.

It also follows from the discussion in the text that the subject of sentences containing *ye/ci* is no longer an *ec* in the sense intended in the formulation of (94), and in fact is not an *ec* at all in the case of French *y* (cf. (104b)). This suggests changing the condition in (94) to "where NP$_i$ is an argument". In regard to this, consider *Ci sono alla festa of* (106b). In the text, we assumed it to be ungrammatical because the NS phenomenon is limited to pre-verbal positions. However, this reason would disappear under the analysis in (iiib) which would be the NS counterpart to (iiia).

(iii) a.   *Io$_i$ ci   sono t$_i$ alla festa
             I   there am   at the party

   b.   *[$_i$e] ci   sono t$_i$ alla festa
             (I)   there am   at the party

Clearly we want to rule out (ib) analogously to (ia). But then the notion *ec* in (94) must be irrelevant altogether. what is relevant is definitely the notion *argument*. what (ia, b) have in common is an argument subject, incompatible with *ci*.

[58] The lexical restrictions which we must independently assume, to limit insertion of *ci* to 'be' and some idioms would actually suffice to prevent insertion of *ci* with Raising verbs. However, these considerations would be ineffective for *ye*, which is equally impossible with Raising verbs, and which is not subject to lexical restrictions.

[59] There is a curious set of exceptions to the impossibility of inversion with *ci* in infinitivals, which has no counterpart in inversion without *ci*. This is illustrated in (i).

(i) a.   Potrebbe esser**ci** del pane senza [esser**ci** dell'acqua]
             There could be some bread without there being some water

   b.   *Potrebbero arrivare dei ragazzi senza   [arrivare delle ragazze]
             could   arrive   some boys   without   arriving some girls

Contrasts like that in (i), for which we have no explanation, have been noted for French in Kayne (1979). Kayne's suggestion is that (ia) is grammatical because the verb (*avoir*, in French) assigns objective Case. However this must be false, given Italian *Ci sono io/*me.*

[60] As we noted in 2.2, French cases like (ia) allow us to establish that past participle agreement is with the subject, not with the i-subject, since it goes together with verb agreement. The same is true of substandard Italian cases like (ib).

(i) a.   Il est arrivé   trois filles.
             it is arrived (sg.) three girls

   b.   Ci   sarebbe $\begin{Bmatrix} \text{stato} \\ \text{*stati} \end{Bmatrix}$ troppi clienti   nel negozio.

             there would be (sg.)   been (sg. only) too many clients in the store
             There would have been . . .

This kind of data is not available in Piedmontese, which independently lacks past participle agreement in these cases, due to enclisis of *ye*, as in **staye** 'been-there' (cf. Note 49).

[61] There appears to be one exception to the generalization captured by (128a) for French, represented by the *Il y a* construction in (i).

(i)   Il y   a   eu   du pain   sur la table
        it there has had ('been') some bread on the table   (A)

In (i) we assume a link between subject clitic *y* and the subject position. This ought to trigger E by (128a). One is led to speculate that this exceptionality of (i) and the fact that French uses 'have' as a main verb in these cases are related, but we will not pursue this matter.

[62] Partial confirmation for this view is provided by the fact that English *It proved that the problem was unsolvable*, under the reading 'It turned out that . . .' is also odd. This case is similar because it too is potentially ambiguous, between the above reading and 'It, i.e. that particular fact, proved that . . .'. However, Italian **Affondarono due navi** 'sank two ships/ they sank two ships' ought also to be relevantly analogous, but it is essentially perfect, though ambiguous.

[63] We may expect that **il** should be analogously confined to base-generated cases of extraposition. This seems true, given (i) (cf. the Italian cases in (27) above).

(i) a.   Il m'est arrivé [de revoir Marie]
          It has happened to me to see again Marie

   b. $\left\{ \begin{array}{c} ?{*}Il \\ \text{Ça} \end{array} \right\}$ m'ennuierait [de revoir Marie]

          It would bother me to see again Marie

However, the fact that *il* is possible with 'be' adjective cases like (ii) is surprising since we assume that in these cases the argument has subject, not object θ-role.

(ii)   Il est facile [de chanter]
          It is easy to sing.

Recall that *il* is never possible with 'be' adjective cases when the argument is an NP, as in (138b), a fact which is predicted precisely by the assumption that, with adjectives, the argument has subject θ-role (cf. Note 13, ch. 1). We are therefore faced with a puzzling difference between S and NP complements. We return to this in Note 73 below.

[64] We note that, within a theory in which null elements were *intrinsically* defined, the text discussion would actually provide an argument against the PRO analysis of null subjects of LGB (cf. 2.1 above). This is because cases like **Ha telefonato il tuo amico** 'Has telephoned your friend' would require insertion of PRO late in the derivation, after NP-movement. But our account of the absence of such cases in French is based specifically on the idea that this kind of 'late' insertion is not possible, and that no insertion is required in Italian. The argument disappears however, if we assume that null elements are *contextually* defined, as in LGB, 6. Under this view, a null element can simply 'become' PRO in the course of the derivation if the contextual conditions obtain, so that no insertion would be required for the above case.

[65] Under the base-generation analysis, the link between SE and the subject position will be the same as with SI. It will simply be a base-generated link, as with all base-generated clitics. The existence of such a link is established, for all variants of the construction with SE, and independently of our discussion in 1.6, by the fact that this construction systematically selects auxiliary E, and must therefore be a case in (128a) above. We thus assume that SE is transmitted θ-role from the subject position. (The assumption that SE has θ-role is supported among other things by the fact that it requires Case in (142).)

Under these assumptions, cases like (140a) imply that our view is correct that *il* is only inserted in D-structure, rather than the conceivable alternative that *il* is only inserted in non-θ positions.

[66] Also, special restrictions hold for sc relatives, in which the predicate must always be somewhat 'complex'. Consider *A student happy, *A student arrested, etc.

[67] 'Be' will be an ergative verb when it takes an NP complement, as in There is a Santa Claus. The lack of *A Santa Claus is requires some special stipulation. Notice that this requirement does not arise from choosing the leftward movement alternative. Rightward movement requires a similar stipulation.

[68] Notice that even with present participles it may be an element other than the D-structure subject which is relativized:

(i)   The boat [PRO$_i$ sinking t$_i$ in the harbor] is mine

The point here is that present participles do not differ from the corresponding verb with respect to θ-role assignment.

[69] Notice however that agreement of the passive participle as in (157a) and in sc's in general is systematic, suggesting that this is in fact a core case even in French. To account for this we might regard subject-object relations within sc's as being more 'local' than they are within other clauses.

[70] Notice that, while the inversion relation of (168), repeated in (i), is ill-formed, the clitic-ec relations of (ii) must be well-formed.

(i)   *[$_i$e] ci$_i$ furono [[e] costruite [molte case]]

(ii) a.   [$_i$e] ne furono [t$_i$ invitati [molti [e]]

            Many of them were invited.

    b.   Maria$_i$ gli fu [t$_i$ presentata t$_i$ [e]]

            Maria was introduced to him.

    c.   Maria$_i$ ne era [t$_i$ affascinata [e]]

            Maria was fascinated by it.

We will return to clitic-ec relations in sc structures, which are problematic independent of our discussion in this section (cf. II. 0.3).

[71] Notice that our account of both (162) and (165) relies on the assumption that inversion relations cannot be established iteratively, since if they could, the D-structure for (162), (165) could be as in (i), where there is no violation of locality conditions.

(i)   [e] ci furono [[e] costruite [molte case]]

[72] Cases like (169) do not necessarily require this particular analysis. In fact the adjective here could be internal to NP, as in [Molte case disabitate] sono in vendita 'Many houses uninhabited (uninhabited houses) are for sale', perhaps as a sc relative. In this case, (169) would be an existential sentence (of the There is a Santa Claus type). However, other cases, like (ia), do require a sc analysis of the material that follows 'be', given the impossibility for (ib).

(i) a.   C'era   [Giovanni ammalato]
            there was   Giovanni sick

    b.   *[Giovanni ammalato] mi ha scritto
            Giovanni sick has written to me

A relevant minimal pair would then be (ia) versus *Ci fu Giovanni arrestato 'There was Giovanni arrested'.

[73] On the assumption that *y*, like English *there*, can only be related to an NP, not to an S, and if 'Il est [sc NP . . .]' is impossible because *y* should be inserted, as argued in the text, then we would expect 'Il est [sc S . . .]' to be possible. This would actually enable us to account for the type 'Il est Adj S' (e.g. **Il est facile de chanter** 'It is easy to sing') which we were unable to account for in Note 63, by regarding the latter as derived from 'Il est [sc S Adj]', via extraposition of the S.

[74] In English, some existentials with verbs like *seem* are found however, as in *There seems little reason to doubt it.*

[75] From this point of view, the alternation *John started the car/The car started* is spurious, not a genuine transitive/ergative alternation. Some analogously spurious cases must be assumed for Italian, given for example (i), pointed out to me by L. Rizzi.

(i) a.   Il   mulo ha girato   la   macina.
         the mule has turned the millstone   (A)

   b.   La macina   ha   girato.
         the millstone has turned   (A)

Milsark also cites contrasts between two different meanings of *grow* and *develop*. The Italian counterparts do not shed light in these cases however.

[76] Insertion of *there* is systematically impossible with the so called 'middle' verbs, e.g. *The car drives nicely* (cf. **There drove (nicely) many cars*), even though an NP-movement analysis of middles would seem plausible. Thus it must be the case that middles somehow differ from ergative verbs. Keyser and Roeper (1984) in fact point out a number of independent differences between middles and ergative, although their analysis of 'ergative' verbs differs from ours.

[77] The hypothesis that *there*, like *il* is only available for insertion in D-structure will furthermore account for its non-occurrence with Control verbs noted in 2.3 above (E.g. for **There tried to be several people at the party/at the party several people*).

[78] There are some exceptions to the generalization that ergative verbs do not allow *-er* affixation, such as for example (?) *He is a slow feeder* in the ergative sense of *feed*. Exceptions of this sort are totally lacking with respect to the Italian counterpart *-ore*. But there would not be much reason to conclude from this that English has a smaller class of ergative verbs, since it is clear that English has a more liberal use of the *-er* affix, given such cases as, for example *A two-hundred and fifty pounder, an eighteen wheeler, A go-getter*, etc., the Romance counterparts of which are completely inconceivable.

[79] Insertion of *there* after rightward movement would lead us to expect cases with transitive verbs. Some such cases are in fact attested, although they seem very rare. Some are cited in Kayne (1979).

CHAPTER 3

ON RECONSTRUCTION AND OTHER MATTERS

3.0. INTRODUCTION

This chapter is a collection of three different topics, which have little in common except the fact that they should best appear here, both because this suits the logic of the presentation, and because if inserted into one of the other chapters, they would constitute very lengthy digressions.

The first topic is the correlation between assignment of θ-role to the subject and assignment of Case to the object. This is subsidiary to the contents of the first two chapters: it presupposes the discussion of inversion and extraposition, and makes further comparison between ergative verbs and passives.

The second is the distribution and syntax of past participial clauses. This relies on and extends our analysis of sc's in 2.7.1. It also provides further evidence for the distinction between ergative and intransitive verbs (in this respect it relates to chapter 1). Its results will be of relevance for Part II, especially chapter 6.

The third topic is the 'reconstruction' of moved phrases in LF. While this is to some extent related to the discussion of *ne*-cliticization in 1.4, it is of crucial importance for Part II, especially chapter 4, where we argue that reconstruction applies to the output of VP-movement.

3.1. SUBJECT θ-ROLE AND CASE

3.1.1. *Minus Accusative*

In this section I will argue that there is a universal correlation between two of the specifications that we must assume for lexical entries of verbs: the one concerning assignment of θ-role to the subject position, and the one concerning assignment of Case: accusative Case, since we assume that verbs assign accusative. I will try to show that all and only the verbs that can assign θ-role to the subject can assign (accusative) Case to an object.

We will begin by considering one half of our claim, the one by which *only* verbs which assign subject θ-role assign accusative Case. This we can express as in (1), where 'θ_s' refers to the property of a verb of assigning θ-role to the subject position, and 'A' to the property of the same verb of assigning accusative Case (the minus sign will have the obvious interpretation).

178

(1) $-\theta_s \rightarrow -A$

The statement in (1) appears to be true empirically. We can see this by exhaustively reviewing the cases in which $-\theta_s$ holds. In each case it will turn out that $-A$ also holds.

Consider the type of structure in (2), where 'NP$_{-\theta}$' is a NP which is not assigned a θ-role.

(2)   NP$_{-\theta}$ V NP

This is the case of ergative verbs. If (1) is true, then the NP to the right of V in (2) will never appear in the accusative. Italian minimal pairs like (3)–(4) show that this is the case.

(3) a. Il   caldo avrebbe   soffocato anche **lui**.
   the   heat   would have choked   also   him

   b. Il   caldo **lo**   avrebbe   soffocato.
   the   heat   him would have choked

   c. Il   caldo avrebbe   soffocato anche $\left\{\begin{matrix} \textbf{me} \\ \textbf{*io} \end{matrix}\right\}$.

   the heat   would have choked   also $\left\{\begin{matrix} me \\ I \end{matrix}\right\}$

(4) a. Sarebbe   soffocato anche **lui**.
   would be   choked   also   he

   He would have choked also.

   b. *****Lo** sarebbe   soffocato.
   him   would be choked

   c. Sarei   soffocato anche $\left\{\begin{matrix} \textbf{*me} \\ \textbf{io} \end{matrix}\right\}$.

   would be choked   also $\left\{\begin{matrix} me \\ I \end{matrix}\right\}$

   I would have choked also.

Recall that our two criteria for detecting accusative Case in Italian are occurrence of third person accusative clitics like *lo, la* etc. (cf. the paradigm in (95), ch. 1) and of accusative forms *me, te* for first and second person non-clitic pronouns contrasting with their nominative counterparts *io, tu*. We must conclude that whereas *lui* of (3a) occurring with transitive *soffocare* must be accusative, given (3b, c), *lui* of (4a) occurring with ergative *soffocare* must be nominative, given (4b, c). However, while this difference would indeed follow from (1), it seems also to follow from other considerations.

There are independent reasons for thinking that in languages like Italian, English and French a non-argument subject must be linked with a post verbal argument, NP or S. If this is true, then the i-subject in (4) must be linked with the subject position and, in general, NP in (2) will have to be linked with $NP_{-\theta}$. But since we are regarding transmission of nominative Case to the i-subject as obligatory if the link is established, as we discussed in 2.2 (cf. also the discussion of (66), ch. 2), this would suffice to account for nominative Case in (4) versus accusative in (3) regardless of whether ergative *soffocare* is a Case assigner. Yet note that the requirement that non-argument subjects always be linked with a post verbal NP or S cannot be very strong given the marginal existence of cases that violate it, like the impersonal passives of (5).[1]

(5) a. (?)?   Gli   fu sparato   addosso.
         (*it*)   *to-him   was fired   upon*

         It was fired on him

   b.   ?   Gli   fu detto   del pericolo.
         (*it*)   *to-him   was told   about the danger*

   c.   ??   Gli   fu parlato   a lungo.
         (*it*)   *to-him   was talked at length*

Lack of accusative objects of ergative verbs is thus still relevant to our claim. For, if ergative verbs could ever assign accusative Case, then at least some impersonal forms like those in (6) ought to have the marginal status of the examples in (5), but none does.

(6) a. *   Gli   cade **me** addosso.
         (*it*)   *to him   falls   me   upon*

         It falls me on him

   b. *   Gli**ele**   scappava.
         (*it*)   *to-him-them   escaped*

         It escaped them from him

   c. *   Arriva **te**.
         (*it*)   *arrives   you*

We assume therefore that the cases in (6) are excluded for two reasons, the second of which is insufficient to account for the severe ungrammaticality: (i) Case fails to be assigned to the phrases in boldface; (ii) The non-argument subject fails to be related to a post verbal argument.

Note that we can eliminate the second of the above reasons, thus isolating the first, by moving from the configuration in (2) to the one in (7).

(7) $NP_{-\theta}$ V NP S

This represents the case of ergative verbs that take sentential complements. In such cases the post verbal NP still fails to appear in the
accusative, as in (8).

(8)   *[e] sarebbe   andato **me** [a prendere il   libro]
        (*it*) *would be* ('*have*') *gone*   *me*   *to fetch*   **the** *book*

But, unlike the ungrammaticality of (6), that of (8) cannot be attributed
to the fact that the post verbal NP must be linked with the subject. For in
this case the requirement that a non-argument subject be related to an
argument could be met if the subject of (8) were related to the sentential
complement; so the ungrammaticality of (8) is in fact unexpected unless
andare fails to assign Case to *me*. The generalization that lies behind (8)
is that in the configuration (7) $NP_{-\theta}$ is never linked with S, always with
NP, as expressed in (9).

(9) a. *$NP_{-\theta}$ V NP S

    b. $NP_{-\theta}$ V NP S

While (9a) is exemplified by (8), (9b) is exemplified by (10).

(10)   [e] sarei   andato io [a prendere il   libro]

        would be gone   I   to fetch   the book

        I would have gone to fetch the book.

The generalization in (9) follows directly from our claim in (1) since the
latter predicts that being linked with the subject position is the only way
for the post verbal NP in (9) to receive Case. (Of course we are assuming
that Ss do not require Case.)

    The correctness of our account of (9a) is emphasized by the fact
that not only (9b), but all other configurations that we predict should
minimally contrast with (9a) do in fact contrast with it. Thus, while the
configuration of (9a) is never found, the one of (11) is amply attested, as
in (12).[2]

(11) $NP_{-\theta}$ V PP S

(12) a. It seems to me [$_S$that you should stay]

    b.   Gli   è capitato [$_S$ di incontrare Giovanni]
            (*it*) *to-him is happened   to meet   Giovanni*

            It has happened to him to run into Giovannni.

c.   Mi   sarebbe convenuto   [s rimanere]
        (*it*) *to-me* *would have been advantageous*   *to stay*

It would have been to my advantage to stay.

d.   Gli   è   spiaciuto [s che tu sia partito]
        (*it*) *to him* *is* (*'has'*) *displeased*   *that you left*

He was sorry that you left.

The contrast between (11) and (9) is due to the fact that in (11) the verb takes, not a direct but an indirect (dative) object, so that its failure to assign accusative will have no effect. The configuration in (13), in which the subject position is assigned a θ-role, also exists, in contrast with (9a), as (14) shows.

(13) $\text{NP}_{+\theta}$ V NP S

(14)   Lo ha sorpreso [s che Giovanni sia   già   partito]
          (*it*) *him has surprised*   *that Giovanni is* (*'has'*) *already left*

It surprised him . . .

Accusative Case in (14) (on *lo*) contrasting with lack of it in (8) is allowed by (1) since the verb in (14), unlike the one in (8), assigns subject θ-role. The difference between the two verbs in (8) and (14) with respect to subject θ-role assignment is independently established for example by the different auxiliaries that the two verbs select (E in (8), (10), A in (14)). Recall the discussion in 2.2, in particular the fact that A always corresponds to a rightward moved, never base-generated, instance of extraposition/inversion.

The truth of (1) is further established by the fact that, while there are cases of accusative assignment across clause boundaries (Exceptional Case Marking, in English) with verbs that assign subject θ-role, there is no such case with verbs that do not assign subject θ-role. This further generalization can be expressed as in (15), where the subject of the infinitive has phonological realization.

(15) a. $\text{NP}_{+\theta}$ V [s NP to VP]

b. *$\text{NP}_{-\theta}$ V [s NP to VP]

The contrast in (15) can be illustrated for example by (16).

(16) a.   John expected [Bill to leave].

b. *It seemed [Bill to leave].

Notice that *seem* is a verb which allows Raising. This means that (given the ECP) it can govern the embedded subject. There is therefore no extrinsic reason (in English) why it could not assign accusative Case to that subject in (16b). Notice also that no difficulty arises from the non-argument subjects of (15b), (16b) occurring with infinitival rather than tensed clauses, since non-arguments can be related to infinitivals unprob-lematically, as shown for example by (12b,c).[3]

There are two classes of cases in which the subject position is not assigned a θ-role: (i) certain non-passive verbs; (ii) all passive forms. Each class breaks down into several subclasses according to the subcate-gorization specifications of the verb. So far, we have considered class (i) with respect to the subcategorizations __NP, __NP S, __PP S, __S, thus essentially exhausting this class.[4] Our discussion can be duplicated in full for class (ii).

For our purposes here, the revision of the traditional analysis of pas-sives which we proposed in 2.7.1 can be considered irrelevant. According to the traditional analysis, it is the passive morphology as a whole which does not assign subject θ-role. According to our revised analysis, this is a property of the passive participle (although it is also a property of 'be'). Under either hypothesis we expect an object of the passive participle never to receive accusative if (1) is true. We may then consider the passive morphology as a whole, as in the traditional analysis, and thus simplify exposition.[5]

Putting aside for the moment the case of double-object constructions in English, the conclusion that passives fail to assign accusative Case appears to hold quite generally. Thus, in the configuration (17a) in which V′ is a verb with passive morphology, parallel to (2), NP will never appear in the accusative, as in (17b) which will contrast with the imper-sonal passives of (5).

(17) a. $NP_{-\theta}$ V′ NP.

    b. *   Fu invitato me
       (*it*) *was invited me*

Parallel to the other generalizations we discussed above, we find there-fore those listed in (18) and (19).[6]

(18) a. *$NP_{-\theta}$ V′ NP S

    b. $NP_{-\theta}$ V′ NP S

    c. $NP_{-\theta}$ V′ (PP) S

(19) a. $NP_{+\theta}$ V [$_S$NP to VP]

    b. *$NP_{-\theta}$ V′ [$_S$NP to VP]

The representations in (18) express the fact that if a passive form has a sentential complement, then a post verbal NP (which is not moved into subject position) cannot fail to be linked with the subject, since this is the only way for it to receive Case, while in the absence of a post verbal NP it will be the S which is linked with the subject. the truth of (18) is illustrated in (20).

(20) a. *[e]   fu informato   me   [che . . .]

        (*it*)   *was informed   me   that* . . .

    b. [e] fui informato io [che . . .]

          was informed I   that . . .

       I was informed that . . .

    c.   [e] mi   fu rivelato   [che . . .]

        (*it*) *to-me was revealed that* . . .

       It was revealed to me that . . .

As for (19), it expressed the lack of Exceptional Case Marking with passives. This is illustrated in (21).

(21) a.   John expected [Bill to leave].

    b. *It was expected [Bill to leave].

We conclude on the basis of this discussion that (1), namely $-\theta_s \rightarrow -A$, is true.

We now turn to the other half of the relation between subject θ-role and accusative Case which we claim exists, namely to the condition in (22).

(22) $-A \rightarrow -\theta_s$

In the above discussion, we attempted to show that the statement in (1) was true empirically. No theoretical reason was provided. The statement in (22) is also true, though this time true necessarily, for precise theoretical reasons. Consider the case of a verb which takes a direct object but does not assign Case to it. This verb will *have to* fail to assign θ-role to the subject position, since the only two possibilities for such a direct object to receive Case will be: (i) that it be linked with a non-argument subject; (ii) that it move into subject position. Both possibilities require $-\theta_s$.

There is actually an exception here, represented by the construction employing Italian SI (and analogously French SE). A verb which did not

Case-mark its direct object would still be able to appear in the SI-construction even if it did not fail to assign subject θ-role. The latter θ-role would be fulfilled by SI and the object could then move into subject position. Yet there are no verbs that can appear only in the SI construction. Given this, we may — not implausibly — assume that the lexicon disallows items which cannot be used productively and can only appear in some specific construction. The condition in (22) will then be predicted to hold quite generally.

While (22) is thus predictable from syntactic principles, (1) and the systematic lack of accusative with $-\theta_s$ verbs, does not appear to be. In fact, as we pointed out, no independent syntactic consideration would prohibit the configurations in (9a) and (15b) (NP$_i$ V NP S$_i$; NP$_i$ V [$_i$NP to VP]) and the corresponding ones in (18a), (19b), which are nevertheless unattested. We must therefore assume that (1) is an autonomous lexical principle, not just a reflex of syntactic factors. Given that (22) also holds, it will be natural to assume that the principle is in fact the conjunction of the two conditions, namely (23).

(23) $\theta_s \longleftrightarrow A$

As far as I can see there is no empirical reason to assume that this lexical principle is further complicated so as to hold only for verbs that are subcategorized for a direct object. We then assume that it holds quite generally, namely that intransitive verbs, like transitives, are potential accusative assigners, although they are not subcategorized for a direct object. This predicts that if there was a way for verbs to occur with direct objects they are not subcategorized for, intransitive verbs should so occur, since they can assign Case, while ergative verbs should not. In 2.7.3 we argued that this is in fact the case with expletive objects in English which give rise to contrasts like *He talked [my head off]/*They arrived [the hell out of the bus terminal]*. (In the text we gave a different interpretation. But see 3.1.2 below.)

Note that the truth of (23), and specifically that of (1), predicts that in the general case NP-traces will not be in Case marked positions. Given locality conditions on relations between NP-traces and their antecedents, we know that the antecedent will always be the subject of the element that governs the trace. But for NP-movement into subject position to be possible, in the general case (the SI-construction aside) the property $-\theta_s$ will have to hold, and given (23) $-A$ will also have to hold for the element that governs the trace, so that rather systematically a trace will be in a Case-less position. This suggests that there is no independent condition requiring that NP-traces be in Case-less positions, only a generalization deriving from (23).[7] The existence of such an independent condition would in any case be difficult to maintain empirically. For example it would be incompatible with our analysis of the SI-construction (cf. 1.6), which provides no means for the verb to lose its accusative-assigning properties when Object Preposing occurs. Also, it would not obviously hold in cases of preposition stranding, like *John was laughed at.* But neither the SI-construction case, nor the preposition stranding case requires any comment under (23), which predicts traces in Case-less positions only rather generally, not always or necessarily.

3.1.2. *Double Objects*

The truth of (23) will enable us to deduce the generalization, which we assumed in 1.8 above (cf. (131), ch. 1), that aside from special cases like the English double object constructions, a verb will never have more than one direct object NP, as expressed by (24).

(24)   *V NP NP

If both of the NPs in (24) are phonologically realized, the generalization follows from the assumption that the verb can assign Case only once. Then one of the NPs will fail to receive Case. The same holds if either or both NPs are *ec*'s related to clitics, since we assume Case requirements to hold for clitic-*ec* chains, just as they do for NPs. If either or both NPs are Wh-traces, i.e. variables, the generalization still follows in the same fashion, since we assume that variables require Case. Given the requirement that PRO must be ungoverned, neither NP can be PRO, thus leaving NP-trace as the only remaining possibility. Because of the binding conditions, if either one of the NPs in (24) is a NP-trace, its antecedent will be the subject of V, and since there is only one subject per verb, it could not be the case that both NPs are traces. If thus either one (never both) of the NPs is a trace, the generalization follows from (23): since NP-movement is always into subject position as we pointed out, it can only appear if the verb is not assigning subject θ-role. But then, by (23) (in particular the portion of it expressed by (1)) the verb will not assign accusative, and the non-moved NP will fail to receive Case.[8] The prediction that there will be no verb with two direct objects will then hold in full, aside from some special cases to which we now turn.
   Consider the following.

(25)   Mary was given a book

Cases like (25) may seem to contradict (23) above ((1) in particular) since no subject θ-role is assigned and yet Case must be assigned to the object, *a book.* However, let us consider the active counterpart to (25) in (26). (These cases are generally referred to as "double object" or "dative shift" constructions.)

(26)   Someone gave [$_{NP_1}$Mary] [$_{NP_2}$a book]

We will postulate, essentially along the lines of Marantz (1981), that NP_1 of (26), which is semantically an indirect object (i.e. which has the semantic role, say 'goal', generally associated with indirect objects) is assigned Case by the verb, whereas NP_2 is assigned Case essentially by the structural configuration. We may presume, adapting Marantz' discussion to our framework, that such exceptional assignment of Case to NP_2 in (26) is related to the fact that the latter occurs in the position, and has the semantic role, which are generally associated with accusative objects.[9]

As we predict for any case in which some exceptional way to assign a second accusative exists, the generalization in (24) does not hold here. However, contrary to what (25) might suggest, (23) still does, as (27) is ungrammatical in most dialects.

(27)   *A book$_i$ was given [$_{NP_1}$Mary] [$_{NP_2}$t$_i$]

The ungrammaticality of cases like (27) (which, according to Marantz is rather general among languages that have double object constructions) is in fact accounted for by (23), since the latter predicts that NP_1 in (27) should fail to receive Case. The grammaticality of (25) will also follow, since we assume that NP_2 of (26) is assigned Case not by the verb but by the structure — say, by this particular configuration involving a transitive verb.[10] This account implies that (23) refers to specifications relative to lexical items rather than to properties of the structure, as we assumed all along (but see also parts of 5.3 below). Thus (23) appears to hold in full, even with English double-object constructions (although we have no account of the dialects that allow (27)).[11]

3.1.3. By-phrases

Our assumption that both passives and ergative verbs are exactly analogous in failing to assign subject θ-role leaves the significant difference between (28a) and (28b) unaccounted for.

(28) a. The ship was sunk by the navy.

b. *The ship sank by the navy.

Concerning this difference we will assume, in agreement with Marantz (1981) that passives do not differ from the corresponding active verbs with respect to 'θ-structure', (or 'Argument structure'), that is, the system of 'thematic' or 'semantic' roles that characterize the verb. Let us see how this idea can be developed.

In order to distinguish on the one hand non-ergative active verbs from passives, and passives from ergative verbs on the other, we will introduce a distinction between 'assignment of θ-role to the subject' (equivalent to 'assignment of subject θ-role', or θ_s), and 'assignment of thematic subject role'. By the first we will mean, as we have done all along, assignment of

θ-role to a configurationally defined position, that of the subject; passives and ergative verbs will be alike in failing to assign θ-role to that position. By the second we will mean assignment of a specific 'thematic' (or 'semantic') role, that of THEMATIC SUBJECT or SEMANTIC SUBJECT, without referring to any structurally defined position. Passives are like the corresponding actives in their ability to assign such thematic subject roles, and unlike ergatives.

We now establish a partial interdependence between the two notions, by supposing that thematic-subject role can be fulfilled in two different ways: (i) by an argument in subject position; (ii) by a *by*-phrase.[12] The choice between (i) and (ii) will be determined by whether or not a θ-role is assigned to the subject position. If it is, (i) will have to be chosen, since we presume that the only θ-role that the subject position can be assigned is the thematic-subject role. If it is not, (ii) will be chosen. The failure of ergative verbs to either assign θ-role to the subject position or appear with a *by*-phrase as in (28b) will be due to the fact that with these verbs there is no thematic-subject role to assign.

We are thus postulating two parameters: plus or minus thematic-subject role, and plus or minus assignment of θ-role to the subject position. If the two were independent we would expect four possibilities. However, since minus thematic-subject role implies minus assignment of θ-role to the subject position as we pointed out, we will have the three possibilities of (29).[13]

(29)

	θ_s	$-\theta_s$
Plus thematic-subject role	Actives	Passives
Minus thematic-subject role		Ergative verbs

The fact that the presence of a *by*-phrase is optional, we will regard as the fact that realization of the thematic-subject role is optional, in contrast with the apparent obligatoriness of the realization of θ-roles that the verb assigns by virtue of subcategorization specifications (i.e. object θ-roles). (Cf. I.0.3). To account for the obligatory presence of an argument subject with active verbs contrasting with the optionality of *by*-phrases, we will assume that what is obligatory is the assignment of θ-role to the subject position by verbs that do assign such a θ-role.[14]

Note that this set of assumptions predicts that if there are cases of VP-complements, namely cases in which the subject position is missing, then in such cases the *by*-phrase ought to be able to occur with the active form of the verb. The reason why the *by*-phrase does not occur with active verbs in sentential structures is that those verbs assign θ-role to the subject position, thus requiring that thematic-subject role be fulfilled

by an argument in that position. A *by*-phrase in such cases is ruled out
by the θ-criterion, since that phrase would represent a second argument
fulfilling thematic-subject role. But this reason disappears if there is no
subject position, so that *by*-phrases ought to occur with active verbs in
VP-structures. We will see that this situation does in fact arise.

In this section we have argued that all and only the verbs that assign
subject θ-role assign accusative Case; that the latter generalization allows
us to deduce the prohibition against more than one direct object in other
than some special cases; and that, while passives do not differ from ergative verbs with respect to assignment of subject θ-role, they do differ
from the latter in allowing a thematic (or 'semantic') subject, being in this
respect analogous to the corresponding active verbs.

3.2. PAST PARTICIPIAL CLAUSES

3.2.0. *Introduction*

In this section we return to the topic of small clauses, introduced in
2.7.1, considering those cases in which the predicate is a past participle.
We will see that there are some past participial clauses that allow both
transitive and intransitive verbs, excluding ergatives, while some others
allow transitives and ergatives, excluding intransitives. We will attempt to
provide an account of these facts, which of course are further evidence
for the distinction between ergative and intransitive verbs. One of the
cases we study is Italian small clause relatives, which will play a role in
later chapters.

We begin by considering the distribution of past participial sc's in
English.

3.2.1. *English*

As we discussed in 2.7.1, in English we find past participial sc's as sc
relatives and as complements of 'be' in passives, as in (30), given in the
analyses we proposed.

(30) a. $[_{NP}$A student $[_{sc}PRO_i$ accepted t_i in the program]] arrived
       yesterday

     b. John$_i$ was $[_{sc}$ t$_i$ accepted t$_i$ in the program]

To simplify discussion we will leave aside a third occurrence of past
participial clauses, represented by complements of *believe, consider*, etc.,
as in *I consider* $[_{sc}him_i$ *accepted* t$_i$ *in the program]*. As far as I can see
the latter complements raise no additional issue. The two types in (30)

cover in their respective distributions the class of transitive verbs, and have somewhat different extensions into the class of verbs that take clausal complements.

Since we take relativization in (30a) to consist of Control by the head, of a PRO subject of the sc, we will predict that the generalization governing the distribution of past participial sc relatives is that there must be, in the complement structure of the past participle, an argument NP that can be placed into subject position of the sc, via NP-movement. This NP could thus be either the direct object, as in (30a), or an argument within a non-tensed complement, as for example in (31).

(31)   [A man [$_{sc}$ PRO$_i$ believed [$_S$ t$_i$ to know the truth]]] was questioned by the police.

This generalization exhausts the distribution of the case in (30a), but will not exhaust that of the case in (30b), i.e. of past participial clauses in passive constructions. This is due to the fact that, in addition to NP-movement, passives can resort to insertion of a non-argument subject, cf. *There was a man arrested, It was believed that* . . . . Given that we assume that non-argument subjects *there* and *it* can only occur if they are related, respectively, to an NP and an S, we can say that past participial sc's will be well formed only if one of (32a, b, c) is true.

(32) a. There is an NP that can move to the subject of the sc.
     b. There is an NP that can be related to *there.*
     c. There is an S that can be related to *it.*

For sc relatives, (32a) must be met, as we showed. For complements of 'be', one of (32a, b, c) must be met. If (32a) holds, the subject of the sc can always move to the subject of 'be', as in (30b). If one of (32b, c) holds, *there/it* can be inserted. However, given our observation, of 2.7.2, that an NP related to *there* is always the subject of the sc complement of 'be', (32b) is actually subsumed under (32a). Finally, (32c) is fulfilled in cases like (33).

(33)   It$_i$ was [$_{sc}$ t$_i$ suggested [$_i$ that he should leave]].

If we now consider intransitive verbs, or more precisely verbs whose complement structure (subcategorization) includes neither an NP nor an S, we expect that they should fail to occur in both passives and past participial relatives, although for somewhat different reasons. Consider (34).

(34) a. *[A student [$_{sc}$[e] applied to the program]] arrived yesterday
     b. *It$_i$ was [$_{sc}$ t$_i$ applied to the program]

As we pointed out in 2.7.1, the case in (34a) is impossible since, as no θ-role is assigned to the subject position, and there is no NP object, there is no argument in the sc that can act as a relativized element. The case in (34b) is ruled out differently, specifically by the syntax of *it*.

All the facts discussed so far thus follow from (32), but others do not. In particular, (32) gives no account of the non-occurrence of ergative verbs, or more generally of verbs that do not assign subject θ-role, in either sc relatives or complements of *be*. Consider (35).

(35) a. ?*[A student [$_{sc}$PRO$_i$ arrived t$_i$ yesterday]] was accepted in the program.

b. *John$_i$ was [$_{sc}$t$_i$ arrived t$_i$ yesterday].

Assuming that English *arrive* is an ergative verb, like its Italian counterpart, its complement structure will be identical to that of transitive *accept* in (30). Analogously, the complement structure of *seem* of (36) will be identical to that of *believe* and *suggest* of (31), (33).

(36) a. *[A man [$_{sc}$PRO$_i$ seemed [$_S$ t$_i$ to know the truth]]] was questioned by the police.

b. *It$_i$ was [$_{sc}$t$_i$ seemed [$_i$ that he should leave]].

It thus seems that what is relevant to the exclusion of this class of verbs from past participial clauses is not the complement structure, or subcategorization specifications, which (32) refers to, but rather specifications concerning subject θ-role assignment. In particular, what is required to rule out (35) and (36) is the assumption that the morphological process that produces past participles from verbs, and which changes lexical specifications from *plus* assignment of subject θ-role to *minus*, is subject to a constraint against vacuous loss of θ-role assignment, so that all the verbs which already fail to assign subject θ-role will be barred from undergoing past participial affixation. From this viewpoint, the near-identical behavior of intransitive and ergative verbs in English past participial clauses (as in, for example, (34a) versus (35a)) is thus fortuitous. By our account, the absence of participles of intransitive verbs is essentially due to the syntax of pleonastics, while the absence of participles of ergative verbs is due to a constraint on a morphological rule. We then expect that, should some of the parameters change as we turn to other languages, we may find cases which allow participles of either intransitives or ergatives but not of both. This expectation is fulfilled, as we see in the next two subsections.

3.2.2. Impersonal Passives

One of the cases in question is that of impersonal passives, which allow intransitives, though not ergatives. The difference between intransitive and ergative verbs with respect to impersonal passives is clear even in languages in which impersonal passives are of limited productivity. Thus, Kayne (1975, p. 247, fn. 56) notes that in French there are contrasts like the one in (37), unaccounted for in his discussion.

(37) a. Il sera parlé de vous par tout le monde.
         '*It will be talked about you by everyone*'.

     b. *Il sera venu chez vous par tout le monde.
         '*It will be come to your place by everyone*'.

But of course the difference will be more tangible in languages in which impersonal passives are productive. Thus Kayne also notes similar contrasts in German, which allows impersonal passives more freely, and Perlmutter (1978) cites contrasts like the one in (38) in Dutch, as evidence for the 'Unaccusative Hypothesis'.

(38) a. Er   wordt hier door de jonge lui   veel gedanst.
         there is   here by   the young people a lot danced

     'It is danced here a lot by the young people'.

     b. *Er   werd door vele   kinderen in de   rook   gestikt.
         there was   by   many children in the smoke   suffocated

     'It was suffocated in the smoke by many children'.

We will attribute the well formedness of cases like (37a), (38a) to a relaxation of the requirement that the non-argument subject (*il, er*) be related to a post verbal argument. As for the ill-formedness of (37b), (38b), our proposal rules out such occurrences of ergative verbs, in a number of ways. First, we do not expect the *by*-phrase since ergative verbs do not assign thematic subject role, as we argued in 3.1.3. If the *by*-phrase is dropped, these examples are still ruled out (correctly) because the verbs appear without the direct objects they are subcategorized for, and furthermore because of the constraint barring (passive) participles of ergative verbs (non-vacuous loss of θ-role assignment).[15] The impersonal forms which are least unexpected within our framework are perhaps those of the type *It arrives me* discussed in 3.1.1. Where impersonal passives are allowed these are ruled out only by lack of accusative Case on the post verbal NP. (See the discussion of (6) above.)

Our claim is thus that the distribution of impersonal passives is essentially governed by the syntax of pleonastic elements, specifically by the presence versus absence of a requirement that such elements be linked with an argument.[16] An apparent alternative to this account of what we may call the 'impersonal passive parameter' would consist of assuming the presence versus absence of a constraint limiting morphological derivation of passive participles to, essentially, transitive verbs. However, this alternative does not seem to me tenable.

First, there would be complications in formulating correctly the constraint for English. For the subcategorization ___NP is not the only one that gives rise to passive participles, ___S does too, as in (33). We would therefore have to assume that the constraint in question allows those two subcategorizations, while excluding, in particular, ___PP, so as to rule out for example (34b). However, exclusion of the latter subcategorization has certain consequences, given cases like (39).

(39) a.   John$_i$ was [t$_i$ talked to t$_i$].

   b.   ?*It$_i$ was [t$_i$ talked [$_{PP}$ to John]].

The assumption that the subcategorization ___PP is excluded from passive participial morphology in English would imply in effect that two different verbs are involved in (39): a transitive verb *talk to* in (39a), and an intransitive verb *talk* in (39b), a conclusion which is not obviously correct.[17]

Secondly, while our constraint on non-argument subjects has the right consequences for the distribution of SI/SE of Italian and French, a constraint on past participial morphology does not: recall how we assume that, while in Italian a non-argument subject can be related to SI, French *il* cannot correspondingly be related to SE, a difference which we attributed to the different distributions of the definiteness restriction in Italian and French (cf. 2.6.3). As we observed, French SE constructions are limited to transitive verbs (as in **Il se construit beaucoup d'immeubles** 'SE builds many buildings'), roughly to the degree that passives are.[18] This parallelism is predicted under the assumption that the relevant constraint is that French *il* must be linked with an argument, while a constraint on passive participial morphology would not carry over to SE cases. Also, from the standpoint of a constraint on morphological derivation of passive participles, the fact that for example English pleonastic *it* never fails to be related to a clausal argument would be quite accidental. We thus reject such an alternative.

3.2.3. *Italian sc Relatives*

A second case in which the distribution of past participial clauses brings to light the difference between intransitive and ergative verbs is represented by Italian sc relatives, which allow ergative verbs on a par with transitives, while not allowing intransitives, as in (40).

(40) a. [Un ragazzo [$_{sc}$PRO$_i$ invitato t$_i$ alla festa]]   non conosceva
      a guy   invited   to the party did not know

   Maria
   Maria

b. [Un ragazzo [$_{sc}$PRO$_i$ arrivato t$_i$ poco fa]]   conosce Maria
   a guy   *arrived   a while ago knows   Maria*

c. *[Un ragazzo [$_{sc}$[e] telefonato a Maria]] non può venire
   a guy   *telephoned to Maria cannot   come*

   alla festa
   to the party

While the account of the transitive and the intransitive cases in (40a,c) will be identical to that of their English counterparts ((30a), (34a)), we will assume that Italian minimally differs from English in permitting past participle formation with vacuous loss of subject θ-role hence permitting (40b). This does not carry over to passives however, as (41) is just as ungrammatical as its English counterpart.

(41)   *Giovanni$_i$ è stato   [$_{sc}$t$_i$ arrivato t$_i$ poco fa].
       Giovanni has been   arrived   a while ago

We must therefore assume that passive constructions universally require non-vacuous loss of subject θ-role or perhaps the possibility of a thematic-subject role. Of course this difference between (40b) and (41) weakens our claim of 2.7.1 above that complements of 'be' have essentially the same structure as sc relatives, but we will assume that the latter stands even so.[19]

The ability of $-\theta_s$ verbs to appear in Italian sc relatives, as in (40b), is not completely general however, since it does not extend to Raising verbs, as in (42).

(42)   *[Un ragazzo [$_{sc}$PRO$_i$ sembrato [$_S$t$_i$ conoscere Maria]]]
       a guy   *seemed   to know   Maria*

   ha   telefonato a Giovanni
   has telephoned to Giovanni

This requires further comment since once we allow vacuous loss of subject θ-role then just as (40b) is expected, on a par with (40a) and (30a), (42) will be expected on a par with examples like (31).

While I will have no formal proposal for distinguishing ergative from Raising verbs here, it seems to me that, if we regard use of $-\theta_s$ verbs in past participial sc relatives as a marked option, as is suggested by the fact that it is possible in some languages and not in others, then it will be intuitively reasonable to expect that the option should be taken in a restrictive way. But what could be the nature of the restriction that excludes Raising verbs? Let us suppose that past participial affixation, beside having access to information concerning subject θ-role, also has access to subcategorization information. Ergative verbs can be distinguished from Raising verbs on the basis of the fact that the subcategorization of the former, ___NP, is one that guarantees that relativization will succeed, i.e. that (32a) above will be fulfilled. The same is not true of the subcategorization ___S, since the possibility of relativizing an NP from a sentential complement will depend on the internal structure of the complement, for example on whether the latter is tensed or not, and in general on factors which are not represented in the lexical entry of the verb. To put it differently, while with verbs that take a direct object, past participial relativization is systematically possible, with verbs that take S-complements it is only sporadically possible. It therefore seems reasonable to expect that if the system is idiosyncratically constrained, it should be constrained to the first class of verbs.

Returning to the contrast in (40) between transitive and ergative verbs on the one hand, and intransitives on the other, we note that this contrast is also reflected in certain nominalizations from past participles. Thus, while we find **l'arrestato** 'the arrested (one)', **i reclusi** 'the confined (ones)', as well as **l'ultimo arrivato l'ultimo venuto** 'the last (one) arrived the last (one) come', **i caduti** 'the fallen (ones)', **i nati** 'the born (ones)', **i sopravvissuti** 'the survived (ones)', **gli accorsi** 'those who rushed in' **l'accaduto** 'the happened (thing) (i.e. the incident)', we find no nominalizations from intransitives, such as *i telefonati 'those who telephoned', *i camminati 'those who walked', etc.

The facts exemplified by (40) are of consequence for the hypothesis which we have rejected, that sc relatives derive from normal relative clauses by deletion of a sequence [Wh-phrase main verb 'be'] by *Wh-be* deletion. While (40a) does have a counterpart with main verb 'be' (cf. 'A guy *who was* invited . . .'), (40b) does not. The latter only has a counterpart involving *auxiliary* 'be', as in (43).

(43)   Un ragazzo **che è**   arrivato poco fa . . .
         a guy   *who is* ('*has*') *arrived a while ago . . .*

Thus *Wh-be* deletion would have to be extended to auxiliary 'be'. Yet such an extension seems untenable. Consider the following.

(44) a. Gli individui **che si erano** presentati al
      The individuals that $\left\{ \begin{array}{l} \textit{SI had introduced} \\ \textit{had introduced themselves} \end{array} \right\}$ *to the*

      direttore furono poi assunti
      director were later hired

    b. Gli individui presentatisi al direttore . . .
      The individuals $\left\{ \begin{array}{l} \textit{self-introduced} \\ \textit{*SI-introduced} \end{array} \right\}$ *to the director . . .*

Example (44a) is ambiguous between a reflexive and an impersonal reading, just like (45), given in the two relevant analyses, and like some of the cases discussed in 1.6.2.

(45) a. Giovanni$_i$ si$_i$ è presentato [e] al direttore.

Giovanni himself is introduced   to the director

Giovanni has introduced himself to the director.

    b. Giovanni$_i$ si è presentato t$_i$ al direttore.
       Giovanni SI is introduced   to the director

    Giovanni has been introduced to the director.

However, (44b) is not ambiguous, and allows only the reflexive reading. This is quite unexpected under a derivation of (44b) from (44a) via *Wh-be* deletion, but can be accounted for under our analysis. While an account of the reflexive reading of (44b) will have to await till 6.3.2 below, we can see right away why a SI reading is not allowed. Under our analysis of SI, the sc relative would have the D-structure in (46a), and the S-structure in (46b), both of which are ill-formed.

(46) a. [[$_{NP}$si] presentati PRO . . .].
    b. [PRO$_i$ presentatisi t$_i$ . . .].

Analysis (46a) is excluded because θ-role fails to be assigned to SI, (46b) because Case fails to be assigned to SI (as in infinitivals; cf. the discussion in 1.6). *Wh-be* deletion would also be problematic with respect to the two different positions of the clitic in (44a,b). Since cliticization on past participles is possible *only* in sc relatives, a derivation of (44b) from (44a) would imply either that *Wh-be* deletion is associated with a process that reattaches clitics to the past participle: a rather awkward complication, or that the conditions that determine the distribution of clitics apply *only* after *Wh-be* deletion. But we will argue that such conditions apply at all levels (see II.0.3 and Part II). Notice also that *Wh-be* deletion extended to auxiliary 'be' would require ad-hoc restrictions to exclude cases like (42) given the grammaticality of ***Un ragazzo che era sembrato conoscere Maria . . .** 'A guy who was ('had') seemed to know Maria . . .'. Furthermore, *Wh-be* deletion would be unenlightening with respect to the distribution of nominalizations from past participles that we noted, as there is no (obvious) possibility for a *Wh-be* deletion derivation of those, cf. **I caduti** 'The fallen (ones)' versus ***I CHE SONO caduti** 'the who are fallen'.

    While we therefore have these and other reasons to reject a *Wh-be* deletion analysis of sc relatives, there does seem to exist some relationship between the fact that Italian ergative verbs appear in past participial relatives, and the fact that they take auxiliary 'be', a relation that *Wh-be* deletion would capture. Thus, French, which is like Italian in assigning auxiliary 'be' to verbs like *arrive* also allows these verbs in past participial relatives, as in (47a), while Spanish which only has auxiliary *haber* 'have' is more like English, as indicated by (47b).

(47) a. Un étudiant arrivé hier soir . . . .   (French)
         A student arrived last night . . .

      b. ?Un estudiante recientemente llegado de Francia . . .   (Spanish)
         A student recently arrived from France . . .

This relationship will not be sufficient for a defense of *Wh-be* deletion
however, essentially for two reasons. First, the various aguments against
Wh-be deletion in general, and against deletion of auxiliary 'be' in particular stand. Secondly, this relationship is too weak. Thus, Spanish speakers vary on the acceptability of (47b), while of course they do not vary
on auxiliary assignment. Some English speakers also do not completely
reject (35a) (?**A student arrived yesterday was accepted in the program*),
and recognize a difference between the latter and (34a) (**A student
applied to the program arrived yesterday*).

We will attempt to account for the relationship in question by suggesting that, while the formal apparatus we are assuming is essentially
correct, so that the ability of ergative verbs to appear in past participial
relatives is determined by a relaxation of the requirement that past participial affixation involve *non-vacuous* loss of subject θ-role, the type of
auxiliary that the verb selects plays a role in triggering such relaxation. In
particular we may suppose that the relaxation is especially favored when
the superficial analogy between transitive pairs like (48) and ergative
pairs like (49) would hold.

(48) a. Uno studente **che era**   ammirato . . .
         a   student   who was   admired . . .

      b. Uno studente ammirato . . .
          a   student   admired . . .

(49) a. Uno studente **che era**   arrivato . . .
         a   student   who was ('had')   arrived . . .

      b. Uno studente arrivato . . .
          a   student   arrived . . .

This superficial analogy will hold only where ergative verbs take auxiliary
'be', so that the relationships between ergative sc relatives and auxiliary
selection will be captured. It would be easy to show that this proposal
has none of the pitfalls of *Wh-be* deletion.

To summarize, in this section we have argued that there are two sets
of factors determining the distribution of passive past participles, one
of a morphological character, the other of a syntactic character. The
morphological factors consist of a requirement that past participial affixation change *non-vacuously* to minus the lexical specification concerning
subject· θ-role assignment. The syntactic factors require that either there
be a NP in the complement structure of the past participle that can move

into subject position, or that there be an argument, NP or S, that can be linked with a pleonastic element. In the general case, for example in English, the morphological factors exclude ergative verbs from past participial clauses, while the syntactic factors exclude intransitive verbs. When the morphological constraints are relaxed, ergative verbs appear in past participial clauses, as in Italian sc relatives. When the syntactic constraints are relaxed, intransitive verbs appear, as in impersonal passives in various languages.

3.3. RECONSTRUCTION

3.3.0. *Introduction*

The notion that moved phrases can be reconstructed in their original position at the level of LF will play a role in the second part of this book, combining with our analyses of causative and restructuring constructions, to provide an explanation for a number of facts. In this section I will argue for the correctness of this notion, independent of the discussion of causative and restructuring constructions.

There are two rather clear cases that suggest that a moved NP can be detected in its original position by interpretive rules, which is to say by rules of the LF component. The first such case involves the element *each* in the structure $[_{NP} Q \overline{N}$ each] where Q is a quantifier-type element, as we see in the next subsection.

3.3.1. *Each Interpretation*

The element *each* and its Italian counterpart *ciascuno* in the construction exemplified here below, appear to require a plural antecedent, as in the synonymous cases in (50a, b).

(50) a.   The kids bought $[_{NP}$one book **each**].

b.   I ragazzi comprarono $[_{NP}$un libro **ciascuno**].

The relation between Italian *ciascuno* and its antecedent is evidenced by gender agreement. Thus, contrasting with the masculine agreement of (1b) we find feminine agreement in **Le ragazze . . . ciascuna** 'The girls . . . each (fem.)'. In the following discussion we will consider English examples for the most part, but the whole discussion may be assumed to carry over to Italian.

The following examples, where judgments are relative to the interpretation suggested by the indices, show that the antecedent must be c-commanding.

(51) a.   *Two girls each$_i$ met us$_i$.

b. We$_i$ were met by two girls each$_i$.

c. *I asked one question each$_i$ about [$_i$the students].

d. I asked [$_i$the students] one question each$_i$.

As we then expect, cases like (52) are ambiguous.

(52)   We$_i$ asked [$_j$the students] one question each$_{\{i \atop j\}}$.

The examples in (53) suggest that the relation between *each* and its antecedent falls under locality conditions of a familiar kind.

(53) a. *We$_i$ expected [$_S$John to read one book each$_i$].

b. *We$_i$ expected [$_S$ that one student each$_i$ would call].

Specifically, (53a,b) look like typical Specified Subject Condition and Nominative Island Condition violations respectively. We may therefore regard the element *each* in the construction [$_{NP}$ Q $\overline{N}$ each] as an anaphor, requiring a plural antecedent.[20] Given that the relation between *each* and its antecedent is part of the interpretation, it is natural to take the well-formedness conditions involved to hold at least at LF.

We must now note that, while in general the plural antecedent to *each* will not be within a prepositional phrase as for example in (51c) above, antecedents of the form *to NP* (and correspondingly *a NP* in Italian) can yield acceptability or near-acceptability, as in (54).

(54) a.   (?)John assigned one interpreter each$_i$ to [$_i$the visitors].

b.   ? John gave one present each$_i$ to [$_i$the kids].

c.   ?·John sent one letter each$_i$ to [$_i$the students].

This kind of exceptionality of *to NP* phrases seems to be rather common. It is found for example in cases like (55).

(55)   John appealed to Bill$_i$ [$_S$PRO$_i$ to leave].

We may therefore assume that *to NP* phrases are rather generally exceptional with respect to the definition of c-command, behaving not like other PPs but rather like NPs, whatever the exact reason.[21]

Our well-formedness conditions on the occurrences of *each* (in particular c-command) predict that a phrase [$_{NP}$Q $\overline{N}$ each] should not be the subject of the sentence containing the plural antecedent. In general, this is true, as for example in (51a), or in (56).

(56)   *One interpreter each$_i$ was friendly to [$_i$the visitors].

Passives however depart noticeably from this prediction. Thus, consider (57), which we represent in the traditional analysis of passives, for simplicity, ignoring here and in further examples the intermediate trace of our analysis of 2.7.1 above.

(57) a. ?[$_i$One interpreter each$_j$] was assigned t$_i$ to [$_j$the visitors].

　　b. ?[$_i$One present each$_j$] was given t$_i$ to [$_j$the kids].

　　c. ?[$_i$One letter each$_j$] was sent t$_i$ to [$_j$the students].

Such passives do not differ very significantly from the corresponding active forms in (54). The contrast between (56) and (57), and the relative lack of contrast between (54) and (57) suggests that at the level at which *each* is required to have a c-commanding antecedent, the phrase containing *each* is represented in direct object position in (57), just as it is in (54). The effect observed for (57) is systematically present in movement cases, and absent in superficially analogous cases in which movement has not occurred, like (56). Of particular relevance are Raising/Control minimal pairs like (58).

(58) a. ?[$_i$One interpreter each$_j$] was likely [$_S$t$_i$ to be assigned t$_i$ to [$_j$those visitors]].

　　b. *[$_i$One interpreter each$_j$] was trying [$_S$PRO$_i$ to be assigned t$_i$ to [$_j$those visitors]].

While (58a,b) are very similar in their S-structure representations, only in (58a) has the phrase containing *each* originated in embedded direct object position, the position which is relevant for the interpretation of *each*. We may note also the contrast betwen (57) and cases like (59).

(59)　　*[$_i$One interpreter each$_j$] assigned himself$_i$ to [$_j$those visitors].

Again, while (59) and (57) are somewhat parallel configurationally (in both cases the direct object is anaphoric to the subject), it is only in (57) that the phrase containing *each* has originated in direct object position.

Somewhat related to the contrast between (59) and (57) is the fact that Italian cases like (60), though never too felicitous, are unambiguous, allowing only the impersonal interpretation associated with the analysis in (60a), not the reflexive interpretation associated with (60b).

(60) a. ?[$_i$ Un evaso　　ciascuno$_j$] si　consegnerà t$_i$　a
　　　　　 one escapee　each　　*SI　will turn in　 to*

　　[$_j$quei carabinieri]
　　 those policemen

　　We will turn in one escapee to each of those policemen.

　　b. *[$_i$Un evaso ciascuno$_j$] si$_i$ consegnerà [e] a [$_j$quei carabinieri]

　　One escapee each will turn himself in to those policemen.

The non-ambiguity of (60) is not surprising since, under our analyses of impersonals and reflexives (cf. 1.5, 1.6 above), the subject, *Un evaso ciascuno* originates in direct object position in (60a), just as it does in (57), while in (60b) it does not, so that the latter is in this respect like its English counterpart in (59).

The generalization therefore seems to be that moved NPs are represented in their original position at LF, which is the level at which *each* is interpreted.[22] Before turning to a theoretical account of this generalization, we will consider another case which appears to confirm it.

3.3.2. *Quantifier Scope*

As has been noted in May (1977), the relative scope of quantifiers is generally (in the unmarked case, as May has discussed in more recent work) predictable from the distribution of clause boundaries. Thus consider (61) (this and others of the following examples are from May (1977.)

(61)   **Some** politician will address **every** rally in John's district.

The case in (61) is ambiguous. In one reading the existential quantifier *some* has scope over the universal quantifier *every*, as in (62a). In the other, *every* has scope over *some*, as in (62b).

(62) a. $(\exists x, x \text{ a politician}) (\forall y, y \text{ a rally}) (x \text{ will address } y)$
There is at least one politician such that he will address each one of the rallies.

   b. $(\forall y, y \text{ a rally}) (\exists x, x \text{ a politician}) (x \text{ will address } y)$
For each one of the rallies, there is at least one politician who will address it.

But consider now (63).

(63)   **Some** politician expected [$_S$ John to address **every** rally].

Unlike (61), (63) is not ambiguous, and allows only the reading in (64a) in which *some* has scope over *every*, not the one in (64b).

(64) a. $(\exists x, x \text{ a politician}) (\forall y, y \text{ a rally}) (x \text{ expected John to address } y)$
There is at least one politician such that he expected John to address each one of the rallies.

   b. *$(\forall y, y \text{ a rally}) (\exists x, x \text{ a politician}) (x \text{ expected John to address } y)$
For each one of the rallies there is at least one politician who expected John to address it.

This correlation between clause membership and relative scope is rather systematic as May has noted, a fact that can be expressed by the generalization in (65).

(65)   Quantifier scope is clause-bounded.

We take (65) to mean that a quantifier will not have scope over material outside the minimal clause that contains it.

May (1977) provides a theoretical account of (65) by assuming that the LF representation of quantifier scope is indeed analogous to the predicate calculus notation of (62), (64), and that there is a rule of Quantifier Raising (QR) that adjoins quantifiers to their minimal Ss. This ensures that quantifiers which are separated by clause boundaries preserve their relative order, so that outer quantifiers will have scope over inner ones, while quantifiers appearing in the same minimal clause could end up in any relative order in the predicate calculus-like notation of LF, whence the ambiguity of cases like (61). For our purposes, the exact way in which (65) is implemented is not particularly relevant. It will be sufficient to assume, as the facts seem to indicate, that there is a process that assigns scope to quantifiers whose effects are captured by (65), and that this process takes place in LF.

As May notes, (65) has a class of exceptions. Consider the Raising case in (66).

(66)   [$_i$**Some** politician] is likely [$_S$t$_i$ to address **every** rally in John's district].

In spite of the fact that *some* and *every* do not appear in the same minimal clause at S-structure, (66) is ambiguous. In particular it allows the interpretation 'It is likely that for each one of the rallies, there is at least one politician who will address it', in which *every* has scope over *some*. This kind of violation of the generalization in (65) is found in all cases in which the quantifier outside the lower clause in S-structure has in fact originated in the latter clause. Note in particular that Raising cases like (66) contrast with parallel Control cases like (67).

(67) a.   [$_i$**Some** politician] is trying [$_S$PRO$_i$ to address **every** rally in John's district].

     b.   [$_i$**Every** musician] wants [$_S$PRO$_i$ to play in **an** orchestra].

Analogously to (63), (67a) does not allow reading in which a different politician is involved for each different rally in the way that (66) does. Correspondingly, (67b) will not allow the reading 'There is one particular orchestra such that all musicians want to play in it', but only a reading in which a different orchestra is intended for each musician (i.e. with *every* having scope over *a*).

Cases like (66) also contrast with cases in which the phrase moved into subject position originates outside the lower clause. Consider for example the pair in (68), in which (a) is structurally parallel to (66) while (b) is not.

(68) a. [$_i$**Two** kids] were expected [$_S$t$_i$ to read **every** book].

    b. [$_i$**Two** kids] were persuaded t$_i$ [$_S$PRO$_i$ to read **every** book].

These two examples differ with respect to quantifier scope. (68a) allows a reading in which *every* has scope over *two*: 'For each individual book there were two kids who were expected to read it' and is in this respect analogous to (66). However, (68b) does not allow the parallel reading 'For each individual book there were two kids who were persuaded to read it', and can only be interpreted as 'There were two kids such that each one of them was persuaded to read every book' with *two* having scope over *every*.[23]

We therefore have a second case of a rule of the LF component with respect to which moved NPs seem to be in their original position. The LF rules involved in these two cases, that is, the one that assigns an antecedent to *each* and the one that assigns scope to quantifiers, would not seem to be related to one another. The fact that two independent LF rules give similar results suggests that this kind of interaction with NP-movement is general and leads us to expect that we may observe it with other interpretive processes, for example the interpretation of reflexives and reciprocals. In this case judgments are less clear, but it seems to me that the facts are essentially in line with this expectation. Thus, one finds that passives like (69a) are more closely comparable to their active counterparts like (69b) than to superficially similar structures in which movement has not applied, like (69c) (although some speakers do not accept (69b), especially with the reciprocal).

(69) a. ? [$_i$Some pictures of $\begin{Bmatrix} \text{each other}_j \\ \text{themselves}_j \end{Bmatrix}$] were given   t$_i$ to $_j$the kids].

    b. ? John gave [some pictures of $\begin{Bmatrix} \text{each other}_i \\ \text{themselves}_i \end{Bmatrix}$] to [$_i$the kids].

    c. ?*[Some pictures of $\begin{Bmatrix} \text{each other}_i \\ \text{themselves}_i \end{Bmatrix}$] amused [$_i$the kids]

While the preceding cases involve NP-movement, the same effects can be observed (perhaps even more clearly) with Wh-movement, as for example in (70).[24]

(70) a. [$_i$How many books each$_j$] did John give t$_i$ to [$_j$the kids]?

    b. [$_i$How many pictures of $\begin{Bmatrix} \text{each other}_i \\ \text{ourselves}_i \end{Bmatrix}$] did he give t$_i$ to us$_j$?

We assume therefore that there is some generalization to the effect that
an element contained in a moved phrase must be present not only in its
final position, but in its original position as well, at the level which is
relevant for interpretation, namely LF.

   Regardless of how exactly we express it, we may note that such a
generalization and the facts we have reviewed provide good evidence for
the existence of the 'original position', namely for the existence of
Move α.

3.3.3. *Reconstruction and the Projection Principle*

In essence, there will be three conceivable ways in which the generalization introduced at the end of the previous section can be captured. These
are described in (71).

   (71) a. LF has access not only to S-structure representation, but to
            D-structure representation as well. This implies a general
            organization of the grammar different from that of the EST
            and more along the lines of the Standard Theory or of the
            theory in Jackendoff (1972).

        b. Traces are not empty categories, but rather full reproductions
            of their antecedents, from which they differ only in not receiv-
            ing phonological realization. Under this view, movement is
            effectively replaced by two operations: copying, and deletion
            (in the phonology) of the original.

        c. Antecedents can be reconstructed into trace position in LF.

It is easy to see how each proposal would account for the facts under
discussion, ensuring that a moved phrase is represented in its original
position at LF.

   At first sight, (71c) may appear to be the least plausible alternative. In
particular the fact that certain elements are detected by LF rules in trace
position though not, for example, in PRO position is automatic under
either (71a) or (71b), but is not under (71c). That is, if reconstruction is
possible into trace position, why is it not possible into PRO position as
well? Thus (71c) alone requires some definition of the relations that
allow reconstruction, so as to exclude for example (58b) above, or for
that matter the simpler (72) here below.

   (72)   *[$_i$One student each$_j$] promised us$_j$ [PRO$_i$ to come].

Yet there are two arguments which show that (71c) is the correct alternative. The first argument is somewhat theoretical and requires a brief
digression.

In some of the above discussion, we presented (near-)grammatical cases instantiating the configuration in (73), where X_A is an element whose antecedent is A, and where t_i is c-commanded by both A and its antecedent $[_i \ldots]$.

(73) $\ldots [_i \ldots X_A \ldots] \ldots A \ldots t_i \ldots$

One such case is the one in (74).

(74)   ?$[_i$One interpreter each$_j]$ was assigned t_i to $[_j$the visitors].

In (74), *each* is the element X_A of (73), and its antecedent *the visitors*, c-commanding the trace t_i, is A.

However, there appear to be cases in which the configuration in (73) is ungrammatical, a fact that can be expressed under (71c), but not under the alternatives, as we will see. One such ungrammatical case was encountered in chapter 1 in the course of our discussion of *ne* (cf. (17), ch. 1), and is given in (75).

(75)   *$[_i$ Molti $[_j$e]] ne$_j$ saranno invitati t_i
         many   *of-them will be   invited*

As we saw in chapter 1, the relation between *ne* and its *ec* is well-formed when *ne* c-commands the latter, as in (76a, b).

(76) a. [e] ne$_i$ saranno invitati molti $[_i$e]]
         of-them will be   invited many

     Many of them will be invited.

     b. Giovanni ne$_i$ inviterà   [molti $[_i$e]]
         Giovanni of-them will invite   many

     Giovanni will invite many of them.

Thus, (75) is indeed relevantly analogous to (74), *ne* being A in (73), and the *ec* being X_A. Let us now see how the difference between (74) and (75), and the fact that (73) is thus only sometimes grammatical, provides an argument for (71c).

In our discussion in 1.4 we regarded clitics as arguments. As such, they must receive a θ-role at all levels, given the projection principle. Under the reconstruction hypothesis, (75) above would be correctly ruled out, since the proper relation between *ne* and its *ec*, allowing θ-role transmission, would obtain at D-structure, as well as at LF after reconstruction, but would fail to obtain at S-structure, in violation of the projection principle.[25] At the same time, cases like (74) will be correctly allowed, since the relation between *each* and its antecedent does not involve θ-role transmission, so that the projection principle will be irrelevant, and the latter relation will not be required to be well-formed (with the antecedent c-commanding *each*) at all levels. It is natural to assume that an antecedent-*each* relation is only required to be well-formed at LF, so that well-formedness can in fact be achieved through reconstruction. Note that our assumption that reconstruction applies in LF (and not in S-structure) is required not just to distinguish (74) from (75), but also, independently, by the fact that it has no 'phonological' effects.

Unlike reconstruction, the alternatives in (71ab) do not account for the difference between (74) and (75). Consider (71b). If the trace t_i in (75) was a full reproduction of its antecedent, i.e. if it was spelled out as [molti [$_i$e]], there would be little reason to assume that a well-formed relation could not be established between *ne* and the *ec*, just as in (76). Consider now (71a). If not only S-structure, but also D-structure entered into LF, then the relation between *ne* and its *ec* in (75) would be well-formed at LF since it is well-formed at D-structure. It would still not be well-formed at S-structure however, so that one might claim that (75) violates the projection principle under (71a) just as it does under the reconstruction hypothesis of (71c). But notice that the assumption that D-structure feeds into LF is massively redundant with trace theory in so far as trace theory aims exactly to carry into LF the aspects of D-structure that are relevant. For example, unlike hypotheses (71b,c), (71a) does not require the trace t_i, to account for the grammaticality of (74). It is therefore reasonable to assume that, under (71a), trace theory would be dispensed with, since motivation for it would be generally lacking. However, without trace theory, there seems to be no form of the θ-criterion that would hold in S-structure (no way for example to assign object θ-role to the phrase *One interpreter each* in (74)). And, without the θ-criterion in S-structure, the difference between (74) and (75) would fail to be captured.

Our view that the configuration in (73) is thus illicit whenever A receives θ-role from X_A as *ne* does from its *ec* in (75), predicts other cases of ungrammaticality. In particular it predicts ungrammaticality for the case in which X_A is an NP-trace (the trace of A) since we assume that NP-traces transmit θ-roles to their antecedents, just like *ec*'s do to clitics. The latter prediction appears to me fulfilled by contrasts like (77), from Rizzi (1982a).

(77) a. È [$_i$PRO$_j$ tornare a casa] che Giovanni$_j$ vuole t$_i$.
         It is to go back home that Giovanni wants.

    b. *È [$_i$ t$_j$ tornare a casa] che Giovanni$_j$ sembra t$_i$.
         '*it is to go back home that Giovanni seems*'.

Although Rizzi gives a different (and not implausible) explanation for the contrast in (77), it seems to me reasonable to regard the latter as in fact instantiating the generalization relative to (73).[26] Thus, while the clefted phrases in (77) can presumably be reconstructed in the position t_i in LF

given the grammaticality of (77a), (77b) will be ungrammatical because
θ-role transmission between t_j and *Giovanni$_j$* fails at S-structure. No
analogous θ-role transmission is required in (77a), since *PRO$_j$* has an
independent θ-role.

Our first argument for (71c) is therefore provided by the fact that,
under the latter, an adequate account for the bifurcation among cases
characterized by (73) is provided by independent principles, the θ-
criterion and the projection principle, while no account is available under
either (71a) or (71b). Our second argument is provided by cases noted in
LGB, which appear to falsify both (71a, b).

As Chomsky notes, there are cases like (78), in which a phrase
appears to be 'reconstructed' into the position of a trace which, derivationally, is not its own trace (LGB, p. 145 n. 79, p. 346 n. 10).

(78) a. [Pictures of each other$_i$] are what$_j$ they like to see t_j.

    b. [PRO$_i$ to be eighteen years old] is what$_j$ everyone$_i$ wants most
t_j.

The phenomenon illustrated by (78) is quite general with 'be' and seems
to extend to the other cases we discussed above, such as *One interpreter
each is what they would like to have*, and *A good orchestra is what every
musician would like to play in* interpretable with *every* having scope over
a. It thus appears that the generalization governing the distribution of
'reconstruction' phenomena is somewhat broader than we have assumed
so far. A broader generalization is compatible in principle with the
reconstruction hypothesis since under that hypothesis, the set of relations
that allow reconstruction must be defined, so that the conclusion that a
phrase can only be reconstructed into its own trace is not a-priori necessary. In contrast, each of (71a,b) must be abandoned in the light of (78)
since it is neither the case that the phrase within brackets is the D-structure object of *see/wants* as (71a) would imply, nor that t_j is its trace
as (71b) would. Each of (71a,b) is thus empirically inadequate in two
respects: in failing to exclude ungrammatical cases like (75), and in
incorrectly excluding grammatical ones like (78).

Given such clear reasons to reject (71a,b), an exact account of (78)
under reconstruction will be less than crucial for selecting among the
three alternatives. Here we will only point to what seem to be the relevant considerations. First, reconstruction in (78) will suggest that there is
coindexation between the reconstructed phrase, the one within brackets,
and the position in which it is reconstructed, namely t_j, and therefore also
with the relative pronoun *what*. The question is then whether there is any
independent reason for assuming such coindexation, and indeed there is.
The gender and number agreement that one finds in cases like *They are
the winners*, **Maria è la vincitrice** 'Maria is the winner (fem.)' makes it

plausible to assume that the two NPs involved are coindexed, which in turn makes it plausible to assume coindexing between the subject phrase and *what* in (78). Furthermore, note that in cases like (78a) in which the subject is plural, singular verb agreement, i.e. 'is' is also possible (though perhaps marginally). This suggests that the singular agreement features of *what* are transmitted to the subject position, through coindexing between the two.[27] That *what* has singular features is independently clear from, for example *Pictures of John ?is/are what pleases/*please me.*

As it is thus reasonably clear that there is coindexing, the remaining problem would be how to allow reconstruction in cases like (78), of the type 'NP$_i$ be what$_i$ ... t$_i$', just as in cases of the type 'NP$_i$ ... t$_i$' (where t$_i$ is the trace of NP$_i$), while excluding it in the type 'NP$_i$ ... PRO$_i$'. The solution seems to me to lie in the fact that, in general, the two NPs in a structure 'NP be NP' do not have independent θ-roles, as for example in *John is the winner: John* and the *winner* do not have independent reference. In this respect, the two NPs in 'NP be NP' in general, and we may presume the subject phrase and *what* of (78) in particular, hold a relation analogous to the one between a NP and its trace, and unlike the one between a NP and a coindexed PRO. Quite plausibly, it is precisely this identity of θ-role that accounts for the coindexation we argued for. Notice that, predictably, where there is no analogous reason to assume identity of θ-role between a NP and *what*, we find neither the verb agreement phenomenon of (78a), as (79a) shows, nor reconstruction, as (79b) shows.

(79) a. [These pictures] $\left\{ \begin{array}{l} \text{get} \\ \text{*gets} \end{array} \right\}$ what$_i$ they deserve t$_i$.

   b. *[Pictures of **each other**$_i$] will show what$_j$ they$_i$ wanted t$_j$.

We may therefore assume that reconstruction is only possible across positions that do not have independent θ-roles, but we will not try to be more precise on this matter.

We thus conclude that the correct way to account for the facts noted in 3.3.1, 3.3.2, is to assume a reconstruction process operating in LF. Our conclusion is based on two arguments. (i) That only reconstruction provides an explanation for the fact that certain elements but not others can fail to be c-commanded by their antecedents in S-structure ((74) versus (75)). (ii) That only reconstruction can account for cases like (78).

NOTES

[1] These cases happen to provide further evidence for the Raising analysis of 'be' of 2.7.1. In so far as they are possible, these passives take auxiliary *essere* (E), like other passives. But since we presume that the complement structure of the past participle contains no

argument with which a non-argument subject could be linked, a relation triggering assignment of E by the system of 1.7 (/2.6.2) exists only under the Raising analysis, as in (i), not under the traditional analysis.

(i)   [e] gli   era   stato [t detto ....]

       (it) to-him was ('had') been   told ...   (E)

[2] None of the verbs in (12) allow accusative pronominalization of the sentential complement. This is also expected from (1). However, in some cases S-pronominalization is impossible altogether, not only in the accusative, as in (i).

(i) a.   ?*Mi sembra questo: che tu debba rimanere.
          It seems to me this: that you should stay.

   b.   *Me lo sembra.
          It seems to me it.

The ungrammaticality of cases like (ib) will thus be irrelevant to our claim, given the comparable ungrammaticality of (ia). In other cases S-pronominalization is possible, though not in the accusative, as in (ii).

(ii) a.   Gli è capitato questo: di vedere Giovanni.
          It happened to him this: to see Giovanni.

   b.   *Glielo è capitato.
          It happened to him it.

These other cases *will* be relevant to our claim that (1) is true, but will simply reduce to the type of case in (6), that is the case of ergative verbs. With the S-complements pronominalized, i.e. replaced by NPs, the verbs in (12) become ergative verbs.

[3] While non-argument subjects are thus found related to both tensed and infinitival clauses, they are never found related to small clauses. We thus have the generalization in (i).

(i) a. $NP_{-\theta}$ V S

   b.   *$NP_{-\theta}$ V sc

This also follows from our claim: Given the truth of (1), sentential complements will be allowed to appear as in (ia) only in two cases. (1) When they are tensed (e.g. *It seems that* ...). In this case the embedded subject is assigned Case internal to the clause. (2) When the embedded subject is PRO (as in (12b,c)). In this case the embedded subject does not require Case. But neither possibility exists with sc's. The first because sc's are never tensed (essentially be definition). The second because sc's never allow PRO subjects when they are complements of verbs (though they do as sc relatives). That sc complements do not allow PRO subjects is clear from the fact that, while there are S/sc alternations generally, there are no such alternations in Control contexts. Compare *I believe [him (to be) sick], John_i seemed [t_i (to be) sick]* with *I_i hope [PRO_i *(to be) well]*. On this we may assume with LGB that sc's are not maximal projections, so that the subject of a sc complement will always be governed, ruling out PRO. (1) above will then account for (ib) by excluding the only remaining alternative, namely that the subject of the sc be lexical, receiving Case from V in (ib) (E.g. *It_i seems [_i John sick]).

[4] $-\theta_s$ verbs with the subcategorization '__PP' do not seem to exist (apart from the one case of Note 10, ch. 1). Consider the D-structure which would correspond to such verbs:

(i)   [e] V [_{PP} P NP]

D-structures of this kind could only surface in two, rather marked, cases: (i) By insertion of a pleonastic element where pleonastics are not required to be linked with NP or S, as in the languages that allow impersonal passives (see 3.2.2 below); (ii) By movement of the NP into subject position where preposition stranding is possible, as for example in English. Yet in English we do not find any cases like *The locks tampered with, contrasting with the corresponding passive cases, like These locks were tampered with. Regarding this apparent gap we may reasonably assume that the lexicon in general rules out items which could only appear if some marked syntactic option was taken.

[5] While we will only consider here passive participles occurring with 'be' as in passive sentences, our conclusions appear to hold for other occurrences of passive participles as well, that is, for passive participles in sc relatives and in sc complements of verbs like believe, consider.

[6] Since there is never a $NP_{+\theta}$ subject with passives, there will be no counterparts to the configurations in (13) and (15a).

[7] Notice that while (23) essentially subsumes the generalization that NP-traces are in Case-less positions, the inverse is not true. In fact the non-existence of the configurations (9), (15b), (18a), (19b) follows from (23) but not from any condition on traces.

[8] Again, this conclusion does not follow for the SI-construction. With that construction, there could in principle be two direct objects: one which would receive Case by moving into subject position, while the other was assigned accusative by the verb. (The verb would assign accusative since it would assign subject θ-role − to SI.) Verbs taking two direct objects could thus exist, but they would only appear in the SI-construction. As before, in the text, we assume the lexicon disallows such verbs.

[9] Notice in fact that if the semantic role of NP_2 changes, as it would if the latter was the subject of a complement, double accusative marking appears impossible, witness the non-existence of the type in (i), where the phrase within brackets is either an infinitival S or a sc.

(i) $\ldots V NP_1 [NP_2 \ldots]$

[10] It is legitimate to ask at this point whether there are double object ergative verbs analogous to the passive in (25). The answer is no, as we will see in the course of 5.3 below, although the reasons for this are not too clear.

[11] An apparent exception to (23) is represented by cases like (ib) in which clitic lo alternates with the predicates of (ia).

(i) a.   Giovanni è $\left\{ \begin{array}{l} \text{felice} \\ \text{il vincitore} \end{array} \right\}$.

           Giovanni is $\left\{ \begin{array}{l} happy \\ the\ winner \end{array} \right\}$.

    b.   Giovanni lo è.
           Giovanni it is

Since we are claiming that 'be' is a $-\theta_s$ verb (cf. 2.7.1), lo of (ib) may seem surprising. However, there is good reason to believe that lo here is not an accusative clitic, but rather a predicate form homophonous with accusative lo. First, lo of (ib) need not be pro-'nominal' since it stands for predicates which are not nominal, like felice 'happy', so that there is no reason to assume Case-marking in those cases. In the cases in which lo stands for a predicate nominal such as il vincitore, there is still no reason to assume Case marking since predicate nominals do not appear to have a θ-role independent of their subject (assuming that Case and θ-roles are associated along the lines of LGB, 6). The special character of lo in (ib) is confirmed by the fact that (ib) lacks the English counterpart *John is it with the meaning of (ia). Lo of (ib) also differs from third person singular accusative lo in that it has no effect on past participle agreement, as (ii) shows.

(ii) a.   Siamo   stati   **giovani** tutti.
           (*we*) *are* *been* (*pl.*) *young*   *all*

           We have all been young.

   b.   **Lo** siamo stati   tutti.
           (*we*) *it*   *are*   *been* (*pl.*) *all*

In (iia), past participle agreement is with the subject. This is predicted by our analysis of 'be' in 2.7.1. The same agreement is present in (iib). If *lo* was a third person accusative clitic we would expect agreement conflict in the manner of (101), chapter 1.

There are other apparent exceptions to (23). One is represented by French cases like **Il me les faut** 'It necessitates them to me' (pointed out to me by R. Kayne) where *les* suggests accusative Case. Some others, from various languages, are noted in Marantz (1981). On these I will have nothing to say beyond remarking that they seem to be rather rare.

The case of English *impress*, as in *John impresses me as intelligent* would constitute an exception to (23) if analyzed as a Raising verb, as proposed in LGB. However, we suspect that the Raising analysis of *impress* can be successfully challenged.

[12] The identity of selectional restrictions and of 'semantic' role between the subject of an active verb and the object of the *by*-phrase, which was captured in the Standard Theory by assuming a movement derivation of the latter from the former (Agent postposing) is thus captured here by an equivalent lexical principle.

[13] According to Marantz (1981), lying behind the fact that passives do not differ from their active counterparts with respect to assignment of thematic-subject role (our terminology) is a generalization to the effect that affixation never alters θ-structure (or 'Predicate Argument structure'), passives being derived from actives via affixation of the abstract morpheme *-en*. This view correctly predicts that no affixation will mediate the relation between transitive *sink* and ergative *sink*, since they differ with respect to θ-structure. As Marantz notes, the claim must be somewhat qualified given for example ergative verbs which appear with a reflexive morpheme in Romance, like *rompersi* etc., discussed in 1.5. The qualified version of the claim is that relating items whose θ-structures differ involves at most the use of an affix which exists independently in the language (as in the case with reflexive morphemes in Romance), never the use of an affix whose use is specific to such relations.

[14] In so far as it is obligatory if there is a subject, assignment of subject θ-role will thus work slightly differently from assignment of accusative Case, which we have been assuming is not intrinsically obligatory if there is an object (cf. 2.2 and discussion of (66), ch. 2).

[15] The account given by Relational Grammarians is rather different. In particular Perlmutter (1978) argues that cases like (38b) are ruled out by the 1 Advancement Exclusiveness Law, a requirement that advancement to 1 (i.e. to subject) can occur at most once, under the assumption that both unaccusative verbs and passivization systematically require advancement to 1. A brief comparison between the *non-vacuous* loss of subject θ-role and the 1 Advancement Exclusiveness Law of Relational Grammar is presented in Marantz (1981) who independently argues for the former.

[16] Actually, for the impersonal passives that one seems to find in French (and Italian), one might hold that the relaxation does not really consist of dropping the requirement that the non-argument subject be related to an argument, but rather of extending to PP the class of arguments to which it can be related. The same view does not seem possible for the impersonal passives of German and Dutch however.

The existence of impersonal passives in which there is no argument that the subject could be related to, is problematic for the attempt in LGB, 6 to find a one-to-one correspondence between Case and θ-roles: the non-argument subject of such impersonal passives still seems to fall under Case requirements (being impossible in infinitivals), absence of a θ-role notwithstanding. To overcome this problem, one might attempt a slightly different approach, along the following lines.

Descriptively, there seem to be three types of elements, as far as Case and θ-roles go, as in (i).

(i) a.   Arguments other than PRO: bear θ-role; have Case.

b.   Non arguments: do not bear θ-role; have Case.

c.   PRO: bears θ-role; does not have Case.

As in LGB, 6, we may supppose that there is a general principle requiring association of Case and θ-roles, call it P. However, still as in LGB, 6, we must assume that (somehow) P does not apply to PRO of (ic), while it must apply to (ia). Since the non-arguments of (ib) are unlike PRO, but like the arguments of (ia) with respect to phonological realization, we may presume that the operative principle, universally, is not P, but rather a principle P' that pays attention to phonological content, thus requiring Case for both (ia) and (ib), to the exclusion of (ic). P' is the old Case Filter, except that now we are relating it to P. P' $-$ unlike P $-$ does not run into problems with respect to impersonal passives. We can now further assume that in languages that do *not* have impersonal passives, in addition to P', P also holds. In these languages, since non-arguments must be Case marked (because of P'), they will also have to be associated with a θ-role, i.e. linked with an argument (because of P): a fact for which LGB did not provide any reason, as far as we can see. The 'impersonal passive' parameter would now be P' versus P' and·P, or more simply *plus or minus* P.

[17] While there is evidence for 'reanalysis' of verb and preposition in cases of preposition stranding, so that it would be appropriate to regard the two as being one constituent at S-structure, it seems to me that it would be incorrect to assume that they could be one even at lexical levels, forming one lexical item. Arguing against such a view is the fact that we never find corresponding nominalizations, e.g. *The talk to* (*of John*), versus *The arrest* (*of John*). Also, while NPs alternate rather generally with Ss when they occur after V, e.g. *He said NP/He said that S*, they never do when they occur after V-P, as far as I can see, e.g. *He talked about NP/*He talked about that S*.

[18] However, there is actually one difference between SE-constructions and passives. Verbs taking sentential complements can be passivized in French, just as in English, but they cannot appear with SE, as shown by (i).

(i)   *Il$_i$ se décida [$_i$d'attendre sa réponse]
          it SE decided to await   his answer

         It was decided . . .

We may account for this fact by assuming that the two intersecting chains that we claimed exist in these cases, (i) subject-SI/SE, and (ii) subject-some post verbal position) must be of the same type, i.e. both involving NP arguments. While we know no precise reason why this should be the case, we note that this in fact provides further support for our claim that there are intersecting chains here.

[19] Small clause complements of *believe*-type verbs behave like sc relatives and unlike passives in this respect, as in **Ritengo Giovanni già partito** 'I believe Giovanni already departed', where *partire* is an ergative verb.

[20] Note however that there are some difficulties in taking principle A of the binding theory as the relevant locality condition. If we take the simpler version of the binding theory, the one in which governing categories are stipulated to be NP and S (as in I.0.3 and LGB, pp. 188 ff.), *each* will be required to be bound within the NP [Q N̄ each], which is obviously incorrect. If we take the more complex version of the theory, the one in which a binding category is a category containing an accessible SUBJECT (as in LGB, pp.

211 ff.), then for example (51b, d) are correctly allowed since [Q $\overline{\text{N}}$ each] does not have a subject, but (53b) would also be allowed incorrectly, as it is parallel to (17a) of chapter 2, repeated in (i), which is well formed for the reasons discussed in 2.2 above.

(i)   They$_i$ expected [$_S$that [pictures of **each other**$_i$] would be on sale].

Assuming that these difficulties could be overcome, perhaps by saying that the anaphor is not *each*, but rather [Q $\overline{\text{N}}$ each], we would then expect non tensed counterparts to (53b), like (ii), to be grammatical, which is not really the case, although there is some contrast between (ii) and (53b).

(ii) a.   ??We$_i$ expected [one student each$_i$ to call].

b.   ??We$_i$ considered [one student each$_i$ guilty].

The exact nature of the locality conditions involved is not crucial to our discussion however. The only crucial consideration is that some form of c-command seems to be required. As an alternative to the text discussion, one may assume that relations NP$_i$-each$_i$ are clause bounded.

[21] The issue actually appears more complex. In particular, the following seem to require a non-relaxed version of c-command.

(i)   *John introduced each other to the kids.

(ii)   ?Bill introduced the girl that John$_i$ liked to him$_i$.

By the relaxed version, (i) should be grammatical while (ii) should be as bad as *Bill introduced him$_i$ to the girl that John$_i$ liked*. We must therefore assume that in some cases the strict version of c-command is at work. It remains unclear how to define the respective domains of the two version, but we note that at least in some cases the degree of embeddedness of the anaphoric element seems to play a role, as (iii) (which will appear in (69b) below) is better than (i).

(iii)   ?John gave some pictures of each other to the kids.

[22] We would expect that ergative verbs should behave like passives with respect to interpretation of *each*. In Italian we do in fact find some contrast, for example, between (ia) and (ib), but parallel English cases are even less clear.

(i) a.   (?)?[$_i$Una lettera ciascuno] arrivava t$_i$ ogni giorno ai prigionieri.
         One letter each arrived every day to the prisoners.

b.   *[Un avvocato ciascuno] telefonava ogni giorno ai prigionieri.
         One lawyer each telephoned every day (to) the prisoners.

[23] May (1977) proposes to account for the exceptionality of Raising contexts (e.g. (66)) with respect to quantifier scope, by allowing quantifier lowering from non-argument positions — in our terms 'non-θ' positions. Beside being rather ad-hoc, this account is falsified by cases like (68b) since, although in the latter the NP *Two kids* is in a non-θ position, it appears that the quantifier *two* cannot be 'lowered' into the lower clause.

[24] As Chomsky (1977), (LGB, 2.4.6) notes, with Wh-movement there is another kind of consideration that suggests some form of reconstruction in LF, namely the fact that for cases like (ia), the interpretation is of the type in (ib).

(i) a.   [$_i$Whose brother] did he see t$_i$?

b.   for which *x*, he saw [*x*'s brother].

[25] French cases of *En-avant* like (i) from Couquaux (1981) may seem to pose a problem for the text discussion (under a Raising analysis of be, (i) may seem relevantly analogous to (75)).

(i)   La préface en   est trop flatteuse
           the preface of-it is too flattering

However, as Couquaux notes, cases involving a quantifier element (in this respect just like (75)) are ungrammatical, even in French *En-avant* contexts, as in (ii) contrasting with (i).

(ii)   *Beaucoup en   sont laides
           many   of-them are   ugly

Couquaux accounts for the ungrammaticality of (ii) somewhat along the lines of our text discussion, and attributes (i) to the possibility of moving only the head noun (*la préface*), rather than the whole NP to the left. It is clear that the correct generalization is that *ne-/en*-cliticization is impossible with respect to the subject, including derived subjects as claimed in the text, and that something special has to be said for (i). We may assume that Couquaux' solution is correct.

There is another apparent problem associated with our discussion in the text, represented by the difference between (75), repeated in (iiia), and cases in which Wh-movement rather than NP-movement is involved as in (iiib).

(iii) a.   *$[_i$ Molti $[_j$e]] ne$_j$ saranno invitati t$_i$
           many   of-them will be invited

   b. $[_i$ Quanti $[_j$e]] [e] ne$_j$ saranno invitati t$_i$?
           how many   of-them will be invited

It seems to me that a solution to this problem ought to take account of the difference which we are independently assuming between t$_i$ of (iiia), and t$_i$ of (iiib). As a NP-trace, the former must transmit θ-role to its antecedent, whereas the latter, as a variable, does not transmit θ-role, but rather fulfils it. In this respect a variable is just like a lexical NP, and indeed the grammaticality of (iiib) would follow if we assumed that t$_i$ is here just like its lexical counterpart *molti* [e] (cf. (76)). However, the execution of this idea still remains difficult. (The issue raised by (iii) is also discussed by Couquaux, who proposes a different account).

[26] Rizzi's account consists of assuming that the trace in (77b) is ungoverned, in violation of the ECP. This view would require some specific assumptions to prevent government from 'be'.

[27] We find it plausible to presume that the same kind of transmission of agreement features to the left is involved in Italian cases like (i) (discussed in Longobardi (1980b)), although we have no proposal on how to exclude their English counterparts.

(i)   Il vincitore sono io.
           the winner am   I

           'The winner is I.'

PART II

COMPLEX PREDICATES

COMPLEX PREDICATES

II.0. INTRODUCTION TO PART II

II.0.1. *Types of Complex Predicates*

In this second part, we examine what we will call COMPLEX PREDICATES, that is structures in which a verb and its infinitival complement appear to form a single unit. There are two major cases of complex predicates discussed in the literature: the 'causative' constructions of Kayne (1975), Rouveret and Vergnaud (1980), and the 'restructuring' constructions of Rizzi (1976a), (1978a). The first are associated with causative and perception verbs like *make, let, see, hear,* the second with various verbs, some of which are semantically 'modals' (like English *want/will, must, can*), some others 'aspectuals' (like *begin, continue*), and some verbs of motion. Perhaps the best known characteristic of these constructions is that objects of the complement verb cliticize to the main verb, as in the causative case in (1a), and the restructuring case in (1b).

(1) a. Giovanni **lo** fa   leggere a Piero.
        Giovanni it makes read   to Piero

    Giovanni makes Piero read it.

     b. Giovanni **lo** vuole leggere.
        Giovanni it wants to read

    Giovanni wants to read it.

Much of the framework of assumptions we developed in Part I will aid us in our investigation here: the hypothesis that there are ergative verbs, the theories of inversion, of auxiliary assignment and past participle agreement, of small clause relatives, the hypothesis that there is reconstruction in LF, will all play crucial roles. In most cases, the interaction between earlier parts and the discussion of complex predicates will be mutual in that, not only will the earlier results enable us to probe more effectively into the syntax of complex predicates, but also the behavior of complex predicates will appear to confirm those results.

While the various analyses of Part I may thus be confirmed by complex predicates, but could nevertheless be put forth independently, our analysis of cliticization relies rather heavily on the analysis of complex predicates, and was not given in full in Part I for this reason. Yet a full discussion of complex predicates cannot be postponed since some

217

assumptions regarding the nature of cliticization are needed to even begin such a discussion. For example, what identifies the structures in (1) as complex predicates is the assumption that cliticization is always in some sense local, so that there must be a closer than usual relation between the two verbs in these cases. Therefore, in the third subsection of this introduction we outline our theory of cliticization in full, giving some arguments, and referring forward to others that will come later.

One of the central claims of this part is that the various types of complex predicates result from a single syntactic process affecting different types of infinitival complements. To prepare the ground for this, in the next subsection we review the typology of infinitival complements and see how this is characterized in GB-theoretical terms.

The overall organization of this part is rather straightforward. In chapter 4 we examine causative constructions and in chapter 5 restructuring constructions. In chapter 6 we examine reflexive clitics, in part considering their interaction with complex predicates, which we claim has consequences for the theory of clitics at large, and in part elaborating on the results of 1.5.

II.0.2. *Verbs with Sentential Complements*

Within the LGB framework, the class of verbs which are subcategorized for a sentential complement breaks down into four subclasses, as determined by two lexical parameters: the ability to trigger $\bar{S}$-deletion, and the ability to assign a θ-role to the subject position (θ_s), as in (2).

(2)

Class	$\bar{S}$-del.	θ_s	
I	+	+	(ECM)
II	+	−	(Raising)
III	−	+	('Equi')
IV	−	−	

All four subclasses are attested empirically. Thus class I is the class of Exceptional Case Marking (ECM) verbs, like English *believe* in (3).

(3)   John believed [$_S$Bill to have left].

If *believe* deletes the $\bar{S}$ (maximal projection) of its complement, it will govern the embedded subject. Since it assigns subject θ-role, we expect, following the discussion in 3.1 relating θ_s to Case assignment (i.e. $\theta_s \leftrightarrow$ A), that it will assign Case to the latter embedded subject. (3) will thus be well-formed.

Class II is the class of Raising verbs, like *seem* in (4).

(4)   John$_i$ seems [$_S$ t$_i$ to have left]

If *seem* triggers $\bar{S}$-deletion, (4) will be well-formed since the trace will be governed, as prescribed by the ECP. On the other hand, cases like **It seems [PRO to talk about ourselves]* will be ungrammatical since PRO is governed, while it must not be (cf. I.0.3). Since *seem* does not assign subject θ-role, we also predict the ungrammaticality of **It seems [John to have left]* (for lack of Case on *John*) as we discussed in 3.1.

Class III is the traditional class of 'Equi' verbs, i.e. of Control verbs like *hope* in (5). (As in Part I, we ignore the distinction between S and $\bar{S}$ in the diagrams. Thus, there is an $\bar{S}$ in (5) since this is an instance of class III).

(5)   John hoped [$_S$ PRO to leave].

Since government of the embedded subject by the main verb does not obtain here, PRO is allowed, while lexical subjects are not, as illustrated by **John hoped [Bill to leave]*, where lack of government prevents Case assignment. (Since *hope* assigns θ_s we assume that it would otherwise assign Case.)

In English, members of Class IV are not very numerous. We find *remain*, as in *It remains [PRO to talk about ourselves]*, although this verb is presumably also in class II, given *This remains to be seen*, which must involve Raising. Another case is *suffice*, as in *It suffices [PRO to meet the requirements]*.[1] But in Italian there are several such verbs. One is *bisognare* of (6a). Others are listed in (6b). (Some of these verbs take indirect objects controlling the embedded subject PRO).

(6) a. [e] bisogna   [$_S$ PRO parlargli]
         (*it*) *is necessary*   *to talk-to-him*

     b. merita,   conviene,   basta,
         (*it*) *is worthwhile* (*it*) *is advantageous* (*it*) *suffices*

         capita,   piace,   sembra,   giova.
         (*it*) *happens* (*it*) *pleases* (*it*) *seems* (*it*) *is helpful*

This characterization of infinitival complements accounts for important similarities in the distribution of Raising and ECM phenomena and for the essentially complementary distribution of Raising-ECM and Control. In particular it accounts for the fact that the verbs that allow ECM as in (3) are (to a large degree) the same that allow passivization with subject-to-subject raising as in (7).[2]

(7)   Bill$_i$ was believed [$_S$ t$_i$ to have left].

The correspondence follows from our assumption that that $\bar{S}$-deletion is involved, since only if a verb triggers $\bar{S}$ deletion will it govern the embedded subject so as to either assign Case as in (3), or satisfy the ECP as in (7). Thus, verbs which do not trigger $\bar{S}$-deletion, like *hope* in (5) will not allow the type of passivization in (7), as shown in (8).

(8)　　*Bill$_i$ was hoped [$_S$ t$_i$ to leave].

The correspondence between ECM and the type of passive in (7) is further confirmed by the fact that in Romance, where, as we will show, ECM cases like (3) are lacking, cases like (7) are also rather generally lacking. Another similarity in the distribution of ECM and subject-to-subject raising is the lack of both in the presence of a filled complementizer, as illustrated by (9).

(9)　a. *John knows [[what] Bill to do].

　　　b. *Bill$_i$ was known [[what] t$_i$ to do].

This can also be naturally captured by our system, provided that we assume that the intervening complementizer prevents government of the embedded subject by the main verb. We may simply say that $\bar{S}$-delelltion is possible only if no lexical material separates the $\bar{S}$ from the S boundary. Then Case assignment will fail in (9a), and the ECP will be violated in (9b), whence the parallel ungrammaticality. The same considerations that rule out (9b) will then account for the fact that we find no Raising verbs that take indirect questions (Cf. *John seems what to read).

While the system thus described, with the two parameters plus-or-minus $\bar{S}$-deletion and plus-or-minus θ_s will account for the relative distribution of the various types of infinitival complements, we assume that in the unmarked case subcategorization for a sentential complement is neutral between the tensed and the infinitival options. Thus, alongside of (3) (ECM) we find John believed [that Bill had left], with (4) (Raising) we find It seems [that John has left], with (5) (Equi) we find John hoped [that he could leave], and with (6a) (of the fourth class) we find **Bisogna [che tu gli parli]** '(It) is necessary that you talk to him'.

Our claim in the chapters that follow will be that the process which forms complex predicates is intrinsically neutral, not formulated to apply to one or the other class in (2).[3] In particular, we will take causative constructions to arise from application of that process to verbs of class I and their infinitival complements, and restructuring constructions to result from its application to verbs of classes II and III and their complements. No complex predicate seems to arise from structures of class IV: a fact which will call for an explanation.

It is obvious, at least for classes II and III (restructuring), that only some members of those classes give rise to complex predicates, so that some sort of constraint must be assumed to govern the process in question. Rizzi (1976a), (1978a), observes that the distinction between restructuring and non-restructuring verbs seems to run along semantic lines, with semantically more impoverished verbs allowing restructuring more readily. A typical minimal pair is the one in (10), where 'want' allows restructuring, while 'wish' does not.

(10) a.   Lo   voglio leggere.
    (*I*) *it* *want* *to read*

  I want to read it.

 b. *   Lo   desidero leggere.
    (*I*) *it* *wish* *to read*

With Rizzi, we will assume that only semantically weak verbs can combine with others to form complex predicates, although we will not attempt to express this idea formallly. (For a discussion of this issue, see Napoli (1981).) As we expect on the basis of our claim that the same process is involved, we find that an analogous constraint, based on the semantics of the verb, is operative within the class of causative-perception verbs, as shown in (11).

(11) a.   Gliel'ho   visto prendere.
    (*I*) *to-him-it have seen take*

  I saw him take it.

 b. ?*   Gliel'ho   osservato prendere.
    (*I*) *to-him-it have observed take*

II.0.3. *The Syntax of Clitics*

There are two major questions that arise in any attempt to characterize the syntax of clitics. One concerns the nature of the locality conditions holding between the clitic and the position which receives the θ-role. The other question is whether clitics are moved or base-generated. Since the two can be regarded as independent, we will consider them separately, in that order.[4]

In the literature, we find two important pieces of evidence that relations between a clitic and the position to which the relevant θ-role is assigned (the relevant θ-position) fall under the binding conditions, specifically the Specified Subject Condition (SSC), which we may use as a descriptive category here. The first piece of evidence has to do specifically with complex predicates. Thus, the literature on causative constructions, in particular Kayne (1975), and analogously the literature on restructuring constructions, in particular Rizzi (1976a), (1978a) shows us that the cases in which an object clitic can appear on a verb higher than the one with which it would normally be associated, are just the cases for which one has independent evidence that no subject is present between the higher and the lower verb. We will see this in detail below.

The second piece of evidence is provided by the discussion of extraction from NP in Italian in Cinque (1980). Cinque observes first that the only constituents that can be 'extracted' from NPs by cliticization are phrases of the form *di NP* 'of NP' which cliticize as *ne*, while cliticization of other phrases, for example of *a NP* 'to NP', is always impossible.[5] He then notes that not all *di NP* phrases can be extracted, and argues that it is only those that represent the subject of the head noun that can, which explains why *a NP* phrases, always being objects, are excluded. We thus have a perfect SSC effect.

If Cinque is correct, the facts he discusses provide a stronger argument for the view that cliticization obeys the SSC than complex predicates do. For, although both Kayne and Rizzi assume the SSC, their discussion does not rule out certain alternatives. One of these consists of regarding cliticization as sensitive to clause boundaries. Another, adopted in fact in the context of a discussion of complex predicates in Radford (1977), has cliticization sensitive to VP boundaries. A third, elaborated in Borer (1981), and essentially also compatible with an analysis of complex pred- icates, consists of assuming that a clitic must govern the θ-position. How- ever, neither S boundaries nor VP boundaries can be invoked to account for the facts Cinque discusses (nor do NP boundaries seem to play any role), so that the first two alternatives are discounted. As for the third, it also fails to extend to Cinque's facts. Consider (12).

(12) a.   Apprezziamo [la generosità [di Giovanni]]
        (*we*) *appreciate*   *the generosity of Giovanni*

     b.   Ne$_i$ apprezziamo [la generosità [$_i$e]]
        (*we*) *of-him appreciate*   *the generosity*

While it is entirely plausible to assume that [e] in (12b) is governed by the head noun *la generosità*, thus satisfying the ECP, it is less plausible to assume that it is governed (across the head noun) by the clitic.[6] Besides, the government alternative would shed little light on the fact that some *di NP* phrases can be cliticized, while others, and other PPs cannot.

Although various questions still arise, as I will briefly discuss below, it seems to me that at the present stage the binding theory remains the best candidate to account for the distribution of cliticization. I will therefore assume that the latter is indeed what is relevant, and that *ec*'s related to clitics are anaphors, like NP-traces.[7]

We now consider the question of movement versus base-generation. Kayne (1975) assumes that clitics are moved. In the context of his discussion and given his theoretical framework, there are strong reasons to assume a movement analysis. For example, the effects of his assump- tion that reflexive cliticization is cyclic while non-reflexive cliticization is post-cyclic, cannot be readily duplicated within a base-generated system (as we will see in the course of the following chapters). While Kayne's analysis has been very influential, more recent studies, in particular Rivas (1977), Jaeggli (1980), Borer (1981) have claimed that Romance object clitics are base-generated. The typical argument that these studies have adduced in favor of the base-generation hypothesis, has to do with clitic-doubling, as in the Spanish example in (13).

(13)   Le   entregué la   carta a él.
            (*I*) *to-him delivered the letter to him*

Under a movement analysis, the clitic in (13) would have no source since the θ-position is occupied by a lexical phrase (*a él*). On the other hand a base-generation analysis will face no problem of principle.

As we mentioned in 1.4 above, we are also claiming that object clitics are base-generated. However, without rejecting the clitic-doubling argument, our argument will be of a rather different type. We will argue that the base-generation and movement hypotheses actually predict different configurations of data with respect to complex predicates, the base-generation hypothesis making the right predictions. In essence, we will argue that, whereas a movement analysis of cliticization requires clitic-*ec* relations to be well-formed only at S-structure, a base-generation analysis requires such relations to be well-formed at D-structure as well, whence the difference in empirical predictions. As we discussed in 1.4, the requirement that clitic-*ec* pairs hold well-formed relations at all levels at which they exist follows from the projection principle, since the latter relations are necessary for transmission of the θ-role to the clitic by the *ec*. It is entirely reasonable to suppose that the well-formedness conditions that hold at D-structure are the same as those that hold at S-structure. Since we assume the binding theory for S-structure, we will assume the binding theory for D-structure as well. This raises a certain question concerning the element PRO.

It is clear that the distribution of PRO is determined exclusively by S-structure. Thus, while in S-structure PRO can only be in subject, and not in object position as shown by (14), its D-structure position is immaterial, as shown by (15a) which must be well-formed to produce (15b).

(14) a. [PRO to invite Bill] would be a good idea.

   b. *[for Bill to invite PRO] would be a good idea.

(15) a. [[e] to be invited PRO] would be nice.

   b. [PRO$_i$ to be invited t$_i$] would be nice.

In the LGB framework, the distribution of PRO and the contrast between (14a, b) is determined by the requirement that PRO be ungoverned at S-structure, which in turn derives from the binding theory (cf. I.0.3 above). The lack of a requirement that PRO be ungoverned at D-structure as well, illustrated by the well-formedness of (15), would

follow from the assumption that the binding theory does not apply in
D-structure. Our claim that it does, may thus seem to rule out (15)
incorrectly.

However, our claim does *not* imply that the binding theory must apply
to PRO in D-structure. In fact the reasons why we assume that it must
apply to clitic-*ec* relations is that those relations must exist, so as to allow
transmission of θ-role to the clitic. But this reasoning does not carry over
to PRO, or for that matter to other elements, like *each other* in (16).

(16)   They$_i$ expected [each other$_i$ to be invited t$_i$].

In (16), *each other* is within a certain local domain of *they* in derived
structure, but it is not in D-structure, showing that the D-structure position of *each other*, like that of PRO, is irrelevant to well-formedness. As
we pointed out in 3.3, our approach here consists of assuming that only
some relations must obtain at all levels, as determined by the requirement
that θ-structure be represented at all levels, that is by the projection
principle. The relations which will be required to obtain at all levels will
then be those that involve θ-role transmission. Others will typically be
required to obtain only at LF. We therefore take the binding theory to be
available at all levels, but to apply at any particular level only to those
relations which must obtain at that level.

We finally consider some doubts and difficulties which remain under
the proposed account of cliticization. One set of problems is represented
by the fact that clitics can be 'extracted', with various degrees of success,
out of small clauses, as in (17), (18). Rather similar facts are brought up
as problematic for the SSC account of cliticization in Kayne (1975, 4.6).

(17) a.   Quel libro$_i$ **gli**   fu   [$_{sc}$ t$_i$ dato t$_i$ [e] da Giovanni]

        that book   to-him was   given   by Giovanni

    b.   Giovanni$_i$ **ne**   pareva [$_{sc}$t$_i$ deluso [e]]

        Giovanni of-it seemed   disappointed
        Giovanni seemed disappointed about it.

(18) a.   ?   **Ne**   considero [$_{sc}$ Giovanni deluso [e]]

        (I) of-it consider   Giovanni disappointed
        I consider Giovanni disappointed about it.

    b.   ??   **Gli**   consideravo [$_{sc}$ Maria fedele [e]]

        (I) to-him considered   Maria faithful
        I considered Maria faithful to him.

Note that in general small clauses behave just like other clauses with respect to the binding conditions, as shown for example by the behavior of the pronoun in (19a) and of the reflexive in (19b).

(19) a. Maria$_i$ considerava [$_{sc}$ Giovanni orgoglioso di lei$_i$]
       Maria considered   Giovanni ·proud   of her

   b. *Maria$_i$ considerava [$_{sc}$ Giovanni orgoglioso di se stessa$_i$]
        Maria considered   Giovanni proud   of herself

The exceptionality of (17), (18) is therefore peculiar to cliticization.

One might attempt to account for (17), (18), by suggesting that locality conditions on cliticization are relaxed when the local domain does not contain an element that takes clitics (i.e. a verb). Results change in fact whenever the sc is replaced by an infinitival complement (which does contain a verb), as shown by the contrast between (17b) and (20a), whose grammatical counterpart is (20b).

(20) a. *Giovanni$_i$ **ne** pareva [$_S$t$_i$ essere deluso [e]]

      Giovanni of-it seemed   to be   disappointed

   b. Giovanni$_i$ pareva [$_S$t$_i$ esser**ne**   deluso [e]]

      Giovanni seemed   to be-of-it disappointed

However, alone, this consideration would incorrectly lead us to expect a relaxation of the conditions in the case of extraction from NP, too. (That is, cliticization out of NPs should be possible not just in the cases noted by Cinque, but generally.) We may then appeal to the fact that a verb taking a sc complement and the predicate in the sc bear a special relation to each other, as evidenced by the existence of selectional dependencies between the two (a matter discussed in Stowell, (1983)). This second consideration (which has no counterpart in the case of extraction from NP), might make it natural to regard the main verb and the predicate in the sc as some sort of discontinuous predicate, and to account in this way for the apparent exceptionality of (17), (18). The first consideration (i.e. the absence of a target for cliticization within the sc) would still be required however, to distinguish the exceptional behavior of clitics from the non exceptional behavior of other elements (cf. (19)). Matters are complicated further by the difference in the level of acceptability between (17) and (18). This difference seems to stem at least in part from the different positions of the lexically realized subject of the sc (within the sc in (18), outside the sc in (17)). For cases like (18) improve if the subject is extracted, as shown by the contrast between (18b) and (21).

(21)   ?Maria$_i$ **gli**   era   considerata [t$_i$ fedele [e]]

Maria   to-him   was   considered   faithful

While it remains unclear how the different role of lexical and non-lexical subjects is to be captured by our grammar, we may note that this phenomenpon stresses the relevance of the notion of subject to the distribution of cliticization.[8]

Another question relates to the evidence in Cinque (1980). Although it achieves a significant degree of explanatory power, Cinque's account of cliticization from NP is in one important respect problematic, as he notes. Cinque shows that the possibility of extracting from NP by cliticization corresponds rather closely to the possibility of extracting by Wh-movement. This suggests of course that analogous factors are at work in the two types of extraction. Yet, as has been argued in recent years (cf. in particular Rizzi (1978b), Chomsky (1980), (LGB), Freidin and Lasnik (1981)), the view that Wh-movement is subject to the binding conditions (specifically, that Wh-traces are anaphors) does not seem tenable (cf. I.0.3, fn. 16, ch. 1).

In spite of the various reservations that the above discussion may suggest, we will continue to assume that cliticization is governed by principle A of the binding theory, i.e., that *ec*'s related to clitics are anaphors. We further assume, pending discussion of the relevant evidence, that object clitics are base-generated and related to their *ec*'s at all levels, under the same locality conditions (i.e. the binding theory) at each level.

NOTES

[1] As for 'be+adjective' cases, like *It is illegal [PRO to park here]*, the considerations of Note 13, ch. 1, Note 63, 73, ch. 2, suggesting that there are no 'ergative' adjectives, would lead us to analyze the sentential argument as having subject rather than object θ-role, so that these cases would not instantiate the subcategorization ___S. On the other hand, infinitivals occurring with Raising adjectives, like the one in *John$_i$ is likely [t$_i$ to win]* cannot be readily analyzed as having subject θ-role. More plausibly, they have object θ-role. The issue raised in the Notes cited above is thus further complicated by these cases.

[2] There are a few exceptions to this generalization, noted and discussed in Marantz (1981, 3.1.1). These are cases like *feel, reason, say*, as in *Elmer was felt to have overstepped his boundaries/*We felt Elmer to have overstepped his boundaries.*

Notice also that, while one finds cases of Raising across indirect objects, as in *John$_i$ seemed to us [t$_i$ to have left]*, there are no cases of ECM across indirect objects (cf. *I proved to him [the problem to be unsolvable]*). This difference follows from the assumption of Stowell (1981), that Case-marking (at least in English) requires linear adjacency (cf. also Note 4, ch. 4).

[3] While the classification in the text does not consider cases in which there is a NP or a ?PP object beside the sentential complement, we will see that restructuring applies to some such cases as well (cf. ergative verbs *andare, venire*).

[4] The two questions are not entirely independent however, since − as we will argue − base-generation entails stronger locality effects than movement.

[5] The term 'extract' is used here for expository convenience, not to imply cliticization by movement.

[6] Following Belletti and Rizzi (1981), we assume however that the *ec* related to *ne* is governed by the verb (and hence, presumably, by *ne*) in the case of quantified nominals, as in (i) (cf. Note 23, ch. 1).

(i) Ne ho visti [due [e]]
    (*I*) *of-them saw two*

Government by V in (i) versus lack of government by V in (12b) is supported by a difference in past participle agreement, as we noted in Note 49, chapter 1.

[7] The text discussion, and especially our reference to relations between clitics and empty categories, is partly misleading since we do *not* presume that the syntax of clitics is substantially different in cases of clitic-doubling, which of course do not involve empty categories.

[8] Contrasts between cases in which the cliticization path crosses a lexical subject and cases in which it only crosses its trace are even stronger with the 'pro-predicate' *lo* (cf. Note 11, ch. 3), as illustrated by the following.

(i) a. Ritengo [Giovanni deluso]
    (*I*) *believe Giovanni disappointed*

   b. * **Lo** ritengo [Giovanni [e]]

    (*I*) *it believe Giovanni*

   c. ?Giovanni$_i$ **lo** era ritenuto [t$_i$[e]]

    Giovanni it was believed

(ii) a. Giovanni$_i$ è [t$_i$ ammalato]
    Giovanni is sick

   b. Giovanni$_i$ **lo** è [t$_i$[e]]

    Giovanni it is

   c. C'è [Giovanni ammalato]
    there is Giovanni sick

   d. *Ce **lo** è [Giovanni [e]]

    there it is Giovanni

We have no explanation for the greater sharpness of the above contrasts compared with those of the text.

CHAPTER 4

CAUSATIVE CONSTRUCTIONS

4.0. INTRODUCTION

In this chapter we consider the various constructions one finds with causative and perception verbs. At a descriptive level, we can recognize three different constructions in which the causative verb **fare** 'make' can occur. These are illustrated in (1).

(1) a. Maria ha fatto riparare la macchina da Giovanni.
    Maria has made repair the car by Giovanni

    Maria had the car repaired by Giovanni.

    b. Maria ha fatto riparare la macchina.
     Maria had the car repaired.

    c. Maria ha fatto riparare la macchina a Giovanni.
     Maria has made repair the car to Giovanni

     Maria had Giovanni repair the car.

We will argue that while the three cases in (1) are structurally similar in some respects, those in (1a,b) are base-generated, whereas (1c) is syntactically derived. In particular, we will argue that in (1a), an instance of the *Faire-par* (FP) construction of Kayne (1975), henceforth 'FS' (French Syntax), the material following *fare* is a base-generated VP complement, so that the relevant structure will be as in (2) at all levels.

(2)

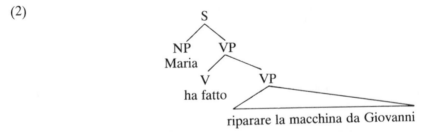

We will argue that the alternation between (1a) and (1b) is due to the rather general optionality of *by*-phrases (as in passives), so that the analysis of (1b) will also be as in (2), less the *by*-phrase. As for (1c), an instance of Kayne's Faire-Infinitive (FI) construction, we will argue for a derivation from a sentential complement of *fare* as in (3a), via movement of the embedded VP ('VP-movement') and the operation of appropriate Case-marking mechanisms, to produce the structure in (3b).

(3) a.

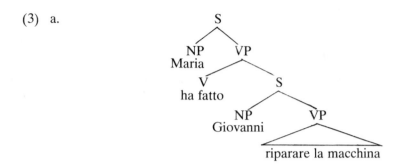

b.

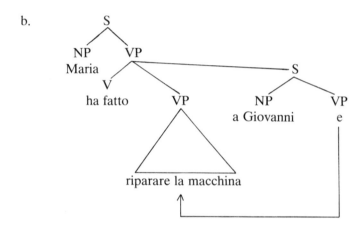

We note that the structure in (3b) is partially similar to the one in (2).

Beside discussing the analyses of the constructions in (1), we will address several issues which relate to the latter analyses in various ways. One concerns the role of reconstruction (cf. 3.3) in the structures in which VP-movement has applied (FI). Another concerns the different behavior of ergative and intransitive verbs when embedded under *fare*. A third concerns the fact that, while the constructions in (1a) are found with both causative verbs **fare, lasciare** 'make, let', as well as with perception predicates **vedere, guardare, osservare, sentire, udire** 'see, look at, observe, hear, hear', the construction in (4) is possible only with perception predicates and — somewhat marginally — with *lasciare*, though not with *fare*.

(4)   Maria ha visto Giovanni riparare la   macchina.
       Maria has seen Giovanni repair   the car

Throughout the chapter we will make comparisons between our theory and the one in Kayne's FS in particular.

4.1. *FAIRE*-INFINITIVE

4.1.0. *Introduction*

In this section we argue for the analysis of the FI construction given in
(3b) and in (5), where we use the notation '— — —' to indicate the trace
of the moved VP.

(5)   Maria ha fatto [$_{VP}$ riparare la macchina] [$_S$ a Giovanni — — —]
        Maria has made   repair   the car   to Giovanni

As suggested by the titles of some of the following subsections, we begin
by arguing that this construction is syntactically derived and not base-
generated; then we proceed to argue that *fare* is subcategorized for a
sentential complement on which it induces S̄-deletion, and finally that a
rule of VP-movement applies to such an underlying structure.

4.1.1. *Syntactic Derivation*

Arguments for a movement derivation of FI are rather strong. One type
of argument, given in FS, 3.2, is based on the observation that phrases
corresponding to *Giovanni* of (5) above act as the subject of the
embedded verb in several important respects, a fact which can be
accounted for naturally if such a phrase *is* the subject of the embedded
verb underlyingly, but which requires a number of ad-hoc stipulations if
the structure is base-generated. There are three major respects in which
the phrase *Giovanni* in (5) acts as the subject of *riparare*: (i) 'semantically', or 'thematically', (ii) with respect to selectional restrictions, (iii) by
functioning as an antecedent to certain phrases. That is, *Giovanni* in (5)
is understood as the thematic subject of *riparare*, it falls under exactly
the same selectional restrictions that *riparare* normally enforces on its
subject, and there are cases like **Con le minacce fecero accusare se
stesso a Giovanni** 'With threats they made Giovanni accuse himself' and
Maria gli fece legare le scarpe con una mano sola 'Maria made him tie
his shoes with one hand', where both *se stesso* and *con una mano sola*
have *Giovanni* as their antecedent, the second of these phrases requiring
specifically a subject antecedent. Within our discussion, (i) above will
follow from the assumption that in (5) *riparare* assigns subject θ-role to
Giovanni in the normal fashion in D-structure, and via the trace of the
VP in S-structure. (ii) will follow from the standard assumption the selectional restrictions apply in D-structure, and (iii) from our hypothesis that
the VP is reconstructed into its original position in LF.

   A second type of argument for a syntactic derivation is provided by
the fact that VP-movement gives rise to the same bifurcation among
anaphoric relations that we noted in 3.3.3 above for established cases of

movement. As we will see in 4.4, 4.6 below, it appears that, while VP-movement is possible when the subject is related to an anaphor of the 'himself' type, it is not possible when the subject is related for example to a trace.

The conclusion that there is a syntactic process at work in the derivation of FI sentences can thus be drawn rather firmly. In fact this point is not too controversial within the literature. Among others, Aissen (1974), FS, Van Tiel Di Maio (1975, 1978), Aissen and Perlmutter (1976), Radford (1977), Quicoli (1980), Rouveret and Vergnaud (1980), all assume a syntactic derivation. Exact determination of the derived structure however, is a different matter, the relevant evidence being more indirect and theory-internal. This is reflected by the little unaniminty one finds in the literature on this other point, which we address in the next few subsections.

4.1.2. *Sentential Complement*

For *fare*, the subcategorization __S (as in the diagrams we ignore the S/$\overline{\text{S}}$ distinction in this notation) is independently attested by the occurrence of this verb with tensed complements as in (6), although such occurrences are more or less confined to exhortations.

(6)   Fa   [$_S$ che Giovanni ritorni]
      make   *that   Giovanni   return*

   Let Giovanni return.

Since no other subcategorization is independently attested, we assume, as the null hypothesis, that the subcategorization __S, and not for example __NP VP, or __NP S, is what is involved in the FI construction, as in (3a) above. In the current framework, in which semantic interpretation derives from S-structure, and in which θ-roles are assigned at all levels, one generally assumes that syntactic operations cause no 'loss' of structure. It is then natural and, strictly speaking, necessary to assume that the S complement and its relevant internal structure, [NP VP], are preserved in derived structure, as in (3b). As we will see below, the sentential structure of the complement is preserved in Kayne's discussion as well. Having thus established that *fare* has a sentential complement at all levels, we may consider whether $\overline{\text{S}}$-deletion applies to that complement.

There are several considerations suggesting that *fare* does trigger $\overline{\text{S}}$-deletion. The first relates to the fact that it never appears in a Control frame, as in (7).

(7)   *Giovanni$_i$ fece   [$_S$ PRO$_i$ riparare la   macchina]
      Giovanni   made   *repair   the   car*

   Giovanni caused himself to repair the car.

The ungrammaticality of (7) under the coreferential interpretation of the two subjects follows from S̄-deletion, since PRO will be governed. As for the grammaticality of (7) under a non coreferential interpretation of the two subjects (as in (1b) above), we will see below that it does not involve PRO as the embedded subject.

A second consideration has to do with the relative acceptability of (8a) compared with (8b).

(8) a. ?Maria lo ha fatto [$_S$[e] riparare la macchina]

       Maria him has made   repair   the car

    b. *Maria ha fatto [$_S$Giovanni riparare la macchina]
      Maria has made Giovanni repair   the car

As is noted in Radford (1979), cases like (8a) or their French counterparts are classified as grammatical in some studies (e.g. Rouveret and Vergnaud (1980)), and ungrammatical in others (e.g. FS). We may presume that, at least in part this difference among linguists reflects dialectal variation. Agreement is quite general however that (8a) is much better than (8b). What this means is that (8a) does not involve a violation of the ECP, or its ungrammaticality ought to be very severe, as with other ECP violations, which are quite comparable to (8b). Putting aside the question of what exactly is involved in (8a) as well as the question of the ungrammaticality of (8b), to which we will return, if the ECP is satisfied in (8a) the *ec* is governed, and therefore S̄-deletion must have occurred.

A third consideration has to do with the well-formedness of (9) which suggests S̄-deletion in the same way as (8a).[1]

(9)   Giovanni$_i$ fu fatto [$_S$ t$_i$ riparare la   macchina]
        Giovanni was made   to repair the car

Note that it is reasonably clear that neither in (8a) nor in (9) has VP-movement applied, and therefore that the analyses are as indicated. For VP-movement in these cases would require dativization of the embedded subject as we will see below, so that in (8a) the latter subject would have to cliticize as *gli* rather than *lo*, and in (9) we would not expect that it could undergo NP-movement since dative phrases ('*a* NP' PPs) never do. Thus in (10), where NP-movement must have applied, given cliticization of the embedded object to the main verb, passivization as in (9) is not possible.

(10) ?*Giovanni lo fu fatto riparare.
      Giovanni was made to repair it.

On the basis of the discussion of (7), (8), (9), we conclude that *fare* triggers S̄-deletion.

We may note that the subcategorization __S, which we assumed at the outset, is confirmed by the ungrammaticality of (11), contrasting with (9).

(11)   *[$_i$e] fu   fatto [$_S$Giovanni$_i$ riparare la macchina]
          was *made* *Giovanni* *repair* *the car*

Under the analysis indicated, the impossibility of inversion in (11) reduces to the impossibility of some of the cases discussed in 2.4 above, e.g. *[$_i$e] **sembra [Giovanni$_i$ riparare la macchina]** 'seems Giovanni to repair the car'. On the other hand, the ungrammaticality of (11) would be surprising if the phrase *Giovanni* was not inside a sentential complement, i.e. if the subcategorization of *fare* were __NP VP, or __NP S, since inversion is not problematic when the i-subject is not within a sentential complement, as in (12).

(12)   [$_i$e] fu $\left\{ \begin{array}{c} \text{costretto} \\ \text{persuaso} \end{array} \right\}$ Giovanni$_i$ [PRO a riparare la macchina]

        was $\left\{ \begin{array}{c} \textit{forced} \\ \textit{persuaded} \end{array} \right\}$ *Giovanni*   *to repair* *the car*

We may also note that, to the extent that it is acceptable, (8a) above confirms our claim of II.0.3 that cliticization is not sensitive to clause boundaries.

If S̄-deletion occurs, then we can account for assignment of accusative Case to the phrase *Giovanni* in (13) while maintaining the view that the sentential structure of the complement is preserved.

(13)   Maria fa [$_{VP}$lavorare] [Giovanni − − −]
        Maria makes Giovanni work.

We can in fact assume that *Giovanni* in (13) is assigned Case by the main verb under government. Case assignment in (13) and the general fact that the embedded subject in FI behaves like an object of the main verb reduces to the treatment of ECM in English (we continue to postpone discussion of (8b)).

Further considerations will have to be appealed to, however, for the cases in which the embedded subject appears in the dative (*a NP*), as in (5) above: *Maria ha fatto [riparare la macchina] [a Giovanni − − −]*. It is clear that in general what determines dative rather than accusative Case on the embedded subject is the presence of a direct object of the embedded verb. We may express this generalization as in (14).

(14)   *Dativization*

        NP NP → NP a NP

Some remarks are in order on the nature of (14). It is rather unlikely that there exists a rule like (14) associated specifically with verbs like *fare* or with the FI construction (as much of the literature on the topic suggests).

For one thing it is hard to imagine that speakers actually learn that causative constructions have such a peculiar property. For another, (14) looks too much like a description of the environment in which datives occur in general. A more plausible hypothesis is that dativization in causative constructions is a reflex of some general mechanisms of Case assignment.[2] While we will not pursue this hypothesis in full and will, in much of our discussion assume a rule like (14), we will consider some of its ramifications. In particular we consider one direct consequence that this hypothesis has. In 3.1.2 above, we claimed that the reason why we do not find sequences of two accusative NP's in general is that one verb will assign only one accusative (cf. 3.1.2 above). However, here we have *two* verbs. It must then be the case that a direct object of the embedded verb is in relevant respects also a direct object of the matrix verb in these complex predicates. More specifically, it would have to be the case that an NP object of the embedded verb neutralizes the ability to assign accusative Case, not only of that verb, but of the main verb as well. We will see that there are other indications that embedded objects are functionally objects of the main verb as well: a conclusion that would have (14) as one of its consequences.[3]

The hypothesis that *fare* induces $\bar{\text{S}}$-deletion on its sentential complement, together with (14), will then account for all the facts so far considered, with the exception of (8b), repeated here.

(15)   *Maria ha fatto [$_\text{S}$ Giovanni riparare la   macchina]
        *Maria has made   Giovanni repair   the car

Previous approaches, including FS, attributed cases like (15) to the inherent obligatoriness of the rule equivalent to our VP-movement. But this is not possible within our theoretical framework, which does not contemplate obligatory rules. We note that in any case such an account appears false empirically, if we are right in regard to the analyses of (8a), (9) above, since VP-movement has not applied in those cases. What we will take (15) to suggest rather, is that in Italian $\bar{\text{S}}$-deletion, though necessary, is not sufficient for Case assignment across sentence boundaries. The next subsection takes up this issue.

4.1.3. *Exceptional Case Marking*

In principle, there are two ways in which one may attempt to account for the general lack of ECM configurations in Italian (cf. *John believes [Bill to have left]/*Giovanni ritiene [Mario esser partito]*): (i) Italian just happens to have a more limited distribution of $\bar{\text{S}}$-deletion than English, (ii) in Italian, $\bar{\text{S}}$-deletion is not sufficient for Case assignment. Of these, the first seems immediately suspicious. While it must be true that Italian has a more limited distribution of $\bar{\text{S}}$-deletion, given that most Italian counterparts of English ECM verbs allow PRO as an embedded subject, this is likely to be a derived rather than a primitive difference. For Italian does not differ significantly from English with respect to the size of the other class of verbs that trigger $\bar{\text{S}}$-deletion, namely Raising verbs (class II of II.0.2 above). Consider in particular the following paradigm.

(16) a. Il governo ha dimostrato [$_\text{S}$che il blocco degli affitti diminuisce
   The government has proved that rent control diminishes

   l'inflazione]
   inflation.

   b. [$_i$Il blocco degli affitti] si è dimostrato [$_\text{S}$ t$_i$ diminuire l'inflazione]
      Rent control   has proved   to diminish inflation

   c. *Il governo ha dimostrato [$_\text{S}$il blocco degli affitti diminuire
      The government has proved rent control to diminish

   l'inflazione]
   inflation.

The pair (16a, b) shows that there is a verb *dimostrare*, subcategorized for a sentential complement, which has both a $+\theta_s$ and a $-\theta_s$ entry (as we noted in 1.5 above). In its $-\theta_s$ entry this verb takes the morpheme *si*, like some ergative verbs (cf. 1.5). The $-\theta_s$ entry gives rise to Raising, as in (16b). This means that this verb, at least in the latter entry, must trigger $\bar{\text{S}}$-deletion. If $\bar{\text{S}}$-deletion was sufficient for Case assignment across clause boundaries in Italian, then indeed there would be no reason why this verb could not trigger $\bar{\text{S}}$-deletion in the other entry as well and why (16c) should be ungrammatical.[4]

The following minimal pair provides further and relatively direct evidence that S boundaries always block Case assignment in Italian.

(17) a. (?)La sua espressione fa   [$_\text{VP}$ sembrare [$_\text{sc}$ Giovanni ammalato]]
         his expression   makes   seem   Giovanni sick

         . . . Giovanni seem sick

   b. *La sua espressione fa   [$_\text{VP}$ sembrare [$_\text{S}$ Giovanni soffrire]]
         his expression   makes   seem   Giovanni suffer

         . . . Giovanni seem to suffer

The structures in (17a, b) are expected under the assumption that *fare* can also take VP complements, as we will argue below in connection with the *Faire-par* construction. In both (17a) and (17b) the only verb that can assign Case is *fare* since *sembrare* is a $-\theta_s$ verb. We must thus assume that in (17a) the phrase *Giovanni* is assigned Case by *fare* across the VP boundary (a fact to which we will return) and the sc boundary. That sc boundaries do not block Case assignment in Italian is independently

clear, given for example **Ritengo** [$_{SC}$**Giovanni soddisfatto**] '(I) believe
Giovanni satisfied'. In (17b) we must assume $\bar{S}$-deletion to have applied
since *sembrare* is a Raising verb. The ungrammaticality of (17b) and the
contrast with (17a) will then force us to conclude that the S boundary
blocks Case assignment in spite of $\bar{S}$-deletion.[5]

We assume therefore that in general Case assignment across S boundaries is not possible in Italian. This accounts for the ungrammaticality of
(15) above, repeated in (18a), but calls into question our account of (13),
repeated in (18b).

(18) a. *Maria ha fatto [$_S$ Giovanni riparare la macchina]
        Maria has made   Giovanni repair   the car

    b. Maria ha fatto [$_{VP}$ lavorare] [$_S$ Giovanni – – –]
        Maria has made   work   Giovanni

Clearly, given our analyses, a distinction between these two cases must
rely on the fact that the complement in (18a) contains a phonologically
realized VP, whereas the one in (18b) does not. It seems rather reasonable in fact to suppose that Case assignment across S boundaries should
become possible when the NP which is assigned Case is the only phonologically realized constituent of that S. The plausibility of this account
comes from the fact that it is independently clear that Case-assignment
mechanisms discriminate between phonologically realized and phonologically non-realized constituents, as phonologically null NPs do not require
Case. If we assume that such mechanisms detect only phonologically
realized material, then in (18b) the S boundaries will in a sense coincide
with the NP boundaries. Let us then postulate that Case assignment
across S boundaries in Italian is possible only if the VP has been
extracted from S (and of course if $\bar{S}$-deletion has applied), as in (18b).

The different distribution of $\bar{S}$-deletion in Italian and English can now
be derived rather than having to be stipulated. Since we are claiming that
in Italian $\bar{S}$-deletion with $+\theta_s$ verbs will result in well-formed sentences
only if the rather marked syntactic process of VP-movement applies, we
predict that the majority of Italian $+\theta_s$ verbs taking S-complement will
not trigger $\bar{S}$-deletion, thus appearing in Control frames (cf. **Giovanni**$_i$
ritiene [$_S$**di PRO**$_i$ **aver finito**] 'Giovanni believes to have finished (that he
has finished)'.

One might attempt to relate the fact that English has looser structural
conditions on Case assignment than Italian to the fact that English
appears to have stricter conditions on linear adjacency, as discussed in
Stowell (1981). Compare **Ho letto attentamente l'articolo** '(I) have read
carefully the article' with its ill-formed English counterpart. Note also the
lack of linear adjacency between the phrase *Giovanni* and its Case
assigner *fare* in (17a) and (18b). One might suppose that languages have

the choice of defining certain locality conditions on Case assignment either linearly on structurally, English choosing one option: linear adjacency, and Italian the other: structural adjacency. Note that this role of S boundaries in distinguishing ECM from non-ECM languages is reminiscent of the role they play in distinguishing the system of auxiliary assignment of Italian from that of French (cf. (128) in 2.6.2 above, and discussion).

This ends our discussion of the sentential complement in the FI construction. We have argued that *fare* triggers $\bar{S}$-deletion and that structural conditions on Case assignment in Italian are stricter than in English. In particular we have argued that Italian allows Case assignment across S boundaries just in case the VP has been extracted. This predicts that VP-movement will be necessary unless the subject is itself phonologically null, as for example in (9), where it is a trace. Under this view there is no need to postulate any process that reanalyzes the embedded subject as an object of *fare*, and we in fact assume that the sentential structure of the complement is preserved in derived structure.

4.1.4. *Cliticization*

In this subsection, we consider some of the interaction between cliticization and the constructions at issue. In part this will serve to confirm our discussion so far, and in part it will allow us to draw certain conclusions regarding the nature of cliticization.

Consider again the contrast in (8), repeated here.

(19) a. *Maria ha   fatto [Giovanni riparare la   macchina]
     Maria has made Giovanni repair   the car.

   b. ?Maria lo   ha   fatto [[e] riparare la   macchina

      Maria him has made   repair   the car

In (19b), we assume that, as always, the chain *lo*-[e] has accusative Case (this chain is the clitic counterpart to, for example, *Giovanni* of (18b)), and that this Case is morphologically realized by the accusative features of *lo*. But given the much more acceptable status of (19b) compared with (19a), it must not be the case that the chain in (19b) has accusative by virtue of *fare* assigning this Case to the embedded subject, or there would be no explanation for the contrast with (19a), where the assignment of accusative to the embedded subject is unsuccessful. Rather, it must be the case that in (19b) the accusative features go to the clitic directly. Therefore, what the contrast in (19) suggests, is what has been argued for independently, for example by Aoun (1979), Borer (1981), namely that clitics are a 'spell out' of the Case assigning features of the verb they appear on.[6] Case assignment will therefore not have to cross the S boundary in (19b).

Something remains to be said about the less than complete acceptability of (19b). Our discussion so far predicts that it should be perfectly grammatical, since the *ec* is governed by the verb, satisfying the ECP, the same *ec* is properly bound by *lo* as required by the binding theory, and *lo* spells out the Case marking features of the verb, as clitics generally do. We may perhaps attribute the status of (19b) to its 'analogy' with (19a). More specifically, we may suppose that there is some tendency, which apparently varies dialectally, to require that a chain headed by an object clitic not extend beyond the Case marking domain of the verb.

Notice that our account of the contrast in (19) confirms again the subcategorization ___S for *fare*, since there would be no account of that contrast under either the subcategorization ___NP VP, or ___NP S. (Both (19a) and (19b) should then be grammatical, since no clause boundary would be involved).

In FI constructions, we find two types of clitics: embedded subjects and embedded objects. Both generally appear on *fare*, as in (20).

(20) a.   Maria lo fa [$_{VP}$ lavorare] [$_S$ [e] − − −]

   Maria makes him work.

   b.   Maria la fa [$_{VP}$ riparare [e]] [$_S$ a Giovanni − − −]

   Maria makes Giovanni repair it.

The theory of cliticization outlined in II.0.3 above requires two different derivations for the two clitics in (20). In particular, it requires that *lo* of (20a) be base-generated on the main verb *fare*, while *la* of (20b) must be base-generated on the embedded verb. This difference stems from our claim that a clitic must be locally related to its *ec* even in D-structure. That is, given this claim, a clitic on the main verb in D-structure can be related to the embedded subject (just as it can in the S-structure of (19b)), but cannot be related to an embedded object (since this yields a violation of the 'SSC' in D-structure.) Clitic *la* of (20b) must therefore be base-generated on the lower verb and moved to the matrix verb later, after (or in conjunction with) VP-movement. We will refer to the process that moves the clitic in this fashion as CLITIC CLIMBING.

Consider now (21), in which the clitics of (20) appear on the embedded verb.

(21) a.   **Maria fa [$_{VP}$ lavorarlo$_i$] [$_S$ [$_i$ e] − − −]

   b.   ??Maria fa [$_{VP}$ ripararla$_i$ [$_i$ e]] [$_S$ a Giovanni − − −]

The contrast in (21) follows naturally from our account. The less than total ungrammaticality of (21b) can be taken to indicate that the factors that determine Clitic Climbing, whatever they are, are not very strong. As for the severe ungrammaticality of (21a), it follows from the ill-formed-ness of the D-structure .... $[_S[_i e]$ lavorarlo$_i]$, due to the independent fact that *lo* cannot function as a subject clitic. The ungrammaticality of (21a) is then parallel to that of ***Lavorarlo sarebbe sorprendente** '(For) him to work would be surprising'. Sentence (21a) may also be ruled out — redundantly — by the fact that the clitic fails to c-command its *ec* in S-structure.[7]

The assumption that Clitic Climbing is required if embedded object clitics are to appear on the main verb, predicts that cases in which a Clitic Climbing derivation is impossible should be ungrammatical. Indeed they are. Consider (22).

(22)   *Maria$_i$ si$_i$ è   fatta $[_{VP}$ accusare $[_i e]] [_S$ a   Giovanni $---]$
     Maria herself has made   accuse   *to Giovanni*

    Maria had Giovanni accuse herself.

A Clitic Climbing derivation of (22) is ruled out by the fact that in D-structure *si* could not have the phrase *Maria* as an antecedent, but only the phrase *Giovanni*. That reflexive (/reciprocal) clitics require antecedents in D-structure is independently established by the fact noted in 2.7.1 above (and in FS) that they do not occur with derived subjects, as shown by (23).

(23)   *I ragazzi$_i$ si sono stati presentati t$_i$ [e]

    The kids have been introduced to each other.

As we briefly mentioned in 2.7.2, and will discuss more in detail in 6.1, we regard the requirement that *si* have a proper antecedent at D-structure as a reflex of a condition that *all* relations involving base-generated clitics be established at D-structure (not only those required by the projection principle). Thus, while a derivation of (22) via Clitic Climbing is ruled out by the fact that *si* would have the wrong antecedent in D-structure, a derivation via base-generation of *si* on the main verb is ruled out by the non-local character of the relation between *si* and the *ec* in D-structure (a binding theory violation).[8] A reflexive/reciprocal clitic coreferential with the matrix subject is not impossible however when, rather than an embedded object, it is an embedded subject, as shown in (24).

(24)   (?)Essi si facevano lavorare (a vicenda).
    They made each other work (reciprocally).

This is predicted by our account. *Si* can be base-generated on the higher verb here, for the same reasons that *lo* of (20a) can. It will thus have a proper antecedent at all levels.

Note that the foregoing account of the ungrammaticality of (22) provides a good argument, additional to those mentioned in 4.1.1, for syntactic derivation of the FI construction. If cases like (22) could be base-generated, there would be no reason for their ungrammaticality. The reflexive could simply be base-generated on the main verb and related to its *ec* locally, at all levels.

The above discussion has dealt only with accusative clitics. As far as dative clitics are concerned, no further comment is required when the dative is the embedded subject. Thus all considerations relative to *lo* in (20a) carry over to *gli* in (25).[9]

(25)   Maria gli fa [$_{VP}$ riparare la macchina] [$_S$[e] — — —]

  Maria makes him repair the car.

But the case of cliticization of dative objects of the embedded verb is more complex, and appears to have a bearing on the exact analysis of the phrase that undergoes movement in these constructions. We therefore address that case in the next subsection, which deals precisely with the nature of the moved phrase.

4.1.5. *VP-movement*

Our formulation of the rule at work in FI constructions differs from the one in FS in that, whereas we assume that the whole VP is moved, Kayne assumes that movement applies to the sequence *verb + direct object* if there is a direct object, and to the verb alone otherwise, leaving indirect objects behind. The VP movement solution is simpler, as well as less problematic from a theoretical standpoint, as we will see below. However there are some rather significant empirical results that the FS solution is intended to capture, which we must consider.

Kayne notes (FS, 4.2) that, while direct objects precede the embedded subject (cf. *Maria ha fatto riparare la macchina a Giovanni* of (1c)), indirect objects follow it. He cites examples like (26).

(26)   Je ferai   écrire mon ami   à   sa   soeur malade.
        I   will make write   my   friend to his sister sick

    I will make my friend write to his sick sister.

The assumption that the FI rule moves V (NP) leaving PP objects behind, will produce the correct linear order of constituents. Kayne further notes that in such cases cliticization of the embedded object is impossible, as in (27).

(27) *Je lui ferai écrire mon ami.
      I *to-her* *will make* *write* *my friend*

Under Kayne's formulation, the ungrammaticality of cases like (27), can be attributed to a violation of the SSC, since the θ-position to which *lui* in (27) is related is inside a clause that has a subject (*mon ami*). Thus (27) would correspond (within a framework in which there are empty categories) to the configuration ... lui$_i$ ... [$_S$mon ami ... [$_i$e]] violating the SSC.

Kayne's assumption that indirect objects remain stranded in the embedded clause will also account for the non-ambiguity of cases like (28).

(28) Paul lui fera porter ces livres à sa femme.
      Paul to-him will make take these books to his wife

      Paul will make him take these books to his wife.

In (28), dative *lui* can only be interpreted as the embedded subject, and not as an embedded dative object. As a consequence, *à sa femme* will be interpreted only as a dative object. This follows from the fact that the impossible reading would correspond to the structure ... lui$_i$ [$_S$à sa femme ... [$_i$e]], violating the SSC, much like (27). The account of (28) cannot be confirmed — Kayne claims — by the linear order of constituents in the absence of cliticization, like the account of (27), since the relevant sentence (29) appears ungrammatical altogether, presumably because of a prohibition on sequences of two datives.

(29) *Paul fera porter ces livres à son fils à sa femme.
      Paul will make his son take these books to his wife.

Kayne's discussion thus rather elegantly correlates two different sets of facts, one concerning linear order, the other cliticization, and explains them directly.

In contrast, if one claims that the whole VP is moved, one must first postulate some late reordering rule so as to produce the correct order of constituents, and second forego the explanation for the ungrammaticality of cases like (27) and for the non-ambiguity of cases like (28). This is essentially what we will do, arguing however for a certain lack of empirical adequacy in Kayne's solution, as well as for the theoretical advantages of ours. We first briefly review the relevant Italian facts.

As one might expect, the facts in Italian are rather similar to those Kayne discusses for French. Although the ungrammaticality resulting from cliticization of dative objects is not very severe in cases like (30), parallel to (27), it is more noticeable in cases like (31).

(30)   ?Gli farò $\left\{ \begin{array}{c} \text{scrivere} \\ \text{telefonare} \end{array} \right\}$ Giovanni.

I will make Giovanni write/phone (to) him.

(31) a. ??   Gli$_i$ fecero sparare $\left\{ \begin{array}{l} \text{un agente addosso } [_ie] \\ \text{addosso } [_ie] \text{ un agente} \end{array} \right\}$.

(*they*) *to-him*   *made*   *fire* $\left\{ \begin{array}{l} \textit{an agent upon} \\ \textit{upon an agent} \end{array} \right\}$

They had an agent fire on him.

b. ??   Gli$_i$ fecero sparare $\left\{ \begin{array}{l} \text{tra i piedi } [_ie] \text{ un agente} \\ \text{un agente tra i piedi } [_ie] \end{array} \right\}$.

(*they*) *to-him*   *made*   *fire* $\left\{ \begin{array}{l} \textit{between the feet an agent} \\ \textit{an agent between the feet} \end{array} \right\}$

They had an agent fire between his feet.

In (31a,b), in which the complements correspond to simple sentences like **Un agente gli sparò addosso** 'An agent fired upon (to) him', **Un agente gli sparò tra i piedi** 'An agent fired between the feet to him (his feet)', the dative is respectively the object of the preposition *addosso*, and a dative of inalienable possession. Corresponding to (28) we find (32) which is also essentially unambiguous, allowing the subject interpretation of the dative clitic, while the object interpretation is at least difficult.

(32)   Giovanni **gli** farà portare questi libri a Maria.
          Giovanni will make him take these books to Maria.

The facts relative to linear order are also similar to those noted for French by Kayne, so that analogous to (26) we find (33a). However, the alternative order, the one predicted by VP-movement, is not completely impossible, as in (33b) (while we find no difference between the two variants of (31a, b)).

(33) a. Farò $\left\{ \begin{array}{c} \text{scrivere} \\ \text{telefonare} \end{array} \right\}$ Giovanni a Maria.

I will make Giovanni write/phone (to) Maria.

b. ?Farò $\left\{ \begin{array}{c} \text{scrivere} \\ \text{telefonare} \end{array} \right\}$ a Maria Giovanni.

As we mentioned, there are certain empirical weaknesses in Kayne's account. Leaving aside the fact that, if extended to Italian, it would predict much stronger violations in (30), (33b), we note that the correlation between linear order and cliticization predicted by Kayne's theory is lacking in certain cases noted by E. Wehrli in work in progress. Wehrli points out (citing Ruwet (1972)) that cases like (34), analogous to (29), are not always ungrammatical, and that to the extent that they are not, they are unambiguous.

(34)   Jean fait porter une lettre à Marie à Paul.
        Jean makes Paul take a letter to Marie.

Speakers who accept (34) will take the first dative as an object and the second as the embedded subject (as in the translation), and never the other way around. The version of (34) given in (35) is also, for the same speakers, unambiguous, allowing only the subject interpretation of *lui.*

(35)   Jean **lui** fait porter une lettre à Marie.
        Jean makes him take a letter to Marie.

The lack of ambiguity of (35) is precisely the one that Kayne notes (cf. (28)) and attributes to the fact that embedded datives remain stranded in the embedded S. But this account is falsified by the fact that in (34) the rightmost dative can only be the embedded subject, as would be predicted by the VP-movement formulation. My own intuitions on Italian concur with Wehrli's discussion of (34) and (35).[10]

   Another kind of difficulty for Kayne's solution derives from the fact that it predicts SSC effects on dative objects in general, and not just with respect to cliticization. But it is far from clear that this prediction is correct. Thus I find coreference in (36) rather difficult, and association of *ciascuno* with the matrix subject in (37) rather free.

(36)   ?*Giovanni$_i$ farà telefonare Maria proprio a lui$_i$.
        Giovanni$_i$ will make Maria telephone exactly (to) him$_i$.

(37)   Abbiamo fatto telefonare la segretaria a tre o quattro studenti
        We$_i$ had the secretary telephone (to) three or four students

        ciascuno.
        each$_i$.

An account of the cliticization facts in (30), (31) based on the SSC would predict rather free coreference in (36) and ungrammaticality on a par with (30), (31) for (37). Kayne of course is aware of this prediction and notes in fact that the behavior of the reciprocal construction in (38) seems to bear it out.

(38)   *Nous ferons écrire notre ami l'un à l'autre.
        We$_i$ will make our friend write one to the other$_i$ (to one another).

While this would seem to support Kayne's analysis, the discrepancy between (30)–(31) and (36)–(37) remains. Cases like (38) in Italian, such as (39), are only mildly ungrammatical, suggesting that some second order factor is involved (probably that of Note 8).[11]

(39)   ?Facciamo sempre telefonare la segretaria l'uno all'altro.
        We$_i$ always make the secretary phone)to) one another$_i$.

A third empirical difficulty, one which Kayne acknowledges, is represented by the fact that indirect objects other than datives are *not* prevented from cliticizing, as in (40).

(40) a.   Cela y fait penser tout le monde.
          That makes everyone think about it.

     b.   On essaiera d'**en** faire parler ton ami.
          We will try to make your friend talk about it.

If only direct objects are moved along with the verb, then all indirect objects ought to behave alike, but this is not the case, given the difference between (40) and (27).[12]

Thus, while we have no satisfactory alternative to propose for the failure of dative object cliticization, there are sufficient doubts about the empirical advantages of the FS solution, to make us want to consider the theoretical advantages of VP-movement.

These advantages are that constituents rather than non-constituents are moved, that there is a maximal degree of structure preservation, and that all θ-roles can be assigned not only in D-structure, but in S-structure as well, in accordance with the projection principle. It is clear that in the current framework these are desiderata, although it is less clear that they are independent of each other. Upon closer examination, they might perhaps all follow from the projection principle.

Considering θ-role assignment in S-structure, under VP-movement all object θ-roles are assigned within the moved VP normally. As for subject θ-role, the VP movement formulation permits assignment of the latter quite straightforwardly, provided that it is VP rather than V that assigns subject θ-role, as argued in LGB and in Marantz (1981). The moved VP will then simply assign θ-role via its trace. Note that assignment of subject θ-role by VP rather than by V poses no threat to our discussion in Part I, where we assumed for simplicity that subject θ-role was assigned by the verb. While the character of the semantic role assigned to the subject is determined compositionally by the various constituents of the VP, as Chomsky and Marantz argue, whether or not *some* θ-role is assigned depends on the verb alone. Since our discussion only aimed to express assignment versus non-assignment of θ-role, the simplification was inconsequential (cf. Note 8, ch. 1).

If the VP-movement formulation meets certain desiderata, Kayne's formulation, involving movement of a string *V-NP* is correspondingly problematic. Under his analysis, movement applies to non-constituents and brings about questionable structural alterations. In particular, the NP which is moved along with the verb will no longer be, after movement, in any reasonable sense, the direct object of that verb, since the VP that dominated both is left behind. Concurrently, certain θ-roles fail to be assigned at S-structure: an embedded direct object will fail to be assigned θ-role to the extent that, in S-structure, it is no longer a dependent of the embedded verb, and an embedded subject will fail to be assigned a θ-role to the extent that it is the whole VP, compositionally, that assigns such θ-role, since that VP has been decomposed. It will also be unclear if and how θ-role can be assigned to stranded indirect objects.

Some of these difficulties may seem ‘overcome by postulating, along the lines of Quicoli (1980), the existence of an intermediate projection of V, $\overline{V}$, dominating verb and direct object if any, to which movement applies. But the latter approach has its share of problems. Consider a VP of the type *write a letter to John*, under the analysis in question, i.e. (41).

(41) $[_{\overline{\overline{V}}} [_{\overline{V}} \text{write a letter}]$ to John$]$

The idea that $\overline{V}$ of (41) is moved would correctly provide for assignment of θ-role to the direct object, since this would be governed by the verb at all levels. But it would be problematic with respect to assignment of θ-role both to the subject and to the indirect object. Subject θ-role would fail to be assigned at S-structure, for the same reasons that it would fail under Kayne's formulation, that is because the VP ($\overline{\overline{V}}$) is scattered at S-structure. As for the indirect object θ-role, this would fail to be assigned at S-structure to the extent that it is the verb that assigns it (the verb would govern the indirect object in (41) under the extended notion of c-command of I.0.3), since the verb is no longer there at S-structure. On the other hand, one might hold the view that it is $\overline{V}$ rather than V that assigns θ-role to the indirect object. θ-role could then be assigned at S-structure via the trace of $\overline{V}$. But this view would in effect be claiming that the semantic role of an indirect object is determined compositionally by the $\overline{V}$, a claim that would seem to us rather questionable. One has no sense that *to John* has a different semantic role in (41) than for example in *write to John*.[13]

We therefore suggest that the correct formulation of the rule operating in FI constructions is VP-movement, and that cases like (33a): *Farò scrivere Giovanni a Maria* are derived via a late reordering rule of the type we discussed in 1.8 above.[14] As for the fact that indirect objects are difficult to cliticize, while we will not have a completely satisfactory solution to propose, we will now consider a possible account compatible with VP-movement.

Note that, although we rejected Kayne's solution, some aspects of it can hardly be incorrect. In particular, the idea that the embedded subject plays a role in blocking cliticization of dative objects is supported (aside from Kayne's arguments) by the fact that in the *Faire-par* construction, which we claim involves a subjectless VP, dative objects cliticize unproblematically, as we will see. Also, the relationship between the failure of datives to cliticize and their occurrence to the right of the embedded subject which Kayne's theory captures, is emphasized by the fact that Italian, which differs from French in marginally allowing cliticization of the dative (cf. (30), (31)), also seems to differ in allowing the dative to the left of the embedded subject more freely (cf. (33b)).

Let us suppose, then, that the output of VP-movement when the embedded verb has an indirect object (e.g. (33b) *Farò [scrivere a Maria] Giovanni*) is anomalous because a dative (the object) precedes an accusative (the embedded subject) whereas in general accusatives precede datives, and that a late rule moving the dative to the right suffices to rectify this anomaly. Suppose further, as seems natural, that clitics can be related only to θ-positions, and thus not to positions that arise via reordering. We would then correctly predict that reordering should inhibit cliticization, and we will in fact expect stronger ungrammaticality from cliticization of the dative where reordering appears more strongly required, as in French versus Italian. We would also correctly predict that, if the embedded subject were dative rather than accusative, no reordering would occur, and would thus account for the interpretation of (34): *Jean fait porter une lettere à Marie à Paul*, which was unaccounted for in Kayne's discussion.[15]

It would remain to account for the non-ambiguity of (28) repeated here below as (42), namely for the fact that in such cases the dative clitic is interpreted as the subject rather than as an object of the embedded verb.

(42)   Paul **lui** fera porter ces livres à sa femme.
        Paul will make him take these books to his wife.

Recall the conclusion reached in 4.1.2 above that an embedded accusative object neutralizes the accusative-assigning properties of the matrix verb. This conclusion was motivated by the fact that in the presence of an embeeded accusative object the embedded subject, which structurally is an object of the matrix verb, appears in the dative (cf. discussion of (14) above). Suppose now that dative is simply another Case, like accusative (along the lines of Note 2), and that, as with accusatives, an embedded dative object neutralizes the ability of the matrix verb to assign dative. This would predict that cases like (43) could not exist, since the embedded subject would fail to receive dative Case.

(43) .   Paul fera [$_{VP}$ porter ces livres à sa femme] [$_S$ à son fils − − −]
          Paul will make his son take these books to his wife.

This prediction is only partially correct since cases like (43) are accepted by some speakers (cf. the discussion of (34) above). We can then assume that what is true categorically for accusatives is true for datives only as a tendency. What would be needed at this point is to assume in addition that the tendency strengthens to an absolute requirement if the first dative in (43) (object) is cliticized, thus accounting for the non-ambiguity of (42), and weakens to no requirement at all when the second dative (subject) is cliticized, thus accounting for the well-formedness of (42). Notice that at least the first part of the assumption is perfectly natural. In fact, since we regard clitics as a spell-out of the Case-marking property of the verb, it is reasonable to assume that an embedded dative object neutralizes the ability of the matrix verb to assign dative more strongly when it is cliticized on that verb than otherwise.[16]

This kind of approach (inspired in part by the cited work in progress of E. Wehrli's)[17] seems to me rather plausible although, as we have seen, questions remain. One further residual question concerns the difference between datives and other indirect objects, for which we have no account. As we saw this was problematic in FS as well. (For further facts, and discussion of cliticization of indirect objects in the FI construction, see Rouveret and Vergnaud (1980).)

In this section we have argued that in the FI construction, the underlying structure is characterized by a sentential complement to which S-deletion applies. *Fare* and the other verbs that appear in this construction are thus verbs of class I in (2) of II.0.2 above. We have argued that a syntactic rule applies to such underlying structures, moving the embedded VP out of the complement. We have defended our formulation against the view that only portions of the embedded VP are moved. We will return to the FI construction and its exact derived structure in 4.3 below, where we discuss its similarities with the *Faire-par* construction. The latter construction is the topic of the next section.

4.2. FAIRE-PAR

4.2.0. *Introduction*

Superficially, instances of the *Faire-par* (FP) construction like (1a) above: *Maria ha fatto riparare la macchina da Giovanni* are very similar to instances of FI discussed in the previous section. They differ only in that the semantic subject of the infinitival is preceded here by the preposition **da** 'by', whereas in corresponding FI constructions it is preceded by **a** 'to', as we have seen. Such superficial similarity is accompanied by a number of similarities at a more formal level. However, Kayne has shown (FS, 3.5) that there are also fundamental differences between the two constructions, and in particular that the infinitival complement in FP differs from that of FI in having many of the properties of passive sentences, which of course suggests that the presence of *by*-phrases in these constructions is not accidental.

In the first of the subsections that follow, we present our analysis of the FP construction, the one we anticipated in 4.0 above. In the other two, we examine certain ramifications that this analysis has. Later in the chapter we will consider both the similarities and the differences between FI and FP, including the facts noted by Kayne. We will also argue that certain cases, which have always been analyzed as instances of FI, must rather be regarded as analogous to FP constructions.

4.2.1. *Base-generation*

As we discussed in 3.1.3, the possibility that the 'thematic subject' of a verb may be represented by a *by*-phrase depends on whether θ-role is assigned to the subject position. If it is, then the role of thematic-subject must be played by an argument in subject position. If it is not, then a *by*-phrase can appear. Within the framework we have adopted, there will be two cases in which assignment of θ-role to the subject position by a $+\theta_s$ verb fails: (i) if the verb has passive morphology, in which case failure of θ-role assignment reflects a property of the morphology, and (ii) if there is no subject position, in which case, the assignment of θ-role is simply impossible. Precisely in these two cases, we will then predict that a *by*-phrase with the value of thematic-subject could be found. Structures like α in (44), in which such a *by*-phrase occurs with the active form of the verb, will thus readily lend themselves to being analyzed as instances of the second case, namely as VP structures.

(44)   Maria fa [$_\alpha$riparare la macchina (da Giovanni)].
         Maria has the car repaired (by Giovanni).

The analysis of the FP construction as involving a base-generated VP complement is formally the simplest. We will attempt to show that it is also the most adequate empirically. An analysis of this kind was also proposed in Strozer (1976).

Within the evolution of EST, such an analysis of FP becomes possible as soon as the *by*-phrase of passives is base-generated rather than being derived by rightward movement ('agent-postposing'). The first time the rule of agent-postposing is explicitly abandoned in Chomsky's work, I believe is Chomsky and Lasnik (1977), where it is assumed that passives are base-generated with an empty subject position. Among other researchers, the assumption that *by*-phrases are base-generated appears for example in Bresnan (1972), and Hornstein (1977), while for example Fiengo (1977) (1980), Jackendoff (1977), Rouveret and Vergnaud (1980) (appeared in manuscript form in 1978) assume a rule of agent-postposing. If *by*-phrases are base-generated, then α in (44) *can* be a VP. The question is whether it *must*. From the fact (which can be easily shown) that the embedded verb in FP can take any type of complement it may be subcategorized for, it is clear that α is not less than a VP. The remaining question is then whether it could be an S. The answer to this is no.

It could not be the case that α is an S in S-structure since there are no SSC effects in S-structure, as shown in (45).

(45)   Maria la$_i$ fa [$_\alpha$riparare [$_i$e] (da Giovanni)].
        Maria has it repaired (by Giovanni).

One might suggest that perhaps VP-movement has applied in (45), and that the complement was an S in D-structure. But this cannot be, since there are no SSC effects in D-structure either. Consider (46a) contrasting with (46b).[18]

(46) a.   Maria si$_i$ è fatta [$_\alpha$accusare [$_i$e] (da Giovanni)].
           Maria had herself accused (by Giovanni).

     b.   *Maria si$_i$ è fatta [$_{VP}$accusare [$_i$e]] [$_S$a Giovanni − − −].
           Maria had Giovanni accuse herself.

In 4.1.4 above, we argued that the FI case in (46b) was ruled out because the relation between *si* and its *ec* would violate the SSC in D-structure (recall that a derivation via Clitic Climbing is excluded.) But since (46a) is grammatical, we must conclude that here *si* can be locally related to its *ec* in D-stucture unproblematically.[19] The fact that (46a) is grammatical whether or not the *by*-phrase is present confirms our claim that the variant in which neither *a* NP, nor *da* NP appears (i.e. (1b) above) is a subcase of FP and not of FI.

Another consideration that points to the conclusion that α in (44) is not an S is that a subject of α would be impossible to characterize within the existing typology of empty elements. Let us consider first the subcase in which there is a *by*-phrase. A subject of α could not have a θ-role. when the *by*-phrase appears, since the role of thematic-subject would be played by that phrase. Then one would have to explain why an active verb fails to assign subject θ-role precisely here, and never in other cases. Assuming for the sake of discussion that one could provide such an explanation, the subject of α would then be a non-argument. But non-argument subjects in Italian are quite generally linked with a post verbal NP or S, whereas here we find cases in which no such NP or S exists, as with **Giovanni fa [$_\alpha$telefonare a Maria da Piero]** 'Giovanni has Maria phoned (to) by Piero' involving intransitive *telefonare*. Furthermore, a non-argument subject could not be an instance of PRO, since PRO never occurs as a non-argument, and not even as a 'quasi' argument, whatever the exact theoretical reasons cf. *[PRO to rain] would be fun.* Therefore

such a subject would presumably have to be an *ec* linked with the infinitival inflection (cf. Note 23, ch. 2). It would also have to be Case-marked,
since non-argument subjects always are (again, for whatever reasons). But
if the subject position is thus a non-θ-position and Case-marked, we will
incorrectly predict that the object could move into such a position, to
produce for example *Maria fa [$_a$la macchina$_i$ riparare t$_i$ da Giovanni].
While the latter derivation might conceivably be blocked if (somehow)
VP-movement *must* apply to a, VP-movement itself would then give rise
to a problem, in that the required relation between the null subject and
the infinitival inflection would fail to obtain at S-structure. The existence
of a subject in the presence of a *by*-phrase is therefore ruled out
altogether.

Let us now consider the case in which the *by*-phrase does not appear.
In such a case, if the subject of a is not assigned a θ-role, all of the
above considerations relative to the presence of a *by*-phrase will apply. If
it is assigned a θ-role, we presume it would be PRO since there is no
antecedent for a trace, and an *ec* linked with inflection would incorrectly
predict a pronominal reading, as with NS sentences. If a in (44) had a
PRO subject, we would expect it to be controlled by the matrix subject
Maria, since 'arbitrary' PRO (PRO$_{arb}$) never occurs when there is a
possible local controller, unless the complement is an indirect question
(see Manzini (1983)). However, the subject of a is plainly not controlled
by *Maria*, the interpretation 'Maria causes herself to repair the car' being
impossible (cf. (9) above). We would thus have to admit a unique case of
PRO$_{arb}$ occurring in the environment of controlled PRO. Yet a subject
of a could not be PRO$_{arb}$ either, since PRO$_{arb}$ cannot be the subject of
a weather verb, cf. *To stay/*To rain would be fun*, while a can contain
such a verb, as in (47).[20]

> (47)   Con questa tecnologia, riusciranno   a far   [$_a$ piovere]
>   *with this technology   (they) will manage to make   (it) rain*

Notice further that if a had a PRO subject only in the absence of the
by-phrase, we would expect radically different behavior depending on
whether the *by*-phrase appears or not. But this is not the case. The fact is
that a in (44) can never contain a phrase anaphoric to the 'subject',
whether or not a *by*-phrase is present, as shown in (48).

> (48)   *Fa [invitare una ragazza ciascuno$_i$ (dai tuoi amici$_i$)]
>   *Have one girl each$_i$ invited (by your friends$_i$).*

The only possible explanation for this is that (44) does not have a PRO
subject, in either variant. Infinitival complements in other constructions
differ from a in this respect, as in (49).

> (49)   Bisognerebbe [PRO$_i$ invitare una ragazza ciascuno$_i$]
>   *It would be necessary to invite one girl each.*

The difference between (48) and (49) will follow from assuming that, while at the relevant level of representation α does not have a subject, other infinitivals do, as indicated in (49). It is for this reason that in general infinitivals will not allow the *by*-phrase with the active form of the verb, whereas α does.

We conclude that α in (44) does not have a subject at any level, namely that it is a base-generated VP. Our conclusion rests in essence on the following arguments:

(i) A subject of α appears impossible to characterize as an *ec*, since its properties would not correspond to those of any of the established types of *ec*'s.

(ii) Phrases anaphoric to the subject are impossible.

(iii) There are neither S-structure, nor D-structure SSC effects.

4.2.2. *Thematic Subject*

In this subsection, we note how the distribution of *by*-phrases in the FP construction provides evidence for the distinction between ergative and intransitive verbs, although it is not entirely accounted for by our discussion.

In English passives, the *by*-phrase occurs only with transitive verbs, or more accurately with verbs that take either an NP object or an S complement. This does not reflect a constraint on the occurrence of the *by*-phrase itself. Rather, it has to do with constraints on passive constructions in English. We recall from 3.2.2 above that in English the non-θ subject position of passives will either be filled by a preposed object, or by a pleonastic element, and that insertion of a pleonastic element requires the presence of a post verbal argument. In the case of the FP construction, since there is no subject position, there will be no constraints of this sort. Consider the D-structures in (50), exemplifying the three basic classes of verbs.

(50) a. Giovanni [VP legge il libro]   (Transitive)
     Giovanni   reads the book

b. Giovanni [VP telefona   a Maria]   (Intransitive)
   Giovanni   telephones to Maria

c. [e] [VP va   Giovanni alla festa]   (Ergative)
       goes Giovanni to the party

Unlike ergatives, transitive and intransitive verbs assign thematic-subject role. Correspondingly, in their active forms they will assign θ-role to the subject position. (Again, for simplicity we assume that V, rather than VP assigns subject θ-role.) From this, the D-structures in (50) follow.

As we discussed before, the thematic-subject role can be played by a
by-phrase provided that no θ-role is assigned to the subject position. If
we now imagine embedding each of the VPs in (50) under *fare* we
expect, since there will be no subject position, that we may find *by*-
phrase counterparts to the phrase *Giovanni* of (50a,b), but not to that of
(50c). This is correct, as (51) shows.

(51) a. Farò   [vp leggere il   libro da Giovanni]
         (I) will make   read   the book by Giovanni

    b. Farò   [vp telefonare a   Maria da Giovanni]
        (I) will make   telephone   to Maria by Giovanni

    c. *Farò   [vp andare alla   festa da Giovanni]
        (I) will make   go   to the party by Giovanni

The case in (51c) is impossible because in (50c) *Giovanni* does not have
the role of thematic-subject but rather that of direct object, and direct
objects are never realized as *by*-phrases. What we rather expect with
ergative verbs, is that the VP of (50c) should occur under *fare* as is, as in
Farò [vp *andare Giovanni alla festa*]. This is correct, as we see in 4.5.

The distribution of *by*-phrases in the FP construction thus provides
further evidence for the distinction between ergative and intransitive
verbs. This evidence is somewhat parallel to that provided by impersonal
passives, which we discussed in 3.2.2.[21] Impersonal passives show that
passive morphology is not universally limited to transitive verbs, though
it is universally limited to non-ergative verbs, just like *by*-phrases.[22]

We may note that the contrast between (51b,c) also provides evidence
for a non-syntactic derivation (i.e. for base-generation) of *by*-phrases.
For, a syntactic derivation would require that the complements in (51)
have subjects, so as to derive (51a,b), but if they did, then nothing
would prevent derivation of (51c) from the well-formed intermediate
structure *Farò* [*Giovanni*$_i$ *andare t*$_i$ *alla festa*], on a par with (51b).

Although it is clear that the *by*-phrase is never possible with ergative
verbs, and that its occurrence is not limited to transitives as our theory
predicts, residual questions remain regarding its exact distribution over
the class of intransitive verbs. In general, the *by*-phrase seems possible
only if some object is present, as shown by the contrast between (52)
and (53).

(52) a.   Farò   [scrivere a Maria   da Giovanni]
         (I) will make   write   to Maria by Giovanni

    b. ?Questo farà   [parlare di voi da tutti]
       this   will make   talk   of you by everyone

(53) * Farò [{ lavorare / camminare / studiare } da Piero]

(*I*) *will make* { *work* / *walk* / *study* } *by Piero*

While it remains unclear how this fact is to be accounted for, we note that without the *by*-phrase, intransitives occur rather freely in FP as we predict, and as shown in (54).

(54) a. Farò [scrivere a Maria]
      (*I*) *will make write *to Maria

   I will have Maria written to.

   b. Questo farà [parlare di voi]
      this will make talk about you

   This will have you talked about.

   c. In quella scuola fanno [{ lavorare / studiare } molto]

      in that school (they) make { *work* / *study* } *much*

   In that school they make you work/study a lot.

   d. Per terapia fanno [camminare]
      for therapy (they) make walk

   As a therapy they make you talk.

   e. Questo fa [ridere]
      this makes laugh

   This is funny.

4.2.3. *On the 'Transformational' Approach*

In this subsection, we first briefly compare the account of passivization provided by the current theoretical model, with the earlier, single rule account of passivization. We then consider the theory of FP proposed in FS. We will argue that the differences between Kayne's theory and ours reflect limitations of the earlier theoretical framework. (Some of our discussion will be similar to that of Jaeggli (1981), as well as closely related to that of LGB, 2.7.)

In the Standard Theory (ST), passivization was attributed to a rule which simultaneously caused three changes: (i) creation of the *by*-phrase (via 'agent postposing'); (ii) introduction of passive morphology; and (iii) movement of the object into subject position (cf. I.0.3). The ST account of passivization is inferior to that of the EST and of the GB theory in particular, in two, related, respects: it provides no explanation for why the three above phenomena cluster, when they do; and it does not allow for the occurrence of such phenomena in isolation. The EST/GB account does provide an explanation for the clustering, and correspondingly allows for occurrence of those phenomena in isolation. Thus, in *John$_i$ was invited t$_i$ (by Bill)*, movement of the phrase *John* is accounted for in terms of the need for such a phrase to receive Case. This allows for the lack of movement where an alternative means of assigning Case may exist. Thus, in Italian, which has a productive inversion strategy, Case can be transmitted to a post verbal NP and movement is unnecessary, as in *Fu invitato Giovanni (da Mario)*.[23] The *by*-phrase in the earlier example *John$_i$ was invited t$_i$ (by Bill)* is possible because no θ-role is assigned to the subject position. This allows for the occurrence of the *by*-phrase in other cases in which assignment of θ-role to the subject position may fail, as in FP. The three properties of English passives are therefore distributed, in the three cases of (55), as indicated.

(55)

	Movement	(by NP)	Passive Morphology
a. John$_i$ was invited (by Bill)	yes	yes	yes
b. Fu invitato Giovanni (da Mario)	no	yes	yes
c. FP construction	no	yes	no

There are other cases in which the three properties of (55a) fail to cluster. For example, we know that NP-movement can occur in isolation with Raising and ergative verbs, as well as with the SI-construction of 1.6 above. Consider further the FI and FP cases here below.

(56) a.   Farà   [$_{VP}$riparare la macchina] [$_{SA}$ Giovanni $---$]
           (*he*) *will make*   *repair   the car   to Giovanni*

    b.   Farà   [$_{VP}$riparare la   macchina (da Giovanni)]
          (*he*) *will make*   *repair   the car   (by Giovanni*)

Both (56a, b) can be passivized with movement of the embedded object into matrix subject position, as in (57).[24]

(57) a. La macchina$_i$ sarà fatta   [$_{VP}$riparare t$_i$] [$_{SA}$ Giovanni $---$]
         the car   will be made   repair   to Giovanni

   .b. La macchina$_i$ sarà fatta   [$_{VP}$ riparare t$_i$ (da Giovanni)]
        the car   will be made   repair   (by Giovanni)

If we now consider the embedded verb in each of (57a,b), we find that (57a) is a case in which NP-movement has applied, while neither passive morphology nor the *by*-phrase appears (of course there could be a *by*-phrase associated with the matrix verb, which has passive morphology.) This case is therefore as characterized in (58a). As for (57b), it represents a case in which (again, with respect to the embedded verb) NP-movement has occurred, a *by*-phrase is present, while there is no passive morphology, thus as in (58b).

(58)

	Movement	(by NP)	Passive Morphology
a. Cases like (57a)	yes	no	no
b. Cases like (57b)	yes	yes	no

The only direct dependency that our framework predicts is one between passive morphology and the optional *by*-phrase, with the former always implying the latter (though not the opposite).[25] It is easy to verify that all of the combinations which are logically possible given this one dependency are instantiated by the empirical facts we have just reviewed. Note that within the ST characterization of passive, which associates NP-movement with passive morphology directly and necessarily, there would be no explanation for why in (57a,b), while movement occurs over two verbs, passive morphology affects only one and not the other or both, a fact which does find adequate explanation within our framework. Thus we know that what makes movement into subject position possible is the non assignment of θ-role to that position, and assignment of θ-role to the matrix subject position will fail here if and only if the *matrix* verb has passive morphology. The embedded verb is irrelevant.

The analysis of the FP construction in FS differs from ours in that it assumes that the complement is underlyingly sentential. It also differs from ours in that it does not quite assimilate the *by*-phrase to that of passives. These two aspects are relatively independent, but they both reflect the ST framework that underlies Kayne's discussion. Let us consider each one of these differences, in order.

With regard to the constituency of the infinitival complement, there is no possibility in Kayne's discussion of analyzing the complement as a base-generated VP, since in ST *by*-phrases are derived via rightward movement from subject position. Kayne's analysis of FP is indeed the simplest, given this premise, since it postulates precisely a sentential complement to which rightward movement of the subject applies, giving rise to the *by*-phrase, and nothing else. But there are several disadvantages of such an analysis compared with ours. Leaving aside the fact that rightward movement would leave a not properly bound trace, a con-

sideration which is internal to our theory, we note in particular that this
analysis does not permit an account of the difference between FI and FP
with respect to the distribution of reflexive clitics illustrated by (46),
since both constructions would now involve sentential complements. It
would also not exclude *by*-phrases with ergative verbs, as we noted in the
discussion of (51) above. Other disadvantages will be pointed out in 4.4
below.[26]

Turning to the second difference between Kayne's analysis and ours,
namely the relation between the *by*-phrase of FP and that of passives,
Kayne assumes that there are two transformations: Passive, involving
formation of the *by*-phrase (via Agent Postposing), insertion of passive
morphology, and object preposing; and *Faire-par*, involving only formation of the *by*-phrase. Thus the *by*-phrase of passives, and that of FP are
produced by two different, though partially similar, processes. This is an
obvious weakness, given Kayne's extensive and convincing discussion of
the similarities between passives and FP. This weakness arises from the
inability of the ST framework to separate the three properties of passives,
as is rather clear from Kayne's own discussion (cf. FS, p. 250—1).

4.3. SIMILARITIES BETWEEN FI AND FP

Under our analyses of FI and FP, these two constructions have different
derivations, but they have rather similar S-structures: in both cases *fare*
has a VP-complement at S-structure. In this section, we consider some
facts which seem to bear out this similarity between the two derived structures, such as the overall pattern of cliticization. We will also consider
from a theoretical perspective the process of Clitic Climbing, namely the
process which we are claiming moves clitics onto the higher verb.

As we have seen, objects of the embedded verb in general cliticize to
the main verb in both FI and FP, as in (59).

(59) a. La$_i$ farò [$_{VP}$ riparare [$_i$ e]] [$_S$ a Giovanni − − −]
         I will make Giovanni repair it.

     b. La$_i$ farò [$_{VP}$ riparare [$_i$ e] (da Giovanni)]
         I will have it repaired (by Giovanni).

As we saw in 4.1.4, the clitic in (59a) (FI) must be base-generated on the
lower verb and then undergo Clitic Climbing (Cl-Cl), so as to be locally
related to the *ec* at all levels. For (59b) (FP), we expect two different
derivations to be possible: base-generation on the lower verb plus Cl-Cl,
as in (59a), and base-generation on the higher verb. Either derivation
would allow the clitic to be locally related to the *ec* at all levels. We
note that, while postulating a Cl-Cl derivation for the FP case may seem
unnecessary, certain empirical facts suggest that it is indeed available, in

particular the fact that cliticization on the lower verb, as in ?? *Farò riparerla* (*da Giovanni*) gives rise to the same mild ungrammaticality as the corresponding FI case ?? *Farò riparerla a Giovanni*. As we saw in 4.1.4, such mild ungrammaticality is characteristic of the failure of Cl-Cl to occur, whereas appearance on the lower verb of clitics that cannot be base-generated on that verb gives rise to more severe ill-formedness.

Most of the literature on this topic, while providing some explanation for why clitics *can* appear on the higher verb in these constructions, provides no explanation for why they *must*. For example, in the FS system, the higher position of object clitics results from a particular formulation of the Clitic Placement rule, which requires that the verb onto which clitics are placed must be to the immediate right of an NP (cf. FS, p. 201). This has a certain empirical adequacy, but is of no explanatory force, in that the requirement that the target verb be adjacent to an NP is given no independent justification, theoretical or empirical.[27] Our account will not fare much better in this respect, as we will also fail to provide an explanatory account of Cl-Cl. We will however attempt to relate this phenomenon to other properties of these constructions.

The facts relative to cliticization are not entirely identical in the two constructions, and it seems to us that the divergence reflects the structural differences which we have already established, and that no further difference is thereby motivated. One of the differences concerns reflexive clitics, as in (46) above, and in the following.

(60) a. *Maria si$_i$ fa [$_{VP}$ accusare [$_i$e]] [$_S$ a Giovanni − − −]
   Maria has Giovanni accuse herself.

   b. Maria si$_i$ fa [$_{VP}$ accusare[$_i$e] (da Giovanni)]
   Maria has herself accused (by Giovanni).

As we pointed out in 4.2.1, this difference follows from the fact that (60b) is base-generated, whereas (60a) is derived by VP-movement.

Another difference concerns cliticization of dative objects, which is problematic in the FI construction as we saw above and as in (61), but not in the FP construction, represented here by (62).

(61) a. ?Gli$_i$ faccio telefonare [$_i$e] Giovanni.
   I will make Giovanni phone (to) him.

   b. ??Gli$_i$ fecero sparare addosso [$_i$e] un agente.
   They had an agent fire upon (to) him.

   c. ??Gli$_i$ fecero sparare tra i piedi [$_i$e] un agente.
   They had an agent fire between the feet to him (his feet).

(62) a. Gli$_i$ faccio telefonare [$_i$e] (da Giovanni)
   I will have him phoned (by Giovanni).

b. Gli$_i$ fecero sparare addosso [$_i$e] (da un agente).
    They had him fired upon (by an agent).

c. Gli$_i$ fecero sparare tra i piedi[$_i$e] (da un agente).
    They had him fired (at) between the feet (by an agent).

To the extent that in 4.1.5 above we failed to provide a precise understanding of the difficulty in (61), we will not be able to provide a precise
understanding of the difference between (61) and (62). However, it
seems reasonable to suppose that this difference too reflects something
we already know about these constructions, and not something new. For
example, the difference would follow from our tentative account of (61)
based on the idea that the dative and accusative arguments are not in
their relative canonical positions (cf. 4.1.5), there being no accusative
argument in (62). We will thus take the basic cliticization facts to be the
same in both constructions.

Another respect in which FI and FP exhibit analogous behavior
concerns the rule of past participle (pp) agreement of 1.7 above.
Consider (63).

(63) a. **La$_i$** ho fatta [$_{VP}$ riparare [$_i$e]] [$_S$ a Giovanni − − −]
         I have made Giovanni repair it.

b. **La$_i$** ho fatta [$_{VP}$ riparare [$_i$e] (da Giovanni)]
    I have had it repaired (by Giovanni).

Our rule of pp agreement prescribes that a pp will agree with an
antecedent to its direct object (cf. (86b), chapter 1). In both (63a) and
(63b) the pp of the main verb *fare* agrees with the feminine singulra clitic
la, which is the antecedent to the object of the embedded verb. Pp agreement thus suggests that in these constructions a direct object of the
embedded verb is also a direct object of the matrix verb. The same
results obtain when the antecedent is a moved NP rather than a clitic, as
in (64) and (65) (analogous to (57) above).[28]

(64) a. **La macchina$_i$** fu fatta   [$_{VP}$ riparare t$_i$]   [$_S$ a Giovanni −−−]
         the car   *was made*   *to repair*   *to Giovanni*

b. **La macchina$_i$** fu fatta   [$_{VP}$ riparare t$_i$ (da Giovanni)]
    the car   *was made*   *to repair*   (*by Giovanni*)

(65) a. **La macchina$_i$** si era fatta [$_{VP}$ riparare t$_i$] [$_S$ a Giovanni − − −]
         the car   *SI had made*   *to repair*   *to Giovanni*

    We made Giovanni repair the car.

b. **La macchina$_i$** si era fatta   [$_{VP}$ riparare t$_i$ (da Giovanni)]
    the car   *SI had made*   *to repair*   (*by Giovanni*)

    We had the car repaired (by Giovanni).

In all cases in (64), (65), the matrix pp *fatta* agrees with the NP *la macchina*, which is the antecedent to the direct object of the embedded verb.[29] Notice that the very fact that in both the passives of (64) and the SI-constructions of (65) NP-movement can apply analogously to FI and FP, emphasizes the structural similarity between the two constructions.

If, with respect to pp agreement, a direct object is defined as the NP governed by the verb, as we assumed in 1.7 above (cf. (87b), ch. 1), then in both FI and FP the matrix verb must govern embedded objects. This conclusion can be drawn independent of pp agreement, on the basis of ergative complements of *fare*. As we will argue in 4.5 below, ergative verbs appear, along with their direct object, in VP complements of *fare*, just like transitive verbs, as for example in (66).

(66)   Maria fa [$_{VP}$intervenire Giovanni]
        Maria makes Giovanni intervene.

Since we know that ergative verbs do not assign Case (cf. 3.1), the direct object of the ergative verb in these cases, e.g. *Giovanni* in (66), will have to be assigned Case by *fare*, which implies that *fare* governs the object of the embedded verb in these structures. We put aside for the moment the difficulty created by postulating government across the VP boundary, which conflicts with the definition of government of I.0.3 (since VP is a maximal projection).

Our discussion up to this point has suggested several ways in which an embedded object in the FI and FP constructions is also an object of the matrix verb. One is pp agreement, as in (63), (64), (65). Another is Case assignment, assuming that *fare* assigns Case to *Giovanni* in (66). A third is what we may call CASE ABSORPTION. With this we will refer to the fact, discussed in 4.1.2 and 4.1.5 above, that an accusative or a dative embedded object appears to neutralize the ability of the matrix verb to assign accusative or dative even if the embedded verb is one that *can* assign such accusative or dative (unlike *intervenire* of (66) which cannot assign accusative). Recall here how the embedded subject in FI, which is assigned Case by the matrix verb, cannot be assigned accusative if there is an accusative embedded object (cf. (14) above and discussion) and the somewhat analogous effect with dative embedded objects (cf. discussion of (43) above). Intuitively, one has a sense that Clitic Climbing is also part of this cluster of phenomena since the clitic appears in the position on the matrix verb normally reserved for its own (cliticized) object. Let us then list all of these phenomena, which we are taking to suggest that an embedded object is also a matrix object, as in (67).

(67) a. Clitic Climbing

  b. Past participle agreement

  c. Case assignment

  d. Case absorption

Of the phenomena in (67), while (a) and (b) obtain in both FI and FP, as we saw, each of the other two obtain only in one construction, but for principled reasons. Thus, (67c) can only arise in cases like (66) which are cases of FP. As for (67d) it is obviously only relevant to FI since the phenomenon of Case absorption concerns the ability of *fare* to assign Case to the embedded subject, and there is no embedded subject in FP. There is therefore, again, no motivation for postulating further structural differences between the two constructions. Notice also that, while (67c) is relative to FP and (67d) to FI, the two phenomena are clearly related conceptually, since (67c) refers to the fact that an embedded object *can* be assigned Case by the higher verb, and (67d) to the fact that, in a sense, it *must*, even in cases in which this would not seem necessary since the lower verb can also assign Case. Thus in effect (67d) subsumes (67c). We can then properly assume that, at a certain level of abstraction, (67) represents a cluster of phenomena common to both FI and FP, supporting our thesis that in derived structure main and embedded verb stand in the same relation in both constructions.

That the phenomena in (67) form a cluster, is also clear from certain interactions. Thus, we know that Cl-Cl may marginally fail. When it does, and only then, pp agreement will also fail, as in (68), to be compared with (63). (We take (68) to be ambiguously cases of FI or FP.)

(68) a.   ??Ho fatt**o** riparar**la** . . .   (no Cl-Cl; no ag't)

   b.   **La** ho fatt**o** riparare . . .   (Cl-Cl; no ag't)

   c.   **Ho fatta** riparar**la** . . .   (no Cl-Cl; ag't)

Like Cl-Cl, dative Case absorption can also marginally fail, so that marginally (or for some speakers) we have cases like (69) (analogous to (43) above), in which a dative object does not prevent the main verb from assigning dative to the embedded subject.

(69)   ??Faccio [$_{VP}$ scrivere una lettera a Giovanni] [$_S$ a Maria — — —]
           I will have Maria write a letter to Giovanni.

However, as we noted in 4.1.5, if the dative object cliticizes to the main verb, as in (70), the sentence is ungrammatical (in the reading of (69)), from which we infer that, if Cl-Cl occurs, dative absorption will not be allowed to fail.[30]

(70)   *Gli$_i$ faccio [$_{VP}$ scrivere una lettera [$_i$e]] [$_S$ a Maria — — —]
           I will have Maria write a letter to him.

Furthermore, to the extent that we assume a general correlation between clitics and Case assigning properties (cf. 4.1.4), we see a certain connection between (67a) and (67c, d). In fact it is tempting to simply deduce the Clitic Climbing phenomenon from Case absorption. That is to say, since we assume that clitics are generally a realization of the Case features of the verb, we could regard Cl-Cl as a reflex of the fact that a certain object is linked with the Case features, not only of the lower verb, but of the higher one as well (it could be linked with both simultaneously if a clitic that has climbed retained a connection with its original position, say by means of a trace). From this point of view, the fact that there is Clitic Climbing, but no Clitic 'Lowering' would simply follow from the asymmetry of the relation between the two verbs, that is, from the fact that the embedded verb is lower in the structure than the matrix verb (cf. the structures in (2), (3b) above). So, while Clitic Climbing would be due to the fact that the matix verb is in a position in which any dependent of the lower verb (embedded objects) can take Case from it, the lack of Clitic 'Lowering' and the ungrammaticality of ****Maria fa lavorarlo** 'Maria makes him work' in (21a) above would be due to the fact that the lower verb is not in a position in which dependents of the matrix verb (embedded subject) could take Case from it. I think this may turn out to be the right approach.

However, doubts and difficulties remain. For one thing, while accusative Cl-Cl can marginally fail, as in ??*Maria fa ripararla a Giovanni* of (21b) above, accusative Case absorption apparently cannot, so that the embedded subject will not appear, with a comparable degree of marginality, in the accusative, as in *Maria fa ripararla Giovanni, *Maria fa riparare la macchina Giovanni*. This is a difficulty for the view that (67d) implies (67a). Another difficulty is represented by Cl-Cl in restructuring constructions. In some restructuring cases, the main verb is a Raising verb and thus not a Case assigner, and yet Cl-Cl occurs, e.g. **Lo potrei leggere** 'I would be able to read it'. It would thus be unclear how Cl-Cl could follow from Case absorption in these cases. It would be analogously unclear how Cl-Cl could follow from Case absorption, for example, in the case of locative clitics, since there is little reason to assume that Case is assigned to locative phrases.

We will leave the theoretical problems posed by the cluster of phenomena in (67) unsolved. In summary, these problems present themselves as follows. While we can account for the fact that Clitic Climbing *can* occur exactly in these constructions and not with regular infinitival complements, we have no account of its near-obligatoriness. The problem of (67a) is not isolated however, since we also have no account of the Case absorption phenomena of (67d). That is, our theory provides no a-priori reason why Case could not be assigned to embedded objects solely by the embedded verb, without affecting the Case-assigning properties of the main verb. The problem posed by (67b,c) consists of the fact that they suggest government across VP boundaries, contrary to the general definition of government. As all of the phenomena in (67) appear related, either because they have something in common at a certain level of characterization, or because they appear to interact, it is plausible to suppose that the reasons why (67b,c) seem to invoke an exceptional notion of government may be related to the account of (67a,b). What ever accounts for the need for clitics to climb and for Case assignment by the lower verb to affect the main verb, could conceivably justify the exceptional government across VP boundaries. (Note that it would be difficult to argue that there are no VP boundaries, especially for the FP construction, given our discussion in 4.2. And if there are VP boundaries in FP, there seems little point in arguing it for the FI construction.) In the absence of an exact theoretical characterization, in further discussion we will continue to assume a largely descriptive characterization of the phenomena in (67), namely, that there is a phenomenon of Clitic Climbing ((67a)), that there is a dativization rule like (14) above ((67d)), and that objects of the embedded verb are objects of the matrix verb as well, with respect to Case assignment and pp agreement ((67c, d)).

The similarities between FI and FP that have been reviewed in this section concern: cliticization and movement of embedded objects, matrix past participle agreement, and certain Case dependencies between the matrix verb and embedded objects.[31]

4.4. SYNTACTIC SUBJECT

In this section we consider a certain class of differences between FI and FP, which we will argue follow from the fact that in FI the thematic (or semantic) subject is also a *syntactic* subject in the configurational sense, whereas in FP the thematic subject, being realized as a *by*-phrase, is not a syntactic subject configurationally. In this respect FP is analogous to passives, whereas FI is like active structures.

As we mentioned in 4.2.0, Kayne (FS, 3.5) notes a number of respects in which FP behaves like passive constructions, while FI resembles actives. We will try to show that a good portion of Kayne's observations fall precisely into the class of facts that our theory explains, although for some of his observations we will have no account.[32]

In the discussion of FI in 4.1 above, we noted that the (*a*) NP phrase of the latter construction functions like a subject of the embedded verb in three respects: (i) semantically; (ii) with respect to selectional restrictions; and (iii) in the role of antecedent. Considering now the *da* NP phrase of FP, we note that the latter appears to function like a subject of the embedded verb as in (i) and (ii) above, but not as in (iii). A *da* NP phrase in FP will function as a semantic subject and will satisfy selectional restrictions that the verb would impose on its subject, for the same reason that it does so in passives, namely because it fulfils the role of thematic-subject, and presumably because selectional restrictions are defined on the latter. But the NP in a *da NP* phrase, will never function as an antecedent, since it does not c-command any other phrase in the sentence.

Consider thus the difference between FI and FP in (71).

(71) a. Giovanni farà   [$_{VP}$invitare una ragazza ciascuno$_i$]
      Giovanni will make   invite   one girl   each

    [$_S$ ai suoi amici$_i$ – – –]
      to his friends

Giovanni will have his friends invite one girl each.

b. *Giovanni farà   [$_{VP}$invitare una ragazza ciascuno$_i$
     Giovanni will make   invite   one girl   each

   (dai suoi amici$_i$)]
   (by his friends)

Giovanni will have one girl each invited (by his friends).

The difference in (71) follows from our hypothesis of 3.3 that moved phrases can be reconstructed in LF. Reconstruction of the moved VP in (71a) will give rise to the structure [$_S$ (a) i suoi amici$_i$ invitare una ragazza ciascuno$_i$], so that the element *ciascuno* will have a proper (c-commanding) antecedent at LF, where we presume the relevant well-formedness conditions apply.[33] In contrast, in (71b) *ciascuno* will not have a proper antecedent at any level. The account of (71b) carries over straightforwardly to corresponding passive cases, which are equally ungrammatical, whether or not they involve NP-movement, as in (72).

(72) a. *Una ragazza ciascuno fu   invitata (dai suoi amici)
     one girl   each   was invited (by his friends)

b. *Fu   invitata una ragazza ciascuno (dai suoi amici)
    was invited one girl   each   (by his friends)

The difference between FI and FP illustrated by (71) is rather systematic, as we would expect, over the class of anaphoric expressions. Thus, we find it with respect to PRO, as in (73), reflexives like *se stesso* as in (74), and the reflexive adjective *proprio*, as in (75).

(73) a.   Ho fatto   [$_{VP}$ affermare [di **PRO**$_i$ averla vista]]
     (I) have made   claim   (of)   to have seen her

    [$_S$ a Giovanni$_i$ – – –]
      to Giovanni

I made Giovanni claim to have seen her.

    b. ?*Ho fatto   [$_{VP}$ affermare [di **PRO**$_i$ averla vista]
         (I) have made   *claim*   *(of)*   *to have seen her*

      (da Giovanni$_i$)]
      (by Giovanni)

      'I had it claimed to have seen her (by Giovanni)'.

(74) a.   Con le minacce, fecero   [$_{VP}$ accusare **se stesso**$_i$]
         with threats,   *(they) made*   *accuse*   *himself*

      [$_S$ a Giovanni$_i$ – – –]
      to Giovanni

      With threats, they made Giovanni accuse himself.

    b. *... fecero   [$_{VP}$ accusare **se stesso**$_i$ (da Giovanni$_i$)]
       ... (they) made   *accuse*   *himself*   *(by Giovanni)*

      ... they had himself accused (by Giovanni).

(75) a.   Faremo   [$_{VP}$ curare   i **propri**$_i$ interessi] [$_S$ ai nostri
         (we) will make   *take care of* *their own interests*   *to our*

      clienti$_i$ – – –]
      customers

      We will make our customers take care of their own interests.

    b. *Faremo   [$_{VP}$ curare   i **propri**$_i$ interessi (dai
       (we) will make   *take care of* *their own interests* *(by*

      nostri clienti$_i$)]
      our   customers)

      We will have their own interests taken care of (by our customers).

Again, the FI cases will be well-formed at LF after reconstruction. But since the *da NP* phrase is not a proper antecedent, the FP cases will be ill-formed, and so will the corresponding passives in (76).

    (76) a. *Fu affermato   [di **PRO**$_i$ averla vista]   (da Giovanni$_i$)
         (it) was claimed *(of)*   *to have seen her* *(by Giovanni)*

     b. *Fu accusato **se stesso**$_i$ (da Giovanni$_i$)
       was accused himself   *(by Giovanni)*

     c. *Saranno curati   i **propri**$_i$ interessi (dai nostri clienti$_i$)
       will be taken care of their own interests (by our   customers)

Note that both the FP cases in (73a) and the passive in (76a) improve, as we expect, with a tensed complement, which will not involve the anaphoric element PRO, as in **?Ho fatto affermare [che la avevi vista] (da Giovanni)** 'I had (it) claimed that you had seen her (by Giovanni)', **?È stato affermato [che la avevi vista] (da Giovanni)** 'It has been claimed that you had seen her (by Giovanni)'.

We now turn to the facts that Kayne discusses, using Italian examples closely equivalent to Kayne's. One of the cases Kayne presents involves possessives in certain idioms, as in (77).

(77) a. Cercherò di fare [$_{VP}$fare il **suo** mestiere] [$_S$a Giovanni − − −]
      (I) will try to make   do his job   to Giovanni

      I will try to have Giovanni do his job.

    b. *Cercherò di fare [$_{VP}$fare il **suo** mestiere (da Giovanni)]
      (I) will try to make   do his job   (by Giovanni)

      I will try to have his job done (by Giovanni).

It is clear that in idioms of this sort the possessive has an anaphoric character, cf. English *John lost his/*her cool.* The contrast in (77) will then be accounted for in the same fashion as the contrasts involving anaphoric elements in (72), (73) etc. Once again, the account of the FP case extends straightforwardly to the corresponding passive case ***Fu fatto il suo mestiere (da Giovanni)** 'Was done his job (by Giovanni)'.

Another one of Kayne's cases involves inalienable possessions, as in (78).

(78) a. Maria ha fatto [$_{VP}$alzare **la mano**] [$_S$a Giovanni − − −]
      Maria has made   raise the hand   to Giovanni

      Maria made Giovanni raise his hand.

    b.*Maria ha fatto [$_{VP}$alzare **la mano** (da Giovanni)]
      Maria has made   raise the hand (by Giovanni)

      Maria had his hand raised (by Giovanni).

This case too can be assimilated to the previous ones quite naturally. The view that phrases expressing inalienable possession are anaphoric to the possessor, beside seeming intuitively plausible, is supported by the fact, which Kayne himself notes (FS, 4.8), that the relation between the two falls under well-known locality conditions (the binding conditions of our framework): ***Maria$_i$ ha detto [che Giovanni alzasse la mano$_i$]** 'Maria said that Giovanni should raise her hand'. Again the passive ***Fu alzata la mano (da Giovanni)** 'Was raised his hand (by Giovanni)' patterns with the FP case as we predict.

Another case noted by Kayne concerns 'non-passivizable' idioms, of the type exemplified in (79), (80).

(79) a. Giovanni **fa** { **il furbo** / **il finto tonto** }.

Giovanni makes { *the smart one* / *the fake idiot* }.

Giovanni tries to be smart/plays dumb.

b. *{ **Il furbo** / **Il finto tonto** } **è fatto** (da Giovanni).

{ *the smart one* / *the fake idiot* } *is made* (*by Giovanni*).

(80) a. Molte famiglie **sbarcano il lunario**   in quel modo.
many   families   make it through the almanac in that way

Many families make ends meet that way.

b. ?*Il **lunario** era **sbarcato**   in quel modo (da molte
the almanac was made it through in that way   (by many

famiglie).
families).

Such idioms, too, discriminate between FI and FP with FP patterning like
passives as usual, as in (81), (82).

(81) a. Maria ha fatto [$_{VP}$ **fare** { **il furbo** / **il finto tonto** }] [$_S$ a Giovanni − − −]

Maria made Giovanni { *try to be smart* / *play dumb* }

b. *Maria ha fatto [$_{VP}$ **fare** { **il furbo** / **il finto tonto** } (da Giovanni)]

Maria had (*it*) { *tried to be smart* / *played dumb* } (*by Giovanni*)

(82) a. Ha fatto [$_{VP}$ **sbarcare il lunario**] [$_S$ a molte famiglie − − −]
He made many families make ends meet.

b. *Ha fatto [$_{VP}$ **sbarcare il lunario** (da molte famiglie)]
He had (*it*) *made ends meet* (*by many families*).

If we are to extend the account of the previous cases to these, we will
have to claim that with such idioms there is an anaphoric relation
between the subject and the idiomatic object. This does not seem too
unreasonable. In fact, in cases like (79), existence of some relation
between the subject and the idiomatic object (which is a predicative
phrase analogous to predicate nominals) is independently suggested by

the gender and number agreement between the two as shown by the feminine agreement in a comparable sentence with feminine subject: *Maria . . . la furba*. For cases like (80), one might assume that the object is inherently possessive, that is, that *il lunario* means 'one's *own* almanac'. Indeed, there does seem to be some general difference in meaning along these lines between nonpassivizable idioms like the one in (79) or **tirare le cuoia** 'pull the skin (i.e. die)' equivalent to English *kick the bucket* and passivizable idioms like **portare assistenza** 'bring assistance', English *take care*. If this view is correct, then the case in (80) reduces to the 'John lost his cool' type of case, and the contrast in (82) reduces to the one in (77).

We note that whether or not our account of cases like (79b), (80b) is correct, what our discussion (as well as Kayne's, in fact) firmly establishes is that the ungrammaticality of passives of nonpassivizable idioms, is not to be attributed to the application of NP-movement, since the corresponding FP cases are also ungrammatical. The FP cases also establish that passive morphology is not the cause of the ungrammaticality. That passives like (80b) do not violate some constraint on NP-movement can also be established by the fact that if NP-movement does not apply, results are equally ungrammatical, as in ***Era sbarcato il lunario in quel modo (da molte famiglie)** 'Was made it through the almanac (by many families)'. This point can be established even further by noting that if NP-movement applies to acceptable FI cases like (82a) in the manner of (83), results are still essentially acceptable.

(83) ?**Il lunario**$_i$ fu fatto [$_{VP}$**sbarcare** t$_i$ in quel modo]
       the almanac was made   to make it through in that way

      [$_S$a molte famiglie $--- $]
        to many families

      (*Approx*:) 'Ends were made to meet on the part of many families.'

As we discussed in 4.2.3 (cf. discussion of (57a) above), cases like (83) isolate one of the properties of English passives, namely NP-movement, as the embedded verb in (83) has neither passive morphology nor a *by*-phrase. If *Il lunario* in (83) is anaphoric to *molte famiglie* as we suggested, then the essential well-formedness of (83) will follow from a two-step reconstruction at LF: of the NP into its original position, and of the VP into its original position, yielding [(*a*) *molte famiglie*$_i$ . . . *il lunario*$_i$ . . .]. This whole discussion of (82a), relying on the evidence provided by (83) etc, and leading to the conclusion that NP-movement is not the cause of the ungrammaticality, can be essentially duplicated for all of the ungrammatical passives discussed above.[34]

This covers those differences between FI and FP noted by Kayne for which our theory provides an explanation. Note that there is no explanation in FS: only a conclusion that FP must be closely related to passives. Nor is any account along the lines of ours foreseeable within the FS framework. While in essence we take the crucial factor to be the syntactic derivation of FI (which allows reconstruction) versus the base-generation of FP, in FS both constructions are syntactically derived: FI by movement of V (NP), and FP by rightward movement of the subject[35]

For some of the facts Kayne notes however, we will have no account. One of these concerns sentences like **Jean quittera ma maison demain** 'Jean will leave my house tomorrow' which can occur as complements in FI, but which have neither passive nor FP counterparts. A relevantly analogous Italian case would possibly be **Giovanni ha lasciato il lavoro alle tre** 'Giovanni left work at three'. Another fact concerns cases like *John will run the 400 meter relay* whose passives, like *The 400 meter relay will be run by John* are deviant (cf. ... *by John, Mark, Bill and Bruce*). As Kayne points out, the FP versions are also deviant, whereas their FI counterparts are well-formed on a par with the simple active sentences. A further type of difference that we will not attempt to account for has to do with certain animacy constraints (cf. Note 8). Kayne notes that, with many verbs taking animate objects, FI is impossible or unnatural, whereas FP is unproblematic, as in (84) (Kayne's examples).

> (84) a. *Pierre a fait matraquer ce garçon à Jean-Jacques.
>   *Pierre made Jean-Jacques bludgeon that boy.*
>
>   b. Pierre a fait matraquer ce garçon par Jean-Jacques.
>   *Pierre had that boy bludgeoned by Jean-Jacques.*

He further notes that when the subject of the causative verb is inanimate, FP is often impossible, while FI is not, as in (85) (also Kayne's examples).

> (85) a. La famine a fait manger des rats aux habitants de la ville.
>   *The famine made the city's inhabitants eat rats.*
>
>   b. *La famine a fait manger des rats par les habitants de la ville.
>   *The famine had rats eaten by the city's inhabitants.*

In these two last sections, we have thus compared the syntactic behavior of the FI and FP constructions, considering separately similarities and differences. We have argued that the similarities reflect the partial equivalence of the two derived structures, while the differences reflect the different ways in which the thematic subject is realized.

4.5. ERGATIVE COMPLEMENTS OF *FARE*

4.5.0. *Introduction*

In 3.3 above, we argued that well-formedness could be achieved via reconstruction only for some anaphoric relations, not for others. On the one hand we have relations involving elements like *ciascuno* and PRO, which are only required to be well formed at LF. But on the other we have for example NP-trace relations, which must be well-formed at S-structure as well, to satisfy the θ-criterion and the projection principle, and for which reconstruction in LF is thus not sufficient.

If in the previous section we were right in claiming that reconstruction plays a role in FI, we should thus expect that, alongside of the constructions that can be successfully embedded in FI which we discussed, all of which involved anaphoric relations of the first type, there should be others, involving relations of the second type (e.g. NP-trace), which cannot be embedded. In this section and in the next, we argue that this is in fact the case, and that a considerable number of constructions fail to appear under *fare* for this reason.

One of the cases that involve NP-trace relations is of course that of ergative verbs. We thus predict that sentences containing ergative verbs could not be embedded in FI. On the other hand, since we have argued in connection with FP that *fare* is subcategorized for VP-complements, we will expect ergative verbs to appear in such complements, as for example in (86).

(86)   Maria fa   [$_{VP}$intervenire Giovanni]
        Maria makes   intervene   Giovanni

        Maria makes Giovanni intervene.

Our discussions of FI and FP will thus jointly make the prediction that ergative complements can only have the analysis of (86), and not that of (87).

(87)   Maria fa   [$_{VP}$intervenire t$_i$] [$_S$Giovanni$_i$ – – –]
        Maria makes   intervene   Giovanni

In this section, we try to show that this prediction is correct. Our arguments fall roughly into two groups, corresponding to each of the first two subsections that follow. Even before we turn to those argument however, we note that our account of the contrast in (17) above, repeated here in (88) provides in itself a rather good argument for our hypothesis.

(88) a. La sua espressione fa   [$_{VP}$sembrare [$_{sc}$Giovanni ammalato]]
         his expression   makes   seem   Giovanni sick

         His expression makes Giovanni seem sick.

     b. *La sua espressione fa   [$_{VP}$sembrare [$_S$Giovanni soffrire]]
         his expression   makes   seem   Giovanni to suffer

         His expression makes Giovanni seem to suffer.

As we discussed above, under the analyses given, the contrast in (88) follows from the hypothesis that S boundaries, unlike sc boundaries, always block Case assignment in Italian, a hypothesis for which we find a fair amount of independent support. Although (88) involves a Raising rather than an ergative verb, it is obvious that the analyses in (88) are correct to the extent that the one in (86) is, whereas if (87) was correct we would expect (89).

(89) a.? ...fa   [$_{VP}$sembrare [$_{sc}$t$_i$ammalato]] [$_S$Giovanni$_i$ − − −]
          makes   *seem*   *sick*   *Giovanni*

   b.* ...fa   [$_{VP}$sembrare [$_{St}$t$_i$soffrire]] [$_S$Giovanni$_i$ − − −]
          makes   *seem*   *to suffer*   *Giovanni*

Even aside from the fact that the linear order in (89a) (... *ammalato Giovanni*) is less acceptable than the one in (88a), we note that the analysis of (89) must be rejected since it provides no means to distinguish the (a) from the (b) case. In (89a,b), unlike (88a,b) the phrase *Giovanni* is exactly in the same structural position, and in the same structural relation to the Case assigning verb *fare*.[36] With (89), we thus reject (87).

4.5.1. *Dative and Reflexive Objects*

In this subsection we show that ergative complements are analogous to complements of FP rather than to those of FI constructions with respect to the behavior of embedded objects.

In 4.3 above, we noted that cliticization of dative objects to *fare* gives rise to near-ungrammaticality in the FI construction as in (90), while it is unproblematic in the FP construction as in (91).

(90) a.   ?Gli$_i$ faccio [$_{VP}$telefonare [$_i$e]] [$_S$Giovanni − − −]
           I will make Giovanni phone (to) him.

   b.   ??Gli$_i$ fecero [$_{VP}$sparare addosso [$_i$e]] [$_S$un agente − − −]
           They had an agent fire upon (to) him.

   c.   ??Gli$_i$ fecero [$_{VP}$sparare tra i piedi [$_i$e]] [$_S$un agente − − −]
           They had an agent fire between his feet.

(91) a.   Gli$_i$ faccio [$_{VP}$telefonare [$_i$e] (da Giovanni)]
           I will have him phoned (by Giovanni).

   b.   Gli$_i$ fecero [$_{VP}$sparare addosso [$_i$e] (da un agente)]
           They had him fired upon (by an agent).

c. Gli$_i$ fecero [$_{VP}$ sparare tra i piedi [$_i$e] (da un agente)]
They had him fired (at) between the feet (by an agent).

With ergative complements, dative objects cliticize freely, as in the FP construction, as shown in (92), given in the analysis we are proposing.

(92) a. Gli$_i$ faccio [$_{VP}$ apparire Giovanni [$_i$e]]
I will make Giovanni appear to him.

b. Gli$_i$ fecero [$_{VP}$ cadere un agente addosso [$_i$e]]
They made an agent fall upon (to) him.

c. Gli$_i$ fecero [$_{VP}$ cadere un agente tra i piedi [$_i$e]]
They made an agent fall between his feet.

The parallel grammaticality of (92) and (91) provides an argument for analyzing the complements in (92) as VPs like those in (91), and against an analysis in which the phrase *Giovanni, un agente* in (92) were embedded subjects as they are in (90). This argument for the VP analysis, while certainly dependent on our analysis of FP, is largely independent of what the exact account of the difficulty in (90) is. In particular, the argument stands whether we assume Kayne's account of (90), in which − contrary to our account − the dative is stranded in the complement and is thus prevented from cliticizing by the SSC (cf. 4.1.5), or whether − as we have suggested − the cases in (90) violate constraints on the relative order of dative and accusative objects. The grammaticality of (92) would follow in one case from the lack of an embedded subject, and in the other from the fact that dative and accusative objects are here in their canonical order.[37]

The difference in the possibility of cliticizing datives of (90) versus (92), is also considered by Kayne (FS, 4.7, 4.8). However, since Kayne's discussion does not recognize the existence of a class of ergative verbs, an account along the lines we are proposing is not available to him. Instead, Kayne argues that, while dative objects of cases like (90) cannot cliticize due to the SSC, those of cases like (92) can cliticize because they are objects not of the embedded verb but of the main verb, and thus not subject to the SSC. Within Kayne's analysis, cases like (93a,b) [Kayne's (36a), p. 283, and (95b), p. 309], analogous to (90a), (92a) respectively, would, prior to cliticization and subsequent to application of the FI rule, have the analyses in (94). (*Mourir* of (93b) is for us an ergative verb by virtue of selecting auxiliary *être*.)

(93) a. *Je lui ferai écrire mon ami.
I will make my friend write to him.

b. On lui fera mourir son chien.
We will make his dog die on him.

(94) a.   Je ferai **écrire** [$_S$mon ami ____ lui]

b.   On fera **mourir** [$_S$son chien ____] lui

Such analyses predict violation of the SSC in (94a), but not in (94b), from which the contrast in (93) would follow. If Kayne's 'sister to *faire*' analysis of datives like the one in (93b) were tenable, it might undercut our argument for a VP analysis of ergative complements.

However, while some of Kayne's arguments are quite reasonable, it appears that there are sufficient reasons to prefer our solution to the 'sister to *faire*' analysis. One reason is that, unlike our account, Kayne's fails to establish any relationship between the apparent exceptionality of certain verbs with respect to dative cliticization under *fare/faire*, and other syntactic properties of these verbs. For example the fact that all such verbs take auxiliary *essere* in Italian.[38] A further reason has to do with cases like (92b,c): *Gli fecero cadere un agente addosso*, *Gli fecero cadere un agente tra i piedi*, for which a 'sister to *faire*' analysis of the dative is particularly difficult to maintain. In these two cases, the phrase introduced respectively by *addosso, tra i piedi* is clearly an object of the *lower* verb, and the dative is clearly related to that phrase. A 'sister to *faire*' analysis here would thus imply, questionably, that the relation between the dative argument position (the *ec*, in our framework) and the *addosso/ tra i piedi* phrase holds across an S boundary; which is precisely what Kayne assumes. But this raises the possibility of an analogous state of affairs in cases like (90b,c), or ?? *Gli fecero sparare un agente addosso*, ?? *Gli fecero sparare un agente tra i piedi*, which however are ungrammatical. The problem for Kayne's analysis at this point is therefore how to account for the difference between (95) and (96) (Kayne's (123), p. 322 and (121a), p. 321).

(95) a.   On fera **tomber** [$_S$Jean ____ dessus] lui ⇒

b.   On lui fera tomber Jean dessus.
We will make Jean fall upon (to) him.

(96) a.   On fera **tirer** [$_S$les soldats ____ dessus] lui ⇒

b.   *?On lui fera tirer les soldats dessus.
We will make the soldiers fire upon (to) him.

Here Kayne argues that the rule that relates *dessus* and *lui* in (95), (96) (and − we would presume − the inalienable *i piedi* and the dative in (90c), (92c)) is sensitive to the SSC, and that the latter condition is relaxed with non-agentive subjects like that of *tomber*. Thus (96a) would violate the SSC, whereas (95a) would be allowed. This further weakens the theory however, as Kayne acknowledges, since there is little independent evidence for such a distinction between agentive and non-agentive subjects with respect to the SSC.

It may also be noted that an account of (95) in terms of non-enforcement of the SSC undercuts the primary argument for the 'sister to *faire*' analysis (though others of Kayne's arguments, which we will not consider, remain unaffected). This is because, given their non-agentive subjects, cases like (93b) will now be predicted to be grammatical by Kayne's theory, regardless of whether the dative originates outside the complement (as in (94b)), or inside. In view of these difficulties, our account of the contrast between (90) and (92) seems clearly preferable, and our argument for the VP analysis of ergative complements will therefore stand.[39]

A further argument for that analysis is provided by the distribution of reflexives. Recall the difference between FI and FP exhibited by (46) above, repeated in (97).

(97) a. *Maria si$_i$ è fatta [$_{VP}$ accusare [$_i$e]] [$_S$ a Giovanni − − −]
      Maria had Giovanni accuse herself.

   b. Maria si$_i$ è fatta [$_{VP}$ accusare [$_i$e] (da Giovanni)]
      Maria had herself accused (by Giovanni).

We have accounted for the contrast in (97) in terms of the reflexive clitic of (97a) failing to be locally related to its *ec* at D-structure. As we expect, similar contrasts arise also when the reflexive clitic is an indirect, or dative object, rather than a direct, or accusative object, as in (98).

(98) a. *Maria si$_i$ è fatta [$_{VP}$ telefonare [$_i$e]] [$_S$ Giovanni − − −]
      Maria had Giovanni phone (to) herself.

   b. Maria si$_i$ è fatta [$_{VP}$ telefonare [$_i$e] (da Giovanni)]
      Maria had herself phoned (by Giovanni).

Since the cases in (98) involve dative clitics, we naturally expect that the ungrammaticality of (98a) will be at least in part of the same nature as that of (90a), the corresponding non-reflexive case. However, we must also assume that it is related to that of (97a), both for empirical and for theoretical reasons. Empirical, because the ungrammaticality of (98a) is, like that of (97a), noticeably more severe than that of (90a) (cf. fn. 19). Theoretical, because our account of (97a) predicts thta (98a) should be equally ill-formed. We thus take the contrast in (98) to be independent, at least in part, from the one between (90) and (91).

While dative reflexive objects thus distinguish FI and FP as in (98), we note that once again ergative complements go with FP, as in (99).

(99) a. Giovanni si$_i$ fa [$_{VP}$ arrivare un libro [$_i$e]]
'*Giovanni has a book arrive to himself*'. (*Giovanni sends for a book.*)

b. Giovanni si$_i$ fa [$_{VP}$ cadere Maria addosso [$_i$e]]
Giovanni makes Maria fall upon himself.

c. Giovanni si$_i$ fa [$_{VP}$ cadere l'acqua in testa [$_i$e]]
Giovanni makes the water fall upon his head.

The well-formedness of (99) is straightforward under the VP analysis of the complement: the reflexive clitic can be locally related to its *ec* at all levels, just as in (98b). On the other hand, an S analysis would predict ill-formedness exactly as in (98a).

We have thus reviewed some cases in which the behavior of embedded objects distinguishes VP complements of *fare* (FP) from S complements (FI). We have seen that ergative complements are consistently like VP complements and unlike S complements.

4.5.2. *Dativized Subjects*

Under the hypothesis that sentences like **Farò intervenire Giovanni** 'I will make Giovanni intervene' result from embedding the VP [*intervenire Giovanni*] under *fare*, the NP *Giovanni* is the embedded direct object, whereas under the alternative hypothesis that they result from embedding the S [*Giovanni$_i$ intervenire t$_i$*], the NP *Giovanni* is the embedded subject. The two hypotheses make different predictions with respect to the possibility that the latter NP may appear in the dative in some cases, which we consider in this subsection.

We note first that, if we assume the existence of a dativization rule like (14) above, which we can give as in (100a), the analysis in (100b) would incorrectly predict the dative *a Giovanni*.

(100) a. NP → a NP / NP ____

b. *Farò [$_{VP}$ intervenire t$_i$] [$_S$ a Giovanni$_i$ – – –]

Cases like (101) ((64a) above) would show that traces do induce dativization, like other NPs.

(101) La macchina$_i$ fu   fatta [$_{VP}$ riparare t$_i$] [$_S$ a Giovanni – – –]
       the car   *was made   repair*   *to Giovanni*

The ungrammaticality of (100b) would thus provide a direct argument against the S analysis of ergative complements. However, it is unclear, and perhaps even unlikely that the argument would stand if, instead of (100a), which we have argued is merely a descriptive generalization, we considered the principles that underlie dativization. For example, under the principle of Case absorption that we suggested above, this will depend on whether we have reasons to postulate that in (100b) the inability of the ergative verb to assign accusative is in effect transmitted to the main verb. Still we note that the VP analysis will exclude the dativization of (100b) without question, while this is not quite so under the S analysis.

In fact, dativization fails even in the presence of a sentential complement of the ergative verb. In such cases, the VP and S analyses predict the S-structures of (102).

(102) a. Farò [$_{VP}$intervenire Giovanni$_i$ [$_S$PRO$_i$ a risolvere il problema]]
I will make Giovanni intervene to solve the problem.

b. ?Farò [$_{VP}$intervenire t$_i$ [$_S$PRO$_i$ a risolvere il problema]]
[$_S$Giovanni$_i$ − − −]

The linear order in (102a) is preferred to the one in (102b). However, in itself this will not suffice to rule out the structure in (102b) since a late reordering rule, whose existence we are independently assuming (cf. 4.1.5), could produce the preferred order from (102b). The question here is whether we expect that the S-complement in the hypothetical structure (102b) should incorrectly induce dativization of the phrase *Giovanni.*

As noted by Kayne (FS, p. 210), there are some clear cases in which a sentential complement induces dativization on a par with a direct object NP. One relevant example is (103a), which we give with the embedded subject cliticized, so as to abstract away from questions of relative ordering of the embedded subject and S-complement. Verbs that pattern comparably to *affermare* of (103a) are those in (1003b). All the verbs of (103) are non-ergative.

(103) a. $\left\{ \begin{array}{c} \textbf{Gli} \\ ?*\textbf{Lo} \end{array} \right\}$ feci affermare di aver letto l'articolo.

I made him claim to have read the article.

b. desiderare, dire, cercare, sostenere, sperare
wish   say   try   claim   hope

With other non-ergative verbs taking S-complements, results are less clear, as in (104a), with the verbs of (104b) yielding roughly comparable judgments.

(104) a. $\left\{ \begin{array}{c} ?\textbf{Gli} \\ ?\textbf{Lo} \end{array} \right\}$ feci acconsentire a studiare la cosa.

I made him consent to study the matter.

b. contribuire, dubitare, esitare, mirare, provare
contribute   doubt   hesitate aim   try

The facts in (103) and (104) will require an extension of the rule of (100a) as in (105), where the S is parenthesized to indicate that S-complements trigger dativization with some variation.

$$(105) \quad NP \to a\ NP\ /\ \left\{ \begin{array}{l} NP \\ (S) \end{array} \right\} \underline{\quad}$$

But in contrast with both the verbs of (103) and those of (104), ergative verbs taking sentential sentential complements never allow dativization of what we may call their 'apparent subject', not even marginally. Note that this generalization is not challenged by a few apparent exceptions like (106), since, as we will see in 5.2 below, these follow from the fact that restructuring has applied to the ergative verb and its complement.

(106)   **Gli** faccio andare a riportare il libro.
        I make him go to return the book.

Again, there would be a direct argument against the S analysis of ergative complements in (102b) if (105) was a formal rule of grammar, since we would then expect dativization at least sometimes or marginally with those complements. But matters are less clear if we try to go beyond the descriptive character of (105). Thus, L. Rizzi has pointed out to me that there is some correspondence between the S-complements that trigger dativization as in (103), and those that can pronominalize in the accusative, compare (103a) with **Giovanni lo afferma** 'Giovanni claims it' and (104a) with **Giovanni vi/*lo acconsente** 'Giovanni consents to it/*it', in which we take the pronouns to refer to propositions. This suggests that, while some S-complements are analogous to direct objects (perhaps because they are dominated by an NP node, cf. Note 40), others are analogous to indirect objects, in general. In so far as ergative verbs have direct objects distinct from their S-complements, we have an independent reason to regard the latter complements as unlike direct objects. It could thus turn out that when all relevant issues are properly understood the lack of dativization in (102) can be assimilated to the (relative) lack of dativization in (104a), in a way that is compatible with the analysis in (102b).[40] Yet again, while the empirical adequacy of the S analysis is at least in doubt, that of the VP analysis is not: in (102a) we will not expect dativization of the phrase *Giovanni* under any circumstance.[41]

There is a third case in which the VP and S analyses make potentially different predictions with respect to dativization. As is known (cf. for example FS, p. 210, Note 9. See also Radford (1977, pp. 230 ff.), and Note 15 above), there are cases in which, at least for some speakers, dativization can be triggered by an indirect object, as in (107).

(107) ?   Gli$_i$ farò   [$_{VP}$telefonare a Maria] [$_S$[$_i$e] — — —]
         (*I*) *to-him will make   telephone   to Maria*

I will make him phone Maria.

This requires a further extension of the rule, as in (108), where the parentheses around *PP* indicate that this portion is applicable only in some cases and/or with dialectal variation.

$$(108) \quad NP \rightarrow a\ NP\ /\ \left\{ \begin{array}{l} NP \\ (S) \\ (PP) \end{array} \right\} \underline{\hspace{1cm}}$$

While the NP of *NP telefona a Maria* can thus be dativized as in (107), the NP of *NP appare a Maria* involving ergative *apparire*, never can. This is quite systematic with ergative verbs: **Lo/*gli farò apparire a Maria** 'I will make him appear to Maria', **Lo/*gli farò andare a Roma** 'I will make him go to Rome', **Lo/*gli farò sottostare alla tua autorità** 'I will make him be submissive to your authority'.[42]

Let us now consider the two competing analyses in (109).

(109) a.   *Gli$_i$ farò [$_{VP}$apparire [$_i$e] a Maria]

      b.   *Gli$_i$ farò [$_{VP}$apparire t$_i$ a Maria] [$_S$[$_i$e] — — —]

In this case an account under the S analysis appears quite unlikely either in terms of (108) or of any underlying principle which we may postulate. The phrases *a Maria* of (109) and (107) are in fact analogous indirect objects in all conceivable syntactic respects. Under the VP analysis, the distinction between (109) and (107) is straightforward, since in (109a) the *ec* related to the clitic is not in a dativizing environment under any of the criteria that we may suggest.

In this subsection we have therefore seen that with ergative complements of *fare* the apparent subject is never dativized. This follows from the VP analysis of the complement, but not from the S analysis.[43]

4.5.3. *Further Remarks and Conclusions*

While the previous subsection noted certain ways in which the apparent subject of an ergative complement is unlike a real subject, there is one respect in which it seems to behave just like a real subject. Consider the severe ungrammaticality of (110).

(110) **Farò [$_{VP}$intervenirlo$_i$[$_i$e]]
      I will make him intervene.

Such ungrammaticality is entirely comparable to that of cases like (111), discussed in 4.1.4 above, in which a real embedded subject cliticizes to the lower verb.

(111) **Farò [$_{VP}$ lavorarlo$_i$] [$_S$ [$_i$ e] — — —]
I will make him work.

Prima facie, the parallelism between (110) and (111) may seem to provide evidence that *lo* in (110) is an embedded subject, just as in (111), since in general cliticization of embedded objects to the lower verb gives rise to only mild ungrammaticality, as in (112) (cf. (21) above and discussion).

(112) ??Faccio [$_{VP}$ leggerlo$_i$ [$_i$ e]] [$_S$ a Giovanni — — —]
I make Giovanni read it.

Yet the different degrees of ungrammaticality of (110) and (112) can be accommodated within our account rather naturally.

As we have seen (cf. 3.1.1), ergative verbs never assign accusative Case. We must therefore assume that in a structure ... fare [$_{VP}$V′ NP ...] in which V′ is an ergative verb, NP is necessarily assigned Case by *fare*. (As we discussed in 4.3 there are indications that objects of the embedded verb function as objects of the matrix verb rather generally in these constructions). But now recall how we argued that clitics are morphological manifestations of the Case assigning properties of the verb (cf. 4.1.4). From this point of view it will be natural to expect that accusative *lo* could not appear on *intervenire* in (110), since this verb does not assign accusative, while it can (marginally) appear on accusative assigning *lavorare* of (112).[44]

The conclusion can then be drawn that ergative complements of *fare* are VPs, like the complements of FP constructions, and not Ss. The arguments we have provided can be summarized as follows:

(i) Only the VP analysis explains why Raising verbs can be embedded under *fare* when they take a sc complement, but not when they take an infinitival.

(ii) Dative and reflexive objects cliticize freely in the case of ergative complements as they do in FP constructions, while they do not in FI constructions.

(iii) Unlike real subjects, the apparent subject of an ergative complement never dativizes.

While ergative complements and FP complements are thus analogous, we will not use the designation FP (*Faire-par*) for the case of ergative complements, since these will never contain a *by/par* phrase, for the reasons discussed in 4.2.2. Rather, we will henceforth use *Fare-VP* to refer to all cases in which *fare* has a VP complement.

The conclusion we have reached in this section (and in fact each of the differences between ergative and intransitive verbs which we noted) strongly confirms the existence of ergative verbs as a separate class. There is one further respect in which complements of *fare* support the distinction between ergatives and intransitives, though unlike the facts discussed earlier this does not bear too directly on the precise analysis of ergative complements. We know that, while verbs can never appear without objects they are subcategorized for, they can appear without subjects in certain constructions (cf. I.0.3). Thus consider (113), which for us are instances of FP without the *by*-phrase (cf. discussion of (54) above).

(113) a. Giovanni farà riparare la macchina.
     Giovanni will have the car repaired.

    b. I suoi commenti fanno ridere.
      His comments make (me) laugh.

    c. Qui fanno lavorare.
     Here they make (you) work.

If verbs that take auxiliary *essere* were intransitive, they too should appear in the manner of *ridere, lavorare* of (113), but they do not, as (114) shows.

(114) a. ??Le bucce di banana fanno cadere.
     Banana peels make (one) fall.

    b. ??Questa medicina fa guarire.
      This medicine makes (one) heal.

    c. ?*La carica della polizia ha fatto fuggire.
      The charge of the police made (people) flee.

The ungrammaticality of the cases in (114) follows from the ergative analysis of the complement verbs since, under the latter, the missing argument is not, the subject but an object which the verb is subcategorized for. Such ungrammaticality will thus be analogous to that of, for example, ?**Giovanni farà riparare** 'Giovanni will make repair', in which the object of *riparare* is missing.[45]

4.6. FI VERSUS RECONSTRUCTION

The same reasons that bar ergative verbs in FI, namely the fact that the NP-trace relation in, for example [*Giovanni$_i$ intervenire t$_i$*] would not be well-formed at S-structure should VP-movement apply, will naturally carry over to other constructions; to some, like Raising and passives, rather obviously.

In this section we review several constructions that fail to appear under *fare*, arguing that each case involves a coindexing relation which is required to be well-formed at S-structure. Comparing all the relations of this type that we will encounter with the relations we discussed in 4.4, for which we saw that reconstruction in LF was sufficient, we will note that the distinction between these two sets corresponds exactly to the distinction between the relations that trigger the system of E-assignment and pp agreement of 1.7 above, and those that do not — a fact which will call for an explanation.

We begin our review with the case of Raising verbs. As we argued in our discussion of (88), (89), Raising verbs never occur in FI. Cases like (115a) thus contrast minimally with Control counterparts like (115b) which will be grammatical because reconstruction is sufficient for establishing Control relations, as we argued in 3.3.3 and 4.4. (Raising/Control contrasts like the one in (115) were noted in FS, 3.7.)

(115) a. *La sua espressione fa [$_{VP}$ sembrare [$_S$ t$_i$ soffrire]]
          [$_S$ (a) Giovanni$_i$ − − −]

          His expression makes Giovanni seem to suffer.

     b. Ho fatto [$_{VP}$ affermare [$_S$ di PRO$_i$ averla vista]]
          [$_S$ a Giovanni$_i$ − − −]

          I made Giovanni claim to have seen her.

As we saw, Raising verbs are also excluded in Fare-VP structures, though only when they take an infinitival complement, not when they take a sc, as in (116a,b), for the reasons we discussed in connection with (17) and (88) above.[46]

(116) a. La sua espressione fa [$_{VP}$ sembrare [$_{sc}$ Giovanni ammalato]]
          His expression makes Giovanni seem sick.

     b. *La sua espressione fa [$_{VP}$ sembrare [$_S$ Giovanni soffrire]]
          His expression makes Giovanni seem to suffer.

Like ergative and Raising constructions, passives are also impossible in FI. Let us consider the passive case in (117a), in the analysis we argued for in 2.7.1 above (following Stowell (1978)), when it occurs as a complement in FI, as in (117b).

(117) a. Piero$_i$ fu [$_{sc}$ t$_i$ invitato t$_i$]
          Piero was invited.

     b. *Giovanni farà [$_{VP}$ essere [$_{sc}$ t$_i$ invitato t$_i$]] [$_S$ (a) Piero$_i$ − − −]
          Giovanni will make Piero be invited.

Clearly, the ill-formedness of (117b) will be analogous to that of Raising cases like (115a).

Kayne (FS, 3.6) notes that not only passives, but 'be' in general fails to appear under *faire*. As far as the FI construction is concerned, this will follow if not only passive 'be', but also copular 'be' of (118a) is a Raising verb, as we argued in 2.7.1. Then the ungrammaticality of cases like (118b) will also be analogous to that of (115a).

(118) a.   Giovanni$_i$ sarà [$_{sc}$ t$_i$ piú attento]
       Giovanni will be more careful.

b.   *Questo farà [$_{VP}$ essere [$_{sc}$ t$_i$ piú attento]] [$_S$ (a) Giovanni$_i$ — — —]
     This will make Giovanni be more careful.

However, if 'be' is a Raising verb taking sc complements, we will then also expect that the latter may occur in the *Fare*-VP construction, on a par with *sembrare* of (116a) above. Yet this is not so, as (119a,b) show.

(119) a.   *Giovanni farà [$_{VP}$ essere [$_{sc}$ Piero$_i$ invitato t$_i$]]
       Giovann will make Piero be invited.

b.   ?*Questo farà [$_{VP}$ essere [$_{sc}$ Giovanni piú attento]]
     This will make Giovanni be more careful.

If our parallel analyses of (116a) and (119a,b) are correct, then some lexical property distinguishing 'be' from other verbs must be playing a role here. This view seems confirmed by the fact that *essere* contrasts minimally not only with *sembrare*, but also with *stare* 'be, stay', a verb closely related to *essere* (*stare* and *essere* share the form of the past participle *stato*.) Thus, compare (118a), (119b) with (120a,b) respectively.

(120) a.   Giovanni starà piú attento.
       Giovanni will be more careful.

b. (?)Questo farà stare Giovanni più attento.
     This will make Giovanni be more careful.

We find it plausible to relate the ungrammaticality of cases lke (119a,b) to our assumption of 2.7.2 above that the sequence *essere NP* where NP is lexical, always demands the presence of pleonastic *ci* (see (170) ch. 2 and discussion). The cases in (119) are thus excluded because *ci* is not present.[47] On the other hand *ci* cannot appear under *fare* for reasons that we will see shortly below.

Among the constructions that cannot occur under *fare* are also all variants of the impersonal-SI construction (the parallel non-occurrence of French SE-moyen under *faire* is noted in Ruwet (1972, 3), FS (5.9)). Consider the "Object Preposing" (O.P.) variant in (121).

(121) a.   I genitori$_i$ si avvertiranno immediatamente t$_i$
           the parents SI will notify   immediately

     The parents will be notified immediately.

  b.   *Il preside farà [$_{VP}$ avvertir**si** immediatamente t$_i$]
       [$_S$ (a)i genitori$_i$ − − −]
       The president will make the parents be notified immediately.

Plainly, the ungrammaticality of (121b) reduces to that of a parallel ergative case, just like that of the Raising and Passive cases in (115a) and (117b). Consider now the variant of (122a) in which O.P. has not applied, when occurring in FI and in *Fare*-VP, as in (122b, c).

(122) a.   [$_i$e] si$_i$ avvertirà   immediatamente i genitori
               SI will notify immediately   the parents

  b.   *Il preside farà [$_{VP}$ avvertir**si**$_i$ immediatamente i genitori]
       [$_S$ [$_i$e] − − −]
       The president will make SI ('one') notify immediately the parents.

  c.   *Il preside farà [$_{VP}$ avvertir**si** immediatamente i genitori]

Examples (122b, c) are both ill-formed because SI fails to receive a θ-role: in (122c) because there is no subject position to transmit such a θ-role; in (122b) because [$_i$e] and SI$_i$ do not stand in the proper relation, as they do in (122a). Note that, if as we argued in 1.6, SI receives a θ-role from the subject position not only in (122a), but also in (121a) where O.P. has applied, then the ill-formedness of (122b) will carry over to (121b), providing a second reason for the ungrammaticality of the latter.[48]

The reasons for the ungrammaticality of (122b) generalize to all subject clitics: any subject clitic will involve a relation between the subject position and an element in the VP, which will be altered by VP-movement. Let us then consider the other subject clitic of Italian, namely *ci* (cf. 2.5.3). This also fails to appear under *fare*, as in (123). (While (123) involves the idiom *volerci*, results with *esserci* are quite similar).

(123) a.   D'ora in poi, [$_i$e] ci$_i$ vorrà   la firma   dell'insegnante.
           from now on   there will want the signature of the teacher

     From now on it will take the teacher's signature.

  b.   *Le nuove disposizioni faranno   [$_{VP}$ voler**ci**$_i$ la firma
       the new regulations   will make   there want the signature

       dell'insegnante] [$_S$ [$_i$e] − − −]
       of the teacher

     The new regulations will require the teacher's signature.

Note that in the case of *ci* there is no θ-role transmission since this clitic is not an argument. However, recall that we assume that *all* relations between clitic and their *ec*'s must obtain at all levels (cf. (93) ch. 2 and discussion). The ill-formedness of (123b) will then indeed be analogous to that of (122b). If we now consider the *Fare*-VP analysis of (123b), that is if we omit the S portion of (123b), its ill-formedness will remain, as analogous to that of (122c). (Note that neither the SI nor the *ci* cases are ungrammatical solely because Clitic Climbing has failed, cf. *Il preside si farà avvertire i genitori/*. . . ci faranno volere la firma . . .*).

The cases we have so far considered involve NP-trace relations and clitic-*ec* relations. These relations must be well-formed at S-structure because of the θ-criterion (an extension of the θ-criterion in the case of *ci*). According to LGB 6, inversion and extraposition relations also invoke the θ-criterion, since they, too, constitute chains: sequences of elements sharing Case and θ-role, like NP-trace and clitic-*ec* relations. That both inversion and extraposition constructions fail to appear under *fare* as we would thus predict is quite clear. It is less clear however whether they may not also be excluded by factors extraneous to this discussion, as we now see.

Consider a simple NS sentence like (124).

(124) [e] ha guidato.
       (*he*) *has* *driven*

As we discussed in 2.1 above, we take the subject of (124) to be an *ec* linked with the tensed inflection, the latter functioning as a clitic. Consider now (125).

(125) Maria lo$_i$ fa [$_{VP}$guidare] [$_S$[$_i$e] − − −]
       Maria makes him drive.

Clitic *lo* of (125) is the accusative counterpart to the NS of (124). In both cases we have an unstressed pronominal subject. In an environment in which tensed inflection is available, like (124), this is realized as a NS, whereas in an environment in which accusative Case is assigned, like (125), it is realized as an accusative clitic (cf. some of 2.1).

One might now expect that, if it were possible to embed inversion constructions like (126a) in FI, (126b) should be grammatical, since the NS of (126a) would correspond to *lo*, or perhaps dative *gli*, of (126b), just as the NS of (124) corresponds to *lo* of (125).

(126) a. [e] ha guidato Giovanni
          (*it*) *has driven* *Giovanni*

   b. *Maria $\left\{ \begin{array}{c} \text{lo}_i \\ \text{gli}_i \end{array} \right\}$ fa [$_{VP}$guidare Giovanni] [$_S$[$_i$e] − − −]

       Maria makes (*it*) *drive Giovanni.*

One would thus be tempted to take the ungrammaticality of (126b) as
due to VP-movement. However, it appears that (126b) is ruled out
independently by the fact (noted in FS, p. 233, and as yet unaccounted
for) that clitics like *lo*, and we presume *gli*, never occur as non-arguments. This fact is illustrated by (127), (128).

(127) a. $[_ie]$ è partito t_i
           He has left.

      b. $[_ie]$ è piovuto t_i
           It has rained.

(128) a. Lo_i ritengo $[_{sc}[_ie]$ partito $t_i]$
           (*I*) *him believe   departed*

           I believe him to have departed.

      b. * Lo_i ritengo $[_{sc}[_ie]$ piovuto $t_i]$
           (*I*) *it   believe   rained*

           I believe it to have rained.

As the auxiliaries in (127) show, both *partire* and *piovere* are ergative
verbs (though *piovere* can also be intransitive, appearing with auxiliary
avere, cf. fn. 20). The only difference in (127) is that, whereas the derived
subject of *partire* is an argument (he), that of *piovere* is a quasi-argument
(weather *it*). As we discussed in 3.2.3, Italian ergative verbs can appear
in past participial sc's in the same way as transitives do. The grammaticality of (128a) is therefore expected, while (128b) can only be
attributed to the fact that clitics like *lo* must be arguments.[49] The same
conclusion is suggested by (129) versus (130), where the subject of (*è*)
ovvio is an argument (argument *it*) in (a), but a non-argument (pleonastic
it), linked with the post-verbal S, in (b).

(129) a.   [e] è ovvio
           (*It*) *is obvious*

      b.   [e] è ovvio [che Giovanni era qui]
           (*It*) *is obvious   that Giovanni was here*

(130) a.   Lo ritengo ovvio.
           I believe it obvious.

      b. *Lo ritengo ovvio che Giovanni era qui.
           I believe it obvious that Giovanni was here.

Cases like (126b) will thus be excluded independent of the status of the
inversion relation.

Things are slightly different in French however, so that we may consider the impossibility of embedding cases like (131a) under *faire*, as in (131b).

(131) a.   Il est arrivé trois filles.
            '*It has arrivd three girls.*'

   b.   *Cela fera [$_{VP}$ arriver trois filles] [$_S$ (a) il − − −]
         '*This will make it arrive three girls.*'

As we argued in 2.6.1, French *il* is not a clitic in the syntactic sense. The factors we discussed in connection with the Italian cases would therefore seem irrelevant here. However, even in this case we cannot exclude the possibility that the ill-formedness may be independent of the effects of VP-movement on the inversion relation. Recall that there is reason to believe that French subject pronouns locally cliticize to the verb in the phonology (see 2.6.1), so that the occurrence of *il* in (131b) might be independently ruled out. Furthermore, in accusative/dative assigning environments one never finds *il*, but rather *le/lui*, and rather than (131b) we may expect (132).

(132)   *Cela $\left\{ \begin{array}{c} \text{le} \\ \text{lui} \end{array} \right\}$ fera arriver trois filles.

But the ungrammaticality of (132) would then be subject to the same account as that of (126b), based on the necessarily argumental status of object clitics, which holds for French as well.

The evidence provided by extraposition constructions is exactly analogous to the evidence just discussed for inversion. Thus, parallel to (126a,b) above, we find **Bisogna che Giovanni parta** 'It is necessary that Giovanni leave' versus *__Questo lo/gli farà bisognare che Giovanni parta__ 'This will make it be necessary that Giovanni leave', and so on.

While we may be unable to establish it on a purely empirical basis, we will nevertheless assume, based on theoretical considerations, that inversion and extraposition relations must be well-formed at S-structure, like NP-trace relations, and therefore that they cannot be altered by VP-movement. The theoretical considerations are that, as we mentioned above, inversion and extraposition relations constitute chains, like NP-trace relations.

In essence, we have therefore considered three classes of relations that constitute chains, listed in (133). Corresponding to each class, we have found a certain set of constructions that fail to appear in FI (and often under *fare*, altogether), as in (134).

(133) a. Antecedent-trace

      b. Clitic-*ec*

      c. Inversion/Extraposition

(134) a. Ergative, Raising, Passive, O.P. constructions

b. Constructions involving subject clitics SI, *ci.*

c. Inversion/Extraposition constructions

Since we have been making comparisons between our theory and Kayne's, we may point out here that, while some of the cases in (134) (in particular Passive, Raising, O.P.) are also noted in FS, Kayne's solutions are systematically different from ours. Whereas we have appealed to well-formedness conditions at S-structure, Kayne consistently relies on extrinsic ordering of rules (cf. FS, ex. 142 p. 251, ex. 147 p. 254, ex. 138 p. 396 and related discussion). This systematic difference results, we believe, from the difference between the two theoretical frameworks, in particular from the fact that Kayne's does not make use of trace theory. On the superiority of the current framework, see Burzio (1983).

Recall that evidence that well-formedness of clitic-*ec* relations cannot be obtained via reconstruction is provided not only by SI and *ci* in the FI construction, but also by the case of *ne* discussed in 3.3.3, in particular by cases like *$*[_i molti \; [_j e]] \; ne_j$ arrivano t_i*. For those clitics which are base-generated we saw that well-formedness of clitic-*ec* relations must obtain not only at S-structure, but at D-structure as well (cf. II.0.3). Thus, in a sense, one can distinguish not two but three classes of relations: (i) those which must be well-formed at three levels, i.e. those of (133b) (for base-generated clitics); (ii) those which must be well-formed at two levels (S-structure, LF), i.e. those of (133a,c); and (iii) those which need only be well-formed at one level (LF), such as those we discussed in 4.4, for example the relation between PRO and its antecedent. We will return to some consequences of this tripartite distinction (cf. 4.8).

There appears to be a close correspondence between the way in which the class of coindexing relations is partitioned by the reconstruction process (at work in FI and in the cases of 3.3), and the way in which the class is partitioned by the system of E assignment/pp agreement of 1.7 above. All of the relations of (133) appear to trigger that system (cf. 1.7, 2.2), while the relations of (135), which we saw in 4.4 can be successfully reconstructed, do not.[50]

(135)   Antecedent-*ciascuno*
                    -PRO
                    -*se stesso*
                    -*proprio*
                    -possessive idiom
                    -inalienable possession

Thus, for example, corresponding to the reconstruction-based contrast between Raising and Control verbs of (115) above, we find the contrast in auxiliary selection of (136).

(136) a. Giovanni$_i$ **era** sembrato [$_S$t$_i$ soffrire]
       Giovanni had seemed   to suffer   (E)

     b. Giovanni$_i$ **aveva** affermato [$_S$di PRO$_i$ averla vista]
       Giovanni had claimed   (of)   to have seen her   (A)

As we argued in 2.6.2, Raising configurations are 'periphery' cases for E assignment in Italian. As a result, some Raising verbs, like *sembrare* of (136a) take auxiliary E, while others do not (cf. Note 50). This contrasts with the systematic lack of auxiliary E in Control configurations like (136b).[51]

Why should there be such a correspondence between the effects of reconstruction and those of E assignment/pp agreement? We know that the partitioning that arises from reconstruction is a reflex of the θ-criterion applying at S-structure. However, so far we have no explanation for why the E assignment/pp agreement system discriminates among binding relations in the way it does. In 1.7 we merely stipulated that the system would be triggered only by '*binding relations*$_1$': essentially the relations that constitute chains. What is needed is therefore an explanation for this curious property of the system of E assignment/pp agreement. In 6.1 below we will see that there is a rather plausible explanation.

4.7. ON PERCEPTION VERBS

The FI and *Fare*-VP constructions are found not only with *fare*, but also with the other causative verb *lasciare*, as well as with perception predicates *vedere, guardare, osservare, sentire, udire*. We will assume that the analyses we discussed above for *fare* also apply when these other verbs are involved. However, as we noted in 4.0, *fare* differs from perception predicates, and in part from *lasciare*, with respect to the possibility of being followed by the sequence NP + *infinitival*, as in (137).

(137) a.   Ho visto Giovanni parlare con Maria.
        I saw Giovanni speak with Maria.

     b.   ?Ho lasciato Giovanni parlare con Maria.
        I let Giovanni speak with Maria.

     c.   *Ho fatto Giovanni parlare con Maria.
        I made Giovanni speak with Maria.

We have already dealt with the ungrammaticality of (137c). We have argued that the material following *fare* is an S, and that such ungrammaticality is due to the general impossibility of assigning Case across S boundaries in Italian. In this section we consider what the exact analysis of cases like (137a, b) should be.

The analyses most frequently proposed are the one in (138a), in which the perception predicate occurs in the frame __S, and the one in (138b) in which it occurs in the frame __NP S.

(138) a. Ho visto [$_S$ Giovanni parlare con Maria]

b. Ho visto Giovanni$_i$ [$_S$PRO$_i$ parlare con Maria]

Under the analysis of (138a), our discussion would face the immediate problem of accounting for the fact that, while Case cannot be assigned across the S boundary in (137c), it can in (138a). We would thus have to postulate that the boundaries involved in the two cases are somewhat different. One might suggest that the complement in (138a) is more analogous to a sc than to other infinitivals. Under the analysis of (138b) there is no immediate problem of this sort. However, on closer scrutiny it appears that both of the analyses in (138) must be rejected.

We will begin by reviewing the arguments against each of (138a,b), and will then consider an alternative. While our discussion will concentrate on Italian and Romance, we see strong reasons to believe that the correct analysis of examples like (137a,b) will shed some light on the corresponding English cases, and quite possibly apply directly to those cases as well. As is well known, the verbs that can occur as in (137a) in Romance are in fact essentially the same class of verbs that can take an infinitival complement without *to* in English. Both in English and in Romance these verbs thus contrast with other verbs taking infinitival complements like *ritenere/believe*, as in (139).[52]

(139) a. $\left\{ \begin{array}{l} \text{Ho visto} \\ \text{*Ritengo} \end{array} \right\}$ Giovanni parlare con Maria.

b. $\left\{ \begin{array}{l} \text{I saw} \\ \text{*I believe} \end{array} \right\}$ John speak with Mary.

One of the arguments against the __S analysis of (138a) is provided by the fact that, unlike tensed/infinitival pairs like *I believe that John delivered the speech I believe John to have delivered the speech*, which are closely synonymous, pairs like (140a, b) are not synonymous.

(140) a. Ho visto che Giovanni ha finito la tesi.
I saw that Giovanni has finished his thesis.

b. Ho visto Giovanni finire la tesi.
I saw Giovanni finish his thesis.

It has been claimed (cf., for example, FS, 232) that in cases like (140b) the phrase corresponding to *Giovanni* is the object of direct perception: a fact which is clearly not true of cases like (140a). Though it appears (cf. Radford (1977, pp. 183 ff.) that the latter claim is to be qualified somewhat, non-synonymy of (140a,b) remains entirely clear, there being *some* implication that I saw Giovanni in (140b), but none at all in (140a).

A closely related argument against the analysis given in (138a) has to do with the non-synonymy of active and passive forms. While S-complements maintain rough synonymy under passivization, as with *I believe [John to have delivered the speech]* versus *I believe [the speech to have been delivered (by John)]*, cases like (141a) are clearly not synonymous with their passive counterparts like (141b), as indicated by the limited acceptability of one of the cases in (141b).[53]

(141) a. Ho $\left\{ \begin{matrix} \text{visto} \\ \text{sentito} \end{matrix} \right\}$ Giovanni pronunciare il discorso.

　　　 I $\left\{ \begin{matrix} saw \\ heard \end{matrix} \right\}$ *Giovanni deliver the speech.*

　　b. Ho $\left\{ \begin{matrix} ?? \text{visto} \\ \text{sentito} \end{matrix} \right\}$ il discorso venire pronunciato (da G.)

　　　 I $\left\{ \begin{matrix} saw \\ heard \end{matrix} \right\}$ *the speech be delivered (by G.)*

The difficulty in the '*vedere*' case in (141b) would lend support to the view that the NP to the right of the perception verb is the 'object of direct perception' (since a speech can be heard, but not very well seen).

Another of the standard tests for distinguishing __NP S from __S: relative scope of quantifiers, also argues against the analysis of (138a). Compare the ambiguity of (142a) with the non ambiguity of (142b).

(142) a. They expected **one** customs official to check **all** passing cars

　　　(i)　They expected that there would be one customs official who would check all passing cars.

　　　(ii)　They expected that, for each passing car, there would be some customs official (or other) who would check it.

　　b. Videro **una** guardia di finanza controllare **tutte** le auto di
　　　They saw one customs official check all passing

　　　passaggio.
　　　cars.

　　　(i)　They saw that there was one customs official who checked all passing cars.

　　　(ii)　??They saw that for each passing car there was some customs official (or other) who checked it.

Under our assumption of 3.3.2 that quantifier scope is clause-bounded, the difference between (142a) and (142b) follows if, unlike (142a),

(142b) has the two quantifiers not contained within the same minimal S, contrary to (138a).

The difference between (143a) and (143b) is also relevant.

(143) a. (?)I expected [$_i$one interpreter **each**$_j$] to be assigned t$_i$ to **those visitors**$_j$

   b. ?? Vidi [un interprete **ciascuno**$_j$] venire assegnato a **quei** visitatori$_j$
      I saw one interpreter each be assigned to those visitors.

We argued in 3.3.1 that the relative well-formedness of cases like (143a) is due to the possibility of reconstructuring the NP containing *each* in its original position in LF. The relative unacceptability of (143b) is thus unaccounted for if the NP containing *each* is the subject of the infinitival as it is in (143a) and as in (138a), while it would be accounted for under the Control analysis of (138b). We must note however, that in this as well as in the other perception verb cases above, results are slightly different from those obtained with established object Control cases. Thus, the ungrammaticality of (144a,b,c) is somewhat more severe than that observed in (141b), (142b), (143b), respectively.

(144) a.   *I forced the speech to be delivered (by John).

   b.   I forced **one** customs official to check **all** passing cars.
        [*For each passing car I forced one customs official (or other) to check it.]

   c.   *I forced one interpreter **each** to be assigned to **those visitors**.

Yet the difference between the perception verb cases and established ___S cases remains significant enough to argue against (138a).

A further argument against (138a) is provided by the contrast between (145) and (146).

(145) a.   Alcuni prigionieri$_i$ furono fatti [$_S$t$_i$lavorare   senza sosta]
           a few prisoners   were made   to work   without stop

   b.   *[$_i$e] furono fatti [$_S$ alcuni prigionieri$_i$ lavorare senza sosta]
             were made   a few prisoners   to work   without stop

(146) a.   Alcuni prigionieri$_i$ furono visti t$_i$ fuggire
           a few prisoners   were seen   to flee

   b.   [$_i$e] furono visti alcuni prigionieri$_i$ fuggire
           were seen   a few prisoners   to flee

Inversion cases like (145b) were discussed in 4.1.2 above, and were taken to support the S analysis of complements of *fare,* indicated in (145). Under that analysis, (145b) is analogous to *[$_i$e] sembrava [$_S$Giovanni$_i$ conoscere la strada] 'seemed Giovanni to know the road' discussed in 2.4 above. The analysis of the complement in (146) must therefore be different. In particular, the grammaticality of (146b) suggests that there is no S boundary between *alcuni prigionieri* and the perception verb. Notice that the hypothesis that complements of perception verbs are not clauses but sc's would offer no solution here, since, as we noted in 2.4, sc boundaries do not differ significantly from clause boundaries with respect to inversion. Compare (145b) with ?*[$_i$e] sembrava [$_{sc}$Giovanni$_i$ ammalato] 'seemed Giovanni sick'.

Note finally that both SI and *ci* constructions fail to appear under perception predicates, a fact which — as we will see below — would follow rather clearly from the Control analysis in (138b), while being problematic for the ___S analysis in (138a). Compare (147) with (148).

(147) a. $\left\{ \begin{array}{l} \text{Si lavora molto.} \\ \text{Si costruisce molte case.} \end{array} \right\}$

$\left\{ \begin{array}{l} \textit{SI ('one') works a lot.} \\ \textit{SI ('one') builds many houses.} \end{array} \right\}$

   b. Queste case si sono costruite rapidamente.
       These houses SI built ('were built') rapidly.

   c. $\left\{ \begin{array}{l} \text{Ci sono due case nuove in questa via.} \\ \text{Ci vogliono molti soldi.} \end{array} \right\}$

$\left\{ \begin{array}{l} \textit{There are two new houses on this street.} \\ \textit{There wants ('it takes') much money.} \end{array} \right\}$

(148) a. *Ho visto $\left\{ \begin{array}{l} \text{lavorar}\mathbf{si} \text{ molto.} \\ \text{costruir}\mathbf{si} \text{ molte case.} \end{array} \right\}$

I have seen $\left\{ \begin{array}{l} \textit{SI work a lot.} \\ \textit{SI build many houses.} \end{array} \right\}$

   b. *Ho visto queste case costruir**si** rapidamente.
       I have seen these houses SI build ('be built') rapidly.

   c. *Ho visto $\left\{ \begin{array}{l} \text{esser}\mathbf{ci} \text{ due case nuove in questa via.} \\ \text{voler}\mathbf{ci} \text{ molti soldi.} \end{array} \right\}$

I have seen $\left\{ \begin{array}{l} \textit{there be two new houses on this street.} \\ \textit{there want ('it take') much money.} \end{array} \right\}$

If perception verbs had a NP controlling the subject of the infinitival as in (138b), then all of (148a,b,c) would follow: (148a,c) would be excluded because the latter NP is missing, and (148b) would be excluded in the manner of (149), i.e. because SI (linked with the subject position, cf. 1.6) lacks Case.

(149)   *Ho costretto [$_i$quei pazienti] [$_S$PRO$_i$ ad esaminarsi t$_i$]
        I have forced those patients to SI examine ('be examined')

However, if perception verbs took bare sentential complements, the material to the right of *vedere* in each of (148a,b,c) would have a sentential structure, which should be well-formed on a par with each of (147a,b,c). Note that, while we do require that both SI and *ci* have Case, Case would be available here since under the ___S hypothesis the perception verb would assign it across the S boundary.[54]

All of the problems we have so far noted for the ___S analysis of (138a) would be dispensed with under the ___NP S analysis of (138b); the analysis given by Kayne in FS.[55] But, as we mentioned, there are good arguments against the latter analysis as well. Some of these are given in Radford (1977, 3.4). Radford correctly notes that there is no independent motivation for the subcategorization ___NP S, while the subcategorization ___S is established by tensed cases like (150).

(150)   Ho visto [$_S$che Giovanni usciva]
        I saw that Giovanni was leaving.

The lack of plausibility for the subcategorization ___NP S is further stressed by the fact that under the latter we would expect tensed alternants to exist which were not like (150), but instead like (151), just as (152a) alternates with (152b).

(151)   *Ho visto   Giovanni [$_S$che Maria era uscita]
        (I)   have seen Giovanni   that Maria had left

(152)   a. I persuaded John$_i$ [$_S$PRO$_i$ to leave]

        b. I persuaded John [$_S$that Mary had left]

In addition, Radford notes that the pattern of nominalization is not the one typical of ___NP S subcategorizations. While, corresponding to (153a) we find (153b), corresponding to (154a) we find (if anything) only (154b).[56]

(153)   a. Ho persuaso   [$_1$Giovanni] [$_2$che era importante
        (I) have persuaded   Giovanni   that it was important

        riconoscere l'errore]
        to recognize the error.

b. Ho persuaso   [₁Giovanni] [₂dell'importanza di
(I) have persuaded   Giovanni   of the importance of

riconoscere l'errore]
recognizing the error.

(154) a. Ho visto   [₁i corridori] [₂partire]
         (I) have seen   the racers   depart.

b. Ho visto   [la partenza dei corridori]
        (I) have seen   the departure of the racers.

Radford also observes that, while in Italian all established cases of __NP S subcategorization exhibit a preposition before the infinitive, perception verb complements do not. This does not provide a very strong argument, we note, since we have no precise understanding of how such prepositions are assigned. Nevertheless the fact is of significance.

Further arguing against the __NP S analysis is the fact — again noted by Radford — that perception verb complements pass (at least some) constituency tests, such as Pseudo-Clefting, Pronominalization, and 'Equative' Deletion, as in (155a, b, c) (from Radford (1977)).

(155) a. Quello che non voglio   vedere è [Maria piangere]
         what   (I) do not want to see   is   Maria cry

                                     Pseudo-clefting.

b. Ho visto   [il cameriere rovesciare   la bottiglia],
       (I) have seen   the waiter   knock over   the bottle,

ma fortunatamente   il proprietario,   questo,
but fortunately   the owner,   this,

non l'ha visto   *Pronominalization.*
(he) did not see it.

c. Ho visto   una cosa molto strana:
        (I) have seen   a very strange thing.

[Maria   inseguire   una capra]   *Equative deletion.*
Maria   chase   a goat.

It is interesting to note however that Akmajian (1977) claims for the tests of (155a,c) that they give negative results in the corresponding English cases. As far as I can see there is no factual difference here between English and Italian, only one of interpretation between Radford and Akmajian. None of the cases in (155) seem to me entirely felicitous as a matter of fact, and simpler cases like (156) are considerably worse than (155a), for reasons which remain unclear. (See also (181), (182) below.)

(156) ??Quello che ho visto   è [Maria piangere]
      what   (*I*) *have seen is Maria cry.*

Still, the evidence in (155) remains significant, as such examples ought to be entirely impossible under a __NP S analysis, as Radford points out. We will assume, therefore, that there is some evidence for constituency.

We will also note that to the extent that Pseudo-Clefting as in (155a) is possible there is a certain tendency for the NP corresponding to *Maria* of that example to trigger verb agreement, as in (157).

(157)   Ciò che non vorremmo   vedere $\left\{ \begin{array}{c} \text{sono} \\ ?\,\text{è} \end{array} \right\}$ [gli anziani

        what   (*we*) *would not want to see* $\left\{ \begin{array}{c} are \\ is \end{array} \right\}$ [*the elderly*

        soffrire]
        suffer]

This fact (noted for the English -*ing* type of complement, as in *I saw Mary crying*, in Akmajian (1977)) is important because it suggests that the NP in such cases is not the subject, but rather the head of the complement. Subjects of Ss never trigger agreement outside of the clause (as Akmajian notes).

It has been noted that the NP preceding the infinitive in English perception verb complements can be a pleonastic element or an idiom chunk. Let us consider the cases in (158), from Gee (1977).

(158) a. We saw **it** rain.

      b. I've never seen **there** be so many complaints from students before.

      c. I would like to see **it** (be) proven that John was there last night.

      d. We heard **all hell** break loose.

      e. Then we saw **the shit** hit the fan.

Under the commonly held view that non-arguments like *it, there,* as well as idiom chunks are systematically incompatible with Control, and assuming that English and Romance perception verb complements have similar analysis, (158) may seem to give one further argument against the Control analysis of (138b). However, notice that cases exist, like

(159a,b), and the French case in (159c) from FS, p. 252, fn. 61, which give results which conflict with this point of view:

(159) a. ?*I saw **there** arrive three girls.

    b. *I hear **it** seem that John will come.

    c. *Il   a   laissé **tort**   leur   être donné par Jean.
       he has let   *blame* *to-them be*   *given* *by* *Jean*

       He let them be blamed by Jean.

Notice further that there is something dubious about the assumption that pleonastics and idiom chunks are necessarily incompatible with Control. Compare (160a, b).

(160) a. [$_i$that John is dishonest] is true [without PRO$_i$ being obvious]

    b.It$_i$ is true [without PRO$_i$ being obvious] [$_i$that John is dishonest]

In both (160a,b), being *obvious* assigns a θ-role to its subject PRO, which will then require an antecedent of comparable θ-role. We take this antecedent to be the S *that John is dishonest* in (160a), and the chain formed by *it* and the same S in (160b): we find nothing theoretically odd about (160b). An unqualified assumption that pleonastic elements cannot occur in PRO-controlling positions is therefore false on both empirical and theoretical grounds, given (160b). On the other hand a general assumption that pleonastic elements can freely appear as subjects of ECM complements as in *I expected [there to arrive three girls]* is true, since there exists no consideration that would exclude them. From this point of view we would rather take the cases in (159a,b) to indicate that some form of Control is involved, before we take (158b,c) to indicate that there is no Control.[57] We see no argument based on weather *it* of (158a), since there is reason to believe that the latter bears some kind of θ-role (cf. LGB, 6, and our Note 15, ch. 2), and we know it can control PRO, as in *It rained without snowing.* The impossibility of **I persuaded it to rain* and similar cases is, I think simply a matter of selectional restrictions (related to the impossibility of persuading the weather). As for the general non-occurrence of idiom chunks in controlling positions, it is also unclear that anything more than selectional restrictions is involved: We know no principle under which NPs like *all hell, the shit* of *All hell broke loose, The shit hit the fan* could not pronominalize as PRO, controlled by an appropriate antecedent. Let us then put aside the evidence based on pleonastics and idiom chunks, given its inconclusive character.

Summarizing, the most significant arguments that we find against each of the analyses in (138), are those listed in (161).

(161) I.   Arguments against ___[$_S$NP infinitival]

        a. Non-synonymy with ___S-tensed cases
        b. Non-synonymy under passivization of the complement
        c. Quantifiers in NP have wide scope
        d. *Each* in NP is never reconstructible into the infinitival
        e. Evidence that NP is not within S, when it is an i-subject
        f. Impossible to embed SI, *ci* constructions
        g. Agreement facts suggest that NP is the head rather than the subject of the complement

    II.   Arguments against ___NP$_i$[$_S$PRO$_i$ infinitival]

        a. No independent justification for this subcategorization (no tensed alternants or nominalizations for S)
        b. Lack of preposition before the infinitive uncharacteristic of object Control cases
        c. Some evidence for constituency (Pseudo-Clefting, Pronominalization, Equative-deletion)

(Note that I.g. argues against the object-Control analysis as well.)

Searching then for a third analysis which might be compatible with both sets of arguments in (161), we consider the construction in (162), also typical of perception predicates. (We will return to the fact that this construction does not exist in English.)

(162)   Ho visto   Giovanni che parlava con Maria.
        (I) have seen Giovanni who spoke   with Maria

        I saw Giovanni speaking with Maria.

This construction is discussed among others in FS (briefly), in Radford (1977), and in Kayne (1981a). It is rather clear that in this case, the complement structure of *vedere* comprises both a NP and an S (as nothing within S or S̄ ever appears to be left of complementizer *che*). The question is then whether these two elements may form a constituent. Kayne (1981a) assumes (differently than in FS) that they do, and that this constituent is a NP. The structure of (162) would thus be as in (163), in which the NP *Giovanni* would be coindexed with the *ec* in subject position, via the complementizer *che*, as Kayne argues.[58]

(163)   Ho visto   [$_{NP}$Giovanni$_i$ [$_S$che$_i$ [$_i$e] parlava con Maria]]
        (I) have seen   Giovanni   who   spoke   with Maria

According to Kayne's analysis these structures are thus somewhat similar to relative clauses, though they cannot be fully assimilated to the latter for various reasons (cf. Note 63), in particular because the *ec* can only be in subject position in these cases. Rather than the normal process of relativization, Wh-movement, one must therefore assume here a special rule operating between the head of the construction and the subject position.

One of the arguments that Kayne gives for the analysis in (163), and for the NP constituency, rests on the observation that such constructions are islands, as (164) shows.

(164)* Con quale ragazza$_i$ hai visto   [$_{NP}$Giovanni [$_S$che [e]
       with which girl   have (you) seen   Giovanni   who

       parlava   [$_i$e]]]?
       was speaking?

Under the given analysis, the ungrammaticality of (164) follows from the Complex NP Constraint, i.e. from Subjacency, given the two boundaries, S and NP. Other arguments of Kayne's are more internal to his discussion and will not be presented here. But there appear to be other arguments, beside Kayne's, for the analysis in (163). One is that such structures can be coordinated with NPs, as in (165).

(165)   Ho visto   [$_{NP}$Maria e   [Giovanni che la seguiva]
      (I) have seen   Maria and   Giovanni who was following her

Another is that they pass the constituency tests of II.c., as in (166), and as noted in Radford (1977).

(166) a. Quello che non vorrei   vedere è [Maria che piange]
       what   (I) would not want to see   is Maria who cries.

                                   Pseudo-clefting.

    b. Ho visto   [il cameriere che   rovesciava
      (I) have seen   the waiter   who was knocking over

      una bottiglia], ma fortunatamente il proprietario,
      a bottle,   but fortunately   the owner,

      questo, non l'ha visto.   *Pronominalization.*
      this,   (he) did not see it.

    c. Ho visto   una cosa molto strana: [Maria
      (I) have seen a very strange thing.   Maria

      che inseguiva   una capra]   *Equative-deletion.*
      who was chasing a goat.

A third is provided by the fact that, under this analysis, the possibility of this construction with perception verbs, its marginality with *lasciare*, and its impossibility with *fare*, as in (167), can be regarded as simply reflecting the distribution of NP objects illustrated by (168).

(167) a.   Ho visto   [$_{NP}$Giovanni che   parlava   con   Maria]
           (I) have seen   *Giovanni who   was speaking   with   Maria*

   b.   ?Lascialo$_i$ [$_{NP}$[$_i$e] che parli   con Maria]
        let-him   *that (may) speak   with Maria*

   c.   *Ho fatto   [$_{NP}$Giovanni che parlasse   con   Maria]
        (I) have made   *Giovanni that would speak with   Maria*

(168) a.   Ho visto   [$_{NP}$Giovanni]
           (I) have seen   *Giovanni.*

   b.   ?Ho lasciato [$_{NP}$Giovanni]
        (I) have left   *Giovanni.*

   c.   *Ho fatto   [$_{NP}$Giovanni]
        (I) have made   *Giovanni.*

The correlation between (167) and (168) is to be partially qualified.
While (167b) is slightly colloquial and the meaning of *lasciare* is here one
between 'leave' and 'let', (168b) is not colloquial and preferred with the
meaning of 'leave'. Cases like (168c) are possible in the sense of making
physically or generating, while cases like (167c) are impossible altogether.
In spite of these qualifications, the correspondence seems to us rather
significant. Given the above arguments, we conclude that Kayne's NP
analysis of the complement in (163) is correct.

If complements like [$_{NP}$ Giovanni$_i$ [$_S$che [$_i$e] *parlava con Maria*]] were
to have infinitival counterparts, the most plausible structure for the latter,
we believe, would be the one in (169).

(169)   [$_{NP}$Giovanni$_i$[$_S$PRO$_i$ parlare con Maria]]

This is precisely the analysis that we will propose for infinitival complements of perception verbs like the one in (137a). The analysis in (169)
has several advantages over the two alternatives we considered above.
First, unlike those alternatives, the analysis of (169) accounts for the
variation of (137) above (i.e. *Ho visto/ ? lasciato/ *fatto Giovanni parlare
con Maria*) on the basis of (168), just as the NP analysis of the tensed
counterpart does for the variation in (167). Secondly, unlike the alternatives, (169) is essentially compatible with both sets of arguments in (161).
All of *Ia, b, c, d, e, f,* which we have taken to indicate that the NP to the
right of the perception verb is not within the same minimal S as the
infinitival, will follow.[59] *I g,* and the indication that the NP is the head of
the construction will also be accounted for, rather obviously. It would be
easy to show that all the facts of *I* relative to the infinitival construction
obtain in analogous fashion for the tensed construction in (163), as we
would expect. Turning to *II, a* will not apply to (169), as the subcate-

gorization __NP is independently justified by (168a,b). And, as tensed alternants we will now correctly expect cases like (163). As for nominalization, we will not expect the S in (169) to have nominal counterparts, any more than we expect the one in (163) or relative clauses to have one. Concerning *II b* and the absence of a preposition before the infinitive, this will seem less puzzling since we are no longer dealing with a case of object Control, although as mentioned we lack a general understanding of how these prepositions function.[60] The difference between perception verb complements and object Control cases with respect to some of the points in *I* will also seem more natural (see the discussion of (144)). The fact that the NP immediately preceding the infinitive (*Giovanni* of (137a)) is, under this analysis, not really the object of the perception verb, but rather the *head* of that object, seems also to do justice to both the claim, which we discussed above and which seems roughly correct, that the latter NP is semantically the object of direct perception, and the counter claim (cf. for example, Radford (1977)) that the latter NP enters only compositionally into what is being perceived.[61] In fact, the semantics of the infinitival cases seems to be rather analogous to that of tensed cases like (163), as we would now predict. Evidence for constituency (*II c*), will follow for the infinitival as it does for the tensed case. Notice that the assumption that infinitival complements of perception verbs in Romance have the same analysis as in English, will not lead us to expect that, contrary to fact, English should also have the construction in (163) **(Ho visto Giovanni che parlava con Maria** 'I saw Giovanni who was talking with Maria'.) It is clear that this construction requires a rather special coindexing rule (as discussed in Kayne (1981a)), while the infinitival relies on normal Control mechanisms. English would then simply lack such a coindexing rule.

The obvious desirability of a parallel account of the two types *Ho visto Giovanni parlare con Maria*, and *Ho visto Giovanni che parlava con Maria*, is reflected in the fact that parallel accounts have been proposed before. Thus, in FS (pp. 126–129, 220–234) both constructions are analyzed as object Control structures, while in Radford (1977) they are both analyzed as involving Raising to object, from an infinitival complement in one case, and a tensed complement in the other. We have already given reasons for rejecting an object Control analysis.[62] As for the Raising to object analysis, first, our theoretical framework does not allow Raising to object, especially in the tensed case. Secondly, while the type *Giovanni che* ... alternates with the type *che Giovanni* ... under perception verbs (cf. (150)) whence the motivation for Raising to object, it does not always do so elsewhere, as is noted in Ruwet (1982, p. 125). Thus, for example (170a) could not be derived via Raising to object since (170b) does not exist.

(170) a.　Con　Giovanni　[che　beve],　Maria　è　disperata.
　　　　　with　Giovanni　that　drinks　Maria　is　desperate

　　　　　With Giovanni drinking . . .

　　　b.　*Con　[che　Giovanni　beve],　Maria　è　disperata.
　　　　　with　that　Giovanni　drinks　Maria　is　desperate

There are a number of syntactic similarities between the two types
in (171) beside those already noted, which will further support the idea
that they have parallel structures. In particular, both allow cliticization,
NP-movement and Clefting of what we now regard as the head of the
complement, as in (172)–(174).[63]

(171) a. Ho visto　　　Giovanni parlare con　Maria.
　　　　　(I) have seen　Giovanni speak　　with　Maria

　　　b. Ho visto　　　Giovanni che　parlava　　　con　Maria.
　　　　　(I) have seen　Giovanni who　was speaking　with　Maria

(172) a.　L'ho visto　　　parlare con　Maria.
　　　　　(I)　him have seen　speak　　with　Maria

　　　b.　L'ho visto　　　che　parlava　　　con　Maria.
　　　　　(I)　him have seen　who　was speaking　with　Maria

(173) a. **Giovanni**　fu visto　　parlare con　Maria.
　　　　　Giovanni　was seen　speak　　with　Maria

　　　b. **Giovanni**　fu visto　che　parlava　　　con　Maria.
　　　　　Giovanni　was seen　who　was speaking　with　Maria

(174) a. È　　　**Giovanni**　che　ho visto　　　parlare con　Maria.
　　　　　(It) is　Giovanni　that (I)　have seen　speak　　with　Maria

　　　b. È　　　**Giovanni**　che ho visto　　che　parlava　　　con Maria.
　　　　　(It) is Giovanni that (I)　have seen who was speaking withMaria

Alongside of such similarities there are however a number of differences, which may seem to argue against our proposal. One difference has
to do with the 'non-island' character of the infinitival case, compared with
the tensed counterpart, as in (175).

(175) a. ?*Il　libro che$_i$　ho visto　　　Giovanni che　leggeva [$_i$e]　è
　　　　　the　book that (I)　have seen　Giovanni who　was reading　is

　　　　Moby Dick.
　　　　Moby Dick

b. Il libro che*i* ho visto Giovanni leggere [*i*e] è Moby
   the book that (I) have seen Giovanni read is Moby

Dick.
Dick

As we discussed above (cf. (164)), the ungrammaticality of cases like (175a) can be taken as a Complex NP Constraint violation, thus supporting the NP constituency of the construction. The relative acceptability of (175b) may then correspondingly be taken as evidence against NP constituency. But the problem for our analysis is not as serious as it seems. While infinitival cases like (175a) are generally accepted in Italian and French, they are not in Spanish, as noted in Bordelois (1974, pp. 103 ff.), to whom (176) is due.

(176) a.   Lo dejé leer el libro.
           (I) him let read the book

           I let him read the book.

b. *El libro que lo dejé leer era Ivanhoe.
   the book that him (I) let read was Ivanhoe

   The book that I let him read was Ivanhoe.

Furthermore, it is known that the Complex NP Constraint holds more weakly for infinitivals than for tensed clauses, whatever the exact theoretical reasons may be, as (177), (178) show.

(177) a.   *Which sink did you send a man who can fix?

b.   ?Which sink did you send a man to fix?

(178) a.   ??The girl that I do not see any possibility that I will meet is Mary.

b.   ?The girl that I do not see any possibility to meet is Mary.

Therefore, it does not seem too implausible to suppose that whatever exact difference there is between tensed and infinitival cases like (175a, b), could be subsumed under a more general difference between tensed and infinitival complements.

Other differences, noted in Akmajian (1977) between the two English cases in (179), appear to carry over to our cases.

(179) a. I saw John speak with Mary.

b. I saw John speaking with Mary.

Generally speaking, it appears that the '-ing' case of (179b) behaves analogously to the tensed case in (171b), while the infinitival in (179a) corresponds to the infinitival in (171a). The discussion in Kayne (1981a) sees in fact a similarity in distribution and behavior between French tensed cases analogous to (171b) and '-ant' cases like (180) (which Italian does not have), which we presume correspond to the English '-ing' cases.[64]

(180)   J'ai vu Jean parlant avec Marie.
        I saw Jean speaking with Marie.

Adapted to our cases, the differences noted by Akmajian are those illustrated in (181)–(184).

(181)   Ciò che ho visto   è   *Pseudo-clefting.*
        what   (I) have seen is

$\left\{ \begin{array}{l} \text{Giovanni che parlava con Maria} \\ \text{??Giovanni parlare con Maria} \end{array} \right\}$

$\left\{ \begin{array}{l} \textit{Giovanni (who was) speaking with Maria} \\ \textit{Giovanni speak with Maria} \end{array} \right\}$

(182)   Abbiamo visto ciò che speravamo di vedere:
        (we) saw   what   (we) hoped to see:

$\left\{ \begin{array}{l} \text{Giovanni che parlava con Maria} \\ \text{??Giovanni parlare con Maria} \end{array} \right\}$ *Equative-deletion.*

$\left\{ \begin{array}{l} \textit{Giovanni (who was) speaking with Maria} \\ \textit{Giovanni speak with Maria} \end{array} \right\}$

(183)   Abbiamo sentito, benché non siamo   riusciti a vedere
        (we) heard,   although (we) did not manage to see

$\left\{ \begin{array}{l} \text{Giovanni che parlava con Maria} \\ \text{??Giovanni parlare con Maria} \end{array} \right\}$ *Right Node Raising.*

$\left\{ \begin{array}{l} \textit{Giovanni (who was) speaking with Maria} \\ \textit{Giovanni speak with Maria} \end{array} \right\}$

(184)   È $\left\{ \begin{array}{l} \text{Giovanni che parlava con Maria} \\ \text{*Giovanni parlare con Maria} \end{array} \right\}$ *Clefting.*

        (it) is $\left\{ \begin{array}{l} \textit{Giovanni (who was) speaking with Maria} \\ \textit{Giovanni speak with Maria} \end{array} \right\}$

        che abbiamo visto.
        that (we) have seen

It will be recalled how we previously assumed, following Radford (1977), that there was a certain similarity in response to Pseudo-clefting and

Equative-deletion (cf. (155a,c), (166a,c)). But (181), (182) now show that the similarity is only partial, since in cases slightly different from those cited by Radford the two constructions diverge. Beside those illustrated by (181)–(184), there are yet other differences in behavior. In particular, there is a difference with respect to the possibility of moving the whole construction into subject position, as in (185) (also discussed in Akmajian (1977)), a difference with respect to coordination with NP (cf. (165)), as in (186), and one with respect to right dislocation, as in (187).[65]

(185)
$$\left\{ \begin{array}{l} \text{?Giovanni\ che parlava con Maria} \\ \text{*Giovanni\ parlare con Maria} \end{array} \right\} \quad \text{è stato visto}$$

$$\left\{ \begin{array}{l} \textit{Giovanni (who was) speaking with Maria} \\ \textit{Giovanni\ speak with Maria} \end{array} \right\} \quad \textit{was seen}$$

da tutti.
by everyone.

(186)   Ho visto [NPMaria] e $\left\{ \begin{array}{l} \text{[Giovanni che la seguiva]} \\ \text{*[Giovanni seguirla]} \end{array} \right\}$.

   (I) saw   Maria and $\left\{ \begin{array}{l} \textit{Giovanni (who was) following her} \\ \textit{Giovanni follow her} \end{array} \right\}$.

(187)   L'ho visto, $\left\{ \begin{array}{l} \text{Giovanni\ che parlava con Maria} \\ \text{*Giovanni\ parlare con Maria} \end{array} \right\}$.

   (I) saw him, $\left\{ \begin{array}{l} \textit{Giovanni (who was) speaking with Maria} \\ \textit{Giovanni\ speak with Maria} \end{array} \right\}$.

We have no account for these differences. However, we must note that the tensed and the infinitival constructions have different distributions not only under the syntactic conditions imposed by the various tests we have been discussing (Wh-movement, pseudo-clefting, etc.), but more generally. For instance, the tensed construction appears in cases like (170), repeated in (188a) here below. Such cases, discussed in Ruwet (1982, 3) have sc alternants like (188b), whose likely analysis is the one indicated, but have no infinitival alternants like (188c).[66]

(188) a.   Con Giovanni$_i$ [$_S$che [$_i$e] beve],   Maria è disperata.
      with Giovanni   (who is) drinking, Maria is desperate

   b.   Con Giovanni$_i$ [$_{sc}$PRO$_i$ ammalato], Maria è disperata.
      with Giovanni   sick,   Maria is desperate

   c.   *Con Giovanni$_i$ [$_S$PRO$_i$bere],   Maria è disperata,
      with Giovanni   to drink, Maria is desperate

Within the present framework, there is no straightforward reason for the ungrammaticality of (188c), which ought to be possible on a par with the sc case (cf. also Note 64.) It is thus not unreasonable to speculate that an account of (188c) versus (188a) would also shed light on the differential behavior of these constructions under the various tests.[67] Concerning the different distributions we also note that the tensed construction (like the English -*ing*, and the French -*ant* constructions) is found with verbs other than perception verbs, such as **incontrare**, **scoprire** 'meet, discover' and others (on this, see Akmajian (1977, p. 441)), while this is not true of the infinitival, as shown in (189).

(189) Ho incontrato { Giovanni che usciva dal cinema / *Giovanni uscire dal cinema } .

(*I*) *have met* { *Giovanni (who was) leaving the movies* / *Giovanni leave the movies* } .

Furthermore the tensed construction can be found in subject position, unlike the infinitival, as in (190). We may in fact presume that the contrast in (190) subsumes the one in (185).

(190) { Giovanni che parla   con la bocca piena / *Giovanni parlare   con la bocca piena }

{ *Giovanni (who is) speaking with his mouth full* / *Giovanni speak   with his mouth full* }

mi fa venire il voltastomaco.
gives me   an upset stomach.

In conclusion, there are certain residual questions, but we find compelling reasons to analyze infinitival complements of perception verbs as NPs, with the head of the NP controlling the subject of the infinitival. In essence, our conclusion rests on the observation that while there are Control effects, an object Control analysis is not tenable. Such an analysis provides the natural infinitival counterpart for the type *Ho visto Giovanni che parlava con Maria* under the analysis of the latter in Kayne (1981a), which seems to us correct.

4.8. CONCLUSION

In this chapter we have provided analyses for the various constructions in which causative and perception predicates can appear. We have argued that the FI construction is syntactically derived via a rule of VP-movement, that the FP construction is base-generated, and that cases in which the complement verb is ergative are to be related to FP rather than to FI. We have analyzed infinitival complements of perception predicates as NPs.

Several conclusions can be drawn from our discussion. One is that causative constructions provide further evidence for our thesis of chapter 1, that there is a class of ergative verbs (Perlmutter's "Unaccusative Hypothesis"), as we noted in 4.5.3. Another is that causative constructions support the general organization of EST, with its three different levels of representation. Consider the well-formedness of the configuration in (191a) versus the ill-formedness of (191b), discussed in 4.4 and 4.6 respectively.

(191) a.   NP fare $[_{VP} \ldots$ se stesso$_i \ldots] [_S(a)NP_i - - -]$

    b.   *NP fare $[_{VP} \ldots t_i \ldots] [_S(a) NP_i - - -]$

The two configurations in (191) are entirely parallel. Thus no distinction can be drawn on the basis of S-structure alone. They can be distinguished however by postulating a level of LF at which the VP can be reconstructed in its original position. Example (191a) will then be well-formed while (191b) is excluded, if we regard *se stesso$_i$* as requiring a proper antecedent only at LF while t_i requires one at S-structure as well, a difference which we have deduced from the projection principle.

While the contrast in (191) thus motivates the LF level of representation, the one in (192), discussed in 4.2 (cf. (46)), will motivate the level of D-structure.

(192) a. $\ldots$ si$_i$ fare $[_{VP} \ldots [_i e] \ldots]$

    b.   *$\ldots$ si$_i$ fare $[_{VP} \ldots [_i e] \ldots] [_S(a)NP - - -]$

Again, no distinction between (192a) and (192b) seems possible on the basis of S-structure, given the exact parallelism. But the distinction is made on the basis of D-structure representation: There, the relation between *si* and the *ec* of (192a) will remain local, while the one of (192b) will not. The requirement that clitic-*ec* relations obtain at D-structure was again deduced from the projection principle.

The contrast of (192) will disappear if instead of a clitic-*ec* relation we consider the antecedent-trace relation of (193), as we saw in connection with (64), (65) above.

(193) a. NP$_i$ fare $[_{VP} \ldots t_i \ldots]$

    b. NP$_i$ fare $[_{VP} \ldots t_i \ldots] [_S(a)NP - - -]$

Yet we assume that antecedent-trace relations are just like clitic-*ec* relations with respect to the projection principle, both being required to obtain at all levels. Where then does the difference between (192) and (193) come from? It comes from the fact that, while si_i is base-generated in its position, NP$_i$ is moved to that position. Thus, while antecedent-trace relations are required to obtain at all levels, just like clitic-*ec* relations, D-structure is irrelevant to (193) since t_i does not exist at that

level. Thus the difference between (192) and (193) motivates the existence of Move α. It also motivates the distinction between D-structure
and LF. In principle one might have attempted to distinguish (192a) and
(192b) on the basis, not of D-structure, but of LF, arguing that in (192b)
si will not be locally related to the *ec* after reconstruction. But this would
have wrongly predicted ill-formedness for (193b) as well. It is thus
D-structure, not LF, which is relevant to (192).[68] Given (193b) and the
assumption that antecedent-trace relations must be well-formed at all
levels, thus also at LF, it must be the case that LF exists both before and
after reconstruction (or perhaps that reconstruction is optional). But this
is quite obvious in general. Consider *They$_i$ expected [[$_i$pictures of each
other$_i$] to be found t$_j$]*, in which *each other* is locally related to its
antecedent before, but not after reconstruction.

We have seen that our discussion of causative constructions has
certain implications for the nature of cliticization. Note that it also
provides strong evidence for the existence of empty categories related to
clitics. While we assume that clitics bear both Case and θ-role, we have
seen that in general they appear on the element that assigns Case, not on
the one that assigns θ-role. This is shown by the examples in (194).

(194) a.   ?Maria lo$_i$ ha fatto   [$_S$[$_i$e] riparare la macchina]
           Maria him has made   repair   the car

      b.   Maria lo$_i$ fa   [$_{VP}$lavorare] [$_S$[$_i$e] – – –]
           Maria him makes   work

      c.   Maria si$_i$ è fatta   [$_{VP}$accusare [$_i$e]]
           Maria herself has made   accuse

      d.   Maria lo$_i$ fa   [$_{VP}$intervenire [$_i$e]]
           Maria him makes   intervene

In each of these cases, the clitic is plainly associated with a θ-role assigned
by the lower verb. This fact essentially excludes lexical analyses of cliticization, namely it falsifies the view, tenable in principle in simple cases,
that clitics are affixes that, say, 'detransitivize' the verb, or more generally
that absorb one argument or θ-role from the item to which they are
affixed. In (194), the connection between clitic and θ-role can only be
established at syntactic, not at lexical levels, since the θ-role in question
pertains to a different lexical item than the one on which the clitic
appears. Note that a claim that such clitics originate on the lower verb
cannot be made, as it can be shown that no 'Clitic Climbing' occurs in
any of (194) (cf. discussions of (20a), (46), (110)). Notice furthermore
that, while in (194) there is a syntactic-configurational generalization,
with the clitics standing in analogous relations to their *ec* in each case,

there is no generalization in terms of one lexical property, since in (a) and (b) the clitic has subject θ-role, while in (c) and (d) it has object θ-role. Any theory will thus have to employ some syntactic apparatus so as to appropriately link at least at some level, each of the clitics in (194) with the position to which θ-role is assigned, while a theory that has the projection principle will have to do so at all levels. If object clitics are base-generated, as we assume, there will therefore have to be an empty category where the θ-role is assigned, so that the θ-role can be transmitted to the clitic (Recall that there is no generalization in terms of the kind of θ-role, while there is one in terms of the position of the *ec* relative to the clitic.) If clitics are moved (as in FS) there will still have to be *ec*'s in S-structure for transmission of θ-role, under the projection principle. Thus, either base-generation, or the projection principle, or both, imply the existence of *ec*'s related to clitics. To the extent that we have evidence for base-generation (such as the fact that under a movement analysis (192b) is predicted well-formed like (193b)), we reach the conclusion that such *ec*'s must exist, even independently of the projection principle.

NOTES

[1] For reasons which remain unclear, this kind of passive is not accepted in French with *faire* and *laisser*, though it is (marginally) with perception predicates like *voir* (see FS, p. 274. Cf. also Note 24).

[2] This hypothesis would seem to lead to the conclusion that the preposition *a* is a Case marker rather generally, and that *a* NP phrases are NPs at the level of subcategorization specifications. For it seems clear that transitive complements of *fare* are not subcategorized for *a* NP subjects. The view that *a* NP phrases are NPs rather than PPs at the level of subcategorization has been put forth independently by Jaeggli (1980), Vergnaud (1974) and others. We will not take this view explicitly in the text for various reasons. One is that, if these phrases are actually NPs, we have no account of their failure to undergo NP movement, whereas if they are PPs this follows from the impossibility of preposition stranding. Another reason is that there would be certain technical problems with respect to our formulation of pp agreement in 1.7, in so far as we have excluded pp agreement with dative clitics by assuming that the latter are in fact PPs.

[3] This discussion leaves unexplained the lack of dative Exceptional Case Marking, i.e. the non-existence of the type *I persuaded John [to Bill to leave]*.

[4] Notice that, in point of fact, the verb of (16c) does *not* trigger $\bar{\text{S}}$-deletion, since passives like (i) are also ungrammatical.

(i)   ?*Il blocco degli affitti$_i$ è stato dimostrato [$_{S}$t$_i$diminuire   l'inflazione]
          rent control   has been proved   to diminish inflation

We may assume that the reason why it does not is precisely that $\bar{\text{S}}$-deletion would not suffice to yield well-formedness for (16c). However, since $\bar{\text{S}}$-deletion would predict that it was well-formed, we must further assume that the distribution of lexical parameters is determined by results with the active, rather than with the passive form of the verb. This conforms with the traditional view that the passive has a derivative character relative to the corresponding active. The primacy of the active form is also supported by the lack of English passives like (ii), which would be well-formed on a par with Raising cases like (iii).

(ii)   John$_i$ was . . . ed to us [$_S$t$_i$ to like it]

(iii)   John$_i$ seemed to us [$_S$t$_i$ to like it]

In contrast to (ii), its active counterpart in (iv) would be ungrammatical through lack of Case on *John*, under Stowell's assumption (1981) that Case assignment (in English) requires linear adjacency.

(iv)   Bill . . . ed to us [$_S$John to like it]

For purposes of $\bar{S}$-deletion, $+\theta_s/-\theta_s$ verbs must therefore be regarded as two different verbs. This contrasts with the fact that they must be regarded as a single verb with respect to the principle governing auxiliary assignment discussed in 2.6.2. Recall how we assumed that, for example, French ergative *couler*, a 'periphery' case for assignment of *être*, takes *avoir* because transitive *couler* does. We see no contradiction here. Adopting for example the view of Marantz (1981) that transitive/ergative pairs (our terminology) represent two sides of one 'branching' lexical entry, we may expect that they behave as a single verb in some respects and as two different verbs in others.

⁵ One might then expect the ungrammaticality of (17b) to disappear under passivization, but the results are not very good, as in (i).

(i)   ??Giovanni$_i$ sarà fatto sembrar t$_i$ soffrire.
          Giovanni will be made to seem to suffer.

However, we find little contrast between (i) and the passive version of (17a) in (ii), suggesting that the difficulty may be due to the complexity of these examples.

(ii)   (?)?Giovanni$_i$ sarà fatto sembrar t$_i$ ammalato.
          Giovanni will be made to seem sick.

The slight difference between (i) and (ii) may be attributed to the prohibition on sequences of infinitives discussed in Longobardi (1980a), and in 5.4 below.

⁶ This generalization does not hold in any obvious way for subject clitics, however, since we assume that with subjects Case is assigned by INFL rather than by the verb. Furthermore, a subject clitic like *ci* need not be contiguous to the Case assigner — the matrix INFL in (i). Cf. 2.5.3.

(i)   [$_i$e] sembrava [$_S$t$_i$ esser**ci** molta gente]
          There seemed to be many people.

⁷ It may actually appear that the clitic in (21a) does c-command the *ec*. Consider the structure of (21a), as in (i).

(i)   [$_{VP_1}$[$_{VP_2}$V . . .] [$_S$NP . . .]]

In (i), *V* would c-command *NP* if the characterization of extended c-command given in I.0.3 (cf. (12) of I.0. and discussion) was taken literally, since VP_1 and VP_2 are of the same category. Then, any clitic attached to *V* would presumably also c-command *NP*, so that *lo$_i$* of (21a) would c-command [$_i$e].

However, we will assume, for empirical reasons, that in (i) c-command does *not* obtain. Our assumption is based on some of the discussion in 5.5 below, where we argue that in (i) NP does not function as an object of V, in particular with respect to E assignment/pp agreement (cf. also Notes 16, 28.) But recall that in 2.2 we concluded that government, and therefore c-command obtains in the configuration (ii).

(ii)   [$_{VP}$[$_{VP}$V . . .]NP]

The structure in (ii) arises in cases of inversion by rightward movement and VP-adjunction (cf. discussion of (26b), ch. 2). We will take the crucial difference between (i) and (ii) to be that in (i) the two VP's are projections of different verbs, whereas in (ii) they are projections of the same verb. The definition of c-command of I.0.3 would there-fore have to be appropriately sharpened to draw this distinction. For a more precise definition, fully compatible with all the facts we are discussing, see LGB, p. 166.

[8] As we expect, cases analogous to (22) in which the reflexive is not a clitic are essen-tially grammatical, though slightly less than perfect, as in (i).

(i)   (?)Maria ha fatto [$_{VP}$accusare se stessa] [$_S$a Giovanni − − −]
        Maria had Giovanni accuse herself.

We may interpret the difficulty in (i) as an effect similar to the SSC though weaker and due to the 'predominance' of the embedded subject among the dependents of *fare*. Such 'predominance' seems to be reflected in the fact that the embedded subject is generally required to be the highest on a certain hierarchy based on animacy. In fact many (though not all, cf. FS, pp. 252 ff.) FI cases like (ii) involving inanimate embedded subjects are ungrammatical, while animate embedded objects are allowed only with a handful of verbs, like *accusare*, as in (iii) (and as we note in the text in 4.4 below), and only if they are in the third person, as shown by (iv).

(ii)   *Giovanni ha fatto disturbare i vicini alla televisione.
        Giovanni made the tv bother the neighbors.

(iii)   Giovanni ha fatto $\left\{ \begin{matrix} \text{accusare} \\ \text{??aiutare} \end{matrix} \right\}$ Maria a Piero.

        Giovanni made Piero $\left\{ \begin{matrix} accuse \\ help \end{matrix} \right\}$ *Maria.*

(iv)   ?*Giovanni $\left\{ \begin{matrix} \text{mi} \\ \text{ti} \end{matrix} \right\}$ ha fatto $\left\{ \begin{matrix} \text{accusare} \\ \text{aiutare} \end{matrix} \right\}$ a Maria.

        Giovanni made Maria $\left\{ \begin{matrix} accuse \\ help \end{matrix} \right\}$ $\left\{ \begin{matrix} me \\ you \end{matrix} \right\}$.

We regard the difference between (iii) and (iv) as due to the higher rank of first and second person NPs on the relevant hierarchy. Recall how first and second person NPs behave differently in other (though not obviously related) respects also: transmission of agreement features when they are i-subjects in the *ci/ye* construction (cf. 2.5.4); failure to prepose in SI constructions (cf. 1.6.2).

[9] Notice that to account correctly for dative *gli* of (25) a 'dative clitic-ec' chain must be regarded as equivalent to a dative NP (i.e. to *a NP*) with respect to the dativization rule in (14). Notice also that, in so far as we regard (14) as a rule at all, it will be more appro-priate to interpret it as a Case checking rather than a Case marking mechanism, so that we can more naturally assume that *gli* of (25) is base-generated as a dative clitic, rather than being dativized in the course of the derivation.

[10] The lack of ambiguity with sequences of two datives is particularly solid when the first one is a dative of inalienable possession related to the direct object, as in (i).

(i)   Fa   stringere la mano   al direttore   a Maria.
        make shake   the hand to the director to Maria

        Make Maria shake the director's hand.

Yet this never corresponds to a possibility for the first dative to cliticize on a par with the second, as shown by (ii).

(ii)   ??Fa**gli** stringere la mano a Maria.
          Make Maria shake the hand to him ('his hand').

          Fa**lle** stringere la mano al direttore.
          Make her shake the director's hand.

[11] Analogous results obtain with non-clitic reflexives, as in (i), which is not significantly worse than (i) of Note 8.

(i)   ?Maria farà telefonare Giovanni a se stessa.
          Maria will make Giovanni phone (to) herself.

[12] Kayne attempts to relate the cases in (40) to extraction of clitics from sc complements of verbs like **croire** 'believe'. Notice that this may seem plausible in view of some of our remarks in II.0.3 above, since in both sc's and in complements of *faire* after FI there is no verbal element to which clitics could be attached. However, this view requires that one find — as Kayne does — a qualitative difference between *y, en* and datives in the *croire* cases, as well as in (40) vs. (27). But we do not see such a difference in Italian (cf. (17), (18) in II.0.3.)

[13] Actually, Quicoli (1980) claims that datives are outside $\overline{V}$ only when the verb has no direct object, and within otherwise. That is, he assumes the structures $[_{\overline{V}}write]$ *to John* and $[_{\overline{V}}write$ *a letter to John]*. But under this additional complication we would find this approach even less convincing.

[14] Some reordering must be assumed in FS too, given cases like (i) (FS, p. 210) which we discuss in 4.5 below.

(i)   Elle a fait admettre à Jean [qu'il avait tort]
          She made Jean admit that he was wrong.

In (i), the bracketed sentential complement induces dativization of the embedded subject on a par with a direct object NP and is thus presumably to the left of the latter at the level relevant to dativization.

[15] Another correct prediction is that in those dialects in which dative objects trigger dativization of the embedded subject on a par with accusative objects (cf. 4.5 below), no reordering should occur. As Wehrli notes, cases like (i) are in fact never ambiguous, the first dative being interpreted as an object, the second as the embedded subject.

(i)   Jean fait télephoner à Paul à Marie.
          Jean makes Marie phone (to) Paul.

[16] An account of the non-ambiguity of (42) along these lines assumes that, while a dependent of the lower verb is also a dependent of the matrix verb, thus absorbing Case from both (especially when cliticized), a dependent of the matrix verb (i.e. the embedded subject) is not also a dependent of the lower verb, thus absorbing Case from the matrix verb only. (*À sa femme* can thus get Case from the lower verb.) The conclusion is therefore that the complex predicate is asymmetrical, as in our analysis, a conclusion also suggested by the existence of Clitic Climbing versus non-existence of Clitic 'Lowering', as we note in 4.3 below. In 5.5 we argue for an analogous asymmetry in restructuring cases.

[17] Wehrli's idea is that all clitics which are not unambiguously non-dative, thus datives as well as first and second person accusatives, must be interpreted as an embedded subject in the FI construction. The proposed generalization has certain advantages over the suggestion in the text. It accounts for the ungrammaticality of (27) and for the non-ambiguity of (28) (equals (42)) in identical fashion. It draws the correct distinction between dative clitics and other indirect object clitics ((27) vs. (40)). Finally, it covers the case of (iv) of fn. 8. However, unlike our suggestion, it says nothing about the linear order of constituents in the absence of cliticization.

[18] Alongside of ungrammatical cases like (46b), there are superficially analogous cases which are grammatical, like the French case in (i), from FS, p. 407.

(i)   Jean se fera connaître à Marie.
        Jean will make himself known to Marie.

We note first that both in French and in Italian examples like (i) are very rare, so that they will not in any case threaten our assumption that the configuration of (46b) is in general ungrammatical. Secondly, there are some reasons to believe that cases like (i) are not really cases of FI, but rather of FP, so that their well-formedness will be expected, on a par with that of (46a). The reasons are that verbs like 'know' allow their thematic subject to be realized as a dative phrase (rather than as a *by*-phrase), cf. the English translation of (i), whence the possibility that (i) may be a variant of FP, with *à Marie* playing the role of *par Marie* of the standard case. The correct account of (i) seems to us to lie along these lines in spite of the fact that a dative phrase with the value of thematic-subject, possible in English as noted, is not possible in French and Italian passives, as in ?***Giovanni sarà conosciuto a tutti** 'Giovanni will be known to everyone', though possible in the corresponding 'unpassive' **Giovanni era sconosciuto a tutti** 'Giovanni was unknown to everyone'.

As Kayne notes (FS, p. 238), French has other cases in which the thematic subject can be realized differently than as a *par*-phrase. These are represented by verbs like **haïr** 'hate', that take a *de*-phrase both in passives and in FP. Italian *da* covers both the *par* and the *de* cases of French.

[19] Contrasts analogous to the one in (46) are found in cases in which indirect rather than direct objects are involved, as in (ia) below, and as our theory predicts. The same facts are recognized, but dealt with rather differently in FS. Kayne assumes in fact (FS, p. 292, fn. 19) that the ungrammaticality of cases like (ia) is subsumed under that of corresponding non-reflexive cases like (ib), discussed in 4.5 above.

(i) a.   *Maria si$_i$ farà [$_{VP}$ scrivere [$_i$e]] [$_S$ Giovanni − − −]
           Maria will make Giovanni write to herself.

   b.   ?Gli$_i$ farò [$_{VP}$ scrivere [$_i$e]] [$_S$ Giovanni − − −]
           I will make Giovanni write to him.

As for the ungrammaticality of cases like (46b) (the direct object case) Kayne assumes (FS, p. 241 f.) that it is of the same nature as that of cases like (ii) (discussed in Note 8) involving first and second person non-reflexive clitics, and presumably due to some animacy constraint on the FI construction.

(ii)   ?*Giovanni $\left\{ \begin{array}{l} mi_i \\ ti_i \end{array} \right\}$ ha fatto [$_{VP}$ accusare [$_i$e]] [$_S$ a Maria − − −]

        Giovanni made Marie accuse $\left\{ \begin{array}{l} me \\ you \end{array} \right\}$.

Like (46b) such cases also turn out to have grammatical FP counterparts, like (iii).

(iii)   Giovanni $\left\{ \begin{array}{l} mi \\ ti \end{array} \right\}$ ha fatto accusare (da Maria).

        Giovanni had $\left\{ \begin{array}{l} me \\ you \end{array} \right\}$ *accused (by Maria).*

We see certain advantages in our account. Unlike ours, Kayne's account does not quite explain the contrast in (46), as both in FS and in our discussion there is no precise understanding of the contrast between (ii) and (iii). Furthermore, our account of (46b) is confirmed by the distribution of reflexives in restructuring constructions, as we see in chapter 6, while the FS accont would shed no light on that distribution. As for the indirect object case, it is clear at least in Italian that cases like (ia) and (ib) have different degrees of ungrammaticality, casting doubt on the FS interpretation. Note that the problem of (ii) does not seem to carry over to indirect objects, as ?**Ti farò scrivere Giovanni** 'I will make Giovanni write to you' seems to be on a par with (ib) rather than with (ii). This suggests that the ungrammaticality of (ia) cannot be subsumed under that of (ii) either.

[20] As discussed in Note 15, chapter 2, we assume weather verbs to be either ergative or intransitive. Cases like (47) would employ the intransitive frame. We attribute the total lack of *by*-phrases in such cases as (47) to the fact that the thematic subject of *piovere* does not have full θ-role, only a 'quasi' θ-role, cf. 3.1.3. To this we also attribute the total failure of such verbs to appear with passive morphology, cf. 3.2.2.

[21] Contrasts like the one between (51b) and (51c) are noted in FS, p. 247, fn. 56. Kayne insightfully relates them to the corresponding contrasts seen in impersonal passives, though no solution is available for either set of contrasts, in his framework.

[22] While our account of the distribution of *by*-phrases is thus quite parallel to that of the distribution of impersonal passives, it seems to me that the Relational Grammar account of impersonal passives in terms of a '1 Advancement Exclusiveness Law' (cf. Note 15, ch. 3) could be extended to account for the distribution of *by*-phrases in FP only at the cost of a rather unlikely analysis of FP constructions.

[23] Notice that even in the theory put forward here there are principles which are stipulated or taken as primitives, and which may eventually turn out to be derivative. One such principle is the conditional '$-\theta_s \rightarrow -A$' of 3.1.1, which underlies the association between passive morphology and NP-movement in the most common type of passive. This principle was shown to be empirically true, while not being entirely predictable theoretically. Another is the principle which states that the role of thematic-subject can be fulfilled in exactly two ways: by a subject NP, and by a *by*-phrase (aside from the few cases of Note 18, involving other phrases).

[24] Cases like (57a,b) are not possible in French (cf. Note 1). Corresponding SE-moyen cases are marginal (cf. FS, p. 396 f.).

[25] Even this dependency does not always hold if we consider as 'passive' the past participles of ergative verbs in Italian sc relatives (see 3.2.3). In fact there is no *by*-phrase with the latter, no 'thematic-subject'.

[26] These deficiencies notwithstanding, we find the FS analysis empirically superior to others, at least in one respect. FS correctly allows intransitive verbs to occur in the FP construction (as in (52), (54), although something would have to be said about the non occurrence of the *by*-phrase in (54), as in our theory). In contrast, the analyses of Radford (1977), and of Rouveret and Vergnaud (1980) both exclude intransitive verbs in principle by going too far in assimilating FP constructions to passives (thus incorrectly excluding both (52) and (54)).

[27] The higher position of clitics in these constructions is derived from independent principles in Rouveret and Vergnaud (1980), who appeal to the principle of the cycle. Within a movement analysis of cliticization, they argue that in cases like (59a), if cliticization applied to the lower cycle and thus with respect to the lower verb, subsequent application of the FI rule (their $\overline{V}$-movement) would produce ill-formed results. For the sake of discussion, we will grant this conclusion, which has to do with the details of their theory. The only remaining possibility will then be for cliticization to apply at the higher cycle. Since they assume that the FI rule moves the relevant phrase ($\overline{V}$) to the left of the embedded subject, but without extracting it from the embedded S, cliticization on the *higher* cycle, but to the *lower* verb would violate strict cyclicity, whence the higher position of the clitic. We have several reasons to doubt such an account, both theoretical and empirical. One is that an account based on the cycle would

not extend to the FP construction if we are right in claiming that the latter does not involve a sentential complement. (Rouveret and Vergnaud assume that it does.) Another is that, while the cycle − in so far as it establishes the order in which rules apply − is conceptually natural in a system like the one of FS, it is not so natural within a system involving trace theory and configurational output conditions such as the one we (as well as Rouveret and Vergnaud) assume. Correspondingly, while it finds adequate empirical motivation in the FS system, the cycle finds none in our system here. On this matter, see also Burzio (1983).

[28] The asymmetry of the derived structure which we presume, cf. Note 16 and discussion below, will lead us to expect that cliticization or NP-movement of the embedded subject (a dependent of the matrix verb) will *not* induce pp agreement on the lower verb in the way that dependents of the lower verb induce pp agreement on the matrix verb (i.e. as in (63)−(65).) The prediction is not really testable, since the lower verb cannot appear with an aspectual auxiliary, a fact which we discuss in 5.8 below. Nevertheless the prediction seems borne out to the extent that it is testable, as in (i).

(i)   **La** faccio $\left\{ \begin{array}{l} \text{?* aver telefonato} \\ \text{** aver telefonata} \end{array} \right\}$ prima delle sei.

     I will make her have phoned before six.

The corresponding prediction is directly testable in the case of restructuring constructions, as we shall see.

[29] Recall that in the formulation of the rule of pp agreement, reference to the direct object is necessary, and that we could not simply say that in (64) and (65) the pp agrees with its own subject. (Analogously, in (63) we could not simply say that the pp agrees with a clitic attached to the same auxiliary-past participle complex.) The reason lies in the contrast in (i).

(i) a. $[_i\text{e}]$ si è andati t_i
       SI has gone.   (E, pp ag't)

   b.   [e] si è telefonato
       SI has phoned.   (E, no pp ag't)

The cases in (i) both take auxiliary *essere*, and can thus only be distinguished for purposes of pp agreement by making reference to the direct object. See 1.7.

We predict that, just as it does with respect to pp agreement, an embedded object should behave as an object of the main verb with respect to E-assignment. (Cf. 1.7.) If we take then traditional analysis of passives which is assumed in the text for simplicity, then this prediction is indeed borne out by auxiliary E of (ii).

(ii)   La macchina$_i$ **era**   stata fatta $[_{VP}\text{riparare } t_i \ldots] \ldots$
       the car   *was ('had')* *been made*   *to repair*

However, under the sc analysis of passives we argued for in 2.7 the prediction cannot be tested. Consider (iii).

(iii)   La macchina$_i$ **era** stata $[_{sc} t_i$ fatta $[_{VP}$ riparare $t_i \ldots] \ldots]$

In (iii) only the intermediate trace, and not the object of the embedded verb is relevant for E-assignment. Auxiliary E in the impersonal cases in (65) is also irrelevant to the point, since impersonal constructions take E independent of the relation involving the direct object (see 1.7). We are thus unable to show that what holds for pp agreement also holds for E-assignment. This will be shown in the case of restructuring constructions.

[30] We may then expect that if Clitic Climbing fails, as in (i), the sentence should be possible at the level of marginality associated with failure of Clitic Climbing.

(i) ?*   Faccio scriver**gli** una lettera a Maria.
            I will have Maria write a letter to him.

Example (i) seems in fact better than (70), but is perhaps slightly worse than other cases in which Clitic Climbing fails (cf. (68a)), although judgements are not very clear.

[31] Another similarity concerns the prohibition on sequences of infinitives discussed in Longobardi (1980a), which we will return to in 5.4 below. As Longobardi notes, sequences of infinitives, not allowed in general, as in (i), are allowed in what we have termed "complex predicates", and in particular in both FI and FP, as in (iia, b).

(i) ??   Giovanni sperava di amare studiare.
            Giovanni hoped   to love   to study

(ii) a.   Maria sperava di fare   riparare la   macchina a   Giovanni.
            Maria hoped   to make repair   the car   to Giovanni

            Maria hoped to make Giovanni repair the car.

    b.   Maria sperava di fare   riparare la   macchina (da Giovanni).
            Maria hoped   to make repair   the car   (by Giovanni)

            Maria hoped to have the car repaired (by Giovanni).

These facts will suggest that (iia, b) have similar structures, although it is not very clear how exactly they bear on the analysis of FI and FP   constructions. See Longobardi (1980a).

[32] Discussions of FP constructions related to Kayne's can be found in Strozer (1976) and Jaeggli (1981) both of whom deal with Spanish. Some of the solutions we propose below are analogous to Jaeggli's.

[33] Recall from 3.3.1 that the prepositon *a* does not in general block c-command. In the light of some of our discussion in this chapter (cf. in particular Note 2), we may now take this as a further indication that *a* is a Case-marker and not a real preposition.

[34] Note however the ungrammaticality of ***Se stesso fu fatto accusare a Giovanni** 'Himself was made accuse to Giovanni', structurally parallel to (83) but based on (74)/ (76b). This and other facts suggest that reconstruction is ineffective when the anaphoric phrase is not embedded. Cf. ?[$_i$*pictures of ourselves] seemed to us* t_i *to be on sale* versus * *ourselves$_i$ seemed to us* t_i *to be happy*. The reasons for this remain unclear.

The text discussion of non-passivizable idioms seems to us to be applicable as well to cases of verbs taking measure-phrase complements, sometimes also noted in the literature as failing to passivize. Consider the paradigm in (i).

(i) a.   La botte conterrà dieci litri di piú.
            The barrel will contain ten extra liters.

    b.   *Dieci litri di piú saranno contenuti (dalla botte).
            Ten extra liters will be contained (by the barrel).

            (NP-movement/pass. morph./ (*by*-phr.))

    c.   *Saranno contenuti dieci litri di piú (dalla botte).
            will be contained   ten extra liters   (by the barrel).

            (no NP-mov./pass. morph./ (*by*-phr.))

    d.   *La modifica farà [$_{VP}$contenere dieci litri di piú (dalla botte)].
            The modification will have ten extra liters contained (by the barrel).

            (no NP-mov./no pass. morph./ (*by*-phr.))

e. La modifica farà b[$_{VP}$ contenere dieci litri di piú] [$_S$ alla botte − − −].
The modification will make the barrel contain ten extra liters.

(no NP-mov./no pass. morph./no (*by*-phr.))

f. ?Dieci litri di piú$_i$ saranno fatti [$_{VP}$ contenere t$_i$] [$_S$ alla botte − − −].
Approx.: *Ten extra liters will be made to contain on the part of the barrel.*

(NP-mov./no pass. morph./no (*by*-phr.))

The paradigm shows that an account of (ib) in terms of a constraint on NP-movement or 'promotion' would be false. Instead, we might assume that in these cases, too, there exists a certain relation between the subject and the post-verbal phrase.

With other measure phrase verbs, such as *cost, last* failure of passivization is − we believe − due to the fact that they are ergative (auxiliary E in Italian). When embedded under *fare*, we then predict that they should only occur in the structure of (ii), as will be clear from our discussion of ergative complements in 4.5 below.

(ii) Questa tassa farà [$_{VP}$ costare tutto il doppio]
     this tax   will make   cost   everything the double

This tax will make everything cost twice as much.

Other verbs, like *become, remain*, which also fail to passivize, do so because they too are ergative. Under *fare* they will then occur as in (iii), whence the absence of either *a* or *da* with the presumed subject, noted in FS, pp. 208ff.

(iii) Questo farà   [$_{VP}$ diventare Giovanni un buon professore]
      this   will make   become   Giovanni a   good professor

This will make Giovanni become a good professor.

[35] In fact, under Kayne's preliminary formulation of the FI rule as moving the subject to the right (FS, p. 205), the FI and FP rules are so similar that they can be partially collapsed (FS, p. 249 f.)

[36] Notice that (89b) would actually violate the prohibition on sequences of infinitives of Note 31. However, our discussion in the text remains correct since the ungrammaticality of (89b) is more severe than that typical of such violations, and furthermore it persists if *sembrare* is replaced by, for example, **finire per** 'end up' (also a Raising verb), in which case the prohibition in question becomes ineffective, due to the presence of the preposition, as Longobardi (1980a) shows.

[37] Our analysis is also confirmed by the fact that, whereas in (90b,c) there is little difference between the order *addosso un agente/tra i piedi un agente* and the order *un agente addosso/un agente tra i piedi* (as we noted for (31) above), the former order is noticeably less acceptable than the latter in (92b, c), as predicted by the VP analysis.

[38] The verbs that Kayne cites (FS, 4.7) as behaving analogously to *mourir* of (93b) are those of (i).

(i) a. se rétrécir, tomber, monter.
       shrink   fall   climb

   b. disparaître, adhérer, rougir, enfler, couler,
      disappear adhere redden swell sink

      battre (e.g. Le coeur lui battait), tourner (e.g. La tête lui tourne)
      beat (e.g. His heart was beating) spin (e.g. His head is spinning)

Of these, the verbs in (1a) take auxiliary *être*, those in (1b) *avoir*. But the Italian counterparts all take auxiliary *essere*, the only exception being *battere* (cf. *battre*), which is odd with either auxiliary. We conclude from this that all of the verbs in (i) are ergative. Auxiliary *avoir* of the verbs in (ib) will follow from the more restrictive character of the E-assignment rule in French compared with its Italian counterpart, as we discussed in 2.6.2.

[39] We also note that cliticization of the dative to the ergative verb yields results typical of the failure of Clitic Climbing, as in (i) to be compared with (92b).

(i)   ??Fecero cader**gli** un agente addosso

Ungrammaticality should be much more extreme if the dative was a dependent of the higher verb. Cf. (21) above and discussion.

[40] Reducing dativization of the embedded subject to Case absorption in the case of sentential complements would imply that such complements are assigned accusative Case. But, since we assume that, in general, Ss do not require Case, we woud have to conclude that such complements are dominated by NP nodes.

[41] The parallel lack of dativization in (102) (contrasting with (103), (104)) and (i), involving inherent-reflexive *pentirsi, vergognarsi* will then argue for the ergative analysis of inherent-reflexive verbs of 1.5 above.

(i)   Questo $\left\{ \begin{array}{l} \textbf{lo} \\ \textbf{*gli} \end{array} \right\}$ farà $\left\{ \begin{array}{l} \text{pentire} \\ \text{vergognare} \end{array} \right\}$ [di non aver studiato]

        This will make him $\left\{ \begin{array}{l} \text{repent} \\ \text{be shamed} \end{array} \right\}$ *for not having studied.*

The non appearance of *si* in cases like (i) will be addressed in 6.3.1 below.

[42] I am grateful to R. Kayne for bringing these facts to my attention.

[43] As we noted in Note 34, the VP analysis also correctly predicts non dativization of the apparent subject in the case of verbs like *become, remain* occurring with predicate nominals.

[44] Note that the status of (110) and (111) is no longer comparable if, rather than *lo, ne* is involved, as in (i).

(i) a.   ??Farò [$_{VP}$ intervenir**ne**$_i$ molti [$_i$e]]
          I will make many of them intervene.

    b.   **Farò [$_{VP}$ lavorar**ne**$_i$] [$_S$ molti [$_i$e] − − −]
          I will make many of them work.

The difference between (ia) and (110) is explicable on the basis of the fact that *ne* is not 'Case-dependent' from the matrix verb like *lo*, since it is clear that, unlike *lo, ne* is not associated with accusative Case. On the other hand the reasons for the ungrammaticality of (111) carry over intact to (ib), both being ruled out because the configurational relation between the clitic and its *ec* is ill-formed, at least in D-structure. (*Ne*, like *lo*, is only an object, and not a subject clitic. cf. 1.4.)

[45] There are some apparent exceptions to the generalization illustrated by (114), such as (i), involving ergative *passare*.

(i)   Fate passare:
          Let (us/them) go by!

Such exceptions are only apparent however, since it is a general fact about imperatives or directions that they allow gaps, for whatever reason, as in *Do not drop ___, Do not play on ___ or around ___.* The gap in these cases is generally interpreted as a deictic ('this', 'this thing' etc.). That a real NP is present in such cases is confirmed by the fact that in FI constructions the latter triggers dativization, as in (ii).

(ii)   **Fagli**   vedere.
              let to-him see
              Let him see (this).

This and other similar examples are presented in Radford (1977, pp. 233 f.) as problematic for the formulation of the dativization rule. Radford also notes, citing observations of G. Lepschy, that verbs that take auxiliary *essere* never appear as in (ii), e.g. ***Fagli salire** 'Let him-dat. go up'. The reasons for this difference are perfectly clear from our discussion: in the ergative case there is no gap or null NP to trigger dativization, and furthermore *gli* would be related, not to the subject, but to the direct object of the embedded verb, which never dativizes.

[46] Note however that we have no account of cases like (i), which ought to be grammatical under the analysis given.

(i)   (?)?La sua expressione fa $[_{VP}$ sembrare $[_S$ che Giovanni soffra$]]$
        His expression makes (it) seem that Giovanni suffers.

Such cases are given as ocmpletely ungrammatical in FS, but we find them noticeably better than (116b).

[47] Note that there is a certain analogy between the two ill-formed types $[_{VP}$ be NP] of (119) and $[_{VP}$ seem that S] of Note 46: both lack the non-argument subject normally linked with the post-verbal argument.

While FS (p. 252, ex. (143a)) regards cases like (119b) as completely ungrammatical, Rizzi (1978a, Note 33) gives a similar example, with the phrase corresponding to *Giovanni* cliticized, as grammatical. While we find Rizzi's example less than perfect, we do notice an improvement, in both (119a) and (119b), if cliticization applies, though the reasons for this remain unclear.

[48] A further reason for the ungrammaticality of (121b), (122b,c) would arise under the suggestion of Note 29, chapter 1 that SI requires not only Case, but nominative Case in particular, since no nominative is available here.

[49] Correspondingly, we find **Lo**$_i$ **faranno** $[_{VP}$ **partire** $[_i$e]] 'They will make him leave' versus ***Lo**$_i$ **faranno** $[_{VP}$ **piovere** $[_i$e]] 'They will make it rain'.

[50] Notice that we are taking the correspondence to be at the level, not of individual relations, but rather of relation types. For there are certain locality conditions that must be fulfilled in order for E-assignment or pp agreement to occur, which play no role in reconstruction. Thus, inversion/extraposition relations trigger E-assignment only when the post-verbal argument is in an A-position, as we saw in 1.7, 2.2; but we assume that all behave alike with respect to reconstruction. Analogously, cl-*ec* relations trigger pp agreement only when the clitic is a direct object (except for reflexives); but again we assume no difference with respect to reconstruction. Also, Italian *ne* triggers pp agreement, while French *en* does not, presumably because of more stringent locality conditions in French, but we see no difference with respect to reconstruction. Finally, while E is selected with only some Raising verbs in Italian, and with none in French (cf. 2.6.2), all Raising structures are alike with respect to reconstruction.

[51] As we know, cases like **Giovanni è venuto a prendere il libro** 'Giovanni has come to fetch the book', in which auxiliary E appears, do not instantiate the configuration of (136b), but must rather be analyzed as in (i) (Cf. 1.8).

(i)   Giovanni$_i$ è venuto t$_i$ [PRO$_i$ a prendere il libro]

[52] There is a difference in the extension of the class, however, in that while English *make, let* behave like the perception predicates, the Italian counterparts differ, as indicated in (137). Of course, English also differs from Italian and Romance in lacking the VP-movement/FI rule.

[53] There is a strong tendency to use *venire* instead of passive *essere* in such cases as (141b). We find no clear explanation for this fact. We note however that, under our analysis of *venire* as an ergative verb in general, and that of passive 'be' as a Raising verb, it seems relatively natural that one may replace the other here. Such preference is reminiscent of the preference for *get* in (i).

(i)   I saw John $\left\{ \begin{array}{l} \text{get} \\ \text{?be} \end{array} \right\}$ arrested.

[54] The SI cases could still be excluded even under the __S analysis if we adopted the suggestion of Note 29, ch. 1 that SI requires not only Case, but *nominative* Case. We would see little reason to extend the suggestion to *ci* however.

[55] One further test which seems to argue for Control and against __S is provided by French *En-avant* constructions like the one in (i).

(i)   Le premier tome **en** a été publié.
        The first volume of it has been published.

Under the __S analysis of perception verb complements, we would expect (iii) below to have the same status as (ii), which is slightly odd since it is generally difficult to embed 'be' under these verbs (cf. Note 53). But, although judgments are not very sharp, this does not seem to be the case.

(ii)   ?J'ai vu le premier tome être publié.
         I saw the first tome be published.

(iii)   ?*J'ai vu le premier tome **en** être publié.
          I saw the first tome of it be published.

The status of (iii) supports a Control analysis of the complement, since under the latter the NP containing *le premier tome* is not (at any level of derivation) in a position from which *en* could cliticize. For discussion of *En*-avant and its interaction with Raising and Control, see Ruwet (1972, 2) Couquaux (1981).

[56] Another citerion for distinguishing the subcategorizations __NP S and __S is of course provided by selectional restrictions. In one case the NP to the right of the verb is an object of the verb, in the other the subject of the infinitival. Thus, __NP S predicts a selectional dependency between the matrix verb and the latter NP, while __S predicts no such dependency at all. Radford in fact claims that there is no dependency, and cites examples like (ia) contrasting with (ib) in which such a dependency clearly exists.

(i) a.   Ho visto il vento muovere le foglie.
           I saw the wind move the leaves.

    b.   *Ho persuaso il vento a muovere le foglie.
           I persuaded the wind to move the leaves.

But I find this argument unconvincing. The difference between (ia) and (ib) is − I think − simply due to the fact that while there is no sense in which one can persuade the wind, there is *some* sense in which one can see it (see also below in the text). Other cases, like (141b) and (ii) here below seem to me to show clearly that there is a selectional dependency.

(ii) a.   Ho visto [che l'indolenza di Giovanni ti irritava]
            I saw that Giovanni's indolence irritated you.

     b.   ?*Ho visto l'indolenza di Giovanni irritarti.
            I saw Giovanni's indolence irrritate you.

Under the ___S hypothesis we would expect no contrasat at all between (iia) and (iib). Selectional dependency seems to me to concur with the other criteria we discussed above, in pointing to Control.

[57] Consider a hypothetical object Control structure like (i), in which NP* is a pleonastic element linked with the argument A.

(i)   ... V $\underline{NP^*_i \ PRO_i}$ ... A ...

The theoretically correct expectation regarding such a structure seems to me to be, not that it could not exist, but only that it must be derived via rightward movement of A. Given the claim of LGB that objects, unlike subjects, never fail to receive a θ-role, A of (i) must be in NP* at D-structure to receive that θ-role. To put it differently, what we predict is that A in (i) will always have the θ-role assigned by V to NP*. If the construction under investigation in the text were a case of object Control, this reasoning would then correctly exclude (159a) since *three girls* is assigned object θ-role by *arrive*; it would correctly exclude (159b) since *that John will come* is assigned object θ-role by *seem*; it could conceivably correctly allow (158c) if *proven* is an adjective rather than a verb and therefore does not assign object θ-role to *that John was there*; while it would still leave (158b) unaccounted for, excluding it in the same way as (159a). But see Note 61.

[58] Kayne (1981a) actually claims that the subject of the S in (163) is PRO. This is largely a matter of what one takes the primary characterization of PRO to be: from the point of view of having an independent θ-role, such an NP is presumably PRO, but from the point of view of government it is presumably not, as the position is governed.

[59] With regard to *If* and the embedding of SI constructions, we may note the paradigm in (i), pointed out to me by L. Rizzi.

(i) a.   *?Ho visto [$_{NP}$quelle case$_i$ [$_S$PRO$_i$ costruirsi t$_i$ rapidamente]]
          (I) saw   those   houses   SI-build ('be built') rapidly

   b.   ?Quelle case   sono state viste costruirsi   rapidamente
          those   houses were seen   to SI-build ('be built') rapidly

   c.   *?[$_i$e] sono state viste [$_{NP}$[$_i$ quelle case]   [$_S$PRO$_i$ costruirsi t$_i$
          were seen   those   houses   SI-build ('be built')
          rapidamente]]
          rapidly

Cases (a) and (c) follow from the analysis given, the SI construction being incompatible with Control, as discussed in the text (no Case on SI). As for (b), note that we are not excluding the subcategorization ___S for perception verbs. The latter is in fact required for (150), and we assume is involved when these verbs appear in the FI construction. The case in (b) is then accounted for under the analysis *Quelle case$_i$ sono state viste* [$_S$t$_i$ *costruirsi t$_i$ rapidamente*], on a par with (77b), chapter 1. (SI has Case because it is linked with the embedded subject which is in a Case-marked chain.) This is somewhat reminiscent of the fact that, under passivization, English perception verbs take regular infinitival clauses for complements, cf. *I saw John leave early/John was seen to leave early*. The cases in (ia,c) continue to be excluded under the S analysis of the complement, (ia) because *quelle case* would fail to be associated with Case, (ic) because i-subjects do not occur in subject position (cf. discussion of (145b)).

[60] As R. Kayne has pointed out to me, the preposition shows up under clefting, as in (i).

(i)   È   [a parlare con Maria] che l'ho visto
        (it) is to speak   with Maria that (I) have seen him

Perhaps clefting (impossible in English) requires that the structure be re-analyzed as an object Control structure.

[61] Note also that, under this analysis, the appearance of pleonastic *there* to the right of the perception verb (as in (158b)) is less problematic than under the object Control analysis (cf. Note 57). For there will now be no paradox between the assumption (of 2.7 above) that *there* only appears in non-θ positions, and the assumption that the perception verb assigns a θ-role to its object, since the latter object will not be the NP immediately dominating *there*, but the larger one, containing the S as well. The nature of the contrast between (158b) and (159a) remains unclear however.

[62] Notice however, that an object Control analysis of the tensed case in (162) (as given in FS) would partially undercut the argument *IIa* of (161) against an object Control analysis of the infinitival case. But (164)–(166) seem to us to provide rather strong reasons to reject such an analysis of the tensed case.

[63] As noted in Radford (1977), these facts distinguish such constructions from relative clauses, which do not allow either NP-movement, cliticization or clefting of the head.

[64] Kayne (1981a) in fact analyzes the gerundive complement of (180), too, as an NP, like the tensed case (i.e. as $[_{NP}\text{Jean}_i \ [_S\text{PRO}_i \ \text{parlant} \ldots]]$). Note that the existence of a gerundive variant alongside of the tensed variant would make the non existence of an infinitival variant of the same construction particularly puzzling. The similarity of the English *-ing* and French *-ant* types is less than complete however, as they seem to differ with respect to Wh-extraction, as in (i), (ii), from Gee (1977), FS, 129, fn. 75 respectively. (See also Kayne (1981a), Note 26.)

(i)   What did the policeman see John crossing?

(ii)   *La fille que je l'ai vu embrassant . . .
         The girl that I have seen him embracing . . .

The non-existence of the *-ing/-ant* construction in Italian may simply reflect the fact that the corresponding suffix *-nte* is not productive. This is found only in nominalized and adjectivalized forms like **studente, decadente** 'student, decadent', etc.

[65] Contrasting with (185) are however the cases in (i) from Brazilian Portuguese, cited in Gee (1977).

(i) a.   Maria roubando o carro foi vista por todos los vizinhos.
         Maria stealing   the car was seen by all   the neighbors

    b.   Maria roubar o carro foi visto por todos los vizinhos.
         Maria steal   the car was seen by all   the neighbors

As Gee notes the two cases differ with respect to verb agreement (cf. *vista/visto*), though we fail to see why.

[66] There is at least one case where we find a construction plausibly similar to (169) outside of perception verb contexts, exemplified in (i). (Notice however, the presence of the preposition *a*.)

(i)   È stato Giovanni a scoprire   l'errore.
         (it) was Giovanni to discover ('who discovered') the error

A candidate for a tensed counterpart of (i) is perhaps (ii).

(ii)   C'è   Giovanni che sta poco bene.
         there is Giovanni who is not very well

The following example, (analogous to examples cited in Ruwet (1982)) seems also somewhat related to the above cases.

(iii)   Giovanni è già   là   che scia come un pazzo.
          Giovanni is already there (who is) skiing like a madman

[67] Akmajian (1977) took the different behavior of the English *-ing* and infinitival constructions under clefting and the other conditions we considered as indicating that the *-ing* construction is a constituent, whereas the infinitival is not. In particular he proposed the analyses in (i).

(i) a.

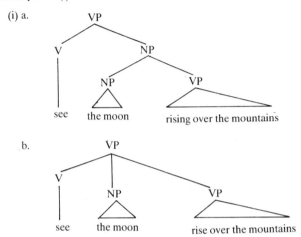

However, Gee (1977, Note 3) citing remarks of Chomsky's, notes that complementizerless Ss can never occur in focus position, as shown in (ii).

(ii) a.   What we wanted was for John to tell the truth for a change.

     b.   ?*What we wanted was John to tell the truth for a change.

This calls into question Akmajian's interpretation of at least some of the differences as valid constituency tests. Gee further notes that both the *-ing* and the infinitival type of complements behave like Ss in significant respects. For example they passivize, as in (iii), and they exhibit SSC effects, as in (iv).

(iii)   I saw John be(ing) questioned by the police.

(iv)   *We saw Mary kiss(ing) each other.

This is unexpected under the analyses of (i), especially under (ib) for the infinitival type. Furthermore, as Kayne (1981a, Note 25) notes, (ia) fails to extend to the tensed type of complement of Romance (i.e. (162)), with which it shares significant distributional properties, since the latter has a complementizer and must therefore involve an S structure. If (ia,b) must thus be rejected, we note that with (ib) Akmajian aimed to account for the lack of *to* before the infinitive, a fact for which our discussion provides no solution.

[68] Note that this account of the difference between (192) and (193) relies crucially on the 'classical' interpretation of D-structure as a separate level of representation, and is incompatible with a more abstract interpretation of D-structure as an aspect of S-structure (from this point of view (122) and (123) woud be on a par). The question of the two possible interpretations of D-structure is addressed but left essentially open in LGB, pp. 90 f.

CHAPTER 5

RESTRUCTURING CONSTRUCTIONS

5.0 INTRODUCTION

In *A Restructuring Rule in Italian Syntax* (Rizzi (1978a) henceforth "RRIS"), Rizzi notes that certain verbs taking infinitival complements like *volere* and a few others behave exceptionally in three major respects, illustrated in (1), (2), (3) below. In (1a), a clitic related to the object of the embedded verb appears on the main verb. This is not possible in general, as (1b) shows.

(1) a. Mario **lo** vuole leggere.
         Mario it wants to read

   Mario wants to read it.

   b. *Mario **lo** odia leggere.
       Mario it hates to read

   Mario hates to read it.

In the SI-construction of (2a), Object Preposing has moved the object of the embedded verb into matrix subject position. This is not possible in the case of normal infinitival complements, as (2b) shows.

(2) a. **Questi libri** si volevano proprio leggere.
         these books SI wanted really to read

   We really wanted to read these books.

   b. ***Questi libri** si odiavano proprio leggere.
       these books SI hated really to read

   We really hated to read these books.

The ill-formedness of both (1b) and (2b) will, given our general assumptions, be due to a violation of the binding theory. In (3a), the main verb *volere*, which normally takes auxiliary *avere*, appears with *essere*, the auxiliary selected by the embedded verb. This behavior is not found in general, as (3b) shows.

(3) a. Mario **sarebbe** proprio voluto andare a casa.
         Mario would be really wanted to go home

   Mario would have really wanted to go home.

   b. *Mario **sarebbe**   proprio odiato andare a casa.
      Mario would be really   hated to go   home

      Mario would have really hated to go home.

Alongside of the exceptional behavior of (1a), (2a), (3a), the verbs in question also exhibit the 'normal' behavior of verbs like *odiare*, as in (4), (5), (6).

  (4) a.   Mario vuole legger**lo**.
         Mario wants to read-it

    b.   Mario odia   legger**lo**.
        Mario hates to read-it

  (5) a.   Si voleva proprio leggere **questi libri**.
        SI wanted really   to read these   books
        We really wanted . . .

    b.   Si odiava proprio leggere **questi libri**.
        SI hated   really   to read these   books
        We really hated . . .

  (6) a.   Mario **avrebbe**   proprio voluto andare a casa.
        Mario would have really   wanted to go   home

    b.   Mario **avrebbe**   **proprio** odiato andare a casa.
        Mario would have really   hated to go   home

We will refer to the three phenomena of (1a), (2a), (3a), as "Clitic Climbing (Cl-Cl)", "Long Object Preposing (Long O.P.)", and "Change of Auxiliary (CA)", respectively.[1]

Rizzi has convincingly shown that these three phenomena are not independent, but are rather determined by common factors. His conclusion rests essentially on the three observations of (7).

  (7) I.   The phenomena of (1a), (2a), (3a) have identical distribution, in that they are found with the same class of verbs.

    II.   Cases like (1a), (2a), (3a) share certain structural peculiarities, as can be shown by employing relevant tests.

   III.   The three phenomena appear to interact, in the sense that if one of them occurs, the others do, also.

Indeed, if (1a), (2a), (3a) represented unrelated idiosyncrasies that verbs like *volere* just happen to have, it would be rather extraordinary that any of I, II, III should hold.[2] Rizzi therefore claims that there is one syntactic rule of 'restructuring', which can (though it need not) apply to verbs like

volere and their infinitival complement to produce a single verbal complex (we will call it a COMPLEX PREDICATE), and that the three phenomena of (1a), (2a), (3a) are simply a reflex of the resulting structure.

In broad terms, the analysis of restructuring constructions which we
will formulate in this chapter agrees with Rizzi's. In particular, we will
share Rizzi's view that the phenomena in (1a), (2a), (3a) all result from
certain anomalies in the syntactic structure of these sentences. Our reasons will be essentially the same as Rizzi's, namely I, II, III above, to
which we will return below. We will also agree with Rizzi that the cases
in question are structurally anomalous as a result of a syntactic process,
and not as a result of base-generation. Here we will expand the arguments that Rizzi gives, as this turns out to be rather crucial for some of
our later discussion.

However, we will also attempt to go beyond the results that Rizzi's
theory achieves, in particular by providing a detailed and hopefully explanatory account of auxiliaries and pp agreement in these constructions,
including the CA of (3a) above. This could not beachieved within Rizzi's
discussion due to his admitted lack of understanding of the general mechanisms of auxiliary assignment, and, if we are right, his failure to recognize the existence of the class of ergative verbs. We will argue that, in
order to achieve these results, it is necessary to postulate that the restructuring rule consists of VP-movement, just like the causative rule discussed
in chapter 4, and here our analysis departs from Rizzi's.

Thus, while we will take the class of restructuring verbs to consist of
the three subclasses in (8), we will claim that the restructuring process
has the effects illustrated for each of those subclasses in (9) (like Rizzi
and others we take verbs like *cominciare, continuare* to appear in both
Raising and Control frames. Cf. RRIS, fn. 7).

(8) a. *Ergative*: andare, venire.
                     go   *come*

   b. *Raising*:   dovere,   potere, cominciare, continuare,
                     have (to) to able begin   *continue*

                   stare (per), sembrare
                   be about   *seem*

   c. *Control*:   volere, sapere,   cominciare, continuare.
                   want   know (how) begin   *continue*

(9) a. Giovanni$_i$ va   t$_i$ [$_S$ PRO$_i$ a prendere il libro] $\Rightarrow$
        Giovanni goes   *to fetch   the book*

        Giovanni$_i$ va [$_{VP}$ a prendere il libro] t$_i$ [$_S$ PRO$_i$ $---$]

b.   Giovanni$_i$ dovrebbe   [$_S$ t$_i$ prendere il libro] ⇒
      Giovanni   would have   to fetch   the book

      Giovanni$_i$ dovrebbe [$_{VP}$ prendere il libro] [$_S$ t$_i$ — — —]

c.   Giovanni$_i$ vorrebbe   [$_S$ PRO$_i$ prendere il libro] ⇒
      Giovanni   would want   to fetch   the book

      Giovanni$_i$ vorrebbe [$_{VP}$ prendere il libro] [$_S$ PRO$_i$ — — —]

Our view is thus that there is one syntactic process of VP-movement that applies to verbs of different classes, and that everything else follows from this maximally simple statement. Recalling the four different classes of II.0.2 above, we note that class I ($+\bar{S}$-deletion, $+\theta_s$) would correspond to verbs like *fare*, whence the FI construction of chapter 4; class II ($+\bar{S}$-deletion, $-\theta_s$) to the Raising verbs of (8b), whence (9b); class III ($-\bar{S}$-del., $+\theta_s$) to the Control verbs of (8c), whence (9c), while class IV ($-\bar{S}$-del., $-\theta_s$) does not correspond to any complex predicate: a fact to which we will return. The verbs of (8a), giving rise to (9a), correspond to the sub-categorization __NP S, not covered by the classification of II.0.2, which only dealt with __S.[3]

In contrast, Rizzi's account, beside not treating (8a) as a separate class but rather as subject Control cases like those of (8c), postulates a derived structure in which main verb and infinitive come to form a single verb, i.e., [$_V$ V V], as we will see in more detail below. Besides, Rizzi specifically claims that the formulation of the restructuring rule must be kept distinct from that of the causative rule on account of important syntactic differences between the two sets of constructions (such as for example the CA of (3a)). While a-priori this might have been a rather reasonable position to take, we will argue that the differences *can* be explained in a way that is compatible with a common VP-movement formulation, by simply appealing to differences in the initial structures to which VP-movement applies. In particular, our idea is that essentially all differences between causative and restructuring constructions are due to the fact that main and embedded subjects are coindexed in restructuring cases, as in all of (9) above, but not in causative cases.

Very roughly, the first part of the chapter will be devoted to providing arguments for VP-movement, the second to accounting for the differences between restructuring and causative constructions. In the first section that follows, we begin by arguing for a syntactic derivation of restructuring constructions. Before turning to that issue however, we will step back to review briefly the observations of (7) above, which, following Rizzi, we take to show that the three phenomena of Cl-Cl, Long O.P., and CA have a common structural cause.

Beginning with I of (7), the three phenomena occur with the same class of verbs: those in (8).[4] Plainly, if they were unrelated, we would expect that some verb should exhibit one or two of these phenomena in isolation, but this is not the case. Notice that the CA (*avere* → *essere*) is not observed with the verbs of (8a) and with *stare* (*per*), *sembrare* of (8b), but this is simply due to the fact that these already take *essere* independently, and is thus irrelevant to our point. As for II, Rizzi shows that whenever any of the three phenomena in question appears, the syntactic structure is in certain ways anomalous, as revealed by certain tests. In particular we find Wh-movement with 'pied piping' of the infinitival, Clefting, Right Node Raising, and Complex-NP Shift. While we refer the reader to RRIS for a more complete discussion, we illustrate the point with the case of clefting, noting that, while the 'normal' cases of (4a), (5a), (6a) above can be successfully clefted, as in (10), the 'exceptional' cases of (1a), (2a), (3a) cannot, as in (11).

(10) a.   È proprio leggerlo   che Mario voleva.
          (*it*) *is really*   *to read-it that Mario wanted*

    b.   È proprio leggere questi libri   che si voleva.
          (*it*) *is really*   *to read these   books that SI wanted*

    c.   È proprio andare a casa che Mario avrebbe   voluto.
          (*it*) *is really*   *to go   home   that Mario would have wanted*

(11) a. *   È proprio leggere che Mario lo voleva.
          (*it*) *is really*   *to read that Mario it   wanted*   (Cl-Cl)

    b. *   È proprio leggere che questi libri   si volevano.
          (*it*) *is really*   *to read that these books SI wanted*
                                                                (Long O.P.)

    c. *   È proprio andare a casa che Mario sarebbe   voluto.
          (*it*) *is really*   *to go   home   that Mario would be wanted*
                                                                (CA)

The parallelism of (9a, b, c) shows, again, that the three phenomena are related, but also that there are specific structural factors associated with them.[5]

Finally, let us consider III and the interaction among the three phenomena. We note that when Long O.P. occurs, Cl-Cl cannot fail, as shown by (12).

(12) a. Questi libri **gli** si vorrebbero proprio dare.
     these books to-him SI would want really to give
                                    (Long O.P.; Cl-Cl)

We would really want to give these books to him.

  b. *Questi libri si vorrebbero proprio dar**gli**.
     these books SI would want really to give-to-him
                                    (Long O.P.; no Cl-Cl)

While Long O.P. thus appears to imply Cl-Cl, note that we would not expect that Cl-Cl should imply Long O.P. since O.P. is in general optional (cf. 1.6). The existence of cases like (13), involving Cl-Cl but not Long O.P. will therefore not call into question the interdependence of the two phenomena.

(13)   Gli si vorrebbe proprio dare questi libri.
      to-him SI would want really to give these books

We would really want to give these books to him.

Cl-Cl interacts with CA as in (14).

(14) a. Mario ci sarebbe proprio voluto andare.
     Mario there would be really wanted to go
                                      (Cl-Cl; CA)

Mario would have really wanted to go there.

  b. Mario avrebbe proprio voluto andarci.
     Mario would have really wanted to go-there
                                    (no Cl-Cl; no CA)

  c. *Mario ci avrebbe proprio voluto andare.
     Mario there would have really wanted to go
                                    (Cl-Cl; no CA)

The ungrammaticality of (14c) versus (14a) shows that Cl-Cl implies CA. The inverse relation, however, does not seem to hold, given examples like (15).

(15)   Mario sarebbe proprio voluto andarci.
      Mario would be really wanted to go-there   (no Cl-Cl, CA)

Example (15) is rather puzzling when compared with (12b), since it suggests that Cl-Cl is optional upon application of restructuring, while (12b) indicates that it is obligatory.[6] Rizzi (RRIS, fn. 26) leaves this problem unsolved. In essence, we will do the same, relating it to our discussion of 4.3 and our incomplete understanding of Clitic Climbing in general. Note that in causative constructions, too, Cl-Cl is strongly obligatory in cases parallel to (12), like (16), while only near-obligatory in some other cases, as we saw (cf. (21b), ch. 4). On this matter, see also Longobardi (1980c).

(16) a. Questi libri gli   si farebbero subito   portare (da Mario).
         these books to-him SI would make immediately take   (by Mario)

   We would have these books immediately taken to him (by Mario).

  b. *Questi libri si farebbero   subito   portargli   (da Mario).
     these books SI would make immediately take-to-him (by Mario)

The interaction between CA and Long O.P. cannot be tested since the SI-construction requires *essere* independently (see 1.7), as Rizzi notes.[7] Thus, once we abstract away from extraneous factors, it appears that the constructions under consideration either behave exceptionally in all respects (Cl-Cl, Long O.P., CA), or in none.

We therefore conclude that the three phenomena in question are all due to the same peculiarity of the syntactic structure involved. Given the nature of the phenomena, it is immediately clear that the peculiarity must consist of a somehow closer than usual relation between main verb and infinitive. Our task in the sections that follow will be to establish what the exact syntactic structure is, and how it arises.

5.1 SYNTACTIC DERIVATION

In this section we argue that restructuring complexes are syntactically derived and not base-generated. Our argument is essentially in the spirit of the arguments given in RRIS 6.3, and is based on the observation that restructuring complexes turn out to be much more similar to their non-restructured counterparts (that is, to the corresponding cases that exhibit the 'normal' behavior of (4)—(6) above) than any base-generation analysis could predict. Consider restructuring verbs *venire, dovere, volere* (representing each of the three classes in (8)), when they occur in normal (i.e. non-restructured) structures, as in (17).

(17) a. Giovanni$_i$ viene t$_i$ [$_S$PRO$_i$ a prendere il   libro]
         Giovanni   comes   to fetch   the book

  b. Giovanni$_i$ dovrebbe   [$_S$t$_i$ prendere il   libro]
      Giovanni   would have   to fetch   the book

c. Giovanni*i* vorrebbe   [sPRO*i* prendere il   libro]
   Giovanni would want   to fetch   the book

Though superficially parallel, the three cases in (17) differ in the range of
phrases that can appear in matrix subject position: a fact which is adequately captured by the different analyses. Thus, in (17b), the matrix subject obeys only selectional restrictions imposed by the embedded
predicate, while the matrix verb plays no role at all. This fact is illustrated
in (18), where inanimates and null analogues to weather *it* and non-argument *it* of English, as selected by the embedded predicate, appear as
matrix subjects.

(18) a. Il   libro dovrebbe   essere portato da Giovanni.
        The book would have to be   brought by Giovanni.

    b. L'acqua   dovrebbe   scorrere.
       The water would have to flow.

    c. Dovrebbe   piovere.
       It would have to rain.

    d. Dovrebbe risultare   che Giovanni non c'era.
       It would   have to appear that Giovanni was not there.

This follows from the Raising analysis of (17b), under the standard
assumption that selectional restrictions apply in D-structure. Then, for
example, in (18b) *l'acqua* is the D-structure subject of the lower verb,
which then undergoes Raising, whence the grammaticality. Equivalently,
we may assume selectional restrictions to be an aspect of θ-role assignment. Since *l'acqua* of (18b) is assigned θ-role by the lower verb exclusively (at all levels, given the projection principle), well-formedness is
again predicted. Such exclusive selectional dependence on the complement verb is in fact a classic argument for Raising. Matters are different
in (17a, c), as (19), (20) show.[8]

(19) a. *Il   libro viene ad essere portato da Giovanni.
        The book comes to be   brought by Giovanni.

    b. *L'acqua   viene   a scorrere.
       The water comes to flow.

    c. *Viene   a piovere.
       It comes to rain.

    d. *Viene   a risultare che Giovanni non c'era.
       It comes to appear   that Giovanni was not there.

(20) a. *Il   libro vuole essere portato da Giovanni.
        The book wants to be   brought by Giovanni.

b. *L'acqua   vuole   scorrere.
   The water   wants   to flow.

c. *Vuole   piovere
   It wants   to rain.

d. *Vuole   risultare   che Giovanni non c'era.
   It wants   to appear   that Giovanni was not there.

The above examples are ungrammatical because *il libro, l'acqua,* the Italian equivalents of weather *it* and pleonastic *it,* are not compatible with the main verb *venire* or *volere,* though they are in each case appropriate subjects for the embedded verb.

In contrast to (17b), in cases like (17a,c), the matrix subject exhibits a *double* dependence: from the main verb, whence (19), (20), and from the embedded verb. The dependence from the embedded verb is established by the ungrammaticality of examples like (21), in which the matrix subject, now compatible with the main verb, is not compatible with the lower one.

(21) a. *Giovanni viene   ad essere letto da Mario.
        Giovanni comes to be   read by Mario.

    b. *Giovanni vuole   piovere.
       Giovanni wants to rain.

These facts follow straightforwardly from the Control analyses of (17a), (17c). Such double dependence constitutes in fact a classic argument for Control (or 'Equi-NP deletion'). In, for example, (17c) the phrase *Giovanni* obeys selectional restrictions imposed by the main verb, because it is its subject. Furthermore, the element PRO will correspondingly have to obey selectional restrictions imposed by the lower verb. But since the latter is anaphoric to (i.e. coreferential with) the matrix subject, it will obey selectional restrictions to the exact extent that its antecedent does. Thus, in effect the matrix subject will have to obey both sets of restrictions. In (17a), the selectional restrictions imposed by the matrix verb are those relative to its object rather than to its subject, but the situation is otherwise entirely parallel to that of (17c).[9]

Our point is now that restructuring complexes do not differ at all from their counterparts in (17) with respect to the selectional restrictions just discussed. This is shown, for example, by the fact that the cases in (22), in which restructuring must have applied given the occurrence of Cl-Cl, are just as grammatical as those in (18), while (19) and (20), which must be taken as ambiguously restructured or not, are ungrammatical altogether, thus also if restructuring has applied.

(22) a. Il libro **gli** dovrebbe essere portato.
the book to-him would have to be brought

The book would have to be brought to him.

b. L'acqua **vi** dovrebbe scorrere.
the water in-it would have to flow

The water would have to flow in it.

c. **Ci** dovrebbe piovere dentro.
(it) there would have to rain within

It would have to rain in it.

This follows only if restructuring complexes are identical to their non-restructured counterparts (i.e. (17)) in those respects relevant to selectional restrictions. In particular it follows if restructured complexes are control (*volere, venire*) or Raising (*potere*) structures underlyingly, as in (9) above. But consider the a-priori conceivable base-generation hypotheses of (23).

(23) a. 'Restructuring' verbs are modals (like English *can, will*, etc.), as in (24a).

b. 'Restructuring' constructions involve VP-complements, as in (24b).

c. 'Restructuring' complexes involve base-generated complex verbs, as in (24c).

(24) a. Giovanni [$_{mod}$ { viene a / dovrebbe / vorrebbe }] prendere il libro.

Giovanni { comes / would have / would want } to fetch the book.

b. Giovanni { viene a / dovrebbe / vorrebbe } [$_{VP}$ prendere il libro]

c. Giovanni [$_V$ { viene a / dovrebbe / vorrebbe } prendere] il libro

Such major properties of restructuring complexes as Cl-Cl and Long O.P. would be accounted for adequately by any of the above hypotheses. (We put aside the CA which poses a greater challenge.) Since we assume that both cliticization and NP-movement are constrained by principle A of the binding theory, we would expect that the object of the embedded verb could successfully either cliticize on the main verb (as in (1a)), or move into matrix subject position (as in (2a)), under any of the analyses in (24). But none of these analyses makes correct predictions on the matter of selectional restrictions.

Under the 'modal' analysis of (24a) we expect the subject to conform with selectional restrictions imposed by the infinitival only. Compare in fact *The book wants to be brought by John, which is ungrammatical for the same reasons as (20a), with The book will be brought by John, grammatical because there are no selectional restrictions associated with modal will. The modal analysis is thus false, at least for the volere and venire cases, given in (20a), (19a). The VP-complement analysis of (24b) would predict no selectional dependence between the subject and the infinitival verb.[10] This is false for all three cases. Compare for example **Giovanni vuole piovere** of (12b) with . . . **riusciranno a far piovere** '(They) will manage to make (it) rain' of (47), ch. 4, for which we argued that the VP analysis of the complement was appropriate. Notice that the analysis of (24b) also falsely predicts that, since the transitive verb fails to assign a θ-role to its subject, a by-phrase may appear. Compare **Maria fa riparare la macchina da Giovanni** 'Maria has the car repaired by Giovanni' of (44), ch. 4, with ***Maria vuole riparare la macchina da Giovanni** 'Maria wants the car repaired by Giovanni'. And, even more obviously, the analysis of (24b) fails to express the fact that Giovanni is understood as the subject of the embedded verb.

As for the complex verb hypothesis of (24c), it is unclear whether under such an analysis we would expect selectional restrictions to be determined by one verb, by the other, or by both. However, we would hardly expect the difference between the dovere case and the venire, volere cases, of (22) versus (19), (20) — a difference which mirrors exactly the one produced by the independent devices of Raising versus Control.

We conclude from this that restructuring constructions are not base-generated, but are rather either Control or Raising structures, like (17a, b, c), at least prior to restructuring. It remains to be determined whether they are Control and Raising structures even after restructuring.

5.2 RESTRUCTURING WITH ANDARE, VENIRE

In this section we consider the effects of the restructuring process in the case of ergative andare and venire. Our claim is that such effects are sufficient to motivate a VP-movement formulation of restructuring.

As we have already noted, restructuring forms like (25) involving andare, venire, differ from their non-restructured counterparts in the manner illustrated by (26), (27), (cf. (59), (60) ch. 2, and discussion).

(25)   Giovanni **lo** $\begin{Bmatrix} \text{va} \\ \text{viene} \end{Bmatrix}$ a prendere.   *restructuring*

Giovanni $\begin{Bmatrix} \textit{goes} \\ \textit{comes} \end{Bmatrix}$ *to fetch it.*

(26) a. *****Lo** viene   Giovanni a prendere.   *restructuring*
         it   comes Giovanni to fetch

   b. [e] viene   Giovanni [a prender**lo**]   *no restructuring*

         comes Giovanni   to fetch-it

(27) a. *****Giovanni **lo** viene   lui   a prendere.   *restructuring*
         Giovanni it   comes himself to fetch

   b. Giovanni viene   lui   [a prender**lo**]   *no restructuring*

         Giovanni comes himself   to fetch-it

We assume, as argued in 2.3, that the phrase Giovanni in (26b), and the emphatic pronoun (ep) *lui* in (27b) occupy the position of direct object of the ergative verb *venire*. We will then take the ungrammaticality of (26a), (27a) to indicate that once restructuring occurs there is no longer a direct object position separating main verb and infinitival. Two possibilities come to mind regarding how this could be so: (i) Restructuring eliminates that position from the structure; (ii) Restructuring changes the linear order of constituents, permuting direct object and infinitival.

There are good indications that (i) is false, and that *andare, venire* of (25) still have a direct object.[11] One indication is provided by the fact that *andare, venire* of (25) take auxiliary *essere* (E), as in (28).

(28)   Giovanni lo é $\begin{Bmatrix} \text{andato} \\ \text{venuto} \end{Bmatrix}$ a prendere.   (E)

Giovanni has $\begin{Bmatrix} \textit{gone} \\ \textit{come} \end{Bmatrix}$ *to fetch it.*

Under the system of auxiliary assignment formulated in 1.7 (and further discussed in 2.6.2), there will be no provision for assignment of E in (28), unless *andare, venire* had a direct object linked with the subject position. (Note that, given the CA phenomenon, it is clear that the rule of auxiliary assignment applies *after* restructuring.)

Another indication that the direct object of *andare, venire* exists in restructured (25) is that this direct object can be relativized in small-clause (sc) relatives. Consider (29a,b).

(29) a. Un vicino   [venuto a chieder**mi**   un favore]
         a   *neighbor*   *come*   *to ask-to-me* *a favor*

         non mi trovò   in casa.
         did not find me *at home*

         A neighbor who had come to ask me a favor . . .

   b. Un vicino   [venuto**mi**   a chiedere un favore] . . .
         a   *neighbor*   *come-to-me*   *to ask*   *a favor*

         A neighbor who had come to ask me a favor . . .

As we argued in 3.2 above, only direct objects can be relativized in sc
relatives, in Italian direct objects of both transitive and ergative verbs.
The internal structure of the relative in (29a) will be $[_{sc}\, \text{PRO}_i\ \text{venuto}\ t_i$
. . .]. Given the position of the clitic, restructuring must have applied in
(29b), and yet the direct object is relativized, just as in (29a).[12] We must
then assume that (i) above is false, and that restructuring changes the
order of constituents, either by moving the infinitival to the left, or by
moving the direct object of the main verb to the right.
    Recall now Fare-VP cases like (30), discussed in 4.5 above.

(30)   **Lo**$_i$ farò $[_{VP}\ \begin{Bmatrix} \text{scendere} \\ \text{andare} \end{Bmatrix}\ [_i e]\ [_S \text{PRO}_i$ a prendere

      (I) him will make $\begin{Bmatrix} \textit{go down} \\ \textit{go} \end{Bmatrix}$ *to fetch*

      il   libro]
      the book

      I will make him go down/go to fetch the book.

As we argued, accusative *lo* rather than dative *gli* in (30) is predicted by
the analysis, since while the environment for dativization is roughly as in
(31), the *ec* to which the clitic is related does not follow, but rather precedes the sentential complement.

(31) $\begin{Bmatrix} \text{NP} \\ \text{S} \end{Bmatrix}$ ____

Consider (32) in the light of this observation:

(32)   **Gli**   farò $\begin{Bmatrix} \text{*scendere} \\ \text{andare} \end{Bmatrix}$ a prendere il libro.

      (I) to-him will make $\begin{Bmatrix} \textit{go down} \\ \textit{go} \end{Bmatrix}$ *to fetch*   *the book*

      I will make him $\begin{Bmatrix} \textit{go down} \\ \textit{go} \end{Bmatrix}$ to fetch the book.

It is clear that the possibility for dative *gli* in (32), contrasting with *lo* of (30) depends on application of restructuring within the complement of *fare*. First, such a possibility exists with restructuring *andare*, but not with non-restructuring *scendere*. Second, cliticization of the object of the right-most verb in (32) results in (33), where Cl-Cl has occurred (actually twice), and therefore restructuring must have too. In contrast, (30) gives rise to (34).

> (33)   Glie**lo** farò andare a prendere.
>   *I will make him go to fetch it.*

> (34)   Lo farò scendere a prender**lo**.
>   *I will make him go down to fetch it.*

It is also clear that dativization in (32) depends on the presence of the NP *li libro*, rather than on that of the sentential complement of *andare*. For, if dativization were due to the sentential complement, we should find it in (35) also.[13]

> (35) ?* $\left\{ \begin{matrix} \textbf{Gli} \\ \textbf{Lo} \end{matrix} \right\}$ farò   andare [a telefonare a Maria]
>
>   (*I*) $\left\{ \begin{matrix} \textit{to-him} \\ \textit{him} \end{matrix} \right\}$ *will make go*   *to telephone to Maria*
>
>   I will make him go to phone Maria.

Since we have attributed dativization to the fact that an embedded object becomes an object of *fare* as well, *il libro* of (32) must then have become an object of *fare*. We take this to indicate that, after restructuring has applied, the infinitival complement of *andare* is no longer sentential. For we would hardly expect *il libro* to act as an object of *fare* if it were separated from it by clause boundaries. Moreover, if the complement of *andare* were sentential, we would not expect cliticization as in (33) to be possible, given the binding theory.

What this means is that the permutation in linear order of direct object and infinitive which we assumed on the basis of (25)–(29) must be due to movement of the infinitival VP to the left, out of its clause, rather than movement of the direct object to the right. We will then take the analysis of restructured (32) to be as in (36), as compared with non-restructured (30).

> (36) Gli_i farò   [$_{VP}$ andare [$_{VP}$ a prendere il libro] [$_i$e]
>   (*I*) *to-him will make*   *go*   *to fetch   the book*
>
>   [$_S$ PRO$_i$ –––]]

In (36), we will assume that just as with causative verbs, *il libro* becomes a direct object of restructuring *andare*. By transitivity, it will then become

an object of *fare* as well. The *ec* related to the clitic will also be an object
of *fare* by virtue of the same principles. And in fact it will be a second
object, whence the dative Case of *gli*.[14] Cliticization of *il libro* to *fare* as
in (33) will also be accounted for.

In this section we have thus provided a first major argument for the
VP-movement formulation. Specifically, we have argued that restructuring
changes a structure like (37a), in which V_1 is an ergative verb, NP_1 its
direct object, and *S* its complement, into (37b).

(37) a. $[_{VP_1} V_1 NP_1 [_S \text{PRO} [_{VP_2} V_2 NP_2]]]$

    b. $[_{VP_1} V_1 [_{VP_2} V_2 NP_2] NP_1 [_S \text{PRO} - - -]]$

Our argument is based on certain empirical evidence which we have
taken to indicate that: (i) After restructuring, NP_1 of (37a) is no longer
between the two verbs, though it is still present in the structure; (ii)
When the structure in (37a) is embedded under *fare*, then if and only if
restructuring applies, NP_2 will induce dativization of NP_1. Under our general assumptions, (ii) will imply that after restructuring NP_2 is both to the
left of NP_1 and no longer within *S*.

5.3 EMBEDDED SUBJECT

In RRIS, the restructuring process is assumed to have the effect illustrated, for the Control subcase, in (38). The Raising subcase would be
exactly analogous (and there is no ergative subcase).

(38)   Giovanni $[_{VP}$ vuole $[_S$ PRO leggere il libro$]]$ ⇒
        Giovanni   *wants*   *to read the book*

    Giovanni $[_{VP} [_V$ vuole leggere$]$ il libro$]$

This formulation differs from ours in two major respects, essentially independent of one another: (i) the two verbs come to form a single verb; (ii)
the embedded subject is deleted. In this section we discuss (ii). We will
refer to this aspect as "subject deletion".

In the previous section, we argued that in the ergative subcase of restructuring, the main verb remained ergative, maintaining its direct object.
If we were correct on this point, we would naturally expect that other
constituents present between the two verbs, in particular the embedded
subject, would not be deleted by restructuring. But there are other, more
specific reasons to suppose that the embedded subject is not deleted.

One reason has to do with the interpretation of restructured complexes. Consider a (non-restructured) Control case like (39a) and a restructured case like (39b).

(39) a. Giovanni$_i$ $\begin{Bmatrix} \text{desidera} \\ \text{vuole} \end{Bmatrix}$ [$_S$ PRO$_i$ prendere il libro]
to fetch

Giovanni $\begin{Bmatrix} \text{wishes} \\ \text{wants} \end{Bmatrix}$ the book

b. Giovanni **lo** vuole prendere.
Giovanni wants to fetch it.

In (39a), *Giovanni* is understood as the subject of both main and em-bedded verbs (i.e. 'Giovanni$_i$ wishes/wants that he$_i$ buy the book'): a fact which is captured precisely by the Control analysis. The point now is that the interpretation of (39b) is quite parallel to that of (39a) and not at all parallel to that of (40) in which, as we argued, the embedded verb does lack a subject (*Fare*-VP).

(40)   Giovanni **lo** ha fatto prendere.
Giovanni it has made fetch

Giovanni has had it fetched.

Cases like (39b) must therefore clearly be Control structures at the level relevant to semantic interpretation. And just as *volere* cases have the se-mantics of Control structures, so *dovere, potere, sembrare* cases of res-tructuring have the semantics of Raising structures, with the surface subject of the main verb interpreted as the subject of the embedded verb only. This type of observation, together with the assumption that seman-tic interpretation draws on S- rather than D-structure, gives rise to a rather obvious argument against subject deletion, since the latter elimi-nates information crucial to semantic interpretation, and in particular crucial to distinguishing between Raising and Control subcases.[15]

Subject deletion is therefore not compatible with the theoretical framework assumed here, in which the semantic component has no access to D-structure. It is also not compatible with the latter framework vis-à-vis the projection principle, which requires that the positions which are subject to θ-role assignment be present at all levels. One must therefore take the discussion in RRIS to presuppose a somewhat dif-ferent theoretical framework, more along the lines of the Standard Theory.

The VP-movement formulation on the other hand is in line with the assumptions of the GB theory. Thus, given that the embedded subject is preserved in S-structure, the desired distinction between Raising and Control cases will be present at that level, and the correct semantic inter-pretation will be derived from that level, under appropriate assumptions. Specifically, we will assume here that the reconstruction rule of 3.3 ap-plies, to provide the correct LF by reconstruction the moved VP into its original position, exactly as in the case of the FI construction discussed in 4.6 above. Aside from a certain set of cases which we consider in 5.6 below, the situation concerning θ-role assignment at S-structure and the projection principle is also exactly as in the FI construction and unproblematic: all θ-roles within the moved VP are assigned straightforwardly. The embedded subject is assigned θ-role by the moved VP, via its trace.

A further argument against subject deletion has to do with the illformedness of cases like (41).

(41)   *I nostri atleti si   vorrebbero vincere.
        our athletes   SI   would want to win

        We would like our athletes to win.

In the absence of restructuring, (41) has the analysis of (42).

(42)   *I nostri atleti$_i$ si vorrebbero [$_S$ t$_i$ vincere]

The ill-formednes of (42) is clearly due to the fact that *volere* is a Control verb, and as such it does not permit Raising. At the theoretical level, (42) will be excluded by whatever device accounts for the essentially complementary distribution of Raising and Control infinitivals, in general. In our theoretical framework, such a device is $\overline{\text{S}}$-deletion, conjoined with the conditions governing the occurrence of PRO and trace at S-structure. Thus the structure in (42) is not well-formed because *volere* does not trigger $\overline{\text{S}}$-deletion, and the embedded subject thus fails to be governed, in violation of the ECP.

But (41) is ungrammatical not only under the anlaysis of (42), but altogether, even if restructuring applies. Under our formulation, the restructured analysis of (41) is as in (43).

(43)   *I nostri atleti$_i$ si vorrebbero [$_{VP}$ vincere] [$_S$ t$_i$ − − −]

This structure is ill-formed because the embedded subject is ungoverned, violating the ECP, just like (42). But if restructuring deleted the embedded subject, there could be no violation of the ECP, and the ungrammaticality of (41) would be unexpected. For, we know that the NP-movement of (42) is allowed as in Raising cases, and we know that restructuring can apply to Raising configurations, so that it ought to be applicable in (42).

A little earlier we noted that under the subject deletion formulation, S-structure was not sufficient to produce the correct semantic or thematic interpretation of restructured complexes, and that D-structure would have had to be resorted to. But cases like (41) constitute a further problem, since their D-structure would be thematically well-formed, on a par with that of, for example **Si vorrebbe che i nostri atleti vincessero** 'We would want that our athletes should win', and will thus be irrelevant to the ungrammaticality.[16] While the former problem was somewhat theory internal, as it would not arise within a theory which allowed the derivation of semantic interpretation from D-structure, the latter one seems to be much less theory internal. Whatever theoretical device is employed to account for the distribution of trace and PRO as subjects of infinitives, it is clear that such a device does not operate on D-structure, both because there are no traces at that level, and because PRO does not appear constrained in its D-structure position, only in its S-structure position.[17] Cases like (41), which we take to indicate that such a device operates on restructured and non-restructured constructions alike, will then be compatible with subject deletion only if the device in question applies at a level which is prior to restructuring, so that the embedded subject is still present, while being different from D-structure, which is irrelevant. But we see little independent motivation for postulating such a level.

Just as we have thus observed that Control verbs appear in Control and never in Raising frames even under restructuring, so we can make the complementary observation, noting the ungrammaticality of (44a), contrasting with (44b).

(44) a. ?*Lo sciopero dei tranvieri   farà
         the strike   of streetcar personnel will make

         [VP dover   comprare più   macchine]
            (people) have to buy   more cars

     b.   Lo sciopero dei tranvieri   farà   [VP vendere
         the strike   of streetcar personnel will make   (one) sell

         più   macchine]
         more cars

In the absence of restructuring, the VP of (44a) has the analysis of (45), in which the subject of *comprare* must be PRO, since there would be no antecedent for a trace.

(45)   [VP dover [S PRO comprare più macchine]]

But *dovere* is a Raising verb, and as such it triggers $\bar{S}$-deletion. PRO will then be governed, and the requirement (complementary to the ECP) that it be always ungoverned will be violated.[18] The fact that (44a) is ungrammatical altogether will then indicate that even under restructuring Raising verbs fail to take Control complements, just as Control verbs fail to take Raising complements. If the restructured version of (45) is (46) as we claim, then the account given for (45) will indeed carry over.

(46)   [VP dover [VP comprare più macchine] [S PRO − − −]]

But if restructuring deleted the embedded subject, then there would be no PRO, and hence, again, no violation; and (44a) ought to be grammatical under its restructured analysis.[19]

Notice that the ungrammaticality of (44a) provides evidence not only against subject deletion, but also against base-generation of restructured complexes. For it is easy to see that the VP of (44a) ought to be well-formed just like that of (44b) under any of the base-generation analyses of (23) above.

On the basis of these arguments we will conclude that in restructured complexes the embedded subject is present at S-structure. This conclusion requires that we now deal with the fact that the embedded subject is never phonologically realized. Consider (47a,b).

(47) a   *Maria vuole [$_S$ me partecipare]
            Maria wants   me to participate

    b   *[e] $\left\{ \begin{array}{l} \text{può} \\ \text{sembra} \end{array} \right\}$ [$_S$ me partecipare]

        (*it*) $\left\{ \begin{array}{l} \text{is possible} \\ \text{seems} \end{array} \right\}$ *me to participate*

Within our framework, the cases in (47) are clearly ungrammatical because the embedded subject is not assigned Case. In (47a) this is because that subject is not governed by the main verb ($-\bar{S}$-deletion; $+A$), in (47b) because the main verb does not assign Case to it, though it governs it ($+\bar{S}$-deletion; $-A$). Our formulation will predict that restructured counterparts, like (48a,b) should be ungrammatical for the same reasons.

(48) a.   *Maria vuole [$_{VP}$ partecipare] [$_S$ me $---$]

    b.   *[e] $\left\{ \begin{array}{l} \text{può} \\ \text{sembra} \end{array} \right\}$ [$_{VP}$ partecipare] [$_S$ me $---$]

Such cases will contrast with (49), in which *fare* is both $+\bar{S}$-deletion and $+A$.

(49)   Maria ha fatto [$_{VP}$ partecipare] [$_S$ me $---$]
            Maria has made me participate.

There will therefore be no difficulty in excluding overt embedded subjects in cases of restructuring when these are accusative. But what about the dativization rule discussed in chapter 4 and the ungrammaticality of (50a, b) versus the grammaticality of (50c)?

(50) a.   *Maria vuole [$_{VP}$ leggere il libro] [$_S$ a Giovanni $---$]
            Maria wants Giovanni to read the book.

    b.   *[e] $\left\{ \begin{array}{l} \text{può} \\ \text{sembra} \end{array} \right\}$ [$_{VP}$ leggere il libro] [$_S$ a Giovanni $---$]

        It is possible/seems Giovanni to read the book.

c.   Maria fa [$_{VP}$ leggere il libro] [$_S$ a Giovanni $- - -$]
        Maria makes Giovanni read the book.

The cases in (50a,b) would be correctly excluded if we assumed that the conditions that govern assignment of dative Case in (50c) are quite parallel to the conditions governing assignment of accusative. Then (50a,b) would be just like (48a,b). Such an assumption could be implemented by restating the environment for dativization as in (51), where we require *1* to govern both *2* and *3*.

$$(51) \qquad \begin{matrix} V \\ [+A] \\ 1 \end{matrix} \quad \begin{Bmatrix} NP \\ S \end{Bmatrix} \quad \underline{\quad} \\ \qquad\quad 2 \quad\;\; 3$$

Under the reformulation, (50a) would be excluded because the main verb does not govern the embedded subject; (50b) because, though it governs it, that verb is not a +A verb; while (50c) would be allowed because *fare* both governs the embedded subject and is a +A verb.[20]

The idea expressed by (51) is essentially that the dative of (50c) is more like a second accusative than a real dative. On the one hand this idea may call for some qualifications to our attempt of 4.1.4 above to view such datives on a par with other datives. On the other, it would seem to be supported by the rather noticeable contrast between (52a) and (52b). ((52a) is the case of (10), ch. 4.)

(52) a,   ?*Mario **lo** fu fatto leggere.
            Mario was made to read it.

b.   *Mario fu telefonato (a).
        Mario was telephoned (to).

Both (52a, b) are derived by moving into subject position a phrase that would otherwise appear in the dative, as in (53a,b).

(53) a.   **Lo** fecero leggere a   Mario.
        (*they*) *it   made   read   to Mario*
            They made Mario read it.

b.   Telefonarono   a   Mario.
        (*they*) *telephoned   to Mario*

The milder ungrammaticality of (52a) suggests indeed that the dative of (53a) is more like a direct object, say like the second object of English double object constructions. The alternation betwen (52a) and (54) here below recalls in fact alternations like *Mary was given the book/The book was given to Mary.*

(54)   Il   libro$_i$ fu   fatto [$_{VP}$ leggere [$_i$e]] [$_S$ a   Giovanni — — —]
            the book was made   to read   to Giovanni

Someone made Giovanni read the book.

Notice however that cases like (54) call into question the adequacy of
(51), since we have been assuming that passive verbs fail to assign accusative, and yet dative does not fail to be assigned in (54). The problem is
how to distinguish (54) from the totally impossible (50b), in which a −A
main verb is involved. Some indication that this problem might have a
solution is in fact provided by English double object constructions. Wasow
(1977) has noted in a different context that, with double object constructions like (55a), one finds passives like (55b) which maintain one of the
direct objects, but never a corresponding ergative (our terms), like (55c).

(55) a.   They dropped John the rope.

     b.   John$_i$ was dropped t$_i$ the rope.

     c.   *John$_i$ dropped t$_i$ the rope.
            (In the interpretation roughly parallel to (55b).)

Note that there is reason to believe that *drop* does indeed exist as an ergative verb, given *They dropped the rope/The rope dropped.* One would
infer from the difference between (55b) and (55c) that ergative verbs and
passives differ in the way in which they fail to assign accusative. Passives
fail with respect to only one of the objects in a double object construction (as we saw in 3.1), while ergatives fail with respect to both objects,
so that (55c) would be ruled out by lack of Case on *the rope.* This difference is presumably related to the different way in which ergatives and
passives are assigned the specification −A: ergatives directly in their lexical entry, passives as a result of a process of derivational morphology.
    Although we fail to see how this difference could be expressed pre-
cisely in our grammar, we note that its mere existence could account for
(54) versus (50b). For it is natural to assume that Raising verbs like *potere, sembrare* are on a par with ergative verbs with respect to their ability to assign accusative, and thus differ from passives along the lines of
(55c) versus (55b). We may then suggest that, while Raising verbs do not
qualify as term 1 in (51), passives do. The latter would simply fail to
assign Case to term 2. The difference betwen (50b) and (54) would then
follow. If this slight reinterpretation of the dativization process is correct
as we will assume, then the fact that in restructuring constructions the
subject of the embedded verb is never phonologically realized will be accounted for in full, in a way fully compatible with our claim that the
latter subject is always syntactically present.
    In 5.1 above and in this section, we have argued that in restructured

complexes the embedded subject is present at all levels. Our arguments were essentially as follows: We infer from their interpretation and from the facts relative to selectional restrictions that restructured constructions are thematically just like their (Raising or Control) non-restructured counterparts. It follows under any version of the general theory that they are essentially like their non-restructured counterparts in D-(eep) structure. This was our argument against base-generation. Under the version of the general theory which we assume, in which the projection principle holds, and in which semantic interpretation derives from S-structure, it also follows that they are thematically like their non-restructured counterparts at other levels as well. This implies the existence of the embedded subject also at other levels. Presence of the embedded subject is furthermore necessary to ensure the correct distribution of Raising and Control complements, even aside from questions of thematic well-formedness. Since this distribution is most likely to be determined at S-structure, the embedded subject must then be present at that level.

If the embedded subject is present, we will not expect the lack of 'SSC' or binding theory effects on the embedded VP, as in *Mario lo$_i$ vuole leggere* [$_i$e] ((1a) above), or in *Questi libri$_i$ si volevano proprio leggere t$_i$* ((2a) above) unless the embedded VP is moved out of its clause. This in effect provides us with a second major argument for VP-movement. The first was the one of 5.2.

5.4. SIMILARITIES BETWEEN RESTRUCTURING AND CAUSATIVE CONSTRUCTIONS

Restructuring constructions behave analogously to causatives in many significant respects, which we review in this section. We will take these similarities to support our common VP-movement analyses, although for the most part the facts of this section do not seem incompatible with alternative analyses of restructuring.

As we have already seen, both sets of constructions exhibit the phenomenon of Clitic Climbing, as in (56).

(56) a.   **Li**$_i$ ho fatti [$_{VP}$ leggere [$_i$e]] [$_S$ a Mario — — —]
            I have had Mario read them.

     b.   **Li**$_i$ ho voluti [$_{VP}$ leggere [e]] [$_S$ PRO$_i$ — — —]
            I have wanted to read them.

We assume that in restructuring, as in causative cases, embedded object clitics are base-generated on the embedded verb, and then moved onto the main verb after, or in conjunction with, application of VP-movement. We still postpone fully justifying this view till chapter 6 below. The rela-

tion between the clitic and the *ec* in each of (56) is well-formed with respect to principle A of the binding theory. This gives us an explanation
of why object clitics *can* appear on the higher verb in these structures.
However, as we pointed out in 4.3 and 5.0, we lack a satisfactory explanation of why they *must* appear on the higher verb and why this requirement is stronger in some cases than in others.

In (56), we also note the similarity between causatives and restructuring constructions with respect to past participle agreement. While in general a past participle agrees with the antecedent to its own direct object,
as in (57), in both (56a) and (56b) the past participle agrees with the antecedent to the direct object of the embedded verb, from which we conclude that in both these constructions the dependents of the embedded
verb are reanalyzed as dependents of the matrix verb as well, as we have
already argued in connection with causatives.

> (57)   **Li$_i$** ho letti [$_i$e]
>   *I have read them.*

Another respect, also already noted, in which restructuring and causative constructions behave alike concerns NP-movement, as in (58).

> (58) a.   Quei libri$_i$ si   faranno   [$_{VP}$ leggere [$_i$e]] [$_S$ a   Mario — — —]
>   *those books SI will make   read   to Mario*
>
>   We will make Mario read those books.
>
>   b.   Quei libri$_i$ si   vorrebbero   [$_{VP}$ leggere [$_i$e] subito]
>   *those books SI would want   to read   immediately*
>
>   [$_S$ PRO — — —]
>   We would like to read those books immediately.

Again, this is predicted by our anlayses. Notice that in (58b) we must assume that SI is a legitimate antecedent for PRO, in spite of the fact that
the subject position is occupied by an NP of different index. Analogously,
in the parallel Raising case in (59), we must assume that SI functions as
the antecedent for the trace t_j.

> (59)   Quei libri$_i$ si$_j$ potrebbero   [$_{VP}$ leggere t$_i$ subito]
>   *those books SI would be able   to read   immediately*
>
>   [$_S$ t$_j$ — — —]
>   We would be able to read those books immediately.

This situation is not problematic for our theory, since it arises independently of our claim that there is an embedded subject in (58), (59), in
cases like (60a,b) (already noted in 2.3 above).

(60) a. Queste disposizioni$_i$ si$_j$ sono adottate t$_i$ [senza
these   provisions   SI have adopted   without

neanche PRO$_j$ informare gli   interessati]
even   informing those concerned

We have adopted these provisions without even informing
those concerned.

b. Certe   cose$_i$ non si$_j$ dicono mai t$_i$ di se stessi$_j$
certain things SI never say   of themselves

We never say certain things of ourselves.

The antecedent for PRO in (60a), and *se stessi* in (60b) is plainly SI,
in spite of the fact that the subject position has been occupied by the
preposed object. The corresponding passive cases are in fact ungrammatical, as in (61). We presume that this is because PRO and *se stessi* lack
antecedents.

(61) a. ?*Queste disposizioni$_i$ sono state adottate t$_i$ [senza neanche
PRO informare gli interessati]
*These provisions have been adopted without even informing
those concerned.*

b. *Queste cose$_i$ non sono mai dette t$_i$ di se stessi$_j$.
These things are never said about ourselves.

If (60) has an ungrammatical passive counterpart like (61), then we will
expect that (59) should too. This is indeed the case, as we see in 5.8.2
below.

Another similarity between restructuring and causative constructions
concerns the prohibition on sequences of infinitives discussed in Longobardi (1980a). Longobardi notes that, when they are not separated by a
preposition, infinitives cannot in general occur in sequence, as in (62): a
fact somewhat reminiscent of the impossibility of sequences of gerunds in
English, noted in Ross (1972).

(62) ?(?)Claudio potrebbe **desiderare finire**   il suo lavoro.
Claudio could   wish   to finish his   work

He also notes however that there are exactly two sets of exceptions to
this prohibition: restructuring constructions, as in (63a), and causative
constructions, as in (63b).

(63) a.   Claudio desidererebbe $\left\{\begin{array}{l}\text{poter finire il suo lavoro.}\\\text{poter\textbf{lo} finire.}\end{array}\right\}$

Claudio would wish $\left\{\begin{array}{l}\textit{to be able to finish his work.}\\\textit{to be able to finish it.}\end{array}\right\}$

b.   Claudio desidererebbe $\left\{\begin{array}{l}\text{fare finire il lavoro a Piero.} \\ \text{far\textbf{lo} finire a Piero.}\end{array}\right\}$

      Claudio would wish $\left\{\begin{array}{l}\textit{to make Piero finish his work.} \\ \textit{to make Piero finish it.}\end{array}\right\}$

Longobardi accounts for this prohibition by postulating the existence of a filter, formulated so as to operate only on normal infinitival complements, and not on causative or restructuring constructions. Though he succeeds in giving a formulation that presupposes two different structures for the two sets of constructions (the analysis of causatives of Rouveret and Vergnaud (1980), and the RRIS analysis of restructuring), it is obvious from his discussion that the task would be simplified if the structures were alike, as we assume.

Restructuring and causative constructions also behave analogously in infinitival relatives and in *Tough*-movement constructions. Descriptively, both infinitival relativization and *Tough*-movement appear to be clause-bounded in Italian, as illustrated by (64), (65).

(64) a.   È una persona da ammirare.
      he is a person to admire.

b.   *È una persona $\left\{\begin{array}{l}\text{da rimpiangere di aver ammirato.} \\ \text{da convincere Maria a invitare.} \\ \text{da suggerire che Maria inviti.}\end{array}\right\}$

      He is a person $\left\{\begin{array}{l}\textit{to regret to have admired.} \\ \textit{to convince Maria to invite.} \\ \textit{to suggest that Maria invite.}\end{array}\right\}$

(65) a.   Questo lavoro è difficile da finire.
      This job is difficult to finish.

b.   *Questo lavoro è difficile $\left\{\begin{array}{l}\text{da cercare di finire.} \\ \text{da imporre a Maria di finire.} \\ \text{da suggerire che lui finisca.}\end{array}\right\}$

      This job is difficult $\left\{\begin{array}{l}\textit{to try to finish.} \\ \textit{to force Maria to finish.} \\ \textit{to suggest that he finish.}\end{array}\right\}$

This limitation is noted, for infinitival relatives in Radford (1977), and for *Tough*-movement in RRIS. These sources also note the apparent exceptionality of causative and restructuring constructions, illustrated in (66), (67).

(66) a.   Ho trovato una cosa da farti vedere.
      I have found something to make you see.

b. È un argomento da continuare a studiare.
   It is a subject to continue to study.

(67) a. Ho trovato una cosa facile da fargli preparare.
      I have found something easy to make him prepare.

b. È un libro difficile da cominciare a leggere proprio adesso.
   It is a book difficult to begin to read just now.

Since we do not have a precise account of the constraint illustrated by (64), (65) (which does not hold for the English counterparts) we will not be able to say exactly how (66) and (67) bear on the derived structure of each construction. But the identical response of the two constructions will of course confirm our view that we are dealing with analogous derived structures.

As we pointed out in 5.0 above, in RRIS it is noted that restructuring constructions give a peculiar response to certain structural tests, such as Clefting, as in (68a). (The CA establishes that restructuring has applied.) Causatives are similar to restructuring constructions in this respect too, as (68b) shows.[21]

(68) a. *È proprio [andare a casa] che sarei voluto.
        It is exactly to go home that I would have (E) wanted.

b. *È proprio [leggere il libro] che gli faccio.
   It is exactly read the book that I will make him.

The parallelism between (68a, b) will again be expected under the present common analyses. However, within our approach, the reason for the ungrammaticality of (68a) will be less obvious than in RRIS.

Under the RRIS account, the material within brackets in (68a) does not form a constituent (cf. (38) above), so that its inability to undergo Clefting is immediately explained. Not so if restructuring is VP-movement, since the material within brackets will then be a VP, thus presumably a constituent. But the potential argument against VP-movement here is in fact defused by (68b), since, as we argued in chapter 4 and as is generally agreed, the bracketed portion of *Gli faccio [leggere il libro]* must have been moved to the left, thus qualifying as a constituent. The RRIS account of (68a) would thus be inapplicable to (68b), while it remains plausible to presume that an account of (68b) would extend to (68a). Yet notice that our discussion, too, allows for some sense in which the bracketed material in (68b) is no longer an autonomous constituent at S-structure, since we must assume that an embedded object becomes an object of the matrix verb as well (though our analysis does not immediately account for this: recall our discussion of Clitic Climbing, Case absorption, etc. in 4.3). We may thus assume that (68b) does indeed violate some constituency requirements, but in our — less obvious — sense. Similar considerations could then apply to (68a).[22]

5.5 AUXILIARIES AND PAST PARTICIPLE AGREEMENT

Superficially, the distribution of auxiliaries and past participle agreement over the sentences we are studying in this chapter is rather puzzling. One major breakthrough towards an understanding comes with the idea that these sentences have been affected by restructuring. But it is only once we have a precise analysis of the mechanisms of auxiliary assignment and past participle agreement in general that we can deal with those phenomnena effectively. Then the peculiarities concerning auxiliaries and past participle agreement not only cease to be puzzling, but become rather effective means to probe into the structure of these constructions. In this section we see how.

As we argued in 1.7, we suppose that *essere* (E) assignment and past participle (pp) agreement function essentially as in (69).

> (69) a. Auxiliary E is assigned when there is a relation of a certain type between the subject and either a clitic or a direct object.
>
> b. A pp will agree with an element holding a relation of a certain type with its direct object.

The two rules in (69) must be taken to be closely related, and in particular to be triggered by exactly the same class of relations: essentially those relations that involve θ-role transmission though as we see below this is not quite accurate. The two rules in (69) wll cover the three cases in (70), determining either E, pp agreement, or both, as indicated.

> (70) a. NP cl V ...   E only
>
> b. ... cl V NP ...   pp agreement only
>
> c. NP V NP ...   Both E and pp agreement

We also assume, as we further argued in 2.6.2, that the notion of 'direct object' involved in both (69a, b) is not a thematic one, but rather a configurational one, based on some notion of government. This explains the fact that subjects of infinitives behave, in some cases, just like true direct objects, so that some Raising verbs like *sembrare* appear with both auxiliary E and pp agreement, just like ergative verbs. In order to distinguish systematic assignment of E with ergative verbs from non systematic assignment with Raising verbs, we distinguish the configuration in (70c), which we take to be a core configuration for E assignment (like the one in (70a)), from the one in (71), which we take to be a periphery configuration.

(71)   NP V [$_S$ NP ...]

We then naturally take all configurations other than (70a), (70c) and (71) to be core configurations for auxiliary *avere* (A). The periphery, i.e. (71) will thus be the area in which variability is allowed, but only, as we argued in 2.6.2, in conformity with principle (72).

(72)   In the periphery, a verb will maintain the auxiliary it takes in the core.

Turning to the way in which this system interacts with restructuring constructions, we first repeat the case of pp agreement with direct object clitics (cf. (56), (57)), illustrated by (73).

(73) a. **Li**$_i$ ho letti [$_i$e]
         I have read them.

     b. **Li**$_i$ ho voluti [$_{VP}$ leggere [$_i$e]] [$_S$ PRO – – –]
         I have wanted to read them.

As we noted, this phenomenon is found with causative constructions as well. However, while causatives do not allow us to test for pp agreement on the lower verb, as they do not allow an auxiliary on that verb, restructuring constructions do, as in (74).

(74)   **Li**$_i$ vorrei [$_{VP}$ aver già letti [$_i$e]] [$_S$ PRO – – –]
        I would want to have already read them.

The outcome of the rule of pp agreement here thus tells us that, under restructuring, an embedded object becomes an object of the main verb, but, as our analysis predicts, without ceasing to be an object of the embedded verb at the same time. Note that simultaneous pp agreement on both main and embedded verbs cannot be obtained because, as is noted in RRIS, restructuring constructions do not allow aspectual auxiliaries on both verbs at once, a fact to which we will return.

Consider now pp agreement in the SI construction, in the simple cases of (75) versus the restructured cases of (76).

(75) a. Gli si è telefonato.
         SI has phoned (to) him   (E; no pp ag't)

     b. Ci si è andati.
         SI has gone there   (E; pp ag't)

(76) a. Gli si **sarebbe** voluto telefonare.
         SI would have wanted to phone (to) him   (E; no pp ag't)

b. Ci si **sarebbe** voluti andare.

SI would have wanted to go there   (E; pp ag't)

Superficially, these facts may seem quite parallel to those illustrated in
(73): the pp agreement of *andare* in (75b) has moved onto the main
verb in (76b), while no agreement appears in (76a) as there is none in
(75a). On closer scrutiny however, these facts turn out to have wider implications.

Recall that pp agreement in (75b) is due to the ergative status of the
verb; that is, to the subject-object relation of (77), while both of the relations indicated induce E.

(77)   . . . [e] si è andati t . . .

Since only the subject-clitic relation of (77) is present with non-ergative
telefonare in (75a), only E and not pp agreement will be found in that
case, and analogously in (76a), which is thus straightforward. But consider the analysis of cases like (76b), as in (78b), derived as we assume
from (78a).

(78) a. $[_ie]$ si$_i$ **sarebbe** voluto $[_S$ PRO$_i$ andare t$_i]$

   b. $[_ie]$ si$_i$ **sarebbe** voluti $[_{VP}$ andare t$_i]$ $[_S$ PRO$_i$ − − −$]$

In order to account for pp agreement in (78b) under (69b), it is not
sufficient to say that the object of the embedded verb (t$_i$) has become
an object of the matrix verb as well. We must also postulate that the
latter object has become related to the matrix subject in the manner
indicated by the dotted line. Then, pp agreement in (78b) will follow in
the same manner as that of (77). But the relation of (78b) is curious
since, derivationally, t$_i$ is the trace of the *embedded* subject, rather than
the matrix one. How can this relation be justified? Recall how we argued
for the FI construction (4.6) that VPs containing a trace could not be
moved, or the trace would fail to have a proper antecedent at S-structure.
If movement applies is to the VP of (78a) however, because of the fact
that matrix and embedded subjects are coindexed, the trace will in effect
have a c-commanding antecedent, represented by the matrix subject.
Putting aside the question of θ-role assignment in cases like (78b), to
which we will return, this relation can therefore be justified in terms of
the same requirement that prohibited ergative complements in the FI
construction: the requirement that traces have c-commanding antecedents
at S-structure.

This account of (76b)−(78b) makes two predictions. One is that since
causative constructions do not allow movement of an ergative VP, no

pp agreement analogous to that of (78b) should be found on a causative main verb. This is correct, as shown by (79), which we analyze as a case of *Fare*-VP.

(79)　$[_i e]$ si$_i$ sarebbe $\begin{Bmatrix} \text{fatto} \\ \text{*fatti} \end{Bmatrix}$ [$_{VP}$ andare Giovanni]

　　SI would have made Giovanni go　　　　　　　(E; no pp ag't only)

Unlike (78b), (79) contains no relation that could trigger pp agreement.

The other prediction is that, since t$_i$ of (78b) is thus related to the matrix subject, the matrix auxiliary should remain E even in the absence of SI. This is also correct. If we replace clitic SI with non-clitic **noi** 'we', the auxiliary of non-restructured (78a) becomes A, as in (80a), but the one of restructured (78b) remains E as in (80b), induced by the subject-object relation.[23]

(80) a.　Noi$_i$ **avremmo** voluto [$_S$ PRO$_i$ andare t$_i$]
　　　　We would have wanted to go.　　　　　　(A; no pp ag't)

　　 b.　Noi$_i$ **saremmo** voluti [$_{VP}$ andare t$_i$] [$_S$ PRO$_i$ — — —]
　　　　We would have wanted to go.　　　　　　(E; pp ag't)

The alternation in (80) is a case of the CA phenomenon (cf. (3a) above), which our analysis of restructuring thus explains: As a result of VP-movement, the direct object of an embedded ergative verb (a trace), comes to bear a direct relation with the matrix subject, which is independently coindexed with it and which c-commands it. Since in complex predicates objects of the embedded verb function as objects of the matrix verb as well, this new relation induces E on the main verb under (69a) (as well as pp agreement under (69b)). It thus seems as if the embedded verb were 'transmitting' its own auxiliary E to the main verb.

Just as we predicted that there would be no agreement in causative cases like (79) superficially parallel to restructuring (78b), so we correctly predict no CA in causative cases like (81), superficially parallel to (80b).

(81)　　Noi $\begin{Bmatrix} \text{avremmo fatto} \\ \text{*saremmo fatti} \end{Bmatrix}$ [$_{VP}$ andare Giovanni]

　　　We would have made Giovanni go.　　　　(A; no pp ag't only)

Unlike (80b), (81) contains no relation that could induce E.

Note that in cases like (80b) the embedded verb maintains its ability to take E, as in (82).

(82)　　Noi$_i$ vorremmo [$_{VP}$ **essere** già andati t$_i$] [$_S$ PRO$_i$ — — —]
　　　We would want to have already gone.　　　(E; pp ag't)

This also follows from our analysis, given the additional assumption that in such cases the matrix subject is reanalyzed as subject of both verbs. Then E of (82) is assigned in the same manner as E of (80b), by (69a). The required reanalysis is natural both because it is complementary to the assumption that an embedded object is reanalyzed as an object of both verbs, and in view of the fact that the matrix subject is now the antecedent to the embedded object.

It must be obvious that no account of this sort of the CA phenomenon could have been forthcoming had we not adopted the ergative analysis of verbs like *andare*. Let us in fact turn to RRIS, which assumes the traditional intransitive analysis of such verbs. The account of CA proposed in RRIS consists of a rule like (83). (Recall that in RRIS restructured sequences are assumed to form a single verb. The 'variables' in (83) play a role in the case of longer sequences, which we will discuss later on).

(83)   **avere** → **essere** / $[_V vbl \_\_ vbl V_k]$
        Where V_k is a verb basically requiring *essere*

The problem with (83) is that it merely describes the phenomenon, without explaining it.[24] In particular, from the standpoint of a rule like (83) there is no principled reason why the CA should only occur from A to E and from right to left as it does. But there are good reasons within our account, which we will now examine. There is also little reason why (83), or a similar rule, could not apply in causative constructions.

Consider restructuring as in (84).

(84) a.   Giovanni$_i$ è andato t$_i$ $[_S$ PRO$_i$ a prendere il libro] $\Rightarrow$
          Giovanni has (E) gone to fetch the book.

     b.   Giovanni$_i$ è andato $[_{VP}$ a prendere il libro] t$_i$ $[_S$ PRO$_i$ — — —]

This is the case of restructuring with *andare* and *venire*, discussed in 5.2, where we noted that the matrix verb in these cases continues to take auxiliary E after restructuring. This fact we attributed to the continued presence of the direct object t$_i$ linked with the subject. Thus while the apparently embedded verb *andare* in (80b) seems to transmit its own auxiliary E to the main verb, transitive *prendere* of (84b) does not appear to transmit its own auxiliary A to main verb *andare*. Under our account, the reason why the CA only goes from A and E and not vice-versa thus follows essentially from the fact that all structure, and in particular t$_i$ of (84a), is preserved under restructuring.

Let us consider now the directional asymmetry of the CA. In our analysis, complex predicates, both in causative and in restructuring constructions are structurally asymmetrical, with the leftmost verb higher in the structure than the rightmost, as in (85a,b).

(85) a.

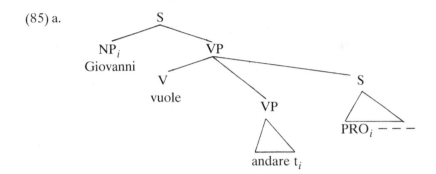

Giovanni wants to go.

b.

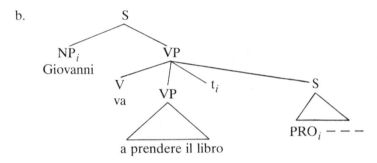

Giovanni goes to fetch the book.

Tree (85a) is essentially the structure of (80b), and (85b) that of (84b). As we have argued, in cases like (85a), the direct object of the embedded verb t_i has become the object of the main verb as well. On the other hand, there is little reason to suppose that in (85b) the object of the main verb t_i has become the object of the embedded verb, since the latter verb does not c-command that object. Thus, while the embedded verb in (85a) will transmit auxiliary E to the main one in the manner we discussed for (80b), we predict that the main verb in (85b) will not correspondingly transmit auxiliary E to the embedded one. While this prediction cannot be verified directly with cases like (85b), since verbs like *andare, venire* do not allow aspectual auxiliaries in their complements (just as in English, we presume for 'semantic' reasons), it can be verified with those Raising verbs of the restructuring class that take auxiliary E (independent of CA), i.e. *sembrare* and *stare* (*per*).

As we argued, the subject of the complement of such Raising verbs behaves like a direct object with respect to E assignment and pp agreement (the periphery configuration of (71) above). The restructured case in (86) would then be relevantly analogous to (85b).

(86)

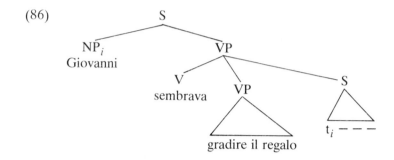

Giovanni seemed to like the present.

In such a case we will be able to verify both that the main verb will continue to take E, as in (87a), and that the transitive embedded verb will
continue to take A, and thus that there is no left-to-right CA, as in (87b).
(The position of the clitic in (87a,b) ensures that restructuring has
occurred.)

(87) a.   Giovanni lo **era** sembrato gradire.
          Giovanni had (E) seemed to like it

     b.   Giovanni lo sembrava **aver** gradito.
          Giovanni seemed to have (A) liked it

From the standpoint of our rule of E assignment, (89a,b) will thus verify
respectively that the embedded subject, a dependent of the main verb, is
still present in the structure (since the main verb takes E), and that this
subject is not reanalyzed as also being a dependent of the embedded
verb for then the embedded verb ought also to take E.[25]

From this, and from the directional asymmetry of the CA phenomenon, we conclude that the complex predicate created by restructuring
is structurally asymmetrical, with the leftmost verb c-commanding the
other but not vice-versa, as our analysis claims. Evidence, though perhaps
less compelling, supporting such asymmetry of the complex predicate was
also found in the case of causative constructions (cf. 4.3 and Note 16, ch.
4). Recall that the analysis in RRIS claims that a restructured pair of
verbs forms a single verb: a structure which cannot be asymmetrical in
any meaningful sense. Within that analysis, the right-to-left direction of
the CA could therefore not be derived, even if the rule of E assignment
of (69a) was available.[26]

Note further that any theoretical device which merely expresses the
observation that the CA goes from right to left is bound to be irrelevant
at best in the case illustrated in (88), where in fact CA appears to go
from left to right.[27]

(88) a. Si vorrebbe **aver** già letto quei libri.
  SI would want to have (A) already read those books.

 b. Quei libri si vorrebbero **esser** già letti.
  those books SI would want to have (E) already read.

In (88a), while the embedded verb takes A, the main one would take E, as always in the SI construction (cf. *Si sarebbe voluto . . .*). Thus, from a strictly observational point of view, in (88b), where O.P. has occurred, one would say that auxiliary E of the main verb has been transmitted to the embedded one. The RRIS rule (83) is thus obviously unenlightening on the alternation in the auxiliaries in (88), while the latter follows straightforwardly from our system. For under the present account, the analysis of (88a) will be as in either of (89a,b), depending on whether restructuring has applied or not, and that of (88b) will be as in (89c) since, given Long O.P., restructuring must have applied.[28]

(89) a. [e] si vorrebbe [$_S$ PRO **aver** già letto quei libri]

 b. [e] si vorrebbe [$_{VP}$ **aver** già letto quei libri] [$_S$ PRO − − −]

 c. Quei libri si vorrebbero [$_{VP}$ **esser** già letti t] [$_S$ PRO − − −]

The distribution of auxiliaries will then follow directly from the existence of the relations diagrammed in (89).

We will now try to show that the overall distribution of auxiliaries can, in itself, fully motivate a VP-movement analysis of restructuring, and exclude conceivable alternatives. Let us consider again the Raising subclass of restructuring verbs. In the absence of restructuring, Raising configurations are schematically as in (90), in which NP_2 is the trace of NP_1.

(90) $NP_1 \ V_1 \ [_S \ NP_2 \ V_2 \ (NP_3) \ldots]$

Consider now non restructured (91a) versus restructured (91b).

(91) a. Giovanni$_i$ **ha** dovuto [$_S$ t$_i$ andare t$'_i$]
  Giovanni has had to go.

 b. Giovanni$_i$ **è** dovuto [$_{VP}$ andare t$'_i$] [$_S$ t$_i$ − − −]

In accordance with our previous discussion, we take auxiliary A of (91a) to depend on *dovere* being one of those cases in which the relation between NP_1 and NP_2 of (90) (the periphery configuration of (71)) does not count for E assignment or, to put it differently, in which NP_2 does not function as a direct object of V_1. The alternation between (91a) and (91b) is an instance of the CA, which affects Raising *dovere* just as it does

Control *volere* of (82) above. As in the Control case, we take the CA to indicate that the direct object of the embedded verb, NP_3 of (90) is, as a result of restructuring, reanalyzed as an object of the main verb. But note that, while NP_3 is so reanalyzed, NP_2 is not. This is shown by (92). (Here and elsewhere we ignore the fact that the clitic, whose only function is to establish that restructuring has occurred, has an *ec* in the embedded VP.)

(92)   Giovanni$_i$ gli **ha** potuto [$_{VP}$ telefonare] [$_S$ t$_i$ — — —]
        Giovanni has (A) been able to phone (to) him.

If restructuring caused NP_2 of (90), and thus t_i of (92) to be reanalyzed as a direct object of the main verb, then *potere* of (92) ought to take E rather than A even though the embedded verb is not ergative. On the other hand NP_2 of (90) is not deleted by restructuring either, as we have argued (cf. 5.3) and as is shown by selection of E in other periphery cases like (87a).

The effects of restructuring on (90) can thus be summarized as in (93).

(93) i.   The relation between V_1 and NP_2 is totally unchanged
          (NP_2 is not deleted).

     ii. NP_3 is reanalyzed as an object of V_1.

But this conclusion excludes virtually all alternatives to the VP-movement analysis. In particular it will be fundamentally incompatible with any view of restructuring that did not involve movement.[29] For, if no movement occurred, we would certainly expect NP_2 of (90) to be reanalyzed before NP_3 is. The distribution of auxiliaries over restructuring constructions thus provides a third major argument for VP-movement. The first two were those of 5.2 and 5.3 above.

5.6 SUBJECT SUBSTITUTION

Our account of the CA phenomenon in the last section relies crucially on the notion that a relation between the embedded subject and a constituent of the embedded VP can, upon application of VP-movement, be reestablished with respect to the matrix subject. We will refer to this notion as SUBJECT SUBSTITUTION. One would expect subject substitution to be possible only in those cases in which the two subjects are coindexed, thus with all three types of candidates for restructuring of (94), but not with causative constructions.

(94) a. NP$_i$ V [$_S$ PRO$_i$ VP]   (*volere*)
     b. NP$_i$ V [$_S$ t$_i$ VP]   (*potere*)
     c. NP$_i$ V t$_i$ [$_S$ PRO$_i$ VP]   (*andare*)

Alongside of the CA, subject substitution makes another important empirical prediction, which we consider in this section. The prediction is that restructuring constructions should show total absence of the bifurcation discussed for the FI construction in 4.6, where we noted that some of the constructions involving relations between the subject and a constituent of the VP could be embedded under *fare*, as in (95a), while others could not, as in (95b).

(95) a. Giovanni ne$_i$ farà   [$_{VP}$ invitare una [$_i$e] **ciascuno$_j$**]
       Giovanni of-them will make   invite one   each

      [$_S$ ai   suoi amici$_j$ – – –]
      to-the his friends

      Giovanni will make his friends invite one of them each.

    b. *Maria gli$_i$ farà   [$_{VP}$ essere presentato t$_j$ [$_i$e]]
       Maria to-him will make   be introduced

      [$_S$ (a)   Giovanni$_j$ – – –]
      (to) Giovanni

      Maria will make Giovanni be introduced to him.

As we have argued, we attribute the contrast in (95) to the fact that the trace of (95b) requires a c-commanding antecedent not only in LF after reconstruction, like *ciascuno* of (95a), but also in S-structure.

The prediction for restructuring is that, given subject substitution, both cases parallel to (95a,b) should be grammatical, since both *ciascuno$_j$* and t$_j$ will take the matrix subject as a proper antecedent at S-structure. This is correct, as shown by (96).

(96) a. I suoi amici **ne** $\left\{ \begin{array}{l} \text{vorrebbero} \\ \text{potrebbero} \\ \text{andrebbero ad} \end{array} \right\}$ invitare una ciascuno.

      His friends would $\left\{ \begin{array}{l} \textit{want} \\ \textit{be able} \\ \textit{go} \end{array} \right\}$ *to invite one of them each.*

    b.   Giovanni **gli** $\left\{ \begin{array}{l} \text{vorrebbe} \\ \text{potrebbe} \\ \text{andrebbe ad} \end{array} \right\}$ essere presentato.

      Giovanni would $\left\{ \begin{array}{l} \textit{want} \\ \textit{be able} \\ \textit{go} \end{array} \right\}$ *to be introduced to him.*

Before turning to the full range of empirical predictions made by subject substitution, we will consider the fact that this phenomenon also raises some theoretical questions. Consider restructuring in the case of ergative and passive complements, with Raising *potere* as in (97), and with Control *volere* as in (98).[30] (As usual, the clitic on the higher verb is

only to ensure that these are restructuring cases. We ignore the *ec* associated with it).

(97) a.   Giovanni$_i$ **ci** potrebbe [$_{VP}$ andare t$_i$] [$_S$ t$_i$ $---$]

   Giovanni would be able to go there.

   b.   Giovanni$_i$ **gli** potrebbe [$_{VP}$ essere presentato t$_i$] [$_S$ t$_i$ $---$]

   Giovanni would be able to be introduced to him.

(98) a.   Giovanni$_i$ **ci** vorrebbe [$_{VP}$ andare t$_i$] [$_S$ PRO$_i$ $---$]

   Giovanni would want to go there.

   b.   Giovanni$_i$ **gli** vorrebbe [$_{VP}$ essere presentato t$_i$] [$_S$ PRO$_i$ $---$]

   Giovanni would want to be introduced to him.

If we assumed that the relation diagrammed in (97), (98), which is the
one created by subject substitution, transmits θ-role, no particular problem would seem to arise for (97), since the correct θ-role of the phrase
Giovanni in (97) is exactly that of object of the embedded verb (as that
phrase was in embedded object position at D-structure.) But in (98) the
same phrase is assigned subject θ-role by the main verb, so that transmission of θ-role by t$_i$ would result in double assignment, and a violation of
the θ-criterion. Main verbs *andare, venire* give rise to essentially the same
problem, as would be easy to show (since they too involve Control). The
question is then whether we must assume that the relation under consideration involves θ-role transmission.

So far, we have assumed that the relations that trigger E assignment
and pp agreement are those that involve θ-role transmission, or that form
chains (cf. 1.7, 4.6). If this view is correct, then the relations in (97), (98)
must involve θ-role transmission since we have seen that they trigger E
assignment and pp agreement in the case of ergative complements, which
is the CA case. (The case of passive complements will be addressed below.) But we will argue that this view, which was useful for providing a
preliminary characterization of the relations that trigger E assignment
and pp agreement, is actually incorrect.

Consider the fact that reflexive clitics induce E, as in (99).

(99)   Giovanni si è guardato.

          Giovanni has (E) watched himself.

The relation in (99), while triggering E assignment, does not involve θ-role
transmission, nor does it represent a chain, as the clitic has object θ-
role. Although in 1.7 we did suggest that a distinguishing criterion based
on θ-roles could be formulated so as to be technically compatible with

(99), we will argue in chapter 6 that the operative principle is in fact of a different nature. Specifically, we will suggest that the system of E-assignment and pp agreement operates at S-structure, and that the reason why certain relations do not trigger the latter system is simply that they do not exist at that level. If this is correct, then it follows only that the relations of (97), (98) must exist at S-structure, not that they must involve θ-role transmission.[31]

This does not solve all the problems. While we can now avoid the conclusion that the phrase *Giovanni* in each of (98) has double θ-role, we still have no account of how the θ-role assigned to t_i is to be transmitted to the relevant phrase, which is PRO_i. This problem we must leave unsolved, noting however that it arises from aspects of our anlaysis for which the empirical evidence is very strong. In particular, it arises from the conjunction of two claims: the one defended in 5.1 that cases like (98a,b) are initially normal Control structures, and the one, supported among other things by the distribution of auxiliaries and pp agreement, that the relations of (98a,b) exist at S-structure.[32] Note that the appropriate distinction between causative and restructuring cases is still made despite this difficulty: in the causative case in (95) (*Maria gli_i farà* [$_{VP}$ *essere presentato* t_j][$_S$ (*a*) *Giovanni_j* − − −]) the trace has no S-structure antecedent at all, while in the restructuring cases in (97) and in (98) it has one, although in (98a,b) this antecedent is not one which is relevant for θ-role assignment. We now return to the empirical predictions of subject substitution.

In 4.6 above we saw that the impossibility of embedding passives in the FI construction as in (95b) carried over to several other cases (listed in (134), ch. 4), which we will now review, comparing causatives with restructuring. We begin with Raising, O.P. and *ci* constructions, each exemplified in (100), which give rise to the ungrammatical causative cases in (101).

(100) a. Molti studenti (**gli**) risultavano [$_S$ t aver già terminato l'esame]

     Many students appeared (to him) to have already completed the exam.

  b. I genitori **si** avvertiranno immediatamente t

     the parents SI will notify immediately
     The parents will be notified immediately.

  c. [e] **ci** vuole la firma dell'insegnante

     there wants the signature of the teacher
     It takes the teacher's signature.

(101) a.   *L'errore di conteggio (**gli**) farà risultare aver già terminato
l'esame (a) molti studenti.
*The counting error will make many students appear (to him) to
have already completed the exam.*

b.   *Il preside $\left\{ \begin{array}{l} \text{farà avvertirsi} \\ \textbf{si } \text{farà avvertire} \end{array} \right\}$ immediatamente (a) i genitori.

The president will have the parents notified immediately.

c.   *Le nuove disposizioni $\left\{ \begin{array}{l} \text{faranno voler}\textbf{ci} \\ \textbf{ci } \text{faranno volere} \end{array} \right\}$ la firma

dell'insegnante.
The new regulations will make it take the teacher's signature.

Since we argued that the ungrammaticality of the cases in (101) was due
to the fact that the relations diagrammed in each of (100) are no longer
well-formed once VP-movement applies, subject substitution will now
predict that under restructuring each of those relations could be reconsti-
tuted with respect to the main subject. Contrasting with causative (101a)
we thus, correctly, expect to find that the restructured (102b) is grammatical, because the relation indicated replaces the one in (102a). Both
cases in (102) are actually slightly odd, due to the sequence of two infinitives (see 5.4), but the contrast with (101a) is clear. (On auxiliaries in
such cases, see 5.7 below.)

(102) a. Molti studenti$_i$ potrebbero [$_S$ t$_i$ risultar**gli** [$_S$ t$_i$ aver già

terminato l'esame]]
*Many students could appear to him to have already completed
the exam.*

b. Molti studenti$_i$ **gli** potrebbero [$_{VP}$ risultare [$_S$ t$_i$ aver già

terminato l'esame]] [$_S$ t$_i$ − − −]

Analogously, we expect the O.P. case in (103b), contrasting with ungrammatical (101b), to be derivable from (103a), with SI undergoing Clitic
Climbing. The example is grammatical, as predicted.

(103) a. I genitori$_i$ dovrebbero [$_S$ t$_i$ avvertir**si** immediatamente t$_i$]

The parents would have to be notified immediately.

b. I genitori$_i$ **si** dovrebbero [$_{VP}$ avvertire immediatamente t$_i$]

[$_S$ t$_i$ − − −]

However note that (103b) can also be derived from (104) (analogous to the Control case in (89b)), via restructuring and Long O.P.[33]

(104) $[_i e]$ si$_i$ dovrebbe $[_S t_i$ avvertire immediatamente i
　　　SI　*would have*　　*to notify*　*immediately*　　　*the*

genitori]
parents

This alternative derivation would not invoke subject substitution in the sense of (103), since (104) does not have any relevant relation between the embedded subject and its VP. Note that (103a) and (104) are derived from the same D-structure: the former via O.P. in the complement and Raising of the preposed object; the latter via Raising of SI (prior to its cliticization). Given the derivation from (104), the grammaticality of (103b) fails to provide further evidence for subject substitution, though it is is entirely compatible with it. (The auxiliaries in (103b) are as discussed in connection with (89c) above, and therefore as predicted by the relation indicated.)

The case of the *ci*-construction of (100c) is illustrated for restructuring in (105).

(105) a. $[_i e]$ dovrebbe $[_S t_i$ voler**ci** la firma dell'insegnante]

　　It would have to take the teacher's signature.

　　b. $[_i e]$ **ci** dovrebbe $[_{VP}$ volere la firma dell'insegnante] $[_S t_i$ − − −]

In 2.5.3 we saw that cases like (105a) are derived via Raising of the *ec* related to *ci*. We also saw that *ci* is never Raised like SI. The higher position of *ci* in (105b) is therefore to be attributed not to Raising, but to Clitic Climbing. The derivation of (105b) will thus involve subject substitution and Clitic Climbing of *ci*, the relation held by *ci* with the embedded subject in (105a) being replaced by the relation with the main subject in (105b). Notice that under the rather reasonable assumption that such a relation is subject to appropriate locality conditions, Clitic Climbing of *ci* can be explained as a reflex of subject substitution. Such an explanation for Clitic Climbing carries over to some other cases, for example the case of SI in (103), if we assume that SI holds a relation with the subject position even after O.P., as we argued in 1.6 above. It will also carry over to the case of reflexive *si* to be discussed in chapter 6. However, it does not extend to the case of clitics that do not hold a relation with the subject, such as non-reflexive object clitics, or to Clitic Climbing in causatives.

The analysis of (105) predicts that this case should instantiate the CA, i.e. that main verb *dovere*, while taking A in the structure of (105a), should take E in (105b). This is correct, as shown by **avrebbe dovuto volerci la firma** versus **Ci sarebbe dovuta volere la firma** 'It would have (A/E) had to take the signature' (The feminine pp agreement of *dovuta* is due to the 'inversion' relation linking the subject with feminine *la firma*. We take this relation also to induce E, redundantly with the relation marked in (105b).)

While thus possible under restructuring verbs of the Raising type as in (105b), the *ci* construction is impossible under the Control type, as illustrated by the contrast in (106).[34]

(106) a.   Ci dovrebbe essere molta gente alla festa.
            There would have to be many people at the party.

     b.   *Ci vorrebbe essere molta gente alla festa.
            There would want to be many people at the party.

The ungrammaticality of (106b) will follow naturally from the fact that *volere*, unlike *dovere*, assigns θ-role to its subject, thus excluding the pleonastic element. The contrast in (106) is further evidence against base-generation analyses, which, as we discussed in 5.1, are bound to miss the fact that different restructured constructions differ in their thematic structure in just the same way as their non-restructured counterparts.

In 4.6 we noted that not only O.P. constructions, but also SI constructions in which O.P. has not occurred, like the one in (107a), cannot be embedded under *fare*, as in (107b), the reason having to do with the subject-clitic relation indicated, as in the *ci* case above.

(107) a.   [e] si telefonerà ai genitori.

            SI will phone (to) the parents.

     b.   *Il preside $\left\{ \begin{array}{l} \text{farà telefonarsi} \\ \text{si farà telefonare} \end{array} \right\}$ ai genitori.
            The president will have the parents called.

Under restructuring, we do find the cases in (108), which may seem parallel to (105b) in that SI appears on the main verb.

(108) a. **Gli** si dovrebbe telefonare.
         SI would have to phone (to) them.

     b. **Gli** si vorrebbe telefonare.
         SI would want to phone (to) them.

However, such cases are derived differently than (105b) and do not bear on subject substitution. The reason is that SI, unlike *ci*, can be on the main verb before restructuring, as in (109) (in (109a) it is Raised, just as in (104).)

(109) a. Si dovrebbe telefonar**gli**.

   b. Si vorrebbe telefonar**gli**.

Beside being unnecessary, as (109) shows, presence of SI on the lower verb is furthermore impossible with Control verbs (for the reasons discussed in 1.6) and very marginal with Raising verbs (as we also saw in 1.6. Cf. fn. 40, ch. 1).

While the difference between causative (107b) and restructuring (108a,b) is therefore not related to subject substitution, there are still some other differences that are. Consider inversion and extraposition constructions, exemplified in (110). (Clitic *ne* in (110a) is related to '__' and thus ensures that the i-subject is in direct object position, which is relevant for what is to follow.)

(110) a. [e] **ne** verranno [molti __]

    Many of them will come.

   b. [e] **gli** sembra [che Giovanni sia qui]

    It seems to him that Giovanni is here.

In 4.6, we argued that these constructions, too, fail to be embedded under *fare*, because of the relation between the subject and the post-verbal argument. (Our claim was based mostly on theoretical rather than empirical considerations. Cf. 4.6.) As we saw in 2.3, cases like (110a) can be embedded under Raising verbs, as in (111a). The same is true of (110b), as in (111b).

(111) a. $[_i e]$ potrebbero $[_S t_i$ venir**ne** [molti __]]

    Many of them would be able to come.

   b. $[_i e]$ potrebbe $[_S t_i$ sembrar**gli** [che Giovanni sia qui]]

    It may seem to him that Giovanni is here.

Such cases remain grammatical if restructuring applies, due once again, we assume, to subject substitution, so that the relations marked in (111) are replaced by those in (112).[35, 36]

(112) a. $[_i e]$ **ne** potrebbero $[_{VP}$ venire [molti __]] $[_S t_i$ − − −]

   b. $[_i e]$ **gli** potrebbe $[_{VP}$ sembrare [che Giovanni sia qui]] $[_S t_i$ − − −]

Given the relations of (112), we correctly predict auxiliary E of **Ne *sarebbero* potuti venire molti** 'Many of them would have been able to come', and **Gli *sarebbe* potuto sembrare che Giovanni fosse qui** 'It may have seemed to him that Giovanni was here'. This exhausts the constructions which we saw in 4.6 to be incompatible with FI. All of those constructions are compatible with restructuring.

In this section we have considered the subject substitution hypothesis in its empirical and theoretical consequences. At the theoretical level we noted, on pages 357–359 some questions concerning θ-role assignment at S-structure for which we have no answer at this point, but which we claimed are inevitable given certain evidence. At the empirical level, we noted that subject substitution explains not only the CA phenomenon, but also a large class of differences between causative and restructuring constructions. In chapter 6 we will examine yet another important case of differential behavior which can be traced to subject substitution: reflexive complements.

5.7 AUXILIARIES IN SOME SPECIAL CASES

In 5.5 above we saw that the interaction between the system of E assignment and pp agreement and our analysis of restructuring predicted the correct distribution of auxiliaries and pp agreement in a number of major cases. In this section we consider some other, more complex cases. Our theory will be essentially on target here as well, although in some of these cases there will be a certain degree of approximation between the predictions and the facts.

As is noted in RRIS, while both ergative verbs (in our terms) and passives take auxiliary E, as in (113), only the former, and not the latter, trigger the CA, as in (114).

(113) a. Giovanni ci è andato.
      Giovanni has (E) gone there.

    b. Giovanni gli è stato presentato.
      Giovanni has (E) been introduced to him.

(114) a. Giovanni ci è voluto andare.
      Giovanni has (E) wanted to go there.

    b. Giovanni gli $\left\{\begin{matrix} \textbf{ha} \\ *\textbf{è} \end{matrix}\right\}$ voluto essere presentato.

      *Giovanni has (A/*E) wanted to be introduced to him.*

Under the classical analysis of passives, which we have assumed for simplicity through much of our discussion, the difference in auxiliary in (114) is indeed puzzling since these two cases would be structurally quite parallel (as in fact in (98) above). However, auxiliary A in (114b), and thus the contrast with (114a), follows quite straightforwardly from the analysis of passives we proposed in 2.7.1. Under the latter, (113b) is as in (115a), while (114b) is as in (115b).

(115) a. Giovanni$_i$ gli è stato [$_{sc}$ t$_i$ presentato t$_i$]

    b. Giovanni$_i$ gli **ha** voluto [$_{VP}$ essere [$_{sc}$ t$_i$presentato t$_i$]

    [$_S$ PRO − − −]

The relations of both (115a,b) cross a clause boundary, therefore such configurations are periphery cases (instances of (71) above.) In such cases, a verb will be free to take either auxiliary, in accordance with its lexical propensity, which we have argued is predictable on the basis of principle (72) (i.e. that the auxiliary be the same as in the core) where applicable. Main verb *essere* has a propensity for auxiliary E, predictable from the fact that it takes E in such core cases as **C'è stato un terremoto** 'There has been an earthquake' (see 2.7.1), whence auxiliary E in (115a), as well as in the configuration of (115b), as shown by (116).

(116)   Giovanni gli vorrebbe **esser** stato presentato.
       Giovanni would want to have (E) been introduced to him.

But, unlike *essere*, *volere* has a propensity for A, since it is a subject Control verb, and subject Control structures are core cases for A. We thus correctly predict that *volere* should take A in (115b). Note that E of (116) indicates that the relation of (115b) does indeed exist, so that A of (115b) cannot be due to absence of the relation.

    The predictions of our analysis are however less on target in the case of 'copular' *essere* which, as is also noted in RRIS, can induce the CA, though with various degrees of marginality. An adequate characterization of the facts seems to me to be that the results are roughly neutral between CA and no CA with *essere* followed by an adjective phrase or a predicate nominal, while CA is somewhat preferred over no CA with *essere* followed by a locative phrase, as in (117) respectively.

(117) a. Giovanni le $\left\{ \begin{array}{l} \textbf{?sarebbe} \\ \textbf{?avrebbe} \end{array} \right\}$ dovuto essere fedele.

    Giovanni would have (?E/?A) had to be faithful to her.

    b. Giovanni ne $\left\{ \begin{array}{l} \textbf{?sarebbe} \\ \textbf{?avrebbe} \end{array} \right\}$ dovuto essere il presidente.

    Giovanni would have (?E/?A) had to be the president of it.

    c. Alcuni passeggeri ci $\left\{ \begin{array}{l} \textbf{sarebbero} \text{ già dovuti} \\ \textbf{??avrebbero} \text{ già dovuto} \end{array} \right\}$ essere.

    Some passengers would have (E/??A) already had to be there.

From the standpoint of our theory, the possibility for E in (117a, b, c), and the difference between the latter and (114b) is unexpected. Since we analyze all instances of main verb 'be' as cases of Raising (recall 2.7.1 and the different auxiliaries in Italian and French), the cases in (117) should correspond to the configuration in (118), which is again a periphery case, given the clause boundary.

(118)   NP dovere [$_{VP}$ essere [$_{sc}$ t $\left\{ \begin{array}{l} \text{Adjective Phrase} \\ \text{Predicate Nominal} \\ \text{Locative Phrase} \end{array} \right\}$]] . . .

Other Raising verbs taking sc-complements such as *risultare, diventare, sembrare* give similar results, though with these the CA option seems to be more noticeably favored than with *essere*, as in (119).

(119) a. Giovanni le $\left\{ \begin{array}{l} \textbf{sarebbe} \\ \textbf{??avrebbe} \end{array} \right\}$ potuto risultare simpatico.

Giovanni would have (E/??A) been able to appear to her likeable.

b. Giovanni ne $\left\{ \begin{array}{l} \textbf{sarebbe} \\ \textbf{?avrebbe} \end{array} \right\}$ presto dovuto diventare il presidente.
Giovanni would have (E/?A) soon had to become the president of it.

c. Giovanni gli $\left\{ \begin{array}{l} \textbf{sarebbe} \\ \textbf{??avrebbe} \end{array} \right\}$ potuto sembrare già ad un buon punto.
Giovanni would have (E/??A) been able to seem to him already at a good point.

Parallel cases involving S rather than sc-complements do not seem to differ fundamentally, as shown in (120).

(120)   Non so quanti studenti gli $\left\{ \begin{array}{l} \textbf{siano} \text{ potuti} \\ \textbf{?abbiano} \text{ potuto} \end{array} \right\}$ risultare essere iscritti.
I don't know how many students may have (E/?A) been able to appear (may have possibly appeared) to him to be enrolled.

Clearly, though they are a residual problem, the above data do not falsify our theory. Thus the possibility for auxiliary E in (117), (119), (120) is evidence for the existence of a relation of the type indicated in (118), and hence for subject substitution. On the other hand, the possibility for A in many of these examples, marginal though it may be, is evidence that this relation crosses a clause boundary. Without such a boundary, all of these cases ought to be core cases for E, with no possibility for A at all.

The residual question then is why the clause boundary of these cases is detected only 'weakly' by our system of E assignment and pp agreement, while that of passive cases like (115b) is detected 'strongly'.

There is another case in which our theory only approximates the actual data. This concerns sequences of more than two restructuring verbs, in particular the configuration which we might refer to as "V_A V_E V_A", represented by a verb normally taking A, followed by a verb normally taking E, and by another verb normally taking A. RRIS claims that in such configurations, the main verb will take A, not E, citing examples like (121).[37]

(121)   Maria li $\left\{ \begin{matrix} \textbf{avrebbe voluti} \\ \textbf{*sarebbe voluti} \end{matrix} \right\}$ andare a prendere lei stessa.

   Maria would have (A/*E) wanted to go to fetch them herself.

This example appears to contrast with (122), in which restructuring between *andare* and *prendere* has not occurred (note the position of clitic **li**), and in which the CA is found as usual.

(122)   Maria **sarebbe** voluta andare a prender**li** lei stessa.
   Maria would have (E) wanted to go to fetch them herself.

Such a characterization of the facts would indeed go against our prediction. For while we analyze (122) as in (123a), with the relation between the main subject and t_i triggering auxiliary E on the main verb, we analyze (121), in which restructuring has applied to *andare* and its complement, as in (123b).

(123) a.

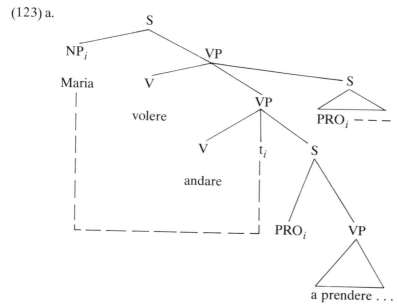

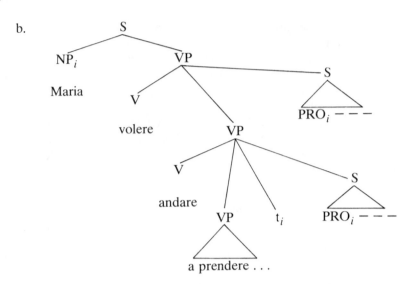

b.

But in (123b) t_i and thus the relation of (123a) is still present, so that E rather than A is expected for the main verb.

However, it appears that the characterization of RRIS is not entirely accurate, since different relevant examples give different results, as in (124).

(124)   Maria gli $\left\{ \begin{matrix} \textbf{avrebbe} \text{ voluto} \\ \textbf{?sarebbe} \text{ voluta} \end{matrix} \right\}$ andare a telefonare lei stessa.

   Maria would have (A/?E) wanted to go to phone (to) him herself.

Why is there such a difference between (121) and (124)? The answer is provided by pp agreement. Restructuring in the case of an ergative verb with a transitive complement gives rise to a configuration like (125), in which the ergative verb V_1 has in fact two direct objects: t_i and NP_j.

(125)

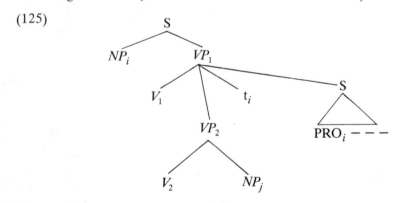

The relation between NP_i and t_i will induce not only E but pp agreement on V_1 as we know. But if we now imagine NP_j of (125) cliticizing to V_1, we will expect a second agreement, conflicting with the first, as occurs in (126).

(126)   Maria **li** è $\left\{ \begin{array}{l} \text{? \textbf{andata}} \\ \text{??\textbf{andati}} \end{array} \right\}$ a prendere.

   Maria has (E) gone (?ag't with Maria/??ag't with li) to fetch them.

When VP_1 of (125) is embedded by VP-movement under another verb, like *volere* of (123b), then the latter will also end up having two direct objects. The difference between (121) and (124) can thus be attributed to the fact that in (121) the E option carries with it the implication that the main pp should agree with *Maria*, in conflict with the agreement induced by *li*, while dative *gli* of (124) does not induce pp agreement, as we know.[38]

The correct characterization concerning auxiliary choice seems therefore to be the one provided by (124), although of course even the latter is not perfectly in line with our predictions. While in the previous case it was the possibility for E which was not predicted, here it is the possibility for A. But as in the previous case, our theory is not falsified by the facts. The possibility for E in (124), though perhaps slighty marginal, will suggest, not only that the relation between main subject and t_i of (123b) exists, but that it exists not as a periphery case, or E should be altogether impossible with *volere*, given principle (72). Moreover, when we consider the fact that restructuring of *andare* and its transitive complement as in (123b) inserts a certain amount of material on the path of the relation in question (at least with respect to linear order) it seems not too unreasonable to expect that the latter relation should become more 'weakly' detectable by our system of E assignment and pp agreement, though formally speaking matters are less clear.[39] Both the facts in (117)–(120), and those given in (124) suggest perhaps that our system of E assignment and pp agreement should be further refined, to allow for some continuity between core and periphery cases, where we have assumed a sharp division.

5.8 MORE ON THE DIFEERENCES BETWEEN CAUSATIVE AND RESTRUCTURING CONSTRUCTIONS

5.8.0 *Introduction*

Attempts to provide a common formulation of the causative and restructuring rules have appeared in the literature before. In particular in Rivas (1974), (1977) Van Tiel-Di Maio (1975), (1978), Aissen and Perlmutter

(1976), and Radford (1977). With reference to these attempts Rizzi (RRIS, 6.1) argues that, while a common formulation would obviously be desirable in principle, it must nevertheless be rejected since it would fail to express some very significant differences between the two types of constructions. The differences he cites are those illustrated by (127)–(129).[40]

(127) a. Giovanni ci $\left\{ \begin{array}{l} \textbf{sarebbe} \\ \textbf{*avrebbe} \end{array} \right\}$ voluto andare.

*Giovanni would have (E/*A) wanted to go there.*

b. Giovanni ci $\left\{ \begin{array}{l} \textbf{*sarebbe} \\ \textbf{avrebbe} \end{array} \right\}$ fatto andare Piero.

*Giovanni would have (*E/A) made go there Piero.*

(128) a.   Giovanni gli vorrebbe **essere presentato**.
            Giovanni would want to be introduced to him.

b.   *Giovanni farebbe   **essere presentato** Piero (da Mario).
      Giovanni would make be introduced   Piero (by Mario)

      Giovanni would make Piero be introduced (by Mario).

(129) a.   Mario **gli** vorrà scrivere.
            Mario will want to write to him.

b.   ??Mario **gli** farà scrivere Piero.
      Mario will make Piero write to him.

Both the difference with respect to the CA of (127) and the one concerning the embedding of passive complements of (128) have already been accounted for in the course of our discussion. They are both due to the fact that subject substitution is applicable in restructuring but not in causative cases. We have also seen that the difference in (128) is part of a more systematic pattern which concerns in analogous fashion ergative, passive, O.P., Raising, *ci*-construction, inversion and extraposition complements, and, as we see in chapter 6, reflexive ones as well. Note that in RRIS it remains unclear how either (127) or (128) could follow from different formulations of the rules for causatives and restructuring. (But see RRIS, fn. 32.)[41]

Let us now consider the contrast in (129). As Rizzi points out, within the account of (129b) given in Kayne's FS, there is a direct argument from this contrast for separate causative and restructuring rules. As we saw in 4.1.5, adapting somewhat Kayne's account to our framework, (129b) would have the analysis in (130), in which the clitic-*ec* relation would violate the 'SSC'.

(130)   Mario gli farà scrivere [$_S$ Piero . . . [e]]

Given the grammaticality of (129a), it would then have to be the case that, unlike FI, restructuring does not cause embedded dative objects to remain stranded in the embedded clause. But (129) will not lead to the same conclusion within our framework. Although we had no definite alternative to propose, in 4.1.5 we argued that Kayne's account of (129b) should be rejected. In the absence of an understanding of (129b), there will be no argument either for or against a different formulation of the two rules based on the contrast in (129). Note however that the contrast in (129) will be accounted for by our theory if we accept the proposal of 4.1.5 that (129b) is ill-formed not because of a violation of the SSC, but because the dative and accusative arguments of the verb, that is the *ec* related to the clitic and the phrase *Piero*, are not in their canonical order. For then the well formedness of (129a) will be due to the fact that there is no corresponding accusative argument here, since in restructuring cases the embedded subject is always null. Thus none of the facts noted in RRIS would appear to constitute an argument against our VP-movement analysis of both constructions.

In the rest of this section we consider yet other superficial differences between the two constructions. We will argue that they too can be accounted for either directly by our analysis, or at least in ways compatible with it.

5.8.1 *Subject Substitution versus VP-Complements*

Rizzi points out that while the embedded passive in (128b) is impossible, there is another type of 'passive' which is possible under *fare*, one which does not involve passive morphology, as in (131).

(131)   Giovanni farebbe   presentare Piero da Mario.
        Giovanni would make introduce   Piero by Mario

        Giovanni would have Piero introduced by Mario.

This represents in fact another difference between causatives and restructuring constructions, which do not allow anything comparable to (131).

In terms of our theory, the difference follows from the fact that causative verbs are subcategorized for VP-complements, which gives rise to the FP construction of (131) as well as to the grammatical variant of (127b) (as argued in 4.2, 4.5), while restructuring verbs are not so subcategorized (as argued in 5.1; see discussion of (24b) above). We may then ask whether, like other differences, this one too could be reduced to some independent difference between the two sets of verbs. There is a not implausible line of reasoning which seems to me to suggest that in fact it can.

Why, after all, should causative verbs and only causative verbs be subcategorized for VP-complements? Note that in some respects such a subcategorization has an effect analogous to that which subject substitution has for restructuring constructions. As we have seen in this chapter, subject substitution allows ergative complements to occur under restructuring verbs (when restructuring applies). In chapter 4 we saw that subcategorization for VP-complements allows ergative complements to occur under causative verbs. Let us suppose that, for some reason, restructuring/causative constructions could only exist if they were 'minimally productive' meaning by this that they must be possible with all three basic classes of complements: transitive, intransitive, ergative. Then, given that subject substitution is not operative with causative constructions, causative verbs would have to take base-generated VPs in order to allow ergative complements and to ensure minimal productivity. Once VP-complements are allowed at the level of subcategorization specifications, then we will naturally expect that, not only ergative verbs, but also transitives and intransitives could appear in such complements as well, whence the FP construction.

We clearly want to regard the possibility of taking VP-complements as a rather marked option. We know however that application of the causative rule is, in effect, obligatory (cf. *Giovanni fa [s Mario leggere], etc.). Thus, provided that the 'minimal productivity' requirement is strong enough, the marked option will have to be taken. This makes the correct prediction that VP-complements, and hence the FP construction, should exist if and only if the FI construction exists also. (English has neither.)

In 4.1.3 we argued that the apparent obligatoriness of the causative rule ought to follow in some fashion from Case theory, specifically from the need of the embedded subject to be assigned Case. From this standpoint we will expect restructuring not to be obligatory, since the embedded subject, being phonologically null, will not require Case. As we know, this is correct. It is easy to see that this makes the further prediction that there should be no analogue to the restructuring or the causative rule in cases in which the embedded subject is phonologically null, but subject substitution is not applicable. A case of this sort is (132).

(132)   [e]   bisogna   [s PRO leggere il libro]
         (it) is necessary   to read the book.

The prediction that VP-movement should not affect structures like (132) comes from the fact that subject substitution would fail to obtain since the two subjects are not coindexed. Consequently, this would make the derived construction not 'minimally productive' since VP-movement could not successfully apply to ergative complements. At the same time the marked option to allow VP-complements would not be warranted since VP-movement is unnecessary when the embedded subject does not require Case.

The prediction is borne out, suggesting that this whole approach is quite possibly correct. As we noted in II.0.2 and in 5.0 above, of the four classes of verbs captured by the interaction of the two lexical parameters of $\pm \bar{S}$-deletion and $\pm \theta_s$, three appear affected by 'restructuring' phenomena, while the fourth one represented by verbs like *bisognare* of (132) ($-\bar{S}$-deletion, $-\theta_s$) seems immune.[42]

Another difference, noted in RRIS, concerns constraints on the distribution of auxiliaries. While either verb in a restructured pair can take an aspectual auxiliary as we have seen, it is impossible for both verbs to appear with an auxiliary at the same time, as shown in (133a), contrasting with non-restructured (133b).

(133) a. *Giovanni lo **avrebbe** voluto **aver** già letto.
      Giovanni would have wanted to have already read it.

    b. Giovanni **avrebbe** voluto **aver**lo già letto.

This constraint may be compared with the one holding in causative constructions. In the latter, the main verb can always take an auxiliary freely, while the embedded one can never appear with an auxiliary at all, as in (134) (analogously in FP).

(134)   ?*Giovanni farà   **aver** letto il   libro a Piero.
      Giovanni will make have read the book to Piero

      Giovanni will make Piero have read the book.

Such a distribution of auxiliaries seems to mirror exactly that of subjects at S-structure. We have argued that in cases of restructuring the main subject becomes the subject of both verbs (see discussion of (82) above). But in causative constructions, while the main verb has a subject, the embedded verb lacks one altogether (in the strict configurational sense we are considering). Since we independently know that the subject plays some role in auxiliary assignment, determining E when it bears a certain type of relation with an element in the VP (cf. (69a)), it seems plausible to suppose that the subject *always* plays a role in auxiliary assignment, and specifically that an auxiliary should be assigned only to the extent that there is a subject present. Thus there will be no embedded auxiliary in (134), and only one auxiliary betwen the two verbs in (133a).[43]

5.8.2 Matrix Passives

Another rather conspicuous difference between the two sets of constructions concerns the possibility of passivizing the matrix verb as in (135), where the embedded object has moved into matrix subject position.[44]

(135) a.   Questo libro è stato   fatto leggere a   Mario (da
           this   book has been made to read to Mario (by

Giovanni).
Giovanni)

Mario has been made to read this book (by Giovanni).

b.   *Questo libro è stato $\left\{ \begin{array}{l} \text{voluto} \\ \text{dovuto} \\ \text{andato a} \end{array} \right\}$ leggere (da Giovanni)

This book has been $\left\{ \begin{array}{l} \textit{wanted to} \\ \textit{had} \\ \textit{gone to} \end{array} \right\}$ *read (by Giovanni)*

Although there are some exceptions to which we will return, the impossibility exemplified by (135b) is rather general among restructuring verbs. The question will be whether this impossibility follows from our analysis.

The cases in (135b) contrast with corresponding O.P. cases such as those in (136) which, as we have seen, are grammatical (Long O.P.)

(136) a.   Questo libro$_i$ si$_j$ è voluto   [$_{VP}$ leggere t$_i$ subito]
           this book   SI   has wanted   to read   immediately

[$_S$ PRO$_j$ − − −]

b.   Questo libro$_i$ si$_j$ è dovuto [$_{VP}$ leggere t$_i$ subito] [$_S$ t$_j$ − − −]
     this book   SI   has had   to read   immediately

c.   Questo libro$_i$ si$_j$ è andato [$_{VP}$ a leggere t$_i$ subito] t$_j$
     this book   SI   has gone   to read   immediately

[$_S$ PRO$_j$ − − −]

As we argued in 5.4 above, we must assume that in cases like (136a,b) SI is the antecedent to the embedded subject PRO$_j$, t$_j$ respectively. Analogously, SI will be the antecedent to t$_j$ in (136c). The cases in (135b) will be essentially parallel in structure to those in (136), but with one difference: the former have no SI. The ungrammaticality of (135b) will then follow directly from the fact that the counterparts to PRO$_j$, t$_j$ of (136) have no antecedent (In fact, there will be no traces corresponding to t$_j$ of (136b, c), only empty categories.) In contrast, (135a) will be grammatical because the embedded subject *Mario*, unlike PRO$_j$, t$_j$ of (136) does not require an antecedent. The difference in (135) would thus once again follow essentially from the single independent difference between the two constructions: coindexation between the two subjects in restructuring cases; no coindexation in causative cases.

Yet other factors seem also to play a role in the ungrammaticality of the examples in (135b). The *dovere* and *andare* cases are in fact also ruled out by our discussion in 3.2 above, in which we concluded that

Raising and ergative verbs were barred from acquiring passive morphology by a constraint against 'vacuous' loss of subject θ-role. As for the case of *volere*, there is some reason to believe that it too independently resists passivization, as the following examples illustrate, though we have no account of this fact.[45]

(137) a.   Tutte le case cinematografiche lo volevano come primo attore.
           All movie producers wanted him as a leading actor.

      b. ?(?)Era voluto come primo attore da tutte le case
           cinematografiche.
           He was wanted as a leading actor by all movie producers.

(138) a.   La voglio ben cotta.
           I want it well done.

      b.   ?*La bistecca sarebbe voluta ben cotta.
           The steak would be wanted well done.

(139) a.   Volevamo che Giovanni partisse.
           We wanted that Giovanni should leave.

      b.   ?*Fu voluto che Giovanni partisse.
           It was wanted that Giovanni should leave.

But we can eliminate the factors associated with the passive morphology of the cases in (135b), while maintaining other relevant aspects, by turning to the corresponding FP cases in (140). (On the relation between passives and FP recall (55) chapter 4 and discusion.)

(140) a. ?*Questa campagna pubblicitaria farà   [$_{VP}$ vedere il   film
          this   advertising campaign   will make   to see   the movie

          [$_S$ PRO − − −] (da tutti)]
                          (*by everyone*)

      b. ?* ... farà   [$_{VP}$ dover [$_{VP}$ vedere il   film] [$_S$ [e] − − −]
             will make   have to   see   the movie

         (da tutti)]
         (*by everyone*)

      c. ?* ... farà   [$_{VP}$ andare [$_{VP}$ a vedere il   film]
             will make   go   to see   the movie

         [e] [$_S$ PRO − − −] (da tutti)]
                            (*by everyone*)

The case in (140a) will now be excluded solely because PRO lacks an antecedent.[46] Correspondingly, the cases in (140b,c) will be excluded because [e] also lacks an antecedent (and, being governed, is not interpretable as PRO, whence a violation of the θ-criterion.) The variant of

(140b,c) with the *by*-phrase (which has a higher degree of ungrammaticality than is indicated) will furthermore be excluded by the fact that
Raising and ergative verbs never have *by*-phrases (since they cannot have
a thematic subject, cf. 3.1.3). But these considerations will now carry over
to the cases in (135b), thus confirming the account of those cases that we
first proposed. In addition however, the factors associated with passive
morphology which we mentioned will also be assumed to play a role in
(135b). This will account for the noticeably more severe ungrammaticality of (135b) compared with (140).

As mentioned above, there are some exceptions to the failure of passivization with restructuring verbs as in (135b). Such exceptions, noted in
Rizzi (1976a), concern 'aspectual' predicates *cominciare, continuare*, as
for example in (141).

(141)   Il   palazzo fu   cominciato a costruire sotto   Carlo V
          the palace was begun   to build   under Charles V

As Rizzi notes, this possibility is somewhat limited even with these verbs,
since a different choice of complement yields rather different results, as
in (142).

(142) ?(?)L'affitto fu   continuato a pagare fino alla fine dell'anno
          the rent   was continued   to pay   till the end   of the year

Still, we may want to consider briefly how such cases should be analyzed.

One hypothesis is that the case in (141) has essentially the same analysis as the *volere* case in (135b), namely the one in (143), and that its
grammaticality is due to the possibility of interpreting PRO of (143) even
in the absence of an overt antecedent. (Note that the Control, rather than
the Raising entry of *cominciare* must be involved here since we would
not expect a Raising verb to appear with passive morphology. See 3.2.1.)

(143)   Il palazzo$_i$ fu cominciato [$_{VP}$ a costruire t$_i$] [$_S$ PRO − − −]

Another hypothesis would consist of assuming that in fact there is no
embedded subject PRO in (141), for example that the latter involves a
base-generated VP-complement, or a base-generated complex verb *cominciare a costruire*. The difference between the *volere* case in (135b) and
(141) would then follow directly. We must note however that the applicability of this second hypothesis would be limited to cases like (141). For
in cases like (144), in which the complement is passivized, it is certainly
more natural, and perhaps necessary, to assume that the complement is
sentential (cf. Note 30).

(144)   Gli ospiti **gli** cominciarono ad essere presentati.
        The guests began to be introduced to him.

In general, with the sole exception of (141), these verbs exhibit exactly the same behavior as other restructuring verbs, so that there will be little reason not to assume that the same restructuring process is generally at work with these verbs also.

One fact that seems relevant to a choice between the two alternatives is that in (141) the embedded subject is construed as coreferential with the matrix thematic subject, that is, the unspecified semantic subject of the passive verb. For, a reading in which somebody did the 'beginning', while somebody else did the 'building' is totally impossible. In this respect cases like (141) differ from FP cases like (145), in which the semantic subject of *fare* and that of *costruire* are quite independent.

(145) Il   palazzo$_i$ fu   fatto [$_{VP}$ costruire t$_i$] sotto Carlo V.
       the palace   was made   to build   under Charles V

Someone had the palace built under Charles V.

Under the analysis in (143), though not under the alternative, we can account for such interpretation by relying on an independently existing device: the one operative in (146) (whatever it is) where the PRO subject of the *per*-clause is also interpreted as controlled by the unexpressed semantic subject of the main verb.[47]

(146) Il palazzo$_i$ fu costruito t$_i$ [per PRO onorare Carlo V]
       The palace was built (for) to honor Charles V.

Another fact that seems relevant is that, in cases in which the embedded subject is not syntactically represented, as in VP-complements of *fare*, it is immaterial whether or not that subject *would* have received a θ-role. Thus, alongside of (145), we find (147), involving ergative *intervenire*.

(147) L'architetto$_i$ fu   fatto [$_{VP}$ intervenire t$_i$]
       The architect   was made   to intervene.

But in cases like (141) it is not at all immaterial, since alongside of (141), we only find the ungrammatical (148).

(148) *L'architetto fu   cominciato ad intervenire.
       The architect was begun   to intervene.

Under the hypothesis of (143), the ungrammaticality of (148) follows from the fact that the embedded subject PRO would fail to receive a θ-role. (Notice that it must be PRO rather than trace as Control *cominciare* does not trigger S̄-deletion. Recall the discussion of (42), (43) above.) But any analysis of (141) not allowing for an embedded subject position would have to feature the rather odd requirement that a certain missing position must be one that would have had a θ-role if in fact it had not been missing. On the basis of this we thus conclude that the correct analysis of (141) is the one in (143).[48]

The FP case in (149), which we expect to be also grammatical, given the assumed parallelism of passives and complements of FP, will correspondingly have the analysis indicated. (Clitic *vi* ensures restructuring.)

(149)   Carlo V **vi**   fece   [$_{VP}$ cominciare [$_{VP}$ a costruire un
         Charles V there made   begin   to build   a

         palazzo] [$_S$ PRO – – –]
         palace

         Charles V made someone begin to build a palace there.

Just as in (143), so in (149) PRO will be interpreted as coreferential with the subject of *cominciare*, even though the latter subject is not represented in the structure.

But why then should (143), (149) be similar to (146) and differ from the *volere* case of (135b) and (140a) with respect to the possibility of interpreting the embedded subject PRO? We will have no precise answer to this question, since we have no precise account of what makes (146) possible. (Recall that, for example, *without*-clauses do not allow for this possibility. See the disscussion of (61a) above.) However, two observations may bear on this question. One is that complements of verbs like *cominciare* behave like adjuncts such as the *per*-clause of (146) and, as we noted in 1.8 (cf. (112b), ch. 1), unlike other infinitival complements, in allowing interpolation of an i-subject, as in (150).

(150) a.   Ha cominciato Giovanni [a costruire lo   steccato]
            has begun   Giovanni to build   the fence

      b.   Ha telefonato Giovanni [per sapere se venivi]
            has phoned   Giovanni to know if you were coming.

      c.   *Ha voluto   Giovanni [sapere se venivi]
            has wanted Giovanni to know if you were coming

The second observation concerns the impossibility for verbs like *cominciare* to take tensed complements, as in (151a) contrasting with (151b).

(151) a.   *Giovanni comincia [che Maria telefoni]
            Giovanni begins   that Maria should phone

      b.   Giovanni vuole [che Maria telefoni]
            Giovanni wants   that Maria should phone

The fact that verbs like *cominciare* are confined to Control structures to the exclusion of (151a) suggests a semantic property, not shared by verbs like *volere*, requiring coreferentiality between the verb's subject and the subject of the complement. We suspect that either of these facts might underlie the difference between *cominciare* and *volere* with respect to passivization as in (141).

5.8.3 *Prepositional Infinitives*

As we have seen, some of the restructuring verbs, specifically those in (152), appear with infinitives preceded by a preposition.

(152)   cominciare (a), continuare (a), stare (per), andare (a),
        begin   *continue*   *be about*   *go*

        venire (a)
        come

In contrast, we have seen that causative and perception verbs take bare infinitives. Two issues arise in this connection.

First, this may seem to be an unexplained difference between the two constructions. Second, the status of the prepositions in (152) has a rather direct bearing on the correctness of the VP-movement analysis of restructuring, as the latter analysis implies that these prepositions *must* be within the infinitival VP. If they were outside, we would incorrectly expect restructuring to permute infinitival and preposition in their linear order. In this subsection we briefly address these two issues. We will not attempt to provide an exhaustive characterization of these prepositions, a task which seems rather complex, but merely argue that our discussion of restructuring is compatible with the evidence so far available.

Concerning the first issue, note that in fact the presence versus absence of a preposition does not represent a systematic difference between causative and restructuring constructions, both because some restructuring verbs appear without a preposition (*dovere, potere, volere, sapere*), and because we find the verb *mandare*, which takes an infinitival preceded by *a*, and which appears in constructions of the FP type as in (153a), and (more marginally) of the FI type as in (153b).

(153) a.   **Lo** mando a prendere (da Giovanni).
            (I) it   send   to fetch   (by Giovanni)

        I will have it picked up (by Giovanni).

    b. ?   **Lo** mando a prendere a   Giovanni
            (I) it   send   to fetch   to Giovanni

        I will have Giovanni pick it up.

It therefore seems reasonable to suppose that these prepositions are only related to lexical factors and not to any syntactic difference between causative and restructuring constructions.

Turning to the second issue, in principle there are three positions in which these prepositions could be: (i) Within the VP (like English *to*); (ii) in complementizer position; (iii) outside the infinitival $\bar{S}$, taking the $\bar{S}$ as a complement. The third possibility is suggested in Rizzi (1982, III.4) for those cases in which the infinitival appears to alternate with NPs, as in (154).

(154) a. Giovanni baderà   a   [fare il proprio dovere]
         Giovanni will pay attention to doing his job.

    b. Giovanni baderà   a   [questo]
         Giovanni will pay attention to this.

Of the cases in (152), *cominciare a, continuare a, stare per* all fail to appear followed by an NP, so that (iii) is presumably ruled out for these cases. *Andare a, venire a* do appear followed by an NP, as in **Giovanni va a Roma** 'Giovanni goes to Rome', but it is unlikely that this instantiates an alternation of the type of (154), since with these verbs we can find both *a*-NP and *a*-infinitive, as in **Giovanni va [a Roma] [a partecipare ad un convegno]** 'Giovanni goes to Rome to participate in a meeting'.

The second possibility (P in COMP), is examined in Kayne (1981c), for the preposition *di*. Kayne argues that if such a preposition is in COMP, then the fact that it never occurs with Raising verbs follows naturally from the general impossibility of Raising over a filled complementizer (see II.0.2 above). Kayne cites the case of Italian *sembrare*, which, though a Raising verb otherwise, can only function as a Control verb (a verb of the same class as *bisognare* of (132) above) when *di* is present, as in (155).

(155) a.   Giovanni sembra gradire il regalo.
      Giovanni seems to like the present.

    b.   *Giovanni sembra **di** gradire il regalo.

    c.   Sembrava   **di** volare.
      (it) seemed to fly

Kayne's discussion thus implies that prepositions that do occur with Raising verbs, such as *a* of *cominciare, continuare* and *per* of *stare (per)* are not in COMP. As for *a* of *andare, venire*, note that *a* of *mandare* in (153a,b) must be in VP if the latter examples are indeed analogous to FP (VP-complement) and FI (VP-movement. Note that some form of $\bar{V}$-movement is overtly supported here by the surface linear order of constituents.) Since *mandare* appears to be closely related to *andare*, being its lexical causative, we have reason to regard *a* of *andare*, and presumably also of *venire*, as like that of *mandare*. In short, we have no reason to believe that any of the prepositions in (152) could not be constituents of the infinitival VP as we have been implicitly assuming.

Note further that Rizzi (1982, III.4) shows clearly that all pre-infinitival prepositions are cliticized to the verb at the surface level, as suggested for example by **Mario pensa che forse potrà partire/Mario pensa di (*forse) poter partire** 'Mario thinks that perhaps he will be able to go/ Mario thinks (perhaps) to be able to go'. This raises the possibility that even (ii) and (iii) above (P in COMP, P outside $\bar{S}$) may be compatible with our theory of restructuring: we could assume that cliticization to V precedes restructuring.

However, there is a curious difference between *di*-infinitivals and others, which might indicate that the difference between a preposition in COMP and a preposition in VP is indeed relevant to the applicability of restructuring. Some verbs taking *di* infinitivals do exhibit some of the properties of restructuring, such as Cl-Cl, and even matrix passivization in the manner discussed for *cominciare, continuare,* as in (156).

(156) a.   **Lo** finirò   di leggere presto.
         (*I*) it   *will finish to read   soon*

   b. Questo libro fu   finito   di stampare nel 1978.
      this   book was finished to print   in   1978

Yet we find that with such verbs the CA is systematically impossible, as in (157).

(157)   Coll'inizio della scuola $\left\{ \begin{array}{l} \textbf{avremo} \text{ finito} \\ \textbf{*saremo} \text{ finiti} \end{array} \right\}$ di andare in spiaggia.

   *With the beginning of school we will have (A/*E) finished go-
   ing to the beach.*

But we will have no specific proposal on how to account for these facts.

5.8.4 *Summary*

In 5.6 above, pursuing the empirical consequences of the subject substitution hypothesis, we noted that the latter correctly predicted several differences between causative and restructuring constructions. In this section, we proceeded in the opposite direction. We started from some observable differences and attempted to determine how these would bear on our theory. We have seen that these differences, too, can be accommodated within our theory. With the differences we have reviewed in this section the overall list of differences is as in (159).

(159) a. *A certain class of complements* is found only under restruc-
         turing: Ergative (if sentential); Passive; O.P.; *ci*-construction;
         Inversion; Extraposition.

b. *Change of Auxiliary*: found only with restructuring.

c. *Dative objects*: fail to cliticize freely only in FI.

d. *VP-complements*: possible only with causative verbs.

e. *Auxiliaries*: free on the main verb and impossible on the embedded verb in causatives; possible only on either verb in restructuring.

f. *Matrix passives*: free in causatives; impossible with some exceptions in restructuring.

g. *Prepositional infinitivals*: Causative and perception predicates take bare infinitivals, while some restructuring verbs take infinitivals preceded by a preposition.

With the exception of (159g) which was regarded as an accidental fact, and not a genuine difference between the two constructions, we have attempted to attribute all of the facts in (159) to independent properties of the structures that undergo VP-movement. To the extent that we have succeeded in doing so, we have provided an explanation for why these differences exist. In contrast, an account based on different formulations of the rules would fail to provide such an explanation, since it would answer the question of why these differences exist only at the cost of raising the new question of why there should be different rules.

There is however one important difference which we have not yet discussed and on which we will have little to say. This is the different distribution of the two sets of constructions over language types. As is noted in Kayne (1980b) and in the references he cites, restructuring constructions are found only in Null Subject (NS) languages, such as Italian and Spanish as well as French up to the seventeenth century, while causative constructions exist in non-NS languages too, like modern French. This of course means that, at the theoretical level, the restructuring process ought to rely on the NS property in some fashion. We may note here that, if our discussion in 5.8.1 above proves correct, and if failure of subject substitution to obtain would indeed be sufficient to exclude restructuring altogether, as with the class of verbs like *bisognare* of (132) above, then, in order to establish the correct typological link it would be sufficient to show that subject substitution is contingent on the NS property. But we will not attempt to put forth a specific proposal.[49]

5.9 CONCLUSION

In this chapter we have attempted to refine the theory proposed in Rizzi's *A Restructuring Rule in Italian Syntax*, integrating it with the theory of causative constructions we developed in chapter 4. While Rizzi's discussion is successful in showing that several diverse phenomena must be attributed to the operation of a single syntactic rule of restructuring, it falls short of an adequate explanation for one of these phenomena: the Change of Auxiliary. We have attempted to show that, within our approach, the latter phenomenon as well as the overall distribution of auxiliaries in restructuring constructions, follows from the conjunction of (i) The VP-movement formulation of the restructuring rule, and (ii) The subject substitution hypothesis. A more fundamental key to our solution of this problem is however the assumption that there exists a class of ergative verbs, i.e. the "Unaccusative Hypothesis".

While both (i) and (ii) above account for are thus motivated by the distribution of auxiliaries, they are also given ample independent motivation. We have in fact provided two other major arguments for VP-movement: one based on the effects of restructuring on ergative complements of *fare* (5.2); a second based on the conclusion that the embedded subject is still present in the structure, while there are no SSC or binding theory effects on the embedded VP (5.3). As for subject substitution we have argued that virtually every difference between restructuring and causative constructions follows from, or is closely related to it (5.8).

In 4.8 above, we concluded that our discussion in chapter 4 provided good evidence for the existence of empty categories. This is true also of our discussion in this chapter. Consider the fact, discussed in chapters 4 and 5, that a set of constructions like Ergative, Passive, O.P., the *ci*-construction, Inversion, and Extraposition can all be embedded in restructuring contexts, but not under causative verbs. From the point of view of our theory featuring *ec*'s and configurational conditions, these constructions fall under one generalization: they all involve a relation between the subject and an element in the VP. But without *ec*'s there will be no generalization.

Whereas in a theory that has *ec*'s constraints are mostly expressed by conditions applying on derived structure, in a theory that has no *ec*'s, constraints are typically expressed by elaborating on the formulation of syntactic rules (see I.0.3). But from the point of view of a system of rules, there will be no particular reason why the rules that give rise to, say, passives, the *ci*-construction, extraposition (whatever they are) should all be applicable under *volere* and inapplicable under *fare*. Surely they will be independent rules. Alternatively, there will be little reason why the causative rule should fail and the restructuring rule succeed whenever the complement is, say, passive, ergative, Raising, or a *ci*-construction. Without *ec*'s, those complements will bear no resemblance to each other. The notion of subject substitution, which plays a crucial role in our account, finds no obvious conceptual or empirical equivalent in a framework that has no *ec*'s, since many of the categories that enter into subject substitution are in fact *ec*'s.

Consider in particular (160a,b).

(160) a. Giovanni$_i$ **sarebbe** venuto t$_i$ alla festa.
    Giovanni would have (E) come to the party.

 b. Giovanni$_i$ **sarebbe** voluto [$_{VP}$ venire t$_i$ alla festa] [$_S$ PRO$_i$ — — —]
    Giovanni would have (E) wanted to come to the party.

Under our analysis, in both (160a,b) auxiliary E is determined by the relation between *Giovanni* and t$_i$. Under a system that has no t$_i$ in (160), it
is possible to give an equivalent formulation of E assignment to handle
the simple case in (160a). Selection of E will be tied in some fashion to
application of NP-movement. However, we have claimed that there is no
relevant application of NP-movement in (160b), since the main subject
Giovanni has not been moved at all. The theory without *ec*'s could thus
only account for (160b) at the cost of claiming that *Giovanni* is in fact
moved, and that the sequence *volere venire* is in fact an ergative verb.
But of course this is false, as we argued in 5.1: restructured *volere* is non-
distinct from non restructured *volere* with respect to semantic interpretation and selectional restrictions, which implies that, like the latter, the
former must be a $+\theta_s$ verb taking a sentential complement.
    The theoretical challenge here is thus represented by the fact that
sequences like *volere venire* behave like ergative verbs in some respects,
as in (160), but not in others. Let us note just one more respect in which
such sequences do not behave like ergative verbs, illustrated by (161).

(161) a.   Il signore [**venuto** alla festa] è Giovanni.
       The gentleman (who has) come to the party is Giovanni.

 b.   *Il signore [**voluto venire** alla festa] è Giovanni.
       The gentleman (who has) wanted to come to the party is
       Giovanni.

While ergative verb *venire* can appear in the 'reduced' relative (i.e. sc
relative, see 3.2.3) in (161a), the sequence *volere venire* cannot correspondingly appear in (161b). Thus, regardless of the exact theory of
'reduced' relatives, (161) fasifies the view that *volere venire* is an ergative
verb. Note that (161) also falsifies a Wh-*be* deletion analysis of 'reduced'
relatives (which we rejected in 2.7.1), since *volere venire* takes auxiliary
'be', just like *venire*, as in (160). Unlike the idea that *volere venire* is an
ergative verb, our theory accounts not only for (160), but also for (161),
under the analyses in (162) (cf. 3.2.3).

(162) a.   ...[PRO$_i$ venuto t$_i$ ...] ...

 b.   ...[PRO$_i$ voluto [$_{VP}$ venire t$_i$] [$_S$ PRO$_j$ — — —] ...] ...

In (162b) PRO$_j$ has no θ-role, just as for example in (163a), and is
furthermore without an antecedent, just as in (163b).

(163) a. *Giovanni$_i$ si$_j$ vorrebbe   [$_{VP}$ venire t$_i$] [$_S$ PRO$_j$ – – –]
           Giovanni   SI   would want   to come

We would want Giovanni to come.

   b. *Il signore [PRO$_i$ voluto [$_{VP}$ invitare t$_i$] [$_S$ PRO$_j$ – – –]] . . . .
           The gentleman (who was) wanted to invite . . .

Our theory thus meets the above challenge.

NOTES

[1] As in chapter 4, CLITIC CLIMBING will be used not only as a descriptive term as in this case, but also as a theoretical term, referring to a syntactic process that moves clitics from one verb to another. It may be useful to point out here that the Clitic Climbing of our discussion has little to do with the rule of Clitic Climbing that Rizzi rejects. For Rizzi only argues against the view — which we do not hold — that cases like (1a) could be characterized by simply postulating movement of the clitic without recognizing deeper structural changes and a relation with the other two major phenomena.

[2] Yet, so far as we know, traditional grammars have always reported these facts separately, precisely as if they were unrelated idiosyncrasies.

[3] *Andare* of (9a) must not induce $\bar{S}$-deletion, given PRO as the embedded subject. We presume this to be predictable from the subcategorization. Let us say that $\bar{S}$-deletion only occurs adjacently to the main verb. We will thus not expect a $+\bar{S}$-deletion counterpart to *andare*. But we may expect *andare* to have a $+\theta_s$ counterpart, also triggering VP-movement. This expectation is in fact fulfilled by the case of **mandare** 'send', briefly discussed in 5.8.3 below, which appears to be the exact $+\theta_s$ counterpart of *andare*.

[4] There are just a few differences between (8) and the class assumed in RRIS. RRIS includes **tornare** 'return', which we find unnatural in restructured contexts, **finire (di)**, which we exclude for the reasons hinted at in Note 5 below, but does not include *sembrare*, which we find natural enough. As Rizzi notes, there is a certain amount of variation among speakers as to the extension of the class. On this matter, see also Napoli (1981).

[5] Note however that the validity of this conclusion is somewhat weakened by the fact, noted in Zubizarreta (1980), that at least some of the tests may fail to bear on the exact structural analysis. For example, Zubizarreta notes that (11a), contrasting with (10a), may simply be ruled out by the failure of the clitic to c-command its *ec* in derived structure. Analogously, in (11b) the NP *questi libri* fails to c-command its trace, i.e. the object of *leggere*.

These reservations do not in my view suffice to alter Rizzi's overall conclusion, which rests on more than one point.

We may note that (i) of (7) is also only true to some approximation, since as we see in 5.8.3 below, verbs taking infinitives preceded by *di* never allow the change of auxiliary, while they sometimes allow Clitic Climbing.

[6] Notice that the hypothesis that the CA can occur in the absence of restructuring would not in any case be tenable, to the extent that I and II of (7) still hold.

[7] Furthermore, the configuration relevant to the CA is one in which the embedded verb takes *essere*, while the configuration relevant to Long O.P. is one in which the embedded verb is transitive, thus one that takes *avere*.

[8] The cases in (19) are impossible only under the intended interpretation of *venire* as a motion verb. They are not impossible under an interpretation of *venire* as in (i).

(i)   Le forze   vennero a mancargli.
           the strength came   to fail-to-him

           It came to pass that his strength failed him.

Under the reading of (i) *venire* appears to be a Raising verb, since the linear order of (ii), typical of ergative verbs and impossible with Raising verbs (cf. 1.8, 2.4), does not allow the reading of (i), but only the nonsensical reading of *venire* as a motion verb.

(ii)   Vennero le forze a mancargli.

The acceptability of (19) under the interpretation of *venire* as in (i) is thus predicted. Raising *venire* appears also to allow restructuring, as in (iii).

(iii)   Le forze **gli** vennero a mancare.

We may also note that (20b,c) are acceptable under certain metaphoric interpretations. This does not affect our point.

[9] A surface subject obeys object selectional restrictions of course, also when the verb is passivized, as in (i), which is thus parallel to (17a).

(i)   John$_i$ was sent t$_i$ [$_S$ PRO$_i$ to fetch the present]

Analogously, the embedded verb will impose object, rather than subject selectional restrictions on the matrix subject, when *it* is passivized as in (18a), or ergative.

[10] An analysis of this type is proposed for Spanish in Strozer (1979), (1980).

[11] Of course i-subject and ep can occur to the right of the infinitival, as in (i), but this does not guarantee that they will be in direct object position, since they could be adjoined to VP (see 2.3 above).

(i) a.   Lo va a prendere **Giovanni**.

    b.   Giovanni lo va a prendere **lui**.

[12] In principle it ought also to be possible to determine whether *andare/venire* of (25) has a direct object on the basis of *ne*-cliticization. If restructured *andare* is analogous to non-restructured *andare* in having a direct object, then we would expect the superficially similar (ia,b) to yield different results with respect to *ne*-cliticization, since the bracketed phrase is possibly a direct object of the main verb in (ia), but not in (ib), *volere* not being an ergative verb.

(i) a.   **Ci**   vanno a studiare |molti stranieri|
           there go   to study   many foreigners

           Many foreigners go to study there.

    b.   **Ci**   vogliono studiare |molti stranieri|
           there want   to study   many foreigners

           Many foreigners want to study there.

Results do not run against this expectation, but relevant contrasts appear rather weak, as in (ii).

(ii) a.   Ce **ne** vanno a studiare molti.
           Many of them go to study there.

     b.   ?Ce **ne** vogliono studiare molti.
           Many of them want to study there.

[13] Sentential complements trigger dativization whether or not they contain a direct object, as in (i).

(i) Questo **gli** farà decidere $\left\{\begin{array}{l} \text{|di leggere il libro|} \\ \text{|di telefonare a Maria|} \end{array}\right\}$.

This will make him (dat.) decide $\left\{\begin{array}{l} \textit{to read the book} \\ \textit{to phone (to) Maria} \end{array}\right\}$.

[14] The direct object of the ergative verb, whose existence we had to argue for in cases like (25), thus shows up overtly in these cases (as *gli* of (36)). However, that this is the direct object is true only internally to our analysis of ergative complements of *fare* (4.5 above). Rejecting our analysis, one might claim that the latter phrase is the subject of *andare/venire*.

[15] The semantic difference between Raising and Control cases which we have just noted is of course quite parallel to the difference with respect to selectional restrictions noted in 5.1: In Control cases, just as the main subject is interpreted as subject of both verbs, so it appears linked to both in terms of selectional restrictions. In Raising cases, the main subject is interpreted as the subject of the embedded verb only, and it correspondingly responds to the selectional restrictions of that verb alone

In 5.1, we noted how selectional restrictions provide an argument against base-generation, and we also briefly noted that semantic interpretation would provide a parallel argument. However, while semantic interpretation also argues against subject deletion as in the text, selectional restrictions do not, provided that one assumes they are enforced at D-structure only, which is compatible with our discussion.

[16] As we would expect, passive cases structurally parallel to (41) are also ungrammatical, as in (i).

(i) *I nostri atleti furono voluti vincere.
    Our athletes were wanted to win.

However, (41) provides a clearer argument than (i), since passivization of these verbs appears independently impossible, as we see in 5.8.2.

[17] The irrelevance of the D-structure position of PRO is illustrated by pairs like (ia, b), which have PRO in the same (governed) D-structure position (as well as (14), (15) II.0).

(i) a. It was necessary $[_S \text{ PRO}_i$ to be invited $t_i]$

 b. *It was likely $[_S \text{ PRO}_i$ to be invited $t_i]$

[18] We note that (44a) under the analysis of (45) would also violate a prohibition on sequences of infinitives that we discuss in 5.4 below. This factor, which generally causes only mild ungrammaticality, can be excluded by considering (i), in which the preposition *per* breaks the sequence.

(i) ?*Il suo atteggiamento farà finire **per** criticarlo.
    His attitude will make (people) end up criticizing him.

As we will see, the prohibition in question does not affect restructured sequences, and will therefore not concern (44a) under its restructured analysis.

[19] As an illustration of this point we may also consider the pair in (i).

(i) Questa sciolina ti farà $\left\{\begin{array}{l} \text{sembrare di volare} \\ \text{*sembrare volare} \end{array}\right\}$.

    this ski-wax to-you will make seem to fly

    This ski-wax will make it seem to you that you are flying.

Sembrare not followed by *di* is a Raising verb. The ungrammatical variant of (i) is thus entirely parallel to that of (44a): our theory, though not one using subject deletion, will correctly exclude a PRO subject of *volare* even under restructuring. The grammatical variant of (i) is due to the fact that *sembrare* followed by *di* is not a Raising verb, and does allow a PRO subject of the complement (as we see in 5.8.3 below).

[20] The case in (i), derived from (50b) via NP-movement would also be excluded along with the latter.

(i)   *Il libro $\left\{\begin{array}{l} \text{può} \\ \text{sembra} \end{array}\right\}$ leggere a Giovanni.

         the book $\left\{\begin{array}{l} \textit{may} \\ \textit{seems} \end{array}\right\}$ *to read to Giovanni.*

The contrast in (ii) would also be accounted for.

(ii) a.   Lo$_i$ farò $|_{VP}$ andare $|_{VP}$ a prendere $[_ie]|$ a Giovanni$_j$ $|_S$ PRO$_j$ $---|$
          I will make Giovanni go to fetch it.

    b.   *Il libro$_i$ va $|_{VP}$ a prendere $[_ie]|$ a Giovanni$_j$ $|_S$ PRO$_j$ $---|$
          the book goes   *to fetch*   *to Giovanni*

          Giovanni goes to fetch the book.

The reason is that in (iib) the phrase *Giovanni* is governed only by $-A$ *andare*, while in (iia) it is governed by $+A$ *fare* as well. Cases like (iia) were discussed in 5.2.
[21] Parallelism with respect to the full range of tests considered in RRIS is shown in Burzio (1978).
[22] There may be more specific reasons for the ungrammaticality of (68a) however, having to do with the fact that the trace in $|_{VP}$ andare t$|$ lacks a proper antecedent. See the discussion of ergative VPs in 5.6 below.
[23] As a matter of fact, (80b) establishes the existence of a direct relation between matrix subject and embedded object more firmly than (78b) does. The pp agreement of (78b) might have followed, technically, even independent of such a relation if one could have claimed that PRO$_i$ was still the antecedent to t$_i$ in S-structure. Then, under a literal, though intuitively not very plausible, interpretation of (69b), the pp would have been required to agree with PRO$_i$ as long as the embedded subject, t$_i$, had become an object of the main verb. But in (80b) t$_i$ *must* be related to the main subject since there is no other way to account for auxiliary E on the main verb.
[24] Rizzi is well aware of this of course, as is clear from the following quote (RRIS, p. 138): "... it would be highly desirable not to have a specific rule at all for these cases, with the paradigms discussed in this paragraph being predicted by some general principle of auxiliary assignment interacting with Restructuring ..." A good portion of this book, and this chapter in particular is the result of having taken the above remark as a program of research.
[25] The evidence for the existence of the embedded subject provided by (87a) is thus additional to the evidence given in 5.3.
[26] The crucial argument of RRIS for regarding the two verbs as forming a single one runs as follows:
    A. The FI rule must move a single verb, to derive (ib) from (ia).

    (i) a.   Piero farà [Mario **andare** a prenderlo]
             Piero will make Mario go to fetch it.

    b.   Piero farà **andare** Mario a prenderlo.

    B. When restructuring applies to *andare* and its complement, the FI rule derives (from (ia)) no longer (ib), but (ii)

    (ii)   Piero lo farà **andare a prendere** a Mario

    C. Therefore **andare a prendere** must have become a single verb.
    But of course from our point of view the premises of this argument are false, in particular A., which is adopted from Kayne's FS. For we regard (ib) as base-generated (*Fare-*

VP), rather than derived from (ia), and (ii) as derived from (ib) in the manner discussed in 5.2, rather than from (ia).

[27] Rizzi suggests (cf. RRIS, fns. 28, 32) that, rather than be stipulated as in (83), the right to left direction of the CA should perhaps follow from the notion that in a restructured complex the rightmost verb is the 'head' of the complex, whence the fact that it imposes its own auxiliary when this is E. But, as the discussion in the text implies, (88b) may then, by the same token, suggest that it is the leftmost verb which is the 'head' of the complex.

[28] The different auxiliaries of (88a, b) were first noted in Rizzi (1976b, fn. 4) where they are presented as an unsolved problem.

[29] For example, with the proposal of Zubizarreta (1980) that restructuring consists of LF reanalysis, without movement.

[30] Note that embedded passives as in (97b), (98b) are likely to be troublesome for base-generation analyses. Under such analyses, the *ec* in embedded object position would have to be derived via movement into main subject position, but then, except under the 'modal' analysis of restructuring verbs ((24a) above) we would expect the main rather than the embedded verb to appear with passive morphology. Under the ergative analysis, the complements in (97a), (98a) would also raise questions for base-generation analyses.

[31] Notice also that such relations do not seem to permit reconstruction, as the ungrammaticality of (i) indicates.

(i)   *$|_i$ Un interprete ciascuno$_i$| vorrebbe |$_{VP}$ essere assegnato t$_j$ a quei visitatori$_i$| |$_S$ PRO$_j$ − − −|

   One interpreter each would want to be introduced to those visitors.

Given our discussion of *ciascuno/each* in 3.3.1, (i) ought to be grammatical if the subject of *volere* could be reconstructed into t$_j$ in LF. Corresponding Raising cases are grammatical, like their non-restructured counterparts.

[32] Notice that the subject substitution hypothesis would be called for even within the discussion in RRIS, although Rizzi does not consider it. For while the case of ergative complements (in our sense) does not arise, the case of passive complements does, with a trace in embedded object position requiring an antecedent in S-structure, just as in our (97b), (98b). And since RRIS deletes the embedded subject, there seems to be no alternative but to take the matrix subject to be the S-structure antecedent to the latter trace.

[33] Control cases parallel to (103b) will allow only one derivation, as there is no Control analogue to (103a) (see 1.6.1).

[34] Presence of the locative phrase *alla festa* is crucial to the ungrammaticality of (106b). Without it, *ci* can be interpreted as a locative pronoun, rather than a pleonastic, implying a different structure.

[35] It is crucial to our discussion that in (112a,b) the post-verbal argument be within the embedded VP rather than adjoined to the matrix VP, which would not invoke subject substitution. In (112a) this is ensured by cliticization of *ne*. In (112b) by the ungrammaticality of *|Che Giovanni sia qui| gli potrebbe sembrare*, since a derivation via rightward movement resulting in VP-adjunction would have no source. The auxiliaries, noted shortly below in the text, would also exclude VP-adjunction, (Recall (26), (27), ch. 2.)

[36] While a case parallel to (112b) involving Control *volere* rather than Raising *potere* is ungrammatical as we might expect, there being no argument to fulfill the subject θ-role, as in (i), a case parallel to (112a) is − perhaps surprisingly − grammatical, as in (ii).

(i)   *Gli vorrebbe sembrare che Giovanni sia qui.
   It would want to seem to him that Giovanni is here.

(ii)   Ne vorrebbero venire molti.
   Many of them would want to come.

Notice that (ii) contrasts minimally with ungrammatical (106b) repeated in (iii), in that both involve restructuring of *volere* and an 'inversion' complement.

(iii)   *Ci vorrebbe essere molta gente alla festa.
          There would want to be may people at the party.

The appropriate theoretical distinction between (ii) and (iii) is not too obvious. It might lie along the following lines. Suppose (ii) is derived from the D-structure (iv).

(iv) |e| vorrebbero |$_S$ |e| veni**rne** molti ___ |

Structure (iv) will be thematically well-formed, provided that the main subject is interpreted as an argument pronominal (NS). Application of VP-movement and Clitic Climbing will then produce (v).

(v) |e| **ne** vorrebbero |$_{VP}$ venire molti ___ | |$_S$ |e| − − −|

The problem is now how to account for the thematic well-formedness of the S-structure (v). It is simply a fact that in (v) 'molti ___', while being in embedded object position (given *ne*-cliticization) is interpreted as the main subject: Many of them would want . . .). It must therefore be the case that the main subject transmits θ-role to the latter phrase via an inversion relation, which is detected by auxiliary E in *Ne* **sarebbero** *voluti venire molti*. Restructuring must therefore cause the main subject to be reinterpreted, from an argument to a non-argument. But then the embedded subject must correspondingly be reinterpreted from a non argument to an argument, namely PRO, which must bear the θ-role assigned by *venire*, and which must be coindexed with the main subject, given the meaning. Structure (v) must therefore actually be as in (vi), while its 'non-inverted' counterpart would be (cf. (98a)) as in (vii).

(vi) |$_i$e| ne vorrebbero |$_{VP}$ intervenire |$_i$molti ___ || |$_S$ PRO$_i$ − − −|

(vii) |$_i$Molti studenti| vorrebbero |$_{VP}$ intervenire t$_i$| |$_S$ PRO$_i$ − − −|

         Many students would want to intervene

The remaining problem in (vi) is how the θ-role that *venire* normally assigns to its object is to be transmitted to PRO$_i$. This problem is in part the same as the one posed by (vii) (cf. discussion of (98a)), but it also has an additional component in that, however a chain linking the object of *venire* and PRO$_i$ may be formed, it will now overlap with the chain linking main subject and 'molti ___'. One theoretical consequence of this analysis would therefore be that we must allow overlapping chains. (On this see also the discussion of SI in 1.6.2 above.) Notice though that this analysis would establish, at least within a subset of cases, a connection between restructuring and the NS property, since it is the latter property that would allow the main subject to be reinterpreted in the course of the derivation. Such a connection is very desirable, as we discuss below.

But how do we exclude a parallel derivation when *ci* is involved, as in (iii)? Consider the D-structure in (viii).

(viii) |e| vorrebbe |$_S$ |e| esser**ci** molta gente alla festa|

This will be thematically well-formed, just like (iv), if the main subject is interpreted as a pronominal argument. But it is natural to assume that VP-movement cannot apply to (viii) since the two subjects are distinct and unrelated, with the embedded subject being neither a trace of the main one nor a coindexed PRO, so that subject substitution will not be applicable. One could argue that the latter is not applicable in (iv) either, for analogous reasons. But subject substitution is unnecessary in (iv), since for the latter we are not forced to assume that the embedded subject is linked with an element in the VP, while we are forced to assume this for (viii). Recall how in 2.5.3 we argued that *ci* must be linked with an *ec* at all levels.

Another possibility is to simply assume that (vi) is derived from a structure like (vii) via rightward movement of the main subject into the already coindexed empty category. This would not alleviate the problems associated with the θ-criterion. On the other hand it would be incompatible with our assumption of 1.4 that clitic *ne* is base-generated, and thus has to c-command its *ec* at all levels. The latter kind of derivation would still allow a distinction between (vi) and (iii), since the *ci* analogue to (vii), i.e. *Molta gente ci vorrebbe essere alla festa*, would be excluded by the requirement that *ci* be related to an *ec* at all levels.

[37] Notice that the rule in (83) above, repeated in (i), is in fact formulated to account for auxiliary A in cases like (121).

(i)   **avere** → **essere** / $[_V \, vbl \underline{\hspace{1em}} vbl \, V_k]$
        Where V_k is a verb basically requiring *essere*

For in (121) the rightmost verb of the complex does not meet the description for V_k. The formulation of (i) would also account for the difference between (114b) (passive 'be') and (117) (copular 'be'), under the assumption — which we do not share — that the sequence 'be-past participle' is parallel to restructured sequences. Then, in (114b) the rightmost verb of the complex would be the past participle of a transitive verb, which does not meet the description for V_k, while in (117) it is main verb *essere*, which does meet such description.

[38] When the two phrases triggering pp agreement have the same features, the difficulty in (126) is attenuated (though perhaps it does not disappear entirely), as we may naturally expect. This is shown in (i).

(i)   (?)**Noi li** siamo andati a prendere.
        *We have (E) gone (agreement with **noi, li**) to fetch them.*

To the same extent, the variant with E of (121) will improve, as we also expect, as in (ii).

(ii)   Noi li $\left\{ \begin{array}{l} \textbf{avremmo voluti} \\ \textbf{?saremmo voluti} \end{array} \right\}$ andare a prendere.

        We would have (A/?E) wanted to go to fetch them.

[39] Of course the intermediate verb in such cases maintains auxiliary E, as in (i). This would be predicted (under principle (72)) even if such configurations were only periphery cases.

(i) a.   Maria li vorrebbe $\left\{ \begin{array}{l} \text{·?\textbf{esser} andata} \\ \text{??\textbf{esser} andati} \\ \text{*\textbf{aver} andato} \end{array} \right\}$ a prendere lei stessa.

        *Maria would want to have (?E/??E/*A) gone to fetch them herself.*

b.   Maria gli vorrebbe $\left\{ \begin{array}{l} \textbf{esser} \text{ già andata} \\ \text{*\textbf{aver} già andato} \end{array} \right\}$ a telefonare.

        *Maria would want to have (E/*A) already gone to phone (to) him.*

[40] The ungrammaticality of cases like (129b) seems to us less severe than Rizzi's "?*" would indicate. Our judgment on comparable examples was '?'. The '??' of (129b) compromises with Rizzi's judgment for the sake of discussion.

[41] Notice that there is a rather direct way, at least in principle, to test whether contrasts like the one in (128) are the result of different formulations of the two rules as suggested in RRIS, or the result of configurational conditions as we are claiming. Consider a case like (i).

(i)   Giovanni$_i$ **vi** vorrebbe ($_{VP}$ essere accompagnato t$_i$] [PRO$_i$ − − −]
           Giovanni would want to be accompanied there.

Our theory will predict that a case of this sort, which we claim is grammatical because subject substitution assigns *Giovanni* as an antecedent to t$_i$, should give rise to ungrammaticality if embedded under *fare*, since the new application of VP-movement would cause t$_i$ to lose its antecedent. On the other hand, the view that it should be stated in the formulation of the two rules that passives are allowed under restructuring but not under causatives would presumably predict the opposite results, since in (i), the main verb is not in the passive. Although the relevant facts are not particularly clear, they do seem to go in the direction of our prediction, as in (ii).

(ii)   *Questo **vi**   farà   voler essere accompagnato (a) Giovanni.
           the   there will make want to be   accompanied (to) Giovanni

           This will make Giovanni want to be accompanied there.

This example must be compared with non-restructured (iii), which we predict should be grammatical (just like (73a) ch. 4), aside from the effects of the prohibition on sequences of infinitives, which we know are absent in restructured cases.

(iii)   ??Questo farà voler esser**vi** accompagnato a Giovanni.

Though (iii) is perhaps slightly worse than we may expect on the basis of the latter prohibition alone, the contrast with (ii) in spite of the compensatory effect of the prohibition seems significant.
[42] If this class of verbs was affected by restructuring, we would expect not only cases like ***Lo bisogna leggere** 'It is necessary to read it' involving Cl-Cl, but also cases like **Quei libri bisognano leggere** 'Those books are necessary to read', derived via NP-movement.
   The impossibility of restructuring with this class is particularly well illustrated by the contrast between Raising *sembrare* in (i), and *sembrare* followed by *di* in (ii), which is a member of this class.

(i) a.   Giovanni sembrava veder**lo**.
           Giovanni seemed   to see-it

   b.   Giovanni **lo** sembrava vedere.

(ii) a.   Sembrava   di veder**lo**.
           (it) seemed to see-it

           We felt like we were seeing it.

   b.   ***Lo** sembrava di vedere.

[43] This account is partially undercut by the fact that causative and perception verbs never allow an auxiliary in their complement, even in the absence of VP-movement, presumably for semantic reasons, as in ?**I will make John have finished*, or ?**Ho visto Giovanni aver mangiato* 'I saw Giovanni have eaten'. But one could still maintain our syntactic account of (134), noting that under VP-movement the syntactic configuration is in fact faithful to the semantics of these sentences.
[44] This difference is also cited as an argument against a common formulation, in Rizzi (1976a), though not in RRIS. In addition, Rizzi (1976a) cites two other differences not mentioned in RRIS: (i) the obligatory character of the causative rule versus the optional character of restructuring: a difference we have dealt with, and (ii) an alleged difference in the degree to which Cl-Cl is obligatory in the two constructions, as in (i).

(i) a.   Maria è dovuta   venir**ci**   molte volte.
           Maria has (E) had to come-here many times

b.   ??Ho   fatto mangiar**lo** a Mario.
     (*I*) *have made eat-it   to Mario*

I made Mario eat it.

On this we note that, in spite of examples like (ia,b), it is very unclear that there is a systematic difference in the overall pattern of cliticization, as is noted in Longobardi (1980c). (See also RRIS, fn. 26.) As we noted in 5.0, both constructions exhibit cases in which Cl-Cl is strongly obligatory.

[45] These results are analogous to those found with English *want*. As for the other Control verbs of the restructuring class, *sapere* also fails to passivize in the manner of (135b), and in other contexts as well, as in **Lo sapevo felice/?*Giovanni era saputo felice** 'I knew him happy/Giovanni was known happy' **Sapevamo che Giovanni era qui/??Fu saputo che Giovanni era qui** 'We knew that Giovanni was here/It was known that Giovanni was here'. *Cominciare, continuare* differ, as we see below.

[46] The case in (140a) must be compared with the FI case in (i), which we predict should be grammatical (see 4.4), and which is in fact noticeably better, though perhaps less than perfect.

(i)   (?)Questa campagna pubblicitaria farà   voler vedere il   film   a
         this   advertising campaign   will make want to see   the   movie to

         tutti.
         everyone.

         . . . will make everyone want to see the movie.

[47] Notice that it would be mistaken to regard PRO of (143) and (146) as 'arbitrary' i.e., not controlled. Consider (ia, b):

(i) a.   Queste cose   saranno cominciate a dire anche { di noi / *di se stessi } .

         these   things will be   begun   to say even { about us / about oneself } .

b.   Queste cose   sono state dette per far piacere { a noi / *a se stessi } .

         these   things have been said   to please { us / oneself } .

The status of (ia,b) is exactly comparable to that of (ii), and differs from that of instances of arbitrary PRO, which do allow anaphors like *se stessi*, as in (iii).

(ii)   Queste cose   sono state dette { di noi / *di se stessi } .

         these   things have been said { about us / about oneself } .

(iii)   Dire   queste cose di   se stessi non è mai opportuno.
         to say these   things about oneself is never   appropriate

The parallelism between (i) and (ii) indeed suggests that PRO of (143) and (146) shares some crucial property with the syntactically unrepresented semantic subject of the passive verb. Note that, given (ib), in which existence of PRO is not in question, (ia) can provide no argument for non-existence of PRO. We may say that this property, which excludes *se stessi*, is some 'indefinitess', or the lack of some feature. We find it conceivable that the difference between (141) and (142), and the limited productivity of such passives may be accounted for by supposing that some predicates (like *build a palace*) more easily accept an 'indefinite' subject than do others (like *pay the rent*).

[48] This makes the prediction that passives like (i) should be possible with these verbs, at least to the extent that passives like (141) are, since PRO of (i) ought to be interpretable in the same fashion as PRO of (143).

(i)   (?)Fu cominciato [$_S$ PRO a costruire il palazzo]
           It was begun to build the palace.

The prediction seems to be essentially correct, as (i) contrasts with (ii) involving *volere* although it is perhaps not as perfect as we would expect.

(ii)   *Fu voluto costruire il palazzo.
           It was wanted to build the palace.

[49] Ideally, one would hope that a solution to this problem may also lead to a solution of the problem of θ-role assignment in cases like (i), discussed in 5.6.

(i)   Giovanni$_i$ vorrebbe   [$_{VP}$ andare t$_i$] [$_S$ PRO$_i$ — — —]
           Giovanni   would want   to go

An idea which seems to me worth considering, though I have not yet found sufficient independent support for it, is that in (i) t$_i$ does transmit θ-role to the subject position, but not to the phrase *Giovanni*, rather to the chain formed by the latter position and verb inflection. This chain, which we independently know can function as a non-argument pro-nominal in NS languages, could then transmit θ-role to PRO$_i$.

A different suggestion on how to link restructuring and the NS property appears in Rizzi (1982, IV. Appendix III.6).

CHAPTER 6

REFLEXIVES

6.0 INTRODUCTION

In this chapter we examine in detail the syntax of reflexive clitics. In the first of the three sections that follow we address the question — thus far unanswered — of why reflexive clitics trigger the rule of E assignment. In the second, we consider the interaction of reflexive clitics with the syntax of complex predicates, causative and restructuring. We will argue that the distribution of reflexive clitics over complex predicates provides the crucial evidence for our view that object clitics are base-generated, and locally related to their *ec*'s at all levels. In the third section we will claim that reflexive clitics can function not only as object clitics, thus receiving object θ-role, but also as lexical affixes which absorb *subject* θ-role. We will argue that in general reflexive clitics are in fact ambiguous between the two possible analyses.

Throughout the discussion, we will compare the behavior of clitic reflexives, with that of non-clitic reflexives, arguing that the differences follow from our theory.

As in previous chapters, we will often refer to clitics of the reflexive series simply as "*si*" even though *si* is only the third person singular and plural form (cf. (43), chapter 1). Also, while the clitic elements we discuss in this chapter allow not only a reflexive but also a reciprocal interpretation, we will for the most part ignore the distinction between the two interpretations, as there appears to be no syntactic difference associated with it.

6.1 REFLEXIVES AND AUXILIARY ASSIGNMENT

In 1.7 above, the noted that some relations, like those of (1a,b) trigger E assignment, while others, like the one of (1c) doe not.

(1) a.   Giovanni è arrivato t

     Giovanni has (E) arrived.

  b.   Giovanni **si**$_i$ è accusato [$_i$e]

     Giovanni has (E) accused himself.

c.   Giovanni ha accusato **se stesso**.

Giovanni has (A) accused himself.

The approach we took in dealing with this fact consisted of postulating that the system of E assignment and pp agreement had a typological distinction built into it, which made it sensitive only to a subset of the binding relations: those we referred to as "*binding relations*₁". As we saw, the appropriate distinction seems to be essentially between relations that involve θ-role transmission or more generally that form chains, and those that do not, whence the different auxiliaries of (1a) and (1c). However, this kind of approach is difficult to maintain, precisely because of cases like (1b), in which a relation which is just like the one of (1c) from the point of view of not involving θ-role transmission or constituting a chain, nevertheless induces E just like that of (1a).

In 1.7 we attempted a solution to this problem based on the definition of *binding relations*₁ as relations between elements that do not have independent θ-roles, regarding *si* of (1b) as not having an independent θ-role by virtue of receiving it from the *ec*. Under this definition, both (1a) and (1b) would involve *binding relations*₁, while (1c) would not, as desired. However, consider now the generalization (noted in 4.6) that NP-PRO relations never trigger E assignment, as for example in (2).

(2)   Giovanni avrebbe odiato   [ₛ PRO invitare Maria]

Giovanni would have (A) hated   to invite Maria.

In order for our proposed account of (1a, b, c) to be compatible with this generalization, it would have to be the case that PRO always has an independent θ-role. This is true of cases like (2), but not of other cases, like (3):

(3)   Giovanni avrebbe odiato   [ₛ PRO$_i$ essere invitato t$_i$

Giovanni would have (A) hated   to be invited

da Maria]
Maria.

In (3), PRO has a θ-role which is not independent, since it is transmitted to it by the *ec*, like the θ-role of *si* in (1b). We may still attempt to distinguish the relation in (3) from the one in (1b) in the definition of *binding relations*₁ by appealing to the fact that, whereas *si* is contiguous to the verb in some relevant sense, PRO is not, since it is not governed by the verb. But the degree of complication that would be involved is such as to suggest rather clearly that this approach is on the wrong track. In contrast, there is another approach which is immune to these difficulties and which provides an immediate solution to the problem of (1b).

This approach consists of postulating that the essential property of the system of E assignment and pp agreement is not that of being sensitive to relations of a certain type, but rather that of operating at S-structure and that the relations which appear to trigger it are all and only the relations which exist at S-structure. Notice that if we can independently establish that the relations of (1a,b) exist at S-structure, while that of (1c) does not, then this approach will in fact provide an explanation for the different auxiliaries in (1a,b) and (1c): something which, at best, the previous approach would have merely described.

That the relation of (1a) exists at S-structure is perfectly clear, since it is established by Move α, and since it is required to exist and be well-formed at S-structure by the projection principle, like all relations that constitute chains. The presence of auxiliary E in (1a), and the fact that E assignment/pp agreement is always triggered by chains are thus accounted for. Unlike the relation of (1a), the one of (1c) is not established by movement, and is not required to exist at S-structure, but only at LF (cf. 4.6). Let us suppose then that, since it is not required, it will not even be permitted to exist at S-structure, and that in general only the relations that are required to obtain at each individual level are represented at that level. This will account for auxiliary A in (1c) and for the fact that in general the relations that do not constitute chains (e.g. those of (2) and (3)) do not trigger E assignment or pp agreement. The question will now be whether we have reasons to believe that the relation of (1b) exists at S-structure. The answer is yes.

As we have noted on several occasions, reflexive *si* only occurs with non-derived antecedents. This is illustrated by the systematic impossibility of *si*, contrasting with the possibility of a corresponding non-reflexive, in every established case of NP-movement: Passive, O.P., Raising, Ergative, as in (4).[1] (In (4b) *si si* → *ci si*.)

(4) a.   I ragazzi$_i$ $\left\{ \begin{array}{c} \text{*si} \\ \text{gli} \end{array} \right\}$ furono posti t$_i$ di fronte [e]

The kids were placed before $\left\{ \begin{array}{c} each\ other \\ him \end{array} \right\}$.

b.   Gli studenti$_i$ $\left\{ \begin{array}{c} \text{*ci} \\ \text{gli} \end{array} \right\}$ si presenteranno t$_i$ [e] domani.

The students SI will introduce ('will be introduced')
$\left\{ \begin{array}{c} to\ each\ other \\ to\ him \end{array} \right\}$ tomorrow.

c.   [$_i$Giovanni e Maria] $\left\{ \begin{matrix} \text{*si} \\ \text{gli} \end{matrix} \right\}$ risultavano [e] [$_S$ t$_i$ essere fuori città]

Giovanni and Maria appeared $\left\{ \begin{matrix} \textit{to each other} \\ \textit{to him} \end{matrix} \right\}$ to be out of town.

d.   [$_i$Maria e Giovanni] $\left\{ \begin{matrix} \text{*si} \\ \text{gli} \end{matrix} \right\}$ venivano spesso t$_i$ in mente [e]

Maria and Giovanni came often to mind $\left\{ \begin{matrix} \textit{to each other} \\ \textit{to him} \end{matrix} \right\}$

('to each other's/his mind')

Reflexive/reciprocal *si* will differ in this respect from non-clitic reflexives and reciprocals which are not subject to such constraint, as (5) shows.

(5) a.   Giovanni fu posto di fronte **a se stesso.**
         Giovanni was placed before himself.

   b.   Giovanni e Maria venivano spesso in mente **l'uno all'altra.**
         Giovanni and Maria came often to mind one to the other ('to
         each other's mind').

We will take the difference between (4) and (5) to indicate that, unlike the relations involved in (5), antecedent-*si* relations must be established at D-structure, (4) being ruled out because *si* lacks a D-structure antecedent. (Note incidentally that (4d) will confirm once again our analysis of ergative verbs.[2]) If this is correct, it follows that antecedent-*si* relations exist at S-structure, thus accounting for E of (1b). But why should antecedent-*si* relations be established at D-structure?

In 1.4 above, we argued that one of the consequences of the projection principle was (6).

(6)   A relation between a base-generated argument clitic and its *ec*
         must exist at all levels.

This will ensure transmission of θ-role from the θ-position to the argument. We have further noted at various points that a principle of wider generality seems in fact to be at work. Thus, in 2.5 above, we argued that the relation between non argument clitic *ci* and its *ec* also had to exist at D-structure, even though the latter relation does not involve θ-role transmission. In 2.7.2 we argued in addition that when *ci* is involved even the inversion relation (i.e. the subject-i-subject relation) appears to be established, under locality conditions, at D-structure, yielding the contrast *There were several houses built/*Ci furono molte case costruite.* (See (161), (162) ch. 2.)[3]

Thus, rather than (6), the principle in (7) seems to hold.

(7)   All relations involving base-generated clitics must exist at all levels.

The principle in (7), a principle derived from the projection principle by generalization over the class of relations involving base-generated clitics, thus provides the theoretical justification for the proposal that antecedent-*si* relations must be established at D-structure, which has a number of desirable empirical consequences.

As we have seen, this idea allows us to interpret the system of E assignment and pp agreement simply as a system that operates at S-structure, detecting binding or coindexing relations without any qualification as to their type, so that we can now dispense with the notion *binding relations*₁ of 1.7.[4] The new interpretation of the system, unlike the old one, explains the bifurcation among coindexing relations that the system gives rise to, and in turn explains the exact correspondence between this bifurcation and the one due to reconstruction, which we noted but were unable to explain in 4.6. It will now be true of all and only the relations that must obtain at S-structure, that reconstruction in LF is not sufficient for their well-formedness, and that they trigger E assignment/pp agreement. The idea that antecedent-*si* relations must obtain at D-structure will furthermore account for a whole cluster of differences between clitic and non-clitic reflexives and reciprocals. In particular it will account for the difference between (4) and (5); for the one between (1b) and (1c); and for the difference with respect to reconstruction which we discuss in the next section.[5]

6.2 REFLEXIVES IN COMPLEX PREDICATES

The behavior of the antecedent-*si* relation which we considered in the previous section, provides an argument for base-generation of *si*, and thus, we presume, of object clitics in general. We saw that a number of phenomena can be accounted for only if we postulate that such a relation is established at D-structure. If this fact is a reflex of principle (7) as we argued, then *si* must be base-generated.

We will now consider the behavior of the *si-ec* relation, and argue that it too provides an argument for base-generation of *si* and of object clitics in general. We will see that the distribution of reflexive clitics over complex predicates can be accounted for only if we postulate that object clitic-*ec* relations are subject to locality conditions not only at S-structure, but at D-structure as well. If this is correct, it trivially follows that object clitics are base-generated since under a movement analysis there would be no clitic-*ec* relation at D-structure.

In 4.1.4 above, we argued that the ungrammaticality of (8a) was due to the ill-formedness of the D-structure (8b), in which the relation indicated violates locality conditions.

(8) a.   *Maria **si**   fa   [$_{VP}$ accusare [e]] [$_S$ a   Giovanni — — —]

        Maria   herself   makes   accuse   to Giovanni

        Maria$_i$ makes Giovanni accuse her$_i$.

   b.   *Maria **si** fa [$_S$ Giovanni accusare [e]]

We now claim that the ungrammaticality of the restructuring case in (9a) is analogously due to the non-local character of the *si-ec* relation in its D-structure (9b).

(9) a.   *I ragazzi$_i$ **si** volevano [$_{VP}$ essere presentati t$_i$ [e]] [$_S$ PRO$_i$ — — —]

        The kids wanted to be introduced to each other.

   b.   *I ragazzi **si** volevano [$_S$ [e] essere presentati PRO [e]]

Note that in both (8) and (9) the antecedent-*si* relation is well-formed at all levels as required by principle (7), so that the ungrammaticality must indeed be attributed to the *si-ec* relation. (In contrast to the Control case in (9), the ergative and Raising cases of restructuring, ***Si andavano ad essere presentati** 'They went to be introduced to each other', ***Si potrebbero essere presentati** 'They would be able to be introduced to each other' would be ungrammatical also because **si** lacks a D-structure antecedent). However, in principle, (8a) and (9a) could be derived not only from the D-structures in (8b), (9b), but also from those in (10a, b), via Clitic Climbing (Cl-Cl).

(10) a.   *Maria fa [$_S$ Giovanni accusar**si** [e]]

    b.   *I ragazzi volevano [$_S$ [e] esser**si** presentati PRO [e]]

To ensure a full account of the ungrammaticality of (8a), (9a) we must therefore rule out not only (8b), (9b), but also (10a,b). But plainly

(10a,b) are also ill-formed, since we expect that the antecedent-*si* relation should also be subject to some locality conditions, say those defined by principle A of the binding theory, like clitic-*ec* relations. Both (10a,b) would then violate the SSC, just like (8b), (9b).

We thus have a full account of the ungrammaticality of (8a), (9a). If it is correct, this account will imply that object clitics are base-generated, since under a movement analysis the ill-formed D-structure relations of (8b), (9b) would not exist; only the well-formed relations of (8a), (9a) would. It will also imply that FI and restructuring constructions are syntactically derived as we argued in chapters 4 and 5. For if they were base-generated, their D-structures would be more like (8a), (9a) than like (8b), (9b) and the clitic-*ec* relations would then be local and well-formed at all levels.

Our theory and the assumption that clitic-*ec* relations are subject to D-structure locality conditions thus predicts that embedded object clitics will, quite generally, not be base-generated on the main verb in those complex predicates which are syntactically derived, namely FI and restructuring. (They will in FP, as discussed in 4.2.1.) This means that when they do appear on the main verb, embedded object clitics must have undergone Cl-Cl. In this connection, consider the Raising and ergative cases of restructuring in (11).

(11) a. I ragazzi **si** dovrebbero parlare.
         The kids would have to talk to each other.

     b. I ragazzi **si** andranno a parlare.
         The kids will go to talk to each other.

From the standpoint of the descriptive generalization that reflexive *si* never occurs with a derived subject, (11a,b) are surprising since they violate that generalization. (Compare these cases with the ungrammatical Raising and ergative cases in (4c,d) above.) But they are not surprising from the standpoint of our theory featuring Cl-Cl. From that standpoint (11a) is derived as in (12), and (11b) has an analogous derivation.

(12) a. I ragazzi$_i$ dovrebbero [$_S$ t$_i$ parlar**si** [e]] $\Rightarrow$

     b. I ragazzi$_i$ **si** dovrebbero [$_{VP}$ parlare [e]] [$_S$ t$_i$ $- - -$]

Under the derivation in (12), (11a) is well-formed at all levels. At D-structure, before Raising gives rise to the intermediate structure (12a), *si* has the phrase *i ragazzi* as its local antecedent. After Raising, the local antecedent is the trace of the latter phrase. It is clear that such a trace is also an appropriate antecedent for *si*, as structures like (12a) are well-formed S-structures. After application of VP-movement, subject substitution and Cl-Cl will give rise to (12b) in which *si* has again *i ragazzi* as a local antecedent. Since the *si-ec* relation is local at all levels, principle (7) above will be satisfied and (11) will be well-formed, in spite of the fact that *si* occurs with a derived subject. Rather similar considerations apply to (11b). The derivation in (12) is parallel to the one we discussed in 5.6 with regard to *ci* (see (105), ch. 5). Note that, as in the case of *ci*, Cl-Cl could be derived here, too, as a reflex of subject substitution, if we assumed, not implausibly, an adjacency requirement on antecedent-*si* relations (see Note 5).

The cases in (11) enable us to make an observation complementary to the one that we can make with regard to (9a) (**I ragazzi si volevano essere presentati.*) That is, while (9a) indicates that in a restructured complex, a reflexive clitic will not appear on the main verb if the embedded verb has a derived subject, even though the main verb does not, the cases in (11) indicate that a reflexive clitic will appear on the main verb provided that the embedded verb does not have a derived subject, even though the main verb does. The overall generalization is thus that reflexive clitics can appear on a restructuring main verb precisely to the extent that they can appear on the lower verb. This generalization can only be accounted for in one of two ways: (i) Such clitics originate on the lower verb and then undergo Cl-Cl, as we assume. Then we may expect a clitic on the higher verb if and only if there is a well-formed source with the clitic on the lower one. (ii) Restructuring verbs add nothing to the thematic structure of the infinitivals that follow them, say like English modals. Then restructuring complexes will have a derived subject if and only if the infinitival does, and the generalization in question would again be predicted. But, as we have argued at length, (ii) is false. As we saw in 5.1, verbs like *dovere* and *volere* have all the thematic properties of Raising and Control verbs respectively. Consequently it must be the case that there is Cl-Cl.[6]

The existence of Cl-Cl is also confirmed by the case of idioms, illustrated in (13), and by 'ergative' *si* of (14).

(13) a.   Giovanni $\left\{\begin{array}{l} \text{me } \textbf{la pagherà} \\ \textbf{la sa} \text{ lunga} \\ \text{non } \textbf{la smette} \text{ mai di scherzare} \\ \textbf{ci metterà} \text{ un secolo} \end{array}\right\}$.

         Giovanni $\left\{\begin{array}{l} \textit{will pay it to me ('will pay for it')} \\ \textit{knows it long ('knows more than he is letting on')} \\ \textit{never stops it to joke ('never stops joking')} \\ \textit{will put a century there ('will take ages')} \end{array}\right\}$

b. Maria glie**la** farà **pagare**.
Maria will make him pay for it.

c. Giovanni $\left\{ \begin{array}{l} \textbf{la} \text{ dovrebbe } \textbf{sapere} \text{ lunga} \\ \textbf{ci} \text{ potrebbe } \textbf{mettere} \text{ un secolo} \end{array} \right\}$.

Giovanni $\left\{ \begin{array}{l} \textit{should know more than he is letting on} \\ \textit{could take ages} \end{array} \right\}$.

(14) a. La finestra **si è rotta**.
The window has broken (itself).

b. La finestra **si** potrebbe **rompere**.
The window could break (itself).

The clitics of (13a) form idioms only with the verbs with which they occur in those examples. Such clitics must therefore bear some lexical relation with those verbs, and only with those verbs. Since we regard D-structure as a direct projection of the lexicon, we must assume that in the D-structures underlying (13b,c) such clitics are on the embedded verb, with which they bear the lexical relation, rather than on the main verb, with which they bear no relation. The S-structures of (13b,c) must therefore be derived via Cl-Cl. The argument for Cl-Cl provided by (13) is in fact a special case of the classical argument for movement based on idiom chunks: one presumes that at D-structure idioms are whole, not scattered. The case in (14) is quite analogous to that of (13) in that *si* here is part of the lexical item *rompersi*, an ergative verb, so that Cl-Cl must have occurred in (14b) too.[7]

We therefore draw the conclusion that embedded object clitics appearing on the main verb in FI and restructuring constructions must have undergone Cl-Cl. This conclusion rests on two observations: (i) cases in which derivation via Cl-Cl is impossible (like (8a) and (9a)) are ungrammatical; (ii) cases in which a derivation without Cl-Cl is impossible (like (11a, b), (13b, c), (14b)) are grammatical. Although most of the evidence for this conclusion is provided by reflexive clitics, we assume that the conclusion holds for all object clitics. The reason why most of the evidence is limited to reflexive clitics is that the considerations that exclude, a-priori, a derivation with or without Cl-Cl (for (8a), (9a), (11a,b)) have to do with the antecedent-*si* relation, which obviously has no counterpart with non-reflexives.

In our discussion of (11) above, we saw that occurrence of reflexive clitic objects of the lower verb in restructuring constructions was contingent on subject substitution, as in (12). This makes the prediction that in the FI construction, where subject substitution is not applicable, such clitics could not occur. That is, given that an antecedent-*si* relation is, by virtue of (7) above, one of those relations that must obtain at S-structure, we expect reflexive-*si* complements to be among those complements that can appear in restructuring constructions (due to subject substitution) but not in FI constructions, like ergative, passive, Raising complements and others discussed in 4.6 and 5.6 above.

If we limit ourselves to Italian, the prediction is borne out straight-forwardly. Thus, contrasting with the grammaticality of (11) or of the other subcase of restructuring **I ragazzi si vorrebbero parlare** 'The kids would want to talk to each other', we find the ungrammaticality of (15).

(15)   *Maria $\left\{ \begin{array}{l} \textbf{si } \text{farà accusare} \\ \text{farà accusar}\textbf{si} \end{array} \right\}$ (a) Giovanni

   Maria will make Giovanni accuse himself.

The overall prediction for the FI construction is therefore that clitic re-flexives should fail to occur as embedded objects altogether. When they are coreferential with the main subject, for the reasons discussed in con-nection with (8a), and when they are coreferential with the embedded subject, for the reasons given for the ungrammaticality of (15).

The case of (15) will contrast with the non-clitic counterpart in (16) which (as we claimed in 4.6) is grammatical because the relation between antecedent and *se stesso* will be well-formed in LF after reconstruction.

(16)   Maria farà accusare **se stesso** a Giovanni.
   Maria will make Giovanni accuse himself.

Like the differences noted in 6.1, the difference between *si* and *se stesso* of (15) versus (16) thus also follows from the principle in (7).

The prediction that reflexive *si* complements should not occur in the FI construction does not seem to be borne out by French, however, which allows (17).

(17)   Marie a fait s'accuser Pierre.
   Marie made Pierre accuse himself.

While our discussion so far does not account for (17), note that this case is puzzling independently of our theory, since it is not the kind of result that one would expect if reflexive clitic complements could be embedded in the FI construction straightforwardly. For one thing, the reflexive clitic in (17) fails to undergo Cl-Cl. For another, the apparent embedded subject, *Pierre*, is not dativized, as it usually is when the embedded verb is transitive. We will return to cases like (17), which motivate rather crucially the theory of reflexive clitics in Kayne's FS, in the next section.

In the remainder of this section we briefly consider the predictions that our analysis of reflexive clitics in restructuring constructions makes with respect to auxiliary assignment and pp agreement. As we discussed in connection with (12), when a structure like (18a) is embedded in a restructuring context, the result will be as in (18b).

(18) a. I ragazzi **si** vedranno [e] piú spesso.

    The kids will see each other more often.

  b. I ragazzi **si** vorrebbero [$_{VP}$ vedere [e] piú spesso] [$_S$ PRO − − −]

    The kids would want to see each other more often.

Given the relation involving the main subject, we correctly predict auxiliary E on the main verb, as in (19).

(19)   I ragazzi si **sarebbero** voluti vedere piú spesso.
        The kids would have (E) wanted to see each other more often.

Descriptively, (19) contrasting with non restructured *I ragazzi* **avrebbero** *voluto vedersi piú spesso*, represents a case of the CA phenomenon, which − like the other cases − our analysis thus accounts for.

    However, the analysis of (18b) does not seem to predict auxiliary E on the embedded verb, as in (20).

(20)   I ragazzi si vorrebbero già $\left\{\begin{matrix} \textbf{esser} \\ \textbf{*aver} \end{matrix}\right\}$ visti.

    The kids would want to already have (E/*A) seen each other.

The reason is that (18b) has no relation between the main subject and the embedded object (Recall that the main subject is the subject of both verbs here. See the discussion of (82), ch. 5.) The relation between the reflexive and the *ec* of (18b) would only predict the pp agreement of *visti* in (20), not auxiliary E; (20) thus suggests that beside the two relations of (18b), the one of (21a) also exists, and therefore that, in general, reflexives must involve the three relations of (21b), rather than the two of (18a).

(21) a. I ragazzi **si** vorrebbero [$_{VP}$ vedere [e] piú spesso] [$_S$ PRO − − −]

  b. I ragazzi **si** vedranno [e] piú spesso.

    Two questions arise at this point. One is whether we can provide theoretical justification for the subject-*ec* relation of (21a,b), for which (20) provides the empirical evidence. The other is whether, given that the latter relation will now be sufficient to account for E and pp agreement in the general case, (analogously to the case of ergative verbs), the other relations can still be justified empirically. Let us consider the second question first.

    There are two facts which confirm the existence of the subject-*si* and the *si-ec* relations of (21b). The first is that indirect object reflexives give rise to 'weaker' pp agreement in Italian, as discussed in 1.7 (i.e. in the presence of another element triggering agreement, no conflict arises), and no pp agreement at all in French (as noted in Note 50, ch 1) as in **Marie s'est fait quelques robes** 'Marie has made (no agreement) herself some dresses'. Given that, as noted in 2.6.2, there is no case in which a subject-object relation triggers pp agreement without also triggering E assignment, or vice-versa, if the subject-object relation was the only one here we would expect, incorrectly, that in such cases as these, E too should be 'weaker' in Italian (i.e. that there might be some possibility for auxiliary A), and impossible in French. The relation between the subject and *si* must therefore also be assumed, so as to trigger E assignment independent of the subject-object relation.

The second fact supporting the existence of the relations involving *si* in (21b) is that, when the reflexive clitic is a direct object, both auxiliary E and pp agreement are systematic, not only in Italian, but in French as well.[8] On the basis of the subject-*ec* relation alone we would expect French relfexives to be periphery cases, and both E and pp agreement to be unsystematic as with ergative verbs (cf. 2.6.2). To account for systematic E and pp agreement in French, both the subject-*si* relation and the *si-ec* relation must then also be assumed. The latter two relations, which are perfectly well justified theoretically, are thus also justified empirically.

Let us now turn to the first question, concerning the theoretical justification for the subject-*ec* relation. Our proposal is that the existence of this third relation merely reflects the fact that the theoretically proper notation is not the linking notation which we are often using for expository purposes, but rather coindexing. Existence of the third relation, while puzzling under the linking notation, follows automatically from the transitivity inherent in coindexing: if the subject is coindexed with *si* and if *si* is coindexed with the *ec*, then the subject is coindexed with the *ec*.[9]

In this section we have thus argued that the distribution of reflexive clitics in FI and restructuring constructions is correctly predicted only if we postulate that object clitics are base-generated. In conjunction with principle (7) above, base-generation makes the general prediction that both antecedent-*si* and clitic-*ec* relations should be local and well-formed both before and after VP-movement. In turn this predicts that in FI constructions embedded object clitics should be impossible altogether, while in restructuring constructions they will be possible only to the extent that they would be possible in the infinitival complement if restructuring did not apply. Aside from a residual problem posed by the FI construction in French, these predictions are correct.

We have seen that when reflexive *si* complements are embedded in restructuring complexes the CA occurs as we predict, and that, quite generally, auxiliaries and pp agreement are as we predict, provided that we take coindexing rather than linking as the relevant notation.

6.3 REFLEXIVES AS LEXICAL AFFIXES

6.3.0 *Introduction*

In the preceding section we saw that our analysis of reflexive clitics did not account for the behavior of such clitics in French causative constructions. In this section we will argue that this and other facts indicate that reflexive *si*, beside occurring as an object clitic, can also occur as an affix absorbing subject *θ*-role, like the other two occurrences of the same morpheme, namely ergative and inherent-reflexive *si*.

We begin by considering precisely ergative and inherent-reflexive *si*, refining the analysis we proposed in 1.5, and examining its interaction with complex predicates.

6.3.1 *Ergative and Inherent-reflexive si*

In 1.5 we argued that verbs occurring with ergative and inherent-reflexive *si* are ergative verbs, so that the cases in (22) would have the analyses indicated.

(22) a.   Le nubi **si** sono dissipate t

        The clouds have dispersed (themselves).

   b.   Giovanni **si** è pentito t

        Giovanni has repented (himself).

We claimed that in such cases *si* is a lexical affix reflecting the inability of the verb to assign subject *θ*-role.

From this point of view we may not have any particular reason to expect *si* to be related to either the object or the subject position. However, it appears that *si* is in fact related to both positions here, just as in the reflexive case. The evidence to this effect is somewhat analogous to that presented just above for reflexives, and has to do with the fact (noted in 2.6.2) that E and pp agreement are systematic over this class of cases not only in Italian, but in French (literary French, cf. Notes 8, 10) as well, as for example in (23) ((23a) from Ruwet (1972, p. 89)).

(23) a   Les nuages **se** sont dissipés.
      The clouds have (E) dispersed (pl.) (themselves).

   b.   Jean s'est repenti.
      Jean has (E) repented (sg.) (himself).

Existence of the relation of (22) would be sufficient for Italian, but again it would predict these cases to be only periphery in French. In order to account for systematic E and pp agreement in French, we must postulate that rather than the analysis in (22), the correct account is as in (24), with *si/se* related to both subject and object. In terms of coindexing, this means that subject, *si/se*, and object are all coindexed.[10]

(24) a.   Les nuages **se** sont dissipés t

b.   Jean s'est repenti t

The relations between *si/se* and both the subject and the object positions are thus motivated by empirical rather than by theoretical considerations. But if we regard *si/se* as the element that in fact withholds assignment of θ-role to the subject and of accusative Case to the object, existence of such relations will not seem particularly unnatural even from the theoretical point of view. It will also be reasonable to expect that *si/se* should be coindexed with the subject because it agrees with it, cf. **Voi vi siete pentiti** 'You repented (yourselves)'.

The two relations involving *si/se*, as in (24), will make the S-structure analysis of these cases quite similar to that of cases of reflexive *si/se* (compare (24) with (21b)). This is a welcome result since the more similar the analyses, the better the explanation for the fact that all of these cases employ the same morpheme. We note incidentally that identity of the morpheme further supports base-generation of reflexive *si/se*. For, if the verbs in (23) are indeed to be analyzed as ergative verbs, it will be rather difficult to provide a movement derivation for *si/se* in those cases.

Given the analysis of (24) we will expect complements involving ergative and inherent-reflexive *si* to be embedded unproblematically under restructuring verbs, with the results exemplified in (25).

(25) a.   Giovanni$_i$ saprebbe [$_S$ PRO$_i$ pentir**si** t$_i$] $\Rightarrow$

Giovanni would know (how) to repent (himself).

b.   Giovanni$_i$ **si** saprebbe [$_{VP}$ pentire t$_i$] [$_S$ PRO$_i$ — — —]

Such cases will be similar in part to the case of simple ergative complements, with subject substitution assigning a new antecedent to t$_i$, and in part to the case of reflexive complements, with the relation of *si* with the embedded subject being replaced by the one with the main subject as a result of subject substitution and Cl-Cl.

Let us now consider the embedding of such complements under causative verbs. As with ergative verbs in general, we expect embedding to be possible only in VP-complements. We will thus analyze the Italian case in (26a), and the French case in (26b) as indicated.[11]

(26) a. Questo farà [$_{VP}$ pentire Giovanni]
         This will make Giovanni repent.

     b. Cela fera [$_{VP}$ **se** repentir Jean]
         This will make Jean repent (himself).

But why should Italian and French differ with respect to the presence of *si/se*?

Given some of our previous discussion, the absence of *si* in the Italian example (26a) seems rather natural. If in these cases *si* is a marker indicating that the subject position is not assigned subject θ-role, it is not too surprising to find that *si* does not appear when there is no subject position. The French case in (26b) is not too troublesome either. While we do have empirical reasons to assume that *si/se* bears a relation with the subject position when there is such a position, we have no strong theoretical or empirical reasons to expect that such a relation must exist under all circumstances, and that thus *si/se* could not appear when there is no subject. For example we do not have the same kind of theoretical reasons that lead us to expect that SE-moyen could not occur under *faire*, as in (27) (from FS, p. 396, analysis our).

(27)   *Les moeurs actuelles font [$_{VP}$ se dire cela surtout pour
        Present-day mores make SE ("one") say that especially to annoy

       ennuyer les gens]
       people

As we discussed in 4.6 in connection with Italian SI, cases like (27) are excluded by the absence of a subject position that could transmit θ-role to SE. (Also, SE fails to receive Case.) But while SI/SE is an argument, which must receive a θ-role, ergative/inherent-reflexives *si/se* is not. Of the latter we assume only that it withholds subject θ-role as a modifier of the lexical properties of the verb, like, for example, a past participial morpheme, not that it receives a θ-role from the subject position.

In sum, our theory does not make any sharp prediction as to whether *si/se* ought to be present in cases like (26a,b). From this point of view the difference between Italian and French may not seem too surprising, and we may assume it reflects some second-order difference between the two languages.[12] Of course we would still want to account for such a difference, ideally relating it to other, independent, differences.

There is in fact a reasonable possibility that the difference in (26) may be related to the difference between the 'inversion' cases in (28).

(28) a. [e] **si**   sono pentiti   molti terroristi

themselves have repented many terrorists

Many terrorists have repented.

   b. Il s'est   repenti   plusieurs terroristes

it itself has repented many   terrorists

Many terrorists have repented.

The three relations indicated in (28a,b) will be exactly analogous to
those of (24). (Recall that we assume a relation between subject and
i-subject, and that the i-subject is in direct object position with ergative
verbs.) Consider then a condition that *si/se* should always agree with both
the subject and the object positions it is related to. This condition would
be fulfilled in (28a) since the subject has the same features as the object
molti terroristi, whence the plural agreement of both verb and past participle. And in fact in Italian it would always be fulfilled (assuming naturally that in such cases as (22) the trace bears the same features as the
subject), so that we may assume it actually holds in this language. But in
French this condition could not be fulfilled in all cases, given (28b). For,
whereas *il* has singular features as shown by singular verb agreement,
plusieurs terroristes is plural. Thus, this condition could not hold in
French, and in (28b) *se* could only agree with either the subject or the
object. Although the form *se* is in itself ambiguous between third person
singular and plural, we can infer that in (28b) it is actually singular,
agreeing with the singular subject. For if it were plural, we would expect
it to induce plural pp agreement, in conflict with the agreement induced
by subject *il*. In fact, if we simply assume for French the weaker condition that *se* should agree with *either* subject *or* object, we will predict that
in (28b) it will agree with the subject, precisely to avoid pp agreement
conflict. The stronger condition of Italian versus the weaker one of
French will now account for the difference in (26). Given the stronger
condition, we expect Italian *si* to be impossible when there is no subject,
as in (26a), while in (26b) French *se* will agree with the object, satisfying
the weaker condition.[13]

Notice that we have sufficient theoretical reasons to correctly expect
no Cl-Cl of *se* in (26b). Since *se* is usually linked with the subject, it will
be natural to expect that it would incorrectly become linked with the
matrix subject should it 'climb'. And, if Cl-Cl of *si* in (25b) above is a

reflex of subject substitution, as suggested for reflexive *si* in 6.2, then failure of *se* to climb in (26b) will be due even more simply to failure of subject substitution in that case.

Since the contrast in (26) is quite parallel to the one between (15) and (17) above, relative to reflexive *si/se*, it is obvious that the latter would be accounted for in the same way as the former, if we could provide an analysis of reflexive *si/se* that rendered it analogous to that of ergative and inherent-reflexive *si/se*. In the next subsection we consider some independent evidence for just such an analysis.

6.3.2. *Inversion and sc Relatives*

The analysis of reflexive clitics as objects is compatible with cases of inversion like (29a), but not with cases like (29b).

(29) a. **Si**   sono uccisi **parecchi prigionieri**.
         themselves have killed several   prisoners

   Several prisoners have killed themselves.

   b. **Se**   **ne**   sono uccisi **parecchi**.
       themselves of-them have killed several

   Several of them have killed themselves.

For (29a), it is possible to assume that the i-subject has originated in subject position and is adjoined to VP. Then the requirement that the reflexive have an appropriate antecedent at all levels would be satisfied, since the antecedent would be the phrase *parecchi prigionieri* at D-structure, and the chain formed by the latter phrase and the subject position at S-structure. But the same cannot be assumed for (29b) since, as we claimed in 1.4 above, *ne*-cliticization implies that the i-subject must have been base-generated in direct object position. From the point of view of the object analysis of *si*, (29b) would thus be odd in two respects: (i) *si* lacks an appropriate antecedent at D-structure; and (ii) the direct object, which we expect to be an *ec* related to clitic *si*, is here occupied by an overt NP.

The case in (29b) is, at the relevant level of abstraction, exactly parallel to the French case in (30a) (from FS, p. 381), and to the Piedmontese case in (30b).

(30) a. Il s'est   dénoncé   **trois mille**   **hommes** ce mois-ci.
         it itself has denounced three thousand men   this month.

   Three thousand men have denounced themselves this month.

    b. A lé masa**se**   **vaire persuné**
       cl has killed-itself several prisoners

    Several prisoners have killed themselves.

As we argued in 2.6.2 above, we take the French *il*-construction of (30a) to be exclusively base-generated, with the i-subject in direct object position, thus just like (29b). As for the Piedmontese case in (30b), on the basis of 2.5 above we can determine from the singular verb agreement that it is not a case of inversion by rightward movement, but rather an instance of the *ye*-construction, also base-generated, like the French *il*-construction. The absence of clitic *ye* we attribute to a phonological rule that deletes it in the presence of clitics like *se* (see 2.5.2).

Therefore, the evidence in (29b) and (30a,b) indicates that reflexive clitics can occur in D-structures analogous to those found with ergative and inherent-reflexive *si* (compare in fact (30a) with (28b)) and with ergative verbs in general, involving an argument in direct object position, and no argument in subject position. The same kind of evidence is provided by the appearance of reflexive *si* in Italian sc relatives, which we now consider.

Recall that the generalization underlying past participial sc relatives is that only direct objects can be relativized. We assume that this generalization results from the fact that, while the sc must have a subject PRO coindexed with the head of the relative, the past participle does not assign a θ-role to the subject position, so that a direct object will have to be moved into that position.

As we saw in 3.2.3, Italian allows sc relativization not only with transitive verbs, but also with ergatives. The two cases in (31a,b) will thus have the parallel analyses indicated and will be well formed, while the cases in (31c,d) will not. Example (31c), involving subject relativization, will be excluded by the failure of PRO to receive a θ-role, and the case in (31d) involving indirect object relativization will be excluded by whatever factors prevent indirect objects from moving into subject position in general.

(31) a. Uno studente [$_{sc}$ PRO$_i$ invitato t$_i$ alla festa] . . .
       A student (who was) invited to the party . . .

    b. Uno studente [$_{sc}$ PRO$_i$ arrivato t$_i$ ieri sera] . . .
       A student (who had) arrived last night . . .

    c. * Uno studente [$_{sc}$ PRO telefonato ieri sera] . . .
       A student (who had) phoned last night . . .

    d. *Uno studente [$_{sc}$ PRO$_i$ telefonato (a) t$_i$ ieri sera] ...
       A student (who was) phoned (to) last night ...

Given these premises, the cases in (32a, b) will be straightforward.

    (32) a. L'auto capovolta**si** nell'incidente era la Ferrari.
         The car (which had) rolled over in the accident was the Ferrari.

       b. Un pilota accorto**si** dell'incidente diede l'allarme.
         A driver (who had) become aware of the accident gave the warning.

Occurrence of ergative and inherent-reflexive *si* as in (32a,b) respectively will simply follow from and confirm our ergative analyses of these cases, ruling out alternative analyses: If, for example, **L'auto si è capovolta** 'The car has rolled over', and **Il pilota si è accorto dell'incidente** 'The driver has become aware of the accident' were intransitive constructions, then (32a,b) should be ruled out just like (31c). The same would be true if they were transitive (say, if *si* was analyzed as an object clitic, as in the FS account of inherent-reflexives. Cf. Note 10) since they would then also involve relativization of the subject.

But precisely the same considerations apply to the reflexive case in (33a), which appears to have the sc relative counterpart in (33b).

    (33) a. Un individuo **si** accusò di aver assassinato il presidente.
         An individual accused himself of having assassinated the president.

       b. Un individuo accusato**si** di aver assassinato il presidente fu creduto pazzo.
         An individual (who had) accused himself of having assassinated the president was deemed insane.

If *si* of (33) were an object clitic, then (33a,b) ought to be parallel to (34a,b).

    (34) a. Un individuo **lo** accusò di aver assassinato il presidente.
         An individual accused him of having assassinated the president.

       b. *Un individuo accusato**lo** di aver assassinato il presidente fu creduto pazzo.
         An individual (who had) accused him of having assassinated the president was deemed insane.

Also, if *si* of (33) were a reflexive object, (33a,b) ought to be parallel to (35a,b).

(35) a. Un individuo accusò **se stesso** di aver assassinato il
         presidente.
         An individual accused himself of having assassinated the
         president.

   b. *Un individuo accusato **se stesso** di aver assassinato il
      presidente fu creduto pazzo.
      An individual (who had) accused himself of having
      assassinated the president was deemed insane.

Therefore *si* of (33) (at least that of (33b)) cannot be an object (in the
sense of having object θ-role). From the standpoint of our theory of sc
relatives, (34b) and (35b) are excluded because they involve subject relativization like (31c), while in order to be as well-formed as (31a,b) (33b)
must have the analysis in (36).[14]

(36)   ... [$_{sc}$ PRO$_i$ accusato**si** t$_i$ ...] ...

Thus both the inversion cases in (29a), (30a, b) and sc relative cases like
(33b) point to the D-structure in (37).[15]

(37)   [e] si-V NP

Taking (37) to be correct, we consider what role *si* plays in it. Note
first that, as in the case of ergative and inherent-reflexive *si/se*, we must
assume here that *si* is related to both the subject and the object positions.
The reason is once again that reflexives are core cases for E assignment
and pp agreement in French. Without those relations, they would be
expected to be only periphery cases. If *si* is indeed present in the
D-structure (37) as we will argue further below, it is then natural to
assume that the relations with the subject and the object exist not only at
S-structure, as implied by their being detected by the rules of E assignment and pp agreement, but at D-structure as well. (Let us say as a reflex
of (7) above.)

    The full representation of the D-structure in (37) would then be as in
(38a), which we may compare with the D-structure we attributed to the
object clitic analysis of *si* in (38b).

(38) a. [e] si-V NP
         ∟┘ └___┘

   b. NP si-V [e]
       └__┘└__┘

One might suggest that (38a) differs from (38b) only in that, while in
(38b) the *si*-object relation involves θ-role transmission, in (38a) it is the
subject-*si* relation that does. That is to say, that *si* of (38a) is now a
subject rather than an object clitic. However, this view, while compatible

with the inversion cases we considered ((29b), (30a,b)), is not compatible with sc relatives like (33b).

The reason is that, while *si/se* behaves like such subject clitics as impersonal-SI/SE-moyen with respect to the inversion cases, as shown by the parallelism between (30a) and the SE-moyen case in (39a), it behaves unlike such subject clitics with respect to the sc relative cases, as shown by the lack of parallelism between (33b) and (39b).

(39) a. Il **se** construit beaucoup d'immeubles dans cette ville.
   it SE builds   many buildings   in   this   city

   Many buildings are built in this city.

   b. *Il regalo [sc PRO*i* compratosi t*i* ieri]   é per Giovanni.
   the present   SI-bought   yesterday is for Giovanni.

The relative in (39b) is to be compared with the non-relative case in (40), which is well-formed.

(40)   Il regalo*i*   **si** è comprato t*i* ieri.
   the present SI has bought   yesterday

   The present was bought yesterday.

We attribute the contrast between (39b) and (40) to the fact that, while active *comprare* of (40) assigns θ-role to the subject position (as does *construire* of (39a)), 'passive' participle *comprato* of (39b) does not, so that SI will fail to receive θ-role. (Also, SI will fail to receive Case in (39b), as it does in infinitivals. See 1.6.) Thus, if *si* of (38a) were transmitted θ-role by the syntactic relation with the subject, we would expect that it too, like SI, should fail to occur in sc relatives, since the morphological process that gives rise to the passive participle from the corresponding verb removes the ability of the verb to assign subject θ-role.

What we must assume for *si* of (38a) is that it is not a subject clitic, but rather a lexical affix, just like ergative and inherent-reflexive *si*. Its effect will be that of absorbing subject θ-role, but at lexical rather than at syntactic levels. We are thus postulating a morphological process that, by affixing *si* to a transitive verb like for example 'accuse', gives rise to a corresponding verb 'self-accuse', which is an ergative verb. Since past participles of ergative verbs are possible in Italian sc relatives in general ('vacuous' loss of subject θ-role being allowed, see 3.2.3), we will expect past participles of ergative verbs derived via *si*-affixation to be possible as well, whence (33b).

In essence, what one must assume is that absorption of subject θ-role by *si* occurs prior to elimination of that θ-role by past participial affixation. And, since we regard the latter as a lexical process, *si*-affixation will have to be a lexical process too. While (33b) thus rules out a subject clitic analysis of reflexive *si*, (32a,b) would analogously rule out a subject clitic analysis of ergative and inherent-reflexive *si*. If *si* of (33b) is thus a lexically inserted affix, then it will clearly be present at D-structure and in (38a) as we have assumed.

Let us now consider how the conclusion that reflexive *si* occurs as a lexical affix, like ergative and inherent-reflexive *si*, bears on our previous analysis of reflexive *si* as an object clitic. Two questions in particular arise in this connection. One is whether the object clitic analysis is still justified once we introduce the lexical analysis. The other is whether the facts that were accounted for under the assumption that reflexive *si* was an object clitic, are still accounted for.

Considering the first question, we note that the object-clitic anlaysis is still required by 'indirect object' cases. That is, while cases like (33a) (**Un individuo si accusò . . .** 'An individual accused himself . . .') can now be derived from a D-structure like (38a) ($[e]$ *si-V NP*) via NP-movement, cases like (41) cannot, since NP-movement does not apply to indirect objects.

(41) a. Giovanni **si** è scritto.
   Giovanni has written to himself.

b. Giovanni **si** è sputato addosso.
   Giovanni has spat upon (to) himself.

c. Giovanni **si** è comprato un'auto.
   Giovanni has bought an automobile to himself.

If cases like (41) could be derived via NP-movement, then the corresponding sc relatives in (42) ought to be well-formed like the one in (33b) analyzed as in (36).

(42) a. *Un individuo $[_{sc}$ PRO$_i$ scritto**si** t$_i$ parecchie volte] . . .
   An individual (who had) written to himself several times . . .

b. *Un individual $[_{sc}$ PRO$_i$ sputato**si** addosso t$_i$] . . .
   An individual (who had) spat upon (to) himself . . .

c. *Un individuo $[_{sc}$ PRO$_i$ comprato**si** un'auto t$_i$] . . .
   An individual (who had) bought an automobile (to) himself . . .

Instead, the cases in (42) will be ruled out just like the case in (31d), that is because NP-movement fails to apply to indirect objects, whatever the exact theoretical reasons. (Example (42c) is also excluded by lack of Case on *un'auto*, cf. fn. 14.)[16] This means that in the cases in (41) the phrase *Giovanni* must be base-generated in subject position, and in turn that *si* is an object clitic here. Thus, the object clitic analysis of reflexive *si*, which is perfectly natural from the theoretical point of view, is still motivated empirically, by indirect object cases. And, if it is available for indirect objects, it is only natural to assume that it is available in general, thus for direct objects as well.

Since not only NP-movement, but, as we saw in 2.4, also inversion fails to apply to indirect objects, we will expect indirect object cases of *si* to fail to appear not only in sc relatives like the one in (33b), but also in inversion cases like (29b), (30a, b). This is correct, as shown by (43).

(43) a. ****Se**   **ne**   sono scritti **(a)** **tre**   (*Italian*)
      to-themselves of-them have written (to) three

   b. **Il s'est   écrit   **(à)** **trois hommes .**   (*French*)
      it to-itself has written (to) three men

   c. **A lè   scriwüse   **(a)** **tre mei amis**   (*Piedmontese*)
      cl has written-to-itself (to) three friends of mine

The cases in (43) are of interest not only for our analysis of *si*, but also in another connection. The ungrammaticality of the indirect object cases in (43), contrasting with the grammaticality of the direct object cases in (29b), (30a,b) provides one further argument for the base-generated character of these types of inversion. For, if the French *il*-construction and its Italian and Piedmontese equivalents were derived by rightward movement, then the cases in (43) should be as grammatical as the direct object cases in (29b), (30a,b), since both sets of cases would have well-formed sources like (44), (45), from which they could be derived in identical fashion.

(44) a. Parecchi prigionieri **si** sono uccisi.   (*Italian*)
         Several prisoners have killed themselves.

   b. Trois mille hommes **se** sont dénoncés.   (*French*)
       Three thousand men have denounced themselves.

   c. Vaire persuné a sun masase.   (*Piedmontese*)
       Several prisoners have killed themselves.

(45) a. Tre prigionieri **si** sono scritti.   (*Italian*)
         Three prisoners have written to themselves.

   b. Trois hommes **se** sont écrit.   (*French*)
       Three men have written to themselves.

   c. Tre mei amis a sun scriwüse.   (*Piedmontese*)
       Three friends of mine have written to themselves.

Still incidental to the main line of discussion we may also note that the difference between direct and indirect object cases of sc relatives, that is the difference between (33b) and (42) provides one further argument against a Wh-*be* deletion derivation of these relatives. For, under Wh-*be* deletion all of these cases should be derivable, from the well-formed sources in (46).

(46) a. Un individuo che **si** era accusato ...
      An individual who had (E) accused himself...

b. Un individuo che **si** era $\left\{\begin{array}{l}\text{scritto}\\ \text{sputato addosso}\\ \text{comprato n'auto}\end{array}\right\}$.

    An individual who had (E) $\left\{\begin{array}{l}\textit{written}\\ \textit{spat upon}\\ \textit{bought an automobile}\end{array}\right\}$

(*to*) *himself.*

Returning now to the main discussion, we consider the second question, namely whether the results we obtained under the object clitic analysis are preserved once the lexical analysis is introduced. We begin by considering the generalization illustrated by (4) above that reflexive *si* never occurs with derived subjects. Stated in these terms, the generalization is now obviously false if cases like *Giovanni si è accusato* can be derived via NP-movement. However, the set of facts that the generalization was intended to capture will continue to follow. Consider the ungrammatical occurrence of *si* with ergative *venire* (*in mente*) of (4d) repeated here.

(47)   *Maria e Giovanni **si** venivano spesso in mente.
     Maria and Giovanni came often to mind to each other ('*to each other's mind*').

As a reflexive object clitic, **si** was excluded from (47) because it lacked a D-structure antecedent. But as an affix, **si** is still excluded. For on the one hand it could not absorb subject θ-role, since with ergative verbs there is no such θ-role. On the other, in (47) there is an indirect object θ-role that must be transmitted to *si* since there is no other element to bear it. The situation for the other cases in question (i.e. in (4)) is analogous. The generalization thus still holds, though it must be rephrased as "Reflexive *si* will not occur in structures which would have a derived subject even aside from the effects of *si*".

Let us now consider our account of the distribution of reflexives over complex predicates, beginning with the ungrammaticality of (8a), repeated here.

(48)   *Maria **si**   fa   accusare a Giovanni.
     Maria herself makes accuse   to Giovanni

Maria makes Giovanni accuse herself.

When *si* is an object clitic, (48) must have the D-structure in (49a), as we discussed. When *si* is an affix, it must have the one in (49b). (Example (48) would then be derived by VP-movement, and NP-movement of *Maria*.)

(49) a.   Maria si fa [$_S$ Giovanni accusare [e]]

    b.   [e] si fa [$_S$ Giovanni accusare Maria]

We argued that (49a) was ill-formed because the relation between *si* and the object position violated locality conditions; (49b) will now be analogously ill-formed, provided that we assume that even in this case the *si*-object relation is subject to locality conditions, which seems natural enough.[17] Base-generation of *si* on the lower verb would not be possible in (49b), just as we argued it was not in (49a). Our assumption that *si* absorbs subject θ-role at lexical levels of representation will exclude absorption of subject θ-role from the main verb when *si* is not base-generated on that verb. Thus (48) will still be completely excluded.

The other cases which we had accounted for under the object clitic analysis of *si* were the ungrammatical example (50a), and the grammatical one in (50b).

(50) a.   *I ragazzi **si** volevano essere presentati.
       The kids wanted to be introduced to each other.

    b.   I ragazzi **si** dovrebbero parlare.
       The kids would have to talk to each other.

The case in (50a), which was ruled out on the basis of the D-structure in (51a), will, under the lexical analysis, be ruled out on the basis of (51b).

(51) a.   I ragazzi si volevano [$_S$ [e] essere presentati PRO [e]]

    b.   [e] si volevano [$_S$ [e] essere presentati PRO [(a) i ragazzi]]

Again, in (51b) the *si*-object relation violates locality conditions, just as it does in (51a). But furthermore a derivation of (50a) from (51b) would be impossible because it would involve movement of an indirect object into subject position. Since *si* is excluded from occurring with passives under the lexical analysis much as it is under the object clitic analysis (as we just saw, cf. discussion of (47)), base-generation of *si* on the lower verb would be impossible in (51b) just as in (51a), and the ungrammaticality of (50a) will thus continue to be expected.

As for (50b), the predictions of the lexical analysis are actually irrelevant, since its grammaticality is predicted under the object clitic analysis anyway, which we know must be available. Considering however the lexical analysis too for the sake of discussion, we note that, while (50b) would be excluded because it is an indirect object case, comparable direct object cases like (52a) would be allowed, as derived from the D-structure (52b), via NP-movement in the complement, Raising, VP-movement and Cl-Cl.

(52) a.   Giovanni **si** dovrebbe vedere.
       Giovani would have to see himself.

  b.   [e] dovrebbe [$_S$ [e] veder**si** Giovanni]

It thus appears that the distribution of reflexive clitics over complex predicates continues to be predicted, and that in general all the facts we had previously accounted for continue to follow once the lexical analysis of *si* is allowed.

To conclude, we have argued that reflexive *si* can function as an object clitic as well as a lexical affix absorbing subject θ-role. This means that cases like (53a) will systematically be ambiguous as to whether they are derived from a D-structure like (53b), or from one like (53c).

(53) a.   Giovanni **si** è accusato.
       Giovanni has accused himself.

  b.   Giovanni si è accusato [e]

  c.   [e] si è accusato Giovanni

Other cases however, will only be possible under one or the other analysis. Thus, indirect object cases superficially similar to (53a) will unambiguously imply a D-structure of the type of (53b) since indirect objects do not move into subject position. Those types of inversion that require an argument in direct object position at D-structure, as well as sc relatives, which require relativization of a direct object argument, will unambiguously imply a D-structure of the type of (53c).

As we have seen, the lexical analysis of reflexive *si* is well justified empirically. Also, this analysis has the desirable consequence of further bridging the gap between reflexive *si* and ergative/inherent-reflexive *si,* thus strengthening the explanation for the presence of the same morpheme in all of these cases.[18] However, from a strictly theoretical point of view, the lexical analysis is only fairly natural, as we do not have any strong theoretical reasons to expect that reflexive *si* should function as an affix.[19] D-structures like (53c) are theoretically natural to the extent that they are in crucial respects similar to the theoretically expected (53b). Thus, from a theoretical standpoint we can at least say that we would not expect that non-reflexive clitics could also function as affixes absorbing subject θ-role, since for those clitics we do not have the reasons provided by (53b) to expect that they will bear a relation with the subject.

6.3.3 *Reflexives under faire*

In this subsection we will argue that the analysis of reflexive clitics as lexical affixes which we proposed above provides a solution to the problem of reflexive clitics in French causatives which we left unsolved in 6.2. We will argue that while the analysis we propose leaves a few questions open, alternative analyses are completely untenable.

Our claim of the previous subsection that reflexives in Italian and French can appear in the D-structures of (54), predicts that the VPs of (54) could be embedded under *fare/faire*, a prediction which must be compared with the results in (55).

(54) a. [e] [$_{VP}$ accusar**si** Piero] (*Italian*)

    b. [e] [$_{VP}$ **s**'accuser Pierre] (*French*)

(55) a. Maria ha fatto [$_{VP}$ accusare Piero] (*Italian*)
        Maria made Piero accuse himself/Maria had Piero accused.

    b. Marie a fait [$_{VP}$ **s**'accuser Pierre] (*French*)
        Marie made Pierre accuse himself.

We will assume, as seems natural, that the absence of *si* in (55a) versus the presence of *se* in (55b) follows in the same fashion as with ergative/inherent-reflexive *si/se* in (26) above, conceivably along the lines we suggested.[20] Given the absence of *si*, cases like (55a) will be ambiguous between the reflexive and the non-reflexive interpretations, while the presence of *se* will make (55b) unambiguous.[21] The French case in (56), parallel to Italian (55a) appears unambiguous too, allowing only a non-reflexive interpretation.

(56)   Marie a fait [$_{VP}$ accuser Pierre] (*French*)
       Marie had Pierre accused.

It seems natural to assume that the non-ambiguity of (56) contrasting with the ambiguity of (55a) is to be related precisely to the fact that French has the non-ambiguously reflexive form in (55b), whereas Italian does not. In this connection, consider a case like (57).

(57)   Le madri fanno sempre [$_{VP}$ parlare dei loro figli] (*Italian*)
       Mothers always make (people) talk about their own kids.

While in (57) the embedded subject can be interpreted rather freely, it cannot be interpreted as coreferential with the main subject. We see no other reason for this than the fact that there is another sentence uniquely associated with that interpretation, namely (58) (which is a case of FI).

(58)   Le madri *si* fanno sempre parlare dei loro figli.   (*Italian*)
        Mothers always make each other talk about their own kids.

But if the non-ambiguity of (57) is due to the existence of (58), then the non-ambiguity of (56) will similarly follow from (55b), as we suggested.

Prior to providing an analysis of cases like (55b), we noted that they are superficially odd in two respects: (i) unlike other clitics, *se* does not 'climb', and (ii) the apparent subject (*Pierre*) is not dativized, as happens when the clitic is non-reflexive, as in (59).

(59)   Marie l'a fait   accuser à Pierre.   (*French*)
        Marie him has made accuse to Pierre

        Marie made Pierre accuse him.

It is clear that both (i) and (ii) follow straightforwardly from our analysis: *se* will fail to climb just as in ergative/inherent-reflexive cases, and essentially because, if it did, it would be incorrectly interpreted as linked with the main subject; and dativization will not apply since the phrase *Pierre* is the embedded object rather than the embedded subject, and thus not in a dativizing environment.

Since *s'accuser* of (55b) is like an ergative verb (in not assigning subject θ-role), we will expect that, like ergative verbs, it will fail to assign Case to its direct object. However, here we attribute this property specifically to the presence of *se*. That is, we assume that affix *si/se* is just like object clitic *si/se* in absorbing the Case that the verb would otherwise assign to its object. In (55b) the embedded object *Pierre* will thus be assigned (accusative) Case by the main verb *faire*, as in general with ergative complements (cf. 4.5). Lack of dativization in (55b) would be very difficult to account for under the analysis of *se* as an object clitic, and is in fact just another piece of evidence supporting the existence of the D-structures in (54).[22] While our analysis thus accounts directly for the two major properties of reflexive complements of *faire*, there remain a few questions and problems to be considered. Before doing so however, we will examine the FS account of such complements.

In FS, reflexive complements of *faire* are taken to provide evidence for the principle of the cycle. Kayne proposes to account for the difference between reflexive (55b) and non-reflexive (59) by assuming, crucially, that object clitics are quite generally the result of movement, and that reflexive cliticization (*Se* placement) is cyclic, while non-reflexive cliticization (clitic placement) is post-cyclic. Within Kayne's framework, in which there are no *ec*'s associated with clitics, derivation of (55b) will then proceed as in (60), while that of (59) will be as in (61).

(60) a. *Underlying*   Marie a fait [$_S$ Pierre accuser **se**]

    b. *1st cycle*   Marie a fait [$_S$ Pierre **s**'accuser]

    c. *2nd cycle*   Marie a fait **s**'accuser [$_S$ Pierre ...]

(61) a. *Underlying*   Marie a fait [$_S$ Pierre accuser **le**]

    b. *2nd cycle*   Marie a fait accuser **le** [$_S$ à Pierre ...]

    c. *post-cycle* Marie **l**'a fait accuser [$_S$ à Pierre ...]

In this system, the account of (i) above (the lower position of *se*) will thus rest on existence of the principle of the cycle, while the account of (ii) (the lack of dativization) rests on non-existence of *ec*'s related to clitics. For if *se* of (60c) had an empty object associated with it, dativization would be expected, just as in the non-reflexive case.

The FS account both of (i) and of (ii) will thus collapse once we move to our own theoretical framework, since we do not assume the cycle, and we do assume *ec*'s. If we had no further reason for ruling out the account in (60), (61), and if we had no alternative to propose, this might simply be taken to indicate that the FS framework is in fact the correct one. But we do have an alternative, the one just given, and we do have further reasons. We note in particular, that the existence of a process of Clitic Climbing, which we argued for above, will make cyclicity of *Se* placement insufficient to account for the lower position of *se*, and post-cyclicity of Clitic placement unnecessary to account for the higher position of non-reflexive *le*.[23, 24]

While our motivation for a principle of Cl-Cl cuts across restructuring and causatives (cf. 4.1.4, 6.2), the strongest motivation is provided by restructuring constructions. And it is indeed the latter constructions which falsify the system of (60), (61) most directly. For within a framework that assumes the cycle, restructuring would be most likely to be cyclic, just like the causative rule, as is argued in fact in RRIS. On the basis of (60)–(61) one would then incorrectly expect, for restructuring constructions, the same differential behavior of reflexives and non-reflexives, with the former cliticized on the embedded verb, and the latter to the main one.[25] And, more generally (as argued in detail in Burzio (1983)), whereas a framework constrained by configurational conditions, such as the GB theory, can account for the several differences between causatives and restructuring rather naturally on the basis of 'subject substitution' applying only with restructuring, a system constrained by ordering of rules has nothing to say about those differences, and is in fact falsified by them since, while the distribution of phenomena over causatives will require a certain order of rules, restructuring constructions too often seem to require just the opposite order.

Returning now to our analysis, two types of comments appear to be in order. The first concerns some divergence between reflexive complements of *faire* on the one hand and inversion and sc relative cases like (29a)–(30), (33b) on the other, which we have assumed are all related to D-structures like (54a,b). The second concerns the p.ediction that reflexive complements of *faire* should behave just like other established cases of *Fare/Faire*-VP (F–VP) and unlike cases of FI.

Beginning with the first, we note that, while inversion and sc relatives are limited to direct object cases, as we saw, complements of *faire* are not, as shown for example by (62) ((62b) from FS, p. 404).

(62) a.   Cela fera **se** téléphoner les enfants.
         That will make the kids telephone (to) each other.

    b.   J'essaierai de faire **s**'acheter des chaussures à mon ami.
         I will try to make my friend buy some shoes to himself.

This is not incompatible with our discussion, however, since the exclusion of indirect objects was attributed to constraints specific to either NP-movement or inversion. Given that neither NP-movement nor inversion is involved here, we may well expect indirect objects to be possible. We will in fact take the analyses of (62a,b) to be as in (63a,b).

(63) a.   Cela fera [$_{VP}$ **se** téléphoner [les enfants]]

    b.   ... faire [$_{VP}$ **s**'acheter des chaussures [à mon ami]]

We will account for the fact that the object of *téléphoner*, which is usually dative, appears in the accusative in (63a), by assuming that *se* absorbs the dative Case that *tèlèphoner* would assign to that object, and that main verb *faire* then assigns accusative. Notice that if this account is correct, what we are observing here is exactly the inverse of the dativization process. This seems to suggest again very strongly — recall 4.1.2 — that there is no dativization rule: there are only general principles, which roduce sometimes one effect, sometimes the opposite one.[26] In (63b) we analogously assume that *se* absorbs the dative that the embedded verb would assign, and that Case is assigned by *faire*. Only this time the Case will be dative, given the presence of the direct object.

There are, however, some other differences between the inversion and sc relative cases of 6.3.2 and reflexive complements of *faire*, for which we will have no account. Thus, inversion cases like (29b), (30a, b) above are not easily accepted by all speakers, and seem quite generally impossible when *si/se* is reciprocal rather than reflexive, cf. **?* Se ne sono incontrati due** 'Two of them met each other'. Sc relatives like (33b) also have a somewhat marked character and are perhaps slightly worse with reciprocal *si*, cf. **? Due amici incontratisi allo stadio non si vedevano da anni** 'Two friends (who had) met each other at the stadium had not seen each other in years'. But no comparable limitations are attested for *se* complements of *faire* (cf. for example the reciprocal of (62a)).

Turning now to a comparison of reflexive complements of *faire* with established cases of F-VP, recall how in 4.5.1 we noted that, unlike FI cases, F-VP cases allow reflexive and dative objects of the embedded verb to cliticize to the main verb, as for example in (64a,b).

(64) a. Jean s_i'est   fait   [$_{VP}$ parvenir un livre [$_i$e]]
       Jean to-himself has made   *arrive*   *a*   *book*

       Jean$_i$ had a book sent to him$_i$.

   b. On **lui**$_i$ fera   [$_{VP}$ mourir son chien [$_i$e]]
       we to-him will make   *die*   *his*   *dog*

       We will make his dog die on him.

This would lead to the expectation that we should find the same behavior with reflexive complements, yet this expectation is not fulfilled, as shown by (65a, b), given in our analysis ((65a) from FS, p. 426).

(65) a. *Sa mère s_i'est fait [$_{VP}$ se présenter [la jeune fille] [$_i$e]]

       Her mother$_i$ made the girl introduce herself to her$_i$.

   b. *Jean **lui**$_i$ a fait [$_{VP}$ se présenter [la jeune fille] [$_i$e]]

       Jean made the girl introduce herself to him.

Although both (65a, b) may be unexpected from the point of view of the VP analysis, we note that they will not provide an argument for analyzing (65a, b) as cases of FI. For the ungrammaticality of (65a, b) seems to reflect a more general prohibition than one finds in FI, since cliticization of non-reflexive direct objects is also impossible here, as in (66a) (from FS, p. 429, analysis ours), while it is unproblematic in FI, as in (66b).

(66) a. *Sa mère est arrivée à **les**$_i$ faire [$_{VP}$ s'acheter [$_i$e] [à la jeune

       Her mother managed to make the girl buy them to (i.e. for)

       fille]]
       herself

   b. Sa mère est arrivée à **les** faire acheter à la jeune fille
       Her mother managed to make the girl buy them.

It seems reasonable to suppose that whatever factors exclude (66a) will exclude (65a, b) also. Failure of cliticization of the embedded objects in (65a, b) contrasts with successful cliticization of the element linked with *se*, which we also regard as an embedded object, as in (67) ((67c) from FS, p. 426, analysis ours).

(67) a. Jean l_i'a fait [$_{VP}$ **se** présenter [$_i$e] à Marie]

        Jean made him introduce himself to Marie.

    b. J'essaierai de **lui**$_i$ faire [$_{VP}$ s'acheter des chaussures [$_i$e]]

        I will try to make him buy some shoes to himself.

    c. Ils **se**$_i$ faisaient [$_{VP}$ **se** laver les mains [$_i$e]]

        They were making each other wash the hands to themselves ('their hands').

Note that, from the standpoint of our analysis, the problem here is not how to account for (67), given (65), (66a). For we predict (67) rather straightforwardly. Since we assume that the element linked with *se* is assigned Case always and necessarily by *faire*, then on the basis of the relation between cliticization and Case assignment discussed in 4.1.5, 4.5 above, we will definitely expect cliticization to the latter verb (cf. discussion of (110), ch. 4). The problem, which we must leave unsolved, is instead how to account for (65), (66a), a problem which we presume arises under an FI analysis as well, given the contrast in (66). The ungrammaticality of (66a) is in fact also unaccounted for in FS.[27]

In summary, the residual problems that our VP analysis has, would not be solved by an FI analysis of reflexive complements of *faire*. On the other hand there are good reasons to reject an FI analysis. One is that since the relation between a subject and a reflexive clitic is one of those relations that must obtain at S-structure, as is established by the fact that it triggers E-assignment, we predict that complements involving reflexive clitics should be among those complements that cannot be embedded in FI constructions. Another is that it would be very difficult under an FI analysis to account for the apparent peculiarities of reflexive complements, especially the lack of dativization of the apparent embedded subject. The analysis in FS succeeds in accounting for those peculiarities, but it is incompatible with our overall discussion at many levels, in particular because it assumes the principle of the cycle, assumes no *ec*'s, would imply non-existence of Clitic Climbing, and would make false predictions for restructuring constructions. The analysis in FS would also shed no light on the behavior of reflexives in Italian causatives (i.e. (55a)).

6.4. CONCLUSION

In this chapter we have argued that, if we regard clitic *si* as a reflexive object, most of the syntactic properties that distinguish it from its non-clitic counterparts like *se stesso* will simply follow from the hypothesis that object clitics in general are base-generated, in conjunction with one single principle requiring that all relations involving base-generated clitics exist at all levels ((7) above), a principle which we have argued in a reflex of the projection principle.

The properties of *si* that we have accounted for in this fashion are those listed in (68).

(68) a. Non-occurrence with NP-movement constructions (e.g. passives).

   b. Selection of auxiliary E.

   c. Peculiar distribution over complex predicates:
      i.   Possible in restructuring constructions precisely to the extent that it would be possible on the complement.
      ii. Impossible altogether in FI constructions.

If this picture were exhaustive, then the only thing speakers would have to learn about *si* would be that it is a reflexive clitic. The syntax of *si* would then be entirely determined by this one piece of knowledge, inter-acting with innate principles such as the projection principle. In turn, the interaction of the syntax of *si* with other components of the grammar, such as the syntax of NP-movement, the syntax of auxiliary assignment, the syntax of complex predicates, would produce the intricate distribution of data captured by (68a, b, c), and the differences with respect to non-clitic reflexives.

The picture is somewhat complicated however by the fact that the object clitic analysis of *si* is not sufficient to account for some aspects of its behavior. In particular for its occurrence in French causatives, in base-generated types of inversion, and in Italian sc relatives. On the basis of this, we have argued that a second, additional analysis must be available: one that has *si* as a lexical affix absorbing subject θ-role and object Case. On the one hand, this second analysis has the desirable effect of estab-lishing the missing link between reflexive *si* and ergative/inherent reflex-ive *si*, but on the other it lacks full theoretical justification. On this point our theory fares in fact only slightly better than Kayne's, which achieved some of the same results by assuming reflexive cliticization to be cyclic and non-reflexive cliticization post-cyclic. Our analysis represents never-theless a step forward because, while from Kayne's theoretical perspec-tive things might have turned out just the opposite, with non-reflexive cliticization cyclic and reflexive cliticization post-cyclic, under the present analysis that is not so: as we noted, affix *si* bears some syntactic analogy only with a reflexive clitic, not with a non-reflexive one. However our analysis fares only slightly better, because in our theoretical world *si* might not have been an affix at all.

Aside from this, note that the discussion in this chapter confirms the general theoretical framework assumed. In particular, our account of (68a) above implies the existence of D-structure, (*si* must have an antecedent at that level). Our account of (68c) also implies the existence of D-structure (*si* must have an antecedent at that level). Our account of (68c) also implies the existence of D-structure, since it relies on D-structure locality conditions on clitic-*ec* relations. Thus consider restructuring in (69a,b).

(69) a *I ragazzi$_i$ **si** volevano [$_{VP}$ essere presentati t$_i$ [e]] [$_S$ PRO$_i$ – – –]

      The kids wanted to be introduced to each other.

  b. Questi libri   si   volevano [$_{VP}$ leggere subito t] [$_S$ PRO – – –]

      These books SI wanted   to read immediately.

      We wanted to read these books immediately.

The relations of (69a, b) are both local at S-structure, thus these two cases cannot be distinguished on the basis of that level alone. But they can on the basis of D-structure, since while the relation of (69a) will be non local at that level, violating general principles, the one of (69b) will not exist, violating no principle. The parallel point for causative constructions was made in 4.8 above.

Our account of the differences between *si* and *se stesso* implies the existence of a level of LF, to the extent that it relies on the assumption that, unlike antecedent-*si* relations, antecedent-*se stesso* relations exist only at LF.

In 5.9 above, we drew the conclusion that only a theory that makes use of *ec*'s and of configurational well-formedness conditions (as opposed to conditions on the application of rules), can appeal to subject substitution and thus account for the systematic differences between restructuring and causative constructions. In this chapter we have strengthened that conclusion in two ways: by considering one more difference, the one relative to reflexive complements, arguing that that too follows from our theory; and by considering one specific instance of a theory not employing *ec*'s and configurational well-formedness conditions (but rather conditions on the application of rules), the theory of reflexives in FS, arguing that that theory would indeed fail to account for the difference.

NOTES

[1] The passive case in (4) is noted in FS, p. 375 ff., where an account based on rule ordering is proposed: cyclic reflexivization (*Se* placement) versus post-cyclic passivization. Reflexivization would thus fail in (4a) because at the point of its application the intended antecedent of *si* would not be in the relevant position (subject position). Some of the other cases in (4) have been noted by L. Rizzi.

The inability of reflexive *si* to occur with ergative verbs has a few apparent exceptions for which at the moment we have no account. Thus, many speakers accept (i).

(i)   ?Giovanni e Maria   si   piacquero subito.
         Giovanni and Maria   to-each other pleased   immediately

         Giovanni and Maria liked each other immediately

And, as R. Kayne informs us, French cases like (ii) are also accepted (the Italian equivalent is also perhaps marginally acceptable).

(ii)   Ils se sont venu en aide.
          They came to each other's aid.

The case in (iii) however, closely corresponding to Italian (4d), is not accepted.

(iii)   *Ils se sont venu à l'esprit.
          They came to each other's mind.

[2] Note that the 'inverted' counterparts to the reflexive cases in (4), such as for example (i), are also impossible.

(i)   *Si furono posti **i ragazzi** di fronte.
          The kids were placed before each other.

Examples like (i) differ from cases of inversion derived by movement, such as (ii), in which we assme that the antecedent to *si* in S-structure is the inversion chain.

(ii)   Si sono già telefonati **Giovanni e Maria.**
          Giovanni and Maria have already phoned each other.

The ungrammaticality of (i) would then seemingly suggest that inversion relations cannot in general be established at D-structure, or (i) should be as grammatical as (ii), although we find no exact theoretical reason for this. Correspondingly, the grammaticality of the ergative cases in (i), (ii) of Note 1 may conceivably be accounted for in terms of a lexically controlled possibility of establishing such relations at D-structure. See also Note 3.

[3] On the basis of the discussion of Note 2, base-generation of the inversion relation with *ci* may predict that reflexive *si* should be possible in *ci* cases, contrary to the evidence in (i).

(i)   * $\left\{ \begin{array}{l} \textbf{Si} \text{ c'erano} \\ \textbf{Ci si} \text{ erano} \end{array} \right\}$ due ragazzi di fronte.

          There were two kids before each other.

At least in part the ungrammaticality of (i) is related to that of its non reflexive counterpart in (ii), which we in turn relate to that of (iid), Note 8, II.0.

(ii)   ?***Gli** c'erano due ragazzi di fronte.
          There were two kids before him.

Concerning the difference in grammaticality between (i) and (ii), we note the ungrammaticality of (iiia), contrasting with (iiib).

(iii) a.   ??There arrived three men |to fix the roof|

  b.   Three men arrived |to fix the roof|

We take (iiia) to indicate that chains involving *there* do not function as argument antecedents. That is, somehow only the subject position, rather than the inversion chain functions as a possible antecedent to the subject of the purposive clause. Although we do not understand exactly why this should be so, the natural assumption that in this respect *ci* is just like *there* will suffice to rule out (i) independent of the issue of the inversion relation obligatorily existing in D-structure, which does not arise with *there*.

[4] There is a residual difficulty here in that in standard contemporary Italian, relations between a Wh-phrase and its trace, which clearly exist at S-structure, do not trigger pp agreement (E assignment is irrelevant). But there is a corresponding difficulty under the alternative hypothesis since these relations, which do not involve θ-role transmission, do trigger pp agreement in certain dialects and styles of Italian as was noted in Note 43, ch. 1, and in French, as in (i).

  (i) a.   La lettre que tu as écrite.
          The letter that you have written (fem.)

  b.   Combien de livres as-tu lus?
          How many books have you read (pl.)?

We will leave this question open.

[5] There is actually a fourth difference for which we have no precise account: the fact that *se stesso*, like English reflexives, can have a non-subject antecedent, while *si* cannot, as in (i).

  (i) a.   Questa situazione metterà Giovanni contro **se stesso**.
          This situation will set Giovanni against himself.

  b.   *Questa situazione **si** metterà Giovanni contro.
          This situation will set Giovanni against himself.

The impossibility for a direct object to be an antecedent for *si* is also implied by the cases in (4). Given that a direct object presumably c-commands clitics, (ib) suggests that conditions tighter than those prescribed by the binding theory hold on antecedent-*si* relations. We might perhaps assume an adjacency requirement, also suggested by some of the discussion in the text below.

[6] Note that the existence of Cl-Cl and the discussion in the text would still be compatible in principle with the view that there is cliticization by movement prior to Cl-Cl. The problem would be how to ensure that cliticization of embedded objects in complex predicates can only occur with respect to the embedded verb, and not with respect to the main verb directly. As far as we can see, this would require extrinsic ordering of rules, with cliticization and the relevant locality conditions applying before VP-movement. Since ordering of rules is not available in our framework, we must reject cliticization by movement altogether. Of course, extrinsic ordering of rules would in any event have a stipulatory character, while our approach is more principled. That is, our D-structure locality conditions on clitic-*ec* relations, which have the same empirical effects as extrinsic ordering of rules, follow from the projection principle.

[7] Notice that, unlike (11a, b) which provide an absolute argument for Cl-Cl, (13), (14) only provide one internal to a base-generation analysis of clitics. Given that the clitics of (13), (14) do not alternate with overt NPs, a movement analysis would have to postulate that cliticization is obligatory here. But, aside from that, all of the cases in (13), (14) could well be derived by single step cliticization.

[8] Actually, pp agreement is obligatory only in literary French, as with other object clitics (see Note 10). But this only provides additional evidence for the clitic-*ec* relation.

[9] Note that the third relation provides an alternative (and perhaps more convincing) account of the contrast in (i), given in Note 8, ch. 1.

(i) a.   Maria, **ti** ho $\left\{ \begin{array}{c} visto \\ vista \end{array} \right\}$.

     Maria, I have seen (no ag't/ag't) you.

     b.   Maria, **ti** sei $\left\{ \begin{array}{c} *visto \\ vista \end{array} \right\}$.

     Maria, you have seen (*no ag't/ag't) yourself.

As we discussed in 1.7, (ia) can be attributed to first and second person pronouns being ambiguous as to whether or not they bear gender and number features. But while the *ec* in direct object position in (ia) only has the pronoun as the antecedent, the one in (ib) will now have both the pronoun and the subject, so that the obligatory agreement will simply follow from the fact that subjects always induce agreement (as we pointed out in Note 48, ch. 1).

[10] This is likely to make our ergative analysis of inherent-reflexives compatible with the fact noted by Kayne (FS, 5.8) that the kind of past participle agreement found with inherent-reflexive *se* is that typical of object clitics, which is obligatory only in literary styles, not in conversational French. This fact motivates Kayne's object clitic analysis of inherent-reflexive *se*.

[11] Notice that evidence that complements of *faire* involving ergative *se* must indeed be analyzed like ergative complements in general is provided among other things by free cliticization of dative objects, as in (i) (from FS, p. 311). On this, recall 4.5.1 above.

(i)   Le soufre **lui** a fait se rétrécir la peau.

     The sulphur has made the skin shrink (itself) to him ('his skin shrink').

[12] As noted in Ruwet (1972, p. 108), and in FS, p. 432, fn. 32, the presence of ergative and inherent-reflexive *se* under *faire* is not always entirely obligatory. This may seem natural given our discussion.

[13] Since this discussion only predicts that the stronger condition *may*, not that it *must* hold in Italian, it is compatible with, though of course it does not explain, the fact that a language which is just like Italian with respect to (28a), namely Spanish, appears to be like French with respect to (26b), as in (i).

(i)   Esto harà arrepenti**rse** a Juan.

     This will make Juan repent (himself).

[14] Examples (34b) and (35b) are also excluded however by the fact that *lo* and *se stesso* fail to receive Case, as passive participles do not assign Case (cf. 3.1).

[15] In contrast to the evidence related to inversion, which was provided also by French and Piedmontese, the evidence related to sc relatives is limited to Italian. The reason is that French does not allow clitics in sc relatives in general, as shown by (ia), contrasting with Italian (ib).

(i) a.   *La fille $\left\{ \begin{array}{c} \textbf{lui } \text{présentée} \\ \text{présentée } \textbf{lui} \end{array} \right\}$ hier soir ...   *(French)*

     The girl (who was) introduced to him last night ...

     b.   La ragazza presentata**gli** ieri sera ...   *(Italian)*

     The girl (who was) introduced to him last night ...

As for Piedmontese, sc relatives are generally rather unnatural in that language. This is very likely related to the fact that passives are also unnatural.

[16] Notice that while failure of NP-movement can in general be reduced to the impossibility of stranding prepositions, this account would not be available here if we are right in assuming, as we do in 6.3.3, that *si* absorbs the preposition. This may in fact explain the significantly milder ungrammaticality of (42a, b) compared with (31d), in which the preposition is not absorbed. It might thus be appropriate to take the failure of NP-movement in (42) as being only 'analogic' in some sense.

[17] Notice however that, while we assume that the locality conditions operating in (49a) consist of principle A of the binding theory, since we regard the *ec* as an anaphor, we cannot assume that the same principle operates in (49b), since the NP *Maria* is not an anaphor. But this problem seems to be exactly the same as the one discussed in 2.3 in connection with inversion, so that we may assume that principle (51) of chapter 2, i.e. "An argument bound by a non-argument is bound in its governing category", is what is at work in (49b).

[18] The distinction between reflexive *si* under the lexical analysis and ergative/inherent-reflexive *si* would be that in contrast with the other two, reflexive *si* occurs productively (but see 6.3.3), and gives rise to reflexive meaning, although one might argue that even some inherent-reflexives, like **divertirsi** 'enjoy oneself', **comportarsi** 'behave (oneself)', have reflexive meaning, witness the fact that the reflexive shows up in the English equivalent.

[19] According to Marantz (1981, 3.1.3), this behavior of reflexive morphemes as affixes absorbing subject θ-role is rather general across languages.

[20] As noted in Ruwet (1972, p. 108), and in FS, p. 432, fn. 32, reflexives differ some-what from ergatives and inherent-reflexives in that, while the latter allow *se* to be some-times omitted (cf. Note 12), the former never do. It may seem reasonable to attribute this difference to the fact that, unlike ergative and inherent-reflexive *se*, reflexive *se* plays a true semantic role here, being responsible for the reflexive meaning of the complement.

[21] The ambiguity of Italian cases like (55a) is sometimes eliminated by extrinsic factors, as for example in (ia,b).

> (i) a.   Giovanni ha fatto riparare l'auto.
>   ?*Giovanni made the car repair itself/
>   Giovanni had the car repaired.
>
>   b.   Maria ha fatto guardare Giovanni allo specchio.
>   Maria made Giovanni look at himself in the mirror/
>   ??Maria had Giovanni looked at in the mirror.

The non-ambiguity of (ia) is due to the fact that the reflexive reading is nonsensical. That of (ib) (as A. Belletti notes) to the fact that the expression *guardare allo specchio* bears an idiomatic association with reflexive interpretation, as shown by (ii).

> (ii) a.   Giovanni si guarda allo specchio.
>   Giovanni looks at himself in the mirror.
>
>   b.   ??Giovanni la guarda allo specchio.
>   Giovanni looks at her in the mirror.

[22] While we discuss in the text the account given in FS, we may note here the one proposed in Grimshaw (1980). The latter consists of regarding *se* also as a lexical affix, but one that detransitivizes the verb, thus eliminating the object argument, or θ-role, rather than the subject θ-role. Lack of dativization as in (55b) would thus follow from the fact that *s'accuser* has no object to trigger such dativization. As I discuss in more detail in Burzio (1981, 5.7.5), Grimshaw is correct in noting that reflexives, inherent reflexives,

inchoatives (our *si/se*-ergatives), SE-moyen, passives, and 'certain verbs' (like *partir* for example) must all be analyzed alike, since for example they all appear to enter into the *il*-construction and, where applicable, they fail to induce dativization under *faire*. From the premise that those 'certain verbs' are the class of intransitives, she would also be correct in drawing the conclusion that all the other constructions must be intransitive too, which would imply among other things that passive constructions involve some lexical process and no NP-movement. She is incorrect however in holding that premise, since those verbs are actually the class of ergatives, from which, by her argument, it follows that those other constructions must be ergative too, involving NP-movement in the normal case, as we have in fact argued for each of them.

Notice also that, while from our point of view of subject θ-role absorption, we do not expect non-reflexive clitics to occur as affixes as we noted in 6.3.2, from Grimshaw's point of view of object θ-role absorption there is little principled reason why they should not.

[23] Of course Kayne understands this perfectly well, and in fact argues specifically against Clitic Climbing (FS, 6.6). The cases he cites are those in (i)–(iv), in which the clitics of (va-d) fail to climb.

(i)   Un malentendu $\left\{\begin{array}{l} \text{?a fait \textbf{y} avoir} \\ \text{*\textbf{y} a fait avoir} \end{array}\right\}$ trop d'enfants à la soirée.

A misunderstanding made there be too many children at the party.

(ii)   Voilà ce qui $\left\{\begin{array}{l} \text{?a fait \textbf{en} vouloir} \\ \text{*\textbf{en} a fait vouloir} \end{array}\right\}$ votre ami à Jean.

That's what made your friend hold a grudge against Jean.

(iii)   Son orgueil $\left\{\begin{array}{l} \text{l'a fait s'\textbf{en} prendre} \\ \text{*l'\textbf{en} a fait se prendre} \end{array}\right\}$ à sa femme.

His pride made him blame his wife.

(iv)   Son orgueil $\left\{\begin{array}{l} \text{l'a fait s'\textbf{en} aller} \\ \text{*l'\textbf{en} a fait s'aller} \end{array}\right\}$.

His pride made him go away.

(v) a.   Il y a trop d'enfants à la soirèe.
       There are too many children at the party.

   b.   Votre ami **en** voulait à Jean.
       Your friend held a grudge against Jean.

   c.   Jean s'**en** prend à sa femme.
       Jean blames his wife.

   d.   Jean s'**en** va.
       Jean goes away.

Our discussion can provide at least a partial understanding of (i)–(iv). Concerning (i), note that we have regarded comparable Italian examples involving *ci* as ungrammatical (cf. (123), ch. 4. Kayne's judgments go from "?" to "??"). To the extent that such cases may be possible, we do predict however that *y* should not climb. For, like *si/se*, *ci/y* is generally related to the subject position. Its climbing would thus cause it to be adjacent to the wrong subject. We also predict that *se* of (iii), (iv) should not climb, for the usual reasons that prevent climbing of *se*. (Note that clitics which are part of idioms such as these must be regarded as just like other clitics, since they too trigger E assignment and pp agreement in the usual fashion, so that they too must be assumed to hold relations with *ec*'s etc.) The failure of the other clitics in (iii), (iv) to climb seems to me to suggest only that Cl-Cl cannot apply selectively, or break a cluster, which is quite compatible with what we have claimed, and seems rather reasonable. Note that *en* must be base-generated on the lower verb here since it is part of the idiom. But we have nothing to say about (ii).

[24] Kayne gives other, independent, arguments for such relative ordering between *Se* placement and Clitic placement. The strongest within his discussion are the following two: I. While *Se* placement must precede passivization to account for the general impossibility of *se* with passives (cf. Note 1), Clitic placement must follow it, given cases like (i) (FS, p. 378).

(i)   *Trois **en** ont été lus par Paul.
         Three of them have been read by Paul.

That is, if Clitic placement could precede passivization, then at the time it applies, the phrase from which *en* originates would be in direct object position, as with well-formed cases, and (i) should be grammatical. II. Since 'NP-extraposition' appears to be generally blocked by the presence of a direct object, *Se* placement must precede it, to allow for (30a) above (*Il s'est dénoncé trois mille hommes ce mois-ci*), while Clitic placement must follow it to exclude (ii).

(ii)   *Il l'a dénoncé trois milles hommes.
         Three thousand men denounced it.

It is obvious that both I and II dissolve under our approach. We have accounted for both the non-occurrence of *se* with passives, and the ungrammaticality of cases like (i), in terms of configurational conditions under the assumption that both *se* and *en* are base-generated. (Cf. discussion of (4) above, and of (17), ch. 1.) As for II, it also dissolves due to our claim that there is no NP-extraposition (cf. 2.6.2, 6.3.2), while the relevant facts continue to follow.

[25] The FS system would actually predict only that reflexives *may* appear on the lower verb in restructuring constructions, not that they *must*, since presumably *Se* placement could occur on the higher cycle as well. But since reflexives *may not* appear on the lower verb under restructuring, the latter system still turns out false. Notice also that second-cycle *Se* placement in restructuring is in any event itself false, given our discussion of (9a), (11a, b) in 6.2 above, leading to the conclusion that only a derivation via Cl-Cl can make the right predictions.

[26] As our discussion of the dativization process in Note 2, ch. 4 did, so our discussion of (63a) suggests that there is no difference in constituency between *a*-NPs and bare NPs, but only one of Case. This means that, as we pointed out in fn. 16, there are unlikely to be strong theoretical reasons for the failure of NP-movement of indirect objects in the sc relatives of (42).

[27] There are actually some further predictions which follow from our discussion of ergative complements in 4.5 above. These appear to be borne out. One concerns the marginal dativization of the embedded subject in the presence of a dative object in FI (as in **Cela lui fait penser à sa mère** 'That makes him think of his mother', from FS, p. 210, fn. 9) versus no comparable dativization of the apparent subject with ergative complements (cf. the discussion of (107), ch. 4.) Reflexive complements behave in this respect like ergative complements, as cases like (63a) appear totally impossible under dativization: *****Cela fera se téléphoner aux enfants**.

Another prediction concerns dativization in the presence of a sentential complement: a respect in which reflexive complements behave again like ergative complements, as in (i) (cf. discussion of (102), ch. 4.)

(i)   Cela fera se persuader $\left\{ \begin{array}{l} \text{*à Jean} \\ \text{Jean} \end{array} \right\}$ |que la terre est ronde|

   That will make Jean persuade himself that the earth is round.

Reflexive complements are also like ergative complements in marginally allowing cliti-cization of *en* to the lower verb in the manner discussed for Italian *ne* in Note 44, ch. 4, as in (ii) (from FS, p. 431).

(ii)   ?Les mauvaises nouvelles ont fait s'**en** tuer une bonne dizaine.
           The bad news made a good ten of them kill themselves.

Compare the analogous inherent-reflexive case **?L'explosion a fait s'en évanouir trente trois** 'The explosion made thirty three of them faint' (FS, p. 431).

CLOSING REMARKS

In this work, we have given an account of various aspects of the syntax of Italian, sometimes extending the discussion to other languages. We have made rather crucial use of ideas and results provided by past research, such as Perlmutter's Unaccusative Hypothesis, Rizzi's analysis of null subjects, Kayne's idea that there is a syntactic rule that produces causative constructions, and Rizzi's idea that there is a syntactic rule of restructuring. We have also made crucial use of the general theoretical framework of the EST and of the GB theory in particular. In fact, following standard methodological guidelines, we have attempted to postulate, for each of the phenomena we have characterized, only a minimal number of language specific properties, relying maximally on the universal properties defined by the GB theory. To the extent that we have been successful in reducing complex sets of phenomena to a small number of principles and rules, we have thus also provided confirmation for the GB framework. Let us consider exactly which aspects of the EST and the GB framework are confirmed by our accunt, by virtue of being crucial to it.

As was already noted in part in 4.8, 5.9, our discussion has confirmed the existence of the three levels of representation of D-structure, S-structure and LF in a rather specific way, by providing evidence that the class of coindexing relations breaks down into the three subclasses (i), (ii), and (iii) of (1).

(1)   Relations that exist, under well-formedness conditions, at:

	D-structure	S-structure	LF
(i)	x	x	x
(ii)		x	x
(iii)	.		x

Class (i) is exemplified by clitic-*ec* relations. We have seen that these relations msut be well-formed both before and after Move α, namely both at D- and at S-structure. (See 6.2, where Move α is VP-movement, but also the discussion of (34b) ch. 1, and (75) ch. 3, where Move α is NP-movement.) We presume that these relations must also be well-formed at LF. Class (ii) is exemplified by NP-trace relations. These do not exist before Move α, since they are created by Move α (cf. 4.8, 5.9). But we have seen that they must be well-formed after Move α. (See 4.6, where Move α is VP-movement, but also the discussion of (77b), ch. 3.) We presume that they must be well-formed at LF. In class (iii) are for example NP-PRO, or NP-*se stesso* relations. These need not be well-formed, and in fact — as we argued — do not even exist, either at D-structure or at S-structure, but only at LF. Their well-formedness can thus be achieved via reconstruction (cf. 4.4, 4.6).

Thus, our discussion has drawn a distinction between (i) and (ii)–(iii) on the basis of the interaction of these relations with Move α, and a distinction between (i)–(ii) and (iii) on the basis of the interaction with reconstruction. But we have also drawn a distinction between (i)–(ii) and (iii) on the basis of the interaction with the system of E assignment and pp agreement, which we argued applies at S-structure, and for this reason is sensitive only to (i) and (ii), not to (iii).

As we have also already seen in part, our discussion has provided evidence that S-structure (as well as D-structure) representation employs ec's, or more generally null elements (thus including PRO). To a good extent the evidence is related to the classification in (1) and to the fact that each of (i), (ii) and (iii) contains cases both with and without null elements. Thus, an antecedent-si relation involving two overt elements falls into class (i), just like clitic-ec relations (cf. 6.1, 6.2). NP-trace relations, in which the second element is null, fall into class (ii), just like inversion and extraposition relations in which only the first element is sometimes null, but sometimes not (cf. 2.2, 4.6). And NP-PRO relations fall into class (iii), just like NP-se $stesso$ relations (cf. 4.6). Thus, if there were no null elements, many of the relations we have postulated could not exist, so that classes (i), (ii), (iii) could not have all the members we attributed them, and those factual generalizations which we have captured could not be captured.

Some of the above will in turn confirm the correctness of the projection principle. In particular, the existence of the tripartite subdivision of coindexing relations in (1) confirms the projection principle because it is in fact the projection principle that predicts it, requiring that relations involving θ-role transmission exist not only at LF, which is the level relevant to interpretation, but also at other levels — at S-structure if Move α is involved, and both at S- and at D-structure if base-generation in a non-θ-position is involved. The existence of null elements will also confirm the projection principle since it is again the projection principle that predicts the existence of null elements and their distribution. The three different levels of representation, the existence of null elements, and the validity of the projection principle have thus all been crucial to our account.

The GB theory is composed of several subtheories, each one of which is built around a certain connfigurationally defined notion of 'locality', in most cases *government*. In this respect, the GB theory makes no provision for the existence of syntactic mechanisms which might be sensitive to thematic relations, i.e. notions like 'agent', 'patient', etc., or for that matter to grammatical relations, i.e. notions like 'subject', '(direct/indirect) object', etc. Rather, it predicts that syntactic mechanisms may well treat alike constituents that bear different thematic or grammatical relations. There are well-known cases where this seems indeed true. Thus, (accusative) Case assignment seems to work in identical fashion with respect to the direct object in (2a) and the subject of the infinitive in (2b).

(2) a.   John invited **him**.

   b.   John expected [$_S$ **him** to come]

Coreference principles also seem to work in identical fashion, since (3a, b) are both ungrammatical, and so does passivization, as (4a, b) show.

(3) a.   *John$_i$ invited him$_i$.

   b.   *John$_i$ expected [$_S$ him$_i$ to come]

(4) a.   He was invited.

   b.   He was expected to come.

Our discussion confirms this aspect of the GB theory too, providing other relevant cases. Consider (5a, b, c).

(5) a.   Il sasso$_i$ è caduto t$_i$
          The stone has (E) fallen.

   b.   Giovanni$_i$ è sembrato [$_S$ t$_i$ gradire il regalo]
          Giovanni has (E) seemed to like the present.

   c.   Giovanni$_i$ è voluto [$_{VP}$ venire t$_i$] [$_S$ PRO$_i$ − − −]
          Giovanni has (E) wanted to come.

The mechanisms of auxiliary assignment operate in the same fashion in each of (5a, b, c), and yet from the point of view of thematic or grammatical relations these cases are very different. In (5a) the subject is related to the direct object. In (5b) it is related to the subject of the complement, and in the CA case in (5c) to the object of the complement. Furthermore, the subject itself bears rather different thematic relations: in (5a) it is presumably a patient (or at least not an agent), in (5b) it is an agent, but with respect to the embedded verb, while in (5c) it is an agent with respect to the main verb. Thus, if our discussion is at all correct, there is clearly no generalization in terms of thematic or grammatical relations behind these cases. But there is one in terms of certain configurational notions, *government* in particular, since, as we have argued, in all of (5a, b, c) the subject (configurationally defined) is related to an element governed by the verb at S-structure.

   While a comparison of (5a,b) with (5c) shows that E assignment is not simply a reflex of NP-movement, since the subject is not moved in

(5c), a comparison between (5a) and (5b) shows that NP-movement, even when it does not occur in conjunction with passivization as in (4), is itself not sensitive to thematic or grammatical relations, since it affects an object in one case and a subject in the other.

As we have seen (cf. 4.8), cliticization is also a case in which thematic/grammatical relations seem to play no role. Thus, clitic *lo* is a direct object in (6a), the subject of the complement in (6b, c), and a direct object of the complement in (6d).

(6) a.   Giovanni **lo**$_i$ ha invitato [$_i$e]
          Giovanni has invited him.

   b.   Giovanni **lo**$_i$ fa [$_{VP}$parlare] [$_S$ [$_i$e] − − −]
          Giovanni makes him talk.

   c.   Giovanni **lo**$_i$ ritiene [$_{sc}$ [$_i$e] onesto]
          Giovanni believes him honest.

   d.   Giovanni **lo**$_i$ fa [$_{VP}$invitare [$_i$e]]
          Giovanni has him invited.

However, in all of (6a, b, c, d) *lo* appears on a verb that can assign accusative Case, and is locally related to an *ec* that receives a θ-role, as we have argued.

Thus, neither auxiliary assignment, nor NP-movement, nor cliticization seem to work on the basis of thematic or grammatical relations. While for expository reasons we have used terms like *subject*, (*direct/indirect*) *object*, it is clear that, quite generally, thematic or grammatical relations per-se have played no role in our discussion.

BIBLIOGRAPHY

Aissen, Judith, 1974, 'Verb Raising', *Linguistic Inquiry* 5, 325—366.

____ and David Perlmutter: 1976, 'Clause Reduction in Spanish', *Berkeley Linguistic Society* II, 1—30, University of California.

Akmajian, Adrian: 1977, 'The Complement Structure of Perception Verbs in an Autonomous Syntax Framework' in P. W. Culicover, T. Wasow, and A. Akmajian (eds.), *Formal Syntax*, Academic Press, New York, pp. 427—460.

Aoun, Youssef: 1979, 'On Government, Case Marking, and Clitic Placement', mimeographed, MIT.

Baltin, Mark: 1978, *Toward a Theory of Movement Rules*, unpublished Ph.D. dissertation, MIT.

Belletti, Adriana: 1980, 'Italian Quantified NPs in LF', *Journal of Italian Linguistics* 5.1/2, 1—18.

____: 1982, '"Morphological" Passive and Pro Drop: The Impersonal Construction in Italian', *Journal of Linguistic Research* 2.4, 1—33.

____ and Luigi Rizzi: 1981, 'The Syntax of *ne*: Some Theoretical Implications', *The Linguistic Review* 1, 117—154.

Besten, Hans den: 1981, 'Government, syntaktische Struktur und Kasus', in M. Kohrt and J. Lenerz (eds.), *Sprache: Formen und Strukturen*, Akten des 15. linguistischen Kolloquiums Münster 1980. Volume 1. Max Niemeyer Verlag, Tübingen. *Linguistische Arbeiten* 98, 97—107.

____: 1982, 'Some Remarks on the Ergative Hypothesis', in *Groninger Arbeiten zur germanistischen Linguistik (GAGL)* 21, 61—81. University of Groningen, German Department.

Bordelois, Ivonne: 1974, *The Grammar of Spanish Causative Complements*, unpublished Ph.D. dissertation, MIT.

Borer, Hagit: 1980, 'Empty Subjects in Modern Hebrew and Constraints on Thematic Relations', in *Proceedings from the 10th Annual Meeting of the North Eastern Linguistic Society*, Ottawa, Canada.

____: 1981, *Parametric Variations in Clitic Constructions*, unpublished Ph.D. dissertation, MIT. Revised and updated in Borer (1984).

____: 1984, *Parametric Syntax*, Foris, Dordrecht.

Bowers, John S.: 1973, *Grammatical Relations*, unpublished Ph.D. dissertation, MIT.

____: 1981, *The Theory of Grammatical Relations*, Cornell University Press, Ithaca and London.

Brandi, Luciana and Patrizia Cordin: 1981, 'Dialetti e Italiano: Un Confronto sul Parametro del Soggetto Nullo', *Rivista di Grammatica Generativa* 6, 33—88.

Bresnan, Joan: 1972, *Theory of Complementation in English Syntax*, unpublished Ph.D. dissertation, MIT.

____ and Jane Grimshaw: 1978, 'The Syntax of Free Relatives in English', *Linguistic Inquiry* 9, 331—391.

Burzio, Luigi: 1978, 'Italian Causative Constructions', *Journal of Italian Linguistics* 3.2, 1—71.

____: 1981, *Intransitive Verbs and Italian Auxiliaries*, unpublished Ph.D. dissertation, MIT.

____: 1982, 'D-structure Conditions on Clitics', *Journal of Linguistic Research* 2.2, 23—54.

440

____: 1983, 'Conditions on Representation and Romance Syntax', *Linguistic Inquiry* **14**, 193—221.

Chomsky, Noam: 1965, *Aspects of the Theory of Syntax*, MIT Press, Cambridge, Mass.

____: 1970, 'Remarks on Nominalization' in R. Jacobs and P. Rosembaum (eds.), *Readings in English Transformational Grammar*, Ginn, Waltham, Mass., pp. 184—221.

____: 1973, 'Conditions on Transformations' in S. R. Anderson and P. Kiparsky (eds.), *A Festschrift for Morris Halle*, Holt, Rinehart and Winston, New York, pp. 232—286.

____: 1977, 'On Wh-movement' in P. Culicover, T. Wasow and A. Akmajian (eds.), *Formal Syntax*, Academic Press, New York, pp. 71—132.

____: 1980, 'On Binding', *Linguistic Inquiry* **11**, 1—46.

____: 1981a, *Lectures on Government and Binding*, Foris, Dordrecht.

____: 1981b, 'A Note on Non-control PRO', *Journal of Linguistic Research* **1**, 1—11.

____: 1981c, *Some Concepts and Consequences of the Theory of Government and Binding*, Linguistic Inquiry monograph 6, MIT Press, Cambridge, Mass.

____ and Howard Lasnik: 1977, 'Filters and Control', *Linguistic Inquiry* **8**, 425—504.

Cinque, Guglielmo: 1976, 'Appropriateness Conditions for the Use of Passives and Impersonals in Italian', *Italian Linguistics* **1**, 11—31.

____: 1980, 'On Extraction from NP in Italian', *Journal of Italian Linguistics* **5**, 1/2, 47—99.

Contreras, Heles: 1973, 'Grammaticality Versus Acceptability: The Spanish *Se* Case', *Linguistic Inquiry* **4**, 83—88.

Couquaux, Daniel: 1981, 'French Predication and Linguistic Theory', in J. Koster and R. May (eds.), *Levels of Syntactic Representation*, Foris, Dordrecht, pp. 33—64.

Engdahl, Elisabet: 1983, 'Parasitic Gaps', *Linguistics and Philosophy* **5**, 5—34.

Fiengo, Robert: 1974, *Semantic Conditions on Surface Structure*, unpublished Ph.D. dissertation, MIT.

____: 1977, 'On Trace Theory', *Linguistic Inquiry* **8**, 35—61.

____: 1980, *Surface Structure: The Interface of Autonomous Components*, Harvard University Press, Cambridge, Mass. and London.

Fillmore, Charles: 1968, 'The Case for Case', in E. Bach and R. Harms (eds.), *Universals in Linguistic Theory*, Holt, Rinehart and Winston, New York, pp. 1—88.

Freidin, Robert and Howard Lasnik: 1981, 'Disjoint Reference and *Wh*-trace', *Linguistic Inquiry* **12**, 39—53.

Gee, James Paul: 1977, 'Comments on the Paper by Akmajian', in P. W. Culicover, T. Wasow and A. Akmajian (eds.), *Formal Syntax*, Academic Press, New York, pp. 461—481.

Grimshaw, Jane: 1980, 'On the Lexical Representation of Romance Reflexive Clitics', Center for Cognitive Science, MIT, Occasional Paper # 5. Reprinted in J. Bresnan (ed.), *The Mental Representation of Grammatical Relations*, MIT Press, Cambridge, Mass., 1982, pp. 87—148.

Groos, Anneke and Henk van Riemsdijk: 1979, 'Matching Effects in Free Relatives', in A. Belletti, L. Brandi, and L. Rizzi (eds.), *Theory of Markedness in Generative Grammar*, Proceedings of the 1979 GLOW Conference, Scuola Normale Superiore, Pisa, pp. 171—216.

Gross, Maurice: 1975, *Méthodes en syntaxe*, Hermann, Paris.

Guéron, Jacqueline: 1980, 'On the Syntax and Semantics of PP Extraposition', *Linguistic Inquiry* **11**, 637—678.

Hall, Barbara: 1965, *Subject and Object in Modern English*, unpublished Ph.D. dissertation, MIT.

Herschensohn, Julia: 1979, 'The French Presentative as a Base-generated Structure', paper presented at the LSA winter meeting.

____: 1982, 'The French Presentational as a Base-generated Structure', *Studies in Language* **6**.2, 193—219.

Hornstein, Norbert: 1977, 'S and the $\overline{\text{X}}$ convention', *Linguistic Analysis* **3**, 137–176.

_____ and Amy Weinberg: 1981, 'Case Theory and Preposition Stranding', *Linguistic Inquiry* **12**, 55–91.

Jackendoff, Ray: 1972, *Semantic Interpretation in Generative Grammar*, MIT Press, Cambridge, Mass.

_____: 1977, $\overline{\text{X}}$ Syntax: A Study of Phrase Structure, Linguistic Inquiry monograph 2, MIT Press, Cambridge, Mass.

Jaeggli, Osvaldo: 1980, *On Some Phonologically Null Elements in Syntax*, Ph.D. dissertation, MIT. Revised and updated in Jaeggli (1982).

_____: 1981, 'A Modular Approach to "Passives" in Romance Agentive Causatives', mimeographed, USC.

_____: 1982, *Topics in Romance Syntax*, Foris, Dordrecht.

Kayne, Richard: 1975, *French Syntax: The Transformational Cycle*, MIT Press, Cambridge, Mass.

_____: 1979, 'Rightward NP Movement in French and English', *Linguistic Inquiry* **10**, 710–719.

_____: 1980a, 'Extension of Binding and Case-Marking', *Linguistic Inquiry* **11**, 75–96.

_____: 1980b, '*Je l'ai voulu lire, j'ai tout voulu lire*', *Langue Française* **46**, 32–40.

_____: 1981a, 'Binding, Quantifiers, Clitics and Control', in F. Heny (ed.), *Binding and Filtering*, Croom Helm, London, pp. 191–211.

_____: 1981b, 'ECP Extensions', *Linguistic Inquiry* **12**, 93–133.

_____: 1981c, 'On Certain Differences between French and English', *Linguistic Inquiry* **12**, 349–371.

_____: 1983, 'Chains, Categories External to S, and French Complex Inversion', *Natural Language and Linguistic Theory* **1**, 107–139.

_____ and Jean-Yves Pollock: 1978, 'Stylistic Inversion, Successive Cyclicity, and Move NP in French', *Linguistic Inquiry* **9**, 595–621.

Keyser, Samuel Jay and Thomas Roeper: 1984, 'On the Middle and Ergative Constructions in English', *Linguistic Inquiry* **15**, 381–416.

Koopman, Hilda and Dominique Sportiche: 1981, 'Variables and the Bijection Principle', paper presented at the GLOW Conference, Göttingen.

Lasnik, Howard: 1976, 'Remarks on Coreference', *Linguistic Analysis* **2**, 1–22.

Lepschy, Anna Laura and Giulio Lepschy: 1977, *The Italian Language Today*, Hutchinson, London.

Longobardi, Giuseppe: 1980a, 'Remarks on Infinitives: A Case for a Filter', *Journal of Italian Linguistics* **5**, 1/2, 101–155.

_____: 1980b, 'Modularity: From a Single Rule to Several Conditions without Loss of Generalization: Evidence from "Identificational Predicates"', paper presented at the GLOW Conference, Nijmegen.

_____: 1980c. 'Postille alla Regola di Ristrutturazione', *Rivista di Grammatica Generativa* **4**, 213–228.

Manzini, Maria Rita: 1982, 'On Italian *si*', mimeographed, MIT.

_____: 1983, 'On Control and Control Theory', *Linguistic Inquiry* **14**, 421–446.

Marantz, Alec: 1981, *On the Nature of Grammatical Relations*, Ph.D. dissertation, MIT. Revised and Updated in Marantz (1984).

_____: 1984, *On the Nature of Grammatical Relations*, Linguistic Inquiry monograph 10, MIT Press, Cambridge, Mass.

May, Robert: 1977, *The Grammar of Quantification*, unpublished Ph.D. dissertation, MIT.

Milsark, Gary: 1974, *Existential Sentences in English*, unpublished Ph.D. dissertation, MIT.

_____: 1977, 'Toward an Explanation of Certain Peculiarities of the Existential Construction in English', *Linguistic Analysis* **3**, 1–29.

Napoli, Donna Jo: 1973, *The Two Si's of Italian*, unpublished Ph.D. dissertation, Harvard University.

____: 1976, 'At Least Two *Si's*', *Italian Linguistics* **2**, 123–148.

____: 1981, 'Semantic Interpretation versus Lexical Governance', *Language* **57**, 841–887.

Obenauer, Hans-Georg: 1976, *Études de syntaxe interrogative du français*, Niemeyer, Tübingen.

Otero, Carlos: 1972, 'Acceptable Ungrammatical Sentences in Spanish', *Linguistic Inquiry* **3**, 233–242.

____: 1976, 'On Acceptable Ungrammaticality: A Rejoinder', *Linguistic Inquiry* **7**, 342–361.

Perlmutter, David: 1971, *Deep and Surface Structure Constraints in Syntax*, Holt, Rinehart and Winston, New York.

____: 1978, 'Impersonal Passives and the Unaccusative Hypothesis', *Berkeley Linguistic Society* **IV**, 157–189. University of California.

Pesetsky, David: 1979, 'Complementizer-trace Phenomena and the Nominative Island Condition', *The Linguistic Review* **1**, 297–343.

Quicoli, Carlos: 1980, 'Clitic Movement in French Causatives', *Linguistic Analysis* **6**, 131–185.

Radford, Andrew: 1977, *Italian Syntax: Transformational and Relational Grammar*, Cambridge University Press, Cambridge (England).

____: 1979, 'Clitics Under Causatives in Romance', *Journal of Italian Linguistics* **4**.1, 137–181.

Reinhart, Tanya: 1976, *The Syntactic Domain of Anaphora*, unpublished Ph.D. dissertation, MIT.

Riemsdijk, Henk van: 1978, *A Case Study in Syntactic Markedness*, Foris Publications, Dordrecht.

Rivas, Alberto: 1974, 'Impersonal Sentences and Their Interaction with Clitic Movement in Spanish', mimeogrpahed, MIT.

____: 1977, *A Theory of Clitics*, unpublished Ph.D. dissertation, MIT.

Rizzi, Luigi: 1976a, 'Ristrutturazione', *Rivista di Grammatica Generativa* **1**, 1–54.

____: 1976b, 'La *Montée du sujet*, le *si* impersonnel et une règle de restructuration dans la syntaxe italienne', *Recherches Linguistiques* **4**, 158–184.

____: 1978a, 'A Restructuring Rule in Italian Syntax' in S. J. Keyser (ed.), *Recent Transformational Studies in European Languages*, MIT Press, Cambridge, Mass. Reprinted with minor revisions in Rizzi (1982b, I).

____: 1978b, 'Violations of the Wh-island Constraint in Italian and the Subjacency Condition', *Journal of Italian Linguistics* **5**, 157–195. Reprinted with minor revisions in Rizzi (1982b, II).

____: 1982a, 'Comments on Chomsky's Chapter: *On the Representation of Form and Function*', in J. Mehler, E. T. C. Walker, and M. Garrett (eds.), *Perspectives on Mental Representation*, Lawrence Erlbaum Associates, London, pp. 441–453.

____: 1982b, *Issues in Italian Syntax*, Foris, Dordrecht.

Rosen, Carol: 1981, *The Relational Structure of Reflexive Clauses: Evidence from Italian*, unpublished Ph.D. dissertation, Harvard University.

Ross, John Robert: 1967, *Constraints on Variables in Syntax*, unpublished Ph.D. dissertation, MIT.

____: 1972, 'Double-ing', *Linguistic Inquiry* **3**, 61–86.

Rouveret, Alain and Jean-Roger Vergnaud: 1980, 'Specifying Reference to the Subject: French Causatives and Conditions on Representations', *Linguistic Inquiry* **11**, 97–202.

Ruwet, Nicolas: 1972, *Théorie syntaxique et syntaxe du français*, Éditions du Seuil, Paris.

____: 1982, *Grammaire des insultes et autres études*, Éditions du Seuil, Paris.

Safir, Kenneth: 1982, *Syntactic Chains and the Definiteness Effect*, unpublished Ph.D. dissertation, MIT.

Siegel, Dorothy: 1973, 'Nonsources of Unpassives', in J. Kimball (ed.), *Syntax and Semantics*, vol. 2, Seminar Press, New York, pp. 301—317.

Stowell, Timothy: 1978, 'What was There before There was There', in D. Farkas et al. (eds.), *Papers from the Fourteenth Regional Meeting*, Chicago Linguistic Society, pp. 457—471.

____: 1981, *Origins of Phrase Structure*, unpublished Ph.D. dissertation, MIT.

____: 1983, 'Subjects Across Categories', *The Linguistic Review* 2, 285—312.

Strozer, Judith: 1976, *Clitics in Spanish*, unpublished Ph.D. dissertation, UCLA.

____: 1980, 'An Alternative to Restructuring in Romance Syntax', paper presented at the Tenth Anniversary Linguistic Symposium on Romance Languages. University of Washington.

Taraldsen, Knut Tarald: 1978, 'On the NIC, vacuous application and the *that-trace* filter', mimeographed, MIT. Distributed by the Indiana University Linguistics Club, Bloomington, Indiana.

____: 1979, 'The Theoretical Interpretation of a Class of Marked Extractions', in A. Belletti, L. Brandi, and L. Rizzi (eds.), *Theory of Markedness in Generative Grammar*, Proceedings of the 1979 GLOW Conference, Scuola Normale Superiore, Pisa, pp. 475—516.

Torrego, Esther: 1984, 'On Inversion in Spanish and Some of Its Effects', *Linguistic Inquiry* 15, 103—129.

Van Tiel-Di Maio, Maria Francesca: 1975, 'Una Proposta per la Sintassi dell'Italiano: V-raising' in *Atti del IX Congresso Annuale della Società di Linguistica Italiana*, Roma 1975.

____: 1978, 'Sur le phénomène dit du déplacement "long" des clitiques, et, en particulier, sur les constructions causatives', *Journal of Italian Linguistics* 3.2, 73—136.

Vergnaud, Jean-Roger: 1974, *French Relative Clauses*, unpublished Ph.D. dissertation, MIT.

Wasow, Thomas: 1977, 'Transformations and the Lexicon', in P. Culicover, T. Wasow, and A. Akmajian (eds.), *Formal Syntax*, Academic Press, New York, pp. 327—360.

Williams, Edwin: 1975, 'Small Clauses in English', in J. Kimball (ed.), *Syntax and Semantics*, vol. 4, Academic Press, New York, pp. 249—273.

____: 1980, 'Passive', mimeographed, University of Massachusetts at Amherst.

Zubizarreta, Maria Luisa: 1980, 'Pour une restructuration thématique', *Recherches Linguistiques*, Université de Paris VIII, 9, 141—187.

INDEX OF NAMES

445

ANALYTICAL INDEX

(References to notes are ordered according to the relevant text page, rather than page of the note. Reference to a text page covers corresponding notes as well.)

447